OCP

Oracle Certified Professional

Java SE 17 Developer
(Exam 1Z0-829)
Programmer's Guide

Volume II

OCP

Oracle Certified Professional

Java SE 17 Developer
(Exam 1Z0-829)
Programmer's Guide

Volume II

Khalid A. Mughal
Vasily A. Strelnikov

P Pearson

Boston • Columbus • New York • San Francisco • Amsterdam • Cape Town
Dubai • London • Madrid • Milan • Munich • Paris • Montreal • Toronto • Delhi • Mexico City
São Paulo • Sydney • Hong Kong • Seoul • Singapore • Taipei • Tokyo

Library of Congress Control Number: 2022951639

ISBN-13: 978-0-13-799364-2
ISBN-10: 0-13-799364-1

1 2023

Pearson's Commitment to Diversity, Equity, and Inclusion

Pearson is dedicated to creating bias-free content that reflects the diversity of all learners. We embrace the many dimensions of diversity, including but not limited to race, ethnicity, gender, socioeconomic status, ability, age, sexual orientation, and religious or political beliefs.

Education is a powerful force for equity and change in our world. It has the potential to deliver opportunities that improve lives and enable economic mobility. As we work with authors to create content for every product and service, we acknowledge our responsibility to demonstrate inclusivity and incorporate diverse scholarship so that everyone can achieve their potential through learning. As the world's leading learning company, we have a duty to help drive change and live up to our purpose to help more people create a better life for themselves and to create a better world.

Our ambition is to purposefully contribute to a world where:

- Everyone has an equitable and lifelong opportunity to succeed through learning.

- Our educational products and services are inclusive and represent the rich diversity of learners.

- Our educational content accurately reflects the histories and experiences of the learners we serve.

- Our educational content prompts deeper discussions with learners and motivates them to expand their own learning (and worldview).

While we work hard to present unbiased content, we want to hear from you about any concerns or needs with this Pearson product so that we can investigate and address them.

- Please contact us with concerns about any potential bias at https://www.pearson.com/report-bias.html.

Note to Reader

For ease of use, this print edition of *OCP Oracle Certified Professional Java SE 17 Developer (Exam 1Z0-829) Programmer's Guide* has been split into two volumes. Both volumes include a complete index of the book.

Contents Overview
Volume II (Chapters 16–Index)

Contents

Volume II

Streams 16

 Chapter Topics

- Understanding the construction of a stream pipeline
- Understanding various aspects of streams: sequential or parallel, ordered or unordered, finite or infinite, and object or numeric
- Creating object streams from various sources; for example, assorted collections, arrays, strings, and I/O classes
- Creating infinite numeric streams using generator functions
- Understanding the various aspects of intermediate stream operations: stream mapping, lazy execution, short-circuit evaluation, and stateless or stateful operations
- Understanding the implications of operation order, and non-interfering and stateless behavioral parameters of intermediate stream operations
- Filtering, skipping, and examining stream elements
- Selecting distinct elements and truncating a stream
- Understanding mapping and flattening a stream
- Sorting stream elements
- Changing the execution mode of a stream and marking a stream as unordered
- Understanding interoperability between stream types
- Understanding the role of the Optional class
- How to create, query, filter, map, and flatten optionals
- Using numeric optionals
- Understanding the implication of invoking a terminal operation on a stream
- Applying consumer actions to elicit side effects in a stream
- Using terminal operations to match, find, and count stream elements

- Understanding functional and mutable reduction, both sequential and parallel
- Collecting stream results in lists, sets, and arrays
- Using functional reduction on numeric streams, including statistical operations
- Understanding the role of a collector in stream execution
- Collecting to a collection, list, set, map, and concurrent map
- Using a collector to join strings
- Using collectors that group and partition stream elements
- Using downstream collectors for functional reduction: counting, finding min/max, summing, averaging, and summarizing
- How to implement collectors for customized reduction
- How to use map-reduce, filtering, flat mapping, and finishing adapters for downstream collectors
- Understanding how to build and execute a parallel stream
- Understanding factors that can affect parallel stream execution
- Understanding the importance of benchmarking parallel stream execution

Java SE 17 Developer Exam Objectives	
[6.1] Use Java object and primitive Streams, including lambda expressions implementing functional interfaces, to supply, filter, map, consume, and sort data ○ *Streams are covered in this chapter.* ○ *For lambda expressions implementing functional interfaces, see Chapter 13, p. 673.*	*§16.3, p. 884* *§16.4, p. 890* *§16.5, p. 905* *§16.7, p. 946*
[6.2] Perform decomposition, concatenation and reduction, and grouping and partitioning on sequential and parallel streams	*§16.7, p. 946* *§16.8, p. 978* *§16.9, p. 1009*
Java SE 11 Developer Exam Objectives	
[6.2] Use Java Streams to filter, transform and process data	*§16.3, p. 884* *§16.4, p. 890* *§16.5, p. 905* *§16.7, p. 946*
[6.3] Perform decomposition and reduction, including grouping and partitioning on sequential and parallel streams	*§16.7, p. 946* *§16.8, p. 978* *§16.9, p. 1009*

The Stream API brings a new programming paradigm to Java: a *declarative* way of processing data using *streams*—expressing *what* should be done to the values and not *how* it should be done. More importantly, the API allows programmers to harness the power of multicore architectures for *parallel* processing of data.

We strongly suggest reviewing the following topics which we consider essential prerequisites for learning about streams:

- Functional-style programming (Chapter 13, p. 673); specially, functional interfaces, lambda expressions, method references, and built-in functional interfaces
- Comparing objects (Chapter 14, p. 741); in particular, the Comparator<E> functional interface (§14.4, p. 761)

16.1 Introduction to Streams

A *stream* allows aggregate operations to be performed on a sequence of elements. An *aggregate operation* performs a task on the stream as a whole rather than on an individual element of the stream. In the context of streams, these aggregation operations are called *stream operations*. Such operations utilize behavior parameterization implemented by functional interfaces for actions performed on the stream elements.

Examples of stream operations accepting implementation of functional interfaces include:

- Generating elements of the stream using a Supplier
- Converting the elements in the stream according to a mapping defined by a Function
- Filtering the elements in the stream according to some criteria defined by a Predicate
- Sorting the elements in the stream using a Comparator
- Performing actions for each of the elements in the stream with the help of a Consumer

Streams can be produced from a variety of sources. Collections and arrays are typical examples of sources for streams. The Collection<E> interface and the Arrays utility class both provide a stream() method that builds a stream from the elements of a collection or an array.

In the loop-based solution below, elements from the values list are processed using a for(:) loop to test whether a year is after the year 2000. The strings in the list are parsed to a Year object before being tested in an if statement.

```
// Loop-based solution:
List<String> values = List.of("2001", "1999", "2021");
for (String s : values) {
  Year y = Year.parse(s);
  if (y.isAfter(Year.of(2000))) {
```

```
        System.out.print(s + " ");                              // 2001 2021
    }
}

// Stream-based solution:
List<String> values2 = List.of("2001", "1999", "2021");
values2.stream()                                          // (1)
        .map(s -> Year.parse(s))                          // (2)
        .filter(y -> y.isAfter(Year.of(2000)))            // (3)
        .forEach(y -> System.out.print(y + " "));         // (4) 2001 2021
```

A stream-based solution for the same problem is also presented above. The stream() operation at (1) generates a stream based on the elements from the collection. The map() operation at (2) parses the string elements to a Year object, as defined by the lambda expression that implements the Function interface. The filter() operation at (3) performs a filtering of the elements in the stream that are after the year 2000, as defined by a lambda expression that implements the Predicate interface. The forEach() operation at (4) performs an action on each stream element, as defined by a lambda expression that implements the Consumer interface.

The loop-based solution specifies how the operations should be performed. The stream-based solution states what operations should be performed, qualified by the implementation of an appropriate functional interface. Stream-based solutions to many problems can be elegant and concise compared to their iteration-based counterparts.

In this chapter we will cover many stream operations in detail, as well as discover other use cases and benefits of using streams.

16.2 Running Example: The CD Record Class

We will use the CD record class and the Genre enum type from Example 16.1 in many of the examples throughout this chapter. The classes are intentionally kept simple for the purposes of exposition, but they will suffice in illustrating the vast number of topics covered in this chapter.

The CD record class declares fields for the following information about a CD: an artist name, a title, a fixed number of tracks, the year the CD was released, and a musical genre. The compiler provides the relevant get methods to access the fields in a CD record, but boolean methods are explicitly defined to determine its musical genre. The compiler also provides implementations to override the toString(), hashCode(), and equals() methods from the Object class. However, the record class provides its own implementation of the toString() method. The record class implements the Comparable<CD> interface with the following comparison order for the fields: artist name, title, number of tracks, year released, and musical genre.

It is important to note the static field declarations in the CD record class, as they will be used in subsequent examples. These include the static references cd0, cd1, cd2, cd3, and cd4 that refer to five different instances of the CD record class. In addition, the fixed-size list cdList contains these five ready-made CDs, as does the array cdArray. The output from Example 16.1 shows the state of the CDs in the cdList. We recommend consulting this information in order to verify the results from examples presented in this chapter.

The simple enum type Genre is used to indicate the style of music on a CD.

Example 16.1 *The* CD *Example Classes*

```java
// The different genres in music.
public enum Genre {POP, JAZZ, OTHER}
```

```java
import java.time.Year;
import java.util.Comparator;
import java.util.List;

/** A record class that represents a CD. */
public record CD(String artist, String title, int noOfTracks,
                 Year year, Genre genre) implements Comparable<CD> {

  // Additional get methods:
  public boolean isPop()   { return this.genre == Genre.POP; }
  public boolean isJazz()  { return this.genre == Genre.JAZZ; }
  public boolean isOther() { return this.genre == Genre.OTHER; }

  // Provide own implementation of the toString() method.
  @Override public String toString() {
    return String.format("<%s, \"%s\", %d, %s, %s>",
        this.artist, this.title, this.noOfTracks, this.year, this.genre);
  }

  /** Compare by artist, by title, by number of tracks, by year, and by genre. */
  @Override public int compareTo(CD other) {
    return Comparator.comparing(CD::artist)
                  .thenComparing(CD::title)
                  .thenComparing(CD::noOfTracks)
                  .thenComparing(CD::year)
                  .thenComparing(CD::genre)
                  .compare(this, other);
  }

  // Some ready-made CDs.
  public static final CD cd0
      = new CD("Jaav",     "Java Jive",      8, Year.of(2017), Genre.POP);
  public static final CD cd1
      = new CD("Jaav",     "Java Jam",       6, Year.of(2017), Genre.JAZZ);
  public static final CD cd2
      = new CD("Funkies",  "Lambda Dancing", 10, Year.of(2018), Genre.POP);
  public static final CD cd3
      = new CD("Genericos", "Keep on Erasing", 8, Year.of(2018), Genre.JAZZ);
  public static final CD cd4
      = new CD("Genericos", "Hot Generics",   10, Year.of(2018), Genre.JAZZ);
```

```
    // A fixed-size list of CDs.
    public static final List<CD> cdList = List.of(cd0, cd1, cd2, cd3, cd4);

    // An array of CDs.
    public static final CD[] cdArray = {cd0, cd1, cd2, cd3, cd4};
}
```

```
import java.util.List;

public final class CDAdmin {
  public static void main(String[] args) {
    List<CD> cdList = CD.cdList;
    System.out.println("    Artist    Title            No. Year Genre");
    for(int i = 0; i < cdList.size(); ++i) {
      CD cd = cdList.get(i);
      String cdToString = String.format("%-10s%-16s%-4d%-5s%-5s",
          cd.artist(), cd.title(), cd.noOfTracks(),
          cd.year(), cd.genre());
      System.out.printf("cd%d: %s%n", i, cdToString);
    }
  }
}
```

Output from the program:

```
     Artist    Title            No. Year Genre
cd0: Jaav      Java Jive        8   2017 POP
cd1: Jaav      Java Jam         6   2017 JAZZ
cd2: Funkies   Lambda Dancing   10  2018 POP
cd3: Genericos Keep on Erasing  8   2018 JAZZ
cd4: Genericos Hot Generics     10  2018 JAZZ
```

16.3 Stream Basics

In this section we introduce the terminology and the basic concepts required to work with streams, and provide an overview of the Stream API.

An example of an aggregate operation is filtering the elements in the stream according to some criteria, where all the elements of the stream must be examined in order to determine the result. We saw a simple example of filtering a list in the previous section. Figure 16.1a shows an example of a *stream-based* solution for filtering a list of CDs to find all pop music CDs. A stream of CDs is created at (1). The stream is filtered at (2) to find pop music CDs. Each pop music CD that is found is accumulated into a result list at (3). Note how the method calls are chained, which is typical of processing elements in a stream. We will fill in the details as we use Figure 16.1 to introduce the basics of data processing using streams.

A stream must be built from a *data source* before operations can be performed on its elements. Streams come in two flavors: those that process *object references*, called

Figure 16.1 *Data Processing with Streams*

```
// Query to create a list of all CDs with pop music.
List<CD> cdList = List.of(CD.cd0, CD.cd1, CD.cd2, CD.cd3, CD.cd4);
List<CD> popCDs = cdList
①  .stream()                                        // Stream creation.
②  .filter(CD::isPop)                               // Intermediate operation.
③  .toList();                                        // Terminal operation.
```

(a) A query for data processing with streams

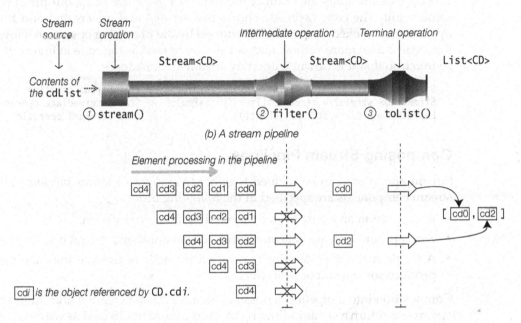

(b) A stream pipeline

(c) Execution of a stream pipeline

object streams; and those that process numeric values, called *numeric streams*. In Figure 16.1a, the call to the stream() method on the list cdList creates an object stream of CD references with cdList as the data source. Building streams from data sources is explored in §16.4, p. 890.

Stream operations are characterized either as *intermediate operations* (§16.5, p. 905) or *terminal operations* (§16.7, p. 946). In Figure 16.1a, there are two stream operations. The methods filter() and collect() implement an intermediate operation and a terminal operation, respectively.

An intermediate operation always returns a new stream—that is, it transforms its *input stream* to an *output stream*. In Figure 16.1a, the filter() method is called at (2) on its input stream, which is the initial stream of CDs returned by the stream() method at (1). The method reference CD::isPop passed as an argument to the filter() method implements the Predicate<CD> functional interface to filter the CDs in the stream. The filter() method returns an output stream, which is a stream of pop music CDs.

A terminal operation either causes a side effect or computes a result. The method collect() at (3) implements a terminal operation that computes a result (§16.7, p. 964). This method is called on the output stream of the filter() operation, which is now the input stream of the terminal operation. Each CD that is determined to be a pop music CD by the filter() operation at (2) is accumulated into a result list by the toList() method at (3). The toList() method (p. 972) creates an empty list and accumulates elements from the input stream—in this case, CDs with pop music.

The code below splits the chain of method calls in Figure 16.1a, but produces the same result. The code explicitly shows the streams that are created and how an operation is invoked on the stream returned by the preceding operation. However, this code is a lot more verbose and not as easy to read as the code in Figure 16.1a— so much so that it is frowned upon by stream aficionados.

```
Stream<CD> stream1 = cdList.stream();            // (1a) Stream creation.
Stream<CD> stream2 = stream1.filter(CD::isPop);  // (2a) Intermediate operation.
List<CD> popCDs2 = stream2.toList();             // (3a) Terminal operation.
```

Composing Stream Pipelines

Stream operations can be chained together to compose a *stream pipeline* in which stream components are specified in the following order:

- An operation on a data source for building the initial stream
- Zero or more intermediate operations to transform one stream into another
- A single mandatory terminal operation in order to execute the pipeline and produce some result or side effect

Composition into a pipeline is possible because stream creation and intermediate operations return a stream, allowing method calls to be chained as we have seen in Figure 16.1a.

The chain of method calls in Figure 16.1a forms the stream pipeline in Figure 16.1b, showing the components of the pipeline. A stream pipeline is analogous to an assembly line, where each operation depends on the result of the previous operation as parts are assembled. In a pipeline, an intermediate operation consumes elements made available by its input stream to produce elements that form its output stream. The terminal operation produces the final result from its input stream. Creating a stream pipeline can be regarded as a fusion of stream operations, where only a single pass of the elements is necessary to process the stream.

Stream operations are typically customized by behavior parameterization that is specified by functional interfaces and implemented by lambda expressions. That is why understanding built-in functional interfaces and writing method references (or their equivalent lambda expressions) is essential. In Figure 16.1a, the Predicate argument of the filter() operation implements the behavior of the filter() operation.

A stream pipeline formulates a query on the elements of a stream created from a data source. It expresses *what* should be done to the stream elements, and not *how* it should be done—analogous to a database query. One important advantage of composing stream pipelines is that the compiler can freely optimize the operations—for example, for parallel execution—as long as the same result is guaranteed.

Executing Stream Pipelines

Apart from the fact that an intermediate operation always returns a new stream and a terminal operation never does, another crucial difference between these two kinds of operations is the way in which they are executed. Intermediate operations use *lazy execution*; that is, they are executed on demand. Terminal operations use *eager execution*; that is, they are executed immediately when the terminal operation is invoked on the stream. This means the intermediate operation will never be executed unless a terminal operation is invoked on the output stream of the intermediate operation, whereupon the intermediate operations will start to execute and pull elements from the stream created on the data source.

The execution of a stream pipeline is illustrated in Figure 16.1c. The stream() method just returns the initial stream whose data source is cdList. The CD objects in cdList are processed in the stream pipeline in the same order as in the list, designated as cd0, cd1, cd2, cd3, and cd4. The way in which elements are successively processed by the operations in the pipeline is shown *horizontally* for each element. The execution of the pipeline only starts when the terminal operation toList() is invoked, and proceeds as follows:

1. cd0 is selected by the filter() operation as it is a pop music CD, and the collect() operation places it in the list created to accumulate the results.

2. cd1 is discarded by the filter() operation as it is not a pop music CD.

3. cd2 is selected by the filter() operation as it is a pop music CD, and the collect() operation places it in the list created to accumulate the results.

4. cd3 is discarded by the filter() operation as it is not a pop music CD.

5. cd4 is discarded by the filter() operation as it is not a pop music CD.

In Figure 16.1c, when the stream is exhausted, execution of the collect() terminal operation completes and execution of the pipeline stops. Note that there was only *one* pass over the elements in the stream. From Figure 16.1c, we see that the resulting list contains only cd0 and cd2, which is the result of the query. Printing the resulting popCDs list produces the following output:

```
[<Jaav, "Java Jive", 8, 2017, POP>, <Funkies, "Lambda Dancing", 10, 2018, POP>]
```

A stream is considered *consumed* once a terminal operation has completed execution. A stream that has been consumed *cannot* be reused, and any attempt to use it will result in a nasty java.lang.IllegalStateException.

The code presented in this subsection is shown in Example 16.2.

Example 16.2 *Data Processing Using Streams*

```java
import java.util.List;
import java.util.stream.Stream;

public class StreamPipeLine {
  public static void main(String[] args) {

    List<CD> cdList = List.of(CD.cd0, CD.cd1, CD.cd2, CD.cd3, CD.cd4);

    // (A) Query to create a list of all CDs with pop music.
    List<CD> popCDs = cdList.stream()            // (1) Stream creation.
        .filter(CD::isPop)                       // (2) Intermediate operation.
        .toList();                               // (3) Terminal operation.
    System.out.println(popCDs);

    // (B) Equivalent to (A).
    Stream<CD> stream1 = cdList.stream();        // (1a) Stream creation.
    Stream<CD> stream2 = stream1.filter(CD::isPop);// (2a) Intermediate operation.
    List<CD> popCDs2 = stream2.toList();         // (3a) Terminal operation.
    System.out.println(popCDs2);
  }
}
```

Output from the program:

```
[<Jaav, "Java Jive", 8, 2017, POP>, <Funkies, "Lambda Dancing", 10, 2018, POP>]
[<Jaav, "Java Jive", 8, 2017, POP>, <Funkies, "Lambda Dancing", 10, 2018, POP>]
```

Comparing Collections and Streams

It is important to understand the distinction between collections and streams. Streams are not collections, and vice versa, but a stream can be created with a collection as the data source (p. 897).

Collections are data structures that can be used to store and retrieve elements. Streams are data structures that do not store their elements, but process them by expressing computations on them through operations like filter() and collect().

Typically, operations are provided to add or remove elements from a collection. However, no elements can be added or removed from a stream—that is, streams are immutable. Because of their functional nature, if a stream operation does remove or discard an element in a stream, a new stream is returned with the remaining elements. A stream operation does not mutate its data source.

A collection can be used in the program as long as there is a reference to it. However, a stream cannot be reused once it is consumed. It must be re-created on the data source in order to be reused.

Operations on a collection are executed immediately, whereas streams can define intermediate operations that are executed on demand—that is, by lazy execution.

Collections are iterable, but streams are *not* iterable. Streams do not implement the Iterable<T> interface, and therefore, a for(:) loop cannot be used to iterate over a stream.

Mechanisms for iteration over a collection are based on an iterator defined by the Collection interface, but must be explicitly used in the program to iterate over the elements; this is called *external iteration*. On the other hand, iteration over stream elements is implicitly handled by the API; this is called *internal iteration* and it occurs when the stream operations are executed.

Collections have a finite size, but streams can be unbounded; these are called *infinite streams*. Special stream operations, such as limit(), exist to compute with infinite streams.

Some collections, such as lists, allow positional access of their elements with an index. However, this is not possible with streams, as only aggregate operations are permissible.

Note also that streams supported by the Stream API are not the same as those supported by the File I/O APIs (§20.1, p. 1233).

Overview of API for Data Processing Using Streams

In this subsection we present a brief overview of new interfaces and classes that are introduced in this chapter. We focus mainly on the Stream API in the java.util .stream package, but we also discuss utility classes from the java.util package.

The Stream Interfaces

Figure 16.2 shows the inheritance hierarchy of the core stream interfaces that are an important part of the Stream API defined in the java.util.stream package. The generic interface Stream<T> represents *a stream of object references*—that is, *object streams*. The interfaces IntStream, LongStream, and DoubleStream are specializations to *numeric streams* of type int, long, and double, respectively. These interfaces provide the static factory methods for creating streams from various sources (p. 890), and define the intermediate operations (p. 905) and the terminal operations (p. 946) on streams.

The interface BaseStream defines the basic functionality offered by all streams. It is recursively parameterized with a stream element type T and a subtype S of the BaseStream interface. For example, the Stream<T> interface is a subtype of the parameterized BaseStream<T, Stream<T>> interface, and the IntStream interface is a subtype of the parameterized BaseStream<Integer, IntStream> interface.

All streams implement the AutoCloseable interface, meaning they should be closed after use in order to facilitate resource management during execution. However, this is not necessary for the majority of streams. Only resource-backed streams need to be closed—for example, a stream whose data source is a file. Such resources are best managed automatically with the try-with-resources statement (§7.7, p. 407).

Figure 16.2   *The Core Stream Interfaces*

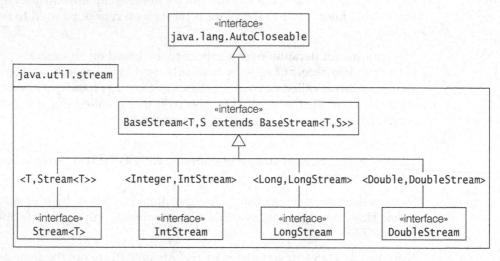

The Collectors Class

A collector encapsulates the machinery required to perform a reduction operation (p. 978). The java.util.stream.Collector interface defines the functionality that a collector must implement. The java.util.stream.Collectors class provides a rich set of predefined collectors for various kinds of reductions.

The Optional Classes

Instances of the java.util.Optional<T> class are containers that may or may not contain an object of type T (p. 940). An Optional<T> instance can be used to represent the absence of a value of type T more meaningfully than the null value. The numeric analogues are OptionalInt, OptionalLong, and OptionalDouble that can encapsulate an int, a long, or a double value, respectively.

The Numeric Summary Statistics Classes

Instances of the IntSummaryStatistics, LongSummaryStatistics, and DoubleSummaryStatistics classes in the java.util package are used by a group of reduction operations to collect summarizing statistics like the count, sum, average, min, and max of the values in a numeric stream of type int, long, and double, respectively (p. 974, p. 1001).

16.4 Building Streams

A stream must have a data source. In this section we will explore how streams can be created from various data sources: collections, arrays, specified values, generator functions, strings, and I/O channels, among others.

Aspects to Consider When Creating Streams

When creating a stream from a data source, certain aspects to consider include whether the stream is:

- Sequential or parallel
- Ordered or unordered
- Finite or infinite
- Object or numeric

Sequential or Parallel Stream

A *sequential stream* is one whose elements are processed sequentially (as in a for loop) when the stream pipeline is executed by a single thread. Figure 16.1 illustrates the execution of a sequential stream, where the stream pipeline is executed by a single thread.

A *parallel stream* is split into multiple substreams that are processed in parallel by multiple instances of the stream pipeline being executed by multiple threads, and their intermediate results combined to create the final result. Parallel streams are discussed in detail later (p. 1009).

The different ways to create a stream on a data source that are illustrated in this section result in a sequential stream. A parallel stream can only be created directly on a collection by invoking the `Collection.parallelStream()` method (p. 897).

The sequential or parallel mode of an existing stream can be modified by calling the `BaseStream.sequential()` and `BaseStream.parallel()` intermediate operations, respectively (p. 933). A stream is executed sequentially or in parallel depending on the execution mode of the stream on which the terminal operation is initiated.

Ordered or Unordered Stream

The *encounter order* of a stream refers to the way in which a stream makes its elements available for processing to an operation in a pipeline. For such data sources as a list, the encounter order of the initial stream is the same as the order of the elements in the list, whereas a stream created with a set of values does not have an encounter order, as the elements of a set are considered to be unordered.

The encounter order of a stream may be changed by an intermediate operation. For example, the `sorted()` operation may impose an encounter order on an unordered stream (p. 929), and the `unordered()` operation may designate a stream unordered (p. 932). Also, some terminal operations might choose to ignore the encounter order; an example is the `forEach()` operation (p. 948).

For ordered sequential streams, an identical result is produced when identical stream pipelines are executed on an identical data source—that is, the execution is deterministic. This guarantee does not hold for unordered sequential streams, as the results produced might be different.

Processing of unordered parallel streams may have better performance than for ordered parallel streams in identical stream pipelines when the ordering constraint is removed, as maintaining the order might carry a performance penalty.

Finite or Infinite Stream

The size of a stream can be finite or infinite depending on how the stream is created. The generate() and iterate() methods of the core stream interfaces create streams with an infinite number of elements (p. 894). Such a stream is said to be *unbounded*. The overloaded ints(), longs(), and doubles() methods of the java.util.Random class create streams with an effectively unlimited number of pseudorandom values (p. 900). An infinite stream must be truncated before the terminal operation is initiated; otherwise, the stream pipeline will never terminate (p. 917).

Object or Numeric Stream

The interface Stream<T> defines the contract for streams of object references—that is, *object streams*. The specialized interfaces IntStream, LongStream, and DoubleStream represent streams of int, long, and double values, respectively—that is, *numeric streams*. The various ways to create streams discussed here will always result in a stream whose element type is either a reference type or a numeric type (int, long, or double). Conversion between these stream types is discussed in §16.5, p. 934.

Table 16.1, p. 904, summarizes selected methods for building streams from various data sources.

The following static factory methods for building streams are defined in the Stream<T> class. Counterparts to these methods are also provided by the IntStream, LongStream, and DoubleStream interfaces for creating numeric streams, unless otherwise noted:

```
static <T> Stream<T> empty()
static <T> Stream<T> of(T t)
static <T> Stream<T> of(T... varargs)
```

The first method creates an *empty* stream—that is, a stream that has no elements.

The second method creates a *singleton* stream—that is, a stream that has a single element.

The third method creates a *finite sequential ordered* stream whose elements are the values specified by the variable arity parameter varargs.

The second and last methods throw a NullPointerException if the argument is null.

```
static <T> Stream<T> ofNullable(T t)          Only in the Stream<T> interface.
```

Creates a *singleton* stream that has a single element, if the argument t is non-null; otherwise, it returns an empty stream.

```
static <T> Stream<T> generate(Supplier<T> supplier)
```

Creates an *infinite sequential unordered* stream where each element is generated by the specified supplier. Typically, this is used for constant streams and streams with random elements.

```
static <T> Stream<T> iterate(T s, UnaryOperator<T> uop)
```

Creates an *infinite sequential ordered* stream produced by the iterative application of the function uop to an initial element seed s, producing a stream consisting of s, e1=uop.apply(s), e2=uop.apply(e1), and so on; that is, uop is applied to the previous element.

```
static <T> Stream<T> concat(Stream<? extends T> a, Stream<? extends T> b)
```

Creates a stream whose elements are all elements of the first stream followed by all elements of the second stream.

The resulting stream is ordered only if both input streams are ordered. If either input stream is parallel, the resulting stream is parallel. As one would expect, the resulting stream is finite only if both input streams are finite.

The Empty Stream

An *empty stream* can be obtained by calling the empty() method of the core stream interfaces. As the name implies, such a stream has no elements.

```
Stream<CD> cdStream = Stream.empty();                     // Empty stream of CD.
System.out.println("Count: " + cdStream.count());        // Count: 0
IntStream iStream = IntStream.empty();                    // Empty stream of int.
System.out.println("Count: " + iStream.count());         // Count: 0
```

The count() method is a terminal operation in the Stream<T> interface (p. 953). It returns the number of elements processed through the stream pipeline.

Using the null value to indicate that a stream is empty may result in a NullPointerException. Therefore, using an explicit empty stream is highly recommended.

Streams from Specified Values

The two overloaded of() methods in the core stream interfaces create finite sequential ordered streams from data values that are specified as arguments.

In the code below, the single-argument of() method is called at (1), and the variable arity of() method is called at (2), both creating a stream of element type CD. The size of the streams created at (1) and (2) is 1 and 3, respectively. The stream pipeline comprising (3) and (4) filters the pop music CDs and prints their title at (4). The forEach() terminal operation at (4) applies its Consumer action to each pop music CD.

```
// From specified objects.
Stream<CD> cdStream1 = Stream.of(CD.cd0);                // (1) Single-arg call.
Stream<CD> cdStream2 = Stream.of(CD.cd0, CD.cd1, CD.cd2); // (2) Varargs call.
cdStream2.filter(CD::isPop)                               // (3)
         .forEach(cd -> System.out.println(cd.title())); // (4)
```

The code below shows examples of using numeric values to create streams. The values specified at (1) and (2) are autoboxed to create a stream of objects. The declaration statements at (3) and (4) avoid the overhead of autoboxing when streams of numeric values are created. However, at (4), an implicit numeric conversion to double is applied to the non-double values.

```
// From specified numeric values.
Stream<Integer> integerStream1 = Stream.of(2017, 2018, 2019);        // (1)
Stream<? extends Number> numStream = Stream.of(100, 3.14D, 5050L);   // (2)
IntStream intStream1 = IntStream.of(2017, 2018, 2019);               // (3)
DoubleStream doubleStream = DoubleStream.of(100, 3.14D, 5050L);      // (4)
```

The variable arity of() method can be used to create a stream whose source is an array. Equivalently, the overloaded Arrays.stream() method can be used for the same purpose. In all cases below, the size of the stream is the same as the size of the array, except at (7). An int array is an object that is passed to the single-argument Stream.of() method (creating a Stream<int[]>), and not the variable arity Stream.of() method. The int array is, however, passed to the variable arity IntStream.of() method at (8). Creating a stream from a numeric array is safer with the numeric stream interfaces or the Arrays.stream() method than the Stream.of() method.

```
// From an array of CDs.
Stream<CD> cdStream3 = Stream.of(CD.cdArray);              // (1)
Stream<CD> cdStream4 = Arrays.stream(CD.cdArray);          // (2)

// From an array of Integer.
Integer[] integerArray = {2017, 2018, 2019};              // (3)
Stream<Integer> integerStream2 = Stream.of(integerArray); // (4)
Stream<Integer> integerStream3 = Arrays.stream(integerArray); // (5)

// From an array of int.
int[] intArray = {2017, 2018, 2019};                      // (6)
Stream<int[]> intArrayStream = Stream.of(intArray);       // (7) Size is 1.
IntStream intStream2 = IntStream.of(intArray);            // (8) Size is 3.
IntStream intStream3 = Arrays.stream(intArray);           // (9) Size is 3.
```

The Stream.of() methods throw a NullPointerException if the argument is null. The ofNullable() method, on the other hand, returns an empty stream if this is the case; otherwise, it returns a singleton stream.

Using Generator Functions to Build Infinite Streams

The generate() and iterate() methods of the core stream interfaces can be used to create infinite sequential streams that are unordered or ordered, respectively.

Infinite streams need to be truncated explicitly in order for the terminal operation to complete execution, or the operation will not terminate. Some stateful intermediate operations must process all elements of the streams in order to produce their results—for example, the sort() intermediate operation (p. 929) and the reduce() terminal operation (p. 955). The limit(maxSize) intermediate operation can be used to limit the number of elements that are available for processing from a stream (p. 917).

Generate

The generate() method accepts a *supplier* that generates the elements of the infinite stream.

```
IntSupplier supplier = () -> (int) (6.0 * Math.random()) + 1;  // (1)
IntStream diceStream = IntStream.generate(supplier);           // (2)
diceStream.limit(5)                                            // (3)
          .forEach(i -> System.out.print(i + " "));           // (4) 2 4 5 2 6
```

The IntSupplier at (1) generates a number between 1 and 6 to simulate a dice throw every time it is executed. The supplier is passed to the generate() method at (2) to create an infinite unordered IntStream whose values simulate throwing a dice. In the pipeline comprising (3) and (4), the number of values in the IntStream is limited to 5 at (3) by the limit() intermediate operation, and the value of each dice throw is printed by the forEach() terminal operation at (4). We can expect five values between 1 and 6 to be printed when the pipeline is executed.

Iterate

The iterate() method accepts a *seed* value and a *unary operator*. The method generates the elements of the infinite ordered stream *iteratively*: It applies the operator to the previous element to generate the next element, where the first element is the seed value.

In the code below, the seed value of 1 is passed to the iterate() method at (2), together with the unary operator uop defined at (1) that increments its argument by 2. The first element is 1 and the second element is the result of the unary operator applied to 1, and so on. The limit() operation limits the stream to five values. We can expect the forEach() operation to print the first five odd numbers.

```
IntUnaryOperator uop = n -> n + 2;                  // (1)
IntStream oddNums = IntStream.iterate(1, uop);      // (2)
oddNums.limit(5)
       .forEach(i -> System.out.print(i + " "));  // 1 3 5 7 9
```

The following stream pipeline will really go bananas if the stream is not truncated by the limit() operation:

```
Stream.iterate("ba", b -> b + "na")
      .limit(5)
      .forEach(System.out::println);
```

Concatenating Streams

The concat() method creates a resulting stream where the elements from the first argument stream are followed by the elements from the second argument stream. The code below illustrates this operation for two unordered sequential streams. Two sets are created at (1) and (2) based on lists of strings that are passed to the set constructors. The two streams created at (3) and (4) are unordered, since they are created from sets (p. 897). These unordered streams are passed to the concat()

method at (5). The resulting stream is processed in the pipeline comprising (5) and
(6). The forEachOrdered() operation at (6) respects the encounter order of the stream
if it has one—that is, if it is ordered (p. 948). The output confirms that the resulting
stream is unordered.

```
Set<String> strSet1                                                          // (1)
    = Set.of("All", " objects", " are", " equal");
Set<String> strSet2                                                          // (2)
    = Set.of(" but", " some", " are", " more", " equal", " than", " others.");
Stream<String> unorderedStream1 = strSet1.stream();                          // (3)
Stream<String> unorderedStream2 = strSet2.stream();                          // (4)
Stream.concat(unorderedStream1, unorderedStream2)                            // (5)
    .forEachOrdered(System.out::print);                                      // (6)
// objectsAll equal are some are others. than equal more but
```

The resulting stream is ordered if both argument streams are ordered. The code
below illustrates this operation for two ordered sequential streams. The two
streams created at (1) and (2) below are ordered. The ordering is given by the specification order of the strings as arguments to the Stream.of() method. These
ordered streams are passed to the concat() method at (3). The resulting stream is
processed in the pipeline comprising (3) and (4). The output confirms that the
resulting stream is ordered.

```
Stream<String> orderedStream1 = Stream.of("All", " objects",                 // (1)
                                          " are", " equal");
Stream<String> orderedStream2 = Stream.of(" but", " some", " are", " more",  // (2)
                                          " equal", " than", " others.");
Stream.concat(orderedStream1, orderedStream2)                                // (3)
     .forEachOrdered(System.out::print);                                     // (4)
// All objects are equal but some are more equal than others.
```

As far as the mode of the resulting stream is concerned, it is parallel if at least one
of the constituent streams is parallel. The code below illustrates this behavior.

The parallel() intermediate operation used at (1) returns a possibly parallel stream
(p. 933). The call to the isParallel() method confirms this at (2). We pass one parallel stream and one sequential stream to the concat() method at (3). The call to the
isParallel() method at (4) confirms that the resulting stream is parallel. The printout from (5) shows that it is also unordered. Note that new streams are created on
the sets strSet1 and strSet2 at (1) and (3), respectively, as we cannot reuse the
streams that were created earlier and consumed.

```
Stream<String> pStream1 = strSet1.stream().parallel();                    // (1)
System.out.println("pStream1 is parallel: " + pStream1.isParallel()); // (2) true
Stream<String> rStream = Stream.concat(pStream1, strSet2.stream());    // (3)
System.out.println("rStream is parallel: " + pStream1.isParallel());  // (4) true
rStream.forEachOrdered(System.out::print);                            // (5)
// objectsAll equal are some are others. than equal more but
```

Streams from Collections

The default methods stream() and parallelStream() of the Collection interface create streams with collections as the data source. Collections are the only data source that provide the parallelStream() method to create a parallel stream directly. Otherwise, the parallel() intermediate operation must be used in the stream pipeline.

The following default methods for building streams from collections are defined in the java.util.Collection interface:

```
default Stream<E> stream()
default Stream<E> parallelStream()
```

Return a *finite sequential* stream or a possibly *parallel* stream with this collection as its source, respectively. Whether it is ordered or not depends on the collection used as the data source.

We have already seen examples of creating streams from lists and sets, and several more examples can be found in the subsequent sections.

The code below illustrates two points about streams and their data sources. If the data source is modified before the terminal operation is initiated, the changes will be reflected in the stream. A stream is created at (2) with a list of CDs as the data source. Before a terminal operation is initiated on this stream at (4), an element is added to the underlying data source list at (3). Note that the list created at (1) is modifiable. The count() operation correctly reports the number of elements processed in the stream pipeline.

```
List<CD> listOfCDS = new ArrayList<>(List.of(CD.cd0, CD.cd1));       // (1)
Stream<CD> cdStream = listOfCDS.stream();                            // (2)
listOfCDS.add(CD.cd2);                                               // (3)
System.out.println(cdStream.count());                               // (4) 3
// System.out.println(cdStream.count());              // (5) IllegalStateException
```

Trying to initiate an operation on a stream whose elements have already been consumed results in a java.lang.IllegalStateException. This case is illustrated at (5). The elements in the cdStream were consumed after the terminal operation at (4). A new stream must be created on the data source before any stream operations can be run.

To create a stream on the entries in a Map, a collection view can be used. In the code below, a Map is created at (1) and populated with some entries. An entry view on the map is obtained at (2) and used as a data source at (3) to create an unordered sequential stream. The terminal operation at (4) returns the number of entries in the map.

```
Map<Integer, String> dataMap = new HashMap<>();                     // (1)
dataMap.put(1, "en"); dataMap.put(2, "to");
dataMap.put(3, "tre"); dataMap.put(4, "fire");
long numOfEntries = dataMap
    .entrySet()                                                     // (2)
```

```
  .stream()                                                          // (3)
  .count();                                                          // (4) 4
```

In the examples in this subsection, the call to the stream() method can be replaced by a call to the parallelStream() method. The stream will then execute in parallel, without the need for any additional synchronization code (p. 1009).

Streams from Arrays

We have seen examples of creating streams from arrays when discussing the variable arity of() method of the stream interfaces and the overloaded Arrays.stream() methods earlier in the chapter (p. 893). The sequential stream created from an array has the same order as the positional order of the elements in the array. As far as numeric streams are concerned, only an int, long, or double array can act as the data source of such a stream.

The code below illustrates creating a stream based on a subarray that is given by the half-open interval specified as an argument to the Array.stream() method, as shown at (1). The stream pipeline at (2) calculates the length of the subarray.

```
Stream<CD> cdStream = Arrays.stream(cdArray, 1, 4);        // (1)
long noOfElements = cdStream.count();                      // (2) 3
```

The following overloaded static methods for building sequential ordered streams from arrays are defined in the java.util.Arrays class:

```
static <T> Stream<T> stream(T[] array)
static <T> Stream<T> stream(T[] array, int startInclusive, int endExclusive)
```

Create a *finite sequential ordered* Stream<T> with the specified array as its source. The stream created by the second method comprises the range of values given by the specified half-open interval.

```
static NumTypeStream stream(numtype[] array)
static NumTypeStream stream(numtype[] array,
                            int startInclusive, int endExclusive)
```

NumType is Int, Long, or Double, and the corresponding *numtype* is int, long, or double.

Create a *finite sequential ordered* NumTypeStream (which is either IntStream, LongStream, or DoubleStream) with the specified array as its source. The stream created by the second method comprises the range of primitive values given by the specified half-open interval.

Building a Numeric Stream with a Range

The overloaded methods range() and rangeClosed() can be used to create *finite ordered* streams of integer values based on a range that can be *half-open* or *closed*, respectively. The increment size is always 1.

The following static factory methods for building numeric streams are defined only in the IntStream and LongStream interfaces in the java.util.stream package.

```
static NumTypeStream range(numtype startInclusive, numtype endExclusive)
static NumTypeStream rangeClosed(numtype startInclusive,
                                        numtype endInclusive)
```

NumType is Int or Long, and the corresponding *numtype* is int or long.

Both methods return a *finite sequential ordered NumType*Stream whose elements are a sequence of numbers, where the first number in the stream is the start value of the range startInclusive and increment length of the sequence is 1. For a *half-open interval*, as in the first method, the end value of the range endExclusive is excluded. For a *closed interval*, as in the second method, the end value of the range endInclusive is included.

The range(startInclusive, endExclusive) method is equivalent to the following for(;;) loop:

```
for (int i = startInclusive; i < endExclusive; i++) {
    // Loop body.
}
```

When processing with ranges of integer values, the range() methods should also be considered on par with the for(;;) loop.

The stream pipeline below prints all the elements in the CD array in reverse. Note that no terminating condition or increment expression is specified. As range values are always in increasing order, a simple adjustment can be done to reverse their order.

```
IntStream.range(0, CD.cdArray.length)                            // (1)
        .forEach(i -> System.out.println(cdArray[CD.cdArray.length - 1 - i]));
```

The following example counts the numbers that are divisible by a specified divisor in a given range of values.

```
int divisor = 5;
int start = 2000, end = 3000;
long divisibles = IntStream
    .rangeClosed(start, end)                                     // (1)
    .filter(number -> number % divisor == 0)                     // (2)
    .count();                                                    // (3)
System.out.println(divisibles);                                  // 201
```

The next example creates an int array that is filled with increment values specified by the range at (1) below. The toArray() method is a terminal operation that creates an array of the appropriate type and populates it with the values in the stream (p. 971).

```
int first = 10, len = 8;
int[] intArray = IntStream.range(first, first + len).toArray();  // (1)
System.out.println(intArray.length + ": " + Arrays.toString(intArray));
//8: [10, 11, 12, 13, 14, 15, 16, 17]
```

The example below shows usage of two nested ranges to print the multiplication tables. The inner arrange is executed 10 times for each value in the outer range.

```
IntStream.rangeClosed(1, 10)                                      // Outer range.
        .forEach(i -> IntStream.rangeClosed(1, 10)               // Inner range.
                    .forEach(j -> System.out.printf("%2d * %2d = %2d%n",
                                                     i, j, i * j)));
}
```

We cordially invite the inquisitive reader to code the above examples in the imperative style using explicit loops. Which way is better is not always that clear-cut.

Numeric Streams Using the Random Class

The following methods for building *numeric unordered* streams are defined in the java.util.Random class:

> *NumType* is Int, Long, or Double, and the corresponding *numtype* is int, long, or double. The corresponding overloaded *numtypes*() methods are ints(), longs(), and doubles().

> *NumType*Stream *numtypes*()
> *NumType*Stream *numtypes*(*numtype* randomNumberOrigin,
>   *numtype* randomNumberBound)
> *NumType*Stream *numtypes*(long streamSize)
> *NumType*Stream *numtypes*(long streamSize, *numtype* randomNumberOrigin,
>   *numtype* randomNumberBound)

> The first two methods generate an *effectively unlimited sequential unordered* stream of pseudorandom *numtype* values. For the zero-argument doubles() method, the double values are between 0.0 (inclusive) and 1.0 (exclusive). For the second method, the *numtype* values generated are in the *half-open* interval defined by the origin and the bound values.

> The last two methods generate a *finite sequential unordered* stream of pseudorandom *numtype* values, where the length of the stream is limited by the specified streamSize parameter.

The examples below illustrate using a *pseudorandom number generator* (PRNG) to create numeric streams. The same PRNG can be used to create multiple streams. The PRNG created at (1) will be used in the examples below.

```
Random rng = new Random();                              // (1)
```

The int stream created at (2) is an *effectively unlimited unordered* stream of int values. The size of the stream is limited to 3 by the limit() operation. However, at (3), the maximum size of the stream is specified in the argument to the ints() method. The values in both streams at (2) and (3) can be any random int values. The contents of the array constructed in the examples will, of course, vary.

```
IntStream iStream = rng.ints();                        // (2) Unlimited, any int value
int[] intArray = iStream.limit(3).toArray();           // Limits size to 3
//[-1170441471, 1070948914, 264046613]
```

```
intArray = rng.ints(3).toArray();                    // (3) Size 3, any int value
//[1011448344, -974832344, 816809715]
```

The unlimited unordered stream created at (4) simulates the dice throw we implemented earlier using the generate() method (p. 895). The values are between 1 and 6, inclusive. The limit() method must be used explicitly to limit the stream. The finite unordered stream created at (5) incorporates the size and the value range.

```
intArray = rng.ints(1, 7)                            // (4) Unlimited, [1, 6]
            .limit(3)                                // Limits size to 3
            .toArray();                              // [5, 2, 4]

intArray = rng.ints(3, 1, 7)                         // (5) Size 3, [1, 6]
            .toArray();                              // [1, 4, 6]
```

The zero-argument doubles() method and the single-argument doubles(streamSize) method generate an unlimited and a limited unordered stream, respectively, whose values are between 0.0 and 1.0 (exclusive).

```
DoubleStream dStream = rng.doubles(3);               // (6) Size 3, [0.0, 1.0)
double[] dArray = dStream.toArray();
//[0.9333794789872794, 0.7037326827186609, 0.2839257522887708]
```

Streams from a CharSequence

The CharSequence.chars() method creates a *finite sequential ordered* IntStream from a sequence of char values. The IntStream must be transformed to a Stream<Character> in order to handle the values as Characters. The IntStream.mapToObj() method can be used for this purpose, as shown at (2). A cast is necessary at (2) in order to convert an int value to a char value which is autoboxed in a Character. Conversion between streams is discussed in §16.5, p. 934.

```
String strSource = "banananana";
IntStream iStream = strSource.chars();               // (1)
iStream.forEach(i -> System.out.print(i + " "));     // Prints ints.
// 98 97 110 97 110 97 110 97 110 97

strSource.chars()
        .mapToObj(i -> (char)i)                      // (2) Stream<Character>
        .forEach(System.out::print);                 // Prints chars.
// banananana
```

The following default method for building IntStreams from a sequence of char values (e.g., String and StringBuilder) is defined in the java.lang.CharSequence interface (§8.4, p. 444):

default IntStream chars()

Creates a *finite sequential ordered* stream of int values by zero-extending the char values in this sequence.

Streams from a `String`

The following method of the `String` class can be used to extract *text lines* from a string:

```
Stream<String> lines()
```
Returns a stream of lines extracted from this string, separated by line terminators.

In the code below, the string at (1) contains three text lines separated by the line terminator (\n). A stream of element type `String` is created using this string as the source at (2). Each line containing the word `"mistakes"` in this stream is printed at (3).

```
String inputLines = "Wise men learn from their mistakes.\n"              // (1)
                  + "But wiser men learn from the mistakes of others.\n"
                  + "And fools just carry on.";
Stream<String> lStream = inputLines.lines();                            // (2)
lStream.filter(l -> l.contains("mistakes")).forEach(System.out::println); // (3)
```

Output from the code:

```
Wise men learn from their mistakes.
But wiser men learn from the mistakes of others.
```

Streams from a `BufferedReader`

A `BufferedReader` allows contents of a text file to be read as lines. A *line* is a sequence of characters terminated by a *line terminator sequence*. Details of using a `Buffered-Reader` are covered in §20.3, p. 1251. A simple example of creating streams on text files using a `BufferedReader` is presented below.

At (1) and (2) in the header of the try-with-resources statement (§7.7, p. 407), a `BufferedReader` is created to read lines from a given file, and a stream of `String` is created at (3) by the `lines()` method provided by the `BufferedReader` class. These declarations are permissible since both the buffered reader and the stream are Auto-Closeable. Both will be automatically closed after the try block completes execution. A terminal operation is initiated at (4) on this stream to count the number of lines in the file. Of course, each line from the stream can be processed depending on the problem at hand.

```
try ( FileReader fReader = new FileReader("CD_Data.txt");          // (1)
      BufferedReader bReader = new BufferedReader(fReader);        // (2)
      Stream<String> lStream = bReader.lines() ) {                // (3)
  System.out.println("Number of lines: " + lStream.count());      // (4) 13
} catch (FileNotFoundException e) {
  e.printStackTrace();
} catch (IOException e) {
  e.printStackTrace();
}
```

The following method for building a `Stream<String>` from a text file is defined in the `java.io.BufferedReader` class:

```
Stream<String> lines()
```

Returns a *finite sequential ordered* Stream of Strings, where the elements are text lines read by this BufferedReader.

The reader position in the file is not guaranteed after the stream terminal operation completes.

The result of the terminal stream operation is undefined if the reader is operated upon during the execution of this operation.

Any operation on a Stream returned by a BufferedReader that has already been closed will throw an UncheckedIOException.

Streams from Factory Methods in the Files Class

A detailed discussion of the NIO2 File API that provides the classes for creating the various streams for reading files, finding files, and walking directories in the file system can be found in Chapter 21, p. 1285.

Analogous to the lines() method in the BufferedReader class, a static method with the same name is provided by the java.nio.file.Files class that creates a stream for reading the file content as lines.

In the example below, a Path is created at (1) to represent a file on the file system. A stream is created to read lines from the path at (2) in the header of the try-with-resources statement (§7.7, p. 407). As streams are AutoCloseable, such a stream is automatically closed after the try block completes execution. As no character set is specified, bytes from the file are decoded into characters using the UTF-8 charset. A terminal operation is initiated at (3) on this stream to count the number of lines in the file. Again, each line in the stream can be processed as desired.

```
Path path = Paths.get("CD_Data.txt");                          // (1)
try (Stream<String> lStream = Files.lines(path)) {             // (2)
  System.out.println("Number of lines: " + lStream.count());   // (3) 13
} catch (FileNotFoundException e) {
  e.printStackTrace();
} catch (IOException e) {
  e.printStackTrace();
}
```

The following static methods for building a Stream<String> from a text file are defined in the java.nio.file.Files class:

```
static Stream<String> lines(Path path)
static Stream<String> lines(Path path, Charset cs)
```

Return a *finite sequential ordered* Stream of String, where the elements are text lines read from a file given by the specified path. The first method decodes the bytes into characters using the UTF-8 charset. The charset to use can be explicitly specified, as in the second method.

Summary of Stream Building Methods

Selected methods for building streams from various data sources are listed in Table 16.1. The first column lists the method names and the reference type that provides them. For brevity, the parameters of the methods are omitted. Note that some methods are overloaded. The prefix *NumType* stands for Int, Long, or Double. A reference is also provided where details about the method can be found. The remaining four columns indicate various aspects of a stream: the type of stream returned by a method, whether the stream is finite or infinite, whether it is sequential or parallel, and whether it is ordered or unordered (p. 891).

Table 16.1 *Summary of Stream Building Methods*

Method	Returned stream type	Finite/ Infinite	Sequential/ Parallel	Ordered/ Unordered
Stream.empty() *NumType*Stream.empty() (p. 893)	Stream<T> *NumType*Stream	Finite	Sequential	Ordered
Stream.of() Stream.ofNullable() *NumType*Stream.of() (p. 893)	Stream<T> Stream<T> *NumType*Stream	Finite	Sequential	Ordered
Stream.generate() *NumType*Stream.generate() (p. 895)	Stream<T> *NumType*Stream	Infinite	Sequential	Unordered
Stream.iterate() *NumType*Stream.iterate (p. 895)	Stream<T> *NumType*Stream	Infinite	Sequential	Ordered
Stream.concat() *NumType*Stream.concat() (p. 895)	Stream<T> *NumType*Stream	Finite if both finite	Parallel if either parallel	Ordered if both ordered
Collection.stream() (p. 897)	Stream<T>	Finite	Sequential	Ordered if collection ordered
Collection.parallelStream() (p. 897)	Stream<T>	Finite	Parallel	Ordered if collection ordered
Arrays.stream() (p. 898)	Stream<T> *NumType*Stream	Finite	Sequential	Ordered
IntStream.range() IntStream.rangeClosed() LongStream.range() LongStream.rangeClosed() (p. 898)	IntStream IntStream LongStream LongStream	Finite	Sequential	Ordered

Table 16.1 *Summary of Stream Building Methods (Continued)*

Method	Returned stream type	Finite/ Infinite	Sequential/ Parallel	Ordered/ Unordered
Random.ints() Random.longs() Random.doubles() (p. 900)	IntStream LongStream DoubleStream	*Finite or infinite, depending on parameters*	*Sequential*	*Unordered*
CharSequence.chars() (p. 901)	IntStream	*Finite*	*Sequential*	*Ordered*
String.lines() (p. 902)	Stream<String>	*Finite*	*Sequential*	*Ordered*
BufferedReader.lines() (p. 902)	Stream<String>	*Finite*	*Sequential*	*Ordered*
Files.lines() (p. 903)	Stream<String>	*Finite*	*Sequential*	*Ordered*

16.5 Intermediate Stream Operations

A stream pipeline is composed of stream operations. The stream operations process the elements of the stream to produce some result. After the creation of the initial stream, the elements of the stream are processed by zero or more intermediate operations before the mandatory terminal operation reduces the elements to some final result. The initial stream can undergo several *stream transformations* (technically called *mappings*) by the intermediate operations as the elements are processed through the pipeline.

Intermediate operations *map* a stream to a new stream, and the terminal operation *reduces* the final stream to some result. Because of the nature of the task they perform, the operations in a stream pipeline are also called *map-reduce transformations*.

Aspects of Streams, Revisited

We now take a closer look at the following aspects pertaining to streams:

- Stream mapping
- Lazy execution
- Short-circuit evaluation
- Stateless and stateful operations
- Order of intermediate operations
- Non-interfering and stateless behavioral parameters of stream operations

Table 16.3, p. 938, summarizes certain aspects of each intermediate operation. Table 16.4, p. 939, summarizes the intermediate operations provided by the Stream API.

Stream Mapping

Each intermediate operation returns a new stream—that is, it maps the elements of its input stream to an output stream. Intermediate operations can thus be easily recognized. Having a clear idea of the *type* of the new stream an intermediate operation should produce aids in customizing the operation with an appropriate implementation of its behavioral parameters. Typically, these behavioral parameters are functional interfaces.

Because intermediate operations return a new stream, calls to methods of intermediate operations can be *chained*, so much so that code written in this *method chaining* style has become a distinct hallmark of expressing queries with streams.

In Example 16.3, the stream pipeline represents the query to create a list with titles of pop music CDs in a given list of CDs. Stream mapping is illustrated at (1). The initial stream of CDs (Stream<CD>) is first transformed by an intermediate operation (filter()) to yield a new stream that has only pop music CDs (Stream<CD>), and this stream is then transformed to a stream of CD titles (Stream<String>) by a second intermediate operation (map(), p. 921). The stream of CD titles is reduced to the desired result (List<CD>) by the terminal operation (collect()).

In summary, the *type of the output stream* returned by an intermediate operation need not be the same as the *type of its input stream*.

Example 16.3 *Stream Mapping and Loop Fusion*

```
import java.util.List;

public class StreamOps {
  public static void main(String[] args) {

    // Query: Create a list with titles of pop music CDs.

    // (1) Stream Mapping:
    List<CD> cdList1 = CD.cdList;
    List<String> popCDs1 = cdList1
        .stream()                      // Initial stream:          Stream<CD>
        .filter(CD::isPop)             // Intermediate operation: Stream<CD>
        .map(CD::title)                // Intermediate operation: Stream<String>
        .toList();                     // Terminal operation: List<String>
    System.out.println("Pop music CDs: " + popCDs1);
    System.out.println();

    // (2) Lazy Evaluation:
    List<CD> cdList2 = CD.cdList;
    List<String> popCDs2 = cdList2
        .stream()                      // Initial stream:          Stream<CD>
```

```
        .filter(cd -> {                    // Intermediate operation:  Stream<CD>
          System.out.println("Filtering: " + cd                      // (3)
                          + (cd.isPop() ? " is pop CD." : " is not pop CD."));
          return cd.isPop();
        })
        .map(cd -> {                        // Intermediate operation: Stream<String>
          System.out.println("Mapping: " + cd.title());         // (4)
          return cd.title();
        })
        .toList();                          // Terminal operation: List<String>
      System.out.println("Pop music CDs: " + popCDs2);
  }
}
```

Output from the program:

```
Pop music CDs: [Java Jive, Lambda Dancing]

Filtering: <Jaav, "Java Jive", 8, 2017, POP> is pop CD.
Mapping: Java Jive
Filtering: <Jaav, "Java Jam", 6, 2017, JAZZ> is not pop CD.
Filtering: <Funkies, "Lambda Dancing", 10, 2018, POP> is pop CD.
Mapping: Lambda Dancing
Filtering: <Genericos, "Keep on Erasing", 8, 2018, JAZZ> is not pop CD.
Filtering: <Genericos, "Hot Generics", 10, 2018, JAZZ> is not pop CD.
Pop music CDs: [Java Jive, Lambda Dancing]
```

Lazy Execution

A stream pipeline does not execute until a terminal operation is invoked. In other words, its intermediate operations do not start processing until their results are needed by the terminal operation. Intermediate operations are thus *lazy*, in contrast to the terminal operation, which is *eager* and executes when it is invoked.

An intermediate operation is *not* performed on all elements of the stream before performing the next operation on all elements resulting from the previous stream. Rather, the intermediate operations are performed back-to-back on *each* element in the stream. In a sense, the loops necessary to perform each intermediate operation on *all* elements successively are fused into a single loop (technically called *loop fusion*). Thus only a single pass is required over the elements of the stream.

Example 16.3 illustrates loop fusion resulting from lazy execution of a stream pipeline at (2). The intermediate operations now include print statements to announce their actions at (3) and (4). Note that we do not advocate this practice for production code. The output shows that the elements are processed *one at a time* through the pipeline when the terminal operation is executed. A CD is filtered first, and if it is a pop music CD, it is mapped to its title and the terminal operation includes this title in the result list. Otherwise, the CD is discarded. When there are no more CDs in the stream, the terminal operation completes, and the stream is consumed.

Short-circuit Evaluation

The lazy nature of streams allows certain kinds of optimizations to be performed on stream operations. We have already seen an example of such an optimization that results in loop fusion of intermediate operations.

In some cases, it is not necessary to process all elements of the stream in order to produce a result (technically called *short-circuit execution*). For instance, the limit() intermediate operation creates a stream of a specified size, making it unnecessary to process the rest of the stream once this limit is reached. A typical example of its usage is to turn an infinite stream into a finite stream. Another example is the takeWhile() intermediate operation that short-circuits stream processing once its predicate becomes false.

Certain terminal operations (anyMatch(), allMatch(), noneMatch(), findFirst(), findAny()) are also short-circuit operations, since they do not need to process all elements of the stream in order to produce a result (p. 949).

Stateless and Stateful Operations

An *stateless* operation is one that can be performed on a stream element without taking into consideration the outcome of any processing done on previous elements or on any elements yet to be processed. In other words, the operation does not retain any *state* from processing of previous elements in order to process a new element. Rather, the operation can be performed on an element independently of how the other elements are processed.

A *stateful* operation is one that needs to retain state from previously processed elements in order to process a new element.

The intermediate operations distinct(), dropWhile(), limit(), skip(), sorted(), and takeWhile() are *stateful* operations. All other intermediate operations are *stateless*. Examples of stateless intermediate operations include the filter() and map() operations.

Order of Intermediate Operations

The order of intermediate operations in a stream pipeline can impact the performance of a stream pipeline. If intermediate operations that reduce the size of the stream can be performed earlier in the pipeline, fewer elements need to be processed by the subsequent operations.

Moving intermediate operations such as filter(), distinct(), dropWhile(), limit(), skip(), and takeWhile() earlier in the pipeline can be beneficial, as they all decrease the size of the input stream. Example 16.4 implements two stream pipelines at (1) and (2) to create a list of CD titles, but skipping the first three CDs. The map() operation transforms each CD to its title, resulting in an output stream with element type String. The example shows how the number of elements processed by the map() operation can be reduced if the skip() operation is performed before the map() operation (p. 921).

Example 16.4 *Order of Intermediate Operations*

```java
import java.util.List;

public final class OrderOfOperations {
  public static void main(String[] args) {

    List<CD> cdList = CD.cdList;

    // Map before skip.
    List<String> cdTitles1 = cdList
        .stream()                    // (1)
        .map(cd -> {                 // Map applied to all elements.
          System.out.println("Mapping: " + cd.title());
          return cd.title();
        })
        .skip(3)                     // Skip afterwards.
        .toList();
    System.out.println(cdTitles1);
    System.out.println();

    // Skip before map preferable.
    List<String> cdTitles2 = cdList
        .stream()                    // (2)
        .skip(3)                     // Skip first.
        .map(cd -> {                 // Map not applied to the first 3 elements.
          System.out.println("Mapping: " + cd.title());
          return cd.title();
        })
        .toList();
    System.out.println(cdTitles2);
  }
}
```

Output from the program:

```
Mapping: Java Jive
Mapping: Java Jam
Mapping: Lambda Dancing
Mapping: Keep on Erasing
Mapping: Hot Generics
[Keep on Erasing, Hot Generics]

Mapping: Keep on Erasing
Mapping: Hot Generics
[Keep on Erasing, Hot Generics]
```

Non-interfering and Stateless Behavioral Parameters

One of the main goals of the Stream API is that the code for a stream pipeline should execute and produce the same results whether the stream elements are processed sequentially or in parallel. In order to achieve this goal, certain constraints are placed on the *behavioral parameters*—that is, on the lambda expressions and method references that are implementations of the functional interface parameters in stream operations. These behavioral parameters, as the name implies, allow the behavior of a stream operation to be customized. For example, the predicate supplied to the filter() operation defines the criteria for filtering the elements.

Most stream operations require that their behavioral parameters are *non-interfering* and *stateless*. A *non-interfering behavioral parameter* does not change the stream data source during the execution of the pipeline, as this might not produce deterministic results. The exception to this is when the data source is *concurrent*, which guarantees that the source is thread-safe. A *stateless behavioral parameter* does not access any state that can change during the execution of the pipeline, as this might not be thread-safe.

If the constraints are violated, all bets are off, resulting in incorrect results being computed, which causes the stream pipeline to fail. In addition to these constraints, care should be taken to introduce side effects via behavioral parameters, as these might introduce other concurrency-related problems during parallel execution of the pipeline.

The aspects of intermediate operations mentioned in this subsection will become clearer as we fill in the details in subsequent sections.

Filtering

Filters are stream operations that select elements based on some criteria, usually specified as a *predicate*. This section discusses different ways of filtering elements, selecting unique elements, skipping elements at the head of a stream, and truncating a stream.

The following methods are defined in the Stream<T> interface, and analogous methods are also defined in the IntStream, LongStream, and DoubleStream interfaces:

```
// Filtering using a predicate.
Stream<T> filter(Predicate<? super T> predicate)
```

Returns a stream consisting of the elements of this stream that match the given non-interfering, stateless predicate.

This is a stateless intermediate operation that changes the stream size, but not the stream element type or the encounter order of the stream.

```
// Taking and dropping elements using a predicate.
default Stream<T> takeWhile(Predicate<? super T> predicate)
default Stream<T> dropWhile(Predicate<? super T> predicate)
```

The takeWhile() method puts an element from the input stream into its output stream, if it matches the predicate—that is, if the predicate returns the value true for this element. In this case, we say that the takeWhile() method *takes* the element.

The dropWhile() method discards an element from its input stream, if it matches the predicate—that is, if the predicate returns the value true for this element. In this case, we say that the dropWhile() method *drops* the element.

For an ordered stream:

The takeWhile() method takes elements from the input stream as long as an element matches the predicate, after which it short-circuits the stream processing.

The dropWhile() method drops elements from the input stream as long as an element matches the predicate, after which it passes through the remaining elements to the output stream.

In short, both methods find the *longest prefix of elements* to take or drop from the input stream, respectively.

For an unordered stream, where the predicate matches some but not all elements in the input stream:

The elements taken by the takeWhile() method or dropped by the dropWhile() method are *nondeterministic*; that is, any subset of matching elements can be taken or dropped, respectively, including the empty set.

If the predicate matches all elements in the input stream, regardless of whether the stream is ordered or unordered:

The takeWhile() method takes all elements; that is, the result is the same as the input stream.

The dropWhile() method drops all elements; that is, the result is the empty stream.

If the predicate matches no elements in the input stream, regardless of whether the stream is ordered or unordered:

The takeWhile() method takes no elements; that is, the result is the empty stream.

The dropWhile() method drops no elements; that is, the result is the same as the input stream.

Note that the takeWhile() method is a *short-circuiting* stateful intermediate operation, whereas the dropWhile() method is a stateful intermediate operation.

```
// Selecting distinct elements.
Stream<T> distinct()
```

Returns a stream consisting of the distinct elements of this stream, where no two elements are equal according to the Object.equals() method; that is, the method assumes that the elements override the Object.equals() method. It also uses the hashCode() method to keep track of the elements, and this method should also be overridden from the Object class.

For ordered streams, the *first* occurrence of a duplicated element is selected in the encounter order—called the *stability guarantee*. This stateful operation is particularly expensive for a parallel ordered stream which entails buffering overhead to ensure the stability guarantee. There is no such guarantee for an unordered stream: Which occurrence of a duplicated element will be selected is not guaranteed.

This stateful intermediate operation changes the stream size, but not the stream element type.

```
// Skipping elements.
Stream<T> skip(long n)
```

Returns a stream consisting of the remaining elements of this stream after discarding the first n elements of the stream in encounter order. If this stream has fewer than n elements, an empty stream is returned.

This stateful operation is expensive for a parallel ordered stream which entails keeping track of skipping the *first* n elements.

This is a stateful intermediate operation that changes the stream size, but not the stream element type.

```
// Truncating a stream.
Stream<T> limit(long maxSize)
```

Returns a stream consisting of elements from this stream, truncating the length of the returned stream to be no longer than the value of the parameter maxSize.

This stateful operation is expensive for a parallel ordered stream which entails keeping track of passing the *first* n elements from the input stream to the output stream.

This is a short-circuiting, stateful intermediate operation.

Filtering Using a Predicate

We have already seen many examples of filtering stream elements in this chapter. The first example of using the Stream.filter() method was presented in Figure 16.1, p. 885.

Filtering a collection using the Iterator.remove() method and the Collection.removeIf() method is discussed in §13.3, p. 691, and §15.2, p. 796, respectively.

The filter() method can be used on both object and numeric streams. The Stream.filter() method accepts a Predicate<T> as an argument. The predicate is typically implemented as a lambda expression or a method reference defining the selection criteria. It yields a stream consisting of elements from the input stream that satisfy the predicate. The elements that do not match the predicate are discarded.

In Figure 16.3, Query 1 selects those CDs from a list of CDs (CD.cdList) whose titles are in a set of popular CD titles (popularTitles). The Collection.contains() method is used in the predicate to determine if the title of a CD is in the set of popular CD titles. The execution of the stream pipeline shows there are only two such CDs (cd0, cd1). CDs that do not satisfy the predicate are discarded.

We can express the same query using the Collection.removeIf() method, as shown below. The code computes the same result as the stream pipeline in Figure 16.3. Note that the predicate in the remove() method call is a negation of the predicate in the filter() operation.

```
List<CD> popularCDs2 = new ArrayList<>(CD.cdList);
popularCDs2.removeIf(cd -> !(popularTitles.contains(cd.title())));
System.out.println("Query 1b: " + popularCDs2);
//Query 1b: [<Jaav, "Java Jive", 8, 2017, POP>, <Jaav, "Java Jam", 6, 2017, JAZZ>]
```

In summary, the `filter()` method implements a stateless intermediate operation. It can change the size of the stream, since elements are discarded. However, the element type of the output stream returned by the `filter()` method is the same as that of its input stream. In Figure 16.3, the input and output stream type of the `filter()` method is `Stream<CD>`. Also, the encounter order of the stream remains unchanged. In Figure 16.3, the encounter order in the output stream returned by the `filter()` method is the same as the order of the elements in the input stream—that is, the insertion order in the list of CDs.

Figure 16.3 *Filtering Stream Elements*

```
// Query 1: Find CDs whose titles are in the set of popular CD titles.
Set<String> popularTitles = Set.of("Java Jive", "Java Jazz", "Java Jam");
List<CD> popularCDs1 = CD.cdList
①    .stream()
②    .filter(cd -> popularTitles.contains(cd.title()))
③    .toList();
```

(a) Query to filter stream elements

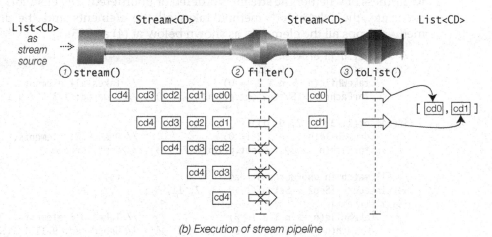

(b) Execution of stream pipeline

Taking and Dropping Elements Using Predicates

Both the `takeWhile()` and the `dropWhile()` methods find the longest prefix of elements to take or drop from the input stream, respectively.

The code below at (1) and (2) illustrates the case for ordered streams. The `take-While()` method takes odd numbers from the input stream until a number is not odd, and short-circuits the processing of the stream—that is, it truncates the rest of the stream based on the predicate. The `dropWhile()` method, on the other hand, drops odd numbers from the input stream until a number is not odd, and passes the remaining elements to its output stream; that is, it skips elements in the beginning of the stream based on the predicate.

```
// Ordered stream:
Stream.of(1, 3, 5, 7, 8, 9, 11)                    // (1)
```

```
        .takeWhile(n -> n % 2 != 0)              // Takes longest prefix: 1 3 5 7
        .forEach(n -> System.out.print(n + " ")); // 1 3 5 7

    Stream.of(1, 3, 5, 7, 8, 9, 11)              // (2)
        .dropWhile(n -> n % 2 != 0)              // Drops longest prefix:  1 3 5 7
        .forEach(n -> System.out.print(n + " ")); // 8 9 11
```

Given an unordered stream, as shown below at (3), both methods return nondeterministic results: Any subset of matching elements can be taken or dropped, respectively.

```
    // Unordered stream:
    Set<Integer> iSeq = Set.of(1, 9, 4, 3, 7);      // (3)
    iSeq.stream()
        .takeWhile(n -> n % 2 != 0)              // Takes any subset of elements.
        .forEach(n -> System.out.print(n + " "));   // Nondeterministic: 1 9 7

    iSeq.stream()
        .dropWhile(n -> n % 2 != 0)              // Drops any subset of elements.
        .forEach(n -> System.out.print(n + " "));   // Nondeterministic: 4 3
```

Regardless of whether the stream is ordered or unordered, if *all* elements match the predicate, the takeWhile() method takes all the elements and the dropWhile() method drops all the elements, as shown below at (4) and (5).

```
    // All match in ordered stream:                 (4)
    Stream.of(1, 3, 5, 7, 9, 11)
        .takeWhile(n -> n % 2 != 0)              // Takes all elements.
        .forEach(n -> System.out.print(n + " ")); // Ordered: 1 3 5 7 9 11

    Stream.of(1, 3, 5, 7, 9, 11)
        .dropWhile(n -> n % 2 != 0)              // Drops all elements.
        .forEach(n -> System.out.print(n + " ")); // Empty stream

    // All match in unordered stream:               (5)
    Set<Integer> iSeq2 = Set.of(1, 9, 3, 7, 11, 5);
    iSeq2.stream()
        .takeWhile(n -> n % 2 != 0)              // Takes all elements.
        .forEach(n -> System.out.print(n + " "));   // Unordered: 9 11 1 3 5 7

    iSeq2.stream()
        .dropWhile(n -> n % 2 != 0)              // Drops all elements.
        .forEach(n -> System.out.print(n + " "));   // Empty stream
```

Regardless of whether the stream is ordered or unordered, if *no* elements match the predicate, the takeWhile() method takes no elements and the dropWhile() method drops no elements, as shown below at (6) and (7).

```
    // No match in ordered stream:                  (6)
    Stream.of(2, 4, 6, 8, 10, 12)
        .takeWhile(n -> n % 2 != 0)              // Takes no elements.
        .forEach(n -> System.out.print(n + " ")); // Empty stream

    Stream.of(2, 4, 6, 8, 10, 12)
        .dropWhile(n -> n % 2 != 0)              // Drops no elements.
        .forEach(n -> System.out.print(n + " ")); // Ordered: 2 4 6 8 10 12
```

```
// No match in unordered stream:                    (7)
Set<Integer> iSeq3 = Set.of(2, 10, 8, 12, 4, 6);
iSeq3.stream()
    .takeWhile(n -> n % 2 != 0)              // Takes no elements.
    .forEach(n -> System.out.print(n + " ")); // Empty stream

iSeq3.stream()
    .dropWhile(n -> n % 2 != 0)              // Drops no elements.
    .forEach(n -> System.out.print(n + " ")); // Unordered: 8 10 12 2 4 6
```

Selecting Distinct Elements

The distinct() method removes all duplicates of an element from the input stream, resulting in an output stream with only unique elements. Since the distinct() method must be able to distinguish the elements from one another and keep track of them, the stream elements must override the equals() and the hashCode() methods of the Object class. The CD objects comply with this requirement (Example 16.1, p. 883).

In Figure 16.4, Query 2 creates a list of unique CDs with pop music. The filter() operation and the distinct() operation in the stream pipeline select the CDs with pop music and those that are unique, respectively. The execution of the stream pipeline shows that the resulting list of unique CDs with pop music has only one CD (cd0).

In Figure 16.4, interchanging the stateless filter() operation and the stateful distinct() operation in the stream pipeline gives the same results, but then the more expensive distinct() operation is performed on *all* elements of the stream, rather than on a shorter stream which is returned by the filter() operation.

Skipping Elements in a Stream

The skip() operation slices off or discards a specified number of elements from the head of a stream before the remaining elements are made available to the next operation. It preserves the encounter order if the input stream has one. Not surprisingly, skipping more elements than are in the input stream returns the empty stream.

In Figure 16.5, Query 3a creates a list of jazz music CDs after skipping the first two CDs in the stream. The stream pipeline uses a skip() operation first to discard two CDs (one of them being a jazz music CD) and a filter() operation afterward to select any CDs with jazz music. The execution of this stream pipeline shows that the resulting list contains two CDs (cd3, cd4).

In the stream pipeline in Figure 16.5, the skip() operation is before the filter() operation. Switching the order of the skip() and filter() operations as in Query 3b in Example 16.5 does not solve the same query. It will skip the first two jazz music CDs selected by the filter() operation.

Figure 16.4   *Selecting Distinct Elements*

```
      // Query 2: Create a list of unique CDs with pop music.
      List<CD> miscCDList = List.of(CD.cd0, CD.cd0, CD.cd1, CD.cd0);
      List<CD> uniquePopCDs1 = miscCDList
①        .stream()
②        .filter(CD::isPop)
③        .distinct()
④        .toList();
```

(a) Selecting distinct elements in a stream

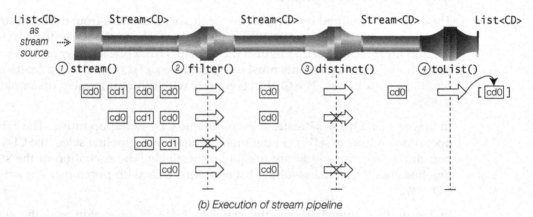

(b) Execution of stream pipeline

Figure 16.5   *Skipping Elements at the Head of a Stream*

```
      // Query 3a: Create a list of jazz CDs, after skipping the first two CDs.
      List<CD> jazzCDs1 = CD.cdList
①        .stream()
②        .skip(2)
③        .filter(CD::isJazz)
④        .toList();
```

(a) Skipping elements in a stream

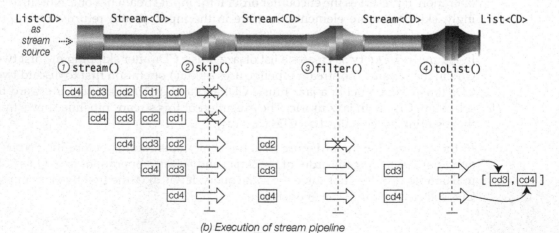

(b) Execution of stream pipeline

Truncating a Stream

The limit() operation returns an output stream whose maximum size is equal to the max size specified as an argument to the method. The input stream is only truncated if its size is greater than the specified max size.

In Figure 16.6, Query 4 creates a list with the first two CDs that were released in 2018. The stream pipeline uses a filter() operation first to select CDs released in 2018, and the limit() operation truncates the stream, if necessary, so that, at most, only two CDs are passed to its output stream. The short-circuit execution of this stream pipeline is illustrated in Figure 16.6, showing the resulting list containing two CDs (cd2, cd3). The execution of the stream pipeline terminates after the limit() operation has reached its limit if there are no more elements left to process. In Figure 16.6, we can see that the limit was reached and execution was terminated. Regardless of the fact that the last element in the initial stream was not processed, the stream cannot be reused once the execution of the pipeline terminates due to a short-circuiting operation.

Figure 16.6 *Truncating a Stream*

```
// Query 4: Create a list with the first 2 CDs that were released in 2018.
List<CD> twoFirstCDs2018 = CD.cdList
①      .stream()
②      .filter(cd -> cd.year().equals(Year.of(2018)))
③      .limit(2)
④      .toList();
```

(a) Truncating a stream

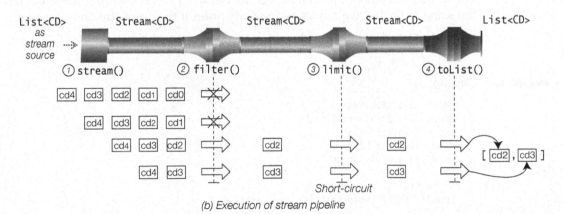

(b) Execution of stream pipeline

The limit() operation is ideal for turning an infinite stream into a finite stream. Numerous examples of using the limit() operation with the iterate() and generate() methods can be found in §16.4, p. 894, and with the Random.ints() method in §16.4, p. 900.

For a given value n, limit(n) and skip(n) are complementary operations on a stream, as limit(n) comprises the first n elements of the stream and skip(n) comprises the remaining elements in the stream. In the code below, the resultList from processing the resulting stream from concatenating the two substreams is equal to the stream source CD.cdList.

```
List<CD> resultList = Stream
    .concat(CD.cdList.stream().limit(2), CD.cdList.stream().skip(2))
    .toList();
System.out.println(CD.cdList.equals(resultList));              // true
```

The skip() operation can be used in conjunction with the limit() operation to process a substream of a stream, where the skip() operation can be used to skip to the start of the substream and the limit() operation to limit the size of the substream. The substream in the code below starts at the second element and comprises the next three elements in the stream.

```
List<CD> substream = CD.cdList
    .stream()
    .skip(1)
    .limit(3)
    .toList();
System.out.println("Query 5: " + substream);
// Query 5: [<Jaav, "Java Jam", 6, 2017, JAZZ>,
//           <Funkies, "Lambda Dancing", 10, 2018, POP>,
//           <Genericos, "Keep on Erasing", 8, 2018, JAZZ>]
```

The limit() operation is a short-circuiting stateful intermediate operation, as it needs to keep state for tracking the number of elements in the output stream. It changes the stream size, but not the stream element type or the encounter order. For an ordered stream, we can expect the elements in the resulting stream to have the same order, but we cannot assume any order if the input stream is unordered.

Example 16.5 contains the code snippets presented in this subsection.

Example 16.5   *Filtering*

```
import java.time.Year;
import java.util.ArrayList;
import java.util.List;
import java.util.Set;
import java.util.stream.Stream;

public final class Filtering {
  public static void main(String[] args) {

    // Query 1: Find CDs whose titles are in the set of popular CD titles.
    Set<String> popularTitles = Set.of("Java Jive", "Java Jazz", "Java Jam");

    // Using Stream.filter().
    List<CD> popularCDs1 = CD.cdList
        .stream()
        .filter(cd -> popularTitles.contains(cd.title()))
        .toList();
    System.out.println("Query 1a: " + popularCDs1);
```

```java
// Using Collection.removeIf().
List<CD> popularCDs2 = new ArrayList<>(CD.cdList);
popularCDs2.removeIf(cd -> !(popularTitles.contains(cd.title())));
System.out.println("Query 1b: " + popularCDs2);

// Query 2: Create a list of unique CDs with pop music.
List<CD> miscCDList = List.of(CD.cd0, CD.cd0, CD.cd1, CD.cd0);
List<CD> uniquePopCDs1 = miscCDList
    .stream()
    .filter(CD::isPop)
    .distinct()                               // distinct() after filter()
    .toList();
System.out.println("Query 2: " + uniquePopCDs1);

// Query 3a: Create a list of jazz CDs, after skipping the first two CDs.
List<CD> jazzCDs1 = CD.cdList
    .stream()
    .skip(2)                                  // skip() before filter().
    .filter(CD::isJazz)
    .toList();
System.out.println("Query 3a: " + jazzCDs1);

// Query 3b: Create a list of jazz CDs, but skip the first two jazz CDs.
List<CD> jazzCDs2 = CD.cdList                 // Not equivalent to Query 3
    .stream()
    .filter(CD::isJazz)
    .skip(2)                                  // skip() after filter().
    .toList();
System.out.println("Query 3b: " + jazzCDs2);

// Query 4: Create a list with the first 2 CDs that were released in 2018.
List<CD> twoFirstCDs2018 = CD.cdList
    .stream()
    .filter(cd -> cd.year().equals(Year.of(2018)))
    .limit(2)
    .toList();
System.out.println("Query 4: " + twoFirstCDs2018);

// limit(n) and skip(n) are complementary.
List<CD> resultList = Stream
    .concat(CD.cdList.stream().limit(2), CD.cdList.stream().skip(2))
    .toList();
System.out.println(CD.cdList.equals(resultList));

// Query 5: Process a substream by skipping 1 and limiting the size to 3.
List<CD> substream = CD.cdList
    .stream()
    .skip(1)
    .limit(3)
    .toList();
System.out.println("Query 5: " + substream);
    }
}
```

Output from the program (*formatted to fit on the page*):

```
Query 1a: [<Jaav, "Java Jive", 8, 2017, POP>, <Jaav, "Java Jam", 6, 2017, JAZZ>]
Query 1b: [<Jaav, "Java Jive", 8, 2017, POP>, <Jaav, "Java Jam", 6, 2017, JAZZ>]
Query 2: [<Jaav, "Java Jive", 8, 2017, POP>]
Query 3a: [<Genericos, "Keep on Erasing", 8, 2018, JAZZ>,
            <Genericos, "Hot Generics", 10, 2018, JAZZ>]
Query 3b: [<Genericos, "Hot Generics", 10, 2018, JAZZ>]
Query 4: [<Funkies, "Lambda Dancing", 10, 2018, POP>,
           <Genericos, "Keep on Erasing", 8, 2018, JAZZ>]
true
Query 5: [<Jaav, "Java Jam", 6, 2017, JAZZ>,
           <Funkies, "Lambda Dancing", 10, 2018, POP>,
           <Genericos, "Keep on Erasing", 8, 2018, JAZZ>]
```

Examining Elements in a Stream

The peek() operation allows stream elements to be examined at the point where the operation is used in the stream pipeline. It does not affect the stream in any way, as it only facilitates a side effect via a non-interfering *consumer* specified as an argument to the operation. It is primarily used for debugging the pipeline by examining the elements at various points in the pipeline.

The following method is defined in the Stream<T> interface, and an analogous method is also defined in the IntStream, LongStream, and DoubleStream interfaces:

Stream<T> peek(Consumer<? super T> action)

Returns a stream consisting of the same elements as those in this stream, but additionally performs the provided non-interfering action on each element as elements are processed from this stream.

This is a stateless intermediate operation that does not change the stream size, the stream element type, or the encounter order.

By using the peek() method, we can dispense with explicit print statements that were inserted in the implementation of the behavioral parameter of the map() operation in Example 16.4, p. 909. Example 16.6 shows how the peek() operation can be used to trace the processing of elements in the pipeline. A peek() operation after each intermediate operation prints pertinent information which can be used to verify the workings of the pipeline. In Example 16.6, the output shows that the skip() operation before the map() operation can improve performance, as the skip() operation shortens the stream on which the map() operation should be performed.

Example 16.6 *Examining Stream Elements*

```
import java.util.List;

public final class OrderOfOperationsWithPeek {
  public static void main(String[] args) {
```

```
        System.out.println("map() before skip():");
        List<String> cdTitles1 = CD.cdList
            .stream()
            .map(CD::title)
            .peek(t -> System.out.println("After map: " + t))
            .skip(3)
            .peek(t -> System.out.println("After skip: " + t))
            .toList();
        System.out.println(cdTitles1);
        System.out.println();

        System.out.println("skip() before map():");            // Preferable.
        List<String> cdTitles2 = CD.cdList
            .stream()
            .skip(3)
            .peek(cd -> System.out.println("After skip: " + cd))
            .map(CD::title)
            .peek(t -> System.out.println("After map: " + t))
            .toList();
        System.out.println(cdTitles2);
    }
}
```

Output from the program:

```
map() before skip():
After map: Java Jive
After map: Java Jam
After map: Lambda Dancing
After map: Keep on Erasing
After skip: Keep on Erasing
After map: Hot Generics
After skip: Hot Generics
[Keep on Erasing, Hot Generics]

skip() before map():
After skip: <Genericos, "Keep on Erasing", 8, 2018, JAZZ>
After map: Keep on Erasing
After skip: <Genericos, "Hot Generics", 10, 2018, JAZZ>
After map: Hot Generics
[Keep on Erasing, Hot Generics]
```

Mapping: Transforming Streams

The map() operation has already been used in several examples (Example 16.3, p. 906, Example 16.4, p. 909, and Example 16.6, p. 920). Here we take a closer look at this essential intermediate operation for data processing using a stream. It maps one type of stream (Stream<T>) into another type of stream (Stream<R>); that is, *each* element of type T in the input stream is mapped to an element of type R in the output stream by the function (Function<T, R>) supplied to the map() method. It defines a *one-to-one mapping*. For example, if we are interested in the *titles* of CDs in the CD stream, we can use the map() operation to transform each CD in the stream to a String that represents the title of the CD by applying an appropriate function:

```
Stream<String> titles = CD.cdList
        .stream()                          // Input stream: Stream<CD>.
        .map(CD::title);                   // Lambda expression: cd -> cd.title()
```

The following methods are defined in the Stream<T> interface, and analogous methods are also defined in the IntStream, LongStream, and DoubleStream interfaces:

<R> Stream<R> map(Function<? super T,? extends R> mapper)

Returns a stream consisting of the result of applying the given non-interfering, stateless function to the elements of this stream—that is, it creates a new stream (Stream<R>) from the results of applying the mapper function to the elements of this stream (Stream<T>).

This is an intermediate operation that does not change the stream size, but it can change the stream element type and does not guarantee to preserve the encounter order of the input stream.

```
// Converting Stream<T> to a Numeric Stream
IntStream     mapToInt(ToIntFunction<? super T> mapper)
LongStream    mapToLong(ToLongFunction<? super T> mapper)
DoubleStream  mapToDouble(ToDoubleFunction<? super T> mapper)
```

Return the numeric stream consisting of the results of applying the given non-interfering, stateless function to the elements of this stream—that is, they create a stream of numeric values that are the results of applying the mapper function to the elements of this stream (Stream<T>).

These operations are all intermediate operations that transform an object stream to a numeric stream. The stream size is not affected, but there is no guarantee that the encounter order of the input stream is preserved.

In Figure 16.7, the query creates a list with CD titles released in 2018. The stream pipeline uses a filter() operation first to select CDs released in 2018, and the map() operation maps a CD to its title (String). The input stream is transformed by the map() operation from Stream<CD> to Stream<String>. The execution of this stream pipeline shows the resulting list (List<String>) containing three CD titles.

The query below illustrates transforming an object stream to a numeric stream. When executed, the stream pipeline prints the years in which the CDs were released. Note the transformation of the initial stream, Stream<CD>. The map() operation first transforms it to a Stream<Year> and the distinct() operation selects the unique years. The mapToInt() operation transforms the stream from Stream<Year> to IntStream—that is, a stream of ints whose values are then printed.

```
CD.cdList.stream()                         // Stream<CD>
        .map(CD::year)                     // Stream<Year>
        .distinct()                        // Stream<Year>
        .mapToInt(Year::getValue)          // IntStream
        .forEach(System.out::println);     // 2017
                                           // 2018
```

Figure 16.7 *Mapping*

```
// Query: Create a list of CD titles released in 2018.
List<String> listOfCDNames = CD.cdList
    .stream()                                              // Stream<CD>
    .filter(cd -> cd.year().equals(Year.of(2018)))         // Stream<CD>
    .map(CD::title)                                        // Stream<String>
    .toList();                                             // List<String>
```

(a) Query using the `Stream.map()` *method*

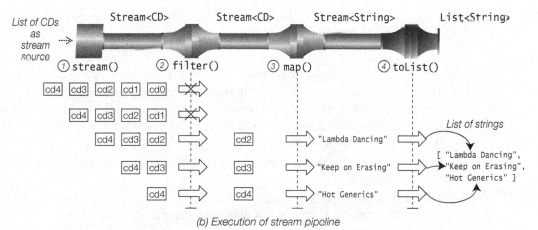

(b) Execution of stream pipeline

In the example below, the `range()` method generates an `int` stream for values in the half-open interval specified by its arguments. The values are generated in *increasing* order, starting with the lower bound of the interval. In order to generate them in *decreasing* order, the `map()` operation can be used to reverse the values. In this case, the input stream and output stream of the `map()` operation are both `IntStreams`.

```
int from = 0, to = 5;
IntStream.range(from, to)                   // [0, 5)
    .map(i -> to + from - 1 - i)            // Reverse the stream values
    .forEach(System.out::print);           // 43210
```

The stream pipeline below determines the number of times the dice value is 6. The `generate()` method generates a value between 1 and 6, and the `limit()` operation limits the max size of the stream. The `map()` operation returns the value 1 if the dice value is 6; otherwise, it returns 0. In other words, the value of the dice throw is mapped either to 1 or 0, depending on the dice value. The terminal operation `sum()` sums the values in the streams, which in this case are either 1 or 0, thus returning the correct number of times the dice value was 6.

```
long sixes = IntStream
    .generate(() -> (int) (6.0 * Math.random()) + 1) // [1, 6]
    .limit(2000)                                     // Number of throws.
    .map(i -> i == 6 ? 1 : 0)                        // Dice value mapped to 1 or 0.
    .sum();
```

Flattening Streams

The flatMap() operation first maps each element in the input stream to *a mapped stream*, and then *flattens* the mapped streams to a *single* stream—that is, the elements of each mapped stream are incorporated into a single stream when the pipeline is executed. In other words, each element in the input stream may be mapped to many elements in the output stream. The flatMap() operation thus defines a *one-to-many mapping* that flattens a multilevel stream by one level.

The following method is defined in the Stream<T> interface, and an analogous method is also defined in the IntStream, LongStream, and DoubleStream interfaces:

```
<R> Stream<R> flatMap(
                Function<? super T,? extends Stream<? extends R>> mapper)
```

The mapper function maps each element of type T in this stream to a *mapped stream* (Stream<R>). The method returns an output stream (Stream<R>) which is the result of replacing each element of type T in this stream with the *elements* of type R from its mapped stream.

If the result of the mapper function is null, the empty stream is used as the mapped stream.

This is an intermediate operation that changes the stream size and the element type of the stream, and does not guarantee to preserve the encounter order of the input stream.

The methods below are defined only in the Stream<T> interface. No counterparts exist in the IntStream, LongStream, or DoubleStream interfaces:

```
IntStream    flatMapToInt(Function<? super T,? extends IntStream> mapper)
LongStream   flatMapToLong(Function<? super T,? extends LongStream> mapper)
DoubleStream flatMapToDouble(
                Function<? super T,? extends DoubleStream> mapper)
```

The mapper function maps each element of type T in this stream to a *mapped numeric stream* (*NumType*Stream). The method returns an output stream (*NumType*Stream), which is the result of replacing each element of type T in this stream with the *values* from its mapped numeric stream. The designation *NumType* stands for Int, Long, or Double.

To motivate using the flatMap() operation, we look at how to express the query for creating a list of unique CDs from two given lists of CDs. Figure 16.8 shows an attempt to express this query by creating a stream of lists of CDs, Stream<List<CD>>, and selecting the unique CDs using the distinct() method. This attempt fails miserably as the distinct() method distinguishes between elements that are lists of CDs, and not individual CDs. Figure 16.8 shows the execution of the stream pipeline resulting in a list of lists of CDs, List<List<CD>>.

The next attempt to express the query uses the map() operation as shown in Figure 16.9. The idea is to map each list of CDs (List<CD>) to a stream of CDs (Stream<CD>), and select the unique CDs with the distinct() operation. The mapper

Figure 16.8 *Incorrect Solution to the Query*

```
// Query: Create a list of unique CDs from two given lists of CDs.
List<List<CD>> listOfListOfCDs =
①    Stream.of(cdList1, cdList2)              // Stream<List<CD>>
②      .distinct()                           // Stream<List<CD>>
③      .toList());                           // List<List<CD>>
```

(a) Incorrect solution using the `Stream.distinct()` *method*

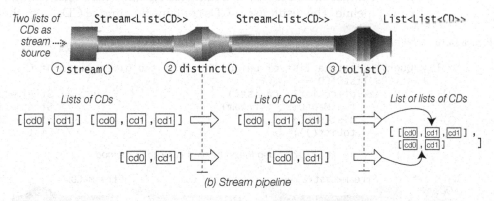

(b) Stream pipeline

Figure 16.9 *Mapping a Stream of Streams*

```
// Query: Create a list of unique CDs from two given lists of CDs.
List<Stream<CD>> listOfStreamOfCD =
①    Stream.of(cdList1, cdList2)              // Stream<List<CD>>
②      .map(List::stream)                    // Stream<Stream<CD>>
③      .distinct()                           // Stream<Stream<CD>>
④      .toList();                            // List<Stream<CD>>
```

(a) Incorrect solution using the `Stream.map()` *method*

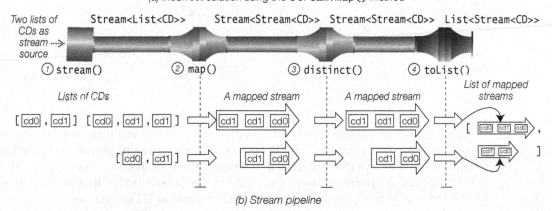

(b) Stream pipeline

function of the map() operation maps each list of CDs to *a mapped stream* that is a stream of CDs, Stream<CD>. The resulting stream from the map() operation is a stream of streams of CDs, Stream<Stream<CD>>. The distinct() method distinguishes between elements that are mapped streams of CDs. Figure 16.9 shows the execution of the stream pipeline resulting in a list of mapped streams of CDs, List<Stream<CD>>.

The flatMap() operation provides the solution, as it flattens the contents of the mapped streams into a single stream so that the distinct() operation can select the unique CDs individually. The stream pipeline using the flatMap() operation and its execution are shown in Figure 16.10. The mapper function of the flatMap() operation maps each list of CDs to a mapped stream that is a stream of CDs, Stream<CD>. The contents of the mapped stream are flattened into the output stream. The resulting stream from the flatMap() operation is a stream of CDs, Stream<CD>. Note how each list in the initial stream results in a flattened stream whose elements are processed by the pipeline. The result list of CDs contains the unique CDs from the two lists.

Figure 16.10 *Flattening Streams*

```
//Query: Create a list of unique CDs from two given lists of CDs.
List<CD> listOfCD =
①    Stream.of(cdList1, cdList2)              // Stream<List<CD>>
②        .flatMap(List::stream)              // Stream<CD>
③        .distinct()                          // Stream<CD>
④        .toList());                          // List<CD>
```

(a) Solution using the Stream.flatMap() *method*

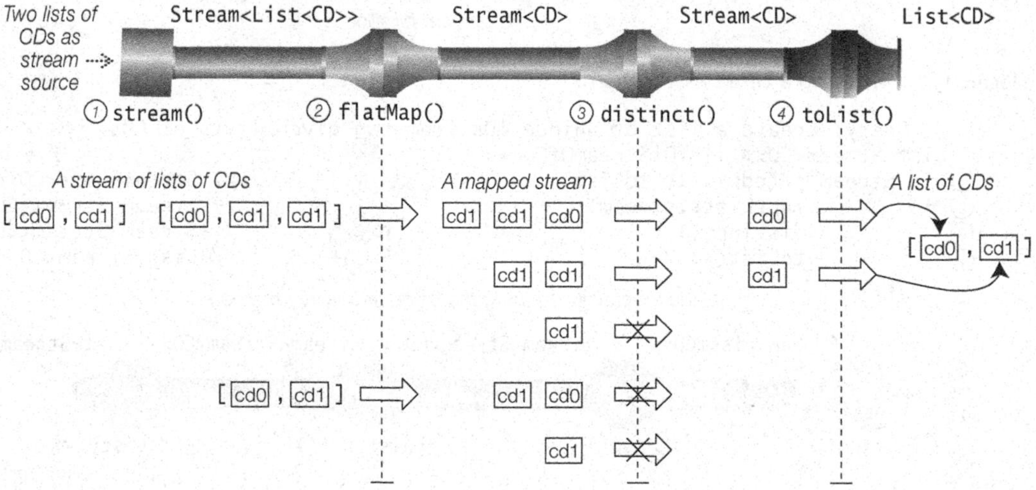

(b) Stream pipeline

The code below flattens a two-dimensional array to a one-dimensional array. The Arrays.stream() method call at (1) creates an object stream, Stream<int[]>, whose elements are arrays that are rows in the two-dimensional array. The mapper of the flatMapToInt() operation maps each row in the Stream<int[]> to a stream of ints (IntStream) by applying the Array.stream() method at (2) to each row. This would result in a stream of mapped streams of ints (Stream<IntStream>), but it is flattened by the flatMapToInt() operation to a final stream of ints (IntStream). The terminal operation toArray() creates an appropriate array in which the int values of the final stream are stored (p. 971).

```
int[][] twoDimArray = { {2017, 2018}, {1948, 1949} };
int[] intArray = Arrays
    .stream(twoDimArray)                    // (1) Stream<int[]>
    .flatMapToInt(row -> Arrays.stream(row)) // (2) mapper: int[] -> IntStream,
                                            // flattens Stream<IntStream> to IntStream.
    .toArray();                             // [2017, 2018, 1948, 1949]
```

Replacing Each Element of a Stream with Multiple Elements

The mapMulti() intermediate operation applies a *one-to-many transformation* to the elements of the stream and flattens the result elements into a new stream. The functionality of the mapMulti() method is very similar to that of the flatMap() method. Whereas the latter uses a Function<T, Stream<R>> mapper to create a *mapping stream* for each element and then flattens the stream, the former applies a BiConsumer<T, Consumer<R>> mapper to each element. The mapper calls the Consumer to accept the replacement elements that are incorporated into a single stream when the pipeline is executed.

The mapMulti() method can be used to perform filtering, mapping, and flat mapping of stream elements, all depending on the implementation of the BiConsumer mapper passed to the method.

The code below shows a *one-to-one transformation* of the stream elements. A BiConsumer is defined at (1) that first filters the stream for pop music CDs at (2), and maps each CD to a string that contains its title and its number of tracks represented by an equivalent number of "*" characters. The resulting string is submitted at (3) to the consumer (supplied by the mapMulti() method). Each value passed to the accept() method of the consumer replaces the current element in the stream. Note that the body of the BiConsumer is implemented in an *imperative* manner using an if statement. The BiConsumer created at (1) is passed to the mapMulti() method at (5) to process the CDs of the stream created at (4). The mapMulti() method passes an appropriate Consumer to the BiConsumer that accepts the replacement elements.

```
// One-to-one
BiConsumer<CD, Consumer<String>> bcA = (cd, consumer) -> {     // (1)
  if (cd.genre() == Genre.POP) {                               // (2)
    consumer.accept(String.format("%-15s: %s", cd.title(),     // (3)
                          "*".repeat(cd.noOfTracks())));
  }
};

CD.cdList.stream()                                             // (4)
        .mapMulti(bcA)                                         // (5)
        .forEach(System.out::println);
```

Output from the code:

```
Java Jive      : ********
Lambda Dancing : **********
```

The code below shows a *one-to-many* transformation of the stream elements. The BiConsumer at (1) iterates through a list of CDs and maps each CD in the list to its title. Each list of CDs in the stream will thus be replaced with the titles of the CDs in the list. The mapMulti() operation with the BiConsumer at (1) is applied at (3) to a stream of list of CDs (Stream<List<CD>>) created at (2). The mapMulti() operation in this case is analogous to the flatMap() operation to achieve the same result.

```java
// One-to-many
List<CD> cdList1 = List.of(CD.cd0, CD.cd1, CD.cd1);
List<CD> cdList2 = List.of(CD.cd0, CD.cd1);
BiConsumer<List<CD>, Consumer<String>> bcB = (lst, consumer) -> {        // (1)
  for (CD cd : lst) {
    consumer.accept(cd.title());
  }
};
List<String> listOfCDTitles = Stream.of(cdList1, cdList2) // (2) Stream<List<CD>>
    .mapMulti(bcB)                                        // (3)
    .distinct()
    .toList();
System.out.println(listOfCDTitles);                           // [Java Jive, Java Jam]
```

The previous two code snippets first defined the BiConsumer with all relevant types specified explicitly, and then passed it to the mapMulti() method. The code below defines the implementation of the BiConsumer in the call to the mapMulti() method. We consider three alternative implementations as exemplified by (2a), (2b), and (2c).

Alternative (2a) results in a compile-time error. The reason is that the compiler cannot unequivocally infer the actual type parameter R of the consumer parameter of the lambda expression. It can only infer that the type of the lst parameter is List<CD> as it denotes an element of stream whose type is Stream<List<CD>>. The compiler makes the safest assumption that the type parameter R is Object. With this assumption, the resulting list is of type List<Object>, but this cannot be assigned to a reference of type List<String>, as declared in the assignment statement. To avoid the compile-time error in this case, we can change the type of the reference to Object or to the wildcard ?.

Alternative (2b) uses the type witness <String> in the call to the mapMulti() method to explicitly corroborate the actual type parameter of the consumer.

Alternative (2c) explicitly specifies the types for the parameters of the lambda expression.

```java
List<String> listOfCDTitles2 = Stream.of(cdList1,cdList2) // (1) Stream<List<CD>>
//   .mapMulti((lst, consumer) -> {                       // (2a) Compile-time error!
//   .<String>mapMulti((lst, consumer) -> {               // (2b) OK.
     .mapMulti((List<CD> lst, Consumer<String> consumer) -> {   // (2c) OK.
       for (CD cd : lst) {
         consumer.accept(cd.title());
       }
     })
     .distinct()
     .toList();
System.out.println(listOfCDTitles2);                         // [Java Jive, Java Jam]
```

The mapMulti() method is preferable to the flatMap() method under the following circumstances:

- When an element is to be replaced with a small number of elements, or none at all. The mapMulti() method avoids the overhead of creating a mapped stream for each element, as done by the flatMap() method.

- When an *imperative approach* for creating replacement elements is easier than using a stream.

The following default method is defined in the Stream<T> interface, and an analogous method is also defined in the IntStream, LongStream, and DoubleStream interfaces:

```
default <R> Stream<R> mapMulti(
            BiConsumer<? super T,? super Consumer<R>> mapper)
```

Returns a stream that is a result of replacing each element of this stream with multiple elements, specifically zero or more elements.

The specified mapper is applied to each element in conjunction with a *consumer* that *accepts* replacement elements. The mapper calls the consumer zero or more times to accept the replacement elements.

Note that the consumer is supplied by the mapMulti() method, and called by the mapper to accept replacement elements. An element of type T is replaced with zero or more elements of type R.

This is an intermediate operation that changes the stream size and the element type of the stream, and does not guarantee to preserve the encounter order of the input stream.

The following default methods are defined only in the Stream<T> interface. No counterparts exist in the IntStream, LongStream, or DoubleStream interfaces:

```
default IntStream
        mapMultiToInt(BiConsumer<? super T,? super IntConsumer> mapper)
default LongStream
        mapMultiToLong(BiConsumer<? super T,? super LongConsumer> mapper)
default DoubleStream
        mapMultiToDouble(BiConsumer<? super T,? super DoubleConsumer> mapper)
```

Return an IntStream, LongStream, and DoubleStream, respectively, consisting of the results of replacing each element of this stream with multiple elements, specifically zero or more elements.

Sorted Streams

The sorted() intermediate operation can be used to enforce a specific encounter order on the elements of the stream. It is important to note that the data source is *not* sorted; only the order of the elements in the stream is affected when a stream is sorted. It is an expensive stateful operation, as state must be kept for all elements in the stream before making them available in the resulting stream.

The following methods are defined in the Stream<T> interface, but only the first method is defined in the IntStream, LongStream, and DoubleStream interfaces:

```
Stream<T> sorted()
Stream<T> sorted(Comparator<? super T> cmp)
```

Return a stream containing the elements of this stream, sorted according to natural order or according to total order defined by the specified comparator, respectively.

The first method requires that the elements implement the Comparable<T> interface.

The sorting operation provides a *stability guarantee* for ordered streams only—that is, duplicates of an element will be in their encounter order in the resulting stream.

This is a stateful intermediate operation that does not change the size of the stream or the stream element type, and enforces the sort order to be the encounter order of the resulting stream.

The Comparable<E> and Comparator<E> interfaces are covered in §14.4, p. 761, and §14.5, p. 769, respectively.

Example 16.7 illustrates the sorted() operation on streams. Printing the array at (1) and executing the stream pipeline at (2) shows that the order of the elements in the array and in the stream is *positional order*, as one would expect. The zero-argument sorted() method sorts in *natural order*, as in the pipeline at (3). It expects the stream elements to implement the Comparable<CD> interface. The sorted() method in the pipeline at (4) uses the *reverse natural order* to sort the elements.

The pipeline at (5) represents the query to find all jazz music CDs and sort them by their title. A comparator to compare by title is passed to the sorted() method. Finally, the pipeline at (6) finds CDs with eight or more tracks, and sorts them according to the number of tracks. An appropriate comparator that compares by the number of tracks is passed to the sorted() method.

It is instructive to compare the output showing the results from each pipeline in Example 16.7. The comparators in Example 16.7 are also implemented as lambda expressions, in addition to their implementation by the methods in the Comparator<E> interface.

- -

Example 16.7 *Sorting Streams*

```
import java.util.Arrays;
import java.util.Comparator;
import java.util.List;

public class Sorting {
  public static void main(String[] args) {

    System.out.println("(1) Positional order in the array:");
```

```
        CD[] cdArray = CD.cdArray;
        System.out.println(Arrays.toString(cdArray));              // (1)

        System.out.println("(2) Positional order in the stream:");
        List<CD> cdsByPositionalOrder =                           // (2)
          Arrays.stream(cdArray)
              .toList();
        System.out.println(cdsByPositionalOrder);

        System.out.println("(3) Natural order:");
        List<CD> cdsByNaturalOrder =                              // (3)
          Arrays.stream(cdArray)
              .sorted()
              .toList();
        System.out.println(cdsByNaturalOrder);

        System.out.println("(4) Reversed natural order:");
        List<CD> cdsByRNO =                                       // (4)
          Arrays.stream(cdArray)
//            .sorted((c1, c2) -> -c1.compareTo(c2))
              .sorted(Comparator.reverseOrder())
              .toList();
        System.out.println(cdsByRNO);

        System.out.println("(5) Only Jazz CDs, ordered by title:");
        List<String> jazzCDsByTitle =                             // (5)
          Arrays.stream(cdArray)
              .filter(CD::isJazz)
//            .sorted((c1, c2) -> c1.title().compareTo(c2.title()))
              .sorted(Comparator.comparing(CD::title))
              .map(CD::title)
              .toList();
        System.out.println(jazzCDsByTitle);

        System.out.println("(6) No. of tracks >= 8, ordered by number of tracks:");
        List<CD> cds =                                            // (6)
          Arrays.stream(cdArray)
              .filter(d -> d.noOfTracks() >= 8)
//            .sorted((c1, c2) -> c1.noOfTracks() - c2.noOfTracks())
              .sorted(Comparator.comparing(CD::noOfTracks))
              .toList();
        System.out.println(cds);
    }
}
```

Output from the program (*formatted to fit on the page*):

```
(1) Positional order in the array:
[<Jaav, "Java Jive", 8, 2017, POP>,
 <Jaav, "Java Jam", 6, 2017, JAZZ>,
 <Funkies, "Lambda Dancing", 10, 2018, POP>,
 <Genericos, "Keep on Erasing", 8, 2018, JAZZ>,
 <Genericos, "Hot Generics", 10, 2018, JAZZ>]
(2) Positional order in the stream:
[<Jaav, "Java Jive", 8, 2017, POP>,
 <Jaav, "Java Jam", 6, 2017, JAZZ>,
```

```
     <Funkies, "Lambda Dancing", 10, 2018, POP>,
     <Genericos, "Keep on Erasing", 8, 2018, JAZZ>,
     <Genericos, "Hot Generics", 10, 2018, JAZZ>]
     (3) Natural order:
     [<Funkies, "Lambda Dancing", 10, 2018, POP>,
      <Genericos, "Hot Generics", 10, 2018, JAZZ>,
      <Genericos, "Keep on Erasing", 8, 2018, JAZZ>,
      <Jaav, "Java Jam", 6, 2017, JAZZ>,
      <Jaav, "Java Jive", 8, 2017, POP>]
     (4) Reversed natural order:
     [<Jaav, "Java Jive", 8, 2017, POP>,
      <Jaav, "Java Jam", 6, 2017, JAZZ>,
      <Genericos, "Keep on Erasing", 8, 2018, JAZZ>,
      <Genericos, "Hot Generics", 10, 2018, JAZZ>,
      <Funkies, "Lambda Dancing", 10, 2018, POP>]
     (5) Only Jazz CDs, ordered by title:
     [Hot Generics, Java Jam, Keep on Erasing]
     (6) No. of tracks >= 8, ordered by number of tracks:
     [<Jaav, "Java Jive", 8, 2017, POP>,
      <Genericos, "Keep on Erasing", 8, 2018, JAZZ>,
      <Funkies, "Lambda Dancing", 10, 2018, POP>,
      <Genericos, "Hot Generics", 10, 2018, JAZZ>]
```

Setting a Stream as Unordered

The unordered() intermediate operation does not actually reorder the elements in the stream to make them unordered. It just removes *the ordered constraint* on a stream if this constraint is set for the stream, indicating that stream operations can choose to ignore its encounter order. Indicating the stream to be unordered can improve the performance of some operations. For example, the limit(), skip(), and distinct() operations can improve performance when executed on unordered parallel streams, since they can process *any* elements by ignoring the encounter order. The removal of the ordered constraint can impact the performance of certain operations on parallel streams (p. 1015).

It clearly makes sense to call the unordered() method on an ordered stream only if the order is of no consequence in the final result. There is no method called ordered to impose an order on a stream. However, the sorted() intermediate operation can be used to enforce a sort order on the output stream.

In the stream pipeline below, the unordered() method clears the ordered constraint on the stream whose elements have the same order as in the data source—that is, the positional order in the list of CDs. The outcome of the execution shows that the titles in the result list are in the same order as they are in the data source; this is the same result one would get without the unordered() operation. It is up to the stream operation to take into consideration that the stream is unordered. The fact that the result list retains the order does not make it invalid. After all, since the stream is set as unordered, it indicates that ignoring the order is at the discretion of the stream operation.

```
//Query: Create a list with the first 2 Jazz CD titles.
List<String> first2JazzCDTitles = CD.cdList
    .stream()
    .unordered()                    // Don't care about ordering.
    .filter(CD::isJazz)
    .limit(2)
    .map(CD::title)
    .toList();                      // [Java Jam, Keep on Erasing]
```

The following method is inherited by the Stream<T> interface from its superinterface BaseStream. Analogous methods are also inherited by the IntStream, LongStream, and DoubleStream interfaces from the superinterface BaseStream.

Stream<T> unordered()

Returns an unordered sequential stream that has the same elements as this stream. The method returns itself if this stream is already unordered. The method can only indicate that the encounter order of this stream can be ignored, and an operation might not comply to this request.

This is an intermediate operation that does not change the stream size or the stream element type. It only indicates that the encounter order can be ignored.

Execution Mode of a Stream

The two methods parallel() and sequential() are intermediate operations that can be used to set the execution mode of a stream—that is, whether it will execute sequentially or in parallel. Only the Collection.parallelStream() method creates a parallel stream from a collection, so the default mode of execution for most streams is sequential, unless the mode is specifically changed by calling the parallel() method. The execution mode of a stream can be switched between sequential and parallel execution at any point between stream creation and the terminal operation in the pipeline. However, it is the *last* call to any of these methods that determines the execution mode for the *entire* pipeline, regardless of how many times these methods are called in the pipeline.

The declaration statements below show examples of both sequential and parallel streams. No stream pipeline is executed, as no terminal operation is invoked on any of the streams. However, when a terminal operation is invoked on one of the streams, the stream will be executed in the mode indicated for the stream.

```
Stream<CD> seqStream1
  = CD.cdList.stream().filter(CD::isPop);                            // Sequential
Stream<CD> seqStream2
  = CD.cdList.stream().sequential().filter(CD::isPop);              // Sequential
Stream<CD> seqStream3
  = CD.cdList.stream().parallel().filter(CD::isPop).sequential(); // Sequential
Stream<CD> paraStream1
  = CD.cdList.stream().parallel().filter(CD::isPop);                // Parallel
Stream<CD> paraStream2
  = CD.cdList.stream().filter(CD::isPop).parallel();                // Parallel
```

The isParallel() method can be used to determine the execution mode of a stream. For example, the call to the isParallel() method on seqStream3 below shows that this stream is a sequential stream. It is the call to the `sequential()` method that occurs last in the pipeline that determines the execution mode.

```
System.out.println(seqStream3.isParallel());                    // false
```

Parallel streams are explored further in §16.9, p. 1009.

The following methods are inherited by the `Stream<T>` interface from its superinterface `BaseStream`. Analogous methods are also inherited by the `IntStream`, `LongStream`, and `DoubleStream` interfaces from the superinterface `BaseStream`.

```
Stream<T> parallel()
Stream<T> sequential()
```

Set the execution mode of a stream. They return a parallel or a sequential stream that has the same elements as this stream, respectively. Each method will return itself if this stream is already parallel or sequential, respectively.

These are intermediate operations that do not change the stream size, the stream element type, or the encounter order.

```
boolean isParallel()
```

Returns whether this stream would execute in parallel when the terminal operation is invoked. The method might yield unpredictable results if called after a terminal operation has been invoked.

It is *not* an intermediate operation.

Converting between Stream Types

Table 16.2 provides a summary of interoperability between stream types—that is, transforming between different stream types. Where necessary, the methods are shown with the name of the built-in functional interface required as a parameter. Selecting a naming convention for method names makes it easy to select the right method for transforming one stream type to another.

Table 16.2   *Interoperability between Stream Types*

Stream types	To Stream<R>	To IntStream	To LongStream	To DoubleStream
From `Stream<T>`	map(Function) flatMap(Function)	mapToInt(ToIntFunction) flatMapToInt(Function)	mapToLong(ToLongFunction) flatMapToLong(Function)	mapToDouble(ToDoubleStream) flatMapToDouble(Function)
From `IntStream`	mapToObj(IntFunction) Stream<Integer> boxed()	map(IntUnary- Operator) flatMap(IntFunction)	mapToLong(IntToLong- Function) asLongStream()	mapToDouble(IntToDouble- Function) asDoubleStream()

Table 16.2 *Interoperability between Stream Types (Continued)*

Stream types	To Stream<R>	To IntStream	To LongStream	To DoubleStream
From LongStream	mapToObj(LongFunction) Stream<Long> boxed()	mapToInt(LongToInt- Function)	map(LongUnary- Operator) flatMap(LongFunction)	mapToDouble(LongToDouble- Function) asDoubleStream()
From DoubleStream	mapToObj(DoubleFunction) Stream<Double> boxed()	mapToInt(DoubleToInt- Function)	mapToLong(DoubleToLong- Function)	map(DoubleUnary- Operator) flatMap(DoubleFunction)

Mapping between Object Streams

The map() and flatMap() methods of the Stream<T> interface transform an object stream of type T to an object stream of type R. Examples using these two methods can be found in §16.5, p. 921, and §16.5, p. 924, respectively.

Mapping an Object Stream to a Numeric Stream

The mapTo*NumType*() methods in the Stream<T> interface transform an object stream to a stream of the designated numeric type, where *NumType* is either Int, Long, or Double.

The query below sums the number of tracks for all CDs in a list. The mapToInt() intermediate operation at (2) accepts an IntFunction that extracts the number of tracks in a CD, thereby transforming the Stream<CD> created at (1) into an IntStream. The terminal operation sum(), as the name implies, sums the values in the IntStream (p. 973).

```
int totalNumOfTracks = CD.cdList
    .stream()                        // (1) Stream<CD>
    .mapToInt(CD::noOfTracks)        // (2) IntStream
    .sum();                          // 42
```

The flatMapTo*NumType*() methods are only defined by the Stream<T> interface to flatten a multilevel object stream to a numeric stream, where *NumType* is either Int, Long, or Double.

Earlier we saw an example of flattening a two-dimensional array using the flatMapToInt() method (p. 924).

The query below sums the number of tracks for all CDs in *two* CD lists. The flatMapToInt() intermediate operation at (1) accepts a Function that maps each List<CD> in a Stream<List<CD>> to an IntStream whose values are the number of tracks in a CD contained in the list. The resulting Stream<IntStream> from the mapper function is flattened into an IntStream by the flatMapToInt() intermediate operation, thus transforming the initial `Stream<List<CD>>` into an `IntStream`. The terminal operation `sum()` sums the values in this `IntStream` (p. 973).

```
List<CD> cdList1 = List.of(CD.cd0, CD.cd1);
List<CD> cdList2 = List.of(CD.cd2, CD.cd3, CD.cd4);
int totalNumOfTracks =
    Stream.of(cdList1, cdList2)                      // Stream<List<CD>>
        .flatMapToInt(                              // (1)
            lst -> lst.stream()                     // Stream<CD>
                .mapToInt(CD::noOfTracks))          // IntStream
                                                    // Stream<IntStream>,
                                                    //   flattened to IntStream.
        .sum();                                     // 42
```

Mapping a Numeric Stream to an Object Stream

The `mapToObj()` method defined by the numeric stream interfaces transforms a numeric stream to an object stream of type `R`, and the `boxed()` method transforms a numeric stream to an object stream of its wrapper class.

The query below prints the squares of numbers in a given closed range, where the number and its square are stored as a pair in a list of size 2. The `mapToObj()` intermediate operation at (2) transforms an `IntStream` created at (1) to a `Stream<List<Integer>>`. Each list in the result stream is then printed by the `forEach()` terminal operation.

```
IntStream.rangeClosed(1, 3)                          // (1) IntStream
    .mapToObj(n -> List.of(n, n*n))                  // (2) Stream<List<Integer>>
    .forEach(p -> System.out.print(p + " "));        // [1, 1] [2, 4] [3, 9]
```

The query above can also be expressed as shown below. The `boxed()` intermediate operation transforms the `IntStream` at (3) into a `Stream<Integer>` at (4); in other words, each `int` value is boxed into an `Integer` which is then mapped by the `map()` operation at (5) to a `List<Integer>`, resulting in a `Stream<List<Integer>>` as before. The compiler will issue an error if the `boxed()` operation is omitted at (4), as the `map()` operation at (5) will be invoked on an `IntStream`, expecting an `IntUnaryFunction`, which is not the case.

```
IntStream.rangeClosed(1, 3)                          // (3) IntStream
    .boxed()                                         // (4) Stream<Integer>
    .map(n -> List.of(n, n*n))                       // (5) Stream<List<Integer>>
    .forEach(p -> System.out.print(p + " "));        // [1, 1] [2, 4] [3, 9]
```

The examples above show that the `IntStream.mapToObj()` method is equivalent to the `IntStream.boxed()` method followed by the `Stream.map()` method.

The `mapToObj()` method, in conjunction with a range of `int` values, can be used to create sublists and subarrays. The query below creates a sublist of CD titles based on a closed range whose values are used as an index in the CD list.

```
List<String> subListTitles = IntStream
    .rangeClosed(2, 3)                               // IntStream
    .mapToObj(i -> CD.cdList.get(i).title())         // Stream<String>
    .toList();                                       // [Lambda Dancing, Keep on Erasing]
```

Mapping between Numeric Streams

In contrast to the methods in the Stream<T> interface, the map() and the flatMap() methods of the numeric stream interfaces transform a numeric stream to a numeric stream of the *same* primitive type; that is, they do *not* change the type of the numeric stream.

The map() operation in the stream pipeline below does not change the type of the initial IntStream.

```
IntStream.rangeClosed(1, 3)                            // IntStream
        .map(i -> i * i)                               // IntStream
        .forEach(n -> System.out.printf("%d ", n));    // 1 4 9
```

The flatMap() operation in the stream pipeline below also does not change the type of the initial stream. Each IntStream created by the mapper function is flattened, resulting in a single IntStream.

```
IntStream.rangeClosed(1, 3)                             // IntStream
        .flatMap(i -> IntStream.rangeClosed(1, 4))      // IntStream
        .forEach(n -> System.out.printf("%d ", n));     // 1 2 3 4 1 2 3 4 1 2 3 4
```

Analogous to the methods in the Stream<T> interface, the mapTo*NumType*() methods in the numeric stream interfaces transform a numeric stream to a stream of the designated numeric type, where *NumType* is either Int, Long, or Double.

The mapToDouble() operation in the stream pipeline below transforms the initial IntStream into a DoubleStream.

```
IntStream.rangeClosed(1, 3)                            // IntStream
        .mapToDouble(i -> Math.sqrt(i))                // DoubleStream
        .forEach(d -> System.out.printf("%.2f ", d));// 1.00 1.41 1.73
```

The methods asLongStream() and asDoubleStream() in the IntStream interface transform an IntStream to a LongStream and a DoubleStream, respectively. Similarly, the method asDoubleStream() in the LongStream interface transforms a LongStream to a DoubleStream.

The asDoubleStream() operation in the stream pipeline below transforms the initial IntStream into a DoubleStream. Note how the range of int values is thereby transformed to a range of double values by the asDoubleStream() operation.

```
IntStream.rangeClosed(1, 3)                            // IntStream
        .asDoubleStream()                              // DoubleStream
        .map(d -> Math.sqrt(d))                        // DoubleStream
        .forEach(d -> System.out.printf("%.2f ", d));// 1.00 1.41 1.73
```

In the stream pipeline below, the int values in the IntStream are first boxed into Integers. In other words, the initial IntStream is transformed into an *object stream*, Stream<Integer>. The map() operation transforms the Stream<Integer> into a Stream<Double>. In contrast to using the asDoubleStream() in the stream pipeline above, note the boxing/unboxing that occurs in the stream pipeline below in the evaluation of the Math.sqrt() method, as this method accepts a double as a parameter and returns a double value.

```
IntStream.rangeClosed(1, 3)                        // IntStream
        .boxed()                                   // Stream<Integer>
        .map(n -> Math.sqrt(n))                    // Stream<Double>
        .forEach(d -> System.out.printf("%.2f ", d));// 1.00 1.41 1.73
```

Summary of Intermediate Stream Operations

Table 16.3 summarizes selected aspects of the intermediate operations.

Table 16.3   *Selected Aspects of Intermediate Stream Operations*

Intermediate operation	Stateful/ Stateless	Can change stream size	Can change stream type	Encounter order
distinct (p. 915)	*Stateful*	*Yes*	*No*	*Unchanged*
dropWhile (p. 913)	*Stateful*	*Yes*	*No*	*Unchanged*
filter (p. 910)	*Stateless*	*Yes*	*No*	*Unchanged*
flatMap (p. 921)	*Stateless*	*Yes*	*Yes*	*Not guaranteed*
limit (p. 917)	*Stateful, short-circuited*	*Yes*	*No*	*Unchanged*
map (p. 921)	*Stateless*	*No*	*Yes*	*Not guaranteed*
mapMulti (p. 927)	*Stateless*	*Yes*	*Yes*	*Not guaranteed*
parallel (p. 933)	*Stateless*	*No*	*No*	*Unchanged*
peek (p. 920)	*Stateless*	*No*	*No*	*Unchanged*
sequential (p. 933)	*Stateless*	*No*	*No*	*Unchanged*
skip (p. 915)	*Stateful*	*Yes*	*No*	*Unchanged*
sorted (p. 929)	*Stateful*	*No*	*No*	*Ordered*
takeWhile (p. 913)	*Stateful, short-circuited*	*Yes*	*No*	*Unchanged*
unordered (p. 932)	*Stateless*	*No*	*No*	*Not guaranteed*

The intermediate operations of the Stream<T> interface (including those inherited from its superinterface BaseStream<T,Stream<T>>) are summarized in Table 16.4. The type parameter declarations have been simplified, where any bounds <? super T> or <? extends T> have been replaced by <T>, without impacting the intent of a method. A reference is provided to each method in the first column. Any type parameter and return type declared by these methods are shown in column two.

The last column in Table 16.4 indicates the function type of the corresponding parameter in the previous column. It is instructive to note how the functional interface parameters provide the parameterized behavior of an operation. For example, the filter() method returns a stream whose elements satisfy a given predicate. This predicate is defined by the functional interface Predicate<T> that is implemented by a lambda expression or a method reference, and applied to each element in the stream.

The interfaces IntStream, LongStream, and DoubleStream also define analogous methods to those shown in Table 16.4, except for the flatMapToNumType() methods, where NumType is either Int, Long, or Double. A summary of additional methods defined by these numeric stream interfaces can be found in Table 16.2.

Table 16.4 *Intermediate Stream Operations*

Method name	Any type parameter + return type	Functional interface parameters	Function type of parameters
distinct (p. 915)	Stream<T>	()	
dropWhile (p. 913)	Stream<T>	(Predicate<T> predicate)	T -> boolean
filter (p. 910)	Stream<T>	(Predicate<T> predicate)	T -> boolean
flatMap (p. 921)	<R> Stream<R>	(Function<T,Stream<R>> mapper)	T -> Stream<R>
flatMapToDouble (p. 921)	DoubleStream	(Function<T,DoubleStream> mapper)	T -> DoubleStream
flatMapToInt (p. 921)	IntStream	(Function<T,IntStream> mapper)	T -> IntStream
flatMapToLong (p. 921)	LongStream	(Function<T,LongStream> mapper)	T -> LongStream
limit (p. 917)	Stream<T>	(long maxSize)	
map (p. 921)	<R> Stream<R>	(Function<T,R> mapper)	T -> R
mapMulti (p. 927)	<R> Stream<R>	(BiConsumer<T,Consumer<R>> mapper)	(T, Consumer<R>) -> void
mapToDouble (p. 921)	DoubleStream	(ToDoubleFunction<T> mapper)	T -> double
mapToInt (p. 921)	IntStream	(ToIntFunction<T> mapper)	T -> int
mapToLong (p. 921)	LongStream	(ToLongFunction<T> mapper)	T -> long
parallel (p. 933)	Stream<T>	()	
peek (p. 920)	Stream<T>	(Consumer<T> action)	T -> void
sequential (p. 933)	Stream<T>	()	
skip (p. 915)	Stream<T>	(long n)	
sorted (p. 929)	Stream<T>	()	
sorted (p. 929)	Stream<T>	(Comparator<T> cmp)	(T,T) -> int

Table 16.4   *Intermediate Stream Operations (Continued)*

Method name	Any type parameter + return type	Functional interface parameters	Function type of parameters
takeWhile (p. 913)	Stream\<T>	(Predicate\<T> predicate)	T -> boolean
unordered (p. 932)	Stream\<T>	()	

16.6   The Optional Class

When a method returns a null value, it is not always clear whether the null value represents a valid value or the *absence of a value*. Methods that can return null values invariably force their callers to check the returned value explicitly in order to avoid a NullPointerException before using the returned value. For example, method chaining, which we have seen for composing stream pipelines, becomes cumbersome if each method call must be checked to see whether it returns a null value before calling the next method, resulting in a cascade of conditional statements.

The concept of an Optional object allows the absence of a value to be handled in a systematic way, making the code robust by enforcing that a consumer of an Optional must also deal with the case when the value is absent. Taking full advantage of Optional wrappers requires using them the right way, primarily to handle situations where the value returned by a method is absent.

The generic class Optional\<T> provides a wrapper that represents either the presence or absence of a non-null value of type T. In other words, the wrapper either contains a non-null value of type T or no value at all.

Example 16.8 illustrates using objects of the Optional\<T> class.

Declaring and Returning an Optional

Example 16.8 illustrates declaring and returning an Optional. A book is represented by the Book class that has an optional blurb of type String; that is, a book may or may not have a blurb. The Optional\<T> class is parameterized with the type String in the declaration, and so is the return type of the method that returns the optional blurb.

```
class Book {
  private Optional<String> optBlurb;

  public Optional<String> getOptBlurb() { return optBlurb; }

  //...
}
```

Creating an Optional

The Optional<T> class models the absence of a value by a special singleton returned by the Optional.empty() method. In contrast to the null value, this singleton is a viable Optional object on which methods of the Optional class can be invoked without a NullPointerException being thrown.

```
static <T> Optional<T> empty()
static <T> Optional<T> of(T nonNullValue)
static <T> Optional<T> ofNullable(T value)
```

The empty() method returns an empty Optional instance; that is, it indicates *the absence of a value*.

The of() method returns an Optional with the specified value, if this value is non-null. Otherwise, a NullPointerException is thrown.

The ofNullable() method returns an Optional with the specified value, if this value is non-null. Otherwise, it returns an empty Optional.

The static Optional.of() factory method creates an Optional that encapsulates the non-null argument specified in the method call, as in the first declaration below. However, if the argument is a null value, a NullPointerException is thrown at runtime, as in the second declaration.

```
Optional<String> blurb0 = Optional.of("Java Programmers tell all!");
Optional<String> xblurb = Optional.of(null);    // NullPointerException
```

The static Optional.ofNullable() factory method also creates an Optional that encapsulates the non-null argument specified in the method call, as in the first declaration below. However, if the argument is a null value, the method returns an *empty* Optional, as in the second declaration—which is effectively the same as the third declaration below.

```
Optional<String> blurb1 = Optional.ofNullable("Program like a Java Pro!");
Optional<String> noBlurb2 = Optional.ofNullable(null);   // Optional.empty()
Optional<String> noBlurb3 = Optional.empty();
```

The blurbs above are used to initialize two Book objects (book0, book1) in Example 16.8. These Book objects with optional blurbs will be used to illustrate how to use Optional objects.

Example 16.8   *Using Optionals*

```
// File: OptionalUsage.java
import java.util.Optional;

// A book can have an optional blurb.
class Book {
  private String bookName;
  private Optional<String> optBlurb;

  public String getBookName() { return bookName; }
  public Optional<String> getOptBlurb() { return optBlurb; }
```

```java
    public Book(String bookName, Optional<String> optBlurb) {
      this.bookName = bookName;
      this.optBlurb = optBlurb;
    }
  }

  // A course can have an optional book.
  class Course {
    private Optional<Book> optBook;
    public Optional<Book> getOptBook() { return optBook; }
    public Course(Optional<Book> optBook) { this.optBook = optBook; }
  }

  public class OptionalUsage {
    public static void main(String[] args) {

      // Creating an Optional:
      Optional<String> blurb0 = Optional.of("Java Programmers tell all!");
      //Optional<String> xblurb = Optional.of(null);    // NullPointerException
      Optional<String> blurb1 = Optional.ofNullable("Program like a Java Pro!");
      Optional<String> noBlurb2 = Optional.ofNullable(null);   // Optional.empty()
      Optional<String> noBlurb3 = Optional.empty();

      // Create some books:
      Book book0 = new Book("Embarrassing Exceptions", blurb0);
      Book book1 = new Book("Dancing Lambdas", noBlurb2);      // No blurb.

      // Querying an Optional:
      if (book0.getOptBlurb().isPresent()) {
        System.out.println(book0.getOptBlurb().get());//Java Programmers tell all!
      }

      book0.getOptBlurb()
            .ifPresent(System.out::println);            //Java Programmers tell all!

//    System.out.println(book1.getOptBlurb().get());  // NoSuchElementException

      String blurb = book0.getOptBlurb()
                          .orElse("No blurb");      // "Java Programmers tell all!"
      System.out.println(blurb);

      blurb = book1.getOptBlurb().orElse("No blurb");            // "No blurb"
      System.out.println(blurb);

      blurb = book1.getOptBlurb().orElseGet(() -> "No blurb"); // "No blurb"
      System.out.println(blurb);

      //blurb = book1.getOptBlurb()                               // RuntimeException
      //             .orElseThrow(() -> new RuntimeException("No blurb"));
    }
  }
```

Output from the program:

```
    Java Programmers tell all!
    Java Programmers tell all!
```

```
Java Programmers tell all!
No blurb
No blurb
```

Querying an Optional

The presence of a value in an Optional can be determined by the isPresent() method, and the value can be obtained by calling the get() method—which is not much better than checking explicitly for the null value, but as we shall see, other methods in the Optional class alleviate this drudgery. The get() method throws a NoSuchElementException if there is no value in the Optional.

```
if (book0.getOptBlurb().isPresent()) {
    System.out.println(book0.getOptBlurb().get());      // Java Programmers tell all!
}
System.out.println(book1.getOptBlurb().get());          // NoSuchElementException
```

The idiom of determining the presence of a value and then handling the value is combined by the ifPresent() method that accepts a Consumer to handle the value if one is present. The ifPresent() method does nothing if there is no value present in the Optional.

```
book0.getOptBlurb().ifPresent(System.out::println); //Java Programmers tell all!
```

T get()

If a value is present in this Optional, the method returns that value; otherwise, it throws a NoSuchElementException.

boolean isPresent()
void ifPresent(Consumer<? super T> consumer)

The first method returns true if there is a value present in this Optional; otherwise, it returns false.

If a value is present in this Optional, the second method invokes the specified consumer with the value; otherwise, it does nothing.

T orElse(T other)
T orElseGet(Supplier<? extends T> other)
<X extends Throwable> T orElseThrow(Supplier<? extends X> exceptionSupplier)
                       throws X extends Throwable

If a value is present in this Optional, all three methods return this value.

They differ in their action when a value is not present in this Optional. The first method returns the other value. The second method invokes the specified supplier other and returns its result. The third method invokes the specified supplier exceptionSupplier and throws the exception created by this supplier.

Note that the type of argument in the first two methods must be compatible with the parameterized type of the Optional on which the method is invoked, or the compiler will issue an error.

Often, a default value should be supplied when an Optional does *not* contain a value. The orElse() method returns the value in the Optional if one is present; otherwise, it returns the value given by the argument specified in the method call.

The orElse() method in the statement below returns the blurb in the book referenced by the reference book0, as this book has a blurb.

```
String blurb = book0.getOptBlurb()
                    .orElse("No blurb");           // "Java Programmers tell all!"
```

The book referenced by the reference book1 has no blurb. Therefore, the orElse() method invoked on the optional blurb returns the argument in the method.

```
blurb = book1.getOptBlurb().orElse("No blurb");    // "No blurb"
```

For an Optional with a value, the orElseGet() method returns the value in the Optional. The orElseGet() method in the statement below returns the object supplied by the Supplier specified as an argument, since the book has no blurb.

```
blurb = book1.getOptBlurb().orElseGet(() -> "No blurb"); // "No blurb"
```

For an Optional with a value, the orElseThrow() method also returns the value in the Optional. The orElseThrow() method in the statement below throws the exception created by the Supplier specified as an argument, since the book has no blurb.

```
blurb = book1.getOptBlurb()                              // RuntimeException
            .orElseThrow(() -> new RuntimeException("No blurb"));
```

Numeric Optional Classes

An instance of the generic Optional<T> class can only encapsulate an object. To deal with optional numeric values, the java.util package also defines the following non-generic classes that can encapsulate primitive numeric values: OptionalInt, OptionalLong, and OptionalDouble. For example, an OptionalInt object encapsulates an int value.

The numeric optional classes provide methods analogous to the static factory methods of the Optional class to create a numeric optional from a numeric value and methods to query a numeric optional. The filter(), map(), and flatMap() methods are *not* defined for the numeric optional classes.

The following methods are defined in the OptionalInt, OptionalLong, and Optional-Double classes in the java.util package. In the methods below, *NumType* is Int, Long, or Double, and the corresponding *numtype* is int, long, or double.

```
static OptionalNumType empty()
static OptionalNumType of(numtype value)
```
These two methods return an empty OptionalNumType instance and an Optional-NumType with the specified value, respectively.

```
boolean isPresent()
void    ifPresent(NumTypeConsumer consumer)
```

If there is a value present in this Optional, the first method returns true. Otherwise, it returns false.

If a value is present in this Optional, the specified consumer is invoked on the value. Otherwise, it does nothing.

numtype getAs*NumType*()

If a value is present in this Optional*NumType*, the method returns the value. Otherwise, it throws a NoSuchElementException.

```
numtype orElse(numtype other)
numtype orElseGet(NumTypeSupplier other)
<X extends Throwable> numtype orElseThrow(Supplier<X> exceptionSupplier)
                                        throws X extends Throwable
```

If a value is present in this Optional*NumType*, all three methods return this value.

They differ in their action when there is no value present in this numeric optional. The first method returns the specified other value. The second method invokes the specified other supplier and returns the result. The third method throws an exception that is created by the specified supplier.

Example 16.9 illustrates using numeric optional values. A recipe has an optional number of calories that are modeled using an OptionalInt that can encapsulate an int value. Declaring, creating, and querying OptionalInt objects is analogous to that for Optional objects.

Example 16.9 *Using Numerical Optionals*

```java
// File: NumericOptionalUsage.java
import java.util.OptionalInt;

class Recipe {
  private String recipeName;
  private OptionalInt calories;    // Optional number of calories.

  public String getRecipeName() { return recipeName; }
  public OptionalInt getCalories() { return calories; }

  public Recipe(String recipeName, OptionalInt calories) {
    this.recipeName = recipeName;
    this.calories = calories;
  }
}

public final class NumericOptionalUsage {
  public static void main(String[] args) {
    // Creating an OptionalInt:
    OptionalInt optNOC0 = OptionalInt.of(3500);
    OptionalInt optNOC1 = OptionalInt.empty();
```

```
        // Creating recipes with optional number of calories:
        Recipe recipe0 = new Recipe("Mahi-mahi", optNOC0);
        Recipe recipe1 = new Recipe("Loco moco", optNOC1);

        // Querying an Optional:
        // System.out.println(recipe1.getCalories()
        //                          .getAsInt());              // NoSuchElementException
        System.out.println((recipe1.getCalories().isPresent()
            ? recipe1.getCalories().getAsInt()
              : "Unknown calories."));          // Unknown calories.

        recipe0.getCalories().ifPresent(s -> System.out.println(s + " calories."));
        System.out.println(recipe0.getCalories().orElse(0) + " calories.");
        System.out.println(recipe1.getCalories().orElseGet(() -> 0) + " calories.");
        // int noc = recipe1.getCalories()                         // RuntimeException
        //             .orElseThrow(() -> new RuntimeException("Unknown calories."));
    }
}
```

Output from the program:

```
Unknown calories.
3500 calories.
3500 calories.
0 calories.
```

16.7 Terminal Stream Operations

A stream pipeline does not execute until a terminal operation is invoked on it; that is, a stream pipeline does not start to process the stream elements until a terminal operation is initiated. A terminal operation is said to be *eager* as it executes immediately when invoked—as opposed to an intermediate operation which is *lazy*. Invoking the terminal operation results in the intermediate operations of the stream pipeline to be executed. Understandably, a terminal operation is specified as the last operation in a stream pipeline, and there can only be one such operation in a stream pipeline. A terminal operation never returns a stream, which is always done by an intermediate operation. Once the terminal operation completes, the stream is consumed and cannot be reused.

Terminal operations can be broadly grouped into three groups:

- *Operations with side effects*

    The Stream API provides two terminal operations, forEach() and forEachOrdered(), that are designed to allow side effects on stream elements (p. 948). These terminal operations do not return a value. They allow a Consumer action, specified as an argument, to be applied to every element, as they are consumed from the stream pipeline—for example, to print each element in the stream.

- *Searching operations*

  These operations perform a search operation to determine a match or find an element as explained below.

  All search operations are *short-circuit operations*; that is, the operation can terminate once the result is determined, whether or not all elements in the stream have been considered.

  Search operations can be further classified into two subgroups:

  o *Matching operations*

  The three terminal operations anyMatch(), allMatch(), and noneMatch() determine whether stream elements match a given Predicate specified as an argument to the method (p. 949). As expected, these operations return a boolean value to indicate whether the match was successful or not.

  o *Finding operations*

  The two terminal operations findAny() and findFirst() find any element and the first element in a stream, respectively, if such an element is available (p. 952). As the stream might be empty and such an element might not exist, these operations return an Optional.

- *Reduction operations*

  A *reduction* operation computes a result from combining the stream elements by successively applying a combining function; that is, the stream elements are *reduced* to a result value. Examples of reductions are computing the sum or average of numeric values in a numeric stream, and accumulating stream elements into a collection.

  We distinguish between two kinds of reductions:

  o *Functional reduction*

  A terminal operation is a functional reduction on the elements of a stream if it reduces the elements to a *single immutable value* which is then returned by the operation.

  The overloaded reduce() method provided by the Stream API can be used to implement customized functional reductions (p. 955), whereas the terminal operations count(), min(), and max() implement specialized functional reductions (p. 953).

  Functional reductions on numeric streams are discussed later in this section (p. 972).

  o *Mutable reduction*

  A terminal operation performs a *mutable reduction* on the elements of a stream if it uses a *mutable container*—for example, a list, a set, or a map—to accumulate values as it processes the stream elements. The operation returns the mutable container as the result of the operation.

  The Stream API provides two overloaded collect() methods that perform mutable reduction (p. 964). One overloaded collect() method can be used to implement customized mutable reductions by specifying the functions (*supplier, accumulator, combiner*) required to perform such a reduction. A second collect() method accepts a Collector that is used to perform a mutable reduction. A *collector* encapsulates the functions required for performing a mutable reduction. The Stream API provides built-in collectors that allow various containers to be used for performing mutable reductions (p. 978). When a terminal operation performs a mutable reduction using a specific container, it is said to *collect to* this container.

The toArray() method implements a specialized mutable reduction that returns an array with the accumulated values (p. 971); that is, the method collects to an array.

Consumer Action on Stream Elements

We have already used both the forEach() and forEachOrdered() terminal operations to print elements when the pipeline is executed. These operations allow side effects on stream elements.

The forEach() method is defined for both streams and collections. In the case of collections, the method iterates over all the elements in the collection, whereas it is a terminal operation on streams.

Since these terminal operations perform an action on each element, the input stream to the operation must be *finite* in order for the operation to terminate.

Counterparts to the forEach() and forEachOrdered() methods for the primitive numeric types are also defined by the numeric stream interfaces.

> void forEach(Consumer<? super T> action)
> This terminal operation performs an action on each element of this stream. This method should not be relied upon to produce deterministic results, as the order in which the elements are processed is not guaranteed.

> void forEachOrdered(Consumer<? super T> action)
> This terminal operation performs an action on each element of this stream, but in the encounter order of the stream if the stream has one.

The difference in behavior of the forEach() and forEachOrdered() terminal operations is that the forEach() method does not guarantee to respect the encounter order, whereas the forEachOrdered() method always does, if there is one.

Each operation is applied to both an ordered sequential stream and an ordered parallel stream to print CD titles with the help of the consumer printStr:

```
Consumer<String> printStr = str -> System.out.print(str + "|");

CD.cdList.stream().map(CD::title).forEach(printStr);                   // (1a)
//Java Jive|Java Jam|Lambda Dancing|Keep on Erasing|Hot Generics|
```

```
CD.cdList.stream().parallel().map(CD::title).forEach(printStr);      // (1b)
//Lambda Dancing|Hot Generics|Keep on Erasing|Java Jam|Java Jive|
```

The behavior of the forEach() operation is nondeterministic, as seen at (1a) and (1b). The output from (1a) and (1b) shows that the forEach() operation respects the encounter order for an ordered sequential stream, but not necessarily for an ordered parallel stream. Respecting the encounter order for an ordered parallel stream would incur overhead that would impact performance, and is therefore ignored.

On the other hand, the forEachOrdered() operation always respects the encounter order in both cases, as seen below from the output at (2a) and (2b). However, it is important to note that, in the case of the ordered parallel stream, the terminal action on the elements can be executed in different threads, but guarantees that the action is applied to the elements in encounter order.

```
CD.cdList.stream().map(CD::title).forEachOrdered(printStr);             // (2a)
//Java Jive|Java Jam|Lambda Dancing|Keep on Erasing|Hot Generics|

CD.cdList.stream().parallel().map(CD::title).forEachOrdered(printStr);   // (2b)
//Java Jive|Java Jam|Lambda Dancing|Keep on Erasing|Hot Generics|
```

The discussion above also applies when the forEach() and forEachOrdered() terminal operations are invoked on numeric streams. The nondeterministic behavior of the forEach() terminal operation for int streams is illustrated below. The terminal operation on the sequential int stream at (3a) seems to respect the encounter order, but should not be relied upon. The terminal operation on the parallel int stream at (3b) can give different results for different runs.

```
IntConsumer printInt = n -> out.print(n + "|");

IntStream.of(2018, 2019, 2020, 2021, 2022).forEach(printInt);          // (3a)
//2018|2019|2020|2021|2022|

IntStream.of(2018, 2019, 2020, 2021, 2022).parallel().forEach(printInt); // (3b)
//2020|2019|2018|2021|2022|
```

Matching Elements

The match operations determine whether any, all, or none of the stream elements satisfy a given Predicate. These operations are not reductions, as they do not always consider all elements in the stream in order to return a result.

Analogous match operations are also provided by the numeric stream interfaces.

```
boolean anyMatch(Predicate<? super T> predicate)
boolean allMatch(Predicate<? super T> predicate)
boolean noneMatch(Predicate<? super T> predicate)
```

These three terminal operations determine whether *any, all,* or *no* elements of this stream match the specified predicate, respectively.

The methods may not evaluate the predicate on all elements if it is not necessary for determining the result; that is, they are *short-circuit* operations.

If the stream is empty, the predicate is *not* evaluated.

The anyMatch() method returns false if the stream is empty.

The allMatch() and noneMatch() methods return true if the stream is empty.

There is no guarantee that these operations will terminate if applied to an infinite stream.

The queries at (1), (2), and (3) below determine whether any, all, or no CDs are jazz music CDs, respectively. At (1), the execution of the pipeline terminates as soon as any jazz music CD is found—the value true is returned. At (2), the execution of the pipeline terminates as soon as a non-jazz music CD is found—the value false is returned. At (3), the execution of the pipeline terminates as soon as a jazz music CD is found—the value false is returned.

```
boolean anyJazzCD = CD.cdList.stream().anyMatch(CD::isJazz);   // (1) true
boolean allJazzCds = CD.cdList.stream().allMatch(CD::isJazz);  // (2) false
boolean noJazzCds = CD.cdList.stream().noneMatch(CD::isJazz);  // (3) false
```

Given the following predicates:

```
Predicate<CD> eq2015 = cd -> cd.year().compareTo(Year.of(2015)) == 0;
Predicate<CD> gt2015 = cd -> cd.year().compareTo(Year.of(2015)) > 0;
```

The query at (4) determines that no CDs were released in 2015. The queries at (5) and (6) are equivalent. If all CDs were released after 2015, then none were released in or before 2015 (negation of the predicate gt2015).

```
boolean noneEQ2015 = CD.cdList.stream().noneMatch(eq2015);       // (4) true
boolean allGT2015 = CD.cdList.stream().allMatch(gt2015);         // (5) true
boolean noneNotGT2015 = CD.cdList.stream().noneMatch(gt2015.negate()); // (6) true
```

The code below uses the anyMatch() method on an int stream to determine whether any year is a leap year.

```
IntStream yrStream = IntStream.of(2018, 2019, 2020);
IntPredicate isLeapYear = yr -> Year.of(yr).isLeap();
boolean anyLeapYear = yrStream.anyMatch(isLeapYear);
out.println("Any leap year: " + anyLeapYear);   // true
```

Example 16.10 illustrates using the allMatch() operation to determine whether a square matrix—that is, a two-dimensional array with an equal number of columns as rows—is an *identity matrix*. In such a matrix, all elements on the main diagonal have the value 1 and all other elements have the value 0. The methods isIdentityMatrixLoops() and isIdentityMatrixStreams() at (1) and (2) implement this test in different ways.

The method isIdentityMatrixLoops() at (1) uses nested loops. The outer loop processes the rows, whereas the inner loop tests that each row has the correct values. The outer loop is a labeled loop in order to break out of the inner loop if an element in a row does not have the correct value—effectively achieving short-circuit execution.

The method isIdentityMatrixStreams() at (2) uses nested numeric streams, where the outer stream processes the rows and the inner stream processes the elements in a row. The allMatch() method at (4) in the inner stream pipeline determines that all elements in a row have the correct value. It short-circuits the execution of the inner stream if that is not the case. The allMatch() method at (3) in the outer stream pipeline also short-circuits its execution if its predicate to process a row returns the value false. The stream-based implementation for the identity matrix test expresses the logic more clearly and naturally than the loop-based version.

Example 16.10 *Identity Matrix Test*

```java
import static java.lang.System.out;

import java.util.Arrays;
import java.util.stream.IntStream;

public class IdentityMatrixTest {
  public static void main(String[] args) {
    // Matrices to test:
    int[][] sqMatrix1 = { {1, 0, 0}, {0, 1, 0}, {0, 0, 1} };
    int[][] sqMatrix2 = { {1, 1}, {1, 1} };
    isIdentityMatrixLoops(sqMatrix1);
    isIdentityMatrixLoops(sqMatrix2);
    isIdentityMatrixStreams(sqMatrix1);
    isIdentityMatrixStreams(sqMatrix2);
  }

  private static void isIdentityMatrixLoops(int[][] sqMatrix) {        // (1)
    boolean isCorrectValue = false;
    outerLoop:
    for (int i = 0; i < sqMatrix.length; ++i) {
      for (int j = 0; j < sqMatrix[i].length; ++j) {
        isCorrectValue = j == i ? sqMatrix[i][i] == 1
                                : sqMatrix[i][j] == 0;
        if (!isCorrectValue) break outerLoop;
      }
    }
    out.println(Arrays.deepToString(sqMatrix)
        + (isCorrectValue ? " is ": " is not ") + "an identity matrix.");
  }

  private static void isIdentityMatrixStreams(int[][] sqMatrix) {      // (2)
    boolean isCorrectValue =
        IntStream.range(0, sqMatrix.length)
                .allMatch(i -> IntStream.range(0, sqMatrix[i].length)  // (3)
                              .allMatch(j -> j == i                    // (4)
                                  ? sqMatrix[i][i] == 1
                                  : sqMatrix[i][j] == 0));
    out.println(Arrays.deepToString(sqMatrix)
        + (isCorrectValue ? " is ": " is not ") + "an identity matrix.");
  }
}
```

Output from the program:

```
[[1, 0, 0], [0, 1, 0], [0, 0, 1]] is an identity matrix.
[[1, 1], [1, 1]] is not an identity matrix.
[[1, 0, 0], [0, 1, 0], [0, 0, 1]] is an identity matrix.
[[1, 1], [1, 1]] is not an identity matrix.
```

Finding the First or Any Element

The findFirst() method can be used to find the first element that is available in the stream. This method respects the encounter order, if the stream has one. It always produces a stable result; that is, it will produce the same result on identical pipelines based on the same stream source. In contrast, the behavior of the findAny() method is nondeterministic. Counterparts to these methods are also defined by the numeric stream interfaces.

Optional<T> findFirst()

This terminal operation returns an Optional describing the *first* element of this stream, or an empty Optional if the stream is empty.

This method may return any element if this stream does not have any encounter order.

It is a *short-circuit* operation, as it will terminate the execution of the stream pipeline as soon as the first element is found.

This method throws a NullPointerException if the element selected is null.

Optional<T> findAny()

This terminal operation returns an Optional describing *some* element of the stream, or an empty Optional if the stream is empty. This operation has nondeterministic behavior.

It is a *short-circuit* operation, as it will terminate the execution of the stream pipeline as soon as any element is found.

In the code below, the encounter order of the stream is the positional order of the elements in the list. The first element returned by the findFirst() method at (1) is the first element in the CD list.

```
Optional<CD> firstCD1 = CD.cdList.stream().findFirst();        // (1)
out.println(firstCD1.map(CD::title).orElse("No first CD."));   // (2) Java Jive
```

Since such an element might not exist—for example, the stream might be empty—the method returns an Optional<T> object. At (2), the Optional<CD> object returned by the findFirst() method is mapped to an Optional<String> object that encapsulates the title of the CD. The orElse() method on this Optional<String> object returns the CD title or the argument string if there is no such CD.

If the encounter order is not of consequence, the findAny() method can be used, as it is nondeterministic—that is, it does not guarantee the same result on the same stream source. On the other hand, it provides maximal performance on parallel streams. At (3) below, the findAny() method is free to return any element from the parallel stream. It should not come as a surprise if the element returned is not the first element in the list.

```
Optional<CD> anyCD2 = CD.cdList.stream().parallel().findAny();   // (3)
out.println(anyCD2.map(CD::title).orElse("No CD."));             // Lambda Dancing
```

The match methods only determine whether any elements satisfy a Predicate, as seen at (5) below. Typically, a find terminal operation is used to find the first element made available to the terminal operation after processing by the intermediate operations in the stream pipeline. At (6), the filter() operation will filter the jazz music CDs from the stream. However, the findAny() operation will return the first jazz music CD that is filtered and then short-circuit the execution.

```
boolean anyJazzCD = CD.cdList.stream().anyMatch(CD::isJazz);          // (5)
out.println("Any Jazz CD: " + anyJazzCD);   // Any Jazz CD: true

Optional<CD> optJazzCD = CD.cdList.stream().filter(CD::isJazz).findAny(); // (6)
optJazzCD.ifPresent(out::println);          // <Jaav, "Java Jam", 6, 2017, JAZZ>
```

The code below uses the findAny() method on an IntStream to find whether any number is divisible by 7.

```
IntStream numStream = IntStream.of(50, 55, 65, 70, 75, 77);
OptionalInt intOpt = numStream.filter(n -> n % 7 == 0).findAny();
intOpt.ifPresent(System.out::println);       // 70
```

The find operations are guaranteed to terminate when applied to a finite, albeit empty, stream. However, for an infinite stream in a pipeline, at least one element must be made available to the find operation in order for the operation to terminate. If the elements of an initial infinite stream are all discarded by the intermediate operations, the find operation will not terminate, as in the following pipeline:

```
Stream.generate(() -> 1).filter(n -> n == 0).findAny();       // Never terminates.
```

Counting Elements

The count() operation performs a functional reduction on the elements of a stream, as each element contributes to the count which is the single immutable value returned by the operation. The count() operation reports the number of elements that are made available to it, which is not necessarily the same as the number of elements in the initial stream, as elements might be discarded by the intermediate operations.

The code below finds the total number of CDs in the streams, and how many of these CDs are jazz music CDs.

```
long numOfCDS = CD.cdList.stream().count();                          // 5
long numOfJazzCDs = CD.cdList.stream().filter(CD::isJazz).count(); // 3
```

The count() method is also defined for the numeric streams. Below it is used on an IntStream to find how many numbers between 1 and 100 are divisible by 7.

```
IntStream numStream = IntStream.rangeClosed(1, 100);
long divBy7 = numStream.filter(n -> n % 7 == 0).count();          // 14
```

```
long count()
```

This terminal operation returns the count of elements in this stream—that is, the length of this stream.

This operation is a special case of a functional reduction.

The operation does not terminate when applied to an infinite stream.

Finding Min and Max Elements

The min() and max() operations are functional reductions, as they consider all elements of the stream and return a single value. They should only be applied to a finite stream, as they will not terminate on an infinite stream. These methods are also defined by the numeric stream interfaces for the numeric types, but without the specification of a comparator.

```
Optional<T> min(Comparator<? super T> cmp)
Optional<T> max(Comparator<? super T> cmp)
```

These terminal operations return an Optional with the minimum or maximum element of this stream according to the provided Comparator, respectively, or an empty Optional if this stream is empty. It throws a NullPointerException if the minimum element is null.

These operations are a special case of a functional reduction.

These operations do not terminate when applied to an infinite stream.

Both methods return an Optional, as the minimum and maximum elements might not exist—for example, if the stream is empty. The code below finds the minimum and maximum elements in a stream of CDs, according to their natural order. The artist name is the most significant field according to the natural order defined for CDs (p. 883).

```
Optional<CD> minCD = CD.cdList.stream().min(Comparator.naturalOrder());
minCD.ifPresent(out::println);        // <Funkies, "Lambda Dancing", 10, 2018, POP>
out.println(minCD.map(CD::artist).orElse("No min CD."));       // Funkies

Optional<CD> maxCD = CD.cdList.stream().max(Comparator.naturalOrder());
maxCD.ifPresent(out::println);        // <Jaav, "Java Jive", 8, 2017, POP>
out.println(maxCD.map(CD::artist).orElse("No max CD."));       // Jaav
```

In the code below, the max() method is applied to an IntStream to find the largest number between 1 and 100 that is divisible by 7.

```
IntStream iStream = IntStream.rangeClosed(1, 100);
OptionalInt maxNum = iStream.filter(n -> n % 7 == 0).max(); // 98
```

If one is only interested in the minimum and maximum elements in a collection, the overloaded methods `min()` and `max()` of the `java.util.Collections` class can be more convenient to use.

Implementing Functional Reduction: The `reduce()` Method

A *functional reduction* combines all elements in a stream to produce a *single immutable value* as its result. The reduction process employs an *accumulator* that repeatedly computes a new partial result based on the current partial result and the current element in the stream. The stream thus gets shorter by one element. When all elements have been combined, the last partial result that was computed by the accumulator is returned as the final result of the reduction process.

The following terminal operations are special cases of functional reduction:

- `count()`, p. 953.
- `min()`, p. 954.
- `max()`, p. 954.
- `average()`, p. 1000.
- `sum()`, p. 1001.

The overloaded `reduce()` method can be used to implement new forms of functional reduction.

`Optional<T> reduce(BinaryOperator<T> accumulator)`

This terminal operation returns an `Optional` with the *cumulative* result of applying the accumulator on the elements of this stream: $e_1 \oplus e_2 \oplus e_3 \ldots$, where each e_i is an element of this stream and $\oplus$ is the accumulator. If the stream is empty, an empty `Optional` is returned.

The accumulator must be *associative*—that is, the result of evaluating an expression is the same, regardless of how the operands are grouped to evaluate the expression. For example, the grouping in the expression below allows the sub-expressions to be evaluated in parallel and their results combined by the accumulator:

$$e_i \oplus e_j \oplus e_k \oplus e_l == (e_i \oplus e_j) \oplus (e_k \oplus e_l)$$

where e_i, e_j, e_k, and e_l are operands, and $\oplus$ is the accumulator. For example, numeric addition, min, max, and string concatenation are associative operations, whereas subtraction and division are nonassociative.

The accumulator must also be a *non-interfering* and *stateless* function (p. 909).

Note that the method reduces a `Stream` of type `T` to a result that is an `Optional` of type `T`.

A counterpart to the single-argument `reduce()` method is also provided for the numeric streams.

```
T reduce(T identity, BinaryOperator<T> accumulator)
```

This terminal operation returns the *cumulative* result of applying the accumulator on the elements of this stream: identity $\oplus\ e_1 \oplus\ e_2 \oplus\ e_3$ ..., where e_i is an element of this stream, and $\oplus$ is the accumulator. The identity value is the initial value to accumulate. If the stream is empty, the identity value is returned.

The identity value must be an *identity* for the accumulator—for all e_i, identity $\oplus\ e_i$ == e_i. The accumulator must be *associative*.

The accumulator must also be a *non-interfering* and *stateless* function (p. 909).

Note that the method reduces a Stream of type T to a result of type T.

A counterpart to the two-argument reduce() method is also provided for the numeric streams.

```
<U> U reduce(
        U identity,
        BiFunction<U,? super T,U> accumulator,
        BinaryOperator<U> combiner)
```

This terminal operation returns the *cumulative* result of applying the accumulator on the elements of this stream, using the identity value of type U as the initial value to accumulate. If the stream is empty, the identity value is returned.

The identity value must be an *identity* for the combiner function. The accumulator and the combiner function must also satisfy the following relationship for all u and t of type U and T, respectively:

$$u \copyright (identity \oplus t) == u \oplus t$$

where $\copyright$ and $\oplus$ are the accumulator and combiner functions, respectively.

The combiner function combines two values during stream processing. It may not be executed for a sequential stream, but for a parallel stream, it will combine cumulative results of segments that are processed concurrently.

Both the accumulator and the combiner must also be *non-interfering* and *stateless* functions (p. 909).

Note that the accumulator has the function type (U, T) -> U, and the combiner function has the function type (U, U) -> U, where the type parameters U and T are always the types of the partial result and the stream element, respectively. This method reduces a Stream of type T to a result of type U.

There is *no* counterpart to the three-argument reduce() method for the numeric streams.

The idiom of using a loop for calculating the sum of a finite number of values is something that is ingrained into all aspiring programmers. A loop-based solution to calculate the total number of tracks on CDs in a list is shown below, where the variable sum will hold the result after the execution of the for(:) loop:

```
int sum = 0;                              // (1) Initialize the partial result.
for (CD cd : CD.cdList) {                  // (2) Iterate over the list.
  int numOfTracks = cd.noOfTracks();       // (3) Get the current value.
  sum = sum + numOfTracks;                 // (4) Calculate new partial result.
}
```

Apart from the for(:) loop at (2) to iterate over all elements of the list and read the number of tracks in each CD at (3), the two necessary steps are:

- Initialization of the variable sum at (1)
- The accumulative operation at (4) that is applied repeatedly to compute a new partial result in the variable sum, based on its previous value and the number of tracks in the current CD

The loop-based solution above can be translated to a stream-based solution, as shown in Figure 16.11. All the code snippets can be found in Example 16.11.

Figure 16.11 *Reducing with an Initial Value*

```
// Query: Find the total number of CD tracks.
int totNumOfTracks = CD.cdList                          // (5)
    .stream()                                           // (6)
    .mapToInt(CD::noOfTracks)                            // (7)
    .reduce(0,                                          // (8)
            (sum, numOfTracks) -> sum + numOfTracks);   // (9)
```

(a) Using the reduce() method with an initial value

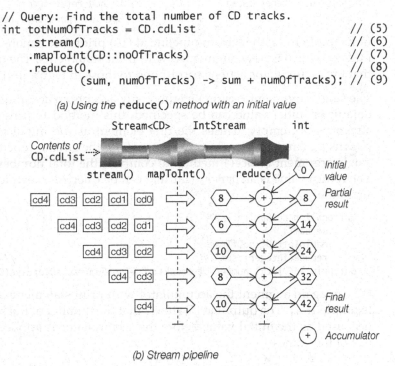

(b) Stream pipeline

In Figure 16.11, the stream created at (6) internalizes the iteration over the elements. The mapToInt() intermediate operation maps each CD to its number of tracks at (7)—the Stream<CD> is mapped to an IntStream. The reduce() terminal operation with two arguments computes and returns the total number of tracks:

- Its first argument at (8) is the *identity* element that provides the initial value for the operation and is also the default value to return if the stream is empty. In this case, this value is 0.
- Its second argument at (9) is the *accumulator* that is implemented as a lambda expression. It repeatedly computes a new partial sum based on the previous partial sum and the number of tracks in the current CD, as evident from

Figure 16.11. In this case, the accumulator is an `IntBinaryOperator` whose functional type is `(int, int) -> int`. Note that the parameters of the lambda expression represent the partial sum and the current number of tracks, respectively.

The stream pipeline in Figure 16.11 is an example of a *map-reduce transformation* on a sequential stream, as it maps the stream elements first and then reduces them. Typically, a filter operation is also performed before the map-reduce transformation.

Each of the following calls can replace the `reduce()` method call in Figure 16.11, as they are all equivalent:

```
reduce(0, (sum, noOfTracks) -> Integer.sum(sum, noOfTracks))
reduce(0, Integer::sum)               // Method reference
sum()                                 // Special functional reduction, p. 1001.
```

In Example 16.11, the stream pipeline at (10) prints the actions taken by the accumulator which is now augmented with print statements. The output at (3) shows that the accumulator actions correspond to those in Figure 16.11.

The single-argument `reduce()` method only accepts an accumulator. As no explicit default or initial value can be specified, this method returns an `Optional`. If the stream is not empty, it uses the first element as the initial value; otherwise, it returns an empty `Optional`. In Example 16.11, the stream pipeline at (13) uses the single-argument `reduce()` method to compute the total number of tracks on CDs. The return value is an `OptionalInt` that can be queried to extract the encapsulated int value.

```
OptionalInt optSumTracks0 = CD.cdList                          // (13)
    .stream()
    .mapToInt(CD::noOfTracks)
    .reduce(Integer::sum);                                     // (14)
out.println("Total number of tracks: " + optSumTracks0.orElse(0));  // 42
```

We can again augment the accumulator with print statements as shown at (16) in Example 16.11. The output at (5) shows that the number of tracks from the first CD was used as the initial value before the accumulator is applied repeatedly to the rest of the values.

Example 16.11 *Implementing Functional Reductions*

```
import static java.lang.System.out;

import java.util.Comparator;
import java.util.Optional;
import java.util.OptionalInt;
import java.util.function.BinaryOperator;

public final class FunctionalReductions {
  public static void main(String[] args) {

// Two-argument reduce() method:
    {
```

```
    out.println("(1) Find total number of tracks (loop-based version):");
    int sum = 0;                              // (1) Initialize the partial result.
    for (CD cd : CD.cdList) {                 // (2) Iterate over the list.
      int numOfTracks = cd.noOfTracks();      // (3) Get the next value.
      sum = sum + numOfTracks;                // (4) Calculate new partial result.
    }
    out.println("Total number of tracks: " + sum);
  }


    out.println("(2) Find total number of tracks (stream-based version):");
    int totNumOfTracks = CD.cdList                            // (5)
        .stream()                                             // (6)
        .mapToInt(CD::noOfTracks)                             // (7)
        .reduce(0,                                            // (8)
                (sum, numOfTracks) -> sum + numOfTracks);     // (9)
    //  .reduce(0, (sum, noOfTracks) -> Integer.sum(sum, noOfTracks));
    //  .reduce(0, Integer::sum);
    //  .sum();
    out.println("Total number of tracks: " + totNumOfTracks);
    out.println();

    out.println("(3) Find total number of tracks (accumulator logging): ");
    int totNumOfTracks1 = CD.cdList                           // (10)
        .stream()
        .mapToInt(CD::noOfTracks)
        .reduce(0,                                            // (11)
            (sum, noOfTracks) -> {                            // (12)
                int newSum = sum + noOfTracks;
                out.printf("Accumulator: sum=%2d, noOfTracks=%2d, newSum=%2d%n",
                           sum, noOfTracks, newSum);
                return newSum;
            }
        );
    out.println("Total number of tracks: " + totNumOfTracks1);
    out.println();

// One-argument reduce() method:

    out.println("(4) Find total number of tracks (stream-based version):");
    OptionalInt optSumTracks0 = CD.cdList                     // (13)
        .stream()
        .mapToInt(CD::noOfTracks)
        .reduce(Integer::sum);                                // (14)
    out.println("Total number of tracks: " + optSumTracks0.orElse(0));
    out.println();

    out.println("(5) Find total number of tracks (accumulator logging): ");
    OptionalInt optSumTracks1 = CD.cdList                     // (15)
        .stream()
        .mapToInt(CD::noOfTracks)
        .reduce((sum, noOfTracks) -> {                        // (16)
            int newSum = sum + noOfTracks;
            out.printf("Accumulator: sum=%2d, noOfTracks=%2d, newSum=%2d%n",
                       sum, noOfTracks, newSum);
            return newSum;
        });
```

```
        out.println("Total number of tracks: " + optSumTracks1.orElse(0));
        out.println();

// Three-argument reduce() method:

        out.println("(6) Find total number of tracks (accumulator + combiner): ");
        Integer sumTracks5 = CD.cdList                          // (17)
//       .stream()                                              // (18a)
         .parallelStream()                                      // (18b)
         .reduce(Integer.valueOf(0),                            // (19) Initial value
                 (sum, cd) -> sum + cd.noOfTracks(),            // (20) Accumulator
                 (sum1, sum2) -> sum1 + sum2);                  // (21) Combiner
        out.println("Total number of tracks: " + sumTracks5);
        out.println();

        out.println("(7) Find total number of tracks (accumulator + combiner): ");
        Integer sumTracks6 = CD.cdList                          // (22)
//       .stream()                                              // (23a)
         .parallelStream()                                      // (23b)
         .reduce(0,
                 (sum, cd) -> {                                 // (24) Accumulator
                    Integer noOfTracks = cd.noOfTracks();
                    Integer newSum = sum + noOfTracks;
                    out.printf("Accumulator: sum=%2d, noOfTracks=%2d, "
                               + "newSum=%2d%n", sum, noOfTracks, newSum);
                    return newSum;
                 },
                 (sum1, sum2) -> {                              // (25) Combiner
                    Integer newSum = sum1 + sum2;
                    out.printf("Combiner: sum1=%2d, sum2=%2d, newSum=%2d%n",
                               sum1, sum2, newSum);
                    return newSum;
                 }
           );
        out.println("Total number of tracks: " + sumTracks6);
        out.println();

// Compare by CD title.
        Comparator<CD> cmpByTitle = Comparator.comparing(CD::title);    // (26)
        BinaryOperator<CD> maxByTitle =
            (cd1, cd2) -> cmpByTitle.compare(cd1, cd2) > 0 ? cd1 : cd2; // (27)

// Query: Find maximum Jazz CD by title:
        Optional<CD> optMaxJazzCD = CD.cdList                   // (28)
            .stream()
            .filter(CD::isJazz)
            .reduce(BinaryOperator.maxBy(cmpByTitle));          // (29a)
//          .reduce(maxByTitle);                                // (29b)
//          .max(cmpByTitle);                                   // (29c)
        optMaxJazzCD.map(CD::title).ifPresent(out::println);// Keep on Erasing
    }
}
```

Possible output from the program:

```
(1) Find total number of tracks (loop-based version):
Total number of tracks: 42
(2) Find total number of tracks (stream-based version):
Total number of tracks: 42

(3) Find total number of tracks (accumulator logging):
Accumulator: sum= 0, noOfTracks= 8, newSum= 8
Accumulator: sum= 8, noOfTracks= 6, newSum=14
Accumulator: sum=14, noOfTracks=10, newSum=24
Accumulator: sum=24, noOfTracks= 8, newSum=32
Accumulator: sum=32, noOfTracks=10, newSum=42
Total number of tracks: 42

(4) Find total number of tracks (stream-based version):
Total number of tracks: 42

(5) Find total number of tracks (accumulator logging):
Accumulator: sum= 8, noOfTracks= 6, newSum=14
Accumulator: sum=14, noOfTracks=10, newSum=24
Accumulator: sum=24, noOfTracks= 8, newSum=32
Accumulator: sum=32, noOfTracks=10, newSum=42
Total number of tracks: 42

(6) Find total number of tracks (accumulator + combiner):
Total number of tracks: 42

(7) Find total number of tracks (accumulator + combiner):
Accumulator: sum= 0, noOfTracks=10, newSum=10
Accumulator: sum= 0, noOfTracks=10, newSum=10
Accumulator: sum= 0, noOfTracks= 8, newSum= 8
Combiner: sum1= 8, sum2=10, newSum=18
Combiner: sum1=10, sum2=18, newSum=28
Accumulator: sum= 0, noOfTracks= 6, newSum= 6
Accumulator: sum= 0, noOfTracks= 8, newSum= 8
Combiner: sum1= 8, sum2= 6, newSum=14
Combiner: sum1=14, sum2=28, newSum=42
Total number of tracks: 42

Keep on Erasing
```

The single-argument and two-argument reduce() methods accept a *binary operator* as the accumulator whose arguments and result are of the *same* type. The three-argument reduce() method is more flexible and can only be applied to objects. The stream pipeline below computes the total number of tracks on CDs using the three-argument reduce() method.

```
Integer sumTracks5 = CD.cdList                 // (17)
    .stream()                                  // (18a)
//  .parallelStream()                          // (18b)
    .reduce(Integer.valueOf(0),                // (19) Initial value
            (sum, cd) -> sum + cd.noOfTracks(),// (20) Accumulator
            (sum1, sum2) -> sum1 + sum2);      // (21) Combiner
```

The reduce() method above accepts the following arguments:

- An *identity* value: Its type is U. In this case, it is an Integer that wraps the value 0. As before, it is used as the initial value. The type of the value returned by the reduce() method is also U.

- An *accumulator*: It is a BiFunction<U,T,U>; that is, it is a binary function that accepts an object of type U and an object of type T and produces a result of type U. In this case, type U is Integer and type T is CD. The lambda expression implementing the accumulator first reads the number of tracks from the current CD before the addition operator is applied. Thus the accumulator will calculate the sum of Integers which are, of course, unboxed and boxed to do the calculation. As we have seen earlier, the accumulator is repeatedly applied to sum the tracks on the CDs. Only this time, the mapping of a CD to an Integer is done when the accumulator is evaluated.

- A *combiner*: It is a BinaryOperator<U>; that is, it is a binary operator whose arguments and result are of the same type U. In this case, type U is Integer. Thus the combiner will calculate the sum of Integers which are unboxed and boxed to do the calculation.

  In the code above, the combiner is not executed if the reduce() method is applied to a *sequential* stream. However, there is no guarantee that this is always the case for a sequential stream. If we uncomment (18b) and remove (18a), the combiner will be executed on the *parallel* stream.

That the combiner in the three-argument reduce() method is executed for a parallel stream is illustrated by the stream pipeline at (22) in Example 16.11, that has been augmented with print statements. There is no output from the combiner when the stream is sequential. The output at (7) in Example 16.11 shows that the combiner accumulates the partial sums created by the accumulator when the stream is parallel.

Parallel Functional Reduction

Parallel execution is illustrated in Figure 16.12. Multiple instances of the stream pipeline are executed in parallel, where each pipeline instance processes a segment of the stream. In this case, only one CD is allocated to each pipeline instance. Each pipeline instance thus produces its partial sum, and the combiner is applied in parallel on the partial sums to combine them into a final result. No additional synchronization is required to run the reduce() operation in parallel.

Figure 16.12 also illustrates why the initial value must be an identity value. Say we had specified the initial value to be 3. Then the value 3 would be added multiple times to the sum during parallel execution. We also see why both the accumulator and the combiner are associative, as this allows for any two values to be combined in any order.

When the single-argument and two-argument reduce() methods are applied to a parallel stream, the accumulator also acts as the combiner. The three-argument reduce() method can usually be replaced with a *map-reduce* transformation, making the combiner redundant.

Figure 16.12 *Parallel Functional Reduction*

```
// Query: Find total number of CD tracks.
Integer sumTracks5 = CD.cdList                        // (17)
    .parallelStream()                                 // (18b)
    .reduce(Integer.valueOf(0),                       // (19) Initial value
            (sum, cd) -> sum + cd.noOfTracks(),       // (20) Accumulator
            (sum1, sum2) -> sum1 + sum2);             // (21) Combiner
```

(a) Using the `Stream.reduce()` *method on a parallel stream*

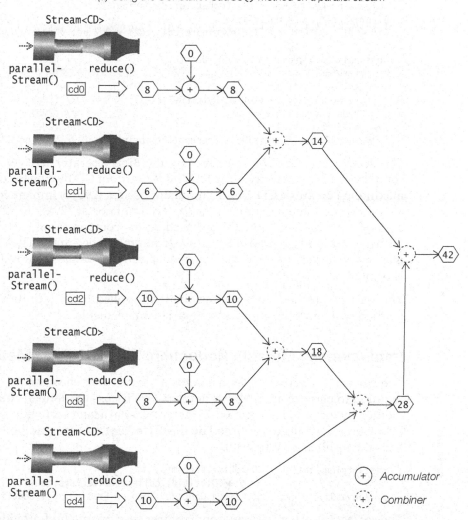

(b) Parallel functional reduction

We conclude the discussion on implementing functional reductions by implementing the max() method that finds the maximum element in a stream according to a given comparator. A comparator that compares by the CD title is defined at (26). A binary operator that finds the maximum of two CDs when compared by title is defined at (27). It uses the comparator defined at (26). The stream pipeline at (28) finds the maximum of all jazz music CDs by title. The method calls at (29a), (29b), and (29c) are equivalent.

```
Comparator<CD> cmpByTitle = Comparator.comparing(CD::title);     // (26)
BinaryOperator<CD> maxByTitle =
    (cd1, cd2) -> cmpByTitle.compare(cd1, cd2) > 0 ? cd1 : cd2; // (27)

Optional<CD> optMaxJazzCD = CD.cdList                           // (28)
    .stream()
    .filter(CD::isJazz)
    .reduce(BinaryOperator.maxBy(cmpByTitle));                  // (29a)
//  .reduce(maxByTitle);                                        // (29b)
//  .max(cmpByTitle);                                           // (29c)
optMaxJazzCD.map(CD::title).ifPresent(out::println);     // Keep on Erasing
```

The accumulator at (29a), returned by the BinaryOperator.maxBy() method, will compare the previous maximum CD and the current CD by title to compute a new maximum jazz music CD. The accumulator used at (29b) is implemented at (27). It also does the same comparison as the accumulator at (29a). At (29c), the max() method also does the same thing, based on the comparator at (26). Note that the return value is an Optional<CD>, as the stream might be empty. The Optional<CD> is mapped to an Optional<String>. If it is not empty, its value—that is, the CD title— is printed.

The reduce() method does not terminate if applied to an infinite stream, as the method will never finish processing all stream elements.

Implementing Mutable Reduction: The collect() Method

The collect(Collector) method accepts a *collector* that encapsulates the functions required to perform a mutable reduction. We discuss predefined collectors implemented by the java.util.stream.Collectors class in a later section (p. 978). The code below uses the collector returned by the Collectors.toList() method that accumulates the result in a list (p. 980).

```
List<String> titles = CD.cdList.stream()
                      .map(CD::title).collect(Collectors.toList());
// [Java Jive, Java Jam, Lambda Dancing, Keep on Erasing, Hot Generics]
```

The collect(supplier, accumulator, combiner) generic method provides the general setup for implementing mutable reduction on stream elements using different kinds of *mutable containers*—for example, a list, a map, or a StringBuilder. It uses one or more mutable containers to accumulate partial results that are combined into a single mutable container that is returned as the result of the reduction operation.

```
<R,A> R collect(Collector<? super T,A,R> collector)
```

This terminal operation performs a reduction operation on the elements of this stream using a `Collector` (p. 978).

A `Collector` encapsulates the functions required for performing the reduction.

The result of the reduction is of type R, and the type parameter A is the intermediate accumulation type of the `Collector`.

```
<R> R collect(
        Supplier<R>              supplier,
        BiConsumer<R,? super T>  accumulator,
        BiConsumer<R,R>          combiner)
```

This terminal operation performs a mutable reduction on the elements of this stream. A counterpart to this method is also provided for numeric streams.

The `supplier` creates a new mutable container of type R—which is typically empty. Elements are incorporated into such a container during the reduction process. For a parallel stream, the supplier can be called multiple times, and the container returned by the supplier must be an *identity container* in the sense that it does not mutate any result container with which it is merged.

The `accumulator` incorporates additional elements into a result container: A stream element of type T is incorporated into a mutable container of type R.

The `combiner` merges two values that are mutable containers of type R. It must be compatible with the `accumulator`. There is no guarantee that the `combiner` is called if the stream is sequential, but definitely comes into play if the stream is parallel.

Both the `accumulator` and the `combiner` must also be *non-interfering* and *stateless* functions (p. 909).

With the above requirements on the argument functions fulfilled, the `collect()` method will produce the same result regardless of whether the stream is sequential or parallel.

We will use Figure 16.13 to illustrate mutable reduction performed on a sequential stream by the three-argument `collect()` method. The figure shows both the code and the execution of a stream pipeline to create a list containing the number of tracks on each CD. The stream of CDs is mapped to a stream of Integers at (3), where each Integer value is the number of tracks on a CD. The `collect()` method at (4) accepts three functions as arguments. They are explicitly defined as lambda expressions to show what the parameters represent and how they are used to perform mutable reduction. Implementation of these functions using method references can be found in Example 16.12.

- *Supplier*: The supplier is a `Supplier<R>` that is used to create new instances of a mutable result container of type R. Such a container holds the results computed by the accumulator and the combiner. In Figure 16.13, the supplier at (4) returns an *empty* `ArrayList<Integer>` every time it is called.

- *Accumulator*: The accumulator is a BiConsumer<R, T> that is used to accumulate an element of type T into a mutable result container of type R. In Figure 16.13, type R is ArrayList<Integer> and type T is Integer. The accumulator at (5) mutates a container of type ArrayList<Integer> by repeatedly adding a new Integer value to it, as illustrated in Figure 16.13b. It is instructive to contrast this accumulator with the accumulator for sequential functional reduction illustrated in Figure 16.11, p. 957.

- *Combiner*: The combiner is a BiConsumer<R, R> that merges the contents of the second argument container with the contents of the first argument container, where both containers are of type R. As in the case of the reduce(identity, accumulator, combiner) method, the combiner is executed when the collect() method is called on a parallel stream.

Figure 16.13 *Sequential Mutable Reduction*

```
// Query: Create a list with the number of tracks on each CD.
List<Integer> tracks = CD.cdList                          // (1)
    .stream()                                             // (2a)
    .map(CD::noOfTracks)                                  // (3)
    .collect(() -> new ArrayList<>(),                     // (4) Supplier
            (cont, noOfTracks) -> cont.add(noOfTracks),// (5) Accumulator
            (cont1, cont2) -> cont1.addAll(cont2));   // (6) Combiner
```

(a) Using the Stream.collect() *method on a sequential stream*

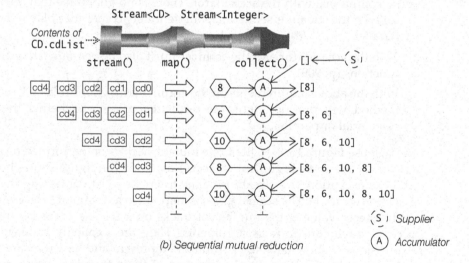

(b) Sequential mutual reduction

Parallel Mutable Reduction

Figure 16.14 shows the stream pipeline from Figure 16.13, where the sequential stream (2a) has been replaced by a parallel stream (2b); in other words, the collect() method is called on a parallel stream. One possible parallel execution of the pipeline is also depicted in Figure 16.14b. We see five instances of the pipeline being executed in parallel. The supplier creates five empty ArrayLists that are used

Figure 16.14 *Parallel Mutable Reduction*

```
// Query: Create a list with the number of tracks on each CD.
List<Integer> tracks = CD.cdList                         // (1)
    .parallelStream()                                    // (2b)
    .map(CD::noOfTracks)                                 // (3)
    .collect(() -> new ArrayList<>(),                   // (4) Supplier
            (cont, noOfTracks) -> cont.add(noOfTracks),  // (5) Accumulator
            (cont1, cont2) -> cont1.addAll(cont2));      // (6) Combiner
```

(a) Using the `Stream.collect()` *method on a parallel stream*

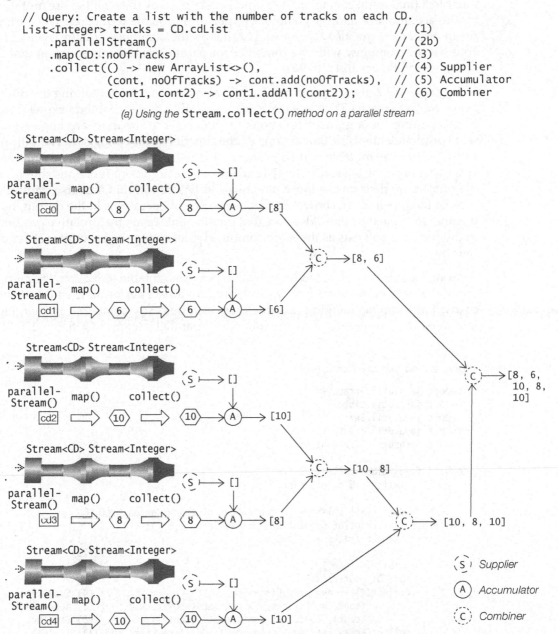

(b) Parallel mutable reduction

as partial result containers by the accumulator, and are later merged by the combiner to a final result container. The containers created by the supplier are mutated by the accumulator and the combiner to perform mutable reduction. The partial result containers are also merged in parallel by the combiner. It is instructive to contrast this combiner with the combiner for parallel functional reduction that is illustrated in Figure 16.12, p. 963.

In Example 16.12, the stream pipeline at (7) also creates a list containing the number of tracks on each CD, where the stream is parallel, and the lambda expressions implementing the argument functions of the collect() method are augmented with print statements so that actions of the functions can be logged. The output from this parallel mutable reduction shows that the combiner is executed multiple times to merge partial result lists. The actions of the argument functions shown in the output are the same as those illustrated in Figure 16.14b. Of course, multiple runs of the pipeline can show different sequences of operations in the output, but the final result in the same. Also note that the elements retain their relative position in the partial result lists as these are combined, preserving the encounter order of the stream.

Although a stream is executed in parallel to perform mutable reduction, the merging of the partial containers by the combiner can impact performance if this is too costly. For example, merging mutable maps can be costly compared to merging mutable lists. This issue is further explored for parallel streams in §16.9, p. 1009.

Example 16.12 *Implementing Mutable Reductions*

```java
import java.util.ArrayList;
import java.util.List;
import java.util.Set;
import java.util.TreeSet;
import java.util.stream.Stream;

public final class Collecting {
  public static void main(String[] args) {

    // Query: Create a list with the number of tracks on each CD.
    System.out.println("Sequential Mutable Reduction:");
    List<Integer> tracks = CD.cdList                              // (1)
        .stream()                                                 // (2a)
//      .parallelStream()                                         // (2b)
        .map(CD::noOfTracks)                                      // (3)
        .collect(() -> new ArrayList<>(),                         // (4) Supplier
                (cont, noOfTracks) -> cont.add(noOfTracks),       // (5) Accumulator
                (cont1, cont2) -> cont1.addAll(cont2));           // (6) Combiner
//      .collect(ArrayList::new, ArrayList::add, ArrayList::addAll); // (6a)
//      .toList();
    System.out.println("Number of tracks on each CD (sequential): " + tracks);
    System.out.println();

    System.out.println("Parallel Mutable Reduction:");
    List<Integer> tracks1 = CD.cdList                             // (7)
```

```
//      .stream()                                          // (8a)
        .parallelStream()                                  // (8b)
        .map(CD::noOfTracks)                               // (9)
        .collect(                                          // (10)
            () -> {                                        // (11) Supplier
                System.out.println("Supplier: Creating an ArrayList");
                return new ArrayList<>();
            },
            (cont, noOfTracks) -> {                        // (12) Accumulator
                System.out.printf("Accumulator: cont:%s, noOfTracks:%s",
                                  cont, noOfTracks);
                cont.add(noOfTracks);
                System.out.printf(", mutCont:%s%n", cont);
            },
            (cont1, cont2) -> {                            // (13) Combiner
                System.out.printf("Combiner: con1:%s, cont2:%s", cont1, cont2);
                cont1.addAll(cont2);
                System.out.printf(", mutCont:%s%n", cont1);
            });
System.out.println("Number of tracks on each CD (parallel): " + tracks1);
System.out.println();

// Query: Create an ordered set with CD titles, according to natural order.
Set<String> cdTitles = CD.cdList                           // (14)
    .stream()
    .map(CD::title)
    .collect(TreeSet::new, TreeSet::add, TreeSet::addAll);// (15)
System.out.println("CD titles: " + cdTitles);
System.out.println();

// Query: Go bananas.
StringBuilder goneBananas = Stream                         // (16)
    .iterate("ba", b -> b + "na")                          // (17)
    .limit(5)
    .peek(System.out::println)
    .collect(StringBuilder::new,                           // (18)
             StringBuilder::append,
             StringBuilder::append);
System.out.println("Go bananas: " + goneBananas);
    }
}
```

Possible output from the program:

```
Sequential Mutable Reduction:
Number of tracks on each CD (sequential): [8, 6, 10, 8, 10]

Parallel Mutable Reduction:
Supplier: Creating an ArrayList
Accumulator: cont:[], noOfTracks:8, mutCont:[8]
Supplier: Creating an ArrayList
Accumulator: cont:[], noOfTracks:6, mutCont:[6]
Combiner: con1:[8], cont2:[6], mutCont:[8, 6]
Supplier: Creating an ArrayList
Accumulator: cont:[], noOfTracks:10, mutCont:[10]
Supplier: Creating an ArrayList
```

```
Accumulator: cont:[], noOfTracks:8, mutCont:[8]
Combiner: con1:[10], cont2:[8], mutCont:[10, 8]
Supplier: Creating an ArrayList
Accumulator: cont:[], noOfTracks:10, mutCont:[10]
Combiner: con1:[10, 8], cont2:[10], mutCont:[10, 8, 10]
Combiner: con1:[8, 6], cont2:[10, 8, 10], mutCont:[8, 6, 10, 8, 10]
Number of tracks on each CD (parallel): [8, 6, 10, 8, 10]

CD titles: [Hot Generics, Java Jam, Java Jive, Keep on Erasing, Lambda Dancing]

ba
bana
banana
bananana
banananana
Go bananas: babanabananabanananabananana
```

Example 16.12 also shows how other kinds of containers can be used for mutable reduction. The stream pipeline at (14) performs mutable reduction to create an ordered set with CD titles. The supplier is implemented by the constructor reference TreeSet::new. The constructor will create a container of type TreeSet<String> that will maintain the CD titles according to the natural order for Strings. The accumulator and the combiner are implemented by the method references TreeSet::add and TreeSet::addAll, respectively. The accumulator will add a title to a container of type TreeSet<String> and the combiner will merge the contents of two containers of type TreeSet<String>.

In Example 16.12, the mutable reduction performed by the stream pipeline at (16) uses a mutable container of type StringBuilder. The output from the peek() method shows that the strings produced by the iterate() method start with the initial string "ba" and are iteratively concatenated with the postfix "na". The limit() intermediate operation truncates the infinite stream to five elements. The collect() method appends the strings to a StringBuilder. The supplier creates an empty StringBuilder. The accumulator and the combiner append a CharSequence to a StringBuilder. In the case of the accumulator, the CharSequence is a String—that is, a stream element—in the call to the append() method. But in the case of the combiner, the CharSequence is a StringBuilder—that is, a partial result container when the stream is parallel. One might be tempted to use a string instead of a StringBuilder, but that would not be a good idea as a string is immutable.

Note that the accumulator and combiner of the collect() method do not return a value. The collect() method does not terminate if applied to an infinite stream, as the method will never finish processing all the elements in the stream.

Because mutable reduction uses the same mutable result container for accumulating new results by changing the state of the container, it is more efficient than a functional reduction where a new partial result always replaces the previous partial result.

Collecting to an Array

The overloaded method `toArray()` can be used to collect or accumulate into an array. It is a special case of a mutable reduction, and as the name suggests, the mutable container is an array. The numeric stream interfaces also provide a counterpart to the `toArray()` method that returns an array of a numeric type.

`Object[] toArray()`

This terminal operation returns an array containing the elements of this stream. Note that the array returned is of type `Object[]`.

`<A> A[] toArray(IntFunction<A[]> generator)`

This terminal operation returns an array containing the elements of this stream. The provided `generator` function is used to allocate the desired array. The type parameter A is the element type of the array that is returned. The size of the array (which is equal to the length of the stream) is passed to the generator function as an argument.

The zero-argument method `toArray()` returns an array of objects, `Object[]`, as generic arrays cannot be created at runtime. The method needs to store all the elements before creating an array of the appropriate length. The query at (1) finds the titles of the CDs, and the `toArray()` method collects them into an array of objects, `Object[]`.

```
Object[] objArray = CD.cdList.stream().map(CD::title)
                            .toArray();                        // (1)
//[Java Jive, Java Jam, Lambda Dancing, Keep on Erasing, Hot Generics]
```

The `toArray(IntFunction<A>)` method accepts a generator function that creates an array of type A, (A[]), whose length is passed as a parameter by the method to the generator function. The array length is determined from the number of elements in the stream. The query at (2) also finds the CD titles, but the `toArray()` method collects them into an array of strings, `String[]`. The method reference defining the generator function is equivalent to the lambda expression (`len -> new String[len]`).

```
String[] cdTitles = CD.cdList.stream().map(CD::title)
                            .toArray(String[]::new);           // (2)
//[Java Jive, Java Jam, Lambda Dancing, Keep on Erasing, Hot Generics]
```

Examples of numeric streams whose elements are collected into an array are shown at (3) and (4). The `limit()` intermediate operation at (3) converts the infinite stream into a finite one whose elements are collected into an int array.

```
int[] intArray1 = IntStream.iterate(1, i -> i + 1).limit(5).toArray();// (3)
// [1, 2, 3, 4, 5]
int[] intArray2 = IntStream.range(-5, 5).toArray();                    // (4)
// [-5, -4, -3, -2, -1, 0, 1, 2, 3, 4]
```

Not surprisingly, when applied to infinite streams the operation results in a fatal `OutOfMemoryError`, as the method cannot determine the length of the array and keeps storing the stream elements, eventually running out of memory.

```
int[] intArray3 = IntStream.iterate(1, i -> i + 1)             // (5)
                  .toArray();                                   // OutOfMemoryError!
```

If the sole purpose of using the toArray() operation in a pipeline is to convert the data source collection to an array, it is far better to use the overloaded Collection.toArray() methods. For one thing, the size of the array is easily determined from the size of the collection.

```
CD[] cdArray1 = CD.cdList.stream().toArray(CD[]::new);      // (6) Preferred.
CD[] cdArray2 = CD.cdList.toArray(new CD[CD.cdList.size()]); // (7) Not efficient.
```

Like any other mutable reduction operation, the toArray() method does not terminate when applied to an infinite stream, unless it is converted into a finite stream as at (3) above.

Collecting to a List

The method Stream.toList() implements a terminal operation that can be used to collect or accumulate the result of processing a stream into a list. Compared to the toArray() instance method, the toList() method is a default method in the Stream interface. The default implementation returns an *unmodifiable* list; that is, elements cannot be added, removed, or sorted. This unmodifiable list is created from the array into which the elements are accumulated first.

If the requirement is an unmodifiable list that allows null elements, the Stream.toList() is the clear and concise choice. Many examples of stream pipelines encountered so far in this chapter use the toList() terminal operation.

```
List<String> titles = CD.cdList.stream().map(CD::title).toList();
// [Java Jive, Java Jam, Lambda Dancing, Keep on Erasing, Hot Generics]
titles.add("Java Jingles");              // UnsupportedOperationException!
```

Like any other mutable reduction operation, the toList() method does not terminate when applied to an infinite stream, unless the stream is converted into a finite stream.

default List<T> toList()

Accumulates the elements of this stream into a List, respecting any encounter order the stream may have. The returned List is *unmodifiable* (§12.2, p. 649), and calls to any mutator method will always result in an UnsupportedOperationException. The unmodifiable list returned allows null values.

See also the toList() method in the Collectors class (p. 980).

The Collectors.toCollection(Supplier) method is recommended for greater control.

Functional Reductions Exclusive to Numeric Streams

In addition to the counterparts of the methods in the Stream<T> interface, the following functional reductions are exclusive to the numeric stream interfaces

IntStream, LongStream, and DoubleStream. These reduction operations are designed to calculate various statistics on numeric streams.

In the methods below, *NumType* is Int, Long, or Double, and the corresponding *numtype* is int, long, or double. These statistical operations do not terminate when applied to an infinite stream:

numtype sum()

This terminal operation returns the sum of elements in this stream. It returns zero if the stream is empty.

OptionalDouble average()

This terminal operation returns an OptionalDouble that encapsulates the arithmetic mean of elements of this stream, or an empty Optional if this stream is empty.

*NumType*SummaryStatistics summaryStatistics()

This terminal operation returns a *NumType*SummaryStatistics describing various summary data about the elements of this stream.

Summation

The sum() terminal operation is a special case of a functional reduction that calculates the sum of numeric values in a stream. The stream pipeline below calculates the total number of tracks on the CDs in a list. Note that the stream of CD is mapped to an int stream whose elements represent the number of tracks on a CD. The int values are cumulatively added to compute the total number of tracks.

```java
int totNumOfTracks = CD.cdList
    .stream()                    // Stream<CD>
    .mapToInt(CD::noOfTracks)    // IntStream
    .sum();                      // 42
```

The query below sums all even numbers between 1 and 100.

```java
int sumEven = IntStream
    .rangeClosed(1, 100)
    .filter(i -> i % 2 == 0)
    .sum();                      // 2550
```

The count() operation is equivalent to mapping each stream element to the value 1 and adding the 1s:

```java
int numOfCDs = CD.cdList
    .stream()
    .mapToInt(cd -> 1)           // CD => 1
    .sum();                      // 5
```

For an empty stream, the sum is always zero.

```java
double total = DoubleStream.empty().sum();    // 0.0
```

Averaging

Another common statistics to calculate is the average of values, defined as the sum of values divided by the number of values. A loop-based solution to calculate the average would explicitly sum the values, count the number of values, and do the calculation. In a stream-based solution, the average() terminal operation can be used to calculate this value. The stream pipeline below computes the average number of tracks on a CD. The CD stream is mapped to an int stream whose values are the number of tracks on a CD. The average() terminal operation adds the number of tracks and counts the values, returning the average as a double value encapsulated in an OptionalDouble.

```
OptionalDouble optAverage = CD.cdList
    .stream()
    .mapToInt(CD::noOfTracks)
    .average();
System.out.println(optAverage.orElse(0.0));          // 8.4
```

The reason for using an Optional is that the average is not defined if there are no values. The absence of a value in the OptionalDouble returned by the method means that the stream was empty.

Summarizing

The result of a functional reduction is a single value. This means that for calculating different results—for example, count, sum, average, min, and max—requires separate reduction operations on a stream.

The method summaryStatistics() does several common reductions on a stream in a single operation and returns the results in an object of type *NumType*SummaryStatistics, where *NumType* is Int, Long, or Double. An object of this class encapsulates the count, sum, average, min, and max values of a stream.

The classes IntSummaryStatistics, LongSummaryStatistics, and DoubleSummaryStatistics in the java.util package define the following constructor and methods, where *NumType* is Int (but it is Integer when used as a type name), Long, or Double, and the corresponding *numtype* is int, long, or double:

*NumType*SummaryStatistics()
Creates an empty instance with zero count, zero sum, a min value as *Num-Type*.MAX_VALUE, a max value as *NumType*.MIN_VALUE, and an average value of zero.

double getAverage()
Returns the arithmetic mean of values recorded, or zero if no values have been recorded.

long getCount()
Returns the count of values recorded.

numtype getMax()

Returns the maximum value recorded, or *NumType*.MIN_VALUE if no values have been recorded.

numtype getMin()

Returns the minimum value recorded, or *NumType*.MAX_VALUE if no values have been recorded.

numtype getSum()

Returns the sum of values recorded, or zero if no values have been recorded. The method in the IntSummaryStatistics and LongSummaryStatistics classes returns a long value. The method in the DoubleSummaryStatistics class returns a double value.

void accept(*numtype* value)

Records a new value into the summary information, and updates the various statistics. The method in the LongSummaryStatistics class is overloaded and can accept an int value as well.

void combine(*NumType*SummaryStatistics other)

Combines the state of another *NumType*SummaryStatistics into this one.

The summaryStatistics() method is used to calculate various statistics for the number of tracks on two CDs processed by the stream pipeline below. Various get methods are called on the IntSummaryStatistics object returned by the summaryStatistics() method, and the statistics are printed.

```
IntSummaryStatistics stats1 = List.of(CD.cd0, CD.cd1)
    .stream()
    .mapToInt(CD::noOfTracks)
    .summaryStatistics();
System.out.println("Count="  + stats1.getCount());     // Count=2
System.out.println("Sum="    + stats1.getSum());       // Sum=14
System.out.println("Min="    + stats1.getMin());       // Min=6
System.out.println("Max="    + stats1.getMax());       // Max=8
System.out.println("Average=" + stats1.getAverage());  // Average=7.0
```

The default format of the statistics printed by the toString() method of the IntSummaryStatistics class is shown below:

```
System.out.println(stats1);
//IntSummaryStatistics{count=2, sum=14, min=6, average=7.000000, max=8}
```

Below, the accept() method records the value 10 (the number of tracks on CD.cd2) into the summary information referenced by stats1. The resulting statistics show the new count is 3 (=2 +1), the new sum is 24 (=14+10), and the new average is 8.0 (=24.0/3.0). However, the min value was not affected but the max value has changed to 10.

```
stats1.accept(CD.cd2.noOfTracks());    // Add the value 10.
System.out.println(stats1);
//IntSummaryStatistics{count=3, sum=24, min=6, average=8.000000, max=10}
```

The code below creates another IntSummaryStatistics object that summarizes the statistics from two other CDs.

```
IntSummaryStatistics stats2 = List.of(CD.cd3, CD.cd4)
    .stream()
    .mapToInt(CD::noOfTracks)
    .summaryStatistics();
System.out.println(stats2);
//IntSummaryStatistics{count=2, sum=18, min=8, average=9.000000, max=10}
```

The combine() method incorporates the state of one IntSummaryStatistics object into another IntSummaryStatistics object. In the code below, the state of the IntSummary-Statistics object referenced by stats2 is combined with the state of the IntSummary-Statistics object referenced by stats1. The resulting summary information is printed, showing that the new count is 5 (=3 +2), the new sum is 42 (=24+18), and the new average is 8.4 (=42.0/5.0). However, the min and max values were not affected.

```
stats1.combine(stats2);                    // Combine stats2 with stats1.
System.out.println(stats1);
//IntSummaryStatistics{count=5, sum=42, min=6, average=8.400000, max=10}
```

Calling the summaryStatistics() method on an empty stream returns an instance of the IntSummaryStatistics class with a zero value set for all statistics, except for the min and max values, which are set to Integer.MAX_VALUE and Integer.MIN_VALUE, respectively. The IntSummaryStatistics class provides a zero-argument constructor that also returns an empty instance.

```
IntSummaryStatistics emptyStats = IntStream.empty().summaryStatistics();
System.out.println(emptyStats);
//IntSummaryStatistics{count=0, sum=0, min=2147483647, average=0.000000,
//max=-2147483648}
```

The summary statistics classes are not exclusive for use with streams, as they provide a constructor and appropriate methods to incorporate numeric values in order to calculate common statistics, as we have seen here. We will return to calculating statistics when we discuss built-in collectors (p. 978).

Summary of Terminal Stream Operations

The terminal operations of the Stream<T> class are summarized in Table 16.5. The type parameter declarations have been simplified, where any bound <? super T> or <? extends T> has been replaced by <T>, without impacting the intent of a method. A reference is provided to each method in the first column.

The last column in Table 16.5 indicates the function type of the corresponding parameter in the previous column. It is instructive to note how the functional interface parameters provide the parameterized behavior of an operation. For example, the method allMatch() returns a boolean value to indicate whether all elements of a stream satisfy a given predicate. This predicate is implemented as a functional interface Predicate<T> that is applied to each element in the stream.

The interfaces IntStream, LongStream, and DoubleStream define analogous methods to those shown for the Stream<T> interface in Table 16.5. Methods that are only defined by the numeric stream interfaces are shown in Table 16.6.

Table 16.5 *Terminal Stream Operations*

Method name (ref.)	Any type parameter + return type	Functional interface parameters	Function type of parameters
forEach (p. 948)	void	(Consumer<T> action)	T -> void
forEachOrdered (p. 948)	void	(Consumer<T> action)	T -> void
allMatch (p. 949)	boolean	(Predicate<T> predicate)	T -> boolean
anyMatch (p. 949)	boolean	(Predicate<T> predicate)	T -> boolean
noneMatch (p. 949)	boolean	(Predicate<T> predicate)	T -> boolean
findAny (p. 952)	Optional<T>	()	
findFirst (p. 952)	Optional<T>	()	
count (p. 953)	long	()	
max (p. 954)	Optional<T>	(Comparator<T> cmp)	(T,T) -> int
min (p. 954)	Optional<T>	(Comparator<T> cmp)	(T,T) -> int
reduce (p. 955)	Optional<T>	(BinaryOperator<T> accumulator)	(T,T) -> T
reduce (p. 955)	T	(T identity, BinaryOperator<T> accumulator)	T -> T, (T,T) -> T
reduce (p. 955)	<U> U	(U identity, BiFunction<U,T,U> accumulator, BinaryOperator<U> combiner)	U -> U, (U,T) -> U, (U,U) -> U
collect (p. 964)	<R,A> R	(Collector<T,A,R> collector)	Parameter is not a functional interface.
collect (p. 964)	<R> R	(Supplier<R> supplier, BiConsumer<R,T> accumulator, BiConsumer<R,R> combiner)	() -> R, (R,T) -> void, (R,R) -> void
toArray (p. 971)	Object[]	()	
toArray (p. 971)	<A> A[]	(IntFunction<A[]> generator)	int -> A[]
toList (p. 972)	List<T>	()	

Table 16.6 *Additional Terminal Operations in the Numeric Stream Interfaces*

Method name (ref.)	Return type
average (p. 949)	Optional*NumType*, where *NumType* is Int, Long, or Double
sum (p. 949)	*numtype*, where *numtype* is int, long, or double
summaryStatistics (p. 974)	*NumType*SummaryStatistics, where *NumType* is Int, Long, or Double

16.8 Collectors

A *collector* encapsulates the functions required for performing reduction: the supplier, the accumulator, the combiner, and the finisher. It can provide these functions since it implements the Collector interface (in the java.util.stream package) that defines the methods to create these functions. It is passed as an argument to the collect(Collector) method in order to perform a reduction operation. In contrast, the collect(Supplier, BiConsumer, BiConsumer) method requires the functions supplier, accumulator, and combiner, respectively, to be passed as arguments in the method call.

Details of implementing a collector are not necessary for our purposes, as we will exclusively use the extensive set of predefined collectors provided by the static factory methods of the Collectors class in the java.util.stream package (Table 16.7, p. 1005). In most cases, it should be possible to find a predefined collector for the task at hand. The collectors use various kinds of containers for performing reduction—for example, accumulating to a map, or finding the minimum or maximum element. For example, the Collectors.toList() factory method creates a collector that performs mutable reduction using a list as a mutable container. It can be passed to the collect(Collector) terminal operation of a stream.

It is a common practice to import the static factory methods of the Collectors class in the code so that the methods can be called by their simple names.

```
import static java.util.stream.Collectors.*;
```

However, the practice adopted in this chapter is to assume that only the Collectors class is imported, enforcing the connection between the static methods and the class to be done explicitly in the code. Of course, static import of factory methods can be used once familiarity with the collectors is established.

```
import java.util.stream.Collectors;
```

The three-argument collect() method is primarily used to implement mutable reduction, whereas the Collectors class provides collectors for both functional and mutable reduction that can be either used in a stand-alone capacity or composed with other collectors.

One group of collectors is designed to collect to a *predetermined container*, which is evident from the name of the static factory method that creates it: toCollection, toList, toSet, and toMap (p. 979). The overloaded toCollection() and toMap() methods allow a specific implementation of a collection and a map to be used, respectively—for example, a TreeSet for a collection and a TreeMap for a map. In addition, there is the joining() method that creates a collector for concatenating the input elements to a String—however, internally it uses a mutable StringBuilder (p. 984).

Collectors can be composed with other collectors; that is, the partial results from one collector can be additionally processed by another collector (called the *downstream collector*) to produce the final result. Many collectors that can be used as a downstream collector perform functional reduction such as counting values, finding the minimum and maximum values, summing values, averaging values, and summarizing common statistics for values (p. 998).

Composition of collectors is utilized to perform *multilevel grouping* and *partitioning* on stream elements (p. 985). The groupingBy() and partitionBy() methods return composed collectors to create *classification maps*. In such a map, the keys are determined by a *classifier function*, and the values are the result of a downstream collector, called the *classification mapping*. For example, the CDs in a stream could be classified into a map where the key represents the number of tracks on a CD and the associated value of a key can be a list of CDs with the same number of tracks. The list of CDs with the same number of tracks is the result of an appropriate downstream collector.

Collecting to a Collection

The method toCollection(Supplier) creates a collector that uses a mutable container of a specific Collection type to perform mutable reduction. A supplier to create the mutable container is specified as an argument to the method.

The following stream pipeline creates an ArrayList<String> instance with the titles of all CDs in the stream. The constructor reference ArrayList::new returns an empty ArrayList<String> instance, where the element type String is inferred from the context.

```
ArrayList<String> cdTitles1 = CD.cdList.stream() // Stream<CD>
  .map(CD::title)                                 // Stream<String>
    .collect(Collectors.toCollection(ArrayList::new));
//[Java Jive, Java Jam, Lambda Dancing, Keep on Erasing, Hot Generics]
```

static <T,C extends Collection<T>> Collector<T,?,C>
        toCollection(Supplier<C> collectionFactory)

Returns a Collector that accumulates the input elements of type T into a new Collection of type C, in encounter order. A new empty Collection of type C is created by the collectionFactory supplier, thus the collection created can be of a specific Collection type.

```
static <T> Collector<T,?,List<T>> toList()
static <T> Collector<T,?,List<T>> toUnmodifiableList()
```

Return a Collector that accumulates the input elements of type T into a new List or an unmodifiable List of type T, respectively, in encounter order.

The toList() method gives no guarantees of any kind for the returned list.

The unmodifiable list returned does not allow null values.

See also the Stream.toList() terminal operation (p. 972).

```
static <T> Collector<T,?,Set<T>> toSet()
static <T> Collector<T,?,Set<T>> toUnmodifiableSet()
```

Return an unordered Collector that accumulates the input elements of type T into a new Set or an unmodifiable Set of type T, respectively.

Collecting to a List

The method toList() creates a collector that uses a mutable container of type List to perform mutable reduction. This collector guarantees to preserve the encounter order of the input stream, if it has one. For more control over the type of the list, the toCollection() method can be used. This collector can be used as a *downstream collector*.

The following stream pipeline creates a list with the titles of all CDs in the stream using a collector returned by the Collectors.toList() method. Although the returned list is modified, this is implementation dependent and should not be relied upon.

```
List<String> cdTitles3 = CD.cdList.stream()        // Stream<CD>
    .map(CD::title)                                 // Stream<String>
    .collect(Collectors.toList());
//[Java Jive, Java Jam, Lambda Dancing, Keep on Erasing, Hot Generics]
titles.add("Java Jingles");                         // OK
```

Collecting to a Set

The method toSet() creates a collector that uses a mutable container of type Set to perform mutable reduction. The collector does not guarantee to preserve the encounter order of the input stream. For more control over the type of the set, the toCollection() method can be used.

The following stream pipeline creates a set with the titles of all CDs in the stream.

```
Set<String> cdTitles2 = CD.cdList.stream()          // Stream<CD>
    .map(CD::title)                                 // Stream<String>
    .collect(Collectors.toSet());
//[Hot Generics, Java Jive, Lambda Dancing, Keep on Erasing, Java Jam]
```

Collecting to a Map

The method toMap() creates a collector that performs mutable reduction to a mutable container of type Map.

```
static <T,K,U> Collector<T,?,Map<K,U>> toMap(
        Function<? super T,? extends K> keyMapper,
        Function<? super T,? extends U> valueMapper)

static <T,K,U> Collector<T,?,Map<K,U>> toMap(
        Function<? super T,? extends K> keyMapper,
        Function<? super T,? extends U> valueMapper,
        BinaryOperator<U>               mergeFunction)

static <T,K,U,M extends Map<K,U>> Collector<T,?,M> toMap(
        Function<? super T,? extends K> keyMapper,
        Function<? super T,? extends U> valueMapper,
        BinaryOperator<U>               mergeFunction,
        Supplier<M>                     mapSupplier)
```

Return a Collector that accumulates elements of type T into a Map whose keys and values are the result of applying the provided key and value mapping functions to the input elements.

The keyMapper function produces keys of type K, and the valueMapper function produces values of type U.

In the first method, the mapped keys cannot have duplicates—an IllegalStateException will be thrown if that is the case.

In the second and third methods, the mergeFunction binary operator is used to resolve collisions between values associated with the same key, as supplied to Map.merge(Object, Object, BiFunction).

In the third method, the provided mapSupplier function returns a new Map into which the results will be inserted.

The collector returned by the method toMap() uses either a default map or one that is supplied. To be able to create an entry in a Map<K,U> from stream elements of type T, the collector requires two functions:

- keyMapper: T -> K, which is a Function to extract a key of type K from a stream element of type T.
- valueMapper: T -> U, which is a Function to extract a value of type U for a given key of type K from a stream element of type T.

Additional functions as arguments allow various controls to be exercised on the map:

- mergeFunction: (U,U) -> U, which is a BinaryOperator to merge two values that are associated with the same key. The merge function must be specified if collision of values can occur during the mutable reduction, or a resounding exception will be thrown.

- mapSupplier: () -> M extends Map<K,V>, which is a Supplier that creates a map instance of a specific type to use for mutable reduction. The map created is a subtype of Map<K,V>. Without this function, the collector uses a default map.

Figure 16.15 illustrates collecting to a map. The stream pipeline creates a map of CD titles and their release year—that is, a Map<String, Year>, where K is String and V is Year. The keyMapper CD::title and the valueMapper CD::year extract the title (String) and the year (Year) from each CD in the stream, respectively. The entries are accumulated in a default map (Map<String, Year>).

What if we wanted to create a map with CDs and their release year—that is, a Map<CD, Year>? In that case, the keyMapper should return the CD as the key—that is, map a CD to itself. That is exactly what the keyMapper Function.identity() does in the pipeline below.

```
Map<CD, Year> mapCDToYear = CD.cdList.stream()
    .collect(Collectors.toMap(Function.identity(), CD::year)); // Map<CD, Year>
```

Figure 16.15 *Collecting to a Map*

```
//Query: Create a map of CD titles and their release year.
Map<String, Year> mapTitleToYear = CD.cdList.stream()
    .collect(Collectors.toMap(CD::title, CD::year));
```

(a) Using the Collectors.toMap() *method*

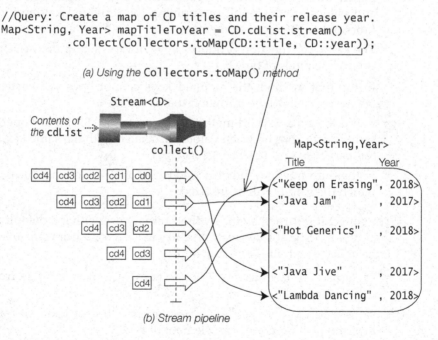

(b) Stream pipeline

As there were no duplicates of the key in the previous two examples, there was no collision of values in the map. In the list dupList below, there are duplicates of CDs (CD.cd0, CD.cd1). Executing the pipeline results in a runtime exception at (1).

```
List<CD> dupList = List.of(CD.cd0, CD.cd1, CD.cd2, CD.cd0, CD.cd1);
Map<String, Year> mapTitleToYear1 = dupList.stream()
    .collect(Collectors.toMap(CD::title, CD::year));        // (1)
// IllegalStateException: Duplicate key 2017
```

The collision values can be resolved by specifying a merge function. In the pipeline below, the arguments of the merge function (y1, y2) -> y1 at (1) have the same value for the year if we assume that a CD can only be released once. Note that y1 and y2 denote the existing value in the map and the value to merge, respectively. The merge function can return any one of the values to resolve the collision.

```
Map<String, Year> mapTitleToYear2 = dupList.stream()
    .collect(Collectors.toMap(CD::title, CD::year, (y1, y2) -> y1));        // (1)
```

The stream pipeline below creates a map of CD titles released each year. As more than one CD can be released in a year, collision of titles can occur for a year. The merge function (tt, t) -> tt + ":" + t concatenates the titles in each year separated by a colon, if necessary. Note that tt and t denote the existing value in the map and the value to merge, respectively.

```
Map<Year, String> mapTitleToYear3 = CD.cdList.stream()
    .collect(Collectors.toMap(CD::year, CD::title,
                              (tt, t) -> tt + ":" + t));
//{2017=Java Jive:Java Jam, 2018=Lambda Dancing:Keep on Erasing:Hot Generics}
```

The stream pipeline below creates a map with the longest title released each year. For greater control over the type of the map in which to accumulate the entries, a supplier is specified. The supplier TreeMap::new returns an empty instance of a TreeMap in which the entries are accumulated. The keys in such a map are sorted in their natural order—the class java.time.Year implements the Comparable<Year> interface.

```
TreeMap<Year, String> mapYearToLongestTitle = CD.cdList.stream()
    .collect(Collectors.toMap(CD::year, CD::title,
                              BinaryOperator.maxBy(Comparator.naturalOrder()),
                              TreeMap::new));
//{2017=Java Jive, 2018=Lambda Dancing}
```

The merge function specified is equivalent to the following lambda expression, returning the greater of two strings:

```
(str1, str2) -> str1.compareTo(str2) > 0 ? str1 : str2
```

Collecting to a ConcurrentMap

If the collector returned by the Collectors.toMap() method is used in a parallel stream, the multiple partial maps created during parallel execution are merged by the collector to create the final result map. Merging maps can be expensive if keys from one map are merged into another. To address the problem, the Collectors class provides the three overloaded methods toConcurrentMap(), analogous to the three toMap() methods, that return a *concurrent collector*—that is, a collector that uses a single *concurrent map* to perform the reduction. A concurrent map is *thread-safe* and *unordered*. A concurrent map implements the java.util.concurrent.ConcurrentMap interface, which is a subinterface of java.util.Map interface (§23.7, p. 1482).

Using a concurrent map avoids merging of maps during parallel execution, as a single map is created that is used concurrently to accumulate the results from the execution of each substream. However, the concurrent map is unordered—any encounter order in the stream is ignored. Usage of the toConcurrentMap() method is illustrated by the following example of a parallel stream to create a concurrent map of CD titles released each year.

```
ConcurrentMap<Year, String> concMapYearToTitles = CD.cdList
    .parallelStream()
    .collect(Collectors.toConcurrentMap(CD::year, CD::title,
                                        (tt, t) -> tt + ":" + t));
//{2017=Java Jam:Java Jive, 2018=Lambda Dancing:Hot Generics:Keep on Erasing}
```

Joining

The joining() method creates a collector for concatenating the input elements of type CharSequence to a single immutable String. However, internally it uses a mutable StringBuilder. Note that the collector returned by the joining() methods performs *functional* reduction, as its result is a single immutable string.

```
static Collector<CharSequence,?,String> joining()
static Collector<CharSequence,?,String> joining(CharSequence delimiter)
static Collector<CharSequence,?,String> joining(CharSequence delimiter,
                                                CharSequence prefix,
                                                CharSequence suffix)
```

Return a Collector that concatenates CharSequence elements into a String. The first method concatenates in encounter order. So does the second method, but this method separates the elements by the specified delimiter. The third method in addition applies the specified prefix and suffix to the result of the concatenation.

The wildcard ? is a type parameter that is used internally by the collector.

The methods preserve the encounter order, if the stream has one.

Among the classes that implement the CharSequence interface are the String, StringBuffer, and StringBuilder classes.

The stream pipelines below concatenate CD titles to illustrate the three overloaded joining() methods. The CharSequence elements are Strings. The strings are concatenated in the stream encounter order, which is the positional order for lists. The zero-argument joining() method at (1) performs string concatenation of the CD titles using a StringBuilder internally, and returns the result as a string.

```
String concatTitles1 = CD.cdList.stream()        // Stream<CD>
    .map(CD::title)                              // Stream<String>
    .collect(Collectors.joining());              // (1)
//Java JiveJava JamLambda DancingKeep on ErasingHot Generics
```

The single-argument joining() method at (2) concatenates the titles using the specified delimiter.

```
String concatTitles2 = CD.cdList.stream()
    .map(CD::title)
    .collect(Collectors.joining(", "));          // (2) Delimiter
//Java Jive, Java Jam, Lambda Dancing, Keep on Erasing, Hot Generics
```

The three-argument `joining()` method at (3) concatenates the titles using the specified delimiter, prefix, and suffix.

```
String concatTitles3 = CD.cdList.stream()
    .map(CD::title)
    .collect(Collectors.joining(", ", "[", "]"));  // (3) Delimiter, Prefix, Suffix
//[Java Jive, Java Jam, Lambda Dancing, Keep on Erasing, Hot Generics]
```

Grouping

Classifying elements into groups based on some criteria is a very common operation. An example is classifying CDs into groups according to the number of tracks on them (this sounds esoteric, but it will illustrate the point). Such an operation can be accomplished by the collector returned by the `groupingBy()` method. The method is passed a *classifier function* that is used to classify the elements into different groups. The result of the operation is a *classification map* whose entries are the different groups into which the elements have been classified. The key in a map entry is the result of applying the classifier function on the element. The key is extracted from the element based on some property of the element—for example, the number of tracks on the CD. The value associated with a key in a map entry comprises those elements that belong to the same group. The operation is analogous to the *group-by* operation in databases.

There are three versions of the `groupingBy()` method that provide increasingly more control over the grouping operation.

```
static <T,K> Collector<T,?,Map<K,List<T>>> groupingBy(
        Function<? super T,? extends K> classifier)

static <T,K,A,D> Collector<T,?,Map<K,D>> groupingBy(
        Function<? super T,? extends K> classifier,
        Collector<? super T,A,D>        downstream)

static <T,K,D,A,M extends Map<K,D>> Collector<T,?,M> groupingBy(
        Function<? super T,? extends K> classifier,
        Supplier<M>                     mapSupplier,
        Collector<? super T,A,D>        downstream)
```

The `Collector` returned by the `groupingBy()` methods implements a *group-by* operation on input elements to create a *classification map*.

The *classifier function* maps elements of type `T` to keys of some type `K`. These keys determine the groups in the classification map.

The collector returned by the single-argument method produces a classification map of type `Map<K, List<T>>`. The keys in this map are the results from applying the specified classifier function to the input elements. The input elements that map to the same key are accumulated into a `List` by the *default downstream collector* `Collector.toList()`.

The two-argument method accepts a downstream collector, in addition to the classifier function. The collector returned by the method is composed with the specified downstream collector that performs a reduction operation on the input elements that map to the same key. It operates on elements of type T and produces a result of type D. The result of type D produced by the downstream collector is the value associated with the key of type K. The composed collector thus results in a classification map of type Map<K, D>.

The three-argument method accepts a map supplier as its second parameter. It creates an empty classification map of type M that is used by the composed collector. The result is a classification map of type M whose key and value types are K and D, respectively.

Figure 16.16 illustrates the groupingBy() operation by grouping CDs according to the number of tracks on them. The classifier function CD::noOfTracks extracts the number of tracks from a CD that acts as a key in the classification map (Map<Integer, List<CD>>). Since the call to the groupingBy() method in Figure 16.16 does not specify a downstream collector, the default downstream collector Collector.to-List() is used to accumulate CDs that have the same number of tracks. The number of groups—that is, the number of distinct keys—is equal to the number of distinct values for the number of tracks on the CDs. Each distinct value for the number of tracks is associated with the list of CDs having that value as the number of tracks.

Figure 16.16 *Grouping*

```
// Query: Group by number of tracks.
Map<Integer, List<CD>> map11 = CD.cdList.stream()
    .collect(Collectors.groupingBy(CD::noOfTracks));   // (1)
```

(a) Using the Collectors.groupBy() *method*

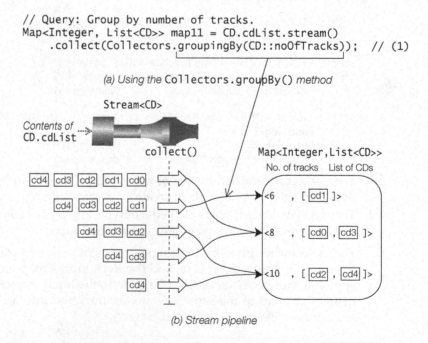

(b) Stream pipeline

The three stream pipelines below result in a classification map that is equivalent to the one in Figure 16.16. The call to the groupingBy() method at (2) specifies the downstream collector explicitly, and is equivalent to the call in Figure 16.16.

```
Map<Integer, List<CD>> map22 = CD.cdList.stream()
    .collect(Collectors.groupingBy(CD::noOfTracks, Collectors.toList()));  // (2)
```

The call to the groupingBy() method at (3) specifies the supplier TreeMap:new so that a TreeMap<Integer, List<CD>> is used as the classification map.

```
Map<Integer, List<CD>> map33 = CD.cdList.stream()
    .collect(Collectors.groupingBy(CD::noOfTracks,                          // (3)
                         TreeMap::new,
                         Collectors.toList()));
```

The call to the groupingBy() method at (4) specifies the downstream collector Collector.toSet() that uses a set to accumulate the CDs for a group.

```
Map<Integer, Set<CD>> map44 = CD.cdList.stream()
    .collect(Collectors.groupingBy(CD::noOfTracks, Collectors.toSet()));    // (4)
```

The classification maps created by the pipelines above will contain the three entries shown below, but only the groupingBy() method call at (3) can guarantee that the entries will be sorted in a TreeMap<Integer, List<CD>> according to the natural order for the Integer keys.

```
{
6=[<Jaav, "Java Jam", 6, 2017, JAZZ>],
8=[<Jaav, "Java Jive", 8, 2017, POP>,
    <Genericos, "Keep on Erasing", 8, 2018, JAZZ>],
10=[<Funkies, "Lambda Dancing", 10, 2018, POP>,
    <Genericos, "Hot Generics", 10, 2018, JAZZ>]
}
```

In general, any collector can be passed as a downstream collector to the groupingBy() method. In the stream pipeline below, the map value in the classification map is a count of the number of CDs having the same number of tracks. The collector Collector.counting() performs a functional reduction to count the CDs having the same number of tracks (p. 998).

```
Map<Integer, Long> map55 = CD.cdList.stream()
    .collect(Collectors.groupingBy(CD::noOfTracks, Collectors.counting()));
//{6=1, 8=2, 10=2}
```

Multilevel Grouping

The downstream collector in a groupingBy() operation can be created by another groupingBy() operation, resulting in a *multilevel grouping* operation—also known as a *multilevel classification* or *cascaded grouping* operation. We can extend the multilevel groupingBy() operation to any number of levels by making the downstream collector be a groupingBy() operation.

The stream pipeline below creates a classification map in which the CDs are first grouped by the number of tracks in a CD at (1), and then grouped by the musical genre of a CD at (2).

```
Map<Integer, Map<Genre, List<CD>>> twoLevelGrp = CD.cdList.stream()
    .collect(Collectors.groupingBy(CD::noOfTracks,              // (1)
             Collectors.groupingBy(CD::genre)));                // (2)
```

Printing the contents of the resulting classification map would show the following three entries, not necessarily in this order:

```
{
6={JAZZ=[<Jaav, "Java Jam", 6, 2017, JAZZ>]},
8={JAZZ=[<Genericos, "Keep on Erasing", 8, 2018, JAZZ>],
    POP=[<Jaav, "Java Jive", 8, 2017, POP>]},
10={JAZZ=[<Genericos, "Hot Generics", 10, 2018, JAZZ>],
    POP=[<Funkies, "Lambda Dancing", 10, 2018, POP>]}
}
```

The entries of the resulting classification map can also be illustrated as a two-dimensional matrix, as shown in Figure 16.16, where the CDs are first grouped into rows by the number of tracks, and then grouped into columns by the musical genre. The value of an element in the matrix is a list of CDs which have the same number of tracks (row) and the same musical genre (column).

Figure 16.17   *Multilevel Grouping as a Two-Dimensional Matrix*

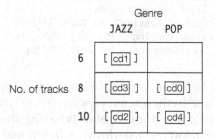

The number of groups in the classification map returned by the above pipeline is equal to the number of distinct values for the number of tracks, as in the single-level groupingBy() operation. However, each value associated with a key in the outer classification map is now an inner classification map that is managed by the second-level groupingBy() operation. The inner classification map has the type Map<Genre, List<CD>>; in other words, the key in the inner classification map is the musical genre of the CD and the value associated with this key is a List of CDs with this musical genre. It is the second-level groupingBy() operation that is responsible for grouping each CD in the inner classification map. Since no explicit downstream collector is specified for the second-level groupingBy() operation, it uses the default downstream collector Collector.toList().

We can modify the multilevel groupingBy() operation to count the CDs that have the same musical genre and the same number of tracks by specifying an explicit downstream collector for the second-level groupingBy() operation, as shown at (3).

The collector `Collectors.counting()` at (3) performs a functional reduction by accumulating the count for CDs with the same number of tracks and the same musical genre in the inner classification map (p. 998).

```
Map<Integer, Map<Genre, Long>> twoLevelGrp2 = CD.cdList.stream()
    .collect(Collectors.groupingBy(CD::noOfTracks,
                Collectors.groupingBy(CD::genre,
                        Collectors.counting()))));    // (3)
```

Printing the contents of the resulting classification map produced by this multi-level `groupingBy()` operation would show the following three entries, again not necessarily in this order:

```
{6={JAZZ=1}, 8={JAZZ=1, POP=1}, 10={JAZZ=1, POP=1}}
```

It is instructive to compare the entries in the resulting classification maps in the two examples illustrated here.

To truly appreciate the `groupingBy()` operation, the reader is highly encouraged to implement the multilevel grouping examples in an imperative style, without using the Stream API. Good luck!

Grouping to a `ConcurrentMap`

If the collector returned by the `Collectors.groupingBy()` method is used in a parallel stream, the partial maps created during execution are merged to create the final map—as in the case of the `Collectors.toMap()` method (p. 983). Merging maps can carry a performance penalty. The `Collectors` class provides the three `groupingBy-Concurrent()` overloaded methods, analogous to the three `groupingBy()` methods, that return a *concurrent collector*—that is, a collector that uses a single *concurrent map* to perform the reduction. The entries in such a map are unordered. A concurrent map implements the `java.util.concurrent.ConcurrentMap` interface (§23.7, p. 1482).

Usage of the `groupingByConcurrent()` method is illustrated by the following example of a parallel stream to create a concurrent map of the number of CDs that have the same number of tracks.

```
ConcurrentMap<Integer, Long> map66 = CD.cdList
    .parallelStream()
    .collect(Collectors.groupingByConcurrent(CD::noOfTracks,
                            Collectors.counting()));
//{6=1, 8=2, 10=2}
```

Partitioning

Partitioning is a special case of grouping. The classifier function that was used for grouping is now a *partitioning predicate* in the `partitioningBy()` method. The predicate function returns the boolean value `true` or `false`. As the keys of the resulting map are determined by the classifier function, the keys are determined by the partitioning predicate in the case of partitioning. Thus the keys are always of type

Boolean, implying that the classification map can have, at most, two map entries. In other words, the partitioningBy() method can only create, at most, two partitions from the input elements. The map value associated with a key in the resulting map is managed by a downstream collector, as in the case of the groupingBy() method.

There are two versions of the partitioningBy() method:

```
static <T> Collector<T,?,Map<Boolean,List<T>>> partitioningBy(
       Predicate<? super T>    predicate)

static <T,D,A> Collector<T,?,Map<Boolean,D>> partitioningBy(
       Predicate<? super T>    predicate,
       Collector<? super T,A,D> downstream)
```

The collector returned by the first method produces a classification map of type Map<Boolean, List<T>>. The keys in this map are the results from applying the partitioning predicate to the input elements. The input elements that map to the same Boolean key are accumulated into a List by the *default downstream collector* Collector.toList().

The second method accepts a downstream collector, in addition to the partitioning predicate. The collector returned by the method is composed with the specified downstream collector that performs a reduction operation on the input elements that map to the same key. It operates on elements of type T and produces a result of type D. The result of type D produced by the downstream collector is the value associated with the key of type Boolean. The composed collector thus results in a resulting map of type Map<Boolean, D>.

Figure 16.18 illustrates the partitioningBy() operation by partitioning CDs according to the predicate CD::isPop that determines whether a CD is a pop music CD. The result of the partitioning predicate acts as the key in the resulting map of type Map<Boolean, List<CD>>. Since the call to the partitioningBy() method in Figure 16.18 does not specify a downstream collector, the default downstream collector Collector.toList() is used to accumulate CDs that map to the same key. The resulting map has two entries or partitions: one for CDs that are pop music CDs and one for CDs that are not. The two entries of the resulting map are also shown below:

```
{false=[<Jaav, "Java Jam", 6, 2017, JAZZ>,
        <Genericos, "Keep on Erasing", 8, 2018, JAZZ>,
        <Genericos, "Hot Generics", 10, 2018, JAZZ>],
  true=[<Jaav, "Java Jive", 8, 2017, POP>,
        <Funkies, "Lambda Dancing", 10, 2018, POP>]}
```

The values in a partition can be obtained by calling the Map.get() method:

```
List<CD> popCDs = map1.get(true);
List<CD> nonPopCDs = map1.get(false);
```

The stream pipeline at (2) is equivalent to the one in Figure 16.18, where the downstream collector is specified explicitly.

```
Map<Boolean, List<CD>> map2 = CD.cdList.stream()
     .collect(Collectors.partitioningBy(CD::isPop, Collectors.toList())); // (2)
```

We could have composed a stream pipeline to filter the CDs that are pop music CDs and collected them into a list. We would have to compose a second pipeline to find the CDs that are *not* pop music CDs. However, the `partitioningBy()` method does both in a single operation.

Figure 16.18   *Partitioning*

```
// Query: Partition by whether it is a pop music CD.
Map<Boolean, List<CD>> map1 = CD.cdList.stream()
    .collect(Collectors.partitioningBy(CD::isPop));        // (1)
```

(a) Using the `Collectors.partitionBy()` *method*

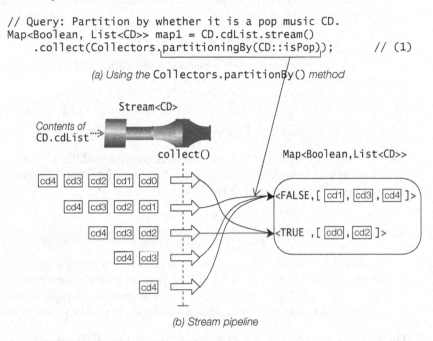

(b) Stream pipeline

Analogous to the `groupingBy()` method, any collector can be passed as a downstream collector to the `partitioningBy()` method. In the stream pipeline below, the downstream collector `Collector.counting()` performs a functional reduction to count the number of CDs associated with a key (p. 998).

```
Map<Boolean, Long> map3 = CD.cdList.stream()
    .collect(Collectors.partitioningBy(CD::isPop, Collectors.counting()));
//{false=3, true=2}
```

Multilevel Partitioning

Like the `groupingBy()` method, the `partitioningBy()` operation can be used in multilevel classification. The downstream collector in a `partitioningBy()` operation can be created by another `partitioningBy()` operation, resulting in a *multilevel partitioning* operation—also known as a *cascaded partitioning* operation. The downstream collector can also be a `groupingBy()` operation.

In the stream pipeline below, the CDs are partitioned at (1): one partition for CDs that are pop music CDs, and one for those that are not. The CDs that are associated with a key are grouped by the year in which they were released. Note that the CDs that were released in a year are accumulated into a List by the default downstream collector Collector.toList() that is employed by the groupingBy() operation at (2).

```
Map<Boolean, Map<Year, List<CD>>> map1 = CD.cdList.stream()
    .collect(Collectors.partitioningBy(CD::isPop,                  // (1)
            Collectors.groupingBy(CD::year)));                     // (2)
```

Printing the contents of the resulting map would show the following two entries, not necessarily in this order.

```
{false={2017=[<Jaav, "Java Jam", 6, 2017, JAZZ>],
        2018=[<Genericos, "Keep on Erasing", 8, 2018, JAZZ>,
            <Genericos, "Hot Generics", 10, 2018, JAZZ>]},
 true={2017=[<Jaav, "Java Jive", 8, 2017, POP>],
        2018=[<Funkies, "Lambda Dancing", 10, 2018, POP>]}}
```

Filtering Adapter for Downstream Collectors

The filtering() method of the Collectors class encapsulates a *predicate* and a *downstream collector* to create an *adapter* for a *filtering* operation. (See also the filter() intermediate operation, p. 912.)

```
static <T,A,R> Collector<T,?,R> filtering(
        Predicate<? super T>       predicate,
        Collector<? super T,A,R> downstream)
```

Returns a Collector that applies the predicate to input elements of type T to determine which elements should be passed to the downstream collector. This downstream collector accumulates them into results of type R, where the type parameter A is the intermediate accumulation type of the downstream collector.

The following code uses the filtering() operation at (2) to group pop music CDs according to the number of tracks on them. The groupingBy() operation at (1) creates the groups based on the number of tracks on the CDs, but the filtering() operation only allows pop music CDs to pass downstream to be accumulated.

```
// Filtering downstream from grouping.
Map<Integer, List<CD>> grpByTracksFilterByPopCD = CD.cdList.stream()
    .collect(Collectors.groupingBy(CD::noOfTracks,                      // (1)
            Collectors.filtering(CD::isPop, Collectors.toList())));  // (2)
```

Printing the contents of the resulting map would show the entries below, not necessarily in this order. Note that the output shows that there was one or more CDs with six tracks, but there were no pop music CDs. Hence the list of CDs associated with key 6 is empty.

```
{6=[],
 8=[<Jaav, "Java Jive", 8, 2017, POP>],
 10=[<Funkies, "Lambda Dancing", 10, 2018, POP>]}
```

However, if we run the same query using the filter() intermediate stream operation at (1) prior to grouping, the contents of the result map are different, as shown below.

```
// Filtering before grouping.
Map<Integer, List<CD>> filterByPopCDGrpByTracks = CD.cdList.stream()
    .filter(CD::isPop)                                        // (1)
    .collect(Collectors.groupingBy(CD::noOfTracks, Collectors.toList()));
```

Contents of the result map show that only entries that have a non-empty list as a value are contained in the map. This is not surprising, as any non-pop music CD is discarded before grouping, so only pop music CDs are grouped.

```
{8=[<Jaav, "Java Jive", 8, 2017, POP>],
 10=[<Funkies, "Lambda Dancing", 10, 2018, POP>]}
```

There are no surprises with partitioning, regardless of whether filtering is done before or after the partitioning, as partitioning always results in a map with two entries: one for the Boolean.TRUE key and one for the Boolean.FALSE key. The code below partitions CDs released in 2018 according to whether a CD is a pop music CD or not.

```
// Filtering downstream from partitioning.
Map<Boolean, List<CD>> partbyPopCDsFilterByYear = CD.cdList.stream()     // (1)
    .collect(Collectors.partitioningBy(CD::isPop,
                Collectors.filtering(cd -> cd.year().equals(Year.of(2018)),
                            Collectors.toList())));  // (2)
```

```
// Filtering before partitioning.
Map<Boolean, List<CD>> filterByYearPartbyPopCDs = CD.cdList.stream()     // (2)
    .filter(cd -> cd.year().equals(Year.of(2018)))
    .collect(Collectors.partitioningBy(CD::isPop, Collectors.toList()));
```

Both queries at (1) and (2) above will result in the same entries in the result map:

```
{false=[<Genericos, "Keep on Erasing", 8, 2018, JAZZ>,
        <Genericos, "Hot Generics", 10, 2018, JAZZ>],
 true=[<Funkies, "Lambda Dancing", 10, 2018, POP>]}
```

Mapping Adapter for Downstream Collectors

The mapping() method of the Collectors class encapsulates a *mapper function* and a *downstream collector* to create an *adapter* for a *mapping* operation. (See also the map() intermediate operation, p. 921.)

```
static <T,U,A,R> Collector<T,?,R> mapping(
        Function<? super T,? extends U> mapper,
        Collector<? super U,A,R>        downstream)
```

Returns a Collector that applies the mapper function to input elements of type T and provides the mapped results of type U to the downstream collector that accumulates them into results of type R.

In other words, the method adapts a downstream collector accepting elements of type U to one accepting elements of type T by applying a mapper function to each input element before accumulation, where type parameter A is the intermediate accumulation type of the downstream collector.

The mapping() method at (1) creates an adapter that accumulates a set of CD titles in each year for a stream of CDs. The mapper function maps a CD to its title so that the downstream collector can accumulate the titles in a set.

```
Map<Year, Set<String>> titlesByYearInSet = CD.cdList.stream()
    .collect(Collectors.groupingBy(
        CD::year,
        Collectors.mapping(                              // (1)
            CD::title,                                   // Mapper
            Collectors.toSet())));                       // Downstream collector
System.out.println(titlesByYearInSet);
// {2017=[Java Jive, Java Jam],
//  2018=[Hot Generics, Lambda Dancing, Keep on Erasing]}
```

The mapping() method at (2) creates an adapter that joins CD titles in each year for a stream of CDs. The mapper function maps a CD to its title so that the downstream collector can join the titles.

```
Map<Year, String> joinTitlesByYear = CD.cdList.stream()
    .collect(Collectors.groupingBy(
        CD::year,
        Collectors.mapping(                              // (2)
            CD::title,
            Collectors.joining(":"))));
System.out.println(joinTitlesByYear);
// {2017=Java Jive:Java Jam,
//  2018=Lambda Dancing:Keep on Erasing:Hot Generics}
```

The mapping() method at (3) creates an adapter that counts the number of CD tracks for each year for a stream of CDs. The mapper function maps a CD to its number of tracks so that the downstream collector can count the total number of tracks.

```
Map<Year, Long> TotalNumOfTracksByYear = CD.cdList.stream()
    .collect(Collectors.groupingBy(
        CD::year,
        Collectors.mapping(                              // (3)
            CD::noOfTracks,
            Collectors.counting())));
System.out.println(TotalNumOfTracksByYear);              // {2017=2, 2018=3}
```

Flat Mapping Adapter for Downstream Collectors

The flatMapping() method of the Collectors class encapsulates a *mapper function* and a *downstream collector* to create an *adapter* for a *flat mapping* operation. (See also the flatMap() intermediate operation, p. 924.)

```
static <T,U,A,R> Collector<T,?,R> flatMapping(
        Function<? super T,? extends Stream<? extends U>> mapper,
        Collector<? super U,A,R>                          downstream)
```

Returns a Collector that applies the specified mapper function to input elements of type T and provides the mapped results of type U to the downstream collector that accumulates them into results of type R.

That is, the method adapts a downstream collector accepting elements of type U to one accepting elements of type T by applying a flat mapping function to each input element before accumulation, where type parameter A is the intermediate accumulation type of the downstream collector.

The flat mapping function maps an input element to a *mapped stream* whose elements are *flattened* (p. 924) and passed downstream. Each mapped stream is closed after its elements have been flattened. An empty stream is substituted if the mapped stream is null.

Given the lists of CDs below, we wish to find all unique CD titles in the lists. A stream of CD lists is created at (1). Each CD list is used to create a stream of CDs whose elements are flattened into the output stream of CDs at (2). Each CD is then mapped to its title at (3), and unique CD titles are accumulated into a set at (4). (Compare this example with the one in Figure 16.9, p. 925, using the flatMap() stream operation.)

```
// Given lists of CDs:
List<CD> cdListA = List.of(CD.cd0, CD.cd1);
List<CD> cdListB = List.of(CD.cd0, CD.cd1, CD.cd1);

// Find unique CD titles in the given lists:
Set<String> set =
  Stream.of(cdListA, cdListB)                          // (1) Stream<List<CD>>
        .collect(Collectors.flatMapping(List::stream,  // (2) Flatten to Stream<CD>
            Collectors.mapping(CD::title,              // (3) Stream<String>
                Collectors.toSet())));                 // (4) Set<String>
```

Set of unique CD titles in the CD lists:

```
[Java Jive, Java Jam]
```

The collectors returned by the flatMapping() method are designed to be used in multilevel grouping operations (p. 987), such as downstream from groupingBy() or partitionBy() operations. Example 16.13 illustrates such a use with the groupingBy() operation.

In Example 16.13, the class RadioPlaylist at (1) represents a radio station by its name and a list of CDs played by the radio station. Three CD lists are constructed at (2) and used to construct three radio playlists at (3). The radio playlists are stored in a common list of radio playlists at (4). A query is formulated at (5) to find the unique titles of CDs played by each radio station. Referring to the line numbers in Example 16.13:

(6) A stream of type Stream<RadioPlaylist> is created from the list radioPlaylists of type RadioPlaylist.

(7) The radio playlists are grouped according to the name of the radio station (String).

(8) Each radio playlist of type RadioPlaylist is used as the source of a stream, which is then flattened into the output stream of type Stream<CD> by the flatMapping() operation.

(9) Each CD in the stream is mapped to its title.

(10) Each unique CD title is accumulated into the result set of each radio station (Set<String>).

The query at (5) uses four collectors. The result map has the type Map<String, List<String>>. The output shows the unique titles of CDs played by each radio station.

- -

Example 16.13 *Flat mapping*

```java
import java.util.List;

// Radio station with a playlist.
public class RadioPlaylist {                                           // (1)
  private String radioStationName;
  private List<CD> Playlist;

  public RadioPlaylist(String radioStationName, List<CD> cdList) {
    this.radioStationName = radioStationName;
    this.Playlist = cdList;
  }

  public String getRadioStationName() { return this.radioStationName; }
  public List<CD> getPlaylist() { return this.Playlist; }
}
```

- -

```java
import java.util.List;
import java.util.Map;
import java.util.Set;
import java.util.stream.Collectors;

public class CollectorsFlatMapping {
  public static void main(String[] args) {
    // Some lists of CDs:                                              // (2)
    List<CD> cdList1 = List.of(CD.cd0, CD.cd1, CD.cd1, CD.cd2);
    List<CD> cdList2 = List.of(CD.cd0, CD.cd0, CD.cd3);
    List<CD> cdList3 = List.of(CD.cd0, CD.cd4);

    // Some radio playlists:                                          // (3)
    RadioPlaylist pl1 = new RadioPlaylist("Radio JVM", cdList1);
    RadioPlaylist pl2 = new RadioPlaylist("Radio JRE", cdList2);
    RadioPlaylist pl3 = new RadioPlaylist("Radio JAR", cdList3);

    // List of radio playlists:                                      // (4)
    List<RadioPlaylist> radioPlaylists = List.of(pl1, pl2, pl3);

    // Map of radio station names and set of CD titles they played:  // (5)
    Map<String, Set<String>> map = radioPlaylists.stream()           // (6)
        .collect(Collectors.groupingBy(RadioPlaylist::getRadioStationName, // (7)
            Collectors.flatMapping(rpl -> rpl.getPlaylist().stream(),     // (8)
                Collectors.mapping(CD::title,                             // (9)
                    Collectors.toSet())))); // (10)
    System.out.println(map);
  }
}
```

Output from the program (*edited to fit on the page*):

```
{Radio JAR=[Hot Generics, Java Jive],
 Radio JVM=[Java Jive, Lambda Dancing, Java Jam],
 Radio JRE=[Java Jive, Keep on Erasing]}
```

Finishing Adapter for Downstream Collectors

The collectingAndThen() method encapsulates a *downstream collector* and a *finisher function* to allow the result of the collector to be adapted by the finisher function.

```
static <T,A,R,RR> Collector<T,A,RR> collectingAndThen(
        Collector<T,A,R> downstream,
        Function<R,RR>    finisher)
```

Returns a Collector that performs the operation of the downstream collector on input elements of type T, followed by applying the finisher function on the result of type R produced by the downstream collector. The final result is of type RR, the result of the finisher function. In other words, the method adapts a collector to perform an additional finishing transformation.

In the call to the collectAndThen() method at (1), the collector Collectors.maxBy() at (2) produces an Optional<Integer> result that is the maximum CD by number of tracks in each group. The finisher function at (3) extracts the value from the Optional<Integer> result, if there is one; otherwise, it returns 0. The collectAndThen() method adapts the Optional<Integer> result of its argument collector to an Integer value by applying the finisher function.

```
Map<Year, Integer> maxTracksByYear = CD.cdList.stream()
    .collect(Collectors.groupingBy(
        CD::year,
        Collectors.collectingAndThen(                                // (1)
            Collectors.maxBy(Comparator.comparing(CD::noOfTracks)),  // (2)
            optCD -> optCD.map(CD::noOfTracks).orElse(0)))           // (3)
    );
System.out.println(maxTracksByYear);                    // {2017=8, 2018=10}
```

In the call to the collectAndThen() method at (4), the collector Collectors.averaging-Double() at (5) produces a result of type Double that is the average number of tracks in each group. The finisher function at (6) maps the Double average value to a string with the specified number format.

```
Map<Genre, String> avgTracksByGenre = CD.cdList.stream()
    .collect(Collectors.groupingBy(
        CD::genre,
        Collectors.collectingAndThen(                     // (4)
            Collectors.averagingDouble(CD::noOfTracks),   // (5)
            d -> String.format("%.1f", d)))               // (6)
    );
System.out.println(avgTracksByGenre);           // {JAZZ=8.0, POP=9.0}
```

Downstream Collectors for Functional Reduction

The collectors we have seen so far perform a *mutable reduction* to some *mutable container*, except for the functional reduction implemented by the joining() method (p. 984). The Collectors class also provides static factory methods that implement collectors which perform *functional reduction* to compute common statistics, such as summing, averaging, finding maximum and minimum values, and the like.

Like any other collector, the collectors that perform functional reduction can also be used in a standalone capacity as a parameter of the collect() method and as a downstream collector in a composed collector. However, these collectors are most useful when used as downstream collectors.

Collectors performing functional reduction have counterparts in terminal operations for streams that provide equivalent reduction operations (Table 16.8, p. 1008).

Counting

The collector created by the Collectors.counting() method performs a functional reduction to count the input elements.

> static <T> Collector<T,?,Long> counting()
>
> The collector returned counts the number of input elements of type T. If there are no elements, the result is Long.valueOf(0L). Note that the result is of type Long.
>
> The wildcard ? represents any type, and in the method declaration, it is the type parameter for the mutable type that is accumulated by the reduction operation.

In the stream pipeline at (1), the collector Collectors.counting() is used in a standalone capacity to count the number of jazz music CDs.

```
Long numOfJazzCds1 = CD.cdList.stream().filter(CD::isJazz)
    .collect(Collectors.counting());              // (1) Standalone collector
System.out.println(numOfJazzCds1);                // 3
```

In the stream pipeline at (2), the collector Collectors.counting() is used as a downstream collector in a grouping operation that groups the CDs by musical genre and uses the downstream collector to count the number of CDs in each group.

```
Map<Genre, Long> grpByGenre = CD.cdList.stream()
    .collect(Collectors.groupingBy(
            CD::genre,
            Collectors.counting()));              // (2) Downstream collector
System.out.println(grpByGenre);                   // {POP=2, JAZZ=3}
System.out.println(grpByGenre.get(Genre.JAZZ));   // 3
```

The collector Collectors.counting() performs effectively the same functional reduction as the Stream.count() terminal operation (p. 953) at (3).

```
long numOfJazzCds2 = CD.cdList.stream().filter(CD::isJazz)
    .count();                                     // (3) Stream.count()
System.out.println(numOfJazzCds2);                // 3
```

Finding Min/Max

The collectors created by the `Collectors.maxBy()` and `Collectors.minBy()` methods perform a functional reduction to find the maximum and minimum elements in the input elements, respectively. As there might not be any input elements, an `Optional<T>` is returned as the result.

```
static <T> Collector<T,?,Optional<T>> maxBy(Comparator<? super T> cmp)
static <T> Collector<T,?,Optional<T>> minBy(Comparator<? super T> cmp)
```

Return a collector that produces an `Optional<T>` with the maximum or minimum element of type T according to the specified `Comparator`, respectively.

The natural order comparator for CDs defined at (1) is used in the stream pipelines below to find the maximum CD. The collector `Collectors.maxBy()` is used as a standalone collector at (2), using the natural order comparator to find the maximum CD. The `Optional<CD>` result can be queried for the value.

```
Comparator<CD> natCmp = Comparator.naturalOrder(); // (1)

Optional<CD> maxCD = CD.cdList.stream()
    .collect(Collectors.maxBy(natCmp));             // (2) Standalone collector
System.out.println("Max CD: "
    + maxCD.map(CD::title).orElse("No CD."));       // Max CD: Java Jive
```

In the pipeline below, the CDs are grouped by musical genre, and the CDs in each group are reduced to the maximum CD by the downstream collector `Collectors.maxBy()` at (3). Again, the downstream collector uses the natural order comparator, and the `Optional<CD>` result in each group can be queried.

```
// Group CDs by musical genre, and max CD in each group.
Map<Genre, Optional<CD>> grpByGenre = CD.cdList.stream()
    .collect(Collectors.groupingBy(
        CD::genre,
        Collectors.maxBy(natCmp)));       // (3) Downstream collector
System.out.println(grpByGenre);
//{JAZZ=Optional[<Jaav, "Java Jam", 6, 2017, JAZZ>],
// POP=Optional[<Jaav, "Java Jive", 8, 2017, POP>]}

System.out.println("Title of max Jazz CD: "
    + grpByGenre.get(Genre.JAZZ)
            .map(CD::title)
            .orElse("No CD."));          // Title of max Jazz CD: Java Jam
```

The collectors created by the `Collectors.maxBy()` and `Collectors.minBy()` methods are effectively equivalent to the `max()` and `min()` terminal operations provided by the stream interfaces (p. 954), respectively. In the pipeline below, the `max()` terminal operation reduces the stream of CDs to the maximum CD at (4) using the natural order comparator, and the `Optional<CD>` result can be queried.

```
Optional<CD> maxCD1 = CD.cdList.stream()
    .max(natCmp);                          // (4) max() on Stream<CD>.
System.out.println("Title of max CD: "
    + maxCD1.map(CD::title)
            .orElse("No CD."));          // Title of max CD: Java Jive
```

Summing

The summing collectors perform a functional reduction to produce the sum of the numeric results from applying a numeric-valued function to the input elements.

```
static <T> Collector<T,?,NumType> summingNumType(
        ToNumTypeFunction<? super T> mapper)
```

Returns a collector that produces the sum of a *numtype*-valued function applied to the input elements. If there are no input elements, the result is zero. The result is of *NumType*.

NumType is Int (but it is Integer when used as a type name), Long, or Double, and the corresponding *numtype* is int, long, or double.

The collector returned by the Collectors.summingInt() method is used at (1) as a standalone collector to find the total number of tracks on the CDs. The mapper function CD::noOfTracks passed as an argument extracts the number of tracks from each CD on which the functional reduction is performed.

```
Integer sumTracks = CD.cdList.stream()
    .collect(Collectors.summingInt(CD::noOfTracks));   // (1) Standalone collector
System.out.println(sumTracks);                         // 42
```

In the pipeline below, the CDs are grouped by musical genre, and the number of tracks on CDs in each group summed by the downstream collector is returned by the Collectors.summingInt() method at (2).

```
Map<Genre, Integer> grpByGenre = CD.cdList.stream()
    .collect(Collectors.groupingBy(
        CD::genre,
        Collectors.summingInt(CD::noOfTracks)));   // (2) Downstream collector
System.out.println(grpByGenre);                    // {POP=18, JAZZ=24}
System.out.println(grpByGenre.get(Genre.JAZZ));    // 24
```

The collector Collectors.summingInt() performs effectively the same functional reduction at (3) as the IntStream.sum() terminal operation (p. 973).

```
int sumTracks2 = CD.cdList.stream()            // (3) Stream<CD>
    .mapToInt(CD::noOfTracks)                  // IntStream
    .sum();
System.out.println(sumTracks2);                // 42
```

Averaging

The averaging collectors perform a functional reduction to produce the average of the numeric results from applying a numeric-valued function to the input elements.

```
static <T> Collector<T,?,Double> averagingNumType(
        ToNumTypeFunction<? super T> mapper)
```

Returns a collector that produces the arithmetic mean of a *numtype*-valued function applied to the input elements. If there are no input elements, the result is zero. The result is of type Double.

NumType is Int, Long, or Double, and the corresponding *numtype* is int, long, or double.

The collector returned by the `Collectors.averagingInt()` method is used at (1) as a standalone collector to find the average number of tracks on the CDs. The mapper function `CD::noOfTracks` passed as an argument extracts the number of tracks from each CD on which the functional reduction is performed.

```
Double avgNoOfTracks1 = CD.cdList.stream()
    .collect(Collectors
        .averagingInt(CD::noOfTracks));          // (1) Standalone collector
System.out.println(avgNoOfTracks1);              // 8.4
```

In the pipeline below, the CDs are grouped by musical genre, and the downstream collector `Collectors.averagingInt()` at (2) calculates the average number of tracks on the CDs in each group.

```
Map<Genre, Double> grpByGenre = CD.cdList.stream()
    .collect(Collectors.groupingBy(
        CD::genre,
        Collectors.averagingInt(CD::noOfTracks)   // (2) Downstream collector
    ));
System.out.println(grpByGenre);                   // {POP=9.0, JAZZ=8.0}
System.out.println(grpByGenre.get(Genre.JAZZ));   // 8.0
```

The collector created by the `Collectors.averagingInt()` method performs effectively the same functional reduction as the `IntStream.average()` terminal operation (p. 974) at (3).

```
OptionalDouble avgNoOfTracks2 = CD.cdList.stream()  // Stream<CD>
    .mapToInt(CD::noOfTracks)                        // IntStream
    .average();                                      // (3)
System.out.println(avgNoOfTracks2.orElse(0.0));      // 8.4
```

Summarizing

The summarizing collector performs a functional reduction to produce summary statistics (count, sum, min, max, average) on the numeric results of applying a numeric-valued function to the input elements.

> static <T> Collector<T,?,*NumType*SummaryStatistics> summarizing*NumType*(
>   To*NumType*Function<? super T> mapper)
>
> Returns a collector that applies a *numtype*-valued mapper function to the input elements, and returns the summary statistics for the resulting values.
>
> *NumType* is Int (but it is Integer when used as a type name), Long, or Double, and the corresponding *numtype* is int, long, or double.

The collector `Collectors.summarizingInt()` is used at (1) as a standalone collector to summarize the statistics for the number of tracks on the CDs. The mapper function `CD::noOfTracks` passed as an argument extracts the number of tracks from each CD on which the functional reduction is performed.

```
IntSummaryStatistics stats1 = CD.cdList.stream()
    .collect(
        Collectors.summarizingInt(CD::noOfTracks)    // (1) Standalone collector
    );
```

```
System.out.println(stats1);
// IntSummaryStatistics{count=5, sum=42, min=6, average=8.400000, max=10}
```

The `IntSummaryStatistics` class provides get methods to access the individual results (p. 974).

In the pipeline below, the CDs are grouped by musical genre, and the downstream collector created by the `Collectors.summarizingInt()` method at (2) summarizes the statistics for the number of tracks on the CDs in each group.

```
Map<Genre, IntSummaryStatistics> grpByGenre = CD.cdList.stream()
  .collect(Collectors.groupingBy(
    CD::genre,
    Collectors.summarizingInt(CD::noOfTracks)));    // (2) Downstream collector
System.out.println(grpByGenre);
//{POP=IntSummaryStatistics{count=2, sum=18, min=8, average=9.000000, max=10},
// JAZZ=IntSummaryStatistics{count=3, sum=24, min=6, average=8.000000, max=10}}

System.out.println(grpByGenre.get(Genre.JAZZ));    // Summary stats for Jazz CDs.
// IntSummaryStatistics{count=3, sum=24, min=6, average=8.000000, max=10}
```

The collector returned by the `Collectors.summarizingInt()` method performs effectively the same functional reduction as the `IntStream.summaryStatistics()` terminal operation (p. 974) at (3).

```
IntSummaryStatistics stats2 = CD.cdList.stream()
    .mapToInt(CD::noOfTracks)
    .summaryStatistics();                          // (3)
System.out.println(stats2);
// IntSummaryStatistics{count=5, sum=42, min=6, average=8.400000, max=10}
```

Reducing

Collectors that perform common statistical operations, such as counting, averaging, and so on, are special cases of functional reduction that can be implemented using the `Collectors.reducing()` method.

static <T> Collector<T,?,Optional<T>> reducing(BinaryOperator<T> bop)

Returns a collector that performs functional reduction, producing an `Optional` with the *cumulative* result of applying the binary operator bop on the input elements: e_1 bop e_2 bop e_3 ..., where each e_i is an input element. If there are no input elements, an empty `Optional<T>` is returned.

Note that the collector reduces input elements of type T to a result that is an `Optional` of type T.

static <T> Collector<T,?,T> reducing(T identity, BinaryOperator<T> bop)

Returns a collector that performs functional reduction, producing the *cumulative* result of applying the binary operator bop on the input elements: identity bop e_1 bop e_2 ..., where each e_i is an input element. The identity value is the initial value to accumulate. If there are no input elements, the identity value is returned.

Note that the collector reduces input elements of type T to a result of type T.

```
static <T,U> Collector<T,?,U> reducing(
    U                                       identity,
    Function<? super T,? extends U> mapper,
    BinaryOperator<U>               bop)
```

Returns a collector that performs a *map-reduce* operation. It maps each input element of type T to a mapped value of type U by applying the mapper function, and performs functional reduction on the mapped values of type U by applying the binary operator bop. The identity value of type U is used as the initial value to accumulate. If the stream is empty, the identity value is returned.

Note that the collector reduces input elements of type T to a result of type U.

Collectors returned by the Collectors.reducing() methods effectively perform equivalent functional reductions as the reduce() methods of the stream interfaces. However, the three-argument method Collectors.reducing(identity, mapper, bop) performs a map-reduce operation using a mapper function and a binary operator bop, whereas the Stream.reduce(identity, accumulator, combiner) performs a reduction using an accumulator and a combiner (p. 955). The accumulator is a BiFunction<U,T,U> that accumulates a partially accumulated result of type U with an element of type T, whereas the bop is a BinaryOperator<U> that accumulates a partially accumulated result of type U with an element of type U.

The following comparators are used in the examples below:

```
// Comparator to compare CDs by title.
Comparator<CD> cmpByTitle = Comparator.comparing(CD::title);          // (1)
// Comparator to compare strings by their length.
Comparator<String> byLength = Comparator.comparing(String::length); // (2)
```

The collector returned by the Collectors.reducing() method is used as a standalone collector at (3) to find the CD with the longest title. The result of the operation is an Optional<String> as there might not be any input elements. This operation is equivalent to using the Stream.reduce() terminal operation at (4).

```
Optional<String> longestTitle1 = CD.cdList.stream()
    .map(CD::title)
    .collect(Collectors.reducing(
        BinaryOperator.maxBy(byLength)));                  // (3) Standalone collector
System.out.println(longestTitle1.orElse("No title"));// Keep on Erasing

Optional<String> longestTitle2 = CD.cdList.stream()  // Stream<CD>
    .map(CD::title)                                  // Stream<String>
    .reduce(BinaryOperator.maxBy(byLength));         // (4) Stream.reduce(bop)
```

The collector returned by the one-argument Collectors.reducing() method is used as a downstream collector at (5) to find the CD with the longest title in each group classified by the year a CD was released. The collector at (5) is equivalent to the collector returned by the Collectors.maxBy(cmpByTitle) method.

```
Map<Year, Optional<CD>> cdWithMaxTitleByYear = CD.cdList.stream()
    .collect(Collectors.groupingBy(
        CD::year,
```

```
            Collectors.reducing(                          // (5) Downstream collector
                BinaryOperator.maxBy(cmpByTitle))
        ));
System.out.println(cdWithMaxTitleByYear);
// {2017=Optional[<Jaav, "Java Jive", 8, 2017, POP>],
//  2018=Optional[<Funkies, "Lambda Dancing", 10, 2018, POP>]}
System.out.println(cdWithMaxTitleByYear.get(Year.of(2018))
                    .map(CD::title).orElse("No title")); // Lambda Dancing
```

The collector returned by the three-argument Collectors.reducing() method is used as a downstream collector at (6) to find the longest title in each group classified by the year a CD was released. Note that the collector maps a CD to its title. The longest title is associated with the map value for each group classified by the year a CD was released. The collector will return an empty string (i.e., the identity value "") if there are no CDs in the stream. In comparison, the collector Collectors.mapping() at (7) also maps a CD to its title, and uses the downstream collector Collectors.maxBy(byLength) at (7) to find the longest title (p. 993). The result in this case is an Optional<String>, as there might not be any input elements.

```
Map<Year, String> longestTitleByYear = CD.cdList.stream()
    .collect(Collectors.groupingBy(
        CD::year,
        Collectors.reducing("", CD::title,               // (6) Downstream collector
            BinaryOperator.maxBy(byLength))
    ));
System.out.println(longestTitleByYear);  // {2017=Java Jive, 2018=Keep on Erasing}
System.out.println(longestTitleByYear.get(Year.of(2018)));       // Keep on Erasing

Map<Year, Optional<String>> longestTitleByYear2 = CD.cdList.stream()
    .collect(Collectors.groupingBy(
        CD::year,
        Collectors.mapping(CD::title,                    // (7) Downstream collector
            Collectors.maxBy(byLength))
    ));
System.out.println(longestTitleByYear2);
// {2017=Optional[Java Jive], 2018=Optional[Keep on Erasing]}
System.out.println(longestTitleByYear2.get(Year.of(2018))
                    .orElse("No title."));               // Keep on Erasing
```

The pipeline below groups CDs according to the year they were released. For each group, the collector returned by the three-argument Collectors.reducing() method performs a map-reduce operation at (8) to map each CD to its number of tracks and accumulate the tracks in each group. This map-reduce operation is equivalent to the collector returned by the Collectors.summingInt() method at (9).

```
Map<Year, Integer> noOfTracksByYear = CD.cdList.stream()
    .collect(Collectors.groupingBy(
        CD::year,
        Collectors.reducing(                             // (8) Downstream collector
            0, CD::noOfTracks, Integer::sum)));
System.out.println(noOfTracksByYear);                    // {2017=14, 2018=28}
System.out.println(noOfTracksByYear.get(Year.of(2018)));// 28
```

```
Map<Year, Integer> noOfTracksByYear2 = CD.cdList.stream()
    .collect(Collectors.groupingBy(
        CD::year,
        Collectors.summingInt(CD::noOfTracks)));    // (9) Special case collector
```

Summary of Static Factory Methods in the Collectors Class

The static factory methods of the Collectors class that create collectors are summarized in Table 16.7. All methods are static generic methods, except for the overloaded joining() methods that are not generic. The keyword static is omitted, as are the type parameters of a generic method, since these type parameters are evident from the declaration of the formal parameters to the method. The type parameter declarations have also been simplified, where any bound <? super T> or <? extends T> has been replaced by <T>, without impacting the intent of a method. A reference is also provided for each method in the first column.

The last column in Table 16.7 indicates the function type of the corresponding parameter in the previous column. It is instructive to note how the functional interface parameters provide the parameterized behavior to build the collector returned by a method. For example, the method averagingDouble() returns a collector that computes the average of the stream elements. The parameter function mapper with the functional interface type ToDoubleFunction<T> converts an element of type T to a double when the collector computes the average for the stream elements.

Table 16.7 *Static Methods in the Collectors Class*

Method name (ref.)	Return type	Functional interface parameters	Function type of parameters
averagingDouble (p. 1000)	Collector<T,?,Double>	(ToDoubleFunction<T> mapper)	T -> double
averagingInt (p. 1000)	Collector<T,?,Double>	(ToIntFunction<T> mapper)	T -> int
averagingLong (p. 1000)	Collector<T,?,Double>	(ToLongFunction<T> mapper)	T -> long
collectingAndThen (p. 997)	Collector<T,A,RR>	(Collector<T,A,R> downstream, Function<R,RR> finisher)	(T,A) -> R, R -> RR
counting (p. 998)	Collector<T,?,Long>	()	
filtering (p. 992)	Collector<T,?,R>	(Predicate<T> predicate, Collector<T,A,R> downstream)	T -> boolean, (T,A) -> R

Table 16.7 *Static Methods in the* Collectors *Class (Continued)*

Method name (ref.)	Return type	Functional interface parameters	Function type of parameters
flatMapping (p. 994)	Collector<T,?,R>	(Function<T, Stream<U>> mapper, Collector<U,A,R> downstream)	T->Stream<U>, (U,A) -> R
groupingBy (p. 985)	Collector<T,?, Map<K,List<T>>>	(Function<T,K> classifier)	T -> K
groupingBy (p. 985)	Collector<T,?,Map<K,D>>	(Function<T,K> classifier, Collector<T,A,D> downstream)	T -> K, (T,A) -> D
groupingBy (p. 985)	Collector<T,?,Map<K,D>>	(Function<T,K> classifier, Supplier<Map<K,D>> mapSupplier, Collector<T,A,D> downstream)	T -> K, ()->Map<K,D>, (T,A) -> D
joining (p. 984)	Collector <CharSequence,?,String>	()	
joining (p. 984)	Collector <CharSequence,?,String>	(CharSequence delimiter)	
joining (p. 984)	Collector <CharSequence,?,String>	(CharSequence delimiter, CharSequence prefix, CharSequence suffix)	
mapping (p. 993)	Collector<T,?,R>	(Function<T,U> mapper, Collector<U,A,R> downstream)	T -> U, (U,A) -> R
maxBy (p. 999)	Collector<T,?,Optional<T>>	(Comparator<T> comparator)	(T,T) -> T
minBy (p. 999)	Collector<T,?,Optional<T>>	(Comparator<T> comparator)	(T,T) -> T
partitioningBy (p. 989)	Collector<T,?, Map<Boolean,List<T>>>	(Predicate<T> predicate)	T -> boolean
partitioningBy (p. 989)	Collector<T,?, Map<Boolean,D>>	(Predicate<T> predicate, Collector<T,A,D> downstream)	T -> boolean, (T,A) -> D

Table 16.7 *Static Methods in the* Collectors *Class (Continued)*

Method name (ref.)	Return type	Functional interface parameters	Function type of parameters
reducing (p. 1002)	Collector<T,?,Optional<T>>	(BinaryOperator<T> op)	(T,T) -> T
reducing (p. 1002)	Collector<T,?,T>	(T identity, BinaryOperator<T> op)	T -> T, (T,T) -> T
reducing (p. 1002)	Collector<T,?,U>	(U identity, Function<T,U> mapper, BinaryOperator<U> op)	U -> U, T -> U, (U,U) -> U
summarizingDouble (p. 1001)	Collector<T,?, DoubleSummaryStatistics>	(ToDoubleFunction<T> mapper)	T -> double
summarizingInt (p. 1001)	Collector<T,?, IntSummaryStatistics>	(ToIntFunction<T> mapper)	T -> int
summarizingLong (p. 1001)	Collector<T,?, LongSummaryStatistics>	(ToLongFunction<T> mapper)	T -> long
summingDouble (p. 978)	Collector<T,?,Double>	(ToDoubleFunction<T> mapper)	T -> double
summingInt (p. 978)	Collector<T,?,Integer>	(ToIntFunction<T> mapper)	T -> int
summingLong (p. 978)	Collector<T,?,Long>	(ToLongFunction<T> mapper)	T -> long
toCollection (p. 979)	Collector<T,?,C>	(Supplier<C> collFactory)	() -> C
toList toUnmodifiableList (p. 980)	Collector<T,?,List<T>>	()	
toMap (p. 981)	Collector<T,?,Map<K,U>>	(Function<T,K> keyMapper, Function<T,U> valueMapper)	T -> K, T -> U
toMap (p. 981)	Collector<T,?,Map<K,U>>	(Function<T,K> keyMapper, Function<T,U> valueMapper, BinaryOperator<U> mergeFunction)	T -> K, T -> U, (U,U) -> U

Table 16.7 *Static Methods in the* Collectors *Class (Continued)*

Method name (ref.)	Return type	Functional interface parameters	Function type of parameters
toMap (p. 981)	Collector<T,?,Map<K,U>>	(Function<T,K> keyMapper, Function<T,U> valueMapper, BinaryOperator<U> mergeFunction, Supplier<Map<K,U>> mapSupplier)	T -> K, T -> U, (U,U) -> U, ()-> Map<K,U>
toSet toUnmodifiableSet (p. 980)	Collector<T,?,Set<T>>	()	

Table 16.8 shows a comparison of methods in the stream interfaces that perform reduction operations and static factory methods in the Collectors class that implement collectors with equivalent functionality.

Table 16.8 *Method Comparison: The Stream Interfaces and the* Collectors *Class*

Method names in the stream interfaces	Static factory method names in the Collectors class
collect (p. 964)	collectingAndThen (p. 997)
count (p. 953)	counting (p. 998)
filter (p. 912)	filtering (p. 992)
flatMap (p. 924)	flatMapping (p. 994)
map (p. 921)	mapping (p. 993)
max (p. 954)	maxBy (p. 999)
min (p. 954)	minBy (p. 999)
reduce (p. 955)	reducing (p. 1002)
toList (p. 972)	toList (p. 980)
average (p. 972)	averagingInt, averagingLong, averagingDouble (p. 1001)
sum (p. 972)	summingInt, summingLong, summingDouble (p. 978)
summaryStatistics (p. 972)	summarizingInt, summarizingLong, summarizingDouble (p. 1001)

16.9   Parallel Streams

The Stream API makes it possible to execute a sequential stream in parallel without rewriting the code. The primary reason for using parallel streams is to improve performance, but at the same time ensuring that the results obtained are the same, or at least compatible, regardless of the mode of execution. Although the API goes a long way to achieve its aim, it is important to understand the pitfalls to avoid when executing stream pipelines in parallel.

Building Parallel Streams

The execution mode of an existing stream can be set to parallel by calling the parallel() method on the stream (p. 933). The parallelStream() method of the Collection interface can be used to create a parallel stream with a collection as the data source (p. 897). No other code is necessary for parallel execution, as the data partitioning and thread management for a parallel stream are handled by the API and the JVM. As with any stream, the stream is not executed until a terminal operation is invoked on it.

The isParallel() method of the stream interfaces can be used to determine whether the execution mode of a stream is parallel (p. 933).

Parallel Stream Execution

The Stream API allows a stream to be executed either sequentially or in parallel— meaning that all stream operations can execute either sequentially or in parallel. A sequential stream is executed in a single thread running on one CPU core. The elements in the stream are processed sequentially in a single pass by the stream operations that are executed in the same thread (p. 891).

A parallel stream is executed by different threads, running on multiple CPU cores in a computer. The stream elements are split into substreams that are processed by multiple instances of the stream pipeline being executed in multiple threads. The partial results from processing of each substream are merged (or combined) into a final result (p. 891).

Parallel streams utilize the Fork/Join Framework (§23.3, p. 1447) under the hood for executing parallel tasks. This framework provides support for the thread management necessary to execute the substreams in parallel. The number of threads employed during parallel stream execution is dependent on the CPU cores in the computer.

Figure 16.12, p. 963, illustrates parallel functional reduction using the three-argument reduce(identity, accumulator, combiner) terminal operation (p. 962).

Figure 16.14, p. 967, illustrates parallel mutable reduction using the three-argument collect(supplier, accumulator, combiner) terminal operation (p. 966).

Factors Affecting Performance

There are no guarantees that executing a stream in parallel will improve the performance. In this subsection we look at some factors that can affect performance.

Benchmarking

In general, increasing the number of CPU cores and thereby the number of threads that can execute in parallel only scales performance up to a threshold for a given size of data, as some threads might become idle if there is no data left for them to process. The number of CPU cores boosts performance to a certain extent, but it is not the only factor that should be considered when deciding to execute a stream in parallel.

Inherent in the total cost of parallel processing is the start-up cost of setting up the parallel execution. At the onset, if this cost is already comparable to the cost of sequential execution, not much can be gained by resorting to parallel execution.

A combination of the following three factors can be crucial in deciding whether a stream should be executed in parallel:

- *Sufficiently large data size*

  The size of the stream must be large enough to warrant parallel processing; otherwise, sequential processing is preferable. The start-up cost can be too prohibitive for parallel execution if the stream size is too small.

- *Computation-intensive stream operations*

  If the stream operations are small computations, then the stream size should be proportionately large as to warrant parallel execution. If the stream operations are computation-intensive, the stream size is less significant, and parallel execution can boost performance.

- *Easily splittable stream*

  If the cost of splitting the stream into substreams is higher than processing the substreams, employing parallel execution can be futile. Collections like Array-Lists, HashMaps, and simple arrays are efficiently splittable, whereas LinkedLists and IO-based data sources are less efficient in this regard.

Benchmarking—that is, measuring performance—is strongly recommended to decide whether parallel execution will be beneficial. Example 16.14 illustrates a simple scheme where reading the system clock before and after a stream is executed can be used to get a sense of how well a stream performs.

The class StreamBenchmarks in Example 16.14 defines five methods, at (1) through (5), that compute the sum of values from 1 to n. These methods compute the sum in various ways. Each method is executed with four different values of n; that is, the stream size is the number of values for summation. The program prints the benchmarks for each method for the different values of n, which of course can vary, as many factors can influence the results—the most significant one being the number of CPU cores on the computer.

- The methods seqSumRangeClosed() at (1) and parSumRangeClosed() at (2) perform the computation on a sequential and a parallel stream, respectively, that are created with the closeRange() method.

```
return LongStream.rangeClosed(1L, n).sum();              // Sequential stream
...
return LongStream.rangeClosed(1L, n).parallel().sum();  // Parallel stream
```

Benchmarks from Example 16.14:

Size	Sequential	Parallel
1000	0.05681	0.11031
10000	0.06698	0.13979
100000	0.71274	0.52627
1000000	7.02237	4.37249

The terminal operation sum() is not computation-intensive. The parallel stream starts to show better performance when the number of values approaches 100000. The stream size is then significantly large for the parallel stream to show better performance. Note that the range of values defined by the arguments of the rangeClosed() method can be efficiently split into substreams, as its start and end values are provided.

- The methods seqSumIterate() at (3) and parSumIterate() at (4) return a sequential and a parallel sequential stream, respectively, that is created with the iterate() method.

```
return LongStream.iterate(1L, i -> i + 1).limit(n).sum();              // Sequential
...
return LongStream.iterate(1L, i -> i + 1).limit(n).parallel().sum();  // Parallel
```

Benchmarks from Example 16.14:

Size	Sequential	Parallel
1000	0.08645	0.34696
10000	0.35687	1.27861
100000	3.24083	11.38709
1000000	29.92285	117.87909

The method iterate() creates an infinite stream, and the limit() intermediate operation truncates the stream according to the value of n. The performance of both streams degrades fast when the number of values increases. However, the parallel stream performs worse than the sequential stream in all cases. The values generated by the iterate() method are not known before the stream is executed, and the limit() operation is also stateful, making the process of splitting the values into substreams inefficient in the case of the parallel stream.

- The method iterSumLoop() at (5) uses a for(;;) loop to compute the sum.

Benchmarks from Example 16.14:

Size	Iterative
1000	0.00586
10000	0.02330
100000	0.22352
1000000	2.49677

Using a for(;;) loop to calculate the sum performs best for all values of n compared to the streams, showing that significant overhead is involved in using streams for summing a sequence of numerical values.

In Example 16.14, the methods measurePerf() at (6) and xqtFunctions() at (13) create
the benchmarks for functions passed as parameters. In the measurePerf() method,
the system clock is read at (8) and the function parameter func is applied at (9). The
system clock is read again at (10) after the function application at (9) has completed. The execution time calculated at (10) reflects the time for executing the
function. Applying the function func evaluates the lambda expression or the method
reference implementing the LongFunction interface. In Example 16.14, the function
parameter func is implemented by method references that call methods, at (1) through
(5), in the StreamBenchmarks class whose execution time we want to measure.

```
public static <R> double measurePerf(LongFunction<R> func, long n) { // (6)
  // ...
  double start = System.nanoTime();                                  // (8)
  result = func.apply(n);                                            // (9)
  double duration = (System.nanoTime() - start)/1_000_000;           // (10) ms.
  // ...
}
```

Example 16.14 *Benchmarking*

```
import java.util.function.LongFunction;
import java.util.stream.LongStream;
/*
 * Benchmark the execution time to sum numbers from 1 to n values
 * using streams.
 */
public final class StreamBenchmarks {

  public static long seqSumRangeClosed(long n) {                     // (1)
    return LongStream.rangeClosed(1L, n).sum();
  }

  public static long paraSumRangeClosed(long n) {                    // (2)
    return LongStream.rangeClosed(1L, n).parallel().sum();
  }

  public static long seqSumIterate(long n) {                         // (3)
    return LongStream.iterate(1L, i -> i + 1).limit(n).sum();
  }

  public static long paraSumIterate(long n) {                        // (5)
    return LongStream.iterate(1L, i -> i + 1).limit(n).parallel().sum();
  }

  public static long iterSumLoop(long n) {                           // (5)
    long result = 0;
    for (long i = 1L; i <= n; i++) {
      result += i;
    }
    return result;
  }
}
```

```
/*
 * Applies the function parameter func, passing n as parameter.
 * Returns the average time (ms.) to execute the function 100 times.
 */
public static <R> double measurePerf(LongFunction<R> func, long n) { // (6)
  int numOfExecutions = 100;
  double totTime = 0.0;
  R result = null;
  for (int i = 0; i < numOfExecutions; i++) {                      // (7)
    double start = System.nanoTime();                             // (8)
    result = func.apply(n);                                       // (9)
    double duration = (System.nanoTime() - start)/1_000_000;      // (10)
    totTime += duration;                                          // (11)
  }
  double avgTime = totTime/numOfExecutions;                       // (12)
  return avgTime;
}


/*
 * Executes the functions in the varargs parameter funcs
 * for different stream sizes.
 */
public static <R> void xqtFunctions(LongFunction<R>... funcs) {   // (13)
  long[] sizes = {1_000L, 10_000L, 100_000L, 1_000_000L};        // (14)

  // For each stream size ...
  for (int i = 0; i < sizes.length; ++i) {                        // (15)
    System.out.printf("%7d", sizes[i]);
    // ... execute the functions passed in the varargs parameter funcs.
    for (int j = 0; j < funcs.length; ++j) {                      // (16)
      System.out.printf("%10.5f", measurePerf(funcs[j], sizes[i]));
    }
    System.out.println();
  }
}

public static void main(String[] args) {                          // (17)

  System.out.println("Streams created with the rangeClosed() method:");// (18)
  System.out.println("  Size   Sequential Parallel");
  xqtFunctions(StreamBenchmarks::seqSumRangeClosed,
               StreamBenchmarks::paraSumRangeClosed);

  System.out.println("Streams created with the iterate() method:"); // (19)
  System.out.println("  Size   Sequential Parallel");
  xqtFunctions(StreamBenchmarks::seqSumIterate,
               StreamBenchmarks::paraSumIterate);

  System.out.println("Iterative solution with an explicit loop:");  // (20)
  System.out.println("  Size   Iterative");
  xqtFunctions(StreamBenchmarks::iterSumLoop);
  }
}
```

Possible output from the program:

```
Streams created with the rangeClosed() method:
  Size   Sequential Parallel
  1000   0.05681    0.11031
  10000  0.06698    0.13979
 100000  0.71274    0.52627
1000000  7.02237    4.37249
Streams created with the iterate() method:
  Size   Sequential Parallel
  1000   0.08645    0.34696
  10000  0.35687    1.27861
 100000  3.24083   11.38709
1000000 29.92285  117.87909
Iterative solution with an explicit loop:
  Size   Iterative
  1000   0.00586
  10000  0.02330
 100000  0.22352
1000000  2.49677
```

Side Effects

Efficient execution of parallel streams that produces the desired results requires the stream operations (and their behavioral parameters) to avoid certain side effects.

- *Non-interfering behaviors*

  The behavioral parameters of stream operations should be non-interfering (p. 909)—both for sequential and parallel streams. Unless the stream data source is concurrent, the stream operations should not modify it during the execution of the stream. See building streams from collections (p. 897).

- *Stateless behaviors*

  The behavioral parameters of stream operations should be stateless (p. 909)—both for sequential and parallel streams. A behavioral parameter implemented as a lambda expression should not depend on any state that might change during the execution of the stream pipeline. The results from a stateful behavioral parameter can be nondeterministic or even incorrect. For a stateless behavioral parameter, the results are always the same.

  Shared state that is accessed by the behavior parameters of stream operations in a pipeline is not a good idea. Executing the pipeline in parallel can lead to *race conditions* in accessing the global state, and using synchronization code to provide thread-safety may defeat the purpose of parallelization. Using the three-argument reduce() or collect() method can be a better solution to encapsulate shared state.

  The intermediate operations distinct(), skip(), limit(), and sorted() are stateful (p. 915, p. 915, p. 917, p. 929). See also Table 16.3, p. 938. They can carry extra performance overhead when executed in a parallel stream, as such an operation can entail multiple passes over the data and may require significant data buffering.

Ordering

An ordered stream (p. 891) processed by operations that preserve the encounter order will produce the same results, regardless of whether it is executed sequentially or in parallel. However, repeated execution of an unordered stream—sequential or parallel—can produce different results.

Preserving the encounter order of elements in an ordered parallel stream can incur a performance penalty. The performance of an ordered parallel stream can be improved if the ordering constraint is removed by calling the unordered() intermediate operation on the stream (p. 932).

The three stateful intermediate operations distinct(), skip(), and limit() can improve performance in a parallel stream that is unordered, as compared to one that is ordered (p. 915, p. 915, p. 917). The distinct() operation need only buffer *any* occurrence of a duplicate value in the case of an unordered parallel stream, rather than the *first* occurrence. The skip() operation can skip *any* n elements in the case of an unordered parallel stream, not necessarily the *first* n elements. The limit() operation can truncate the stream after *any* n elements in the case of an unordered parallel stream, and not necessarily after the *first* n elements.

The terminal operation findAny() is intentionally nondeterministic, and can return *any* element in the stream (p. 952). It is specially suited for parallel streams.

The forEach() terminal operation ignores the encounter order, but the forEachOrdered() terminal operation preserves the order (p. 948). The sorted() stateful intermediate operation, on the other hand, enforces a specific encounter order, regardless of whether it executed in a parallel pipeline (p. 929).

Autoboxing and Unboxing of Numeric Values

As the Stream API allows both object and numeric streams, and provides support for conversion between them (p. 934), choosing a numeric stream when possible can offset the overhead of autoboxing and unboxing in object streams.

As we have seen, in order to take full advantage of parallel execution, composition of a stream pipeline must follow certain rules to facilitate parallelization. In summary, the benefits of using parallel streams are best achieved when:

- The stream data source is of a sufficient size and the stream is easily splittable into substreams.
- The stream operations have no adverse side effects and are computation-intensive enough to warrant parallelization.

Review Questions

16.1 Given the following code:

```
import java.util.*;

public class RQ1 {
    public static void main(String[] args) {
        List<String> values = Arrays.asList("X", "XXX", "XX", "XXXX");
        int value = values.stream()
                          .mapToInt(v -> v.length())
                          .filter(v -> v != 4)
                          .reduce(1, (x, y) -> x * y);
        System.out.println(value);
    }
}
```

What is the result?
Select the one correct answer.

(a) 4
(b) 6
(c) 24
(d) The program will throw an exception at runtime.

16.2 Which statement is true about the `Stream` methods?

(a) The `filter()` method discards elements from the stream that match the given `Predicate`.
(b) The `findFirst()` method always returns the first element in the stream.
(c) The `reduce()` method removes elements from the stream that match the given `Predicate`.
(d) The `sorted()` method sorts the elements in a stream according to their natural order, or according to a given `Comparator`.

16.3 Given the following code:

```
import java.util.stream.*;

public class RQ3 {
    public static void main(String[] args) {
        IntStream values = IntStream.range(0, 5);
        // (1) INSERT CODE HERE
        System.out.println(sum);
    }
}
```

Which of the following statements when inserted independently at (1) will result in a compile-time error?
Select the two correct answers.

(a) `int sum = values.reduce(0, (x, y) -> x + y);`
(b) `int sum = values.parallel().reduce(0, (x, y) -> x + y);`

```
(c)  int sum = values.reduce((x, y) -> x + y).orElse(0);
(d)  int sum = values.reduce(0, (x, y) -> x + y).orElse(0);
(e)  int sum = values.parallel().reduce((x, y) -> x + sum).orElse(0);
(f)  int sum = values.sum();
```

16.4   Given the following code:

```
import java.util.stream.*;

public class RQ4 {
  public static void main(String[] args) {
    IntStream values = IntStream.range(0, 5);
    // (1) INSERT CODE HERE
    System.out.println(value);
  }
}
```

Which of the following statements, when inserted independently at (1), will result
in the value 4 being printed?
Select the two correct answers.

```
(a)  int value = values.reduce(0, (x, y) -> x + 1);
(b)  int value = values.reduce((x, y) -> x + 1).orElse(0);
(c)  int value = values.reduce(0, (x, y) -> y + 1);
(d)  int value = values.reduce(0, (x, y) -> y);
(e)  int value = values.reduce(1, (x, y) -> y + 1);
(f)  long value = values.count();
```

16.5   Given the following code:

```
import java.util.*;
import java.util.stream.*;

public class RQ5 {
  public static void main(String[] args) {
    List<String> values = List.of("AA", "BBB", "C", "DD", "EEE");
    Map<Integer, List<String>> map = null;
    // (1) INSERT CODE HERE
    map.forEach((i, s) -> System.out.println(i + " " + s));
  }
}
```

Which statement when inserted independently at (1) will result in the output
1 [C]?
Select the one correct answer.

```
(a)  map = values.stream()
                  .collect(Collectors.groupingBy(s -> s.length(),
                          Collectors.filtering(s -> !s.contains("C"),
                              Collectors.toList())));
(b)  map = values.stream()
                  .collect(Collectors.groupingBy(s -> s.length(),
                          Collectors.filtering(s -> s.contains("C"),
                              Collectors.toList())));
```

```
(c) map = values.stream()
              .filter(s -> !s.contains("C"))
              .collect(Collectors.groupingBy(s -> s.length(),
                            Collectors.toList()));
(d) map = values.stream()
              .filter(s -> s.contains("C"))
              .collect(Collectors.groupingBy(s -> s.length(),
                            Collectors.toList()));
```

16.6   Given the following code:

```
import java.util.stream.*;

public class RQ7 {
  public static void main(String[] args) {
    Stream<String> values = Stream.generate(() -> "A");
    boolean value = values.peek(v -> System.out.print("B"))
                          .takeWhile(v -> !v.equals("A"))
                          .peek(v -> System.out.print("C"))
                          .anyMatch(v -> v.equals("A"));
    System.out.println(value);
  }
}
```

What is the result?
Select the one correct answer.

(a) Btrue
(b) Ctrue
(c) BCtrue
(d) Bfalse
(e) Cfalse
(f) BCfalse

16.7   Given the following code:

```
import java.util.stream.*;

public class RQ9 {
  public static void main(String[] args) {
    IntStream.range('a', 'e')
              .mapToObj(i -> String.valueOf((char) i).toUpperCase())
              .filter(s -> "AEIOU".contains(s))
              .forEach(s -> System.out.print(s));
  }
}
```

What is the result?
Select the one correct answer.

(a) A
(b) AE
(c) BCD
(d) The program will fail to compile.

16.8 Given the following code:

```java
import java.util.stream.*;

public class RQ10 {
  public static void main(String[] args) {
    IntStream.range(0, 5)
             .filter(i -> i % 2 != 0)
             .forEach(i -> System.out.println(i));
  }
}
```

Which of the following statements will produce the same result as the program? Select the two correct answers.

(a)
```java
IntStream.rangeClosed(0, 5)
         .filter(i -> i % 2 != 0)
         .forEach(i -> System.out.println(i));
```
(b)
```java
IntStream.range(0, 10)
         .takeWhile(i -> i < 5)
         .filter(i -> i % 2 != 0)
         .forEach(i -> System.out.println(i));
```
(c)
```java
IntStream.range(0, 10)
         .limit(5)
         .filter(i -> i % 2 != 0)
         .forEach(i -> System.out.println(i));
```
(d)
```java
IntStream.generate(() -> {int x = 0; return x++;})
         .takeWhile(i -> i < 4)
         .filter(i -> i % 2 != 0)
         .forEach(i -> System.out.println(i));
```
(e)
```java
var x = 0;
IntStream.generate(() -> return x++)
         .limit(5)
         .filter(i -> i % 2 != 0)
         .forEach(i -> System.out.println(i));
```

16.9 Given the following code:

```java
import java.util.function.*;
import java.util.stream.*;

public class RQ11 {
  public static void main(String[] args) {
    Stream<String> abc = Stream.of("A", "B", "C");
    Stream<String> xyz = Stream.of("X", "Y", "Z");
    String value = Stream.concat(xyz, abc).reduce((a, b) -> b + a).get();
    System.out.println(value);
  }
}
```

What is the result?
Select the one correct answer.

(a) ABCXYZ
(b) XYZABC

   (c) ZYXCBA
   (d) CBAZYX

16.10   Which statement produces a different result from the other statements?
        Select the one correct answer.

   (a) ```
        Stream.of("A", "B", "C", "D", "E")
              .filter(s -> s.compareTo("B") < 0)
              .collect(Collectors.groupingBy(s -> "AEIOU".contains(s)))
              .forEach((x, y) -> System.out.println(x + " " + y));
        ```
   (b)  ```
        Stream.of("A", "B", "C", "D", "E")
              .filter(s -> s.compareTo("B") < 0)
              .collect(Collectors.partitioningBy(s -> "AEIOU".contains(s)))
              .forEach((x, y) -> System.out.println(x + " " + y));
        ```
   (c) ```
        Stream.of("A", "B", "C", "D", "E")
              .collect(Collectors.groupingBy(s -> "AEIOU".contains(s),
                            Collectors.filtering(s -> s.compareTo("B") < 0,
                                         Collectors.toList())))
              .forEach((x, y) -> System.out.println(x + " " + y));
        ```
   (d)  ```
        Stream.of("A", "B", "C", "D", "E")
              .collect(Collectors.partitioningBy(s -> "AEIOU".contains(s),
                            Collectors.filtering(s -> s.compareTo("B") < 0,
                                         Collectors.toList())))
              .forEach((x, y) -> System.out.println(x + " " + y));
        ```

16.11   Given the following code:

```
import java.util.stream.*;

public class RQ13 {
  public static void main(String[] args) {
    Stream<String> strings = Stream.of("i", "am", "ok").parallel();
    IntStream chars = strings.flatMapToInt(line -> line.chars()).sorted();
    chars.forEach(c -> System.out.print((char)c));
  }
}
```

   What is the result?
   Select the one correct answer.

   (a) iamok
   (b) aikmo
   (c) amiok
   (d) The result from running the program is unpredictable.
   (e) The program will throw an exception at runtime.

16.12   Which of the following statements are true about the Stream methods?
        Select the two correct answers.

   (a) The filter() method accepts a Function.
   (b) The peek() method accepts a Function.
   (c) The peek() method accepts a Consumer.

(d) The forEach() method accepts a Consumer.
(e) The map() method accepts a Predicate.
(f) The max() method accepts a Predicate.
(g) The findAny() method accepts a Predicate.

16.13 Which Stream methods are terminal operations?
Select the two correct answers.

(a) peek()
(b) forEach()
(c) map()
(d) filter()
(e) sorted()
(f) min()

16.14 Which Stream methods have short-circuit execution?
Select the two correct answers.

(a) collect()
(b) limit()
(c) flatMap()
(d) anyMatch()
(e) reduce()
(f) sum()

16.15 Given the following code:

```
import java.util.stream.*;

public class RQ17 {
  public static void main(String[] args) {
    Stream<String> values = Stream.of("is", "this", "", null, "ok", "?");
    // (1) INSERT CODE HERE
    System.out.println(c);
  }
}
```

Which statement inserted independently at (1) produces the output 6?
Select the one correct answer.

(a) `long c = values.count();`
(b) `long c = values.collect(Collectors.counting());`
(c) `int c = values.mapToInt(v -> 1).reduce(0, (x, y) -> x + 1);`
(d) `long c = values.collect(Collectors.reducing(0L, v -> 1L, Long::sum));`
(e) `int c = values.mapToInt(v -> 1).sum();`
(f) Insert any of the above.

16.16 Which code produces identical results?
Select the two correct answers.

(a) `Set<String> set1 = Stream.of("XX", "XXXX", "", null, "XX", "X")`
                    `.filter(v -> v != null)`
                    `.collect(Collectors.toSet());`

```
        set1.stream()
            .mapToInt(v -> v.length())
            .sorted()
            .forEach(v -> System.out.print(v));
(b) Set<Integer> set2 = Stream.of("XX", "XXXX", "", null, "XX", "X")
                                   .map(v -> (v == null) ? 0 : v.length())
                                   .filter(v -> v != 0)
                                   .collect(Collectors.toSet());
        set2.stream()
            .sorted()
            .forEach(v -> System.out.print(v));
(c) List<Integer> list1 = Stream.of("XX", "XXXX", "", null, "XX", "X")
                                   .map(v -> (v == null) ? 0 : v.length())
                                   .filter(v -> v != 0)
                                   .toList();
        list1.stream()
            .sorted()
            .forEach(v -> System.out.print(v));
(d) List<Integer> list2 = Stream.of("XX", "XXXX", "", null, "XX", "X")
                                   .map(v -> (v == null) ? 0 : v.length())
                                   .filter(v -> v != 0)
                                   .distinct()
                                   .toList();
        list2.stream()
            .sorted()
            .forEach(v -> System.out.print(v));
```

Date and Time 17

 Chapter Topics

- Overview of the new Date and Time API in the java.time package
- Understanding the temporal concepts represented by the LocalTime, LocalDate, LocalDateTime, ZonedDateTime, Instant, Period, and Duration classes
- Creating and using temporal objects
- Accessing temporal objects using temporal units and temporal fields
- Comparing temporal objects
- Creating modified instances of temporal objects
- Performing temporal arithmetic with temporal objects
- Using time zones and daylight savings with ZonedDateTime objects.
- Interoperability between date/time values and legacy dates

Java SE 17 Developer Exam Objectives	
[1.3] Manipulate date, time, duration, period, instant and time-zone objects using Date-Time API	§17.1, p. 1024 to §17.7, p. 1072

Java 8 introduced a new and comprehensive API for date and time. This chapter provides comprehensive coverage of essential topics regarding the Date and Time API. Coverage of formatting and parsing of date and time values is deferred to §18.6, p. 1127.

17.1 Date and Time API Overview

The java.time package provides the main support for dealing with dates and times. It contains the main classes that represent date and time values, including those that represent an amount of time.

- LocalDate: This class represents a date in terms of *date fields* (year, month, day). A *date* has no time fields or a time zone. (This class is not to be confused with the java.util.Date legacy class.)
- LocalTime: This class represents time in a 24-hour day in terms of *time fields* (hour, minute, second, nanosecond). A *time* has no date fields or a time zone.
- LocalDateTime: This class represents the concept of date and time combined, in terms of *both* date and time fields. A *date-time* has no time zone.
- ZonedDateTime: This class represents the concept of a date-time with a time zone—that is, a *zoned date-time*.
- Instant: This class represents a measurement of time as a point on a timeline starting from a specific origin (called the *epoch*). An *instant* is represented with nanosecond precision and can be a negative value.
- Period: This class represents an amount or quantity of time in terms of number of days, months, and years, which can be negative. A *period* is a *date-based* amount of time. It has no notion of a clock time, a date, or a time zone.
- Duration: This class represents an amount or quantity of time in terms of number of seconds and nanoseconds, which can be negative. A *duration* is a *time-based* amount of time. As with instants, durations have no notion of a clock time, a date, or a time zone.

We will use the term *temporal objects* to mean objects of classes that represent temporal concepts.

The temporal classes implement *immutable* and *thread-safe* temporal objects. The state of an immutable object cannot be changed. Any method that is supposed to modify such an object returns a modified copy of the temporal object. It is a common mistake to ignore the object returned, thinking that the current object has been modified. Thread-safety guarantees that the state of such an object is not compromised by concurrent access.

Table 17.1 summarizes the fields in selected classes from the Date and Time API. The table shows the relative size of the objects of these classes in terms of their fields; for example, a LocalTime has only time fields, whereas a ZonedDateTime has time-, date-, and zone-based fields. The three asterisks *** indicate that this information can be derived by methods provided by the class, even though these fields do not exist in an object of the Duration class.

The information in Table 17.1 is crucial to understanding how the objects of these classes can be used. A common mistake is to access, format, or parse a temporal object that does not have the required temporal fields. For example, a LocalTime object has only time fields, so trying to format it with a formatter for date fields will result in a java.time.DateTimeException. Many methods will also throw an exception if an invalid or an out-of-range argument is passed in the method call. It is important to keep in mind which temporal fields constitute the state of a temporal object.

Table 17.1   *Fields in Selected Classes in the Date and Time API*

Classes	Year	Month	Day	Hours	Minutes	Seconds /Nanos	Zone offset	Zone ID
LocalTime (p. 1027)				+	+	+		
LocalDate (p. 1027)	+	+	+					
LocalDate-Time (p. 1027)	+	+	+	+	+	+		
ZonedDate-Time (p. 1072)	+	+	+	+	+	+	+	+
Instant (p. 1049)						+		
Period (p. 1057)	+	+	+					
Duration (p. 1064)			***	***	***	+		

Table 17.2 provides an overview of the method naming conventions used in the temporal classes LocalTime, LocalDate, LocalDateTime, ZonedDateTime, and Instant. This method naming convention makes it easy to use the API, as it ensures method naming is standardized across all temporal classes. Depending on the method, the suffix *XXX* in a method name can be a specific field (e.g., designate the Year field in the getYear method name), a specific unit (e.g., designate the unit Days for number of days in the plusDays method name), or a class name (e.g., designate the class type in the toLocalDate method name).

Apart from the methods shown in Table 17.2, the selected methods shown in Table 17.3 are common to the temporal classes LocalTime, LocalDate, LocalDateTime, ZonedDateTime, and Instant.

Subsequent sections in this chapter provide ample examples of how to create, combine, convert, access, and compare temporal objects, including the use of temporal arithmetic and dealing with time zones and daylight savings. For formatting and parsing temporal objects, see §18.6, p. 1127.

Table 17.2 *Selected Method Name Prefixes in the Temporal Classes*

Prefix (parameters not shown)	Usage
at*XXX*()	Create a new temporal object by combining this temporal object with another temporal object. Not provided by the ZonedDateTime class.
of() of*XXX*()	Static factory methods for constructing temporal objects from constituent temporal fields.
get() get*XXX*()	Access specific fields in this temporal object.
is*XXX*()	Check specific properties of this temporal object.
minus() minus*XXX*()	Return a copy of this temporal object after subtracting an amount of time.
plus() plus*XXX*()	Return a copy of this temporal object after adding an amount of time.
to*XXX*()	Convert this temporal object to another type.
with() with*XXX*()	Create a copy of this temporal object with one field modified.

Table 17.3 *Selected Common Methods in the Temporal Classes*

Method (parameters not shown)	Usage
now()	Static method that obtains the current time from the system or specified clock in the default or specified time zone.
from()	Static method to obtain an instance of this temporal class from another temporal.
until()	Calculate the amount of time from this temporal object to another temporal object.
toString()	Create a text representation of this temporal object.
equals()	Compare two temporal objects for equality.
hashCode()	Returns a hash code for this temporal object.

Table 17.3 *Selected Common Methods in the Temporal Classes (Continued)*

Method (parameters not shown)	Usage
compareTo()	Compare two temporal objects. (The class ZonedDateTime does not implement the Comparable<E> interface.)
parse()	Static method to obtain a temporal instance from a specified text string (§18.6, p. 1127).
format()	Create a text representation of this temporal object using a specified formatter (§18.6, p. 1127). (Instant class does not provide this method.)

17.2 Working with Dates and Times

The classes LocalTime, LocalDate, and LocalDateTime in the java.time package represent time-based, date-based, and combined date-based and time-based temporal objects, respectively, that are all time zone agnostic. These classes represent *human time* that is calendar-based, meaning it is defined in terms of concepts like year, month, day, hour, minute, and second, that humans use. The Instant class can be used to represent *machine time*, which is defined as a point measured with nanosecond precision on a continuous timeline starting from a specific origin (p. 1049).

Time zones and daylight savings are discussed in §17.7, p. 1072.

Creating Dates and Times

The temporal classes in the java.time package do not provide any public constructors to create temporal objects. Instead, they provide overloaded static factory methods named of which create temporal objects from constituent temporal fields. We use the term *temporal fields* to mean both time fields (hours, minutes, seconds, nanoseconds) and date fields (year, month, day). The of() methods check that the values of the arguments are in range. Any invalid argument results in a java.time.DateTimeException.

```
// LocalTime
static LocalTime of(int hour, int minute)
static LocalTime of(int hour, int minute, int second)
static LocalTime of(int hour, int minute, int second, int nanoOfSecond)
static LocalTime ofSecondOfDay(long secondOfDay)
```

These static factory methods in the LocalTime class return an instance of Local-Time based on the specified values for the specified time fields. The second and nanosecond fields are set to zero, if not specified.

The last method accepts a value for the secondOfDay parameter in the range [0, 24 * 60 * 60 − 1] to create a LocalTime.

```
// LocalDate
static LocalDate of(int year, int month, int dayOfMonth)
static LocalDate of(int year, Month month, int dayOfMonth)
static LocalDate ofYearDay(int year, int dayOfYear)
```

These static factory methods in the LocalDate class return an instance of LocalDate based on the specified values for the date fields. The java.time.Month enum type allows months to be referred to by name—for example, Month.MARCH. Note that month numbering starts with 1 (Month.JANUARY).

The last method creates a date from the specified year and the day of the year.

```
// LocalDateTime
static LocalDateTime of(int year, int month, int dayOfMonth,
                        int hour, int minute)
static LocalDateTime of(int year, int month, int dayOfMonth,
                        int hour, int minute, int second)
static LocalDateTime of(int year, int month, int dayOfMonth, int hour,
                        int minute, int second, int nanoOfSecond)
static LocalDateTime of(int year, Month month, int dayOfMonth,
                        int hour, int minute, int second)
static LocalDateTime of(int year, Month month, int dayOfMonth,
                        int hour, int minute)
static LocalDateTime of(int year, Month month, int dayOfMonth,
                        int hour, int minute, int second, int nanoOfSecond)
```

These static factory methods in the LocalDateTime class return an instance of LocalDateTime based on the specified values for the time and date fields. The second and nanosecond fields are set to zero, if not specified. The java.time.Month enum type allows months to be referred to by name—for example, Month.MARCH (i.e., month 3 in the year).

```
static LocalDateTime of(LocalDate date, LocalTime time)
```

Combines a LocalDate and a LocalTime into a LocalDateTime.

All code snippets in this subsection can be found in Example 17.1, p. 1031, ready for running and experimenting. An appropriate import statement with the java.time package should be included in the source file to access any of the temporal classes by their simple name.

The LocalTime Class

The declaration statements below show examples of creating instances of the LocalTime class to represent time on a 24-hour clock in terms of hours, minutes, seconds, and nanoseconds.

```
LocalTime time1 = LocalTime.of(8, 15, 35, 900);      // 08:15:35.000000900
LocalTime time2 = LocalTime.of(16, 45);              // 16:45
// LocalTime time3 = LocalTime.of(25, 13, 30);       // DateTimeException
```

The ranges of values for time fields hour (0–23), minute (0–59), second (0–59), and nanosecond (0–999,999,999) are defined by the ISO standard. The toString() method of the class will format the time fields according to the ISO standard as follows:

```
HH:mm:ss.SSSSSSSSS
```

Omitting the seconds (ss) and fractions of seconds (SSSSSSSSS) in the call to the of() method implies that their value is zero. (More on formatting in §18.6, p. 1134.) In the second declaration statement above, the seconds and the nanoseconds are not specified in the method call, resulting in their values being set to zero. In the third statement, the value of the hour field (25) is out of range, and if the statement is uncommented, it will result in a DateTimeException.

The LocalDate *Class*

Creating instances of the LocalDate class is analogous to creating instances of the LocalTime class. The of() method of the LocalDate class is passed values for date fields: the year, month of the year, and day of the month.

```
LocalDate date1 = LocalDate.of(1969, 7, 20);              // 1969-07-20
LocalDate date2 = LocalDate.of(-3113, Month.AUGUST, 11);// -3113-08-11
// LocalDate date3 = LocalDate.of(2021, 13, 11);          // DateTimeException
// LocalDate date4 = LocalDate.of(2021, 2, 29);           // DateTimeException
```

The ranges of the values for date fields year, month, and day are (–999,999,999 to +999,999,999), (1–12), and (1–31), respectively. The month can also be specified using the enum constants of the java.time.Month class, as in the second declaration statement above. A DateTimeException is thrown if the value of any parameter is out of range, or if the day is invalid for the specified month of the year. In the third declaration, the value of the month field 13 is out of range. In the last declaration, the month of February cannot have 29 days, since the year 2021 is not a leap year.

The toString() method of the LocalDate class will format the date fields according to the ISO standard (§18.6, p. 1134):

```
uuuu-MM-dd
```

The year is represented as a *proleptic year* in the ISO standard, which can be negative. A year in CE (Current Era, or AD) has the same value as a proleptic year; for example, 2021 CE is the same as the proleptic year 2021. However, for a year in BCE (Before Current Era, or BC), the proleptic year 0 corresponds to 1 BCE, the proleptic year –1 corresponds to 2 BCE, and so on. In the second declaration in the preceding set of examples, the date -3113-08-11 corresponds to 11 August 3114 BCE.

The LocalDateTime *Class*

The class LocalDateTime allows the date and the time to be combined into one entity, which is useful for representing such concepts as appointments that require both a time and a date. The of() methods in the LocalDateTime class are combinations of the of() methods from the LocalTime and LocalDate classes, taking values of both time and date fields as arguments. The toString() method of this class will format the temporal fields according to the ISO standard (§18.6, p. 1134):

```
uuuu-MM-ddTHH:mm:ss.SSSSSSSSS
```

The letter T separates the values of the date fields from those of the time fields.

```
// 2021-04-28T12:15
LocalDateTime dt1 = LocalDateTime.of(2021, 4, 28, 12, 15);
```

```
// 2021-08-19T14:00
LocalDateTime dt2 = LocalDateTime.of(2021, Month.AUGUST, 19, 14, 0);
```

The LocalDateTime class also provides an of() method that combines a LocalDate object and a LocalTime object. The first declaration in the next code snippet combines a date and a time. The static field LocalTime.NOON defines the time at noon. In addition, the LocalTime class provides the instance method atDate(), which takes a date as an argument and returns a LocalDateTime object. The second declaration combines the time at noon with the date referred to by the reference date1. Conversely, the LocalDate class provides the overloaded instance method atTime() to combine a date with a specified time. In the last two declarations, the atTime() method is passed a LocalTime object and values for specific time fields, respectively.

```
// LocalDate date1 is 1969-07-20.
LocalDateTime dt3 = LocalDateTime.of(date1, LocalTime.NOON); // 1969-07-20T12:00
LocalDateTime dt4 = LocalTime.of(12, 0).atDate(date1);       // 1969-07-20T12:00
LocalDateTime dt5 = date1.atTime(LocalTime.NOON);            // 1969-07-20T12:00
LocalDateTime dt6 = date1.atTime(12, 0);                     // 1969-07-20T12:00
```

As a convenience, each temporal class provides a static method now() that reads the system clock and returns the values for the relevant temporal fields in an instance of the target class.

```
LocalTime currentTime = LocalTime.now();
LocalDate currentDate = LocalDate.now();
LocalDateTime currentDateTime = LocalDateTime.now();
```

Example 17.1 includes the different ways to create temporal objects that we have discussed so far.

```
// LocalTime
LocalDateTime atDate(LocalDate date)
```
Returns a LocalDateTime that combines this time with the specified date.

```
// LocalDate
LocalDateTime atTime(LocalTime time)
LocalDateTime atTime(int hour, int minute)
LocalDateTime atTime(int hour, int minute, int second)
LocalDateTime atTime(int hour, int minute, int second, int nanoOfSecond)
LocalDateTime atStartOfDay()
```
Return a LocalDateTime that combines this date with the specified values for time fields. The second and nanosecond fields are set to zero, if their values are not specified. In the last method, this date is combined with the time at midnight.

```
// LocalDateTime
ZonedDateTime atZone(ZoneId zone)
```
Returns a ZonedDateTime by combining this date-time with the specified time zone (p. 1072).

```
// LocalTime, LocalDate, LocalDateTime, respectively.
static LocalTime now()
static LocalDate now()
static LocalDateTime now()
```

Each temporal class has this static factory method, which returns either the current time, date, or date-time from the system clock.

Example 17.1 *Creating Local Dates and Local Times*

```java
import java.time.LocalDate;
import java.time.LocalDateTime;
import java.time.LocalTime;
import java.time.Month;

public class CreatingTemporals {

  public static void main(String[] args) {

    // Creating a specific time from time-based values:
    LocalTime time1 = LocalTime.of(8, 15, 35, 900);// 08:15:35.000000900
    LocalTime time2 = LocalTime.of(16, 45);         // 16:45
//  LocalTime time3 = LocalTime.of(25, 13, 30);     // DateTimeException
    System.out.println("Surveillance start time: " + time1);
    System.out.println("Closing time: " + time2);

    // Creating a specific date from date-based values:
    LocalDate date1 = LocalDate.of(1969, 7, 20);            // 1969-07-20
    LocalDate date2 = LocalDate.of(-3113, Month.AUGUST, 11);// -3113-08-11
//  LocalDate date3 = LocalDate.of(2021, 13, 11);          // DateTimeException
//  LocalDate date4 = LocalDate.of(2021, 2, 29);           // DateTimeException
    System.out.println("Date of lunar landing:       " + date1);
    System.out.println("Start Date of Mayan Calendar: " + date2);

    // Creating a specific date-time from date- and time-based values.
    // 2021-04-28T12:15
    LocalDateTime dt1 = LocalDateTime.of(2021, 4, 28, 12, 15);
    // 2021-08-17T14:00
    LocalDateTime dt2 = LocalDateTime.of(2021, Month.AUGUST, 17, 14, 0);
    System.out.println("Car service appointment: " + dt1);
    System.out.println("Hospital appointment:    " + dt2);

    // Combining date and time objects.
    // 1969-07-20T12:00
    LocalDateTime dt3 = LocalDateTime.of(date1, LocalTime.NOON);
    LocalDateTime dt4 = LocalTime.of(12, 0).atDate(date1);
    LocalDateTime dt5 = date1.atTime(LocalTime.NOON);
    LocalDateTime dt6 = date1.atTime(12, 0);
    System.out.println("Factory date-time combo: " + dt3);
    System.out.println("Time with date combo:    " + dt4);
    System.out.println("Date with time combo:    " + dt5);
    System.out.println("Date with explicit time combo: " + dt6);
```

```
        // Current time:
        LocalTime currentTime = LocalTime.now();
        System.out.println("Current time:     " + currentTime);

        // Current date:
        LocalDate currentDate = LocalDate.now();
        System.out.println("Current date:     " + currentDate);

        // Current date and time:
        LocalDateTime currentDateTime = LocalDateTime.now();
        System.out.println("Current date-time: " + currentDateTime);
    }
}
```

Possible output from the program:

```
Surveillance start time: 08:15:35.000000900
Closing time: 16:45
Date of lunar landing:        1969-07-20
Start Date of Mayan Calendar: -3113-08-11
Car service appointment: 2021-04-28T12:15
Hospital appointment:     2021-08-17T14:00
Factory date-time combo: 1969-07-20T12:00
Time with date combo:     1969-07-20T12:00
Date with time combo:     1969-07-20T12:00
Date with explicit time combo: 1969-07-20T12:00
Current time:     10:55:41.296744
Current date:     2021-03-05
Current date-time: 2021-03-05T10:55:41.299318
```

Accessing Fields in Dates and Times

A temporal object provides get methods that are tailored to access the values of specific temporal fields that constitute its state. The LocalTime and LocalDate classes provide get methods to access the values of time and date fields, respectively. Not surprisingly, the LocalDateTime class provides get methods for accessing the values of both time and date fields.

```
// LocalTime, LocalDateTime
int getHour()
int getMinute()
int getSecond()
int getNano()
```

Return the value of the appropriate time field from the current LocalTime or LocalDateTime object.

```
// LocalDate, LocalDateTime
int        getDayOfMonth()
DayOfWeek  getDayOfWeek()
int        getDayOfYear()
Month      getMonth()
int        getMonthValue()
int        getYear()
```

Return the value of the appropriate date field from the current LocalDate or LocalDateTime object. The enum type DayOfWeek allows days of the week to be referred to by name; for example, DayOfWeek.MONDAY is day 1 of the week. The enum type Month allows months of the year to be referred to by name—for example, Month.JANUARY. The month value is from 1 (Month.JANUARY) to 12 (Month.DECEMBER).

```
// LocalTime, LocalDate, LocalDateTime
int get(TemporalField field)
long getLong(TemporalField field)
boolean isSupported(TemporalField field)
```

The first two methods return the value of the specified TemporalField (p. 1046) from this temporal object as an int value or as a long value, respectively. To specify fields whose value does not fit into an int, the getLong() method must be used.

The third method checks if the specified field is supported by this temporal object. It avoids an exception being thrown if it has been determined that the field is supported.

Using an invalid field in a get method will result in any one of these exceptions: DateTimeException (field value cannot be obtained), UnsupportedTemporalType-Exception (field is not supported), or ArithmeticException (numeric overflow occurred).

Here are some examples of using the get methods; more examples can be found in Example 17.2. Given that time and date refer to a LocalTime (08:15) and a LocalDate (1945-08-06), respectively, the code below shows how we access the values of the temporal fields using specifically named get methods and using specific temporal fields.

```
int minuteOfHour1 = time.getMinute();                   // 15
int minuteOfHour2 = time.get(ChronoField.MINUTE_OF_HOUR); // 15

int monthVal1 = date.getMonthValue();                   // 8
int monthVal2 = date.get(ChronoField.MONTH_OF_YEAR);    // 8
```

The temporal class LocalDateTime also provides two methods to obtain the date and the time as temporal objects, in contrast to accessing the values of individual date and time fields.

```
LocalDateTime doomsday = LocalDateTime.of(1945, 8, 6, 8, 15);
LocalDate date = doomsday.toLocalDate();                // 1945-08-06
LocalTime time = doomsday.toLocalTime();                // 08:15
```

```
// LocalDateTime
LocalDate toLocalDate()
LocalTime toLocalTime()
```

These methods can be used to get the LocalDate and the LocalTime components of this date-time object, respectively.

The following two methods return the number of days in the month and in the year represented by a LocalDate object.

```
LocalDate foolsday = LocalDate.of(2022, 4, 1);
int daysInMonth = foolsday.lengthOfMonth();     // 30
int daysInYear = foolsday.lengthOfYear();        // 365 (2022 is not a leap year.)
```

```
// LocalDate
int lengthOfMonth()
int lengthOfYear()
```

These two methods return the number of days in the month and in the year represented by this date, respectively.

Comparing Dates and Times

It is also possible to check whether a temporal object represents a point in time before or after another temporal object of the same type. In addition, the LocalDate and LocalDateTime classes provide an isEqual() method that determines whether a temporal object is equal to another temporal object of the *same* type. In contrast, the equals() method allows equality comparison with an *arbitrary* object.

```
LocalDate d1 = LocalDate.of(1948, 2, 28);        // 1948-02-28
LocalDate d2 = LocalDate.of(1949, 3, 1);         // 1949-03-01
boolean result1 = d1.isBefore(d2);               // true
boolean result2 = d2.isAfter(d1);                // true
boolean result3 = d1.isAfter(d1);                // false
boolean result4 = d1.isEqual(d2);                // false
boolean result5 = d1.isEqual(d1);                // true
boolean result6 = d1.isLeapYear();               // true
```

The temporal classes implement the Comparable<E> interface, providing the compareTo() method so that temporal objects can be compared in a meaningful way. The temporal classes also override the equals() and the hashCode() methods of the Object class. These methods make it possible to both search for and sort temporal objects.

```
// LocalTime
boolean isBefore(LocalTime other)
boolean isAfter(LocalTime other)
```

Determine whether this LocalTime represents a point on the timeline before or after the other time, respectively.

```
// LocalDate
boolean isBefore(ChronoLocalDate other)
boolean isAfter(ChronoLocalDate other)
boolean isEqual(ChronoLocalDate other)
boolean isLeapYear()
```

The first two methods determine whether this LocalDate represents a point on the timeline before or after the other date, respectively. The LocalDate class implements the ChronoLocalDate interface.

The third method determines whether this date is equal to the specified date.

The last method checks for a leap year according to the ISO proleptic calendar system rules.

```
// LocalDateTime
boolean isBefore(ChronoLocalDateTime<?> other)
boolean isAfter(ChronoLocalDateTime<?> other)
boolean isEqual(ChronoLocalDateTime<?> other)
```

The first two methods determine whether this LocalDateTime represents a point on the timeline before or after the specified date-time, respectively. The Local-DateTime class implements the ChronoLocalDateTime<LocalDateTime> interface.

The third method determines whether this date-time object represents the same point on the timeline as the other date-time.

```
int compareTo(LocalTime other)                 // LocalTime
int compareTo(ChronoLocalDate other)           // LocalDate
int compareTo(ChronoLocalDateTime<?> other)    // LocalDateTime
```

Compare this temporal object to another temporal object. The three temporal classes implement the Comparable<E> functional interface. The compareTo() method returns 0 if the two temporal objects are equal, a negative value if this temporal object is less than the other temporal object, and a positive value if this temporal object is greater than the other temporal object.

Creating Modified Copies of Dates and Times

An immutable object does not provide any set methods that can change its state. Instead, it usually provides what are known as with methods (or *withers*) that return a copy of the original object where exactly one field has been set to a new value. The LocalTime and LocalDate classes provide with methods to set the value of a time or date field, respectively. Not surprisingly, the LocalDateTime class provides with methods to set the values of both time and date fields individually. A with method changes a specific property in an absolute way, which is reflected in the state of the new temporal object; the original object, however, is not affected. Such with methods are also called *absolute adjusters*, in contrast to the *relative adjusters* that we will meet later (p. 1040).

```
// LocalTime, LocalDateTime
LocalTime/LocalDateTime withHour(int hour)
LocalTime/LocalDateTime withMinute(int minute)
LocalTime/LocalDateTime withSecond(int second)
LocalTime/LocalDateTime withNano(int nanoOfSecond)
```

Return a copy of this LocalTime or LocalDateTime with the value of the appropriate time field changed to the specified value. A DateTimeException is thrown if the argument value is out of range.

```
// LocalDate, LocalDateTime
LocalDate/LocalDateTime withYear(int year)
LocalDate/LocalDateTime withMonth(int month)
LocalDate/LocalDateTime withDayOfMonth(int dayOfMonth)
LocalDate/LocalDateTime withDayOfYear(int dayOfYear)
```

Return a copy of this LocalDate or LocalDateTime with the value of the appropriate date field changed to the specified value. A DateTimeException is thrown if the specified value is out of range or is invalid in combination with the values of the other time or date fields in the temporal object.

The first and second methods will adjust the day of the month to the *last valid day* of the month, if the day of the month becomes invalid when the year or the month is changed (e.g., the month value 2 will change the date 2020-03-31 to 2020-02-29).

In contrast, the third method will throw a DateTimeException if the specified day of the month is invalid for the month-year combination (e.g., the day of month 29 is invalid for February 2021), as will the last method if the day of the year is invalid for the year (e.g., the day of year 366 is invalid for the year 2021).

```
// LocalTime, LocalDate, LocalDateTime
LocalTime/LocalDate/LocalDateTime with(TemporalField field, long newValue)
```

Returns a copy of this temporal object with the specified TemporalField (p. 1046) set to a new value. The ChronoField enum type implements the TemporalField interface, and its enum constants define specific temporal fields (p. 1046).

Using an invalid field in the with() method will result in any one of these exceptions: DateTimeException (field value cannot be set), UnsupportedTemporalTypeException (field is not supported), or ArithmeticException (numeric overflow occurred).

The code lines below are from Example 17.2. In the second assignment statement, the method calls are chained. Three instances of the LocalDate class are created consecutively, as each with method is called to set the value of a specific date field. The last assignment shows the use of temporal fields in the with() method for the same purpose.

```
LocalDate date2 = LocalDate.of(2021, 3, 1);                 // 2021-03-01
date2 = date2.withYear(2024).withMonth(2).withDayOfMonth(28); // 2024-02-28
```

```
LocalDate date3 = LocalDate.of(2021, 3, 1);              // 2021-03-01
date3 = date3
    .with(ChronoField.YEAR, 2024L)
    .with(ChronoField.MONTH_OF_YEAR, 2L)
    .with(ChronoField.DAY_OF_MONTH, 28L);                // 2024-02-28
```

The following code contains a logical error, such that the last two LocalDate instances returned by the with methods are ignored, and the reference date2 never gets updated.

```
date2 = date2.withYear(2022);                    // 2022-03-01
date2.withMonth(2).withDayOfMonth(28);           // date2 is still 2022-03-01.
```

In the next code examples, each call to a with method throws a DateTimeException. The minute and hour values are out of range for a LocalTime object. Certainly the month value 13 is out of range for a LocalDate object. The day of month value 31 is not valid for April, which has 30 days. The day of year value 366 is out of range as well, since the year 2021 is not a leap year.

```
LocalTime time = LocalTime.of(14, 45);     // 14:45
time = time.withMinute(100);      // Out of range. DateTimeException.
time = time.withHour(25);         // Out of range. DateTimeException.

LocalDate date = LocalDate.of(2021, 4, 30);  // 2021-04-30
date = date.withMonth(13);        // Out of range. DateTimeException.
date = date.withDayOfMonth(31);   // Out of range for month. DateTimeException.
date = date.withDayOfYear(366);   // Out of range for year. DateTimeException.
```

The code snippets below illustrate how the withYear() and withMonth() methods adjust the day of the month, if necessary, when the year or the month is changed, respectively.

```
LocalDate date3 = LocalDate.of(2020, 2, 29);  // Original: 2020-02-29
date3 = date3.withYear(2021);                 // Expected: 2021-02-29
System.out.println("Date3: " + date3);        // Adjusted: 2021-02-28

LocalDate date4 = LocalDate.of(2021, 3, 31);  // Original: 2021-03-31
date4 = date4.withMonth(4);                   // Expected: 2021-04-31
System.out.println("Date4: " + date4);        // Adjusted: 2021-04-30
```

The year in the date 2020-02-29 is changed to 2021, resulting in the following date: 2021-02-29. Since the year 2021 is not a leap year, the month of February cannot have 29 days. The withYear() method adjusts the day of the month to the last valid day of the month (i.e., 28). Similarly, the month in the date 2021-03-31 is changed to 4 (i.e., April), resulting in the following date: 2021-04-31. Since the month April has 30 days, the withMonth() method adjusts the day of the month to the last valid day of the month (i.e., 30).

- -

Example 17.2 *Using Local Dates and Local Times*

```
import java.time.DayOfWeek;
import java.time.LocalDate;
import java.time.LocalDateTime;
import java.time.LocalTime;
```

```java
import java.time.Month;
import java.time.temporal.ChronoField;

public class UsingTemporals {

  public static void main(String[] args) {
    // Date-Time: 1945-08-06T08:15
    LocalDateTime doomsday = LocalDateTime.of(1945, 8, 6, 8, 15);
    LocalDate date = doomsday.toLocalDate();                      // 1945-08-06
    LocalTime time = doomsday.toLocalTime();                      // 08:15
    System.out.println("Date-Time: " + doomsday);
    System.out.println();

    // Time: 08:15
    int hourOfDay      = time.getHour();                          // 8
    int minuteOfHour1  = time.getMinute();                        // 15
    int minuteOfHour2  = time.get(ChronoField.MINUTE_OF_HOUR);    // 15
    int secondOfMinute = time.getSecond();                        // 0
    System.out.println("Time of day:      " + time);
    System.out.println("Hour-of-day:      " + hourOfDay);
    System.out.println("Minute-of-hour 1: " + minuteOfHour1);
    System.out.println("Minute-of-hour 2: " + minuteOfHour2);
    System.out.println("Second-of-minute: " + secondOfMinute);
    System.out.println();

    // Date: 1945-08-06
    int year        = date.getYear();                            // 1945
    int monthVal1   = date.getMonthValue();                      // 8
    int monthVal2   = date.get(ChronoField.MONTH_OF_YEAR);       // 8
    Month month     = date.getMonth();                           // AUGUST
    DayOfWeek dow   = date.getDayOfWeek();                       // MONDAY
    int day         = date.getDayOfMonth();                      // 6
    System.out.println("Date:         " + date);
    System.out.println("Year:         " + year);
    System.out.println("Month value 1: " + monthVal1);
    System.out.println("Month value 2: " + monthVal2);
    System.out.println("Month-of-year: " + month);
    System.out.println("Day-of-week:      " + dow);
    System.out.println("Day-of-month:     " + day);
    System.out.println();

    // Ordering
    LocalDate d1 = LocalDate.of(1948, 2, 28);                    // 1948-02-28
    LocalDate d2 = LocalDate.of(1949, 3, 1);                     // 1949-03-01
    boolean result1 = d1.isBefore(d2);                           // true
    boolean result2 = d2.isAfter(d1);                            // true
    boolean result3 = d1.isAfter(d1);                            // false
    boolean result4 = d1.isEqual(d2);                            // false
    boolean result5 = d1.isEqual(d1);                            // true
    boolean result6 = d1.isLeapYear();                           // true

    System.out.println("Ordering:");
    System.out.println(d1 + " is before "   + d2 + ": " + result1);
    System.out.println(d2 + " is after "    + d1 + ": " + result2);
    System.out.println(d1 + " is after "    + d1 + ": " + result3);
    System.out.println(d1 + " is equal to " + d2 + ": " + result4);
```

```java
        System.out.println(d1 + " is equal to " + d1 + ": " + result5);
        System.out.println(d1.getYear() + " is a leap year: " + result6);
        System.out.println();

        System.out.println("Using absolute adjusters:");
        LocalDate date2 = LocalDate.of(2021, 3, 1);
        System.out.println("Date before adjusting: " + date2);     // 2021-03-01
        date2 = date2.withYear(2024).withMonth(2).withDayOfMonth(28);
        System.out.println("Date after adjusting:  " + date2);     // 2024-02-28
        System.out.println();

        System.out.println("Using temporal fields:");
        LocalDate date3 = LocalDate.of(2021, 3, 1);
        System.out.println("Date before adjusting: " + date3);     // 2021-03-01
        date3 = date3
            .with(ChronoField.YEAR, 2024L)
            .with(ChronoField.MONTH_OF_YEAR, 2L)
            .with(ChronoField.DAY_OF_MONTH, 28L);
        System.out.println("Date after adjusting:  " + date3);     // 2024-02-28
    }
}
```

Output from the program:

```
Date-Time: 1945-08-06T08:15

Time of day:      08:15
Hour-of-day:      8
Minute-of-hour 1: 15
Minute-of-hour 2: 15
Second-of-minute: 0

Date:   1945-08-06
Year:   1945
Month value 1: 8
Month value 2: 8
Month-of-year: AUGUST
Day-of-week:   MONDAY
Day-of-month:  6

Ordering:
-1004-03-01 is before 1004-03-01: true
1004-03-01 is after -1004-03-01: true
-1004-03-01 is after -1004-03-01: false
-1004-03-01 is equal to 1004-03-01: false
-1004-03-01 is equal to -1004-03-01: true
1004 is a leap year: true

Using absolute adjusters:
Date before adjusting: 2021-03-01
Date after adjusting:  2024-02-28

Using temporal fields:
Date before adjusting: 2021-03-01
Date after adjusting:  2024-02-28
```

Temporal Arithmetic with Dates and Times

The temporal classes provide *plus* and *minus* methods that return a copy of the original object that has been *incremented or decremented by a specific amount of time*— for example, by number of hours or by number of months.

The LocalTime and LocalDate classes provide plus/minus methods to increment/decrement a time or a date by a specific amount in terms of a *time unit* (e.g., hours, minutes, and seconds) or a *date unit* (e.g., years, months, and days), respectively. The LocalDateTime class provides plus/minus methods to increment/decrement a date-time object by an amount that is specified in terms of either a time unit or a date unit. For example, the plusMonths(m) and plus(m, ChronoUnit.MONTHS) method calls to a LocalDate object will return a new LocalDate object after adding the specified number of months passed as an argument to the method. Similarly, the minusMinutes(mm) and minus(mm, ChronoUnit.MINUTES) method calls on a LocalTime class will return a new LocalTime object after subtracting the specified number of minutes passed as an argument to the method. The change is relative, and is reflected in the new temporal object that is returned. Such plus/minus methods are also called *relative adjusters*, in contrast to *absolute adjusters* (p. 1035). The ChronoUnit enum type implements the TemporalUnit interface (p. 1044).

```
// LocalTime, LocalDateTime
LocalTime/LocalDateTime minusHours(long hours)
LocalTime/LocalDateTime plusHours(long hours)

LocalTime/LocalDateTime minusMinutes(long minutes)
LocalTime/LocalDateTime plusMinutes(long minutes)

LocalTime/LocalDateTime minusSeconds(long seconds)
LocalTime/LocalDateTime plusSeconds(long seconds)

LocalTime/LocalDateTime minusNanos(long nanos)
LocalTime/LocalDateTime plusNanos(long nanos)
```

Return a copy of this LocalTime or LocalDateTime object with the specified amount either subtracted or added to the value of a specific time field. The calculation always wraps around midnight.

For the methods of the LocalDateTime class, a DateTimeException is thrown if the result exceeds the date range.

```
// LocalDate, LocalDateTime
LocalDate/LocalDateTime minusYears(long years)
LocalDate/LocalDateTime plusYears(long years)

LocalDate/LocalDateTime minusMonths(long months)
LocalDate/LocalDateTime plusMonths(long months)

LocalDate/LocalDateTime minusWeeks(long weeks)
LocalDate/LocalDateTime plusWeeks(long weeks)

LocalDate/LocalDateTime minusDays(long days)
LocalDate/LocalDateTime plusDays(long days)
```

Return a copy of this LocalDate or LocalDateTime with the specified amount either subtracted or added to the value of a specific date field.

All methods throw a DateTimeException if the result exceeds the date range.

The first four methods will change the day of the month to the *last valid day* of the month if necessary, when the day of the month becomes invalid as a result of the operation.

The last four methods will adjust the month and year fields as necessary to ensure a valid result.

```
// LocalTime, LocalDate, LocalDateTime
LocalTime/LocalDate/LocalDateTime minus(long amountToSub,
                                        TemporalUnit unit)
LocalTime/LocalDate/LocalDateTime plus(long amountToAdd, TemporalUnit unit)
boolean isSupported(TemporalUnit unit)
```

The minus() and plus() methods return a copy of this temporal object with the specified amount subtracted or added, respectively, according to the TemporalUnit specified. The ChronoUnit enum type implements the TemporalUnit interface, and its enum constants define specific temporal units (p. 1044).

The isSupported() method checks if the specified TemporalUnit is supported by this temporal object. It avoids an exception being thrown if it has been determined that the unit is supported.

The minus() or the plus() method can result in any one of these exceptions: DateTimeException (the amount cannot be subtracted or added), Unsupported-TemporalTypeException (unit is not supported), or ArithmeticException (numeric overflow occurred).

```
// LocalTime, LocalDate, LocalDateTime
LocalTime/LocalDate/LocalDateTime minus(TemporalAmount amountToSub)
LocalTime/LocalDate/LocalDateTime plus(TemporalAmount amountToAdd)
```

Return a copy of this temporal object with the specified temporal amount subtracted or added, respectively. The classes Period (p. 1057) and Duration (p. 1064) implement the TemporalAmount interface.

The minus() or the plus() method can result in any one of these exceptions: DateTimeException (the temporal amount cannot be subtracted or added) or ArithmeticException (numeric overflow occurred).

```
// LocalTime, LocalDate, LocalDateTime
long until(Temporal endExclusive, TemporalUnit unit)
```

Calculates the amount of time between two temporal objects in terms of the specified TemporalUnit (p. 1044). The start and the end points are this temporal object and the specified temporal argument endExclusive, where the end point is excluded. The result will be negative if the other temporal is before this temporal.

The until() method can result in any one of these exceptions: DateTime-Exception (the temporal amount cannot be calculated or the end temporal cannot be converted to the appropriate temporal object), UnsupportedTemporalType-Exception (unit is not supported), or ArithmeticException (numeric overflow occurred).

```
// LocalDate
Period until(ChronoLocalDate endDateExclusive)
```

Calculates the amount of time between this date and another date as a Period (p. 1057). The calculation excludes the end date. The LocalDate class implements the ChronoLocalDate interface.

Example 17.3 demonstrates what we can call *temporal arithmetic*, where a LocalDate object is modified by adding or subtracting an amount specified as days, weeks, or months. Note how the value of the date fields is adjusted after each operation. In Example 17.3, the date 2021-10-23 is created at (1), and 10 months, 3 weeks, and 40 days are successively added to the new date object returned by each plus method call at (2), (3), and (4), respectively, resulting in the date 2022-10-23. We then subtract 2 days, 4 weeks, and 11 months successively from the new date object returned by each minus() method call at (5), (6), and (7), respectively, resulting in the date 2021-10-23. The method calls at (5), (6), and (7) are passed the temporal unit explicitly. In Example 17.3, several assignment statements are used to print the intermediate dates, but the code can be made more succinct by method chaining.

```
LocalDate date = LocalDate.of(2021, 10, 23);          // 2021-10-23
date = date.plusMonths(10).plusWeeks(3).plusDays(40); // Method chaining
System.out.println(date);                             // 2022-10-23
date = date.minus(2, ChronoUnit.DAYS)
           .minus(4, ChronoUnit.WEEKS)
           .minus(11, ChronoUnit.MONTHS);             // Method chaining
System.out.println(date);                             // 2021-10-23
```

The following code snippet illustrates the wrapping of time around midnight, as one would expect on a 24-hour clock. Each method call returns a new LocalTime object.

```
LocalTime witchingHour = LocalTime.MIDNIGHT           // 00:00
    .plusHours(14)                                    // 14:00
    .plusMinutes(45)                                  // 14:45
    .plusMinutes(30)                                  // 15:15
    .minusHours(15)                                   // 00:15
    .minusMinutes(15);                                // 00:00
```

The next code snippet illustrates how the plusYears() method adjusts the day of the month, if necessary, when the year value is changed. The year in the date 2020-02-29 is changed to 2021 by adding 1 year, resulting in the following date: 2021-02-29. The plusYears() method adjusts the day of the month to the last valid day of the month, 28; as the year 2021 is not a leap year, the month of February cannot have 29 days.

```
LocalDate date5 = LocalDate.of(2020, 2, 29);  // Original: 2020-02-29
date5 = date5.plusYears(1);                   // Expected: 2021-02-29
System.out.println("Date5: " + date5);        // Adjusted: 2021-02-28
```

A temporal can also be adjusted by a *temporal amount*—for example, by a Period (p. 1057) or a Duration (p. 1064). The methods plus() and minus() accept the temporal amount as an argument, as shown by the code below.

```
LocalTime busDep = LocalTime.of(12, 15);                // 12:15
Duration d1 = Duration.ofMinutes(30);                   // PT30M
LocalTime nextBusDep = busDep.plus(d1);                 // 12:45

LocalDate birthday = LocalDate.of(2020, 10, 23);        // 2020-10-23
Period p1 = Period.ofYears(1);                          // P1Y
LocalDate nextBirthday = birthday.plus(p1);             // 2021-10-23
```

The until() method can be used to calculate the amount of time between two compatible temporal objects. The code below calculates the number of days to New Year's Day from the current date; the result, of course, will depend on the current date. In the call to the until() method at (1), the temporal unit specified is ChronoUnit.DAYS, as we want the difference between the dates to be calculated in days.

```
LocalDate currentDate = LocalDate.now();
LocalDate newYearDay = currentDate.plusYears(1).withMonth(1).withDayOfMonth(1);
long daysToNewYear = currentDate.until(newYearDay, ChronoUnit.DAYS); // (1)
System.out.println("Current Date: " + currentDate); // Current Date: 2021-03-08
System.out.println("New Year's Day: " + newYearDay);// New Year's Day: 2022-01-01
System.out.println("Days to New Year: " + daysToNewYear);// Days to New Year: 299
```

The statement at (1) below is meant to calculate the number of minutes until midnight from now, but throws a DateTimeException because it is not possible to obtain a LocalDateTime object from the end point, which is a LocalTime object.

```
long minsToMidnight = LocalDateTime.now()              // (1) DateTimeException!
        .until(LocalTime.MIDNIGHT.minusSeconds(1), ChronoUnit.MINUTES);
```

However, the statement at (2) executes normally, as both the start and end points are LocalTime objects.

```
long minsToMidnight = LocalTime.now()                  // (2)
        .until(LocalTime.MIDNIGHT.minusSeconds(1), ChronoUnit.MINUTES);
```

- -

Example 17.3 *Temporal Arithmetic*

```
import java.time.LocalDate;
import java.time.temporal.ChronoUnit;

public class TemporalArithmetic {

  public static void main(String[] args) {

    LocalDate date = LocalDate.of(2021, 10, 23);        // (1)
    System.out.println("Date:            " + date);     // 2021-10-23
    date = date.plusMonths(10);                         // (2)
    System.out.println("10 months after: " + date);     // 2022-08-23
    date = date.plusWeeks(3);                           // (3)
    System.out.println("3 weeks after:   " + date);     // 2022-09-13
```

```
    date = date.plusDays(40);                         // (4)
    System.out.println("40 days after:     " + date); // 2022-10-23

    date = date.minus(2, ChronoUnit.DAYS);            // (5)
    System.out.println("2 days before:     " + date); // 2022-10-21
    date = date.minus(4, ChronoUnit.WEEKS);           // (6)
    System.out.println("4 weeks before:    " + date); // 2022-09-23
    date = date.minus(11, ChronoUnit.MONTHS);         // (7)
    System.out.println("11 months before: " + date);  // 2021-10-23
  }
}
```

Output from the program:

```
Date:              2021-10-23
10 months after:   2022-08-23
3 weeks after:     2022-09-13
40 days after:     2022-10-23
2 days before:     2022-10-21
4 weeks before:    2022-09-23
11 months before: 2021-10-23
```

17.3 Using Temporal Units and Temporal Fields

Temporal units and temporal fields allow temporal objects to be accessed and manipulated in a human-readable way.

For temporal units and temporal fields supported by the Period and Duration classes, see §17.5, p. 1057, and §17.6, p. 1064, respectively.

Temporal Units

The java.time.temporal.TemporalUnit interface represents a *unit* of measurement, rather than an amount of such a unit—for example, the unit *years* to qualify that an amount of time should be interpreted as number of years. The java.time.temporal .ChronoUnit enum type implements this interface, defining the temporal units by constant names to provide convenient unit-based access to manipulate a temporal object. Constants defined by the ChronoUnit enum type include the following temporal units, among others: SECONDS, MINUTES, HOURS, DAYS, MONTHS, and YEARS.

The output from Example 17.4 shows a table with all the temporal units defined by the ChronoUnit enum type. It is not surprising that not all temporal units are valid for all types of temporal objects. The time units, such as SECONDS, MINUTES, and HOURS, are valid for temporal objects that are time-based, such as LocalTime, LocalDateTime, and Instant. Likewise, the date units, such as DAYS, MONTHS, and YEARS, are valid units for temporal objects that are date-based, such as LocalDate, LocalDateTime, and ZonedDateTime.

A `ChronoUnit` enum constant can be queried by the following selected methods:

`Duration getDuration()`

Gets the estimated duration of this unit in the ISO calendar system. For example, `ChronoUnit.DAYS.getDuration()` has the duration `PT24H` (i.e., 24 hours).

`boolean isDateBased()`
`boolean isTimeBased()`

Check whether this unit is a date unit or a time unit, respectively. For example, `ChronoUnit.HOURS.isDateBased()` is `false`, but `ChronoUnit.SECONDS.isTimeBased()` is `true`.

`boolean isSupportedBy(Temporal temporal)`

Checks whether this unit is supported by the specified temporal object. For example, `ChronoUnit.YEARS.isSupportedBy(LocalTime.MIDNIGHT)` is `false`.

`static ChronoUnit[] values()`

Returns an array containing the unit constants of this enum type, in the order they are declared. This method is called at (2) in Example 17.4.

The temporal classes provide the method `isSupported(unit)` to determine whether a temporal unit is valid for a temporal object. In Example 17.4, this method is used at (3), (4), and (5) to determine whether each temporal unit defined by the `ChronoUnit` enum type is a valid unit for the different temporal classes.

The following methods of the temporal classes all accept a temporal unit that qualifies how a numeric quantity should be interpreted:

- `minus(amount, unit)` and `plus(amount, unit)`, (p. 1040)

```
LocalDate date = LocalDate.of(2021, 10, 23);
System.out.print("Date " + date);
date = date.minus(10, ChronoUnit.MONTHS).minus(3, ChronoUnit.DAYS);
System.out.println(" minus 10 months and 3 days: " + date);
// Date 2021-10-23 minus 10 months and 3 days: 2020-12-20

LocalTime time = LocalTime.of(14, 15);
System.out.print("Time " + time);
time = time.plus(9, ChronoUnit.HOURS).plus(70, ChronoUnit.MINUTES);
System.out.println(" plus 9 hours and 70 minutes is " + time);
// Time 14:15 plus 9 hours and 70 minutes is 00:25
```

- `until(temporalObj, unit)`, (p. 1040)

```
LocalDate fromDate = LocalDate.of(2021, 3, 1);
LocalDate xmasDate = LocalDate.of(2021, 12, 25);
long tilChristmas = fromDate.until(xmasDate, ChronoUnit.DAYS);
System.out.println("From " + fromDate + ", days until Xmas: " + tilChristmas);
// From 2021-03-01, days until Xmas: 299
```

Temporal Fields

The `java.time.temporal.TemporalField` interface represents a specific field of a temporal object. The `java.time.temporal.ChronoField` enum type implements this interface, defining the fields by constant names so that a specific field can be conveniently accessed. Selected constants from the `ChronoField` enum type include `SECOND_OF_MINUTE`, `MINUTE_OF_DAY`, `DAY_OF_MONTH`, `MONTH_OF_YEAR`, and `YEAR`.

The output from Example 17.4 shows a table with all the temporal fields defined by the `ChronoField` enum type.

Analogous to a `ChronoUnit` enum constant, a `ChronoField` enum constant can be queried by the following selected methods:

```
TemporalUnit getBaseUnit()
```
Gets the unit that the field is measured in. For example, `ChronoField.DAY_OF_MONTH.getBaseUnit()` returns `ChronoUnit.DAYS`.

```
boolean isDateBased()
boolean isTimeBased()
```
Check whether this field represents a date or a time field, respectively. For example, `ChronoField.HOUR_OF_DAY.isDateBased()` is `false`, but `ChronoField.SECOND_OF_MINUTE.isTimeBased()` is `true`.

```
boolean isSupportedBy(TemporalAccessor temporal)
```
Checks whether this field is supported by the specified temporal object. For example, `ChronoField.YEAR.isSupportedBy(LocalTime.MIDNIGHT)` is `false`.

```
static ChronoField[] values()
```
Returns an array containing the field constants of this enum type, in the order they are declared. This method is called at (7) in Example 17.4.

The temporal classes provide the method `isSupported(field)` to determine whether a temporal `field` is valid for a temporal object. In Example 17.4, this method is used at (8), (9), and (10) to determine whether each temporal field defined by the `ChronoField` enum type is a valid field for the different temporal classes.

The following methods of the temporal classes all accept a temporal field that designates a specific field of the temporal object:

- `get(field)`, (p. 1032)

```
LocalDate date = LocalDate.of(2021, 8, 13);
int monthValue = date.get(ChronoField.MONTH_OF_YEAR);
System.out.print("Date " + date + " has month of the year: " + monthValue);
// Date 2021-08-13 has month of the year: 8
```

- `with(field, amount)`, (p. 1035)

```
LocalDateTime dateTime = LocalDateTime.of(2021, 8, 13, 20, 20);
System.out.print("Date-time " + dateTime);
dateTime = dateTime.with(ChronoField.DAY_OF_MONTH, 11)
                   .with(ChronoField.MONTH_OF_YEAR, 1)
                   .with(ChronoField.YEAR, 2022);
```

```
System.out.println(" changed to: " + dateTime);
// Date-time 2021-08-13T20:20 changed to: 2022-01-11T20:20
```

In Example 17.4, the code at (1) and at (6) prints tables that show which ChronoUnit and ChronoField constants are valid in which temporal-based object. A LocalTime instance supports time-based units and fields, and a LocalDate instance supports date-based units and fields. A LocalDateTime or a ZonedDateTime supports both time-based and date-based units and fields. Using an invalid enum constant for a temporal object will invariably result in an UnsupportedTemporalTypeException being thrown.

Example 17.4 *Valid Temporal Units and Temporal Fields*

```
import java.time.Instant;
import java.time.LocalDate;
import java.time.LocalDateTime;
import java.time.LocalTime;
import java.time.ZonedDateTime;
import java.time.temporal.ChronoField;
import java.time.temporal.ChronoUnit;

public class ValidTemporalUnitsAndFields {

  public static void main(String[] args) {

    // Temporals:
    LocalTime time = LocalTime.now();
    LocalDate date = LocalDate.now();
    LocalDateTime dateTime = LocalDateTime.now();
    ZonedDateTime zonedDateTime = ZonedDateTime.now();
    Instant instant = Instant.now();

    // Print supported units:                                        // (1)
    System.out.printf("%29s %s %s %s %s %s%n",
        "ChronoUnit", "LocalTime", "LocalDate", "LocalDateTime",
        " ZDT ", "Instant");
    ChronoUnit[] units = ChronoUnit.values();                        // (2)
    for (ChronoUnit unit : units) {
      System.out.printf("%28S: %7b %9b %10b %9b %7b%n",
          unit.name(), time.isSupported(unit), date.isSupported(unit),   // (3)
          dateTime.isSupported(unit), zonedDateTime.isSupported(unit),   // (4)
          instant.isSupported(unit));                                    // (5)
    }
    System.out.println();

    // Print supported fields:                                      // (6)
    System.out.printf("%29s %s %s %s %s %s%n",
        "ChronoField", "LocalTime", "LocalDate", "LocalDateTime",
        " ZDT ", "Instant");
    ChronoField[] fields = ChronoField.values();                    // (7)
    for (ChronoField field : fields) {
      System.out.printf("%28S: %7b %9b %10b %9b %7b%n",
          field.name(), time.isSupported(field), date.isSupported(field),// (8)
```

```
                dateTime.isSupported(field), zonedDateTime.isSupported(field), // (9)
                instant.isSupported(field));                                    // (10)
        }
        System.out.println();
    }
}
```

Output from the program (ZDT *stands for* ZonedDateTime *in the output*):

ChronoUnit	LocalTime	LocalDate	LocalDateTime	ZDT	Instant
NANOS:	true	false	true	true	true
MICROS:	true	false	true	true	true
MILLIS:	true	false	true	true	true
SECONDS:	true	false	true	true	true
MINUTES:	true	false	true	true	true
HOURS:	true	false	true	true	true
HALF_DAYS:	true	false	true	true	true
DAYS:	false	true	true	true	true
WEEKS:	false	true	true	true	false
MONTHS:	false	true	true	true	false
YEARS:	false	true	true	true	false
DECADES:	false	true	true	true	false
CENTURIES:	false	true	true	true	false
MILLENNIA:	false	true	true	true	false
ERAS:	false	true	true	true	false
FOREVER:	false	false	false	false	false

ChronoField	LocalTime	LocalDate	LocalDateTime	ZDT	Instant
NANO_OF_SECOND:	true	false	true	true	true
NANO_OF_DAY:	true	false	true	true	false
MICRO_OF_SECOND:	true	false	true	true	true
MICRO_OF_DAY:	true	false	true	true	false
MILLI_OF_SECOND:	true	false	true	true	true
MILLI_OF_DAY:	true	false	true	true	false
SECOND_OF_MINUTE:	true	false	true	true	false
SECOND_OF_DAY:	true	false	true	true	false
MINUTE_OF_HOUR:	true	false	true	true	false
MINUTE_OF_DAY:	true	false	true	true	false
HOUR_OF_AMPM:	true	false	true	true	false
CLOCK_HOUR_OF_AMPM:	true	false	true	true	false
HOUR_OF_DAY:	true	false	true	true	false
CLOCK_HOUR_OF_DAY:	true	false	true	true	false
AMPM_OF_DAY:	true	false	true	true	false
DAY_OF_WEEK:	false	true	true	true	false
ALIGNED_DAY_OF_WEEK_IN_MONTH:	false	true	true	true	false
ALIGNED_DAY_OF_WEEK_IN_YEAR:	false	true	true	true	false
DAY_OF_MONTH:	false	true	true	true	false
DAY_OF_YEAR:	false	true	true	true	false
EPOCH_DAY:	false	true	true	true	false
ALIGNED_WEEK_OF_MONTH:	false	true	true	true	false
ALIGNED_WEEK_OF_YEAR:	false	true	true	true	false
MONTH_OF_YEAR:	false	true	true	true	false
PROLEPTIC_MONTH:	false	true	true	true	false
YEAR_OF_ERA:	false	true	true	true	false
YEAR:	false	true	true	true	false

```
           ERA:  false     true      true      true   false
INSTANT_SECONDS:  false     false     false     true   true
 OFFSET_SECONDS:  false     false     false     true   false
```

17.4 Working with Instants

The temporal classes LocalTime, LocalDate, LocalDateTime, and ZonedDateTime are suitable for representing human time in terms of year, month, day, hour, minute, second, and time zone. The Instant class can be used for representing computer time, specially *timestamps* that identify to a higher precision when an event occurred on the timeline. Instants are suitable for persistence purposes—for example, in a database.

An Instant represents *a point on the timeline*, measured with nanosecond precision from a starting point or origin which is defined to be at 1970-01-01T00:00:00Z—that is, January 1, 1970, at midnight—and is called the *epoch*. Instants before the epoch have negative values, whereas instants after the epoch have positive values. The Z represents the time zone designator for the *zero UTC offset*, which is the time zone offset for all instants in the UTC standard (p. 1072). The text representation of the epoch shown above is in the ISO standard format used by the toString() method of the Instant class.

An Instant is modeled with two values:

- A long value to represent the *epoch-second*
- An int value to represent the *nano-of-second*

The nano-of-second must be a value in the range [0, 999999999]. This representation is reflected in the methods provided for dealing with instants. The Instant class shares many of the method name prefixes and the common method names in Table 17.2, p. 1026, and Table 17.3, p. 1026, with the other temporal classes, respectively. Although the Instant class has many methods analogous to the other temporal classes, as we shall see, there are also differences. Instant objects are, like objects of the other temporal classes, immutable and thread-safe.

Creating Instants

The Instant class provides the following predefined instants:

```
static Instant EPOCH
static Instant MAX
static Instant MIN
```

These static fields of the Instant class define constants for the epoch (1970-01-01T00:00:00Z), the maximum (1000000000-12-31T23:59:59.999999999Z), and the minimum instants (-1000000000-01-01T00:00Z), respectively.

Following are selected methods for creating and converting instances of the Instant class:

```
static Instant now()
```
Returns the current instant based on the system clock.

```
static Instant ofEpochMilli(long epochMilli)
static Instant ofEpochSecond(long epochSecond)
static Instant ofEpochSecond(long epochSecond, long nanoAdjustment)
```
These static factory methods return an Instant based on the millisecond, second, and nanosecond specified.

Nanoseconds are implicitly set to zero. The argument values can be negative. Note that the amount is specified as a long value.

```
String toString()
```
Returns a text representation of this Instant, such as "2021-01-11T14:18:30Z". Formatting is based on the ISO instant format for date-time:
```
uuuu-MM-ddTHH:mm:ss.SSSSSSSSSZ
```
where Z designates the UTC standard (also known as *Coordinated Universal Time*).

```
static Instant parse(CharSequence text)
```
Returns an Instant parsed from a character sequence, such as "2021-04-28T14:18:30Z", based on the ISO instant format. A DateTimeParse-Exception is thrown if the text cannot be parsed to an instant.

```
ZonedDateTime atZone(ZoneId zone)
```
Returns a ZonedDateTime by combining this instant with the specified time zone (p. 1072).

Analogous to the other temporal classes, the Instant class also provides the now() method to obtain the current instant from the system clock.

```
Instant currentInstant = Instant.now();       // 2021-03-09T10:48:01.914826Z
```

The Instant class provides the static factory method ofEpoch*UNIT*() to construct instants from seconds and nanoseconds. There is no method to construct an instant from just nanoseconds.

```
Instant inst1 = Instant.ofEpochMilli(-24L*60*60*1000);// Date 1 day before epoch.
Instant inst2 = Instant.ofEpochSecond(24L*60*60);     // Date 1 day after epoch.
Instant inst3 = Instant.ofEpochSecond(24L*60*60 - 1,  // Date 1 day after epoch.
                       1_000_000_000L);
out.println("A day before: " + inst1); // Date 1 day before: 1969-12-31T00:00:00Z
out.println("A day after:  " + inst2); // Date 1 day after : 1970-01-02T00:00:00Z
out.println("A day after:  " + inst3); // Date 1 day after : 1970-01-02T00:00:00Z
```

Note that the amount specified is a long value. The last statement above also illustrates that the nanosecond is adjusted so that it is always between 0 and 999,999,999. The adjustment results in the nanosecond being set to 0 and the second being incremented by 1.

The toString() method of the Instant class returns a text representation of an Instant based on the ISO standard. The code shows the text representation of the instant 500 nanoseconds after the epoch.

```
Instant inst4 = Instant.ofEpochSecond(0, 500);
out.println("Default format:  " + inst4);          // 1970-01-01T00:00:00.000000500Z
```

The Instant class also provides the parse() static method to create an instant from a string that contains a text representation of an instant, based on the ISO standard. Apart from treating the value of the nanosecond as optional, the method is strict in parsing the string. If the format of the string is not correct, a DateTimeParseException is thrown.

```
Instant instA = Instant.parse("1970-01-01T00:00:00.000000500Z");
Instant instB = Instant.parse("1949-03-01T12:30:15Z");
Instant instC = Instant.parse("-1949-03-01T12:30:15Z");
Instant instD = Instant.parse("-1949-03-01T12:30:15"); // DateTimeParseException!
```

The code below illustrates creating an Instant by combining a LocalDateTime object with a time zone offset. Three different zone-time offsets are specified at (2), (3), and (4) to convert the date-time created at (1) to an Instant on the UTC timeline, which has offset zero. Note that an offset ahead of UTC is subtracted and an offset behind UTC is added to adjust the values of the date/time from the LocalDateTime object to the UTC timeline.

```
LocalDateTime ldt = LocalDate.of(2021, 12, 25).atStartOfDay();  //(1)
Instant i1 = ldt.toInstant(ZoneOffset.of("+02:00"));     // (2) Ahead of UTC
Instant i2 = ldt.toInstant(ZoneOffset.UTC);              // (3) At UTC
Instant i3 = ldt.toInstant(ZoneOffset.of("-02:00"));     // (4) Behind UTC
System.out.println("ldt: " + ldt);
System.out.println("i1:  " + i1);
System.out.println("i2:  " + i2);
System.out.println("i3:  " + i3);
```

Output from the code:
```
ldt: 2021-12-25T00:00
i1:  2021-12-24T22:00:00Z
i2:  2021-12-25T00:00:00Z
i3:  2021-12-25T02:00:00Z
```

```
// LocalDateTime
default Instant toInstant(ZoneOffset offset)
```

Converts a date-time to an instant by combining this LocalDateTime object with the specified time zone. The valid offset in Java is in the range from −18 to +18 hours. The absolute value of the offset is added to or subtracted from the date-time depending on whether it is specified as a negative or positive value, respectively, keeping in mind that an Instant represents a point in time on the UTC timeline.

This method is inherited by the LocalDateTime class from its superinterface java.time.chrono.ChronoLocalDateTime.

Accessing Temporal Fields in an Instant

The Instant class provides the following selected methods to access temporal fields in an instance of the class:

```
int getNano()
long getEpochSecond()
```

Return the number of nanoseconds and the number of seconds represented by this instant from the start of the epoch, respectively. Note that the method names are without the s at the end.

```
int  get(TemporalField field)
long getLong(TemporalField field)
```

The get(field) method will return the value of the specified field in this Instant as an int. Only the following ChronoField constants are supported: NANO_OF_SECOND, MICRO_OF_SECOND, MILLI_OF_SECOND, and INSTANT_SECONDS (p. 1046). The first three fields will always return a valid value, but the INSTANT_SECONDS field will throw a DateTimeException if the value does not fit into an int. All other fields result in an UnsupportedTemporalTypeException.

As the getLong(field) method returns the value of the specified field in this Instant as a long, there is no problem with overflow in returning a value designated by any of the four fields mentioned earlier.

```
boolean isSupported(TemporalField field)
```

The isSupported(field) determines whether the specified field is supported by this instant.

```
long toEpochMilli()
```

Returns the number of milliseconds that represent this Instant from the start of the epoch. The method throws an ArithmeticException in case of number overflow.

The code below shows how the getNano() and getEpochSecond() methods of the Instant class read the value of the nanosecond and the epoch-second fields of an Instant object, respectively.

```
Instant inst = Instant.ofEpochSecond(24L*60*60,    // 1 day and
                                     555_555_555L);// 555555555 ns after epoch.
out.println(inst);                  // 1970-01-02T00:00:00.555555555Z
out.println(inst.getNano());        // 555555555 ns
out.println(inst.getEpochSecond()); // 86400 s
```

Reading the nanosecond and epoch-second fields of an Instant *in different units* can be done using the get(field) method. Note the value of the nanosecond field expressed in different units using ChronoField constants. To avoid a DateTimeException when number overflow occurs, the getLong(field) method is used instead of the get(field) method in accessing the epoch-second field.

```
out.println(inst.get(ChronoField.NANO_OF_SECOND));    // 555555555 ns
out.println(inst.get(ChronoField.MICRO_OF_SECOND));   // 555555 micros
```

```
out.println(inst.get(ChronoField.MILLI_OF_SECOND));       // 555 ms
out.println(inst.getLong(ChronoField.INSTANT_SECONDS));   // 86400 s
//out.println(inst.get(ChronoField.INSTANT_SECONDS));     // DateTimeException
//out.println(inst.get(ChronoField.HOUR_OF_DAY));         // UnsupportedTemporal-
                                                          // TypeException
```

The Instant class provides the toEpochMilli() method to derive the position of the instant measured in milliseconds from the epoch; that is, the second and nanosecond fields are converted to milliseconds. Converting 1 day (86400 s) and 555555555 ns results in 86400555 ms.

```
out.println(inst.toEpochMilli());                         // 86400555 ms
```

Comparing Instants

The methods isBefore() and isAfter() can be used to determine if one instant is before or after the other on the timeline, respectively.

```
// instA is  1970-01-01T00:00:00.000000500Z
// instB is  1949-03-01T12:30:15Z
// instC is -1949-03-01T12:30:15Z
out.println(instA.isBefore(instB));           // false
out.println(instA.isAfter(instC));            // true
```

The Instant class also overrides the equals() method and the hashCode() method of the Object class, and implements the Comparable<Instant> interface. Instants can readily be used in collections. The code below illustrates comparing instants.

```
out.println(instA.equals(instB));             // false
out.println(instA.equals(instC));             // false

List<Instant> list = Arrays.asList(instA, instB, instC);
Collections.sort(list);                // Natural order: position on the timeline.
// [-1949-03-01T12:30:15Z, 1949-03-01T12:30:15Z, 1970-01-01T00:00:00.0000005Z]
```

```
boolean isBefore(Instant other)
boolean isAfter(Instant other)
```
Determine whether this Instant is before or after the other instant on the timeline, respectively.

```
boolean equals(Object other)
```
Determines whether this Instant is equal to the other instant, based on the timeline position of the instants.

```
int hashCode()
```
Returns a hash code for this Instant.

```
int compareTo(Instant other)
```
Compares this Instant with the other instant, based on the timeline position of the instants.

Creating Modified Copies of Instants

The Instant class provides the with(field, newValue) method that returns a copy of this instant with either the epoch-second or the nano-of-second set to a new value, while the other one is unchanged.

Instant with(TemporalField field, long newValue)

Returns a copy of this instant where either the epoch-second or the nano-of-second is set to the specified value. The value of the other is retained.

This method only supports the following ChronoField constants: NANO_OF_SECOND, MICRO_OF_SECOND, MILLI_OF_SECOND, and INSTANT_SECONDS (p. 1046). For the first three fields, the nano-of-second is replaced by appropriately converting the specified value, and the epoch-second will be unchanged in the copy returned by the method. For the INSTANT_SECONDS field, the epoch-second will be replaced and the nanosecond will be unchanged in the copy returned by the method. Valid values that can be specified with these constants are [0–999999999], [0–999999], [0–999], and a long, respectively.

This method throws a DateTimeException if the field cannot be set, an Unsupported-TemporalTypeException if the field is not supported, and an ArithmeticException if number overflow occurs.

In the code below, the three instants i1, i2, and i3 will have the nano-of-second set to 5,000,000,000 nanoseconds using the with() method, but the epoch-second will not be changed.

```
Instant i0, i1, i2, i3;
i0 = Instant.now();
out.println(i0);                             // 2021-02-28T08:43:35.864Z
i1 = i0.with(ChronoField.NANO_OF_SECOND,  500_000_000);// 500000000 ns.
i2 = i0.with(ChronoField.MICRO_OF_SECOND, 500_000);    // 500000x1000 ns.
i3 = i0.with(ChronoField.MILLI_OF_SECOND, 500);        // 500x1000000 ns.
out.println(i1);                             // 2021-02-28T08:43:35.500Z

out.println(i1.equals(i2));                  // true
out.println(i1.equals(i3));                  // true
```

In the code below, oneInstant has the nano-of-second set to 500,000,000 nanoseconds and the epoch-second set to 1 day after the epoch.

```
Instant oneInstant = Instant.now()
                     .with(ChronoField.MILLI_OF_SECOND, 500)
                     .with(ChronoField.INSTANT_SECONDS, 24L*60*60);
out.println(oneInstant);                     // 1970-01-02T00:00:00.500Z
```

Temporal Arithmetic with Instants

The Instant class provides *plus* and *minus* methods that return a copy of the original instant that has been *incremented or decremented by a specific amount* specified in terms of either seconds, milliseconds, or nanoseconds. Each amounts below is explicitly designated as a `long` to avoid problems if the amount does not fit into an int.

```
Instant event =
    Instant.EPOCH                //              1970-01-01T00:00:00Z
        .plusSeconds(7L*24*60*60) // (+7days)    1970-01-08T00:00:00Z
        .plusSeconds(6L*60*60)    // (+6hrs)     1970-01-08T06:00:00Z
        .plusSeconds(5L*60)       // (+5mins)    1970-01-08T06:05:00Z
        .plusSeconds(4L)          // (+4s)       1970-01-08T06:05:04Z
        .plusMillis(3L*100)       // (+3ms)      1970-01-08T06:05:04.003Z
        .plusNanos(2L*1_000)      // (+2micros)  1970-01-08T06:05:04.003002Z
        .plusNanos(1L);           // (+1ns)      1970-01-08T06:05:04.003002001Z
```

However, it is more convenient to express the above calculation using the `plus(amount, unit)` method, which also allows the amount to be qualified by a unit. This is illustrated by the statement below, which is equivalent to the one above.

```
Instant ptInTime =
    Instant.EPOCH                        // 1970-01-01T00:00:00Z
        .plus(7L, ChronoUnit.DAYS)       // 1970-01-08T00:00:00Z
        .plus(6L, ChronoUnit.HOURS)      // 1970-01-08T06:00:00Z
        .plus(5L, ChronoUnit.MINUTES)    // 1970-01-08T06:05:00Z
        .plus(4L, ChronoUnit.SECONDS)    // 1970-01-08T06:05:04Z
        .plus(3L, ChronoUnit.MILLIS)     // 1970-01-08T06:05:04.003Z
        .plus(2L, ChronoUnit.MICROS)     // 1970-01-08T06:05:04.003002Z
        .plus(1L, ChronoUnit.NANOS);     // 1970-01-08T06:05:04.003002001Z
```

The code below shows the `plus()` method of the `Instant` class that takes a `Duration` (p. 1064) as the amount to add.

```
Instant start = Instant.EPOCH
                    .plus(20, ChronoUnit.MINUTES);// 1970-01-01T00:20:00Z
Duration length = Duration.ZERO.plusMinutes(90);  // PT1H30M (90 mins)
Instant end = start.plus(length);                 // 1970-01-01T01:50:00Z
```

The `until()` method calculates the amount of time between two instants in terms of the unit specified in the method.

```
long eventDuration1 = start.until(end, ChronoUnit.MINUTES); // 90 minutes
long eventDuration2 = start.until(end, ChronoUnit.HOURS);   // 1 hour
```

As an `Instant` does not represent an amount of time, but a point on the timeline, it cannot be used in temporal arithmetic with other temporal objects. Although an `Instant` incorporates a date, it is not possible to access it in terms of year and month.

```
Instant plusSeconds/minusSeconds(long seconds)
Instant plusMillis/minusMillis(long millis)
Instant plusNanos/minusNanos(long nanos)
```

Return a copy of this instant, with the specified amount added or subtracted. Note that the argument type is `long`.

The methods throw a `DateTimeException` if the result is not a valid instant, and an `ArithmeticException` if numeric flow occurs during the operation.

```
Instant plus(long amountToAdd, TemporalUnit unit)
Instant minus(long amountToSub, TemporalUnit unit)
```

Return a copy of this instant with the specified amount added or subtracted, respectively, where the specified TemporalUnit qualifies the amount (p. 1044).

The following units, defined as constants by the ChronoUnit class, can be used to qualify the amount: NANOS, MICROS, MILLIS, SECONDS, MINUTES, HOURS, HALF_DAYS, and DAYS (p. 1044).

A method call can result in any one of these exceptions: DateTimeException (if the operation cannot be performed), UnsupportedTemporalTypeException (if the unit is not supported), or ArithmeticException (if numeric overflow occurs).

```
Instant isSupported(TemporalUnit unit)
```

Returns true if the specified unit is supported (p. 1044), in which case, the unit can be used in plus/minus operations on an instant. If the specified unit is not supported, the plus/minus methods that accept a unit will throw an exception.

```
Instant plus(TemporalAmount amountToAdd)
Instant minus(TemporalAmount amountToSubtract)
```

Return a copy of this instant, with the specified amount added or subtracted. The amount is typically defined as a Duration.

A method call can result in any one of these exceptions: DateTimeException (if the operation cannot be performed) or ArithmeticException (if numeric overflow occurs).

```
long until(Temporal endExclusive, TemporalUnit unit)
```

Calculates the amount of time between two temporal objects in terms of the specified TemporalUnit (p. 1044). The start and end points are this temporal object and the specified temporal argument, where the end point is excluded.

The start point is an Instant, and the end point temporal is converted to an Instant, if necessary.

The following units, defined as constants by the ChronoUnit class, can be used to indicate the unit in which the result should be returned: NANOS, MICROS, MILLIS, SECONDS, MINUTES, HOURS, HALF_DAYS, and DAYS (p. 1044).

The until() method can result in any one of these exceptions: DateTimeException (the temporal amount cannot be calculated or the end temporal cannot be converted to the appropriate temporal object), UnsupportedTemporalTypeException (the unit is not supported), or ArithmeticException (numeric overflow occurred).

Converting Instants

Each of the classes LocalTime, LocalDate, LocalDateTime, and ZonedDateTime provides the ofInstant() method to obtain a temporal object from an Instant. The code below shows how instants can be converted to other temporal objects for a given time zone. For date/time represented by this particular instant, the offset for the time zone "America/New_York" is -4 hours from UTC.

```
Instant instant = Instant.parse("2021-04-28T03:15:00Z");
ZoneId zid = ZoneId.of("America/New_York");
LocalTime lt = LocalTime.ofInstant(instant, zid);          // 10:18:30
LocalDate ld = LocalDate.ofInstant(instant, zid);          // 2021-04-27
LocalDateTime ldt = LocalDateTime.ofInstant(instant, zid); // 2021-04-27T23:15
ZonedDateTime zdt = ZonedDateTime.ofInstant(instant, zid);
    // 2021-04-27T23:15-04:00[America/New_York]
```

static *TemporalType* ofInstant(Instant instant, ZoneId zone)

Creates a *TemporalType* object from the given Instant and ZoneId (p. 1072), where *TemporalType* can be LocalTime, LocalDate, LocalDateTime, or ZonedDateTime.

17.5 Working with Periods

For representing *an amount of time*, the Date and Time API provides the two classes Period and Duration. We will concentrate on the Period class in this section and discuss the Duration class in §17.6, p. 1064.

The Period class essentially represents a *date-based amount of time* in terms of years, months, and days, whereas, the Duration class represents a *time-based amount of time* in terms of seconds and nanoseconds.

The date-based Period class can be used with the LocalDate class, and not surprisingly, the time-based Duration class can be used with the LocalTime class. Of course, the LocalDateTime class can use both temporal amount classes.

The Period and Duration classes are in the same package (java.time) as the temporal classes, and the repertoire of methods they provide should look familiar, as they share many of the method prefixes with the temporal classes (Table 17.2, p. 1026).

The mantra of immutable and thread-safe objects also applies to both the Period and the Duration classes.

Creating Periods

Like the temporal classes, the Period class does not provide any public constructors, but rather provides an overloaded static factory method of() to construct periods of different lengths, based on date units.

```
Period p = Period.of(2, 4, 8);          // (1)
System.out.println(p);                  // (2) P2Y4M8D (2 Years, 4 Months, 8 Days)
Period p1 = Period.ofYears(10);         // P10Y, period of 10 years.
Period p2 = Period.ofMonths(14);        // P14M, period of 14 months.
Period p3 = Period.ofDays(40);          // P40D, period of 40 days.
Period p4 = Period.ofWeeks(2);          // P14D, period of 14 days (2 weeks).
```

The most versatile of() method requires the amount of time for all date units: years, months, and days, as at (1). Other of() methods create a period based on a particular date unit, as shown in the examples above.

The toString() method of the Period class returns a text representation of a Period according to the ISO standard: P*y*Y*m*M*d*D—that is, *y* Years, *m* Months, and *d* Days. The output from (2) above, P2Y4M8D, indicates a period of 2 years, 4 months, and 8 days.

The code snippet below does *not* create a period of 3 years, 4 months, and 5 days— it creates a period of only 5 days. The first method call is invoked with the class name, and the subsequent method calls are on the new Period object returned as a consequence of the previous call. The of() method creates a new Period object based on its argument.

```
Period period = Period.ofYears(3).ofMonths(4).ofDays(5);   // P5D. Logical error.
```

As we would expect, we can create a period that represents the amount of time between two dates by calling the static method between() of the Period class.

```
LocalDate d1 = LocalDate.of(2021, 3, 1);  // 2021-03-01
LocalDate d2 = LocalDate.of(2022, 3, 1);  // 2022-03-01
Period period12 = Period.between(d1, d2); // P1Y
Period period21 = Period.between(d2, d1); // P-1Y
```

The Period class also provides the static method parse() to create a period from a string that contains a text representation of a period in the ISO standard. If the format of the string is not correct, a java.time.format.DateTimeParseException is thrown.

```
Period period2 = Period.parse("P1Y15M20D"); // 1 year, 15 months, 20 days
Period period3 = Period.parse("P20D");      // 20 days
Period period4 = Period.parse("P5W");       // 35 days (5 weeks)
//  Period pX = Period.parse("P24H"); // java.time.format.DateTimeParseException
```

```
static Period ZERO
```

This constant defines a Period of length zero (P0D).

```
static Period of(int years, int months, int days)
static Period ofYears(int years)
static Period ofMonths(int months)
static Period ofWeeks(int weeks)
static Period ofDays(int days)
```

These static factory methods return a Period representing an amount of time equal to the specified value of a date unit. Date units that are implicit are set to zero. A week is equal to 7 days. The argument value can be negative.

```
static Period between(LocalDate startDateInclusive,
                      LocalDate endDateExclusive)
```

This static method returns a Period consisting of the number of years, months, and days between the two dates. The calculation excludes the end date. The result of this method can be a negative period if the end date is before the start date.

```
String toString()
```

Returns a text representation of a Period according to the ISO standard. Typical formats are P*y*Y*m*M*d*D and P*n*W—that is, *y* Years, *m* Months, and *d* Days, or *n* Weeks.

```
static Period parse(CharSequence text)
```

This static method returns a Period parsed from a character sequence—for example, "P3Y10M2D" (3 years, 10 months, 2 days). A java.time.format.Date-TimeParseException is thrown if the text cannot be parsed to a period.

Accessing Date Units in a Period

The Period class provides the obvious get*XXX*() methods to read the values of date units of a Period object, where *XXX* can be Years, Months, or Days.

```
Period period5 = Period.of(2, 4, -10);
System.out.println("Period: " + period5);            // Period: P2Y4M-10D
System.out.println("Years:  " + period5.getYears());  // Years:  2
System.out.println("Months: " + period5.getMonths()); // Months: 4
System.out.println("Days:   " + period5.getDays());   // Days:   -10
```

Reading the value of date units of a Project object can also be achieved using the get(unit) method, where only the date units shown in the code below are allowed. A list of these valid temporal units can be obtained by calling the getUnits() method of the Period class.

The class also has methods to check if *any* date unit of a period has a negative value or if *all* date units of a period have the value zero.

```
System.out.println("Years:  " + period5.get(ChronoUnit.YEARS)); // Years:  2
System.out.println("Months: " + period5.get(ChronoUnit.MONTHS));// Months: 4
System.out.println("Days:   " + period5.get(ChronoUnit.DAYS));  // Days: -10
List<TemporalUnit> supportedUnits = period5.getUnits(); // [Years, Months, Days]

System.out.println("Total months: " + period5.toTotalMonths()); // 28 months
System.out.println(period5.isNegative());                       // true
System.out.println(period5.isZero());                           // false
```

The class Period provides the method toTotalMonths() to derive the *total* number of months in a period. However, this calculation is solely based on the number of years and months in the period; the number of days is *not* considered. A Period just represents an amount of time, so it has no notion of a date. Conversion between months and years is not a problem, as 1 year is 12 months. However, conversion between the number of days and the other date units is problematic. The number of days in a year and in a month are very much dependent on whether the year is a leap year and on a particular month in the year, respectively. A Period is oblivious to both the year and the month in the year, as it represents an *amount* of time and *not* a *point* on the timeline.

```
int getYears()
int getMonths()
int getDays()
```

Return the value of a specific date unit of this period, indicated by the name of the method.

`long get(TemporalUnit unit)`

Returns the value of the specified unit in this Period. The only supported date ChronoUnits are YEARS, MONTHS, and DAYS (p. 1044). All other units throw an exception.

`List<TemporalUnit> getUnits()`

Returns the list of date units supported by this period: YEARS, MONTHS, and DAYS (p. 1044). These date units can be used in the get(TemporalUnit) method.

`long toTotalMonths()`

Returns the total number of months in this period, based on the values of the years and months units. The value of the days unit is not considered.

`boolean isNegative()`

Determines whether the value of any date units of this period is negative.

`boolean isZero()`

Determines whether the values of all date units of this period are zero.

Comparing Periods for Equality

The Period class overrides the equals() and hashCode() methods of the Object class, but the class does *not* implement the Comparable<E> interface. The value of each date unit is compared individually, and must have the same value to be considered equal. A period of 1 year and 14 months is not equal to a period of 2 years and 2 months, or to a period of 26 months. For this reason, Period objects do not implement the Comparable<E> interface.

```
Period px = Period.of(1, 14, 0);
Period py = Period.of(2, 2, 0);
Period pz = Period.ofMonths(26);
System.out.println(px.equals(py));        // false
System.out.println(px.equals(pz));        // false
System.out.println(px.equals(Period.ZERO)); // false
```

`boolean equals(Object obj)`

Determines whether this period is equal to another period, meaning that each corresponding date unit has the same value.

`int hashCode()`

Returns a hash code for this period.

Creating Modified Copies of Periods

The Period class provides with methods to set a new value for each date unit individually, while the values of the other date units remain unchanged. Note that each method call returns a new Period object, and chaining method calls work as expected.

```
Period p5 = Period.of(2, 1, 30) // P2Y1M30D
   .withYears(3)                // P3Y1M30D, sets the number of years
   .withMonths(16)             // P3Y16M30D, sets the number of months
   .withDays(1);               // P3Y16M1D, sets the number of days
```

```
Period withYears(int years)
Period withMonths(int months)
Period withDays(int days)
```

Return a copy of this period where a specific date unit is set to the value of the argument. The values of the other date units are not affected.

Temporal Arithmetic with Periods

The Period class provides *plus* and *minus* methods that return a copy of the original object that has been *incremented or decremented by a specific amount* specified in terms of a date unit—for example, as a number of years, months, or days. As the following code snippets show, only the value of a specific date unit is changed; the values of other date fields are unaffected. There is no implicit normalization performed, unless the normalized() method that normalizes only the months is called, adjusting the values of the months and years as necessary.

```
Period p6 = Period.of(2, 10, 30)  // P2Y10M30D
   .plusDays(10)                  // P2Y10M40D
   .plusMonths(8)                 // P2Y18M40D
   .plusYears(1)                  // P3Y18M40D
   .normalized();                 // P4Y6M40D
```

We can do simple arithmetic with periods. The code examples below use the plus() and the minus() methods of the Period class that take a TemporalAmount as an argument. Both the Period and the Duration classes implement the TemporalAmount interface. In the last assignment statement, we have shown the state of both new Period objects that are created.

```
Period p7 = Period.of(1, 1, 1);      // P1Y1M1D
Period p8 = Period.of(2, 12, 30);    // P2Y12M30D
Period p9 = p8.minus(p7);            // P1Y11M29D
p8 = p8.plus(p7).plus(p8);           // P3Y13M31D, P5Y25M61D
```

```
Period plusYears/minusYears(long years)
Period plusMonths/minusMonths(long months)
Period plusDays/minusDays(long days)
```

Return a copy of this period, with the specified value for the date unit added or subtracted. The values of other date units are unaffected.

```
Period plus(TemporalAmount amount)
Period minus(TemporalAmount amount)
```

Return a copy of this period, with the specified temporal amount added or subtracted. The amount is of the interface type TemporalAmount that is implemented by the classes Period and Duration, but only Period is valid here. The operation is performed separately on each date unit. There is no normalization performed. A DateTimeException is thrown if the operation cannot be performed.

```
Period normalized()
```

Returns a copy of this period where the years and months are normalized. The number of days is not affected.

```
Period negated()
Period multipliedBy(int scalar)
```

Return a new instance of `Period` where the value of each date unit in this period is individually negated or multiplied by the specified `scalar`, respectively.

We can also do simple arithmetic with dates and periods. The following code uses the `plus()` and `minus()` methods of the `LocalDate` class that take a `TemporalAmount` as an argument (p. 1040). Note the adjustments performed to the month and the day fields to return a valid date in the last assignment statement.

```
Period p10 = Period.of(1, 1, 1);          // P1Y1M1D
LocalDate date1 = LocalDate.of(2021, 3, 1);   // 2021-03-01
LocalDate date2 = date1.plus(p10);        // 2022-04-02
LocalDate date3 = date1.minus(p10);       // 2020-01-31
```

We can add and subtract periods from `LocalDate` and `LocalDateTime` objects, but not from `LocalTime` objects, as a `LocalTime` object has only time fields.

```
LocalTime time = LocalTime.NOON;
time = time.plus(p10);        // java.time.temporal.UnsupportedTemporalTypeException
```

Example 17.5 is a simple example to illustrate implementing period-based loops. The method `reserveDates()` at (1) is a stub for reserving certain dates, depending on the period passed as an argument. The `for(;;)` loop at (2) uses the `Local-Date.isBefore()` method to terminate the loop, and the `LocalDate.plus()` method to increment the current date with the specified period.

Example 17.5 *Period-Based Loop*

```
import java.time.LocalDate;
import java.time.Period;

public class PeriodBasedLoop {
  public static void main(String[] args) {
    reserveDates(Period.ofDays(7),
                LocalDate.of(2021, 10, 20), LocalDate.of(2021, 11, 20));
    System.out.println();
    reserveDates(Period.ofMonths(1),
                LocalDate.of(2021, 10, 20), LocalDate.of(2022, 1, 20));
    System.out.println();
    reserveDates(Period.of(0, 1, 7),
                LocalDate.of(2021, 10, 20), LocalDate.of(2022, 1, 21));
  }

  public static void reserveDates(Period period,           // (1)
                                  LocalDate fromDate,
                                  LocalDate toDateExclusive) {
    System.out.println("Start date: " + fromDate);
    for (LocalDate date = fromDate.plus(period);           // (2)
        date.isBefore(toDateExclusive);
```

```
            date = date.plus(period)) {
        System.out.println("Reserved (" + period + "): " + date);
      }
      System.out.println("End date: " + toDateExclusive);
    }
  }
```

Output from the program:

```
Start date: 2021-10-20
Reserved (P7D): 2021-10-27
Reserved (P7D): 2021-11-03
Reserved (P7D): 2021-11-10
Reserved (P7D): 2021-11-17
End date: 2021-11-20

Start date: 2021-10-20
Reserved (P1M): 2021-11-20
Reserved (P1M): 2021-12-20
End date: 2022-01-20

Start date: 2021-10-20
Reserved (P1M7D): 2021-11-27
Reserved (P1M7D): 2022-01-03
End date: 2022-01-21
```

We conclude this section with Example 17.6, which brings together some of the methods of the Date and Time API. Given a date of birth, the method birthdayInfo() at (1) calculates the age and the time until the next birthday. The age is calculated at (2) using the Period.between() method, which computes the period between two dates. The date for the next birthday is set at (3) as the birth date with the current year. The if statement at (4) adjusts the next birthday date by 1 year at (5), if the birthday has already passed. The statement at (6) calculates the time until the next birthday by calling the LocalDate.until() method. We could also have used the Period.between() method at (6). The choice between these methods really depends on which method makes the code more readable in a given context.

Example 17.6 *More Temporal Arithmetic*

```
import java.time.LocalDate;
import java.time.Month;
import java.time.Period;

public class ActYourAge {

  public static void main(String[] args) {
    birthdayInfo(LocalDate.of(1981, Month.AUGUST, 19));
    birthdayInfo(LocalDate.of(1935, Month.JANUARY, 8));
  }

  public static void birthdayInfo(LocalDate dateOfBirth) {        // (1)
    LocalDate today = LocalDate.now();
    System.out.println("Today:        " + today);
```

```
    System.out.println("Date of Birth: " + dateOfBirth);
    Period p1 = Period.between(dateOfBirth, today);                    // (2)
    System.out.println("Age:           " +
                        p1.getYears()  + " years, " +
                        p1.getMonths() + " months, and " +
                        p1.getDays()   + " days");

    LocalDate nextBirthday = dateOfBirth.withYear(today.getYear()); // (3)
    if (nextBirthday.isBefore(today) ||                             // (4)
        nextBirthday.isEqual(today)) {
      nextBirthday = nextBirthday.plusYears(1);                     // (5)
    }
    Period p2 = today.until(nextBirthday);                          // (6)
    System.out.println("Birthday in " + p2.getMonths() + " months and " +
                        p2.getDays()   + " days");
  }
}
```

Possible output from the program:

```
Today:          2021-03-05
Date of Birth: 1981-08-19
Age:            39 years, 6 months, and 14 days
Birthday in 5 months and 14 days
Today:          2021-03-05
Date of Birth: 1935-01-08
Age:            86 years, 1 months, and 25 days
Birthday in 10 months and 3 days
```

17.6 Working with Durations

The java.time.Duration class implements a *time-based amount of time* in terms of *seconds* and *nanoseconds*, using a long and an int value for these time units, respectively. Although the Duration class models an amount of time in terms of seconds and nanoseconds, a duration can represent an amount of time in terms of days, hours, and minutes. As these time units have fixed lengths, it makes interoperability between these units possible. The time-based Duration class can be used with the LocalTime and LocalDateTime classes, as these classes have time fields. In contrast, the Period class essentially represents a *date-based amount of time* in terms of years, months, and days (p. 1057).

The Period and Duration classes are in the same package (java.time) as the temporal classes. The Period and the Duration classes provide similar methods, as they share many of the method prefixes and common methods with the temporal classes (Table 17.2, p. 1026, and Table 17.3, p. 1026). Their objects are immutable and thread-safe. However, there are also differences between the two classes (p. 1072). Familiarity with one would go a long way toward understanding the other.

Creating Durations

Like the Period class, the Duration class provides the static factory methods of*UNIT*() to construct durations with different units.

```
Duration d1 = Duration.ofDays(1L);                          // PT24H
Duration d2 = Duration.ofHours(24L);                        // PT24H
Duration d3 = Duration.ofMinutes(24L*60);                   // PT24H
Duration d4 = Duration.ofSeconds(24L*60*60);               // PT24H
Duration d5 = Duration.ofMillis(24L*60*60*1000);          // PT24H
Duration d6 = Duration.ofSeconds(24L*60*60 - 1, 1_000_000_000L); // (1) PT24H
Duration d7 = Duration.ofNanos(24L*60*60*1_000_000_000); // (2) PT24H
Duration d8 = Duration.ofNanos(24*60*60*1_000_000_000);  // (3) PT-1.857093632S
```

The durations created above all have a length of 1 day, except for the one in the last declaration statement. Note that the amount specified should be a long value. It is a good defensive practice to always designate the amount as such in order to avoid inadvertent problems if the amount does not fit into an int. The designation L should be placed such that there is no danger of any previous operation in the expression causing a rollover. This problem is illustrated at (3), where the int value of the argument expression is rolled over, as it is greater than Integer.MAX_VALUE.

The statement at (1) above also illustrates that the value of the nanoseconds is adjusted so that it is always between 0 and 999,999,999. The adjustment at (1) results in the value 0 for nanoseconds and the number of seconds being incremented by 1.

Calling the toString() method on the first seven declarations above, the result is the string "PT24H" (a duration of 24 hours), whereas for the last duration at (3), the result string is "PT-1.857093632S", which clearly indicates that the int amount was not interpreted as intended.

The previous declarations are equivalent to the ones below, where the amount is *qualified* with a specific unit in the call to the of(value, unit) method.

```
Duration d11 = Duration.of(1L, ChronoUnit.DAYS);           // P24H
Duration d22 = Duration.of(24L, ChronoUnit.HOURS);         // P24H
Duration d33 = Duration.of(24L*60, ChronoUnit.MINUTES);    // P24H
Duration d44 = Duration.of(24L*60*60, ChronoUnit.SECONDS); // P24H
Duration d88 = Duration.of(24L*60*60*1000, ChronoUnit.MILLIS);// P24H
Duration d77 = Duration.of(24L*60*60*1_000_000_000,
                           ChronoUnit.NANOS);              // P24H
```

The code snippet below does *not* create a duration of 8 days—it creates a duration of 24 hours. The first method call is invoked with the class name, and the subsequent method call is on the new Duration object returned as a consequence of the first call. The of() method creates a new Duration object based on its argument.

```
Duration duration = Duration.ofDays(7).ofHours(24);   // PT24H. Logical error.
```

Like the Period class, we can create a duration that represents the amount of time between two temporal objects by calling the static method between() of the Duration class.

```
LocalTime startTime = LocalTime.of(14, 30);               // 14:30
LocalTime endTime   = LocalTime.of(17, 45, 15);           // 17:45:15
```

```
Duration interval1 = Duration.between(startTime, endTime);   // PT3H15M15S
Duration interval2 = Duration.between(endTime, startTime);   // PT-3H-15M-15S
```

Note the exception thrown in the last statement below because a `LocalDateTime` object *cannot* be derived from a `LocalTime` object, whereas the converse is true.

```
LocalDateTime dateTime = LocalDateTime.of(2021, 4, 28,
                                          17, 45, 15);       // 2021-04-28T17:45:15
Duration interval3 = Duration.between(startTime, dateTime);  // PT3H15M15S
Duration interval4 = Duration.between(dateTime, startTime);  // DateTimeException!
```

The `Duration` class also provides the `parse()` static method to create a duration from a text representation of a duration based on the ISO standard. If the format of the string is not correct, a `DateTimeParseException` is thrown. Formatting according to the `toString()` method is shown in parentheses.

```
Duration da = Duration.parse("PT3H15M10.1S");// 3hrs. 15mins. 10.1s.(PT3H15M10.1S)
Duration db = Duration.parse("PT0.999S");    // 999000000 nanos.   (PT0.999S)
Duration dc = Duration.parse("-PT30S");      // -30 seconds.       (PT-30S)
Duration dd = Duration.parse("P-24D");       // -24 days           (PT-576H)
Duration dd = Duration.parse("P24H");        // Missing T. DateTimeParseException!
```

static Duration ZERO

This constant defines a `Duration` of length zero (PT0S).

static Duration ofDays(long days)
static Duration ofHours(long hours)
static Duration ofMinutes(long minutes)
static Duration ofMillis(long millis)
static Duration ofSeconds(long seconds)
static Duration ofSeconds(long seconds, long nanoAdjustment)
static Duration ofNanos(long nanos)

These static factory methods return a `Duration` representing an amount of time in seconds and nanoseconds that is equivalent to the specified amount, depending on the method. Nanoseconds are implicitly set to zero. The argument value can be negative. Standard definitions of the units are used. Note that the amount is specified as a `long` value.

static Duration of(long amount, TemporalUnit unit)

This static factory method returns a `Duration` representing an amount of time in seconds and nanoseconds that is equivalent to the specified amount in the specified temporal unit. The amount is specified as a `long` value, which can be negative.

Valid `ChronoUnit` constants to qualify the amount specified in the method call are the following: NANOS, MICROS, MILLIS, SECONDS, MINUTES, HOURS, HALF_DAYS, and DAYS (p. 1044). These units have a standard or an estimated duration.

static Duration between(Temporal startInclusive, Temporal endExclusive)

This static method returns the duration between two temporal objects that must support the seconds unit and where it is possible to convert the second temporal argument to the first temporal argument type, if necessary. Otherwise, a `DateTimeException` is thrown. The result of this method can be a negative period if the end temporal is before the start temporal.

```
String toString()
```

Returns a text representation of a `Duration` according to the ISO standard: PT*h*H*m*M*d*.*d*S—that is, *h* Hours, *m* Minutes, and *d.d* Seconds, where the nanoseconds are formatted as a fraction of a second.

```
static Duration parse(CharSequence text)
```

This static method returns a `Duration` parsed from a character sequence. The formats accepted are based on the ISO duration format PTnHnMn.nS—for example, "PT2H3M4.5S" (2 hours, 3 minutes, and 4.5 seconds). A `java.time.format.Date-TimeParseException` is thrown if the text cannot be parsed to a duration.

Accessing Time Units in a Duration

The `Duration` class provides the get*UNIT*() methods to read the *individual* values of its time units. The class also has methods to check if the period has a negative value or if its value is zero.

```
Duration dx = Duration.ofSeconds(12L*60*60, 500_000_000L); // PT12H0.5S
out.println(dx.getNano());                                 // 500000000
out.println(dx.getSeconds());                              // 43200 (i.e. 12 hrs.)
```

Reading the *individual values* of time units of a `Duration` object can also be done using the `get(unit)` method, where only the NANOS and SECONDS units are allowed. A list of temporal units that are accepted by the `get(unit)` method can be obtained by calling the `getUnits()` of the `Duration` class.

```
out.println(dx.get(ChronoUnit.NANOS));     // 500000000
out.println(dx.get(ChronoUnit.SECONDS));   // 43200
out.println(dx.get(ChronoUnit.MINUTES));   // UnsupportedTemporalTypeException
out.println(dx.getUnits());                // [Seconds, Nanos]
```

The class `Duration` provides the method to*UNIT*() to derive the *total length* of the duration in the unit designated by the method name. The seconds and the nanoseconds are converted to this unit, if necessary.

```
out.println("Days:    " + dx.toDays());    // Days:    0
out.println("Hours:   " + dx.toHours());   // Hours:   12
out.println("Minutes: " + dx.toMinutes()); // Minutes: 720
out.println("Millis:  " + dx.toMillis());  // Millis:  43200500
out.println("Nanos:   " + dx.toNanos());   // Nanos:   43200500000000
```

```
int getNano()
long getSeconds()
```

Return the number of nanoseconds and seconds in this duration, respectively—*not* the total length of the duration. Note that the first method name is getNano, without the s.

```
long get(TemporalUnit unit)
```

Returns the value of the specified unit in this Duration—*not* the total length of the duration. The only supported ChronoUnit constants are NANOS and SECONDS (p. 1044). Other units result in an UnsupportedTemporalTypeException.

```
List<TemporalUnit> getUnits()
```

Returns the list of time units supported by this duration: NANOS and SECONDS (p. 1044). These time units can be used with the get(unit) method.

```
long toDays()
long toHours()
long toMinutes()
long toMillis()
long toNanos()
```

Return the *total* length of this duration, converted to the unit designated by the method, if necessary. Note that there is no toSeconds() method. Also, the method name is toNanos—note the s at the end.

The methods toMillis() and toNanos() throw an ArithmeticException in case of number overflow.

```
boolean isNegative()
```

Determines whether the total length of this duration is negative.

```
boolean isZero()
```

Determines whether the total length of this duration is zero.

Comparing Durations

The Duration class overrides the equals() method and the hashCode() method of the Object class, and implements the Comparable<Duration> interface. Durations can readily be used in collections. The code below illustrates comparing durations.

```
Duration eatBreakFast = Duration.ofMinutes(20L);             // PT20M
Duration eatLunch    = Duration.ofSeconds(30L*60);          // PT30M
Duration eatSupper   = Duration.of(45L, ChronoUnit.MINUTES); // PT45M

out.println(eatBreakFast.equals(eatLunch));                 // false
out.println(Duration.ofSeconds(0).equals(Duration.ZERO));   // true

List<Duration> ld = Arrays.asList(eatSupper, eatBreakFast, eatLunch );
Collections.sort(ld);                       // Natural order.
out.println(ld);                            // [PT20M, PT30M, PT45M]
```

```
boolean equals(Object otherDuration)
```

Determines whether the *total length* of this duration is equal to the total length of the other duration.

```
int hashCode()
```

Returns a hash code for this duration.

```
int compareTo(Duration otherDuration)
```

Compares the *total length* of this duration to the total length of the other duration.

Creating Modified Copies of Durations

The Duration class provides withUNIT() methods to set a new value for each time unit individually, while the value of the other time unit is retained. Note that each method call returns a new Duration object, and chaining method calls works as expected.

```
Duration oneDuration =  Duration.ZERO                  // PT0S
                       .withNanos(500_000_000)         // New copy: PT0.5S
                       .withSeconds(12L*60*60);        // New copy: PT12H0.5S
```

```
Duration withNanos(int nanoOfSecond)
Duration withSeconds(long seconds)
```

Return a copy of this duration where either the nanosecond or the seconds are set to the value of the argument, respectively. The value of the other time unit is retained.

Temporal Arithmetic with Durations

The Duration class provides *plus* and *minus* methods that return a copy of the original object that has been *incremented or decremented by a specific amount* specified in terms of a unit—for example, as a number of days, hours, minutes, or seconds.

```
Duration max20H = Duration.ZERO                        // PT0S
                 .plusHours(10)                        // PT10H
                 .plusMinutes(10*60 + 30)              // PT20H30M
                 .plusSeconds(6*60*60 + 15)            // PT26H30M15S
                 .minusMinutes(2*60 + 30)              // PT24H15S
                 .minusSeconds(15);                    // PT24H
```

The plus() and the minus() methods also allow the amount to be qualified by a unit that has a standard or an estimated duration, as illustrated by the statement below, which is equivalent to the one above.

```
Duration max20H2 =
    Duration.ZERO                                      // PT0S
            .plus(10L,              ChronoUnit.HOURS)   // PT10H
            .plus(10*60 + 30,       ChronoUnit.MINUTES) // PT20H30M
            .plus(6*60*60L + 15, ChronoUnit.SECONDS)    // PT26H3015S
            .minus(2*60 + 30,       ChronoUnit.MINUTES) // PT24H15S
            .minus(15,              ChronoUnit.SECONDS); // PT24H
```

The code below shows the plus() and the minus() methods of the Duration class that take a Duration as the amount to add or subtract.

```
Duration eatBreakFast = Duration.ofMinutes(20L);              // PT20M
Duration eatLunch     = Duration.ofSeconds(30L*60);           // PT30M
Duration eatSupper    = Duration.of(45L, ChronoUnit.MINUTES); // PT45M
```

```
Duration totalTimeForMeals = eatBreakFast                    // PT20M
    .plus(eatLunch)                                          // PT50M
    .plus(eatSupper);                                        // PT1H35M
```

The statement below shows other arithmetic operations on durations and how they are carried out, together with what would be printed if the intermediate results were also written out.

```
Duration result = Duration.ofSeconds(-100, -500_000_000) // -100.5 => PT-1M-40.5S
                    .abs()              // abs(-100.5) = 100.5  => PT1M40.5S
                    .multipliedBy(4) // 100.5*4 = 402 => PT6M42S
                    .dividedBy(2);   // 402 / 2 = 201 => PT3M21S
```

```
Duration plusDays/minusDays(long days)
Duration plusHours/minusHours(long hours)
Duration plusMinutes/minusMinutes(long minutes)
Duration plusSeconds/minusSeconds(long seconds)
Duration plusMillis/minusMillis(long millis)
Duration plusNanos/minusNanos(long nanos)
```

Return a copy of this duration, with the specified value of the unit designated by the method name added or subtracted, but converted first to seconds, if necessary. Note that the argument type is long.

```
Duration plus(long amountToAdd, TemporalUnit unit)
Duration minus(long amountToSub, TemporalUnit unit)
```

Return a copy of this duration with the specified amount added or subtracted, respectively, according to the TemporalUnit specified (p. 1044).

Valid ChronoUnit constants to qualify the amount specified in the method call are the following: NANOS, MICROS, MILLIS, SECONDS, MINUTES, HOURS, HALF_DAYS, and DAYS (p. 1044). These units have a standard or an estimated duration. Other units result in an UnsupportedTemporalTypeException.

```
Duration plus(Duration duration)
Duration minus(Duration duration)
```

Return a copy of this duration, with the specified duration added or subtracted.

```
Duration abs()
```

Returns a copy of this duration with a positive length.

```
Duration negated()
```

Returns a copy of this duration where the length has been negated.

```
Duration dividedBy(long divisor)
Duration multipliedBy(long multiplicand)
```

The first method returns a new instance with the result of dividing the length of this duration by the specified divisor. Division by zero would bring down untold calamities.

The second method returns a new instance with the result of multiplying the length of this duration by the specified multiplicand.

We can perform arithmetic operations on durations and temporal objects. The following code uses the `plus()` and `minus()` methods of the `LocalTime` and `LocalDateTime` classes that take a `TemporalAmount` as an argument (p. 1040). We can add and subtract durations from `LocalTime` and `LocalDateTime` objects, but not from `LocalDate` objects, as a `LocalDate` object only supports date units.

```
LocalTime timeA = LocalTime.of(14,45,30);                   // 14:45:30
LocalDate dateA = LocalDate.of(2021, 4, 28);               // 2021-04-28
LocalDateTime dateTimeA = LocalDateTime.of(dateA, timeA); // 2021-04-28T14:45:30

Duration amount = Duration.ofMinutes(20);                  // PT20M

timeA = timeA.plus(amount);                                 // 15:05:30
dateTimeA = dateTimeA.minus(amount);                       // 2021-04-28T14:25:30

dateA = dateA.minus(amount);              // UnsupportedTemporalTypeException
```

Example 17.7 illustrates implementing duration-based loops. The program prints the showtimes, given when the first show starts, the duration of the show, and when the theatre closes. The `for(;;)` loop at (1) uses the `LocalTime.isBefore()` method and the `LocalTime.plus(duration)` method to calculate the showtimes.

Example 17.7 *Duration-Based Loop*

```
import java.time.LocalTime;
import java.time.Duration;

public class DurationBasedLoop {
  public static void main(String[] args) {
    Duration duration = Duration.ofHours(2).plusMinutes(15);    // PT2H15M
    LocalTime firstShowTime = LocalTime.of(10, 10);            // 10:10
    LocalTime endTimeExclusive = LocalTime.of(23, 0);         // 23:00
    for (LocalTime time = firstShowTime;                       // (1)
         time.plus(duration).isBefore(endTimeExclusive);
         time = time.plus(duration)) {
      System.out.println("Showtime (" + duration + "): " + time);
    }
    System.out.println("Closing time: " + endTimeExclusive);
  }
}
```

Output from the program:

```
Showtime (PT2H15M): 10:10
Showtime (PT2H15M): 12:25
Showtime (PT2H15M): 14:40
Showtime (PT2H15M): 16:55
Showtime (PT2H15M): 19:10
Closing time: 23:00
```

Differences between Periods and Durations

Table 17.4 summarizes the differences between selected methods of the Period and the Duration classes, mainly in regard to the temporal units supported, representation for parsing and formatting, and comparison. *N/A* stands for *Not Applicable*.

Table 17.4   *Some Differences between the* Period *Class and the* Duration *Class*

Methods	The Period class	The Duration class
of(amount, unit)	*N/A*	Valid ChronoUnits: NANOS, MICROS, MILLIS, SECONDS, MINUTES, HOURS, HALF_DAYS, DAYS (p. 1065).
parse(text) toString()	Representation based on: PnYnMnD and PnW (p. 1057).	Representation based on: PnDTnHnMn.nS (p. 1065).
get(unit)	Supported ChronoUnits: YEARS, MONTHS, DAYS (p. 1059).	Supported ChronoUnits: NANOS, SECONDS (p. 1067).
getUnits()	Supported ChronoUnits: YEARS, MONTHS, DAYS (p. 1059).	Supported ChronoUnits: NANOS, SECONDS (p. 1067).
equals(other)	Based on values of individual units (p. 1059).	Based on total length (p. 1067).
compareTo(other)	*N/A*	Natural order: total length (p. 1067).
minus(amount, unit) plus(amount, unit)	*N/A*	Valid ChronoUnits: NANOS, MICROS, MILLIS, SECONDS, MINUTES, HOURS, HALF_DAYS, DAYS (p. 1069).
abs()	*N/A*	Returns copy with positive length (p. 1069).
dividedBy(divisor)	*N/A*	Returns copy after dividing by divisor (p. 1069).
normalized()	Only years and months normalized (p. 1061).	*N/A*

17.7 Working with Time Zones and Daylight Savings

The following three classes in the java.time package are important when dealing with date and time in different time zones and daylight saving hours: ZoneId, ZoneOffset, and ZonedDateTime.

UTC (*Coordinated Universal Time*) is the primary *time standard* used for keeping time around the world. *UTC/Greenwich* is the time at Royal Observatory, Greenwich, England. It is the basis for defining time in different regions of the world.

Time Zones and Zone Offsets

A *time zone* defines a region that observes the same standard time. The time observed in a region is usually referred to as *the local time*. A time zone is described by a *zone offset from UTC/Greenwich* and any *rules* for applying daylight saving time (DST). Time zones that practice DST obviously have variable offsets during the year to account for DST.

In Java, each time zone has a zone ID that is represented by the class java.time.ZoneId. The class java.time.ZoneOffset, which extends the ZoneId class, represents a zone offset from UTC/Greenwich. For example, the time zone with US/Eastern as the zone ID has the offset -04:00 during daylight saving hours—that is, it is 4 hours behind UTC/Greenwich when DST is in effect.

The time zone offset at UTC/Greenwich is represented by ZoneOffset.UTC and, by convention, is designated by the letter Z. GMT (*Greenwich Mean Time*) has zero offset from UTC/Greenwich (UTC+0), thus the two are often used as synonyms; for example, GMT-4 is equivalent to UTC-4. However, GMT is a time zone, whereas UTC is a time standard.

Java uses the IANA Time Zone Database (TZDB) maintained by the Internet Assigned Numbers Authority (IANA) that updates the database regularly, in particular, regarding changes to the rules for DST practiced by a time zone (p. 1073).

A set with names of available time zones can readily be obtained by calling the ZoneId.getAvailableZoneIds() method. Time zones have unique names of the form *Area/Location*—for example, US/Eastern, Europe/Oslo. The following code prints a very long list of time zones that are available to a Java application.

```
ZoneId.getAvailableZoneIds()                      // Prints a long list of zone names.
    .stream()
    .sorted()
    .forEachOrdered(System.out::println);   // Output not shown intentionally.
```

The ZoneId.of() method creates an appropriate zone ID depending on the format of its argument:

- *UTC-equivalent ID*, if only "Z", "UTC", or "GMT" is specified. As these designations are equivalent, the result is ZoneOffset.UTC; that is, it represents the offset UTC+0.
- *Offset-based ID*, if the format is "+hh:mm" or "-hh:mm"—for example, "+04:00", "-11:30". The result is an instance of the ZoneOffset class with the parsed offset.
- *Prefix offset-based ID*, if the format is the prefix UTC or GMT followed by a numerical offset—for example, "UTC+04:00", "GMT-04:00". The result is a time zone represented by a ZoneId with the specified prefix and a parsed offset.

- *Region-based ID*, if the format is *"Area/Location"*—for example, "US/Eastern", "Europe/Oslo". The result is a ZoneId that can be used, among other things, to look up the underlying zone rules associated with the zone ID. In the examples in this section, a zone ID is specified in the format of a region-based ID.

The code below creates a region-based zone ID. The method ZoneId.systemDefault() returns the system default zone ID.

```
ZoneId estZID = ZoneId.of("US/Eastern");              // Create a time zone ID.
System.out.println(estZID);                           // US/Eastern
System.out.println(ZoneId.systemDefault());           // Europe/Oslo
```

Selected methods in the ZoneId abstract class are presented below. The concrete class ZoneOffset extends the ZoneId class.

```
static ZoneId of(String zoneId)
```
Returns an appropriate zone ID depending on the format of the zone ID string. See the previous discussion on zone ID.

```
String           toString()
abstract String getId()
```
Return a string with the zone ID, typically in one of the formats accepted by the of() method.

```
abstract ZoneRules getRules()
```
Retrieves the associated time zone rules for this zone ID. The rules determine the functionality associated with a time zone, such as daylight savings (p. 1082).

```
static Set<String> getAvailableZoneIds()
```
Returns a set with the available time zone IDs.

```
static ZoneId systemDefault()
```
Returns the zone ID of the default time zone of the system.

The ZonedDateTime **Class**

The ZonedDateTime class represents a date-time with time zone information, and an instance of the class is referred to as a *zoned date-time* (Table 17.1, p. 1025). The date and time fields are stored with nanosecond precision. The time zone information is represented by a time zone with a zone offset from UTC/Greenwich. In essence, a zoned date-time represents an instant on a specific timeline determined by its zone ID and its zone offset from UTC/Greenwich. This timeline is referred to as the *local timeline*, whereas the timeline at UTC/Greenwich is referred to as the *instant timeline*.

A majority of the methods in the ZonedDateTime class should be familiar from the temporal classes discussed earlier in this chapter (p. 1027). Both Table 17.2, p. 1026, and Table 17.3, p. 1026, showing the common method name prefixes and common methods, apply to the ZonedDateTime class as well. The LocalDateTime class is the closest equivalent of the ZonedDateTime class.

Issues relating to daylight savings are covered later in this section (p. 1082). In particular, the methods of(), with(), minus(), and plus() take into consideration daylight savings.

The methods get(), with(), plus(), minus(), and until() throw an UnsupportedTemporal-TypeException when an unsupported field is accessed, and a DateTimeException when the operation cannot be performed for any other reason.

Objects of the ZonedDateTime class are also immutable and thread-safe. The class also overrides the equals() and the hashCode() methods of the Object class, but in contrast to the LocalDateTime class, its objects are *not* comparable.

With that overview, we turn our attention to dealing with zoned date-times as represented by the ZonedDateTime class.

Creating Zoned Date-Time

Analogous to the other temporal classes, the current zoned date-time can be obtained from the system clock in either the default time zone or a specific time zone by calling the now() method of the ZonedDateTime class. The zoned date-times created at (1a), (2a), and (3a) represent the same date-time locally in the default time zone Europe/Oslo, at UTC/Greenwich (UTC), and in the US/Eastern time zone, respectively.

The text representation of the zoned date-times from (1a), (2a), and (3a) is shown below at (1b), (2b), and (3b), respectively. The text representation of a zoned date-time returned by the toString() method shows the date and the time separated by the letter T, followed by the zone offset and the time zone.

```
ZonedDateTime defaultZDT = ZonedDateTime.now();                          // (1a)
ZonedDateTime utcZDT    = ZonedDateTime.now(ZoneId.of("UTC"));           // (2a)
ZonedDateTime edtZDT    = ZonedDateTime.now(ZoneId.of("US/Eastern"));    // (3a)
System.out.println("Default Zone Date-time: " + defaultZDT);
System.out.println("UTC Date-time:          " + utcZDT);
System.out.println("EDT Zone Date-time:     " + edtZDT);
```

Output from the print statements:

```
Default Zone Date-time: 2021-07-11T11:35:20.008+02:00[Europe/Oslo]      // (1b)
UTC Date-time:          2021-07-11T09:35:20.023Z[UTC]                    // (2b)
EDT Zone Date-time:     2021-07-11T05:35:20.023-04:00[US/Eastern]        // (3b)
```

The local time in the Europe/Oslo time zone has the zone offset +02:00—meaning it is 2 hours *ahead* of UTC/Greenwich, as it is east of Greenwich. The date-time at UTC/Greenwich (UTC) has no zone offset, just the letter Z instead of an offset. The local time in the US/Eastern time zone has the zone offset -04:00—meaning it is 4 hours *behind* UTC/Greenwich, as it is west of Greenwich. On this particular date, the time difference between the Europe/Oslo time zone and the US/Eastern time zone is 6 hours, where daylight saving time is in effect in both time zones (p. 1082).

One convenient way to create a zoned date-time is to assemble it from its constituent parts. We will use the following declarations to create zoned date-times.

```
LocalTime concertTime = LocalTime.of(00, 10);                    // 00:10
LocalDate concertDate = LocalDate.of(1973, Month.JANUARY, 14); // 1973-01-14
LocalDateTime concertDT = LocalDateTime.of(concertDate,
                                       concertTime);   // 1973-01-14T00:10
ZoneId hwZID = ZoneId.of("US/Hawaii");                          // US/Hawaii
Instant instantZ = Instant.ofEpochSecond(95854200);            // 1973-01-14T10:10:00Z
```

The code below creates three zoned date-times from constituent parts. The arguments in the method call comprise the parts of a zoned date-time in each case. We note that the zone offset of the US/Hawaii time zone is -10:00—that is, 10 hours behind UTC/Greenwich. Note how the ofInstant() method converts the time in the instant to the correct local time in the specified time zone.

```
ZonedDateTime concertZDT0 = ZonedDateTime.of(concertDate, concertTime, hwZID);
ZonedDateTime concertZDT1 = ZonedDateTime.of(concertDT, hwZID);
ZonedDateTime concertZDT2 = ZonedDateTime.ofInstant(instantZ, hwZID);
// 1973-01-14T00:10-10:00[US/Hawaii]
boolean areEqual = concertZDT0.equals(concertZDT1)
                && concertZDT0.equals(concertZDT2);       // true
```

The LocalDateTime and the Instant classes also provide the atZone() method that combines a date-time or an instant, respectively, with a time zone to create a zoned date-time. The two zoned date-times created below are equal to the three created earlier.

```
ZonedDateTime concertZDT3 = concertDT.atZone(hwZID);
ZonedDateTime concertZDT4 = instantZ.atZone(hwZID);
// 1973-01-14T00:10-10:00[US/Hawaii]
```

We can also use the parse() method to create a zoned date-time from a text string that is compatible with the ISO format (p. 1129).

```
ZonedDateTime concertZDT5
   = ZonedDateTime.parse("1973-01-14T00:10-10:00[US/Hawaii]");
```

```
static ZonedDateTime now()
static ZonedDateTime now(ZoneId zone)
```

Return a ZonedDateTime containing the current date-time from the system clock in the default time zone or in the specified time zone, respectively.

```
static ZonedDateTime of(int year, int month, int dayOfMonth, int hour,
                        int minute, int second, int nanoOfSecond, ZoneId zone)
static ZonedDateTime of(LocalDate date, LocalTime time, ZoneId zone)
static ZonedDateTime of(LocalDateTime localDateTime, ZoneId zone)
static ZonedDateTime ofInstant(Instant instant, ZoneId zone)
```

Return a ZonedDateTime formed from the specified arguments. Note the zone argument that is required. The methods throw a DateTimeException when the operation cannot be performed for some reason.

Note that these methods take into consideration any adjustments because of daylight savings (p. 1082).

```
static ZonedDateTime parse(CharSequence text)
```
Returns a ZonedDateTime by parsing the text string according to DateTimeFormatter.ISO_ZONED_DATE_TIME (p. 1129)—for example, "2021-07-03T16:15:30+01:00 [Europe/Oslo]".

```
String toString()
```
Returns a string comprising the text representation of the constituent parts: the LocalDateTime, typically followed by the zone offset and the time zone—for example, 2021-07-11T05:35:20.023-04:00[US/Eastern].

Accessing Fields of Zoned Date-Time

The ZonedDateTime class provides many get methods to access the values of various fields of a zoned date-time. The most versatile is the get(field) method, which supports all the constants defined by the ChronoField enum type (p. 1046). In addition, there are get methods for specific fields, and methods for extracting the different constituent parts of a zoned date-time.

```
// Using ChronoField constants:
int theDay       = concertZDTO.get(ChronoField.DAY_OF_MONTH);    // 14
int theMonthValue = concertZDTO.get(ChronoField.MONTH_OF_YEAR);  // 1
int theYear      = concertZDTO.get(ChronoField.YEAR);            // 1973

// Using specific get methods:
int theMonthValue2 = concertZDTO.getMonthValue();                // 1
Month theMonth     = concertZDTO.getMonth();                     // JANUARY

// Extracting constituent parts:
LocalTime theTime      = concertZDTO.toLocalTime();        // 00:10
LocalDate theDate      = concertZDTO.toLocalDate();        // 1973-01-14
LocalDateTime theDT    = concertZDTO.toLocalDateTime();    // 1973-01-14T00:10
ZoneId theZID          = concertZDTO.getZone();            // US/Hawaii
ZoneOffset theZoffset  = concertZDTO.getOffset();          // -10:00
```

```
int getFIELD()
```
Gets the value of the field designated by the suffix *FIELD*, which can be DayOfMonth, DayOfYear, MonthValue, Nano, Second, Minute, Hour, or Year.

```
DayOfWeek getDayOfWeek()
Month     getMonth()
```
Get the value of the day-of-week and month-of-year field, respectively.

```
ZoneId     getZone()
ZoneOffset getOffset()
```
Gets the time zone ID (e.g., US/Central) and the time zone offset from UTC/ Greenwich (e.g., -04:00), respectively (p. 1073).

```
int  get(TemporalField field)
long getLong(TemporalField field)
boolean isSupported(TemporalField field)
```

The first two methods return the value of the specified TemporalField (p. 1046) as an int value or as a long value, respectively. The value of the ChronoField enum constants NANO_OF_DAY, MICRO_OF_DAY, EPOCH_DAY, PROLEPTIC_MONTH, and INSTANT_SECONDS will not fit into an int, and therefore, the getLong() method must be used.

The third method checks if the specified field is supported by this zoned date-time. All ChronoField enum constants are supported by the ZonedDateTime class (p. 1046).

```
LocalTime      toLocalTime()
LocalDate      toLocalDate()
LocalDateTime toLocalDateTime()
```

Return the respective part of this zoned date-time.

```
Instant toInstant()
```

Converts a zoned date-time to an instant representing the same point as this date-time. This method is inherited by the ZonedDateTime class from its super-interface java.time.chrono.ChronoZonedDateTime.

Conversion of a zoned date-time to an instance of the java.util.Date legacy class can be done via this method (p. 1088).

Creating Modified Copies of Zoned Date-Time

Individual fields of a zoned date-time can be set to a new value in a copy of a zoned date-time as illustrated by the following code.

```
ZonedDateTime theZDT = concertZDT0           // 1973-01-14T00:10-10:00[US/Hawaii]
    .withYear(1977)                          // 1977-01-14T00:10-10:00[US/Hawaii]
    .with(ChronoField.MONTH_OF_YEAR, 8)      // 1977-08-14T00:10-10:00[US/Hawaii]
    .withDayOfMonth(16)                      // 1977-08-16T00:10-10:00[US/Hawaii]
    .with(ChronoField.HOUR_OF_DAY, 9)        // 1977-08-16T09:10-10:00[US/Hawaii]
    .with(ChronoField.MINUTE_OF_HOUR, 30);   // 1977-08-16T09:30-10:00[US/Hawaii]
```

The withField() methods behave analogous to the with() method with a corresponding field argument, taking into consideration the time gap and the time overlap that occur when daylight saving time starts and ends (p. 1082).

The withZoneSameLocal() method can be used to change the time zone, while retaining the date-time. The code at (1) below changes the time zone from US/Hawaii to US/Central, while retaining the date-time. Note that the two zoned date-times, theZDT and zdtSameLocal, do *not* represent the same instant according to UTC/Greenwich, as shown by the output from the print statements.

```
ZoneId cTZ = ZoneId.of("US/Central");
ZonedDateTime zdtSameLocal = theZDT.withZoneSameLocal(cTZ);            // (1)
```

```
System.out.printf("%23s %25s%n", "ZonedDateTime", "Instant");
System.out.printf("%-35s %s%n", theZDT, theZDT.toInstant());
System.out.printf("%-35s %s%n", zdtSameLocal, zdtSameLocal.toInstant());
```

Output from the print statements:

```
              ZonedDateTime                        Instant
1977-08-16T09:30-10:00[US/Hawaii]    1977-08-16T19:30:00Z
1977-08-16T09:30-05:00[US/Central]   1977-08-16T14:30:00Z
```

The local time 09:30 in the US/Hawaii time zone is 10 hours (offset -10:00) behind UTC/Greenwich, whereas the same local time in the US/Central time zone (offset -05:00) is 5 hours behind UTC/Greenwich on the date 1977-08-16, resulting in different instants at UTC/Greenwich for the same local time.

The withZoneSameInstant() method can be used to change the time zone *and* adjust the date-time to the new time zone. We see in the code below at (2) that the adjusted local time 14:30 in the US/Central time zone is 5 hours behind UTC/Greenwich, resulting in both zoned date-times representing the same instant at UTC/Greenwich.

```
ZonedDateTime zdtSameInstant = theZDT.withZoneSameInstant(cTZ);        // (2)
System.out.printf("%23s %25s%n", "ZonedDateTime", "Instant");
System.out.printf("%-35s %s%n", theZDT, theZDT.toInstant());
System.out.printf("%-35s %s%n", zdtSameInstant, zdtSameInstant.toInstant());
```

Output from the print statements:

```
              ZonedDateTime                        Instant
1977-08-16T09:30-10:00[US/Hawaii]    1977-08-16T19:30:00Z
1977-08-16T14:30-05:00[US/Central]   1977-08-16T19:30:00Z
```

ZonedDateTime with*FIELD*(int amount)

Returns a copy of this zoned date-time with the field designated by the suffix *FIELD* set to the specified value, where the suffix *FIELD* can be DayOfMonth, DayOfYear, MonthValue, Nano, Second, Minute, Hour, or Year.

Note that these methods take into consideration the time gap and the time overlap that can occur due to daylight savings (p. 1082).

ZonedDateTime with(TemporalField field, long newValue)

Returns a copy of this zoned date-time with the specified TemporalField set to the specified value. All constants of the ChronoField enum type (p. 1046) can be used to specify a particular field.

ZonedDateTime withZoneSameLocal(ZoneId zone)
ZonedDateTime withZoneSameInstant(ZoneId zone)

The first method returns a copy of this zoned date-time with the specified time zone, but normally retaining the date-time.

The second method returns a copy of this zoned date-time with the specified time zone, but retaining the instant; that is, it results in the date-time being adjusted according to the specified time zone.

Temporal Arithmetic with Zoned Date-Time

Temporal arithmetic with zoned date-times is analogous to temporal arithmetic with date-times (p. 1040). However, it is important to note the differences that are due to time zones and daylight savings (p. 1082).

Example 17.8 illustrates calculating flight times. The code at (1) creates a flight departure time for a flight to London from New York at 8:30 pm on July 4, 2021. The flight time is 7 hours and 30 minutes. The code at (2) calculates the local time of arrival at London, first by calling the withZoneSameInstant() method to find the local time in London at the time the flight departs from New York, and then adding the flight time to obtain the local arrival time in London.

In Example 17.8, the code at (3) calculates the flight duration by calling the Duration.between() method with the departure and arrival times as arguments. The code at (4) calls the until() method to calculate the flight time in minutes from the departure time to the arrival time.

Finally, the code at (5) and (6) calculates the local time at the departure airport at the time the flight arrives in London in two different ways. At (5), the plusMinutes() method adds the flight time to the departure time. At (6), the withZoneSameInstant() method converts the arrival time to its equivalent in the departure time zone.

Example 17.8 *Flight Time Information*

```java
import java.time.DateTimeException;
import java.time.Duration;
import java.time.LocalDateTime;
import java.time.Month;
import java.time.ZoneId;
import java.time.ZonedDateTime;
import java.time.temporal.ChronoUnit;

public class FlightTimeInfo {
  public static void main(String[] args) {
    try {
      // Departure from New York at 8:30pm on July 4, 2021.           (1)
      LocalDateTime departure = LocalDateTime.of(2021, Month.JULY, 4, 20, 30);
      ZoneId departureZone = ZoneId.of("America/New_York");
      ZonedDateTime departureZDT = ZonedDateTime.of(departure, departureZone);

      // Flight time is 7 hours and 30 minutes.
      // Calculate local arrival time at London:                      (2)
      ZoneId arrivalZone = ZoneId.of("Europe/London");
      ZonedDateTime arrivalZDT
          = departureZDT.withZoneSameInstant(arrivalZone)
                .plusMinutes(7*60 + 30);
      System.out.printf("DEPARTURE:  %s%n", departureZDT);
      System.out.printf("ARRIVAL:    %s%n", arrivalZDT);

      // Flight time as a Duration:                                   (3)
      Duration flightduration = Duration.between(departureZDT, arrivalZDT);
      System.out.println("Flight duration:    " + flightduration);
```

```
                    // Flight time in minutes:                              (4)
                    long flightTime = departureZDT.until(arrivalZDT, ChronoUnit.MINUTES);
                    System.out.println("Flight time (mins.): " + flightTime);

                    System.out.printf(                                      // (5)
                        "Time at departure airport on arrival: %s%n",
                        departureZDT.plusMinutes(7*60 + 30));

                    System.out.printf(                                      // (6)
                        "Time at departure airport on arrival: %s%n",
                        arrivalZDT.withZoneSameInstant(departureZone));

                } catch (DateTimeException e) {
                    e.printStackTrace();
                }
            }
        }
```

Output from the program:

```
DEPARTURE:  2021-07-04T20:30-04:00[America/New_York]
ARRIVAL:    2021-07-05T09:00+01:00[Europe/London]
Flight duration:     PT7H30M
Flight time (mins.): 450
Time at departure airport on arrival: 2021-07-05T04:00-04:00[America/New_York]
Time at departure airport on arrival: 2021-07-05T04:00-04:00[America/New_York]
```

Selected methods from the ZonedDateTime class for temporal arithmetic are presented below.

```
ZonedDateTime plusUNIT(long amount)
ZonedDateTime minusUNIT(long amount)
```

Return a copy of this zoned date-time with the specified amount either added or subtracted, respectively, where the unit is designated by the suffix *UNIT*, which can be Nanos, Seconds, Minutes, Hours, Days, Weeks, Months, or Years.

With the time units (Nanos, Seconds, Minutes, Hours), the operation is on the instant timeline, where a Duration of the specified amount is added or subtracted.

With the date units (Days, Weeks, Months, Years), the operation is on the local timeline, adding and subtracting the amount from the date-time corresponding to this zoned date-time.

```
ZonedDateTime plus(long amountToAdd, TemporalUnit unit)
ZonedDateTime minus(long amountToSubtract, TemporalUnit unit)
boolean isSupported(TemporalUnit unit)
```

Return a copy of this zoned date-time with the specified amount added or subtracted, respectively, according to the TemporalUnit specified. The methods support all ChronoUnit enum constants, except FORVER (p. 1044).

Time units operate on the instant timeline, but date units operate on the local timeline, when performing these operations.

The isSupported() method checks if the specified TemporalUnit is supported by this zoned date-time (p. 1044).

```
ZonedDateTime plus(TemporalAmount amountToAdd)
ZonedDateTime minus(TemporalAmount amountToSubtract)
```

Return a copy of this zoned date-time with the specified temporal amount added or subtracted, respectively. The classes Period (p. 1057) and Duration (p. 1064) implement the TemporalAmount interface.

If the amount is a Duration, the time units operate on the instant timeline. However, if the amount is a Period, the date units operate on the local timeline.

```
long until(Temporal endExclusive, TemporalUnit unit)
```

Calculates the amount of time between this zoned date-time and the specified temporal object in terms of the specified TemporalUnit (p. 1044). The end point is excluded. An exception is thrown if the specified temporal object cannot be converted to a zoned date-time.

This method supports all ChronoUnit enum constants, except FOREVER (p. 1044).

Date units operate on the local timeline, but time units operate on the instant timeline when performing this operation.

Daylight Savings

If a time zone practices daylight savings, the time zone offset of a ZonedDateTime can be different depending on whether daylight saving time (DST) or standard time (for the rest of the year) is in effect. Zone rules associated with the zone ID of a zoned date-time are used to determine the right zone offset for time zones that practice daylight savings.

A *time gap* occurs when the clock is moved *forward* at the start of DST, and a *time overlap* occurs when the clock is moved *backward* at the end of DST. Usually the gap and the overlap are 1 hour. In that case, when the time gap occurs, an hour is lost and that day has only 23 hours, whereas when a time overlap occurs, an hour is gained and that day has 25 hours. Care should be exercised when dealing with zoned date-times that can involve crossovers to and from DST. Luckily, the methods of(), with(), plus(), and minus() of the ZonedDateTime class take daylight savings into consideration.

As an example to illustrate daylight savings, we will use the US/Central time zone. For this time zone, DST starts at 02:00:00 on 14 March in 2021, when the clocks are moved forward by 1 hour, resulting in the hour between 02:00:00 and 03:00:00 being lost. The gap in this case is 1 hour. The day on 2021-03-14 will only be 23 hours long.

DST for the US/Central time zone ends at 02:00:00 on 7 November in 2021, when clocks are moved backward by 1 hour, resulting in the hour before 02:00:00 being repeated twice. The overlap in this case is 1 hour. The day on 2021-11-07 will be 25 hours long.

The following output from Example 17.9 illustrates what happens when the plusHours() method increments a zoned date-time across the time gap.

```
Daylight Savings in US/Central starts at 2021-03-14T02:00 (spring forward 1 hour).
                          _____ZonedDateTime_____
                          Date      Time  Offset     TZ       DST   UTC
(1) Before gap:     2021-03-14 01:30 -06:00 US/Central false 07:30
    + 1 hour
(2) After gap:      2021-03-14 03:30 -05:00 US/Central true  08:30
```

Line (1) above shows the following information about a zoned date-time that is before the gap: Date (2021-03-14), Time (01:30), Offset (-06:00), TZ (US/Central), DST that indicates whether it is in effect (false), and UTC equivalent of the time (07:30). Note that the time 01:30 is before the gap. Adding 1 hour to the zoned date-time in line (1) puts the resulting time (02:30) in the gap, which does not exist. The plusHours() method increments the expected time 02:30 by the gap length to 03:30 and increments the offset -6:00 by the gap length to -05:00 to comply with DST. Line (2) shows the final result of the operation. DST is now in effect. The UTC equivalent time is now 08:30, an hour after 07:30, as we would expect.

The following output from Example 17.9 illustrates what happens when the plusHours() method increments a zoned date-time successively across the time overlap.

```
Daylight Savings in US/Central ends at 2021-11-07T02:00 (fall back 1 hour).
                          _____ZonedDateTime_____
                          Date      Time  Offset     TZ       DST   UTC
(1) Before overlap: 2021-11-07 00:30 -05:00 US/Central true  05:30
    + 1 hour
(2) In overlap:     2021-11-07 01:30 -05:00 US/Central true  06:30
    + 1 hour
(3) In overlap:     2021-11-07 01:30 -06:00 US/Central false 07:30
    + 1 hour
(4) After overlap:  2021-11-07 02:30 -06:00 US/Central false 08:30
```

Line (1) shows a zoned date-time before the overlap with the following information: Date (2021-11-07), Time (00:30), Offset (-05:00), TZ (US/Central), DST that indicates whether it is in effect (true), and UTC equivalent of the time (05:30). Again note that the time 00:30 is before the time overlap. Lines (2), (3), and (4) show the result of successively adding 1 hour to the resulting zoned date-time from the previous operation, starting with the zoned date-time in line (1).

Adding 1 hour to the time 00:30 in line (1) with DST in effect changes the time to 01:30, which is in the overlap, but before the DST crossover at 02:00. The result is shown in line (2).

Adding 1 hour to the time 01:30 in line (2) with DST in effect does *not* change the time. The operation only decrements the offset -05:00 by the overlap length (1 hour) to -06:00, as the time 01:30 is still in the overlap after the DST crossover because it is repeated, but now the standard time is in effect. The result is shown in line (3).

Adding 1 hour to the time 01:30 in line (3) with standard time in effect changes the time to 02:30. The resulting time 02:30 is not in the overlap. The result is shown in line (4). The result would have been the same if we had added 3 hours to the zoned date-time in line (1): the time would be incremented by 2 hours (3 – overlap length) and the offset decremented by the overlap length (1 hour).

The last column, UTC, also shows that the time at UTC/Greenwich changed successively by 1 hour as a result of the plus operations.

In Example 17.9, the methods adjustForGap() at (1a) and adjustForOverlap() at (1b) create the scenarios for DST crossovers discussed above. The method printInfo() at (7) prints the result of each plus operation. The essential lines of code are (4a) and (4b) that perform the plus operations, with the rest of the code creating zoned date-times (2a, 3a, 2b, 3b) and printing formatted output (5a, 5b).

The method isDST() at (8) determines if DST is in effect for a zoned date-time. The method localTimeAtUTC() at (9) returns the UTC equivalent of the time in a zoned date-time. These auxiliary methods are simple but instructive examples of operations on zoned date-times.

The zone rules associated with a time zone can be obtained by calling the ZoneId.getRules() method on a zone ID. The zone rules are represented by the java.time.zone.ZoneRules class that provides the isDaylightSavings() method to determine whether an instant is in daylight savings. A zoned date-time can be converted to an instant by the toInstant() method.

```
// java.time.zone.ZoneRules
boolean isDaylightSavings(Instant instant)
```
Determines whether the specified instant is in daylight savings.

- -

Example 17.9 *Adjusting for DST Crossovers*

```
import java.time.LocalDate;
import java.time.LocalDateTime;
import java.time.LocalTime;
import java.time.ZoneId;
import java.time.ZoneOffset;
import java.time.ZonedDateTime;

public class DSTAdjustment {
  public static void main(String[] args) {
    adjustForGap();
    adjustForOverlap();
  }

  /**
   * Adjustment due to the time gap at DST crossover.             (1a)
   * DST starts in US/Central TZ: 2021-03-14T02:00:00,
   * clocks are moved forward 1 hour, resulting in a time gap of 1 hour.
   */
  static void adjustForGap() {
    // Start date and time for DST in US/Central in 2021.         (2a)
```

```java
        ZoneId cTZ = ZoneId.of("US/Central");
        LocalDate dateStartDST = LocalDate.of(2021, 3, 14);
        LocalTime timeStartDST = LocalTime.of(2, 0);
        LocalDateTime ldtStartDST = LocalDateTime.of(dateStartDST, timeStartDST);
        ZonedDateTime zdtStartDST = ZonedDateTime.of(ldtStartDST, cTZ);

        // Time before the gap.                                              (3a)
        LocalTime timeBeforeGap = LocalTime.of(1, 30);
        LocalDateTime ldtBeforeGap = LocalDateTime.of(dateStartDST, timeBeforeGap);
        ZonedDateTime zdtBeforeGap = ZonedDateTime.of(ldtBeforeGap, cTZ);

        // Add 1 hour.                                                       (4a)
        ZonedDateTime zdtAfterGap = zdtBeforeGap.plusHours(1);

        // Print a report.                                                   (5a)
        System.out.printf("Daylight Savings in %s starts at %s "
            + "(spring forward 1 hour).%n", cTZ, ldtStartDST);
        System.out.println("                              _____ZonedDateTime_____");

        System.out.printf("%27s %7s %7s %5s %9s %5s%n",
                    "Date", "Time", "Offset", "TZ", "DST", "UTC");
        printInfo("(1) Before gap:     ", zdtBeforeGap);
        System.out.println("     + 1 hour");
        printInfo("(2) After gap:      ", zdtAfterGap);
        System.out.println();

        // Add 3 hours:                                                      (6a)
        ZonedDateTime zdtPlus3Hrs = zdtBeforeGap.plusHours(3);
        System.out.printf("%s + 3 hours = %s%n", zdtBeforeGap, zdtPlus3Hrs);
        System.out.println();
    }

    /**
     * Adjustment due to the time overlap at DST crossover.                  (1b)
     * DST ends in US/Central TZ: 2021-11-07T02:00:00,
     * clocks are moved backward 1 hour, resulting in a time overlap of 1 hour.
     */
    static void adjustForOverlap() {
        // End date and time for DST in US/Central in 2021.                  (2b)
        ZoneId cTZ = ZoneId.of("US/Central");
        LocalDate dateEndDST = LocalDate.of(2021, 11, 7);
        LocalTime timeEndDST = LocalTime.of(2, 0);
        LocalDateTime ldtEndDST = LocalDateTime.of(dateEndDST, timeEndDST);
        ZonedDateTime zdtEndDST = ZonedDateTime.of(ldtEndDST, cTZ);

        // Time before the overlap:                                         (3b)
        LocalTime timeBeforeOverlap = LocalTime.of(0, 30);
        LocalDateTime ldtBeforeOverlap = LocalDateTime.of(dateEndDST,
                                                timeBeforeOverlap);
        ZonedDateTime zdtBeforeOverlap = ZonedDateTime.of(ldtBeforeOverlap, cTZ);

        // Add 1 hour:                                                      (4b)
        ZonedDateTime zdtInOverlap1 = zdtBeforeOverlap.plusHours(1);
        ZonedDateTime zdtInOverlap2 = zdtInOverlap1.plusHours(1);
        ZonedDateTime zdtAfterOverlap = zdtInOverlap2.plusHours(1);
```

```java
    // Print a report.                                                     (5b)
    System.out.printf("Daylight Savings in %s ends at %s (fall back 1 hour).%n",
                cTZ, ldtEndDST);
    System.out.println("                     _____ZonedDateTime_____");

    System.out.printf("%27s %7s %7s %5s %9s %5s%n",
                "Date", "Time", "Offset", "TZ", "DST", "UTC");
    printInfo("(1) Before overlap: ", zdtBeforeOverlap);
    System.out.println("    + 1 hour");
    printInfo("(2) In overlap:     ", zdtInOverlap1);
    System.out.println("    + 1 hour");
    printInfo("(3) In overlap:     ", zdtInOverlap2);
    System.out.println("    + 1 hour");
    printInfo("(4) After overlap:  ", zdtAfterOverlap);
    System.out.println();

    // Add 3 hours:                                                        (6b)
    ZonedDateTime zdtPlus3Hrs = zdtBeforeOverlap.plusHours(3);
    System.out.printf("%s + 3 hours = %s%n", zdtBeforeOverlap, zdtPlus3Hrs);
    System.out.println();
}

/**
 * Print info for a date-time.                                            (7)
 * @param leadTxt Text to lead the information.
 * @param zdt     Zoned date-time whose info is printed.
 */
static void printInfo(String leadTxt, ZonedDateTime zdt) {
    System.out.printf(leadTxt + "%10s %5s %6s %5s %-5s %5s%n",
                zdt.toLocalDate(), zdt.toLocalTime(),
                zdt.getOffset(), zdt.getZone(),
                isDST(zdt), localTimeAtUTC(zdt));
}

/**
 * Determine if DST is in effect for a zoned date-time.                   (8)
 * @param zdt  Zoned date-time whose DST status should be determined.
 * @return     true, if DST is in effect.
 */
static boolean isDST(ZonedDateTime zdt) {
    return zdt.getZone().getRules().isDaylightSavings(zdt.toInstant());
}

/**
 *  Find local time at UTC/Greenwich equivalent to local time in          (9)
 *  the specified zoned date-time.
 * @param zdt   Zoned date-time to convert to UTC/Greenwich.
 * @return      Equivalent local time at UTC/Greenwich.
 */
static LocalTime localTimeAtUTC(ZonedDateTime zdt) {
    return zdt.withZoneSameInstant(ZoneOffset.UTC).toLocalTime();
}
}
```

Analogous to the plus() methods, the of() methods also make adjustments at DST crossings. Sticking to the DST information from Example 17.9, if we try to create a zoned date-time with a time that is in the gap, the of() method typically moves the time by the length of the gap (1 hour) into DST.

```
ZonedDateTime zdt1 = ZonedDateTime.of(
    LocalDate.of(2021, 3, 14),
    LocalTime.of(2, 30),                   // Time 02:30 is in the gap.
    ZoneId.of("US/Central"));
System.out.println(zdt1);                  // 2021-03-14T03:30-05:00[US/Central]
```

For a time in the overlap, the offset is ambiguous—it can be -05:00 for DST or -06:00 for standard time. Typically, the of() methods return a zoned date-time with the DST offset, as shown in the following code:

```
ZonedDateTime zdt2 = ZonedDateTime.of(
    LocalDate.of(2021, 11, 7),
    LocalTime.of(1, 30),                   // Time 01:30 in the overlap.
    ZoneId.of("US/Central"));
System.out.println(zdt2);                  // 2021-11-07T01:30-05:00[US/Central]
```

The withField() methods behave analogously to the to() methods when it comes to DST crossings. If we try to create a zoned date-time with the time 02:00 that is in the gap, the withHour() method typically moves the time by the length of the gap (1 hour) into DST.

```
ZonedDateTime zdt3 = ZonedDateTime.of(
    LocalDate.of(2021, 3, 14), LocalTime.of(0, 0), ZoneId.of("US/Central")
    ).withHour(2);                         // Time 02:00 is in the gap.
System.out.println(zdt3);                  // 2021-03-14T03:00-05:00[US/Central]
```

For a time in the overlap, the withMinute() method returns a zoned date-time with the DST offset, as shown in the following code:

```
ZonedDateTime zdt4 = ZonedDateTime.of(
    LocalDate.of(2021, 11, 7), LocalTime.of(1, 0), ZoneId.of("US/Central")
    ).withMinute(30);                      // Time 01:30 is in the overlap.
System.out.println(zdt4);                  // 2021-11-07T01:30-05:00[US/Central]
```

Finally, the result of temporal arithmetic with zoned date-times can depend on whether date units or time units are involved. We illustrate the behavior using the following zoned date-time that is before the crossover from DST to standard time.

```
ZonedDateTime zdtBeforeOverlap = ZonedDateTime.of(
    LocalDate.of(2021, 11, 7),
    LocalTime.of(0, 30),                   // Time 00:30 is before the DST crossover.
    ZoneId.of("US/Central"));
```

We add 1 day with the plusDays() method and 24 hours with the plusHours() method to the zoned date-time using the code below. Number of days is measured by the date unit *days*, and number of hours by the time unit *hours*. From the output we see that the results are different. The day was added to the date-time and converted back to a zoned date-time with the offset adjusted, without affecting the time part; that is, date units operate on the *local* timeline. Adding 24 hours results in a zoned-based time that is exactly a duration of 24 hours later, taking the DST crossover into consideration; that is, time units operate on the *instant* timeline.

```
// Date units and time units.
System.out.printf("%s + 1 day   = %s%n",
    zdtBeforeOverlap, zdtBeforeOverlap.plusDays(1));        // (1) Add 1 day.
System.out.printf("%s + 24 hours = %s%n",
    zdtBeforeOverlap, zdtBeforeOverlap.plusHours(24));      // (2) Add 24 hours.
```

Output from the print statements:

```
2021-11-07T00:30-05:00[US/Central] + 1 day    = 2019-11-04T00:30-06:00[US/Central]
2021-11-07T00:30-05:00[US/Central] + 24 hours = 2021-11-07T23:30-06:00[US/Central]
```

By the same token, adding a Period (that has only date fields) and a Duration (that has only time fields) using the plus(Period.ofDays(1)) and the plus(Duration .ofHours(24)) method calls instead at (1) and (2) above, respectively, will give the same results.

17.8 Converting Date and Time Values to Legacy Date

An object of the java.util.Date legacy class represents time, date, and time zone. The class provides the method from() to convert a java.time.Instant (p. 1049) to a Date. In order to convert dates and times created using the new Date and Time API, we need to go through an Instant to convert them to a Date object.

The java.time.ZonedDateTime class provides the toInstant() method to convert a ZonedDateTime object to an Instant, which is utilized by the zdtToDate() method of the ConvertToLegacyDate utility class in Example 17.10 at (1).

A java.time.LocalDateTime object lacks a time zone in order to convert it to a Date. The ldtToDate() method at (2) adds the system default time zone to create a Zoned-DateTime object which is then converted to an Instant.

A LocalDate object lacks time and a time zone in order to convert it to a Date. The ldToDate() method at (3) adds a fictive time (start of the day), and the resulting LocalDateTime object is added the system default time zone to create a ZonedDateTime object which is then converted to an Instant.

A LocalTime object lacks a date and a time zone in order to convert it to a Date. The ltToDate() method at (4) adds a fictive date (2021-1-1), and the resulting LocalDate-Time object is added to the system default time zone to create a ZonedDateTime object which is then converted to an Instant.

For an example, see Example 18.8, p. 1143.

Example 17.10 *Converting to Legacy Date*

```java
import java.time.*;
import java.util.Date;

public class ConvertToLegacyDate {
  /** Convert a ZonedDateTime to Date. */
  public static Date zdtToDate(ZonedDateTime zdt) {                    // (1)
    return Date.from(zdt.toInstant());
  }

  /** Convert a LocalDateTime to Date. */
  public static Date ldtToDate(LocalDateTime ldt) {                    // (2)
    return Date.from(ldt.atZone(ZoneId.systemDefault()).toInstant());
  }

  /** Convert a LocalDate to Date. */
  public static Date ldToDate(LocalDate ld) {                          // (3)
    return Date.from(ld.atStartOfDay()
                       .atZone(ZoneId.systemDefault())
                       .toInstant());
  }

  /** Convert a LocalTime to Date. */
  public static Date ltToDate(LocalTime lt) {                          // (4)
    return Date.from(lt.atDate(LocalDate.of(2021, 1, 1))
                       .atZone(ZoneId.systemDefault())
                       .toInstant());
  }
}
```

 Review Questions

17.1   Given the following code:

```java
import java.time.LocalDate;

public class RQ1 {
  public static void main(String[] args) {
    LocalDate d1 = LocalDate.of(2021, 1, 31);
    LocalDate d2 = d1.plusMonths(1);
    LocalDate d3 = d2.minusMonths(1);
    System.out.println(d1.getDayOfYear() + " " + d2.getDayOfYear() + " " +
                       d3.getDayOfYear());
  }
}
```

What is the result?
Select the one correct answer.

(a) 31 61 31
(b) 31 59 28

(c) 31 59 31

(d) The program will throw an exception at runtime.

17.2   Given the following code:

```
import java.time.LocalDate;

public class RQ2 {
  public static void main(String[] args) {
    LocalDate d1 = LocalDate.of(2021, 1, 1);
    d1 = d1.withDayOfMonth(d1.lengthOfMonth()).withMonth(2);
    System.out.println(d1);
  }
}
```

What is the result?

Select the one correct answer.

(a) 2021-02-28

(b) 2021-02-31

(c) 2021-03-03

(d) The program will throw an exception at runtime.

17.3   Given the following code:

```
import java.time.*;

public class RQ3 {
  public static void main(String[] args) {
    LocalDateTime d1 = LocalDate.of(2021, 4, 1).atStartOfDay();
    Instant i1 = d1.toInstant(ZoneOffset.of("+18:00"));
    LocalDate d2 = LocalDate.ofInstant(i1, ZoneId.of("UTC"));
    System.out.println(d2);
  }
}
```

What is the result?

Select the one correct answer.

(a) 2021-04-1

(b) 2021-04-2

(c) 2021-03-30

(d) 2021-03-31

17.4   Given the following code:

```
import java.time.*;

public class RQ4 {
  public static void main(String[] args) {
    LocalDateTime dt = LocalDate.of(2021, 4, 1).atStartOfDay();
    ZonedDateTime zdt1 = dt.atZone(ZoneId.of("Europe/Paris"));
    ZonedDateTime zdt2 = dt.atZone(ZoneId.of("Europe/London"));
    Duration d = Duration.between(zdt1.minusMinutes(30), zdt2.plusMinutes(30));
    System.out.println(d);
  }
}
```

What is the result, given that the time difference between Paris and London is 1 hour?
Select the one correct answer.

(a) PT0H
(b) PT1H
(c) PT2H
(d) PT-2H
(e) PT-1H

17.5 Which statement is false?
Select the one correct answer.

(a) Instant objects can represent points in time with nanosecond precision.
(b) Instant objects and LocalTime objects have same precision.
(c) Duration objects can express the amount of time between two LocalDate objects.
(d) Period objects can express the number of days between two Instant objects.

17.6 Given the following code:

```java
import java.time.*;

public class RQ6 {
  public static void main(String[] args) {
    LocalTime t = LocalTime.of(8, 15);
    LocalDate d = LocalDate.of(2021, 4, 1);
    LocalDateTime dt = d.atTime(t);
    dt.minusMinutes(30).withDayOfMonth(12);
    System.out.println(dt);
  }
}
```

What is the result?
Select the one correct answer.

(a) 2021-04-12T08:45
(b) 2021-04-12T07:45
(c) 2021-04-01T08:15
(d) 2021-04-01T07:15

17.7 Which statement is true?
Select the one correct answer.

(a) Adding a Duration and adding a Period to a ZonedDateTime object produces the same result.
(b) A Duration of 36,000 seconds is the same as a Period of 1 hour.
(c) Daylight savings is taken into consideration by LocalTime and LocalDateTime objects.
(d) A Period of 1 day is always equivalent to a Duration of 24 hours.
(e) Period and Duration objects can have positive and negative values.

17.8   Given the following code:

```
import java.time.*;

public class RQ8 {
  public static void main(String[] args) {
    Period d  = Period.parse("P2D");
    LocalDate ld = LocalDate.of(2021, 4, 1);
    LocalDateTime ldt = ld.plus(d);
    System.out.println(ldt);
  }
}
```

What is the result?
Select the one correct answer.

(a) 2021-04-01T00:30
(b) 2021-04-01T23:30
(c) 2021-03-31T00:30
(d) 2021-03-31T23:30
(e) The program will fail to compile.

17.9   Given the following code:

```
import java.time.*;

public class RQ9 {
  public static void main(String[] args) {
    Duration d  = Duration.parse("PT-24H");
    LocalDate ld = LocalDate.of(2021, 4, 1).plus(d);
    System.out.println(ld);
  }
}
```

What is the result?
Select the one correct answer.

(a) 2021-03-31
(b) 2021-04-01
(c) 2021-04-02
(d) The program will throw an exception at runtime.
(e) The program will fail to compile.

17.10   Given the following code:

```
import java.time.*;

public class RQ10 {
  public static void main(String[] args) {
    LocalDate ld = LocalDate.of(2021, 4, 1);
    // (1) INSERT CODE HERE
    System.out.println(ldt);
  }
}
```

Which of the following statements, when inserted independently at (1), will print
the following result: 2021-04-03T00:30?

Select the two correct answers.
(a) `LocalDateTime ldt = ld.atTime(LocalTime.of(0, 30))`
                             `.plus(Duration.ofHours(48));`
(b) `LocalDateTime ldt = ld.plus(Duration.ofHours(48))`
                             `.atTime(LocalTime.of(0, 30));`
(c) `LocalDateTime ldt = ld.atTime(LocalTime.of(48,30));`
(d) `LocalDateTime ldt = ld.plusDays(3).atTime(LocalTime.of(-23,30));`
(e) `LocalDateTime ldt = ld.atTime(0, 30).plus(Duration.ofHours(48));`

17.11   Given the following code:

```
import java.time.*;

public class RQ11 {
  public static void main(String[] args) {
    LocalDate now = LocalDate.now();
    LocalDate foolsDay = LocalDate.of(2021, Month.APRIL, 1);
    LocalDateTime tomorrowAfternoon = now.plusDays(1)
                          .atTime(LocalTime.of(12, 01));
    LocalDate anotherDay = foolsDay.withDayOfMonth(2).minusDays(1);
  }
}
```

How many `LocalDate` objects are created in this example?
Select the one correct answer.
(a) 3
(b) 4
(c) 5
(d) 6

17.12   Given the following code:

```
import java.time.*;

public class RQ13 {
  public static void main(String[] args) {
    LocalTime lt = LocalTime.of(17,30);
    LocalDateTime ldt = LocalDateTime.of(2021, Month.APRIL, 2, 15, 15);
    Duration d = Duration.between(lt, ldt);
    System.out.println(d);
  }
}
```

What is the result?
Select the one correct answer.
(a) PT-1H-45M
(b) PT1H-45M
(c) PT2H-15M
(d) PT-2H-15M
(e) The program will throw an exception at runtime.

17.13   Given the following code:

```
import java.time.*;
import static java.time.temporal.ChronoUnit.DAYS;

public class RQ14 {
  public static void main(String[] args) {
    LocalDateTime ldt = LocalDateTime.of(2021, Month.APRIL, 2, 15, 15);
    // (1) INSERT CODE HERE
    System.out.println(ldt);
  }
}
```

Which statement inserted at (1) will *not* give the following result: 2021-04-03T16:15?
Select the one correct answer.

(a) ldt = ldt.plusHours(1).with(LocalDate.of(2021, Month.APRIL, 3));

(b) ldt = ldt.plusDays(1).with(LocalTime.of(16, 15));

(c) ldt = ldt.plus(Duration.of(2, DAYS)).minus(Duration.parse("PT23H"));

(d) ldt = ldt.plus(Duration.of(2, DAYS))
                .minus(Duration.ofMinutes(15).ofHours(16));

(e) ldt = ldt.plus(Duration.parse("PT25H"));

(f) ldt = ldt.plus(Duration.ofMinutes(25 * 60));

Localization 18

 Chapter Topics

- Understanding localization of applications
- Understanding the role and purpose of locales as embodied by the `java.util.Locale` class
- Understanding how to specify a properties file
- Creating and using resource bundles with the `java.util.Resource-Bundle` class for storing and retrieving locale-specific information for the purpose of localization
- Using formatters provided by the `java.text.NumberFormat` class and its subclass, `java.text.DecimalFormat`, for locale-specific formatting and parsing of number, currency, and percentage values, including compact number and accounting currency formatting
- Using formatters provided by the `java.time.format.DateTimeFormatter` class for locale-specific formatting and parsing of date and time values
- Using formatters provided by the `java.text.MessageFormat` class for locale-specific formatting and parsing of messages
- Using the `java.text.ChoiceFormat` class for implementing choice patterns for conditional formatting and parsing of messages

Java SE 17 Developer Exam Objectives	
[11.1] Implement localization using locales, resource bundles, parse and format messages, dates, times, and numbers including currency and percentage values	§18.1, p. 1096, to §18.7, p. 1139
Java SE 11 Developer Exam Objectives	
[12.1] Implement Localization using Locale, resource bundles, and Java APIs to parse and format messages, dates, and numbers	§18.1, p. 1096, to §18.7, p. 1139

Often, applications have to work across borders and cultures, and thus must be capable of adjusting to a variety of local requirements. For example, an accounting system for the US market is obviously not going to function well in the Norwegian market. Not only is the formatting of dates, times, numbers, and currency different, but the languages in the two markets are different as well. Developing programs so that they have global awareness of such differences is called *internationalization*—also known as *i18n* (the 18 refers to the 18 characters deleted in the word *internationalization*).

Java provides the concept of a *locale* to create applications that adhere to cultural and regional preferences necessary in order to make an application truly international—a process called *localization*. Localization of applications enhances the user experience by being culturally sensitive to the user and minimizing misinterpretation of information on the part of the user. The user dialogue is an obvious candidate for localization in an application. Identifying and factorizing to isolate locale-sensitive data and code facilitates localization. Understanding cultural issues is important in this regard. Other examples of resources that might require localization are messages, salutations, graphics, measurement systems, postal codes, and phone numbers. Hard-coding such locale-sensitive information is certainly not a good idea. Once an application is properly set up for internationalization, it is relatively straightforward to localize it for multiple locales without too much effort.

This chapter covers support provided by the Java SE Platform APIs to aid localization of applications: locales to access particular cultural and regional preferences, properties files as resource bundles to store locale-specific information, and formatters to format numbers, currencies, dates, times, and messages according to locale rules.

18.1 Using Locales

A *locale* represents a specific geographical, political, or cultural region. Its two most important attributes are *language* and *country*. Certain classes in the Java standard library provide *locale-sensitive* operations. For example, they provide methods to format values that represent *dates*, *currencies*, and *numbers* according to a specific locale. Adapting a program to a specific locale is called *localization*.

A locale is represented by an instance of the class `java.util.Locale`. A locale object can be created using the following constructors:

```
Locale(String language)
Locale(String language, String country)
```

The language string is normalized to lowercase and the country string to uppercase. The language argument is an ISO-639 Language Code (which uses two lowercase letters), and the country argument is an ISO-3166 Country Code (which uses two uppercase letters) or a UN M.49 three-digit area code—although the constructors do not impose any constraint on their length or perform any syntactic checks on the arguments.

For the one-argument constructor, the country remains undefined.

Examples of selected language codes and country codes are given in Table 18.1 and Table 18.2, respectively.

Table 18.1 *Selected Language Codes*

Language code	Language
"en"	English
"no"	Norwegian
"fr"	French

Table 18.2 *Selected Country/Region Codes*

Country/Region code	Country/Region
"US"	United States (U.S.)
"GB"	Great Britain (GB)
"NO"	Norway
"FR"	France
"003"	North America

The Locale class also has predefined locales for certain *languages,* irrespective of the region where they are spoken, as shown in Table 18.3.

Table 18.3 *Selected Predefined Locales for Languages*

Constant	Language
Locale.ENGLISH	Locale with English (new Locale("en"))
Locale.FRENCH	Locale with French (new Locale("fr"))
Locale.GERMAN	Locale with German (new Locale("de"))—that is, Deutsch

The Locale class also has predefined locales for certain *combinations of countries and languages,* as shown in Table 18.4.

Table 18.4 *Selected Predefined Locales for Countries*

Constant	Country
Locale.US	Locale for U.S. (new Locale("en","US"))
Locale.UK	Locale for United Kingdom/Great Britain (new Locale("en","GB"))
Locale.CANADA_FRENCH	Locale for Canada with French language (new Locale("fr","CA"))

Normally a program uses the *default locale* on the platform to provide localization. The Locale class provides a get and a set method to manipulate the default locale.

```
static Locale getDefault()
static void    setDefault(Locale newLocale)
```

The first method returns the default locale, and the second one sets a specific locale as the default locale.

```
static Locale[] getAvailableLocales()
```

Returns an array of all installed locales.

```
static Locale forLanguageTag(String languageTag)
```

Returns a locale for the specified IETF BCP 47 language tag string, which allows extended locale properties, such as a calendar or a numeric system. An example would be creating a locale based on the language tag "zh-cmn-Hans-CN", which stands for Mandarin Chinese, Simplified script, as used in China. Note that the *locale qualifiers* (also called *subtags*) in the language tag are separated by hyphens (-).

```
String getCountry()
```

Returns the country/region code for this locale, or null if the code is not defined for this locale.

```
String getLanguage()
```

Returns the language code of this locale, or null if the code is not defined for this locale.

```
String getDisplayCountry()
String getDisplayCountry(Locale inLocale)
```

Returns a name for the locale's country that is appropriate for display, depending on the default locale in the first method or the inLocale argument in the second method.

```
String getDisplayLanguage()
String getDisplayLanguage(Locale inLocale)
```

Return a name for the locale's language that is appropriate for display, depending on the default locale in the first method or the inLocale argument in the second method.

```
String getDisplayName()
String getDisplayName(Locale inLocale)
```

Return a name for the locale that is appropriate for display.

```
String toString()
```

Returns a text representation of this locale in the format "*languageCode-_countryCode*". Language is always lowercase and country is always uppercase. If either of the codes is not specified in the locale, the _ (underscore) is omitted.

A locale is an immutable object, having *two sets* of get methods to return the *display name* of the country and the language in the locale. The first set returns the display name of the current locale according to the default locale, while the second set returns the display name of the current locale according to the locale specified as an argument in the method call.

Methods that require a locale for their operation are called *locale-sensitive*. Methods for formatting numbers, currencies, dates, and the like use the locale information to determine how such values should be formatted. A locale does not provide such services. Subsequent sections in this chapter provide examples of locale-sensitive classes (Figure 18.1, p. 1115).

Example 18.1 illustrates the use of the get methods in the Locale class. The call to the getDefault() method at (1) returns the default locale. The method call locNO.getDisplayCountry() returns the country display name (Norwegian) of the Norwegian locale according to the default locale (which in this case is United States), whereas the method call locNO.getDisplayCountry(locFR) returns the country display name (Norvège) of the Norwegian locale according to the French locale.

Example 18.1 also illustrates that an application can change its default locale programmatically at any time. The call to the setDefault() method at (2) sets the default locale to that of Germany. The name of the Norwegian locale is displayed according to this new default locale.

Example 18.1 *Understanding Locales*

```java
import java.util.Locale;
public class LocalesEverywhere {

    public static void main(String[] args) {

        Locale locDF = Locale.getDefault();                  // (1)
        Locale locNO =  new Locale("no", "NO");              // Locale: Norwegian/Norway
        Locale locFR =  new Locale("fr", "FR");              // Locale: French/France

        System.out.println("Default locale is: " + locDF.getDisplayName());
        System.out.println("Display country (language) for Norwegian locale:");

        System.out.printf("In %s: %s (%s)%n", locDF.getDisplayCountry(),
            locNO.getDisplayCountry(locDF), locNO.getDisplayLanguage(locDF));

        System.out.printf("In %s: %s (%s)%n", locNO.getDisplayCountry(),
            locNO.getDisplayCountry(locNO), locNO.getDisplayLanguage(locNO));

        System.out.printf("In %s: %s (%s)%n", locFR.getDisplayCountry(),
            locNO.getDisplayCountry(locFR), locNO.getDisplayLanguage(locFR));

        System.out.println("\nChanging the default locale.");
        Locale.setDefault(Locale.GERMANY);                   // (2) Locale: German/Germany
        locDF = Locale.getDefault();
        System.out.println("Default locale is: " + locDF.getDisplayName());
```

```
System.out.printf("Interpreting %s locale information in %s locale.%n",
                  locNO.getDisplayName(), locDF.getDisplayName());
    }
}
```

Output from the program:

```
Default locale is: English (United States)
Display country (language) for Norwegian locale:
In United States: Norway (Norwegian)
In Norway: Norge (norsk)
In France: Norvège (norvégien)

Changing the default locale.
Default locale is: Deutsch (Deutschland)
Interpreting Norwegisch (Norwegen) locale information in Deutsch (Deutschland)
locale.
```

18.2 Properties Files

Applications need to customize their behavior and access information about the runtime environment. This could be about getting configuration data to run the application, tailoring the user interface to a specific locale, accessing the particulars for a database connection, customizing colors and fonts, and many other situations. It is not a good idea to hard-code such information in the application, but instead making it available externally so that the application can access it when needed, and where it can be modified without having to compile the application code.

Creating a Property List in a Properties File

A *property list* contains *key–value pairs* that designate *properties*, where a key is associated with a value, analogous to the entries in a map. Such a list can be created in a *properties file*, where a key–value pair is defined on each line according to the following syntax:

    <key> = <value>

Following are some examples of properties that define information about the Java SE 17 Developer exam:

```
cert.name = OCP, Java SE 17 Developer
exam.title = Java SE 17 Developer
exam.number = 1Z0-829
```

Alternatively, we can use the colon (:) instead of the equals sign (=). In fact, whitespace can also be used to separate the key and the value. Any leading whitespace on a line is ignored, as is any whitespace around the equals sign (=).

Both the key and the value in a properties file are interpreted as String objects. The value string comprises all characters on the right-hand side of =, beginning with the first non-whitespace character and ending with the last non-whitespace character. Here are some examples:

```
company = GLOBUS
greeting=Hi!
            gratitude                    =Thank you!
```

We do not need to escape the metacharacter = or : in a value string. However, key names can be specified by escaping any whitespace in the name with the backslash character (\). Metacharacters = and : in a key name can also be escaped in the same way. In the first example below, the key string is "fake smiley" and the value string is ":=)". In the second example below, the key string is ":=)" and the value string is "fake smiley".

```
fake\ smiley = :=)
\:\=) = fake smiley
```

A backslash (\) at the end of a line can also be used to break the property specification across multiple lines, and any leading whitespace on a continuation line is ignored. The value in the following property specification is "Au revoir!" and not "Au   revoir!":

```
farewell = Au \
            revoir!
```

If only the key is specified and no value is provided, the empty string ("") is returned as the value, as in the following example:

```
KeyWithNoValue
```

If necessary, any conversion of the value string must be explicitly done by the application.

In the case of a duplicate key in a properties file, the last key–value pair with a duplicate key supersedes any previous resource specifications with this key.

If the first non-whitespace character on a line is the hash sign (#), the whole line is treated as a comment, and thereby ignored—as are blank lines. The exclamation mark (!) can also be used for this purpose.

```
# Any comments so far?
```

If the character encoding of a properties file does not support Unicode characters, then these must be specified using the \uxxxx encoding in the file. For example, to specify the property euro = €, we can encode it as:

```
euro = \u20AC
```

Since a properties file is a text file, it can conveniently be created in a text editor, and appropriate file permissions set to avoid unauthorized access. Although the name of a properties file can be any valid file name, it is customary to append the file extension .properties.

The Java Standard library provides classes to utilize the properties defined in a properties file.

- The java.util.ResourceBundle class can be used to implement a *resource bundle* based on the properties in a property (resource) file (p. 1102).

- The java.util.Properties class can be used to implement a Properties *table* based on the properties defined in a properties file—but this will not be discussed here, as this class is beyond the scope of this book.

18.3 Bundling Resources

Locale-specific data (messages, labels, colors, images, etc.) must be customized according to the conventions and customs for each locale that an application wishes to support. A *resource bundle* is a convenient and efficient way to store and retrieve locale-specific data in an application. The abstract class java.util.ResourceBundle is the key to managing locale-specific data in a Java application.

Resource Bundle Families

A *resource bundle* essentially defines *key–value pairs* that are associated with a specific locale. The synonyms *resources* and *properties* are also used for *key–value pairs*, depending on how a resource bundle is implemented. The application can retrieve locale-specific resources from the appropriate resource bundle.

A specific naming convention is used to create resource bundles. This naming convention allows resource bundles to be associated with specific locales, thereby defining *resource bundle families*. All bundles in a resource bundle family have a common *base name*, along with other locale-specific extensions, but the language and country extensions are the important ones to consider. Best practice is to use the following name for a resource bundle that defines all country-specific resources:

   baseName_languageCode_countryCode

and to use the following name for a resource bundle that defines all language-specific resources:

   baseName_languageCode

In addition, it is also recommended to include a *default resource bundle* that has only the common base name. The underscore (_) is mandatory. The extensions with the language and country codes are according to locale conventions discussed earlier (p. 1096). The following resource bundle family, used in Example 18.3, has the common base name BasicResources:

BasicResources	Default resource bundle
BasicResources_no_NO	Resource bundle for Norwegian (Norway) locale
BasicResources_fr	Resource bundle for all locales with French language

An application need not store all resources associated with a locale in a single resource bundle family. The resources can be organized in different resource bundle families for a given locale.

This naming scheme allows a resource bundle to be associated with a specific locale. Note that an application provides a version of each resource bundle for every locale supported by the application, unless they are shared. An example of such sharing is shown above: the locales for France and French-Canada both share the BasicResources_fr resource bundle. We have not defined separate BasicResources bundles for these two locales. We will have more to say on this matter later when we discuss how resources are located for a given locale in a resource bundle family.

Creating Resource Bundles

A resource bundle can be a *property resource file* (as shown in Example 18.2) or a *resource bundle class*, which is a *subclass of the abstract class* java.util.ResourceBundle. A resource bundle class can be used to implement resources that are not strings. We will not discuss resource bundle classes here as they are beyond the scope of this book.

Property Resource Files

A *property resource file* is a *properties file*, in which each line defines a *key–value pair* that designates a *property*. The discussion on properties files (p. 1100) also applies to a property resource file. However, note that a property resource file must be named according to the resource bundle naming scheme outlined above, and has the mandatory file extension .properties in addition.

Example 18.2 shows the three property resource files used by Example 18.3. The property resource file BasicResources.properties defines the default resource bundle for the resource bundle family BasicResources that applies for all locales. The property resource files BasicResources_no_NO.properties and BasicResources_fr.properties define resource bundles for the Norwegian (Norway) locale and the French locale, respectively. Note the appending of the language/country code to the bundle family name using the underscore (_).

The first line in each of the three property resource files in Example 18.2 is a comment documenting the name of the file. Typically, the property resource files are placed in a directory, usually called resources, which is in the same location as the application.

Note also that we use the same key name for a property in *all* property resource files of a resource bundle family. The greeting, gratitude, and the farewell messages are designated by their respective key names in all property resource files. In Example 18.2, the astute reader will notice that the key name company is only specified in the default property resource file BasicResources.properties, but not in the other property resource files. If the default resource bundle for a resource bundle family is provided, it is always in the search path when locating the value associated with a key.

Modifying an existing property resource file or adding a new property resource file may not require recompiling of the application, depending on the implication of the changes made to the property resource file.

Example 18.2   *The* `BasicResources` *Bundle Family (See Also Example 18.3)*

```
# File: BasicResources.properties
company = GLOBUS
greeting = Hi!
gratitude = Thank you!
farewell = See you!
```

```
# File: BasicResources_no_NO.properties
greeting = Hei!
gratitude = Takk!
farewell = Ha det!
```

```
# File: BasicResources_fr.properties
greeting = Bonjour!
gratitude = Merci!
farewell = Au revoir!
```

Locating, Loading, and Searching Resource Bundles

Once the necessary resource bundle families have been specified, the application can access the resources in a specific resource bundle family for a particular locale using the services of the java.util.ResourceBundle class. First, a locale-specific resource bundle is *created* from a resource bundle family using the getBundle() method—an elaborate process explained later in this section.

```
static ResourceBundle getBundle(String baseName)
static ResourceBundle getBundle(String baseName, Locale locale)
```
Return a resource bundle using the specified base name for a resource bundle family, either for the default locale or for the specified locale, respectively.

The resource bundle returned by this method is *chained* to other resource bundles (called *parent resource bundles*) that are searched if the key-based lookup in this resource bundle fails to find the value of a resource.

An unchecked java.util.MissingResourceException is thrown if no resource bundle for the specified base name can be found.

Also, it should be noted that bundles are loaded by the classloader, and thus their bundle names are treated exactly like fully qualified class names; that is, the package name needs to be specified when a resource bundle is placed in a package, such as "resources.BasicResources".

If the resource bundle found by the getBundle() method was defined as a *property resource file*, its contents are read into an instance of the concrete class PropertyResourceBundle (a subclass of the abstract ResourceBundle class) and this instance is returned.

The resource bundle instances returned by the getBundle() methods are immutable and are cached for reuse.

```
Object getObject(String key)
String getString(String key)
```
The first method returns an object for the given key from this resource bundle.

The second method returns a string for the given key from this resource bundle. This is a convenience method, if the value is a string. Calling this method is equivalent to (String) getObject(key). A ClassCastException is thrown if the object found for the given key is not a string.

An unchecked java.util.MissingResourceException is thrown if no value for the key can be found in this resource bundle or any of its parent resource bundles. A NullPointerException is thrown if the key is null.

```
Set<String> keySet()
```
Returns a Set of all keys contained in this ResourceBundle.

```
Locale getLocale()
```
Returns the locale of this resource bundle. The locale is derived from the naming scheme for resource bundles.

We will use Example 18.3 to illustrate salient features of localizing an application using resource bundles. The application has the following data, which should be localized:

```
Company: GLOBUS
Greeting: Hi!
Gratitude: Thank you!
Farewell: See you!
```

The example illustrates how the application can localize this data for the following locales: default ("en_US"), Norway ("no_NO"), French-Canada ("fr_CA"), and France ("fr_FR"). The company name is the same in every locale. The greeting, gratitude, and farewell messages are all grouped in one resource bundle family (BasicResources). For each locale, the application reads this data from the appropriate resource bundles and prints it to the terminal (see the output from Example 18.3).

- -

Example 18.3 *Using Resource Bundles (See Also Example 18.2)*

```
import java.util.Locale;
import java.util.ResourceBundle;
public class UsingResourceBundles {

  // Supported locales:                                              // (1)
  public static final Locale[] locales = {
```

```
        Locale.getDefault(),                            // Default: US (English)
        new Locale("no", "NO"),                         // Norway (Norwegian)
        Locale.FRANCE,                                  // France (French)
        Locale.CANADA_FRENCH                            // Canada (French)
    };

    // Localized data from property resource files:              // (2)
    private static String company;
    private static String greeting;
    private static String gratitude;
    private static String farewell;

    public static void main(String[] args) {                     // (3)
        for (Locale locale : locales) {
            setLocaleSpecificData(locale);
            printLocaleSpecificData(locale);
        }
    }

    private static void setLocaleSpecificData(Locale locale) {    // (4)
        // Get resources from property resource files:
        ResourceBundle properties =
            ResourceBundle.getBundle("resources.BasicResources", locale);   // (5)
        company = properties.getString("company");                // (6)
        greeting = properties.getString("greeting");
        gratitude = properties.getString("gratitude");
        farewell = properties.getString("farewell");
    }

    private static void printLocaleSpecificData(Locale locale) {  // (7)
        System.out.println("Resources for " + locale.getDisplayName() + " locale:");
        System.out.println("Company: " + company);
        System.out.println("Greeting: " + greeting);
        System.out.println("Gratitude: " + gratitude);
        System.out.println("Farewell: " + farewell);
        System.out.println();
    }
}
```

Output from running the program:

```
Resources for English (United States) locale:
Company: GLOBUS
Greeting: Hi!
Gratitude: Thank you!
Farewell: See you!

Resources for Norwegian (Norway) locale:
Company: GLOBUS
Greeting: Hei!
Gratitude: Takk!
Farewell: Ha det!

Resources for French (France) locale:
Company: GLOBUS
Greeting: Bonjour!
```

```
Gratitude: Merci!
Farewell: Au revoir!

Resources for French (Canada) locale:
Company: GLOBUS
Greeting: Bonjour!
Gratitude: Merci!
Farewell: Au revoir!
```

In Example 18.3, the static method getBundle() of the ResourceBundle class is called
at (5) to create a resource bundle for the specified locale from the resource bundle
family with the base name BasicResources. In Example 18.3, the resource bundle family is located in the resources directory, which is also the location of the package
with the same name.

```
String company;
...
ResourceBundle properties =
    ResourceBundle.getBundle("resources.BasicResources", locale);   // (5)
company = properties.getString("company");                          // (6)
```

Since all the resource bundles in the resource bundle family BasicResources are
property resource files, both the key and the value are String objects. It is convenient to use the getString() method in the ResourceBundle class to do lookup for
resources, as shown at (6). The key is passed as an argument. Searching the
resource for a given key is explained later in this section.

Locating Locale-Specific Resources

A broad outline of the steps is given below to locate and create the resource bundle
(and its parent bundles) returned by the getBundle() static method of the abstract
class java.util.ResourceBundle for a specific locale. For the nitty-gritty details of
locating resource bundles, we recommend consulting the Java SE API documentation for the java.util.ResourceBundle class.

Exactly which resource bundle (and its parent bundles) will be returned by the
getBundle() static method depends on the following factors:

- The *resource bundles included in the resource bundle family* specified by its fully
  qualified base name in the call to the getBundle() method
- The *specified locale* in the call to the getBundle() method
- The *current default locale* of the application

For the explanation given below, assume that the default local is "en_US" and the
following resource files (from Example 18.2) in the resource bundle family with the
base name BasicResources reside in a directory named resources:

```
BasicResources.properties
BasicResources_no_NO.properties
BasicResources_fr.properties
```

Also assume the following call is made to the getBundle() method to retrieve the resource bundle (and its parent resource bundles) for the baseName bundle family and the specified locale:

```
ResourceBundle resources = ResourceBundle.getBundle(baseName, specifiedLocale);
```

Step 1: Create a list of candidate bundle names based on the specified locale.

The getBundle() method first generates a list of *candidate bundle names* by appending the attributes of the locale argument (specified language code, specified country code) to the base name of the resource bundle family that is passed as an argument. Typically, this list would have the following candidate bundle names, where the order in which the names are generated is important in locating resources:

```
baseName_specifiedLanguageCode_specifiedCountryCode
baseName_specifiedLanguageCode
```

For example, if the base name is BasicResources and the locale that is passed as an argument is "fr_CA" in the call to the getBundle() method, the list of candidate bundle names generated would be as follows:

```
BasicResources_fr_CA
BasicResources_fr
```

Note that more specific bundles are higher in this list, and more general ones are lower in the list. The bundle BasicResources_fr_CA is more specific than the bundle BasicResources_fr, as the former is only for France (French), whereas the latter is for all French-speaking countries.

A candidate bundle name in this list is a *parent* resource bundle for the one above it.

Step 2: Find the result bundle that can be instantiated in the candidate bundle list.

The getBundle() method then iterates over the list of candidate bundle names from the beginning of the list to find the *first* one (called the *result bundle*) for which it can instantiate an actual resource bundle.

Finding the result bundle depends on whether it is possible to instantiate a resource bundle class or load the contents of a property resource file into an instance of the PropertyResourceBundle class, where the resource bundle class or the property resource file has the same name as the candidate bundle name.

In our example regarding the "fr_CA" locale, the candidate resource name BasicResources_fr_CA in the list of candidate resource names does not qualify as a result resource bundle because it cannot be created based on any resource bundles in the resource bundle family BasicResources. Only the candidate resource name BasicResources_fr can be created and is the result resource bundle, as there is a resource bundle named BasicResources_fr.properties in the resource bundle family.

Once a result resource bundle has been found, its *parent chain* is constructed and returned (p. 1109). In our example with the "fr_CA" locale, the parent chain for the result source bundle named BasicResources_fr.properties is created and returned.

Step 3: If no result resource bundle is found in Step 2, the search for a result bundle is conducted with the default locale.

It is possible that no result resource bundle is found in the previous step. Only in that case is the search for a result resource bundle repeated with the current *default locale* (default language code, default country code). A new list of candidate bundle names is generated, which will typically include the following names, and is instantiated to find a result bundle name:

```
baseName_defaultLanguageCode_defaultCountryCode
baseName_defaultLanguageCode
```

In our example, this second step is not performed since a result resource bundle (BasicResources_fr) was found in the previous step.

Once a result resource bundle using the default locale has been found, its *parent chain* is constructed and returned (p. 1109).

Step 4: If no result resource bundle is found in Step 3 using the current default locale either, an attempt is made to instantiate the default resource bundle designated by baseName.

If successful, this instantiation of the default resource bundle is returned by the getBundle(baseName, specifiedLocale) method.

In our example, this step with the bundle name BasicResources is not performed since a result resource bundle (BasicResources_fr) was already found.

Step 5: If the steps above do not yield a result resource bundle, an unchecked java.util.MissingResourceException *is thrown.*

In our example, no exception is thrown since a result resource bundle (BasicResources_fr) was found in Step 2.

Constructing the Parent Chain of a Result Resource Bundle

Once a result resource bundle is identified (see Step 2 and Step 3 in the previous section), a *parent chain* for the result source bundle is constructed and returned by the getBundle() method as follows:

- All candidate bundle names that are below the result bundle name in the candidate bundle list are iterated over, and those candidate bundles that can be instantiated are *chained* in the order in which they appear in the list.

  In our example, the result resource bundle BasicResources_fr was found last in the list of candidate bundle names, and therefore does not get any parent according to this step.

- Lastly, an attempt is also made to chain the *default resource bundle* (with the base name) into the parent chain of the result resource bundle which is then returned by the getBundle(baseName, specifiedLocale) method.

  In our example, the default resource bundle BasicResources is provided and is therefore set as the parent bundle to the result resource bundle Basic-Resources_fr.

```
BasicResources_fr.properties
BasicResources.properties (parent)
```

This will result in the parent chain being searched, if necessary, when a lookup is performed for a resource in this result bundle for the "fr_CA" locale, where the most specific bundle (BasicResources_fr.properties) is researched first and the most general one (BasicResources.properties) last.

Note that an attempt is also made to include the default resource bundle when no result resource bundle can be found in the candidate bundle list, as shown in Step 4 earlier.

Best practice recommends including a default resource bundle as *fallback* in a resource bundle family. This bundle will then always be searched last to find the value associated with a key.

Table 18.5 shows the result resource bundles with the parent bundle chain from the resource bundle family BasicResources that will be located and loaded for each locale supported by Example 18.3. We have shown property resource file names in the table and indicated the parent resource bundle. Actually, resource bundle classes are instantiated at runtime, based on the contents of the property resource files. Note that the resource bundle BasicResources_fr.properties is searched for both the "fr_FR" locale and the "fr_CA" locale.

Table 18.5 *Result and Parent Bundles (See Example 18.3)*

Specified locale	Result resource bundles	Step that creates the parent chain:
Locale("en", "US")	BasicResources.properties	*Step 4*
Locale("no", "NO")	BasicResources_no_NO.properties BasicResources.properties *(parent)*	*Step 2*
Locale("fr", "FR")	BasicResources_fr.properties BasicResources.properties *(parent)*	*Step 2*
Locale("fr", "CA")	BasicResources_fr.properties BasicResources.properties *(parent)*	*Step 2*

Searching in Resource Bundles

Example 18.4 is instructive in understanding which resource bundles for a given locale will be searched when performing key-based lookups for locale-specific values. Each resource bundle in the resource family MyResources has only one key, and the name of the key is different in all resource bundles. The value of the key in each file is the name of the resource bundle. The program prints the value of all the keys found in the resource bundles for a given locale. The method keySet(), called at (1), returns a set with all the keys from the resource bundles that can be searched for the locale specified in the getBundle() method. Any value written out will be the name of the resource bundle that is searched. Since a key set is returned, the key order in the set is not guaranteed. However, this key set is converted to a sorted key set to reflect the hierarchy of resource bundles for each locale.

From the program output, we can see that the default resource bundle is always searched (for all the locales in Example 18.4). Only if no corresponding resource bundle for the given locale can be found in the resource bundle family will the resource bundle for the current default locale be searched ("no_NO" locale in Example 18.4). For a language-country locale, both the country and the language resource bundles are included, if any of them are in the resource bundle family (the "fr_CA" locale in Example 18.4). For a language locale, only the language resource bundle is included, if it is in the resource bundle family ("fr" locale in Example 18.4).

Example 18.4 *Locating Resource Bundles*

```
# MyResources_fr_CA.properties
file1 = MyResources_fr_CA
```

```
# MyResources_fr.properties
file2 = MyResources_fr
```

```
# MyResources_en_US.properties
file3 = MyResources_en_US
```

```
# MyResources_en.properties
file4 = MyResources_en
```

```
# MyResources.properties
file5 = MyResources
```

```java
import java.util.Locale;
import java.util.ResourceBundle;
import java.util.TreeSet;

public class LocatingBundles {
  public static void main(String[] args) {

    Locale[] locales = {
        new Locale("no", "NO"),                          // Norway
        Locale.CANADA_FRENCH,                            // Canada (French)
        Locale.FRENCH,                                   // French
        Locale.getDefault(),                             // Default: en_US
    };

    for (Locale locale: locales) {
      System.out.println("Locating resource bundles for " + locale + " locale:");
      ResourceBundle resources = ResourceBundle.getBundle("resources.MyResources",
                                                    locale);
      for (String key : new TreeSet<>(resources.keySet())) {            // (1)
        System.out.println(resources.getString(key));
      }
```

```
            System.out.println();
        }
      }
    }
```

Output from the program:

```
    Locating resource bundles for no_NO locale:
    MyResources_en_US
    MyResources_en
    MyResources

    Locating resource bundles for fr_CA locale:
    MyResources_fr_CA
    MyResources_fr
    MyResources

    Locating resource bundles for fr locale:
    MyResources_fr
    MyResources

    Locating resource bundles for en_US locale:
    MyResources_en_US
    MyResources_en
    MyResources
```

 Review Questions

18.1   Given the following resource bundle in the pkg package directory:

```
    # File: MyResources_en_US.properties
    greeting = Howdy!
    gratitude = Thank you!
    farewell = See ya!
    farewell = Bye!
```

Assume that the current default locale is "en_US". What will be the result of compiling and running the following program?

```
    import java.util.*;
    public class TestResourceBundles {
      public static void main(String[] args) {
        ResourceBundle resources = ResourceBundle.getBundle("pkg.MyResources",
                                                     Locale.FRANCE);

        for (String key : resources.keySet()) {
          System.out.println(resources.getString(key));
        }
      }
    }
```

Select the one correct answer.

    (a) The program output will contain the following lines:
```
Howdy!
Bye!
Thank you!
```
    (b) The program output will contain the following lines:
```
Howdy!
See ya!
Thank you!
```
    (c) When run, the program will throw a `MissingResourceException`.

    (d) When run, the program will terminate normally without printing anything.

18.2   Given the following three resource bundles in the pkg3 package:

```
# MyResources_en_US.properties
farewell = See ya!
```

```
# MyResources_en.properties
farewell = Have a good one!
```

```
# MyResources.properties
farewell = Goodbye!
```

Assume that the current default locale is "en_US". What will be the result of compiling and running the following program?

```
import java.util.*;
public class TestResourceBundles3 {
  public static void main(String[] args) {
    ResourceBundle resources = ResourceBundle.getBundle("pkg3.MyResources",
                                                   Locale.ENGLISH);
    System.out.println(resources.getString("farewell"));
  }
}
```

Select the one correct answer.

    (a) See ya!

    (b) Have a good one!

    (c) Goodbye!

    (d) When run, the program will throw a `MissingResourceException`.

    (e) When run, the program will terminate normally without printing anything.

18.3   Given the following code:

```
import java.util.*;

public class RQ4_2 {
  public static void main(String[] args) {
    ResourceBundle rb = ResourceBundle.getBundle("resources", new Locale("en"));
    for (String key : new TreeSet<String>(rb.keySet())) {
      System.out.print(key+"="+rb.getString(key)+" ");
    }
  }
}
```

and the file `resources.properties`

```
k1=a
k2=b
```

and the file `resources_en.properties`

```
k1=c
```

and the file `resources_en_GB.properties`

```
k1=d
k2=e
```

What is the result?

Select the one correct answer.

(a) k1=d k2=e

(b) k1=c k2=b

(c) k1=a k2=b

(d) k1=d k2=e

(e) The program will throw an exception at runtime.

18.4   Given the following code:

```
import java.util.*;

public class RQ4_3 {
  public static void main(String[] args) {
    Locale.setDefault(new Locale("ru"));
    ResourceBundle rb = ResourceBundle.getBundle("resources",new Locale("en"));
    for (String key : new TreeSet<String>(rb.keySet())) {
      System.out.print(key+"="+rb.getString(key)+" ");
    }
  }
}
```

and the file `resources.properties`

```
k1=a
k2=b
```

and the file `resources_en.properties`

```
k1=c
```

and the file `resources_ru.properties`

```
k1=A
k2=B
```

What is the result?

Select the one correct answer.

(a) k1=c k2=B

(b) k1=c k2=b

(c) k1=A k2=B

(d) The program will throw an exception at runtime.

18.4 Core API for Formatting and Parsing of Values

The abstract class Format and its subclasses in the java.text package provide support for formatting and parsing of dates, times, numbers, currencies, and percentages (Figure 18.1).

Figure 18.1   *Core Classes for Formatting in the* java.text *Package*

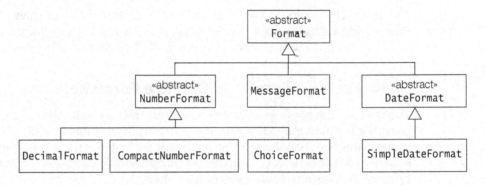

A *formatter* has two primary functions. The first is to create a human-readable text representation of a value, called *formatting*. The second is to create a value from a character sequence, such as a string, containing a text representation of the value, called *parsing*.

In the rest of this chapter, we emphasize the *locale-sensitive* nature of formatting and parsing of different kinds of values.

- *Formatting numbers, currencies, and percentages (p. 1116)*

  The support for formatting numbers, currencies, and percentages is provided by the abstract class java.text.NumberFormat and its subclasses java.text .DecimalFormat and java.text.CompactNumberFormat.

- *Formatting dates and times (p. 1127)*

  The support provided for formatting dates and times by the abstract class java.text.DataFormat and its subclass java.text.SimpleFormat is aimed at objects of the java.util.Date legacy class, and is *not* covered in this book.

  Support for the new Date and Time API is provided by the java.time package, which is covered extensively in Chapter 17, p. 1023. The class java.time.format .DateTimeFormatter provides the support for formatting date and time values created using the new Date and Time API.

- *Formatting messages (p. 1139)*

  The support for formatting *messages* containing numbers, currencies, dates, and times is provided by the concrete class java.text.MessageFormat. The class java.text.ChoiceFormat allows a choice of formatting dependent on numerical values, and is typically used for *conditional formatting* of messages.

  The support provided by the MessageFormat class for date and time values is aimed at objects of the legacy class Date, but there are a number of ways that the

MessageFormat class can be utilized with formatting objects of the new Date and Time API, and they are discussed later (p. 1139).

18.5 Formatting and Parsing Number, Currency, and Percentage Values

The abstract class java.text.NumberFormat and its subclasses java.text.Decimal-Format and java.text.CompactNumberFormat provide methods for locale-sensitive formatting and parsing of *number*, *currency*, and *percentage* values.

Static Factory Methods to Create a Formatter

The abstract class NumberFormat provides static factory methods for creating locale-sensitive formatters for number, currency, and percentage values. However, the locale cannot be changed after the formatter is created. The factory methods return instances of the concrete classes DecimalFormat and CompactNumberFormat for formatting number, currency, and percentage values.

```
static NumberFormat getNumberInstance()
static NumberFormat getNumberInstance(Locale locale)
```
Return a general formatter for numbers—that is, a number formatter.

```
static NumberFormat getCurrencyInstance()
static NumberFormat getCurrencyInstance(Locale locale)
```
Return a formatter for currency values—that is, a currency formatter.

```
static NumberFormat getPercentInstance()
static NumberFormat getPercentInstance(Locale locale)
```
Return a formatter for percentages—that is, a percentage formatter.

```
static NumberFormat getCompactNumberInstance()
static NumberFormat getCompactNumberInstance(Locale locale,
                                   NumberFormat.Style formatStyle)
```
Return a compact number formatter with the default compact format style or a specific compact format style, respectively (p. 1120). For example, the value 2_345_678 can be formatted by a compact number formatter as "2M" with the SHORT compact form style and as "2 million" with the LONG compact form style, respectively, for the US locale.

In all cases, a locale can be specified to localize the formatter.

Formatting Number, Currency, and Percentage Values

A number formatter can be used to format a double, a long value, or an object. The abstract class NumberFormat provides the following concrete methods for this purpose. Depending on the number formatter, the formatting is locale-sensitive, determined by the default or a specific locale.

```
String format(double d)
String format(long l)
```

Formats the specified number and returns the resulting string.

```
String format(Object obj)            // inherited from the Format class.
```

Formats the specified object and returns the resulting string. For example, it can be used to format BigInteger and BigDecimal numbers.

The following code shows how we can create a *number formatter* for the Norwegian locale and one for the US locale, and use them to format numbers according to rules of the locale. The number formatted is a double (1a) or a BigDecimal (1b), giving the same results. Note that the grouping of the digits and the decimal separator used in formatting is according to the locale.

```
double num = 12345.6789;                              // (1a)
// BigDecimal num = new BigDecimal("12345.6789");     // (1b)

Locale locNOR = new Locale("no", "NO");               // Norway
NumberFormat nfNOR = NumberFormat.getNumberInstance(locNOR);
System.out.println(nfNOR.format(num));                // 12 345,679

NumberFormat nfUS = NumberFormat.getNumberInstance(Locale.US);
System.out.println(nfUS.format(num));                 // 12,345.679
```

The following code shows how we can create a *currency* formatter for the Norwegian locale, and use it to format currency values according to this locale. Note the currency symbol and the grouping of the digits, with the amount being rounded to two decimal places. Also note that the delimiter between the currency symbol and the first digit is a *non-breaking space* (nbsp), having the unicode \u00a0; that is, it is not a normal space (\u0020). The grouping of digits is also with a nbsp. Such use of a nbsp is also locale-specific—formatting for the US locale has no nbsp, as can be seen below.

```
NumberFormat cfNOR = NumberFormat.getCurrencyInstance(locNOR);
String formattedCurrStr = cfNOR.format(num);
System.out.println(formattedCurrStr);          // kr 12 345,68 (with 2 nbsp)

NumberFormat cfUS = NumberFormat.getCurrencyInstance(Locale.US);
String formattedCurrStrUS = cfUS.format(num);
System.out.println(formattedCurrStrUS);        // $12,345.68
```

The value 1.0 is equivalent to 100%. A value is converted to a percentage by multiplying it by 100, and by default rounding it to an integer. By default, the result is rounded up only if the decimal part is *equal to or greater than* 0.5 after multiplying by 100. However, both the number of decimal places and the rounding behavior for the percentage value can be changed (p. 1122).

The following code shows how we can create a *percentage* formatter for the Norwegian locale, and use it to format percentage values according to this locale. Also note that the delimiter between the percentage number and the currency symbol is a *non-breaking space*. Again, such use of a nbsp is also locale-specific—formatting percentages for the US locale has no nbsp, as can be seen below. Note the rounding of the percentage values.

```
double rebate = 0.746;
NumberFormat pfNOR = NumberFormat.getPercentInstance(locNOR);
String formattedPStr = pfNOR.format(rebate);
System.out.println(formattedPStr);                    // 75 % (with nbsp)

NumberFormat pfUS = NumberFormat.getPercentInstance(Locale.US);
String formattedPStrUS = pfUS.format(rebate);
System.out.println(formattedPStrUS);                  // 75%

System.out.println(pfUS.format(0.745));               // 74%
```

Accounting Currency Formatting

By default, the minus sign (-) is used as a prefix when formatting negative numbers using a currency formatter returned by the NumberFormat.getCurrencyInstance() method.

```
NumberFormat df0 = NumberFormat.getCurrencyInstance(Locale.US);
System.out.println(df0.format(-9.99));                // -$9.99
```

However, in accountancy, it is a common practice to enclose a negative currency value in parentheses, (). For example, ($9.99) is interpreted as -$9.99. One way to format negative currency values with parentheses for a given locale is to create the locale so that it allows this style for currency formatting. The code below illustrates how this can be achieved for the US locale.

A US locale is created at (1) below that formats negative currency values with parentheses. The Locale.forLanguageTag() method creates a locale from the specified language tag en-US-u-cf-account that consists of several subtags separated by a hyphen:

- en: Represents the English language
- US: Represents the United States
- u: Indicates that a *Unicode locale/language extension* is specified as a *key–value* pair
- cf-account: The key–value pair, where the key cf stands for *currency format*, and the value account means to use parentheses for negative numbers

The language tag en-US-u-cf-standard will result in a US locale that is the same as Locale.US. For further details, kindly consult the Unicode Locale Data Markup Language (LDML).

The currency formatter created at (2) for the locale created at (1) will now use parentheses for negative currency values.

```
Locale loc = Locale.forLanguageTag("en-US-u-cf-account");  // (1)
NumberFormat df = NumberFormat.getCurrencyInstance(loc);   // (2)
System.out.println(df.format(-9.99));                      // ($9.99)
```

Parsing Strings to Number, Currency, and Percentage Values

A *number* formatter can be used to parse strings that contain text representations of *numeric* values. The abstract class NumberFormat provides the following concrete methods for this purpose.

Number parse(String str) throws ParseException

Parses the text in the specified string from the beginning of the string to produce a Number. No leading whitespace is allowed. Any trailing characters after the parsed text are ignored. This method throws the checked java.text.Parse-Exception if unsuccessful.

void setParseIntegerOnly(boolean intOnly)
boolean isParseIntegerOnly()

Set or get the status if this formatter should only parse integers.

The class DecimalFormat specifically provides the following concrete methods to customize the formatter to parse BigDecimal numbers.

void setParseBigDecimal(boolean newValue)
boolean isParseBigDecimal()

Set or get the status if this formatter should parse BigDecimal numbers.

The code calling the parse() method must be prepared to handle a checked Parse-Exception—for brevity, exception handling is omitted in the code below.

The following code shows the Norwegian number formatter from earlier being used to parse strings. At (1), the result is a long value because the dot (.) in the input string is a delimiter and not a legal character according to the number format used in the Norwegian locale. At (2), the result is a double value because the comma (,) in the input string is the decimal separator in the Norwegian locale. Note that the print statement prints the resulting number according to the *default* locale (U.S., in this case). For the US locale, the dot (.) and the comma (,) are interpreted as the decimal separator and the group separator, respectively.

```
System.out.println(nfNOR.parse("9876.598"));    // (1) 9876
System.out.println(nfNOR.parse("9876,598"));    // (2) 9876.598

System.out.println(nfUS.parse("9876.598"));     // (3) 9876.598
System.out.println(nfUs.parse("9876,598"));     // (4) 9876598
```

In order to parse a string to a BigDecimal, we can proceed via a DecimalFormat that is customized to parse a BigDecimal. The overloaded parse() method below returns a Number, which is actually a BigDecimal in this case.

```
DecimalFormat dfUS = (DecimalFormat) nfUS;
dfUS.setParseBigDecimal(true);
BigDecimal bd = (BigDecimal) dfUS.parse("9876,598");
```

The following code demonstrates using a *currency* formatter as a parser. Note that the currency symbol is interpreted according to the locale in the currency formatter.

In the Norwegian locale, the decimal symbol is not a period (.) when parsing numbers; it is a *delimiter* in the input string, as can be seen at (1) below. For some locales, a *non-breaking space* (\u00a0) may be required between the currency symbol and the first digit, as can be seen at (2).

```
System.out.println(cfNOR.parse("kr\u00a09876.59"));            // (1) 9876
System.out.println(cfNOR.parse("kr\u00a09876,59"));            // (2) 9876.59
System.out.println(cfNOR.parse("kr\u00a09 876,59"));           // (3) 9
System.out.println(cfNOR.parse("kr\u00a09\u00a0876,59"));      // (4) 9876.59

System.out.println(cfUS.parse("$9876.59"));                    // (5) 9876.59
```

When parsing percentages, a *nbsp* might be required between the percentage value and the percent sign (%) in the input string, as can be seen at (1) below for the Norwegian locale. For parsing a percentage value according to the US locale, no such consideration is necessary, as can be seen at (2). However, the format of the percentage value is according to the locale used by the formatter, as can be seen at (1) and (2).

```
System.out.println(pfNOR.parse("15,75\u00a0%"));              // (1) 0.1575
System.out.println(pfUS.parse("25.5%"));                      // (2) 0.255
```

Compact Number Formatting

A *compact number formatter* creates a textual representation that represents the *compact form* of a number. This formatter is an instance of the CompactNumberFormat that can be created by calling the getCompactNumberInstance() factory method of the NumberFormat class. For example, the value 1_000_000 can be formatted in a compact form as "1M" or "1 million".

The compact form can be specified by the constants of the enum type NumberFormat.Style, shown in Table 18.6. The compact form has a suffix, depending on the value of the number and the locale. Suffixes for the US locale are shown in Table 18.6. The compact form of numbers below 1000 is without any suffix.

Table 18.6   *Compact Number Styles*

Styles for compact number form	Verbosity	Suffix for the US locale in compact form
NumberFormat.Style.SHORT	Short number format style (default)	T (Trillion), B (Billion), M (Million), K (Thousand) Examples: 2T, 2.5M, 1.5K
NumberFormat.Style.LONG	Long number format style	trillion, billion, million, thousand Examples: 2 trillion, 2.5 million, 1.5 thousand

The code below creates two compact number formatters for the US locale that use the SHORT and the LONG compact number styles, respectively, to format numbers to their compact form.

```
NumberFormat shortCompactFormat = NumberFormat.getCompactNumberInstance(
    Locale.US, NumberFormat.Style.SHORT)
NumberFormat longCompactFormat = NumberFormat.getCompactNumberInstance(
    Locale.US, NumberFormat.Style.LONG);
```

The compact number formatters are used on different numerical values to create their compact form, as shown in Table 18.7.

```
System.out.println(shortCompactFormat.format(9_400_000));    // 9M
System.out.println(longCompactFormat.format(9_400_000));     // 9 million
```

The second row in Table 18.7 shows the compact form generated after the number of maximum fraction digits is set to 2 (p. 1122):

```
shortCompactFormat.setMaximumFractionDigits(2);
longCompactFormat.setMaximumFractionDigits(2);
```

Note the rounding that takes place depending on the value of the number. By default, RoundingMode.HALF_EVEN is used (see Table 18.9).

Table 18.7 *Formatting Numbers to Compact Form*

Number n	Compact form returned by shortCompactFormatter.format(n) method	Compact form returned by longCompactFormatter.format(n) method
9_400_000 9_500_000 12_500 12_510 999	"9M" "10M" "12K" "13K" "999"	"9 million" "10 million" "12 thousand" "13 thousand" "999"
9_400_000 9_500_000 12_500 12_510 999	*(Max fraction digits = 2)* "9.4M" "9.5M" "12.5K" "12.51K" "999"	*(Max fraction digits = 2)* "9.4 million" "9.5 million" "12.5 thousand" "12.51 thousand" "999"

Compact Number Parsing

The parse() method of the compact number formatter can be used to parse a string that contains a compact form to a numerical value.

```
try {
  System.out.println(shortCompactFormat.parse("9M"));          // 9000000
  System.out.println(longCompactFormat.parse("9 million"));    // 9000000
} catch (ParseException pe) {
  System.out.println(pe);
}
```

The compact number formatters above are used to parse different compact forms to numerical values, as shown in Table 18.8. Note that parsing requires that the compact form ends in an appropriate suffix; otherwise, the suffix is ignored, as we can see in Table 18.8.

Table 18.8 *Parsing Compact Form to Numbers*

Compact form string s	Number returned by `shortCompactFormatter.parse(s)` method	Number returned by `longCompactFormatter.parse(s)` method
"9M"	9000000	9
"9.5M"	9500000	9.5
"2K"	2000	2
"1.5K"	1500	1.5
"999"	999	999
"9 million"	9	9000000
"9.5 million"	9.5	9500000
"2 thousand"	2	2000
"1.5 thousand"	1.5	1500

Specifying the Number of Digits

The following methods of the `NumberFormat` abstract class and its subclass `Decimal-Format` allow formatting of numbers to be further refined by setting the number of digits to be allowed in the integral and the decimal part of a number. This also applies for `BigDecimal` numbers. However, a concrete number formatter can enforce certain limitations on these bounds. In addition, a rounding mode can be set as explained below.

```
void setMinimumIntegerDigits(int n)
int  getMinimumIntegerDigits()

void setMaximumIntegerDigits(int n)
int  getMaximumIntegerDigits()

void setMinimumFractionDigits(int n)
int  getMinimumFractionDigits()

void setMaximumFractionDigits(int n)
int  getMaximumFractionDigits()
```

Set or get the minimum or maximum number of digits to be allowed in the integral or decimal part of a number.

```
void setRoundingMode(RoundingMode roundingMode)
```

Sets the *rounding mode* used in this number formatter—that is, how the resulting value is rounded by the formatter. The enum type `java.math.RoundingMode` defines constants for such modes (see Table 18.9).

Table 18.9 *Selected Rounding Modes*

Enum type java.math. RoundingMode constants	Description
CEILING	Rounds toward *positive infinity.* 1.1 -> 2 (same as UP) -1.8 -> -1 (same as DOWN)
FLOOR	Rounds toward *negative infinity.* 1.8 -> 1 (same as DOWN) -1.1 -> -2 (same as UP)
UP	Rounds *away from zero.* Never *decreases* the *magnitude* of the calculated value. 1.1 -> 2 -1.1 -> -2
DOWN	Rounds *toward zero.* Never *increases* the *magnitude* of the calculated value. 1.8 -> 1 -1.8 -> -1
HALF_UP	Rounds toward the nearest neighboring value, unless both neighboring values are equidistant, in which case it rounds *up.* This is the same as *normal rounding.* 1.5 -> 2 (same as UP, if discarded fraction is >= 0.5) 1.4 -> 1 (same as DOWN, if discarded fraction is < 0.5) -1.4 -> -1 (same as DOWN, if discarded fraction is < 0.5) -1.5 -> -2 (same as UP, if discarded fraction is >= 0.5)
HALF_DOWN	Rounds toward the nearest neighboring value, unless both neighboring values are equidistant, in which case it rounds *down.* 1.6 -> 2 (same as UP, if discarded fraction is > 0.5) 1.5 -> 1 (same as DOWN, if discarded fraction is <= 0.5) -1.5 -> -1 (same as DOWN, if discarded fraction is <= 0.5) -1.6 -> -2 (same as UP, if discarded fraction is > 0.5)
HALF_EVEN	Rounds toward the nearest neighboring value, unless both neighboring values are equidistant, in which case it rounds toward the even neighbor. This rounding policy is used in floating-point arithmetic in Java. 2.5 -> 2 (same as HALF_DOWN, if digit left of discarded fraction is even) 1.5 -> 2 (same as HALF_UP, if digit left of discarded fraction is odd) -1.5 -> -2 (same as HALF_UP, if digit left of discarded fraction is odd) -2.5 -> -2 (same as HALF_DOWN, if digit left of discarded fraction is even)

Example 18.5 demonstrates the rounding modes defined by the enum type java.math.RoundingMode. The examples in Table 18.9 are computed in Example 18.5. A number format is created at (1) for the US locale. The maximum number of digits in the fraction part is set to 0 at (2); that is, the floating-point value will be rounded to an integer before formatting.

The method roundIt() at (3) does the rounding and the formatting when passed a formatter, the maximum number of digits (0) required in the fraction part, the rounding mode, and the two values to round and format. The method sets the maximum number of digits required in the fraction part and the rounding mode at (4) and (5), respectively, in the formatter. The formatting of the values is done by calling the format() method at (6) and (7). We encourage checking the output against the rules for rounding for each mode shown in Table 18.9.

Example 18.5 *Rounding Modes*

```java
import java.math.RoundingMode;
import java.text.NumberFormat;
import java.text.ParseException;
import java.util.Locale;

public class Rounding {

    public static void main(String[] args) {
        System.out.println(" Rounding:    v1          v2");
        NumberFormat nfmtUS = NumberFormat.getNumberInstance(Locale.US);        // (1)
        int maxFractionDigits = 0;                                             // (2)
        roundIt(nfmtUS, maxFractionDigits, RoundingMode.CEILING,   1.1, -1.8);
        roundIt(nfmtUS, maxFractionDigits, RoundingMode.FLOOR,     1.8, -1.1);
        roundIt(nfmtUS, maxFractionDigits, RoundingMode.UP,        1.1, -1.1);
        roundIt(nfmtUS, maxFractionDigits, RoundingMode.DOWN,      1.8, -1.8);
        roundIt(nfmtUS, maxFractionDigits, RoundingMode.HALF_UP,   1.5, 1.4);
        roundIt(nfmtUS, maxFractionDigits, RoundingMode.HALF_UP,   -1.4, -1.5);
        roundIt(nfmtUS, maxFractionDigits, RoundingMode.HALF_DOWN, 1.6, 1.5);
        roundIt(nfmtUS, maxFractionDigits, RoundingMode.HALF_DOWN, -1.5, -1.6);
        roundIt(nfmtUS, maxFractionDigits, RoundingMode.HALF_EVEN, 2.5, 1.5);
        roundIt(nfmtUS, maxFractionDigits, RoundingMode.HALF_EVEN, -1.5, -2.5);
    }

    static void roundIt(NumberFormat nf, int maxFractionDigits, RoundingMode rMode,
                        double v1, double v2) {                     // (3)
        nf.setMaximumFractionDigits(maxFractionDigits);            // (4)
        nf.setRoundingMode(rMode);                                 // (5)
        System.out.printf("%9s: ", rMode);
        System.out.printf("%5s -> %2s ", v1, nf.format(v1));       // (6)
        System.out.printf("%5s -> %2s%n", v2, nf.format(v2));      // (7)
    }
}
```

Output from the program:

```
    Rounding:    v1          v2
    CEILING:   1.1 ->  2  -1.8 -> -1
      FLOOR:   1.8 ->  1  -1.1 -> -2
         UP:   1.1 ->  2  -1.1 -> -2
       DOWN:   1.8 ->  1  -1.8 -> -1
    HALF_UP:   1.5 ->  2   1.4 ->  1
    HALF_UP:  -1.4 -> -1  -1.5 -> -2
  HALF_DOWN:   1.6 ->  2   1.5 ->  1
  HALF_DOWN:  -1.5 -> -1  -1.6 -> -2
  HALF_EVEN:   2.5 ->  2   1.5 ->  2
  HALF_EVEN:  -1.5 -> -2  -2.5 -> -2
```

Customizing Decimal Number Formatting

The java.text.DecimalFormat class formats and parses numbers (including BigDecimal) according to a *string pattern*, specified using special *pattern symbols* (Table 18.10) and taking into account any locale considerations. It can format numbers as integers (1234), fixed-point notation (3.14), scientific notation (2.99792458E8), percentages (60%), and currency amounts ($64.00).

Although the DecimalFormat class defines constructors, the Java API recommends using the factory methods of its abstract superclass NumberFormat to create an instance of this class.

```
NumberFormat df = NumberFormat.getNumberInstance(Locale.US);
if (nf intanceof DecimalFormat) {
  DecimalFormat df = (DecimalFormat) nf;
  df.applyPattern(pattern);              // Supply the pattern.
  String output = df.format(number);     // Format the number.
}
```

The idiom is to create a DecimalFormat object as shown above, localized if necessary, and customizing it with a pattern using the method shown below. The overloaded format() methods inherited by the DecimalFormat class from its superclass Number-Format can now be called to format a number. The pattern can also be changed on the fly.

void applyPattern(String pattern)

Applies the given pattern to this DecimalFormat object.

Table 18.10 *Selected Number Format Pattern Symbols for the United States*

Pattern symbol	Purpose
0 (Zero)	Placeholder for a digit. Can result in leading and/or trailing zeroes. Can result in rounding up of the fractional part of a number.
# (Hash sign)	Placeholder for a digit. Leading and/or trailing zeroes may be absent. Can result in rounding up of the fractional part of a number.
. (Dot)	Placeholder for *decimal separator*. If omitted, a floating-point number is rounded up to the nearest integer. Can be different for other countries. For example, in Germany, the decimal separator is the comma (,).
, (Comma)	Placeholder for *grouping separator* (a.k.a. *thousands separator*). Can be different for other countries. For example, in Germany, the grouping separator is the period (.).

Example 18.6 shows formatting of a number, either a double at (1a) or a BigDecimal at (1b), using different patterns at (2) and different locales at (3). Decimal formatters are created at (4), as explained above. A decimal formatter is customized with

a pattern at (5) and the number is formatted at (6). In particular, note how the decimal and group separators are localized for each locale. The currency amounts are also formatted according to the particulars of each locale, and not according to the currency symbol that is specified in the currency patterns.

Example 18.6 *Using the* DecimalFormat *class*

```java
import java.math.BigDecimal;
import java.text.DecimalFormat;
import java.text.NumberFormat;
import java.util.ArrayList;
import java.util.List;
import java.util.Locale;

public class FormattingDecimalNumbers {

  public static void main(String[] args) {
    // The number to format.
    double number = 1234.567;                                    // (1a)
//  BigDecimal number = new BigDecimal("1234.567");              // (1b)

    // Formats to use:
    String[] patterns = {                                        // (2)
      "#",
      "###,###.##",
      "###.##",
      "00000.00",
      "BTC ###,###.##",                                // BTC: Bitcoin
    };

    // Locales to consider:
    Locale[] locales = { Locale.US, Locale.GERMANY };            // (3)

    // Create localized DecimalFormats:                             (4)
    List<DecimalFormat> dfs = new ArrayList<>(locales.length);
    for (int i = 0; i < locales.length; i++) {
      NumberFormat nf = NumberFormat.getNumberInstance(locales[i]);
      if (nf instanceof DecimalFormat) {
        dfs.add((DecimalFormat) nf);
      }
    }

    // Write the header:
    System.out.printf("%15s", "Patterns");
    for (Locale locale : locales) {
      System.out.printf("%15s", locale);
    }
    System.out.println();

    // Do formatting and print results:
    for (String pattern : patterns) {
      System.out.printf("%15s", pattern);
      for (DecimalFormat df : dfs) {
        df.applyPattern(pattern);                                // (5)
```

```
            String output = df.format(number);                    // (6)
            System.out.printf("%15s", output);
        }
        System.out.println();
    }
  }
}
```

Output from the program:

```
    Patterns         en_US         de_DE
           #          1235          1235
  ###,###.##      1,234.57      1.234,57
     ###.##       1234.57       1234,57
    00000.00      01234.57      01234,57
BTC ###,###.##  BTC 1,234.57  BTC 1.234,57
```

18.6 Formatting and Parsing Date and Time

The class java.time.format.DateTimeFormatter provides the support for locale-sensitive formatting and parsing of *date* and *time* values.

In this section we take a closer look at formatting temporal objects and parsing character sequences for temporal objects. In particular, we consider the following formatters, which provide increasing flexibility in customizing formatting and parsing:

- *Default formatters* are implicitly used by such methods as the toString() method of the temporal classes.
- *Predefined formatters* are ready-made formatters provided as constants by the java.time.format.DateTimeFormatter class, such as those that adhere to the ISO standard (Table 18.11, p. 1130).
- *Style-based formatters* are formatters that use the format styles defined by the constants of the java.time.format.FormatStyle enum type (Table 18.12, p. 1132). These formatters are created by the static factory methods ofLocalized*Type*() of the DateTimeFormatter class, where *Type* is either Time, Date, or DateTime (Table 18.13, p. 1132).
- *Pattern-based formatters* use customized format styles defined by *pattern letters* (Table 18.15, p. 1135). These formatters are created by the static factory method ofPattern() of the DateTimeFormatter class.

The DateTimeFormatter class provides static factory methods for obtaining a formatter. The idiom for using a formatter is to obtain a formatter first, localize it if necessary, and then pass it to the methods responsible for formatting and parsing temporal objects. Each of the temporal classes LocalTime, LocalDate, LocalDateTime, and ZonedDateTime provides the following methods: an instance method format() and a static method parse(). These two methods do the formatting and the parsing according to the rules of the formatter that is passed as an argument, respectively.

Analogous methods for formatting and parsing temporal objects passed as an arguments are also provided by the DateTimeFormatter class (see below). For example, the following code lines give the same result string, where date and df refer to a LocalDate object and a DateTimeFormatter object for formatting dates, respectively:

```
String resultStr1 = date.format(df);
String resultStr2 = df.format(date);
boolean eqStr = resultStr1.equals(resultStr2);      // true
```

From the method headers of the format() and the parse() methods of the temporal classes, we can see that these methods will readily compile with *any* DateTimeFormatter. The validity of the formatter for a given temporal object is resolved at runtime, resulting in a resounding exception if it is not valid.

```
// Defined by LocalTime, LocalDate, LocalDateTime, and ZonedDateTime
String format(DateTimeFormatter formatter)
```

Formats this temporal object using the specified formatter, and returns the resulting string. Each temporal class provides this method. The temporal object is formatted according to the rules of the formatter. The method throws a java.time.DateTimeException if formatting is not successful.

```
static TemporalType parse(CharSequence text)
static TemporalType parse(CharSequence text, DateTimeFormatter formatter)
```

Each temporal class provides these two static methods, where *TemporalType* can be any of the temporal classes LocalTime, LocalDate, LocalDateTime, or ZonedDateTime.

The first method returns an instance of the *TemporalType* from a character sequence, using the default parsing rules for the *TemporalType*.

The second method obtains an instance of the *TemporalType* from a character sequence using the specified formatter.

Both methods return an object of a specific temporal class, and both throw a java.time.format.DateTimeParseException if parsing is not successful.

Formatters supplied by the DateTimeFormatter class are immutable and thread-safe. All formatters created using static methods provided by the DateTimeFormatter class can be localized by the localizedBy() method in this class. The DateTimeFormatter class provides methods that can be used to format and parse temporal objects.

```
// Defined by DateTimeFormatter
DateTimeFormatter localizedBy(Locale locale)
```

Returns a copy of this formatter that will use the specified locale (§18.1, p. 1096). Although the formatters in the examples presented in this section use the default locale (the US locale in this case), we encourage the reader to experiment with changing the locale of a formatter with this method in the examples.

```
String format(TemporalAccessor temporal)
```

Formats a temporal object using this formatter. The main temporal classes implement the TemporalAccessor interface.

This method throws an unchecked java.time.DateTimeException if an error occurs during formatting.

```
TemporalAccessor parse(CharSequence text)
```

This method fully parses the text to produce a temporal object. It throws an unchecked java.time.DateTimeException if an error occurs during parsing.

```
DateTimeFormatter withZone(ZoneId zone)
```

Returns a copy of this formatter with a new override zone—that is, a formatter with similar state to this formatter but with the override zone set.

Default Formatters for Date and Time Values

Default formatters rely on the toString() method of the individual temporal classes for creating a text representation of a temporal object. The default formatter used by the toString() method applies the formatting rules defined by the ISO standard.

In the following code, the result of formatting a LocalTime object is shown at (1):

```
LocalTime time = LocalTime.of(12, 30, 15, 99);
String strTime = time.toString();              // (1) 12:30:15.000000099
LocalTime parsedTime = LocalTime.parse(strTime); // (2)
System.out.println(time.toString().equals(parsedTime.toString())); // true
```

Each temporal class provides a static method parse(CharSequence text) that parses a character sequence using a default formatter that complies with the ISO standard. In the preceding code, the text representation created at (1) is parsed at (2) to obtain a new LocalTime object. Not surprisingly, the text representations of the two LocalTime objects referred to by the references time and parsedTime are equal.

The line of code below shows that the argument string passed to the parse() method is not in accordance with the ISO standard, resulting in a runtime exception:

```
LocalTime badTime = LocalTime.parse("12.30.15");  // DateTimeParseException
```

The examples in this section make heavy use of the toString() method to format temporal objects according to the ISO standard.

Predefined Formatters for Date and Time Values

The DateTimeFormatter class provides a myriad of predefined formatters for temporal objects, the majority of which comply with the ISO standard. Table 18.11 shows selected ISO-based predefined formatters from this class. We have also indicated in the last column which temporal classes a formatter can be used with for formatting and parsing.

For example, the row for the ISO_LOCAL_DATE formatter in Table 18.11 indicates that this formatter can be used for formatting a LocalDate and for formatting the date part of a LocalDateTime or a ZonedDateTime. It can parse the text representation of a LocalDate. In contrast, the row for the ISO_LOCAL_DATE_TIME formatter indicates that this formatter can be used for formatting a LocalDateTime and for formatting the date-time part of a ZonedDateTime. It can parse the text representation of a Local-DateTime. In addition, the text representation of a LocalDateTime can be parsed by this formatter to a LocalTime or a LocalDate by the parse(text, formatter) method of the appropriate class.

Table 18.11 *Selected ISO-Based Predefined Formatters for Date and Time*

DateTimeFormatter	Examples	Formatting	Parsing
ISO_LOCAL_TIME	12:30:15	LocalTime *Time part of:* LocalDateTime ZonedDateTime	LocalTime
BASIC_ISO_DATE	20210428	LocalDate *Date part of:* LocalDateTime ZonedDateTime	LocalDate
ISO_LOCAL_DATE	2021-04-28	LocalDate *Date part of:* LocalDateTime ZonedDateTime	LocalDate
ISO_LOCAL_DATE_TIME	2021-04-28T12:30:15	LocalDateTime *Date-time part of:* ZonedDateTime	LocalTime LocalDate LocalDateTime
ISO_ZONED_DATE_TIME	2021-04-28T12:30:15+01:00 [Europe/Paris]	ZonedDateTime	LocalTime LocalDate LocalDateTime ZonedDateTime
ISO_INSTANT	2021-04-28T12:30:15.000000500Z	Instant	Instant

An example of using an ISO-based predefined formatter is given next. Note that the formatter obtained at (1) is a formatter for date fields. It can be used only with temporal objects that have date fields—in other words, the LocalDate, LocalDate-Time, and ZonedDateTime classes. This formatter is passed at (2) to the format() method, to create a text representation of a date. The resulting string is parsed at (3) by the parse() method that uses the same formatter. The resulting date is also formatted using the same formatter at (4). It is hardly surprising that the text representations of both dates are equal.

```
DateTimeFormatter df = DateTimeFormatter.ISO_LOCAL_DATE;      // (1)
LocalDate date = LocalDate.of(1935, 1, 8);
String strDate = date.format(df);                            // (2) 1935-01-08
LocalDate parsedDate = LocalDate.parse(strDate, df);         // (3)
System.out.println(strDate + "|" +
                   parsedDate.format(df));                   // (4) 1935-01-08|1935-01-08
```

As this code shows, a formatter can be reused, both for formatting and for parsing. The code at (4) in the code below applies the formatter from (1) in the preceding code snippet to format a LocalDateTime object. It should not come as a surprise that the resulting text representation of the LocalDateTime object pertains to only date fields in the temporal object; the time fields of the LocalDateTime object are ignored. Parsing this text representation back with the same formatter at (5) will yield only a LocalDate object.

```
LocalDateTime dateTime = LocalDateTime.of(1935, 1, 8, 12, 45);
String strDate2 = dateTime.format(df);                    // (4) 1935-01-08
LocalDate parsedDate2 = LocalDate.parse(strDate2, df);    // (5) LocalDate
```

To summarize, the DateTimeFormatter.ISO_LOCAL_DATE can be used to format and parse a LocalDate, but can only format the date part of a LocalDateTime object (or a ZonedDateTime object).

Using this date formatter with a LocalTime object is courting disaster, as shown by the following code. Formatting with this formatter results in an unchecked java.time.temporal.UnsupportedTemporalTypeException, and parsing results in an unchecked java.time.format.DateTimeParseException.

```
String timeStr2 = LocalTime.NOON.format(df);   // UnsupportedTemporalTypeException
LocalTime time2 = LocalTime.parse("12:00", df);// DateTimeParseException
```

The DateTimeFormatter.ISO_INSTANT predefined formatter shown in Table 18.11 is implicitly used by the parse(text) and toString() methods of the Instant class.

Style-Based Formatters for Date and Time Values

For more flexible formatters than the predefined ISO-based formatters, the Date-TimeFormatter class provides the static factory methods ofLocalized*Type*(), where *Type* is either Time, Date, or DateTime. These methods create formatters that use a specific format style. However, the format style cannot be changed after the formatter is created. Format styles are defined by the enum type java.time.format.Format-Style, and are shown in Table 18.12. The styles define format patterns that vary in their degree of verbosity.

The format style in a style-based formatter can be made locale-specific by setting the desired locale in the formatter using the localizedBy() method of the DateTime-Formatter class (p. 1128).

```
static DateTimeFormatter ofLocalizedTime(FormatStyle timeStyle)
static DateTimeFormatter ofLocalizedDate(FormatStyle dateStyle)
static DateTimeFormatter ofLocalizedDateTime(FormatStyle dateTimeStyle)
static DateTimeFormatter ofLocalizedDateTime(FormatStyle dateStyle,
                                             FormatStylse timeStyle)
```

These static factory methods of the DateTimeFormatter class create a formatter that will format a time, a date, or a date-time, respectively, using the specified format style. The formatter can also be used to parse a character sequence for a time, a date, or a date-time, respectively.

Table 18.12   *Format Styles for Date and Time*

Styles for date/time	Verbosity	Example formatting a date (default locale: United States)
FormatStyle.SHORT	Short-style pattern	1/11/14
FormatStyle.MEDIUM	Medium-style pattern	Jan 11, 2014
FormatStyle.LONG	Long-style pattern	January 11, 2014
FormatStyle.FULL	Full-style pattern	Saturday, January 11, 2014

In the discussion below, we will make use of the following temporal objects.

```
LocalTime time = LocalTime.of(14, 15, 30);              // 14:15:30
LocalDate date = LocalDate.of(2021, 12, 1);             // 2021-12-01
LocalDateTime dateTime = LocalDateTime.of(date, time);  // 2021-12-01T14:15:30
// 2021-12-01T14:15:30-06:00[US/Central]
ZonedDateTime zonedDateTime = ZonedDateTime.of(dateTime, ZoneId.of("US/Central"));
```

Table 18.13 shows which temporal classes can be formatted by a combination of a format style from Table 18.12 and an ofLocalized*Type*() method of the DateTimeFormatter class, where *Type* is either Time, Date, or DateTime. For example, in Table 18.13 we can see that the method call DateTimeFormatter.ofLocalizedDate(FormatStyle.SHORT) will return a formatter that can be used to format instances of the LocalDate class, but will only format the date part of a LocalDateTime or a ZonedDateTime instance, as can be seen in the code below. This particular formatter requires date fields in the temporal object, and instances of these three temporal classes fit the bill.

```
DateTimeFormatter dfs = DateTimeFormatter.ofLocalizedDate(FormatStyle.SHORT);
String str1 = date.format(dfs);           // 12/1/21
String str2 = dateTime.format(dfs);       // Date part: 12/1/21
String str3 = zonedDateTime.format(dfs);  // Date part: 12/1/21
```

Table 18.13   *Using Style-Based Formatters*

Format-Style	Using formatters created by factory methods of the DateTimeFormatter class: *temporalReference*.format(formatter)		
	ofLocalizedTime(style)	ofLocalizedDate(style)	ofLocalizedDateTime(style)
SHORT MEDIUM	LocalTime *Time part of:* LocalDateTime ZonedDateTime	LocalDate *Date part of:* LocalDateTime ZonedDateTime	LocalDateTime *Date-time part of:* ZonedDateTime
LONG FULL	*Time part of:* ZonedDateTime	LocalDate *Date part of:* LocalDateTime ZonedDateTime	ZonedDateTime

Similarly, the method call DateTimeFormatter.ofLocalizedTime(FormatStyle.LONG) will return a formatter that will only format temporal objects that have a time part *and* are compatible with the rules of FormatStyle.LONG. Only instances of the Zoned-DateTime class fit the bill. The code below shows that we can format the time part of a ZonedDateTime instance with this formatter.

```
DateTimeFormatter tff = DateTimeFormatter.ofLocalizedTime(FormatStyle.FULL);
String str4 = zonedDateTime.format(tff);  // Time part:
                                          //   2:15:30 PM Central Standard Time
String str5 = time.format(tff);           // java.time.DateTimeException
String str6 = date.format(tff);           // java.time.temporal.
                                          //      UnsupportedTemporalTypeException
String str7 = dateTime.format(tff);       // java.time.DateTimeException
```

In summary, a style-based formatter will only format a temporal object (or its constituent parts) if the temporal object has the temporal parts required by the formatter *and* is compatible with the rules of the format style of the formatter.

Table 18.14 shows how the style-based formatters can be used as parsers. As in Table 18.13, this table also shows the combination of a format style from Table 18.12 and an ofLocalized*Type*() method of the DateTimeFormatter class, where *Type* is either Time, Date, or DateTime. From the table, we can read which temporal objects can be parsed from a character sequence that is compatible with the rules of a formatter for a given combination of the format style and a specific factory method.

Table 18.14 *Using Style-Based Parsers*

| Format-Style | Using parsers created by factory methods of the DateTimeFormatter class: *TemporalClass*.parse(characterSequence,formatter) | | |
	ofLocalizedTime(style)	ofLocalizedDate(style)	ofLocalizedDateTime(style)
SHORT MEDIUM	LocalTime	LocalDate	LocalTime LocalDate LocalDateTime
LONG FULL	LocalTime	LocalDate	LocalTime LocalDate LocalDateTime ZonedDateTime

For any format style, the two methods ofLocalizedTime() and ofLocalizedDate() return formatters that can be used to parse a compatible character sequence to a LocalTime or a LocalDate instance, respectively.

In the code that follows, the date formatter created at (1) is used at (3) to parse the input string at (2) to create a LocalDate object.

```
DateTimeFormatter df = DateTimeFormatter.ofLocalizedDate(FormatStyle.SHORT);// (1)
String inputStr = "2/29/21";                         // (2) en_US date, SHORT style
LocalDate parsedDate = LocalDate.parse(inputStr, df);  // (3)
System.out.println(parsedDate);                      // (4) 2021-02-28
```

In the above code, the input string "2/29/21" is specified in the short style of the default locale (which in our case is the US locale). The input string is parsed by the date formatter (using the SHORT format style) to create a new LocalDate object.

Although the value 29 is invalid for the number of days in February for the year 2021, the output shows that it was adjusted correctly. The contents of the input string (in this case, "2/29/21") must be compatible with the rules of the format style in the date formatter (in this case, FormatStyle.SHORT). If this is not the case, a DateTimeParse-Exception is thrown. Note that in the print statement at (4), the LocalDate object from the parsing is converted to a string by the LocalDate.toString() method using the implicit ISO-based formatter.

A formatter returned by the ofLocalizedDateTime() method can parse a character sequence to instances of different temporal classes, as shown in the rightmost column of Table 18.14. This is illustrated by the code below. Such a formatter is created at (1) and localized to the locale for France. It is first used to format a zoned date-time object at (2) to obtain a character string that we can parse with the formatter. At (3), (4), (5), and (6), this sequence is parsed to obtain a LocalTime, a Local-Date, a LocalDateTime, and a ZonedDateTime, respectively, as these temporal objects can be constructed from the format of the character string representing a zoned date-time.

```
DateTimeFormatter dtff
    = DateTimeFormatter.ofLocalizedDateTime(FormatStyle.FULL)
                    .localizedBy(Locale.FRANCE);            // (1)

// "mercredi 1 décembre 2021 à 14:15:30 heure normale du centre nord-américain"
String charSeq = zonedDateTime.format(dtff);               // (2)
LocalTime pTime = LocalTime.parse(charSeq, dtff);          // (3) 14:15:30
LocalDate pDate = LocalDate.parse(charSeq, dtff);          // (4) 2021-12-01

// 2021-12-01T14:15:30
LocalDateTime pDateTime = LocalDateTime.parse(charSeq, dtff);        // (5)

// 2021-12-01T14:15:30-06:00[America/Chicago]
ZonedDateTime pZonedDateTime = ZonedDateTime.parse(charSeq, dtff);   // (6)
```

In summary, a character sequence can be parsed to a temporal object by a style-based formatter if the character sequence is in the format required by the formatter to create the temporal object.

Pattern-Based Formatters for Date and Time Values

For more fine-grained formatting and parsing capabilities for temporal objects, we can use the ofPattern() method of the DateTimeFormatter class. This method creates immutable formatters that interpret temporal objects according to a string pattern that is defined using the *pattern letters* shown in Table 18.15.

```
static DateTimeFormatter ofPattern(String pattern)
```
This static method creates a formatter using the specified pattern. The set of temporal objects it can be used with depends on the pattern letters used in the specification of the pattern. The letter pattern defines the rules used by the formatter. The method throws an IllegalArgumentException if the pattern is invalid.

Table 18.15 provides an overview of selected pattern letters. All letters are reserved when used in a letter pattern. A sequence of characters can be escaped by enclosing it in single quotes (e.g., "EEEE 'at' HH:mm"). Non-letter characters in the string are interpreted verbatim and need not be escaped using single quotes (e.g., "uuuu.MM.dd @ HH:mm:ss"). The number of times a pattern letter is repeated can have a bearing on the interpretation of the value of the corresponding date or time field. The uppercase letter M (Month of the year) should not be confused with the lowercase letter m (minutes in the hour).

Table 18.15 *Selected Date/Time Pattern Letters*

Date or time component	Pattern letter	Examples
Year (2: two rightmost digits) Proleptic year: use u Year of era (AD/BC): use y	u uu uuu uuuu uuuuu	2021; -2000 (2001 BC) 15; 0 (i.e., 1 BC); -1 (i.e., 2 BC) 2021; -2021 (i.e., 2022 BC) 02021 (padding)
Month in year (1–2: number) (3: abbreviated text form) (4: full text form)	M MM MMM MMMM	8 08 Aug August
Day in month	d dd	6 06
Day name in week (1–3: abbreviated text form) (4: full text form)	E EE EEE EEEE	Tue Tue Tue Tuesday
Hour in day (0–23)	H HH	9 09
Hour in am/pm (1–12) (does not include the AM/PM marker, but required for parsing)	h hh	7 07
Minute in hour (0–59)	m mm	6 06
Second in minute (0–59)	s ss	2 02
Fraction of a second (S)	SSS SSSSSS SSSSSSSSS	123 123456 123456789
Era designator (AD/BC)	G	AD
Time zone name (1 to 4)	z zzzz	CST Central Standard Time
Time zone offset (1 to 5)	Z ZZZZ ZZZZZ	-0600 GMT-06:00 -06:00
Time zone ID (must be two)	VV	US/Central

Table 18.15   *Selected Date/Time Pattern Letters (Continued)*

Date or time component	Pattern letter	Examples
AM/PM marker	a	AM
Period-of-day (used with temporal values having time units)	B	at night in the morning noon in the afternoon in the evening
Escape for text	'	'T' prints as T
Single quote	' '	'

A letter pattern can be used to format a temporal object if the temporal object has the temporal fields required by the pattern. The pattern "'Hour': HH" can be used to format the hour part of any LocalTime object or a LocalDateTime object, but not a LocalDate.

A letter pattern can be used to parse a string if the string matches the pattern *and* the letter pattern specifies the mandatory parts needed to construct a temporal object. The pattern "MM/dd/uuuu" can be used to parse the string "08/13/2009" to obtain a LocalDate object, but not a LocalDateTime object. The latter requires the time part as well.

Example 18.7 demonstrates both formatting temporal objects and parsing character sequences for temporal objects using letter patterns. The main() method at (1) calls four methods to format and parse different temporal objects. The formatting of the temporal object can be localized by specifying the desired locale in the main() method.

- The method usingTimePattern() at (2) demonstrates using a letter pattern for the time part to both format a LocalTime and parse a text representation of a LocalTime, respectively. The same pattern is used to format only the time part of a Local-DateTime and a ZonedDateTime, respectively.

- The method usingDatePattern() at (3) demonstrates using a letter pattern for the date part to both format a LocalDate and parse a text representation of a Local-Date, respectively. The same pattern is used to format only the date part of a LocalDateTime and a ZonedDateTime, respectively.

- The method usingDateTimePattern() at (4) demonstrates using a letter pattern for the date and time parts to both format a LocalDateTime and parse a text representation of a LocalDateTime, respectively. The same pattern is also used to parse the text representation of a LocalDateTime to obtain a LocalDate and a LocalTime, respectively.

- The method usingZonedDateTimePattern() at (5) demonstrates using a letter pattern for the date, time, and zone parts to both format a ZonedDateTime and parse a text representation of a ZonedDateTime, respectively. The same pattern is also used to parse the text representation of a ZonedDateTime to obtain a LocalDate-Time, a LocalDate, and a LocalTime, respectively.

The usage of letter patterns with the ofPattern() method in Example 18.7 is analogous to the usage of style-based formatters provided by the ofLocalized*Type*() methods (Table 18.13, p. 1132). The main difference is that letter patterns provide great flexibility in creating customized format styles.

Example 18.7 *Formatting and Parsing with Letter Patterns*

```java
import java.time.*;
import java.time.format.*;
import java.util.Locale;

public class FormattingParsingWithPatterns {

  /** Temporals */
  private static LocalTime time = LocalTime.of(12, 30, 15, 99);
  private static LocalDate date = LocalDate.of(2021, 4, 28);
  private static LocalDateTime dateTime = LocalDateTime.of(date, time);
  private static ZoneId zID = ZoneId.of("US/Central");
  private static ZonedDateTime zonedDateTime = ZonedDateTime.of(dateTime, zID);

  public static void main(String[] args) {                              // (1)
    Locale locale = Locale.US;
    usingTimePattern(locale);
    usingDatePattern(locale);
    usingDateTimePattern(locale);
    usingZonedDateTimePattern(locale);
  }

  /** Pattern with time part. */
  public static void usingTimePattern(Locale locale) {                  // (2)
    String timePattern = "HH::mm::ss:SSS";
    DateTimeFormatter timeFormatter = DateTimeFormatter.ofPattern(timePattern)
                                              .localizedBy(locale);
    String strTime = time.format(timeFormatter);
    LocalTime parsedTime = LocalTime.parse(strTime, timeFormatter);
    String strTime2 = dateTime.format(timeFormatter);
    String strTime3 = zonedDateTime.format(timeFormatter);

    System.out.printf("Time pattern: %s%n", timePattern);
    System.out.printf("LocalTime (formatted): %s%n", strTime);
    System.out.printf("LocalTime (parsed):    %s%n", parsedTime);
    System.out.printf("LocalDateTime (formatted time part): %s%n", strTime2);
    System.out.printf("ZonedDateTime (formatted time part): %s%n%n", strTime3);
  }

  /** Pattern with date part. */
  public static void usingDatePattern(Locale locale) {                  // (3)
    String datePattern = "EEEE, uuuu/MMMM/dd";
    DateTimeFormatter dateFormatter = DateTimeFormatter.ofPattern(datePattern)
                                              .localizedBy(locale);
    String strDate = date.format(dateFormatter);
    LocalDate parsedDate = LocalDate.parse(strDate, dateFormatter);
    String strDate2 = dateTime.format(dateFormatter);
    String strDate3 = zonedDateTime.format(dateFormatter);
```

```java
        System.out.printf("Date pattern: %s%n", datePattern);
        System.out.printf("LocalDate (formatted): %s%n", strDate);
        System.out.printf("LocalDate (parsed)    : %s%n", parsedDate);
        System.out.printf("LocalDateTime (formatted date part): %s%n", strDate2);
        System.out.printf("ZonedDateTime (formatted date part): %s%n%n", strDate3);
    }

    /** Pattern with date and time parts. */
    public static void usingDateTimePattern(Locale locale) {          // (4)
        String dtPattern = "EE, HH::mm::ss 'on' uuuu/MM/dd";
        DateTimeFormatter dtFormatter = DateTimeFormatter.ofPattern(dtPattern)
                                             .localizedBy(locale);
        String strDateTime = dateTime.format(dtFormatter);
        LocalDateTime parsedDateTime = LocalDateTime.parse(strDateTime,
                                                  dtFormatter);
        LocalDate parsedDate3 = LocalDate.parse(strDateTime, dtFormatter);
        LocalTime parsedTime3 = LocalTime.parse(strDateTime, dtFormatter);

        System.out.printf("DateTime pattern: %s%n", dtPattern);
        System.out.printf("LocalDateTime (formatted):   %s%n", strDateTime);
        System.out.printf("LocalDateTime (parsed):      %s%n", parsedDateTime);
        System.out.printf("LocalDate (parsed date part): %s%n", parsedDate3);
        System.out.printf("LocalTime (parsed time part): %s%n%n", parsedTime3);
    }

    /** Pattern with time zone, date and time parts. */
    public static void usingZonedDateTimePattern(Locale locale) {       // (5)
        String zdtPattern = "EE, HH::mm::ss 'on' uuuu/MM/dd VV";
        DateTimeFormatter zdtFormatter = DateTimeFormatter.ofPattern(zdtPattern)
                                              .localizedBy(locale);
        String strZonedDateTime = zonedDateTime.format(zdtFormatter);
        ZonedDateTime parsedZonedDateTime
            = ZonedDateTime.parse(strZonedDateTime, zdtFormatter);
        LocalDateTime parsedDateTime2
            = LocalDateTime.parse(strZonedDateTime, zdtFormatter);
        LocalDate parsedDate4 = LocalDate.parse(strZonedDateTime,
                                           zdtFormatter);
        LocalTime parsedTime4 = LocalTime.parse(strZonedDateTime,
                                           zdtFormatter);

        System.out.printf("ZonedDateTime pattern: %s%n", zdtPattern);
        System.out.printf("ZonedDateTime (formatted):   %s%n", strZonedDateTime);
        System.out.printf("ZonedDateTime (parsed):      %s%n", parsedZonedDateTime);
        System.out.printf("LocalDateTime (parsed):      %s%n", parsedDateTime2);
        System.out.printf("LocalDate (parsed date part): %s%n", parsedDate4);
        System.out.printf("LocalTime (parsed time part): %s%n", parsedTime4);
    }
}
```

Probable output from the program:

```
Time pattern: HH::mm::ss:SSS
LocalTime (formatted): 12::30::15:000
LocalTime (parsed):    12:30:15
LocalDateTime (formatted time part): 12::30::15:000
ZonedDateTime (formatted time part): 12::30::15:000
```

```
Date pattern: EEEE, uuuu/MMMM/dd
LocalDate (formatted): Wednesday, 2021/April/28
LocalDate (parsed)   : 2021-04-28
LocalDateTime (formatted date part): Wednesday, 2021/April/28
ZonedDateTime (formatted date part): Wednesday, 2021/April/28

DateTime pattern: EE, HH::mm::ss 'on' uuuu/MM/dd
LocalDateTime (formatted):   Wed, 12::30::15 on 2021/04/28
LocalDateTime (parsed):      2021-04-28T12:30:15
LocalDate (parsed date part): 2021-04-28
LocalTime (parsed time part): 12:30:15

ZonedDateTime pattern: EE, HH::mm::ss 'on' uuuu/MM/dd VV
ZonedDateTime (formatted):   Wed, 12::30::15 on 2021/04/28 US/Central
ZonedDateTime (parsed):      2021-04-28T12:30:15-05:00[US/Central]
LocalDateTime (parsed):      2021-04-28T12:30:15
LocalDate (parsed date part): 2021-04-28
LocalTime (parsed time part): 12:30:15
```

18.7 Formatting and Parsing Messages

A *compound message* may contain various kinds of data: strings, numbers, currencies, percentages, dates, and times. The locale-sensitive values in such messages should be formatted according to an appropriate locale. In this section we first consider a solution provided by the java.text.MessageFormat class for formatting compound messages. Later we consider the java.text.ChoiceFormat class that supports conditional formatting (p. 1145).

An overview of various other support in the Java SE APIs for formatting compound messages can be found at the end of this section (p. 1152).

Format Patterns

The modus operandi of formatters provided by the MessageFormat class is a classic one, as exemplified by the printf() method called on the System.out static field (§1.9, p. 24). A *string pattern* designating *placeholders* for values is specified. MessageFormat takes a list of values and formats them, and then inserts their text representation into the respective placeholders in the pattern to create the final result. The simple example below illustrates the basic use of the MessageFormat class.

```
String pattern = "At {3} on {2} Elvis landed at {0} and was greeted by {1} fans.";
String output = MessageFormat.format(pattern, "Honolulu", 3000,
                          LocalDate.of(1961,3,25), LocalTime.of(12,15));
System.out.println(output);
```

Output from the code:

```
At 12:15 on 1961-03-25 Elvis landed at Honolulu and was greeted by 3,000 fans.
```

The pattern specifies placeholders (called *format elements*) using curly brackets {} to designate where text representations of values are to be inserted. The number specified in a format element is the *argument index* of a particular argument in the list of arguments submitted to the formatter. In the code above, the pattern has four format elements.

The variable arity static method `MessageFormat.format()` is passed the pattern and a list of arguments to format. Below, we can see which argument in the method call is indicated by the argument index in a format element that is specified in the pattern above.

```
Format element:     {0}        {1}           {2}                        {3}
Arguments:       "Honolulu", 3000, LocalDate.of(1961,3,25), LocalTime.of(12,15)
```

Care must be taken that an argument index in a format element designates the right argument. The same argument index in multiple format elements just means that the argument it designates is applied to all of those format elements.

Note that the text outside of the format elements is copied verbatim to the result string. A single quote (') can be used to quote arbitrary characters, and two single quotes ('') can be used to escape a single quote in a pattern. For example, the pattern `"'{1}'"` represents the string `"{1}"`, and not a format element.

The flexibility of the `MessageFormat` class will become clear as we dig into its functionality.

The general syntax of a format element is shown below:

```
{ Argument_Index }
{ Argument_Index, Format_Type }
{ Argument_Index, Format_Type, Format_Style }
```

The format type and the format style allow further control over the formatting. The *format type* indicates what kind of argument (e.g., number, date, or time) is to be formatted, and the *format style* indicates how the argument will be formatted (e.g., currency format for a number, short format for a date). Legal combinations of format type and format style are shown in Table 18.16.

Table 18.16 *Format Type and Format Style Combinations for Format Elements*

Format type value	Format style value that can be specified for a format type
none	*none*
number	*none,* integer, currency, percent, *subformat pattern*
date *or* time	*none,* short, medium, long, full, *subformat pattern*
choice (p. 1145)	*subformat pattern*

The first variant of the format element (first row in Table 18.16) was used in the code earlier, where neither format type nor format style is specified. In this case, the text representation of the argument as defined by the `toString()` method is used in the pattern to create the final result. We will explore other combinations from Table 18.16 in this section.

When format type and format style values are used in a format element, an appropriate formatter is implicitly created to format the argument corresponding to that particular format element. The formatters created are instances of the formatter classes shown in Figure 18.1, p. 1115. For example, the format element {3,time,short} results in a locale-specific formatter being created implicitly by the following method call:

```
DateFormat.getTimeInstance(DateFormat.SHORT, getLocale())
```

This formatter will format a java.util.Date object (which represents both date and time) by extracting its time components and formatting them according to the format defined by DateFormat.SHORT and taking the locale into consideration. If a MessageFormat instance does not specify the locale, then the default locale is used.

Format elements that specify the format types date and time are compatible with the java.util.Date legacy class, with subsequent reliance on the DateFormat class to provide an appropriate formatter. This presents a slight problem when we want to format date and time values of the new Date and Time API. We will use the static methods of the utility class ConvertToLegacyDate (§17.8, p. 1088) to convert LocalDate, LocalTime, LocalDateTime, and ZonedDateTime objects to Date objects in order to leverage the format element handling functionality of the MessageFormat class.

The pattern that we saw earlier with just vanilla format elements (i.e., format elements with just the argument index) is now shown at (1) below to include the specification of the type and style of the format elements. A MessageFormat instance that is based on the pattern at (1) is created at (2) using a constructor of the MessageFormat class. The arguments that we want to format are included in the Object array at (3). Note that the element index in this array corresponds to an argument index in the format elements specified in the pattern. We use the methods from the utility class ConvertToDate to convert LocalTime and LocalDate values to Date values (§17.8, p. 1088). Finally, at (4), the argument array is passed for formatting to the format() method inherited by the MessageFormat class from its superclass Format. The code below also outlines the pertinent steps that are involved when using a MessageFormat instance to format compound messages.

```
// Specify the pattern:                                                        (1)
String pattern2 = "At {3,time,short} on {2,date,medium} Elvis landed at {0} "
              + "and was greeted by {1,number,integer} fans.";

// Create a MessageFormat based on the given pattern:                          (2)
MessageFormat mf2 = new MessageFormat(pattern2);

// Create the array with the arguments to format:                             (3)
Object[] messageArguments = {
    "Honolulu",                                      // argument index 0
    3000,                                            // argument index 1
    ConvertToDate.ldToDate(LocalDate.of(1961,3,25)), // argument index 2
    ConvertToDate.ltToDate(LocalTime.of(12,15))      // argument index 3
};
```

```
// Format the arguments:                                        (4)
String output2 = mf2.format(messageArguments);
System.out.println(output2);
```

Output from the code:

```
At 12:15 PM on Mar 25, 1961 Elvis landed at Honolulu and was greeted by 3,000 fans.
```

This output is different from the output we saw earlier when using vanilla format elements. In this case, appropriate formatters are implicitly created for each format element that apply the format style and take into consideration the locale (in this case, it is the default locale, which happens to be the US locale).

The following constructors defined by the MessageFormat class are used in the examples in this section:

```
MessageFormat(String pattern)
MessageFormat(String pattern, Locale locale)
```

Create a message formatter to apply the specified pattern. The created formatters will format or parse according to the default locale or the specified locale, respectively.

Selected methods are provided by the MessageFormat class, many of which are used in the examples in this section:

```
final String format(Object obj)         // Inherited from the Format class.
```

Returns a string that is the result of formatting the specified object. Passing an Object[] formats the elements of the array individually.

```
static String format(String pattern, Object... arguments)
```

This static method implicitly creates a one-time formatter with the given pattern, and returns the result of using it to format the variable arity arguments.

```
void setLocale(Locale locale)
```

Sets the locale to be used when creating subformats. Subformats already created are not affected.

```
Locale getLocale()
```

Returns the locale used by this formatter.

```
void applyPattern(String pattern)
```

Sets the pattern used by this formatter by parsing the pattern and creating the necessary subformats.

```
String toPattern()
```

Returns a pattern that represents the current state of this formatter.

```
void setFormat(int formatElementIndex, Format newFormat)
void setFormats(Format[] newFormats)
```

The first method sets the format to use for the format element indicated by the formatElementIndex in the previously set pattern string.

The second method sets the formats to use for the format elements in the previously set pattern string. Note that the order of formats in the newFormats array corresponds to *the order of format elements in the pattern string.* Contrast this method with the setFormatsByArgumentIndex() method.

More formats provided than needed by the pattern string are ignored. Fewer formats provided than needed by the pattern string results in only the provided formats being inserted.

```
void setFormatByArgumentIndex(int argumentIndex, Format newFormat)
void setFormatsByArgumentIndex(Format[] newFormats)
```

The first method sets the format to use for the format element indicated by the argumentIndex in the previously set pattern string.

The second method sets the formats to use for the format elements in the previously set pattern string. However, note that the order of formats in the newFormats array corresponds to *the order of elements in the arguments array* passed to the format methods or returned by the parse methods. Contrast this method with the setFormats() method.

Any argument index not used for any format element in the pattern string results in the corresponding new format being ignored.

Fewer formats being provided than needed results in only the formats for provided argument indices being replaced.

Formatting Compound Messages

If the application is intended for an international audience, we need to take the locale into consideration when formatting compound messages.

Example 18.8 illustrates formatting compound messages for different locales, where locale-sensitive data is contained in resource bundles (p. 1102). The program output shows stock information about an item according to the requested locale, showing how formatting of number, currency, date, and time is localized. A resource bundle file is created for each locale. The resource bundle for the US locale is shown in Example 18.8. The program output shows stock information for the US locale and the locale for Spain.

Example 18.8 *Formatting Compound Messages*

```
# File: StockInfoBundle.properties
pattern = Stock date: {3,time,short}, {4,date,long}\n\
          Item name: {0}\n\
          Item price: {1,number,currency}\n\
          Number of items: {2,number,integer}
item.name = Frozen pizza
item.price = 9.99
```

```java
import java.text.*;
import java.time.*;
import java.util.*;

public class CompoundMessageFormatting {
  static void displayStockInfo(Locale requestedLocale) {              // (1)
    System.out.println("Requested Locale: " + requestedLocale);

    // Fetch the relevant resource bundle:                            (2)
    ResourceBundle bundle =
        ResourceBundle.getBundle("resources.StockInfoBundle", requestedLocale);

    // Create a formatter, given the pattern and the locale:          (3)
    MessageFormat mf = new MessageFormat(bundle.getString("pattern"),
                                         requestedLocale);

    // Argument values:                                               (4)
    String itemName = bundle.getString("item.name");
    double itemPrice = Double.parseDouble(bundle.getString("item.price"));
    int numOfItems = 1234;
    Date timeOnly = ConvertToLegacyDate.ltToDate(LocalTime.of(14,30));
    Date dateOnly = ConvertToLegacyDate.ldToDate(LocalDate.of(2021,3,1));

    // Create argument array:                                         (5)
    Object[] messageArguments = {
        itemName,        // {0}
        itemPrice,       // {1,number,currency}
        numOfItems,      // {2,number,integer}
        timeOnly,        // {3,time,short}
        dateOnly,        // {4,date,long}
    };

    // Apply the formatter to the arguments:                          (6)
    String result = mf.format(messageArguments);
    System.out.println(result);
  }

  public static void main(String[] args) {
    displayStockInfo(Locale.US);
    System.out.println();
    displayStockInfo(new Locale("es", "ES"));
    System.out.println();
  }
}
```

Output from the program:

```
Requested Locale: en_US
Stock date: 2:30 PM, March 1, 2021
Item name: Frozen pizza
Item price: $9.99
Number of items: 1,234

Requested Locale: es_ES
Fecha de stock: 14:30, 1 de marzo de 2021
```

```
Nombre del artículo: Pizza congelada
Precio del artículo: 8,99 ?
Número de artículos: 1.234
```

In Example 18.8, the method `displayStockInfo()` at (1) epitomizes the basic steps for using `MessageFormat` for formatting compound messages. The method is passed the requested locale for which the stock information should be displayed. It goes without saying that the stock information is printed only if the relevant resource bundle files can be found.

The `MessageFormat` instance created at (2) is locale-specific. The pattern is read from the resource bundle. It is composed of several lines, and appropriate format elements for each kind of value in the pattern are specified, as shown in the resource bundle for the US locale. The `MessageFormat` instance implicitly creates the necessary formatters for type and style specified in the format elements, and applies them to the corresponding arguments.

The arguments to format are set up at (4). We convert `LocalTime` and `LocalDate` instances to `Date` instances. Another solution is to convert these instances to their text representation beforehand using an appropriate `DateTimeFormatter`. It is also possible to set specific formatters for any argument that is to be formatted. We leave the curious reader to explore these solutions for formatting compound messages.

At (5), an `Object` array is initialized with the arguments. Finally, at (6), the `format()` method is invoked on the formatter, passing the argument array. Again note that the currency delimiter for ? (euro) is a nbsp in the formatted output, as discussed earlier (p. 1116).

Keep in mind that a `MessageFormat` can be reused, with a new locale, a new pattern, and new arguments:

```
MessageFormat mf = new MessageFormat(previousPattern);
mf.setLocale(newLocale);
mf.applyPattern(newPattern);
String output = mf.format(newMessageArguments);
```

Conditional Formatting

Consider *contiguous half-open intervals* on the number line, as shown below. The (lower and upper) *limits* of these intervals can be any numbers, which will always be in ascending order as they are on the number line. Below we see two half-open intervals with limits 0.0, 1.0, and 2.0.

```
limits:        0.0           1.0           2.0
        <-----[----------)[----------)-----> number line
                 vᵢ            vᵢ₊₁
```

If a value *v* falls in the half-open interval $[v_i, v_{i+1})$, then we select the (lower) limit v_i. So, if *v* is any number in the half-open interval $[0.0, 1.0)$, the limit 0.0 is selected. Similarly, if v is any number in the half-open interval [1.0, 2.0), the limit 1.0 will be selected, and so on.

From Table 18.16, we see that the format element having the format type choice requires a *subformat pattern*. This subformat pattern specifies a *choice format*. The general syntax of the choice format is shown below, where limit v_i and its associated subformat pattern f_i are separated by the hash sign (#). Each $v_i\#f_i$ constitutes *a choice*, and choices are separated by the vertical bar (|). Two consecutive limits constitute a half-open interval: $[v_i, v_{i+1})$. Note that the last choice uses <, meaning any value greater than or equal to v_n. Also, the limits $v_1, v_2, ..., v_n$ must be in ascending order for the choice format to work correctly.

$$v_1\#f_1 \mid v_2\#f_2 \mid \ ... \ \mid v_n{<}f_n$$

The choice format thus defines the limits and the corresponding choices. When a value is supplied for formatting, the choice format determines the limit, as explained above, and the formatter uses the choice associated with this limit— hence the term *conditional formatting*.

Below is a pattern that uses a choice format. The pattern's only format element has *argument index* 0 and *format type* choice, and its subformat pattern specifies a *choice format* (underlined below, but see also Table 18.16). The argument index 0 in the pattern designates the value that is used to determine the limit, and thereby, select the corresponding choice in the choice format.

```
"There {0,choice,0#are no bananas|1#is only one banana|\
                        2<are {1,number,integer} bananas}."
```

The choice format above has three choices, separated by the vertical bar (|). Its limits are 0, 1, and 2. Each limit in a choice is associated with a subformat pattern. For limits 0 and 1, the subformat pattern is just text. The subformat pattern for limit 2 specifies a format element to format a number as an integer, as it expects an argument to be supplied for this format element. Note that the argument index in this embedded format element is 1.

Example 18.9 uses a pattern that includes the choice format above to illustrate handling of plurals in messages. Resource bundles for different locales contain the pattern with the choice format. An appropriate resource bundle for a locale is fetched at (1). The choice pattern is read from the resource bundle and a MessageFormat is created at (2), based on the choice pattern and the requested locale. For each locale, the formatter is tested for three cases, exemplified by the rows of two-dimensional array messageArguments at (3). Each row of arguments is passed to the format() method at (5) for formatting. The program output shows the arguments passed and the corresponding result.

In the argument matrix, the first row, {0.5}, specifies the argument 0.5, which falls in the half-interval [0, 1). Limit 0 is chosen, whose choice is selected. This results in the following pattern to be applied:

```
"There are no bananas."
```

Similarly for the second row, {1.5}, the limit is determined to be 1, resulting in the following pattern to be applied:

"There <u>is only one banana</u>."

For the third row, {2.5, 2}, the argument 2.5 determines the limit 2, resulting in the pattern below to be applied. The second element (value 2) in this row is the argument that is formatted according to the format element in this pattern.

"There <u>are {1,number,integer} bananas</u>."

We see from the program output that the correct singular or plural form is selected depending on the value of the argument passed to the formatter. It is instructive to experiment with passing different values to the formatter.

Example 18.9　*Using Choice Pattern*

```
# File: ChoiceBundle.properties
choice.pattern = There {0,choice,0#are no bananas|1#is only one banana|\
                           2<are {1,number,integer} bananas}.
...
```

```
import java.text.*;
import java.util.*;

public class ChoicePatternUsage {

  static void displayMessages(Locale requestedLocale) {
    System.out.println("Requested Locale: " + requestedLocale);

    // Fetch the resource bundle:                                        (1)
    ResourceBundle bundle =
        ResourceBundle.getBundle("resources.ChoiceBundle", requestedLocale);

    // choice.pattern = There {0,choice,0#are no bananas|1#is only one banana
    //                         |2#are {1,number,integer} bananas}.
    // Create formatter for specified choice pattern and locale:         (2)
    MessageFormat mf =
        new MessageFormat(bundle.getString("choice.pattern"), requestedLocale);

    // Create the message argument arrays:                               (3)
    Object[][] messageArguments = { {0.5}, {1.5}, {2.5, 2} };

    // Test the formatter with arguments:                               (4)
    for (int choiceNumber = 0;
         choiceNumber < messageArguments.length; choiceNumber++) {
      String result = mf.format(messageArguments[choiceNumber]);        // (5)
      System.out.printf("Arguments:%-10sResult: %s%n",
              Arrays.toString(messageArguments[choiceNumber]),result);
    }
  }

  public static void main(String[] args) {
    displayMessages(new Locale("en", "US"));
```

```
        System.out.println();
        displayMessages(new Locale("es", "ES"));
    }
}
```

Output from the program:

```
Requested Locale: en_US
Arguments:[0.5]      Result: There are no bananas.
Arguments:[1.5]      Result: There is only one banana.
Arguments:[2.5, 2]   Result: There are 2 bananas.

Requested Locale: es_ES
Arguments:[0.5]      Result: Ahí no hay plátanos.
Arguments:[1.5]      Result: Ahí es solo un plátano.
Arguments:[2.5, 2]   Result: Ahí son 2 plátanos.
```

Example 18.9 illustrates using a choice format for handling plurals. Example 18.10 illustrates an alternative approach where the choice format is created programmatically using the ChoiceFormat class.

The class ChoiceFormat provides the following constructors for creating a choice format either programmatically or using a pattern.

ChoiceFormat(double[] limits, String[] formats)

Creates a ChoiceFormat with the limits specified in ascending order and the corresponding formats.

ChoiceFormat(String newPattern)

Creates a ChoiceFormat with limits and corresponding formats based on the specified pattern string.

The ChoiceFormat class is locale-agnostic—that is, providing no locale-specific operations. However, the class MessageFormat implements locale-specific operations, and allows formats to be set for individual format elements in its pattern. By setting a ChoiceFormat as a format for a choice format element in a locale-sensitive MessageFormat, it is possible to achieve locale-specific formatting behavior in a ChoiceFormat. This approach is illustrated in Example 18.10. The numbers below correspond to the numbers on the lines in the source code for Example 18.10.

(1) The locale-specific resource bundle with resources for the pattern and for constructing the choice format is fetched. See the listing of the resource bundle file in Example 18.10.

(2) A locale-specific MessageFormat is created based on the pattern ("There {0}.") which is read from the resource bundle.

(3) To create a ChoiceFormat programmatically requires two equal-length arrays that contain the limits and the corresponding subformats, respectively. The double array limits is created with the limit values 0, 1, and 2. A String array messageFormats is created by reading the values of the keys none, singular, and

plural from the resource bundle. These are the subformats corresponding to the limits that we saw in the choice format in Example 18.9.

(4) Given the arrays for the limits and the subformats, the ChoiceFormat constructor creates the choice format.

(5) and (6) One way to set customized formats for individual format elements in a MessageFormat is by first creating an array of Format (superclass of format classes in java.text package). The order of the formats in this array must be the same as either *the order of format elements in the pattern string* or *the order of elements in the argument array passed to the format methods*. There is only one format element in the pattern ("There {0}."). The array of Format thus has only one element which is the choice format for this format element, and therefore, both orders are valid in this case. We can use either the setFormats() or the setFormatsByArgumentIndex() method, as shown at (6a) and (6b), respectively. Either method will associate the choice format with the format element having the argument index 0 in the pattern.

However, the format for the format element at the argument index 0 in the pattern can easily be set by calling the setFormat() method, as shown at (6c).

(7) through (9) The behavior of the program is exactly the same as for Example 18.9. Experimenting with other limits and arguments is recommended.

Example 18.10 *Using the* ChoiceFormat *Class*

```
# File: ChoiceBundle.properties
...
pattern = There {0}.
none = are no bananas
singular = is only one banana
plural = are {1,number,integer} bananas
```

```
import java.text.*;
import java.util.*;

public class ChoiceFormatUsage {

  static void displayMessages(Locale requestedLocale) {
    System.out.println("Requested locale: " + requestedLocale);

    // Fetch the resource bundle:                                         (1)
    ResourceBundle bundle =
        ResourceBundle.getBundle("resources.ChoiceBundle", requestedLocale);

    // Create formatter for specified pattern and locale:                (2)
    MessageFormat mf = new MessageFormat(
        bundle.getString("pattern"),        // pattern = There {0}.
        requestedLocale
        );
```

```
        // Create the limits and the formats arrays:                    (3)
        double[] limits = {0,1,2};                                  // (3a)
        String [] grammarFormats = {                                // (3b)
            bundle.getString("none"),        // none = are no bananas
            bundle.getString("singular"),    // singular = is only one banana
            bundle.getString("plural")       // plural = are {1,number,integer} bananas
        };

        // Create the choice format:                                    (4)
        ChoiceFormat choiceForm = new ChoiceFormat(limits, grammarFormats);

        // Create the formats:                                          (5)
        Format[] formats = {choiceForm};

        // Set the formats in the formatter:                            (6)
        mf.setFormats(formats);                                     // (6a)
//      messageForm.setFormatsByArgumentIndex(formats);             // (6b)
//      mf.setFormat(0, choiceForm);                                // (6c)

        // Create the arguments arrays:                                 (7)
        Object[][] messageArguments = { {0.5}, {1.5}, {2.5, 2} };

        // Test the formatter with arguments:                           (8)
        for (int choiceNumber = 0;
            choiceNumber < messageArguments.length; choiceNumber++) {
          String result = mf.format(messageArguments[choiceNumber]);    // (9)
          System.out.printf("Arguments:%-10sResult: %s%n",
            Arrays.toString(messageArguments[choiceNumber]),result);    }
    }

    public static void main(String[] args)    {
        displayMessages(new Locale("en", "US"));
        System.out.println();
        displayMessages(new Locale("es", "ES"));
    }
}
```

Output from the program:

```
Requested Locale: en_US
Arguments:[0.5]      Result: There are no bananas.
Arguments:[1.5]      Result: There is only one banana.
Arguments:[2.5, 2]   Result: There are 2 bananas.

Requested locale: es_ES
Arguments:[0.5]      Result: Ahí no hay plátanos.
Arguments:[1.5]      Result: Ahí es solo un plátano.
Arguments:[2.5, 2]   Result: Ahí son 2 plátanos.
```

Parsing Values Using Patterns

An instance of the MessageFormat class can be used both for formatting and for parsing of values. The class provides the parse() methods for parsing text. We will primarily use the one-argument method shown below to demonstrate parsing with the MessageFormat class.

```
Object[] parse(String source) throws ParseException
Object[] parse(String source, ParsePosition position)
```

The first method parses text from the beginning of the string source to return an Object array with the parsed values.

The second method parses from the position in the string source where the parsing should start.

Both methods may not use the entire text of the given string source.

The parse() methods return an Object array with the parsed values, which means that the parsed values must be extracted from the array and cast to the appropriate type in order to compute with them. The cast to the appropriate type must be done safely—typically by determining the type with the instanceof operator before applying the cast.

As the one-argument parse() method throws a checked ParseException when an error occurs under parsing, the code snippets in this subsection must be executed in a context that handles this exception.

The round trip of formatting values and then parsing the formatted result to obtain the same values back is illustrated below. It should not come as a surprise that this round trip always works, as demonstrated by the code below. We see that the argument of type double that was formatted and the value of type double that was parsed according to the pattern at (1) are equal.

```
String pattern = "foo {0,number,currency} bar";              // (1)
MessageFormat mfp = new MessageFormat(pattern, Locale.US);
Object[] arguments = new Object[] {10.99};           // [10.99]
String formattedResult = mfp.format(arguments);      // "foo $10.99 bar"
Object[] parsedResult = mfp.parse(formattedResult);  // [10.99]
System.out.println((double)arguments[0] == (double)parsedResult[0]); // true
```

A vanilla format element, {*i*}, in a pattern matches a string in the source, as no format type or style is specified for such a format element. The source at (3) matches the format element in the pattern at (2), as is evident from the parse result at (4).

```
String patternA = "{0}";                                     // (2)
MessageFormat mfpA = new MessageFormat(patternA, Locale.US);
Object[] parsedResultA = mfpA.parse("One Two Three");        // (3)
System.out.println(parsedResultA[0] instanceof String);   // true
System.out.println(Arrays.toString(parsedResultA));       // (4) [One Two Three]
```

Any text in a pattern must be matched verbatim in the source. Note how the text in the pattern at (5) is matched in the source at (6), with the string "2" being returned as the result of parsing.

```
String patternB = "One {0} Three";                           // (5)
MessageFormat mfpB = new MessageFormat(patternB, Locale.US);
Object[] parsedResultB = mfpB.parse("One 2 Three");          // (6)
System.out.println(parsedResultB[0].equals("2"));         // true
System.out.println(Arrays.toString(parsedResultB));       // [2]
```

The code below illustrates that the parse() method may not use the entire text in the source, only what is necessary to declare a match. Parsing stops after the word Three in the source at (7) when a match for the pattern has been found in the source.

```
Object[] parsedResultC = mfpB.parse("One 2 Three whatever");       // (7)
System.out.println(Arrays.toString(parsedResultC));                // [2]
```

In order for the parse to succeed, the source must contain text that is compatible with the pattern so that it can be parsed according to any type or style specified in the format elements defined in the pattern. At (8) below, the pattern contains two format elements that require an integer and a currency value specified according to the US locale. The source at (9) meets the requirements to match the pattern. The parse result shows that an int value and a double value were parsed.

```
String patternD = "foo {0,number,integer} {1,number,currency} bar";  // (8)
MessageFormat mfpD = new MessageFormat(patternD, Locale.US);
Object[] parsedResultD = mfpD.parse("foo 2021 $64.99 bar");           // (9)
System.out.println(Arrays.toString(parsedResultD));           // [2021, 64.99]
```

We have seen earlier in this chapter that a *nbsp* is necessary in the source in order to parse certain currencies (p. 1119). That is also the case when parsing such currency values with the MessageFormat class, and is illustrated below for the Norwegian locale. Unless a *nbsp* is the delimiter between the currency symbol and the first digit of the amount, as shown at (10b), parsing will result in a checked ParseException being thrown.

```
Locale locale = new Locale("no", "NO");
String pattern1 = "foo {0,number,currency} bar";
MessageFormat mfp1 = new MessageFormat(pattern1, locale);
// String parseSource = "foo kr 10,99 bar";         // (10a) ParseException
String parseSource = "foo kr\u00a010,99 bar";       // (10b) nbsp. OK.
Object[] parsedResults = mfp1.parse(parseSource);
if (parsedResults[0] instanceof Double dValue) {
  System.out.println(dValue);                       // 10.99
}
```

Additional Support for Formatting in the Java SE Platform APIs

In this subsection we mention additional support for formatting values that is provided by various classes in the Java SE Platform APIs.

The class java.util.Formatter provides the core support for *formatted text representation* of primitive values and objects through its overloaded format() methods. See the Java SE Platform API documentation for the nitty-gritty details on how to specify the format.

```
format(String format, Object... args)
format(Locale loc, String format, Object... args)
```

Write a string that is a result of applying the specified format string to the values in the variable arity parameter args. The resulting string is written to the *destination object* that is associated with the formatter.

The destination object of a formatter is specified when the formatter is created. The destination object can, for example, be a String, a StringBuilder, a file, or any OutputStream.

Return the current formatter.

The classes java.io.PrintStream and java.io.PrintWriter also provide an overloaded format() method with the same signature for formatted output. These streams use an associated Formatter that sends the output to the PrintStream or the PrintWriter, respectively. We have used the printf() method of the PrintStream class for sending output to the terminal every time this method is invoked on the System.out field (§1.9, p. 24).

The String class also provides an analogous format() method, but it is static. This method also uses an associated Formatter for formatting purposes. Unlike the format() method of the classes mentioned earlier, this static method returns the resulting string after formatting the values (§8.4, p. 457).

The java.io.Console only provides the first form of the format() and the printf() methods (without the locale specification). These methods too use an associated Formatter. They write the resulting string to the console's output stream, and return the current console (§20.4, p. 1256).

Review Questions

18.5 Given the following code:

```java
import java.text.DecimalFormat;
import java.text.NumberFormat;
import java.util.Locale;

public class DecimalNumberPatternsRQ {
  public static void main(String[] args) {
    // (1) INSERT CODE HERE
    double value = 0.456;
    DecimalFormat df = (DecimalFormat) NumberFormat.getNumberInstance(Locale.US);
    df.applyPattern(pattern);
    String output = df.format(value);
    System.out.printf("|%s|", output);
  }
}
```

Which code, when inserted independently at (1), will result in the following output: |.46|?

Select the five correct answers.

(a) `String pattern = ".00";`
(b) `String pattern = ".##";`
(c) `String pattern = ".0#";`
(d) `String pattern = "#.00";`

```
(e)  String pattern = "#.0#";
(f)  String pattern = "#.##";
(g)  String pattern = ".#0";
```

18.6   Given the following code:

```
import java.math.*;
import java.text.*;
import java.util.*;

public class RQ7 {
  public static void main(String[] args) {
    NumberFormat nf = NumberFormat.getCurrencyInstance(Locale.US);
    nf.setMaximumFractionDigits(2);
    nf.setRoundingMode(RoundingMode.HALF_DOWN);
    double value = 9876.54321;
    String s1 = nf.format(value);
    nf.setRoundingMode(RoundingMode.HALF_UP);
    String s2 = nf.format(value);
    System.out.println(s1 + " " + s2);
  }
}
```

What is the result?
Select the one correct answer.

(a) $9,876.54 $9,876.55
(b) $9,876.53 $9,876.53
(c) $9,876.54 $9,876.54
(d) $9,876.53 $9,876.55
(e) The program will throw an exception at runtime.

18.7   Given the following code:

```
import java.math.*;
import java.text.*;
import java.util.*;

public class RQ7Alt {
  public static void main(String[] args) {
    BigDecimal value = new BigDecimal("9876.545");
    NumberFormat nf = NumberFormat.getCurrencyInstance(Locale.US);
    nf.setMaximumFractionDigits(2);
    nf.setRoundingMode(RoundingMode.HALF_DOWN);
    String s1 = nf.format(value);
    System.out.println();
    nf.setRoundingMode(RoundingMode.HALF_UP);
    String s2 = nf.format(value);
    System.out.println(s1+" "+s2);
  }
}
```

What is the result?

Select the one correct answer.

(a) $9,876.55 $9,876.55
(b) $9,876.54 $9,876.54
(c) $9,876.55 $9,876.54
(d) $9,876.54 $9,876.55
(e) The program will throw an exception at runtime.

18.8 Given the following code:

```java
import java.time.*;
import java.time.format.*;
import java.util.*;

public class RQ8 {
  public static void main(String[] args) {
    LocalDate foolsDay = LocalDate.of(2021, Month.APRIL, 1);
    DateTimeFormatter df = DateTimeFormatter
                                .ofLocalizedDateTime(FormatStyle.SHORT)
                                .localizedBy(Locale.UK);
    System.out.print(df.format(foolsDay));
  }
}
```

What is the result?
Select the one correct answer.

(a) 04/01/2021
(b) 01/04/2021
(c) The program will throw an exception at runtime.
(d) The program will fail to compile.

18.9 Given the following code:

```java
import java.time.*;
import java.time.format.*;
import java.util.*;

public class RQ9 {
  public static void main(String[] args) {
    LocalDateTime foolsDay = LocalDateTime.of(2021, Month.APRIL, 1, 14, 30, 0);
    DateTimeFormatter df = DateTimeFormatter.ofPattern("day")
                                            .localizedBy(Locale.UK);
    System.out.print(df.format(foolsDay));
  }
}
```

What is the result?
Select the one correct answer.

(a) 1
(b) 01
(c) 1am
(d) 1am21

(e) 1am2021

(f) 1pm

(g) 1pm21

(h) 1pm2021

(i) The program will throw an exception at runtime.

18.10   Given the following code:

```
import java.time.*;
import java.time.format.*;
import java.util.*;

public class RQ10 {
  public static void main(String[] args) {
    LocalDate d = LocalDate.of(2021, Month.APRIL, 1);
    Locale.setDefault(Locale.UK);
    DateTimeFormatter df = DateTimeFormatter.ofLocalizedDate(FormatStyle.MEDIUM);
    String s1 = df.format(d);
    Locale.setDefault(Locale.FRANCE);
    String s2 = df.format(d);
    df.localizedBy(Locale.US);
    String s3 = df.format(d);
    if("Apr 1, 2021".equals(s1)) {
      System.out.print("UK ");
    }
    if("1 avr. 2021".equals(s2)) {
      System.out.print("FR ");
    }
    if("1 Apr 2021".equals(s3)) {
      System.out.println("US");
    }
  }
}
```

What is the result?

Select the one correct answer.

(a) UK FR US

(b) UK US

(c) UK FR

(d) FR US

(e) UK

(f) FR

(g) US

18.11   Given the following code:

```
import java.text.*;
import java.util.*;

public class RQ11 {
  public static void main(String[] args) {
    double x = 0.987654321;
    NumberFormat nf = NumberFormat.getPercentInstance(Locale.US);
```

```
      System.out.println(nf.format(x));
    }
  }
```

What is the result?

Select the one correct answer.

(a) 0.98%

(b) 0.99%

(c) 98%

(d) 99%

(e) 0.987654321%

(f) 987654321%

18.12   Given the following code:

```
import java.text.*;
import java.time.*;
import java.time.format.*;

public class RQ12 {
  public static void main(String[] args) {
    ZoneId london = ZoneId.of("Europe/London");
    ZoneId paris = ZoneId.of("Europe/Paris");
    LocalDateTime date1 = LocalDateTime.parse("2021-01-01T01:01:01",
                                    DateTimeFormatter.ISO_DATE_TIME);
    ZonedDateTime date2 = date1.atZone(london);
    DateTimeFormatter df1 = DateTimeFormatter.ofPattern("hz")
                                    .withZone(london);
    DateTimeFormatter df2 = DateTimeFormatter.ofPattern("hz")
                                    .withZone(paris);
    String result = MessageFormat.format("{0} {1} {2} {3}",
                              df1.format(date1), df1.format(date2),
                              df2.format(date1), df2.format(date2));
    System.out.println(result);
  }
}
```

Given that London (GMT) and Paris (CET) time zones are exactly one hour apart, what is the result?

Select the one correct answer.

(a) 1GMT 1GMT 1CET 2CET

(b) 1GMT 2GMT 1CET 2CET

(c) 1GMT 1CET 1CET 2CET

(d) 1GMT 2CET 1GMT 2CET

(e) 1GMT 1GMT 2CET 2CET

18.13   Given the following code:

```
import java.text.MessageFormat;

public class RQ13 {
  public static void main(String[] args) {
    String a = "A", b = "B";
```

```
      String result = MessageFormat.format("{0}-'{1}'-{3}-{0}-{1}-'{2}'", a, b);
      System.out.println(result);
    }
  }
```

What is the result?
Select the one correct answer.

(a) A-{1}--A-B-{2}

(b) A-B--A-B-{2}

(c) A-B-{3}-A-B-

(d) A-{1}-{3}-A-B-{2}

(e) The program will throw an exception at runtime.

18.14   Given the following code:

```
import java.text.*;

public class RQ14 {
  public static void main(String[] args) {
    double[] limits = {0,1,2,3,4};
    String[] formats = {"zero","{1}st","{1}nd","{1}rd","{1}th"};
    ChoiceFormat cf = new ChoiceFormat(limits, formats);
    MessageFormat mf = new MessageFormat("{0}");
    mf.setFormat(0, cf);
    Object[] values = {4,5};
    System.out.println(mf.format(values));
  }
}
```

What is the result?
Select the one correct answer.

(a) 4th

(b) 5th

(c) {1}th

(d) The program will throw an exception at runtime.

18.15   Given the following code:

```
import java.text.*;

public class RQ15 {
  public static void main(String[] args) {
    double[] limits = {0,-1,1};
    String[] formats = {"zero","negative","positive"};
    ChoiceFormat cf = new ChoiceFormat(limits, formats);
    MessageFormat mf = new MessageFormat("{0}");
    mf.setFormat(0, cf);
    Object[] values = {0.9};
    System.out.println(mf.format(values));
  }
}
```

What is the result?

Select the one correct answer.

(a) zero
(b) negative
(c) positive
(d) The program will throw an exception at runtime.

18.16   Given the following code:

```
import java.time.*;
import java.time.format.*;
import java.util.*;

public class RQ16 {
  public static void main(String[] args) {
    Locale.setDefault(Locale.US);
    DateTimeFormatter dtf = DateTimeFormatter.ofLocalizedDate(FormatStyle.MEDIUM);
    LocalDate d = LocalDate.parse("Apr 1, 2021", dtf);   // (1)
    d = LocalDate.parse("2021-04-01");                   // (2)
    String s = d.format(dft);                            // (3)
    System.out.println(s);
  }
}
```

What is the result?
Select the one correct answer.

(a) Apr 1, 2021
(b) 2021-04-01
(c) The program will throw a runtime exception at (1).
(d) The program will throw a runtime exception at (2).
(e) The program will throw a runtime exception at (3).

18.17   Given the following code:

```
import java.time.*;
import java.time.format.*;
import java.util.*;

public class RQ17 {
  public static void main(String[] args) {
    Locale.setDefault(Locale.US);
    DateTimeFormatter dtf = DateTimeFormatter.ofLocalizedDate(FormatStyle.SHORT);
    LocalDate d = LocalDate.parse("2021-04-01");    // (1)
    d = LocalDate.parse("4/1/21", dtf);             // (2)
    System.out.println(d);
  }
}
```

What is the result?
Select the one correct answer.

(a) Apr 1, 2021
(b) 4/1/21
(c) 2021-04-01

(d) The program will throw a runtime exception at (1).

(e) The program will throw a runtime exception at (2).

18.18 Which statement is true about localization?
Select the one correct answer.

(a) The default locale is `Locale.US`.

(b) The default locale is `Locale.ISO`.

(c) The default format for the `LocalDate` object is `DateTimeFormatter.BASIC_ISO_DATE`.

(d) The default format for the `LocalDate` object is `DateTimeFormatter.ISO_DATE`.

Java Module System   19

 Chapter Topics

- Understanding the issues the modules address and the benefits they provide
- Understanding the most important goals of the Java Module System: strong encapsulation, reliable configuration, and better performance
- Understanding how the modular JDK is organized, and how to discover and use its salient modules
- Writing a module declaration that specifies the properties of a module: its module name, and the requires and exports directives in such a declaration
- Understanding the module graph of an application
- Differentiating between readability of a module and accessibility of public types in an exported package of a required module
- Understanding the accessibility rules for members of a public type whose package is exported
- Understanding how implied dependencies are introduced in the module graph by the requires transitive directive, and its implication
- Creating the directory structure of a modular application, where an exploded module contains the source code for all packages in a module
- Compiling and running a multi-module application
- Creating modular JARs as repositories of compiled modules
- Running an application from its modular JARs
- Implications of open modules and the opens directives for reflection at runtime
- Creating, loading, and using services with provides-with and uses directives: specifying a service interface, and implementing service provider, service locator, and service consumer

- Creating and executing runtime images
- Differentiating between different kinds of modules: unnamed, automatic, and named modules
- Applying code migration strategies to modularize plain code
- Exploring modular JARs: listing JAR contents, extracting JAR contents, listing observable modules, describing the module descriptor, and viewing module-level, package-level, and class-level dependencies
- Providing a summary of relevant options accepted by the JDK command-line tools (javac, java, jar, jdeps, and jlink)

Java SE 17 Developer Exam Objectives	
[7.1] Define modules and their dependencies, expose module content including for reflection. Define services, producers, and consumers	§19.1, p. 1163 to §19.5, p. 1179 §19.8, p. 1191 §19.9, p. 1196
[7.2] Compile Java code, produce modular and non-modular jars, runtime images, and implement migration using unnamed and automatic modules	§19.6, p. 1186 §19.7, p. 1189 §19.10, p. 1204 to §19.14, p. 1218
Java SE 11 Developer Exam Objectives	
[7.1] Deploy and execute modular applications, including automatic modules	§19.2, p. 1164 §19.6, p. 1186 §19.7, p. 1189 §19.10, p. 1204 to §19.13, p. 1214
[7.2] Declare, use, and expose modules, including the use of services	§19.3, p. 1168 §19.4, p. 1177 §19.5, p. 1179 §19.8, p. 1191 §19.9, p. 1196

The *Java Platform Module System* (JPMS) provides the software engineering technology that makes it possible to efficiently build, deploy, maintain, and evolve very large software systems. It was successfully used to modularize the JDK before finally being released in Java 9.

This chapter discusses how the language, the JDK tools, and the runtime environment provide the support for creating modular applications in Java.

19.1 Making the Case for Modules

We begin by briefly examining the issues that modules address and the benefits they provide.

Stronger Encapsulation

Modules in Java provide a new level of encapsulation above packages. Whereas a package encapsulates classes and interfaces, a module encapsulates a set of packages and any other resources required by the module. An application is thus composed of reusable and related modules, where each module groups a set of packages and each package groups a set of classes and interfaces.

Fine-Grained Visibility of Public Types

The need for modules in Java arose from many concerns. For programming in the large, the concept of packages has many shortcomings, particularly in providing more fine-grained visibility of public types which are accessible in *all* packages, with no possibility of curtailing the accessibility of such a public type. A module can provide stronger encapsulation with a well-defined public API that other modules can use, and packages that are meant to be internal to a module are now guaranteed to be inaccessible to other modules.

Reusability, Maintainability, and Optimization

Applying the principles of encapsulation at each encapsulation level increases the reusability and aids the maintainability of the code, resulting in modules that can be optimized independently.

Reliable Configuration

Prior to modules, the Java language did not support any notion of *dependencies* between artifacts that comprise an application. Ad hoc use of JARs (Java Archives) proved inadequate for such relationships, as the compiler and the JVM saw the JAR files merely as containers of types and resources.

Now there is better encapsulation of modules in JARs, with one module in each JAR. The Java Module System explicitly utilizes the dependencies between modules to reason and maintain these dependencies both at compile time and at runtime, resulting in reliable application configurations. Before an application is launched, all modules needed by the application are resolved in order to avoid problems relating to missing modules or types during execution.

Better Performance

Modules in Java contribute to developing scalable systems with improved performance, as modules can be optimized independently. The module system guarantees that all classes of the same package are in the same module—that is, there are no *split packages*, and the modules describe explicit dependencies. The class loader thus knows which module to look into when loading a class, improving the start-up time of applications.

Scalable Applications

As the packages in the Java API are now organized into modules, it is possible for an application to include only those modules that are needed, thus reducing the binary footprint of the application. The modular JDK now caters to customized Java builds that can be scaled to small devices, and can also be shipped with the runtime environment included.

Improved Security

Organizing an application in modules can also improve security as critical code can be strongly encapsulated in modules, potentially decreasing the attack surface of an application.

Backward Compatibility

Modules are not a mandatory requirement for an application to run in the modular JDK. However, the benefits of using modules for large-scale application development are substantial as mentioned in this section. The modular JDK provides support to incrementally migrate legacy code into modules.

19.2 The Modular JDK

Support for modules is provided by the Java language and the JDK. The concept of a *module* is incorporated into the language. Existing tools in the JDK, such as javac, java, jar, and jdeps, have been enhanced to aid module-based development. Support for modules provided by these tools is covered in later sections. This section provides an overview of how the modular JDK is organized and what it has to offer.

Reasons for Modularity

The need to modularize the JDK arose from many reasons, among them the following:

- A monolithic runtime library (epitomized by the `rt.jar` file) was not conducive to the maintainability and evolution of the Java ecosystem with its ever-increasing APIs.

- Bloat of obsolete technologies could not be addressed properly, and was often at the risk of breaking backward compatibility.

- Maintaining backward compatibility in the face of ever-evolving packages made this goal more difficult.

- The one-size-fits-all runtime library started to incur a penalty in terms of increased space, more memory at runtime, and a need for lower consumption of CPU resources.

- JARs as containers of Java code were inadequate to elicit relationships between packages, having no means to expose their dependencies other than by resorting to third-party solutions (e.g., Maven and OSGi).

- The class-path solution to specify the location of package repositories was not optimal in locating types, leading to unforeseen problems when loading them and often throwing an exception at runtime because some type was missing.

Goals of the Modular JDK

Specific goals of the modular JDK, not surprisingly, align with the benefits of modules extolled in §19.1, p. 1163.

- *Stronger encapsulation*: This results in well-defined communication boundaries between modules and stricter encapsulation of their internal implementation.

- *Reliable configuration*: Any combination of modules must satisfy all dependencies both at compile time and runtime.

- *Enhanced performance*: Modularized code is more amiable to program optimizations.

- *Improved scalability*: The evolution of the Java platform can continue in a modularized fashion, as modules can be worked on in parallel.

- *Better security*: Modularized code decreases the attack surface, and access through *reflection* is strictly controlled at runtime.

Overview of the Modular JDK

The monolithic library of the JDK has now been split into many modules, with each module defining a specific functionality of the JDK. The installation directory of the JDK, shown in Figure 19.1, gives an overview of how the JDK is organized. The path of the installation directory will vary depending on the OS platform.

- The `bin` directory: This is where the executables are found—the Java Runtime Environment (JRE), which includes the Java Virtual Machine (JVM), and the

JDK command-line tools, among others, that are necessary to develop and run Java programs.

- The jmods directory: This directory epitomizes the modular JDK. It contains the *platform modules* of the JDK. These are compiled modules used to create custom runtime images of applications.

Each platform module is archived in a file having the name of the module and the extension .jmod—for example, java.base.jmod, java.se.jmod, and jdk.jartool.jmod. The modules beginning with the prefix "java." implement the Java SE specification, often called *standard modules*. These are present in all implementations of the Java SE platform. The modules beginning with the prefix "jdk." are platform specific, often called *non-standard modules*. These are not necessarily available for all implementations of the Java SE platform.

JMOD archives use a special archive format reserved for the platform modules, that are created using the JDK tool jmod. All JDK tools understand JMOD archives. The platform modules can be explored like any other application module. Examples of exploring such modules can be found in §19.13, p. 1211. There is seldom any need to create a JMOD archive or change the contents of the jmods directory.

Note that modules can be packaged both as JARs and as JMOD archives.

- The lib directory: This directory contains additional class libraries and support required by the JDK. These files are not meant for external use.

Figure 19.1   *Structure of JDK 17 Installation*

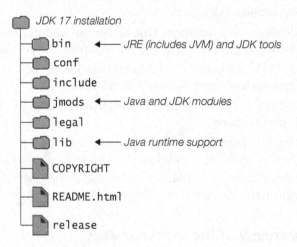

Module Graph of the JDK

The modules in the JDK define *dependencies* on other modules. These dependencies can be viewed as a graph in which the modules are the *nodes* and the *unidirectional edges* between the nodes define the dependencies between the modules. A partial *module graph* of the JDK is shown in Figure 19.2. The complete module graph of the JDK is of course substantially larger, but Figure 19.2 will suffice to convey its modular structure. It is also a *reduced graph* where by redundant dependencies, like the *implicit dependencies* on the java.base module (p. 1167), have been omitted.

A unidirectional edge, for example, from the module java.se to the java.desktop module signifies that the former has a dependency on the latter. The (complete) module graph of the JDK allows us to read which modules any given module depends on. The structure of the module graph in Figure 19.2 highlights two important modules: java.se at the zenith and java.base at the base of the graph, showing that the former depends on each module in the Java SE platform configuration and the latter on none of them.

Module graphs visualize the modular structure of an application, providing insights into its architecture and in discovering any anomalies. Such graphs can be built using the JDK tool jdeps (p. 1214). Other JDK tools, such as javac and java, perform analysis on the module graph of the application to ensure that all module dependencies are satisfied.

Figure 19.2   *Partial Module Graph of Java SE 17 Modules*

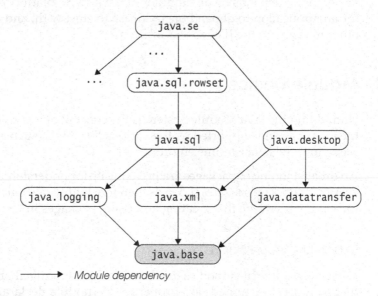

The java.base **Module**

The java.base module implements the *fundamental* APIs of the Java SE platform. It is necessary for any Java program to function, and deemed necessary for every configuration of the Java platform. Not surprisingly, it is required by every module in the JDK. In fact, *every* application module has an *implicit dependence* on the java.base module. However, it is seldom necessary for a module to explicitly specify a dependence on the java.base module.

Typically when constructing a module graph, dependency on the java.base module is only shown for a module that does not depend on any other module. Otherwise, this dependency is implicit.

The java.base module contains many important packages, such as java.lang, java.util, and java.io. The java.lang package, which contains the primordial class java.lang.Object, is imported automatically by every Java compilation unit.

Even though every module depends on the java.base module, this does not mean that all packages in it are also automatically *imported*. This only applies to the java.lang package. To use simple names of types in the source code, the relevant packages must be explicitly imported.

The java.se Module

The java.se module represents the *core* Java platform. It depends on each module in the Java SE platform configuration. Technically called an *aggregate module*, it does not contain any packages, but acts as a conduit to channel dependencies on other modules. Any module that depends on the java.se module would effectively imply that it depends on all modules of the Java SE platform. A typical scenario is for an application to depend on java.base to start with, and add dependencies to other modules in the JDK as and when needed.

19.3 Module Basics

Underlying the Java Module System is the concept of a *module* which is defined in the language and supported by the various JDK tools (such as javac, java, jar, and jdeps) and the Java runtime environment.

An understanding of packages is a prerequisite for understanding modules. The discussion of packages in §6.3, p. 326, is therefore highly relevant to this chapter. Going forward, we assume that creating and using packages in Java is well understood.

Module Declaration

A *module declaration* embodies the definition of a module that contains packages—that is, it specifies a module's properties. A module declaration must specify the *name* of the module and can declare the following in its declaration:

- *Dependencies* the module has on other modules—that is, modules it *requires* to implement its functionality
- Packages it *exports* for other modules to use
- Packages it *opens* for *reflection* to other modules (p. 1191)
- Services it *provides* (p. 1196)
- Services it *consumes* (p. 1196)

In essence, a modular declaration specifies any modules its packages (and hence their classes) require to implement their functionality, and any packages that are provided for the benefit of other modules. Unless otherwise specified, other packages in the module are internal to the module—that is, they are not accessible to other modules.

The *basic form* of a module declaration is shown below. A module has a unique *name*. The *body* of the modular declaration can include *module directives*. The requires and exports *directives* are shown in the module declaration below. The modules required by a module for its internal implementation are specified using a requires directive, and the packages that other modules can utilize from it are specified using an exports directive. The latter is called an *unqualified export* as the exported package is available to any module that requires this module. (See §19.4, p. 1177, for an overview of all module directives.)

```
module moduleName {
  // Body:
  requires moduleName₁;        // A requires directive.
  ...
  requires moduleNameₙ;
  exports packageName₁;        // An exports directive.
  ...
  exports packageNameₘ;
}
```

There can be zero or more such directives in such a module declaration. So a module declaration with no directive is valid, as it neither requires any modules (bar the java.base module) nor exports any of its packages.

The same directive cannot be duplicated. The directives can occur in any order, but conventionally they are grouped with requires directives preceding exports directives. In a module declaration, the word module is treated as a keyword only in the context of specifying the module name, and the words requires and exports are treated as keywords only in the context of specifying a module directive. They can be used as normal identifiers in all other contexts.

Only one module declaration can be specified in a file, which must be named module-info.java. No other declarations can be included in this file, and there can be no package statement either, but the import statement is allowed. This file also cannot be empty. As any other Java source code file, the module-info.java file with the module declaration is compiled and its bytecode is placed in a class file named module-info.class, called the *module descriptor*.

The graphical notation in Figure 19.3(a) and (b) shows two modules, client and seller, with their corresponding module declarations in Figure 19.3(c) and (d), respectively.

- *The name of the module*: This is the unique *name* of the module to distinguish it from other modules.

Figure 19.3 *Modules and Module Declarations*

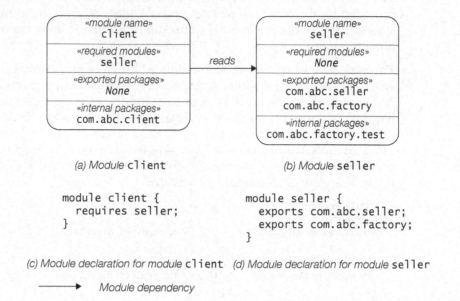

(a) Module client   (b) Module seller

```
module client {              module seller {
  requires seller;             exports com.abc.seller;
}                              exports com.abc.factory;
                             }
```

(c) Module declaration for module client (d) Module declaration for module seller

⟶ *Module dependency*

In Figure 19.3(a) and (b), the names of the modules are client and seller, respectively. These module names are used in the respective module declaration in Figure 19.3(c) and (d).

- *The required modules*: These are the modules that a module *requires* for the types (i.e., classes and interfaces) in its packages.

In Figure 19.3(a) and (b), the client module requires the seller module and the seller module does not require any module, respectively. This is reflected in the respective module declarations in Figure 19.3(c) and (d): The module declaration for client has a requires directive specifying the seller module, but the module declaration for seller has no requires directive. The requires directive states that the specified module is required at compile time and runtime by the declared module.

The client module has a dependence on the seller module, called a *module dependency*, shown with a directed arrow from client module to seller module in Figure 19.3. Technically, the client module is said *read* the seller module. Often, we say module client *depends on* module seller, or module client *requires* module seller, or module seller *is readable* by module client. Although technically not correct, for the purpose of this discussion, they are all synonyms.

- *The exported packages*: These are packages that a module *exports* so other modules can utilize them for their own implementation. Exported packages define the *public API* of the declared module, where *accessibility rules* govern what types (and hence which members in these types) in an exported package are accessible to other modules (p. 1174).

In Figure 19.3(a) and (b), the client module does not export any packages and the seller module exports packages com.abc.seller and com.abc.factory. This is reflected in the respective module declarations: The module declaration for client has no exports directive, but the module declaration for seller has two exports directives that specify the exported packages.

Although the package com.abc.factory in module seller is exported, it does *not* imply that the package com.abc.factory.test is exported as well. This is analogous to the import statement, where packages must be imported individually.

- *The internal packages*: These are the packages that are *internal* to the module and therefore not accessible to other modules.

In Figure 19.3(a) and (b), the client module has an internal package com.abc.client and the seller module has an internal package com.abc.factory.test. However, there is no directive to specify an internal package in the module declaration. The question of how we implement a module and its packages in the file system is answered in §19.5, p. 1179.

Module Name

A legal module name can consist of one or more (by convention, lowercase) legal identifiers separated by a . (dot), as in the case of a package name. Module names and package names are in different *namespaces*. From the context in which such a name occurs, the compiler can deduce which namespace it belongs to. For example, the name com.abc.seller is a module name if used with the context-dependent keyword module in a module declaration, but it is a package name when used in an exports directive.

Analogous to package names, reverse DNS (*Domain Name System*) notation can be used to form unique module names. The convention is to use the name of the *principal exported package* (if there is one) in a module as its module name. When naming a module, it is recommended that the name should reflect the *structure* of the module—that is, its package hierarchy. For example, the module declarations in Figure 19.3(c) and (d) can be written as follows, respectively:

```
module com.abc.client {          module com.abc.seller {
    requires com.abc.seller;          exports com.abc.seller;
}                                      exports com.abc.factory;
                                   }
```

If care is not exercised in naming modules and packages, distinguishing between module names and package names can become a problem when reading the code, as we can see in the module declarations above, where the name com.abc.seller is used both as a module name and as a package name. For brevity, we will not adhere to the naming scheme described above and will continue to use simple names for modules, as in Figure 19.3.

A package is implemented in the file system by a directory hierarchy that mirrors its name. For example, a package named com.abc.seller is implemented by its source code files being located under the directory ./com/abc/seller. As we shall see in §19.5, p. 1181, a module named com.abc.seller is implemented by a directory whose name is com.abc.seller under which all its packages are located.

Some examples of legal module names (as well as legal package names):

    my.big.fat.module, com.passion.controller, org.geek.gui, view

Some examples of illegal module names (as well as illegal package names):

    net.soda.7up, org:factory, com-factory-gizmo

Module Graph

The structure of an application is reflected by its module graph constructed from dependencies between its modules. An important aspect of the module system is to perform *module resolution* at compile time and runtime to ensure that the application has a *reliable configuration*. This process *resolves* all dependencies, making sure that they are satisfied—that is, the requires directives are matched by exports directives with all types required being accessible.

The module resolution mandates that the module graph is *acyclic*, meaning that the graph cannot have *dependency cycles* where a module depends on itself, either directly or indirectly. The module system also does not allow a package to be split between different modules, primarily because this would mean searching in several modules to locate a type in a split package. Therefore, all code in a package must be in the same module.

Every module depends on the proverbial java.base module in the JDK. Its packages are available to all modules—for example, the package java.lang containing classes like Object and String. Specifying java.base in a requires directive is optional in a module declaration. If not specified explicitly, an *implicit dependency* on java.base is automatically applied.

Figure 19.4(a) shows the module graph from Figure 19.3 augmented by the two dependencies on java.base. The declarations of module client and module seller in Figure 19.4(b) and (c) include explicit requires directives specifying java.base. The convention is to leave the dependency on java.base implicit. Showing all implicit dependencies from all modules on java.base in a module graph can quickly make the graph look like spaghetti. Often this dependency is only shown for modules that do not depend on other modules (a.k.a. *sink nodes* in graph terminology).

Figure 19.4   *Module Graph and Implicit Dependencies*

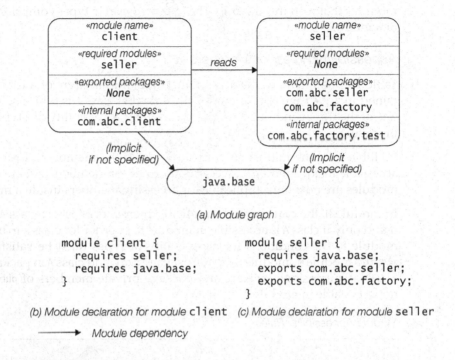

(a) Module graph

```
module client {                    module seller {
    requires seller;                   requires java.base;
    requires java.base;                exports com.abc.seller;
}                                      exports com.abc.factory;
                                   }
```

(b) Module declaration for module client   *(c) Module declaration for module* seller

───────▶ *Module dependency*

Readability and Accessibility

A *readability* relationship is implied by the requires directive. Module client *reads* module seller, since the module declaration of client specifies the following requires directive:

    requires seller;   // (1)

This requires directive alone is not enough to allow code in module client to access types in packages contained in module seller. Module seller must reciprocally *export* the relevant packages required by module client, as in the following exports directive in the declaration of module seller:

    exports com.abc.seller;   // (2)

What if the code in module client wants to access the class GizmoSeller in the package com.abc.seller of module seller? In this case, this class is only accessible to module client if it is declared public in the package com.abc.seller:

    public class GizmoSeller { /*...*/ }   // (3)

The three conditions, as exemplified by (1), (2), and (3) above, must be satisfied for the accessibility relationship. The module system ensures, both at compile time and runtime, that these conditions are met before allowing access to code from other modules.

We see that only a public type in an exported package of a module is accessible by modules that read this module. The exported public types comprise the *public API* of a module.

Accessibility Rules for Members

Table 19.1 summarizes the accessibility rules for *members* of a public class A contained in a package pkg1 of module M. Note that class A is public so that it satisfies one of the three conditions discussed earlier for accessibility of a type from another module.

In Table 19.1, the middle column shows how the members of public class A are accessible inside module M. Accessibility rules for members that are applied before modules are now only applicable for accessing members inside a module.

In module N, the public and the protected members of public class A are accessible if and only if class A is accessible in module N. In order for class A to be accessible in module N, the conditions for accessibility of types must be satisfied: Module N *requires* module M, module M *exports* package pkg1, and class A in package pkg1 is public. Not surprisingly, private and package-private members of public class A are not accessible in module N.

Table 19.1   *Module Accessibility Rules*

Access modifier for members in public class A inside package pkg1 of module M	Inside module M	Inside module N
public	Accessible in all packages in module M	Accessible in all packages in module N, if and only if module N *requires* module M and module M *exports* pkg1
protected	Accessible in package pkg1, and accessible only by subclasses of class A in other packages in module M	Accessible by subclasses of class A in all packages in module N, if and only if module N *requires* module M and module M *exports* pkg1
package-private	Only accessible in package pkg1	Not accessible
private	Only accessible in class A	Not accessible

Implied Module Dependencies

As an example of refactoring modules, we will refactor the seller module in
Figure 19.3(b). We decide to move the package com.abc.factory and its subpackage
com.abc.factory.test to a new module called factory. The effects of this factoring
are illustrated in Figure 19.5. Now both client and seller require factory, as can be
seen from their module declarations in Figure 19.5(d) and (e). The package
com.abc.factory is now exported by the module factory in Figure 19.5(f). Apart
from fixing the module declarations and moving the relevant packages from seller
to factory, no other changes are necessary.

The module graph in Figure 19.5 shows the dependencies between the modules
after refactoring. Note that there are two paths from client to factory in the module
graph. One might be tempted to think that since client requires seller and seller
requires factory, then client requires factory transitively, and we could omit the
requires directive on factory in client. However, the compiler will diligently flag
an error. Dependencies specified by the requires directive are *not* transitive.

Figure 19.5   *Module Declarations and Module Graph*

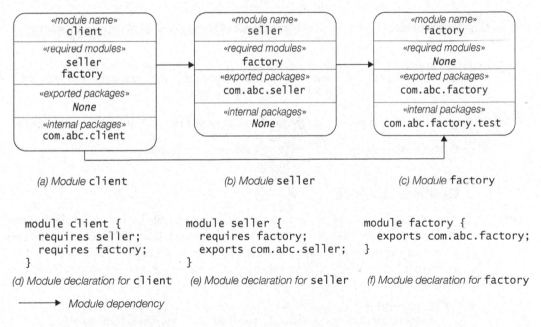

```
module client {            module seller {            module factory {
  requires seller;           requires factory;           exports com.abc.factory;
  requires factory;          exports com.abc.seller;    }
}                          }
```

(d) Module declaration for client   *(e) Module declaration for* seller   *(f) Module declaration for* factory

⟶ *Module dependency*

The requires transitive *Directive*

Implied dependencies can be created by the requires transitive directive. This is illustrated in Figure 19.6. If it is the case that all modules that require seller will also
require factory, we can omit the requires directive on factory in client and use a
requires transitive directive in seller. In Figure 19.6, client no longer requires
factory, but seller specifies factory in a requires transitive directive. All changes

are confined to the module declarations in Figure 19.6(d) and (e), so no other changes are required in the code. Implications of using a requires transitive directive are that any module that requires seller now will also implicitly require factory. This implied dependency is shown from client to factory in the module graph in Figure 19.6.

Figure 19.6   *Implied Module Dependencies*

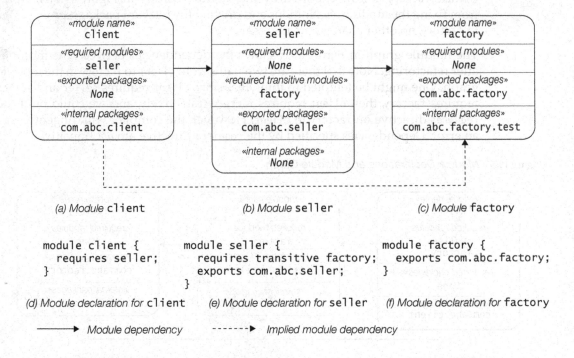

```
module client {          module seller {                       module factory {
  requires seller;          requires transitive factory;          exports com.abc.factory;
}                           exports com.abc.seller;             }
                          }
```

(d) Module declaration for client   *(e) Module declaration for* seller   *(f) Module declaration for* factory

──────▶ *Module dependency*   ------▶ *Implied module dependency*

Qualified Export

Any package that is exported by a module is readable by any module that requires its module. However, sometimes it is necessary that only certain modules can access an exported package. This can be achieved by using the exports-to directive, as shown below at (1), where packageOne in moduleX is *only* exported to moduleA and moduleB:

```
module moduleX {
  exports packageOne to moduleA, moduleB;   // (1) Qualified export.
  exports packageTwo;                       // (2) Unqualified export.
}
```

This is known as *qualified export*. Apart from moduleA and moduleB, no other module can access packageOne in moduleX. The compiler will issue an error if an attempt is made by any other module. Qualified export does not prevent the modules in the to clause to access other packages that are exported. Unqualified export of packageTwo, shown at (2), allows *any* module that requires moduleX to access packageTwo. Qualified export should be used judiciously, as its usage results in tight coupling between modules that can increase the degree of dependency between modules—a hallmark of poor software design.

Figure 19.7 shows how the module declaration of the factory module that uses the exports-to directive allows its package com.abc.factory to be accessible only by the seller and the client module. Any other module that requires module factory will not be able to access the com.abc.factory package in the factory module.

Figure 19.7 *Qualified Export*

```
module client {            module seller {             module factory {
  requires seller;           requires factory;            exports com.abc.factory
  requires factory;          exports com.abc.seller;         to seller, client;
}                          }                           }
```

(d') Module declaration for client   *(e') Module declaration for* seller   *(f') Module declaration for* factory *with qualified export of its package*

19.4 Overview of Module Directives

An overview of all module directives is given in Table 19.2, together with references to where they are covered in this chapter.

Modules add 10 restricted keywords to the language: exports, module, open, opens, provides, requires, to, transitive, uses, and with. The words open (see Table 19.3) and module are keywords only in the header of a module declaration, and the remaining in a particular context of a specific directive. The word static is already a keyword, but has a different meaning in the requires static directive.

Table 19.2 *Overview of Module Directives*

Directive	Description
requires *module* (p. 1170)	The current module specifies a dependence on the specified *module*, allowing the current module to access exported public types in the specified *module*.
requires transitive *module* (p. 1175)	Any module that requires the current module will have an implicit dependence on the specified *module*, and can access exported public types in the specified *module* on par with the current module.
requires static *module*	The current module has a mandatory dependence on the specified *module* at compile time, but is optional at runtime. This is known as *optional dependency*. It is not discussed in this book.

Table 19.2   *Overview of Module Directives (Continued)*

Directive	Description
exports *package* *(p. 1170)*	The specified *package* exported by the current module is available to other modules that require the current module—that is, they can access public types in the specified *package*. This is called an *unqualified export*.
exports *package* to *module1*, ... *(p. 1176)*	The specified *package* exported by the current module is solely available to the modules specified in the to clause. That is, only those modules in the to clause that require the current module can access public types in the specified *package*. This is called a *qualified export*.
opens *package* *(p. 1191)*	Access to the specified *package* is only granted through *reflection* (§25.6, p. 1587) at runtime for code in other modules. This is called an *unqualified opens directive*.
opens *package* to *module1*, ... *(p. 1195)*	Access to the specified *package* is only granted through *reflection* at runtime solely for code in modules specified in the to clause. This is called a *qualified opens directive*.
provides *type* with *type1*, ... *(p. 1196)*	The current module specifies that it provides a *service* (specified by *type*) that is implemented by one or more *service providers* (*type1*, ... in the with clause implement the service). The current module is said to be a *service provider*. The service provided can be consumed by other modules that want to use this service.
uses *type* *(p. 1196)*	The current module specifies that it uses a *service* (specified by *type*) and that a *service provider* that implements it may be discoverable at runtime. Typically, the current module is said to be a *service locator*, but can also be a *service consumer* if the locator is merged with the consumer.

Table 19.3   *The open Modifier for Modules*

Modifier	Description
open module *module* { ... } *(p. 1196)*	Unrestricted access to *all* packages in the *module* is granted through *reflection* at runtime for code in other modules.

19.5 Creating a Modular Application

After understanding the basic role of a module declaration, we can proceed to create a modular application. As support for Java modules is not quite up to par at present in integrated development environments (IDEs), we will use the command-line tools provided by the JDK. Using the command-line tools also provides a deeper understanding of the Java Module System. We will be using the following JDK tools in the rest of this chapter:

- *Java language compiler: the* `javac` *command (p. 1186)*
- *Java application launcher: the* `java` *command (p. 1186)*
- *Java Archive tool: the* `jar` *command (p. 1189)*
- *Java Class Dependency Analyzer tool: the* `jdeps` *command (p. 1214)*
- *Java Linker tool: the* `jlink` *command (p. 1204)*

The JDK tools are versatile tools with numerous features and many capabilities. The myriad of options for each tool can be overwhelming. Tables with summaries of selected options for each tool are provided, starting with Table 19.6 on page 1218.

As a running example, we will develop an elementary multi-module application that is based on a very simplified Model-View-Controller (MVC) design pattern. Prior knowledge of the MVC design pattern is not essential. To keep things manageable, the emphasis is more on the mechanics of creating a modular application than on providing an industrial-strength implementation of the MVC design pattern.

To make it less tedious in experimenting with the modular application code, a file with the relevant commands is provided, together with the source code of the application, all of which can readily be downloaded from the book's website. Hands-on coding of a modular application is highly encouraged, to understand both the Java modules and the tools essential for creating modular applications.

Running Example: Dispensing Canned Advice

In the MVC design pattern, the controller handles the user requests. The model provides the business logic and manages the data in the application. The view creates the response to the user, usually by updating the data display. Simplified, the interaction in an MVC-based application proceeds as follows:

1. A user sends a request to the controller.
2. The controller interacts with the model and with the view.

   First it requests the model to update its data according to the user request, and then it requests the view to create a response. The view accesses the model and updates the data display accordingly.

The dispensing canned advice application (called `adviceApp`) embodies the simplified MVC design pattern outlined above. It comprises four modules: the `model`, view, controller, and main modules, shown in Figure 19.8. The main module in Figure 19.8 simulates the user mentioned above. From the notation used for a module in Figure 19.8, we can read the name of the module, the modules it requires, the packages it exports, and any packages that are internal to the module. Based on the modules required by each module, the resulting *module graph* is also shown in Figure 19.8, with *dependencies* between them. For example, the controller module requires the modules view and model, thus there are two dependencies from the controller module to the view and the model modules, respectively.

Figure 19.8   *Module Graph of the* adviceApp *Application*

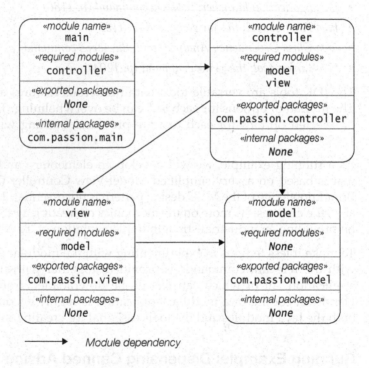

Module dependency

Creating the Application Directory Structure

Typically, the code for a modular application is organized in a *directory structure*, similar to the one shown in Figure 19.9. The modules are created in the src directory and compiled into the mods directory. The compiled modules are bundled into modular JARs and placed in the mlib directory. The different JDK tools can thus operate on the relevant directories.

The application root directory for the adviceApp application bears the same name. It is also the *working directory* in which all commands are issued to the JDK tools. Under the adviceApp directory, the following command creates the directories shown in Figure 19.9:

```
>mkdir mlib mods src
```

Figure 19.9   *Application Directory Structure*

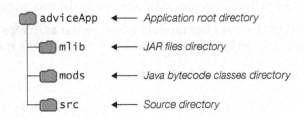

Creating an Exploded Module Directory

The model module does not require any user-defined modules—that is, it does not depend on any user-defined module, and can therefore be implemented first. Its module declaration is straightforward, as it exports its only package, com.passion.model (shown in Figure 19.10). The directory layout for the model module is created manually under the src directory as shown in Figure 19.10, and referred to as the *exploded module*.

Referring to Figure 19.10, (1) shows that the module name and that of the *module root directory* must be the same, and (2) shows that the module-info.java file containing the module declaration must reside immediately under the module root directory.

Figure 19.10   *Exploded Module Structure for the model Module*

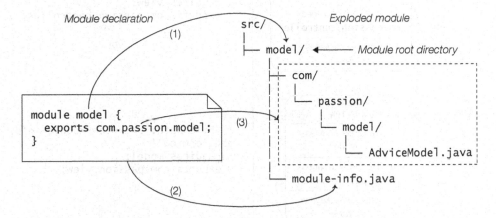

Packages were discussed in §6.3, p. 326. Any package (or subpackage) that a module contains is mapped to a corresponding directory hierarchy under the module root directory. In Figure 19.10, (3) shows how the package com.passion.model of the module is laid out under the module root directory, with the directory hierarchy com/passion/model mirroring its package name. It also shows that the package has only one source file, AdviceModel.java. If the package had any other source files, they would also be placed in the same location.

A package is included in a module by virtue of its location in the module root directory. The organization of the module root directory, as in Figure 19.10, defines what constitutes a module. Similarly, any other packages in the module are mapped to their directory structure under the module root directory.

Figure 19.11 shows the module graph of the adviceApp application together with the module declaration of each module that is in the module graph. Each module

Figure 19.11 *Module Graph and Module Declarations*

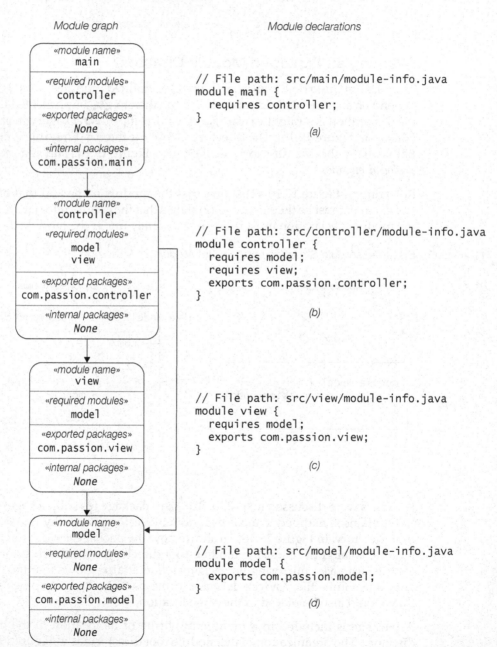

Module graph

«module name»
main

«required modules»
controller

«exported packages»
None

«internal packages»
com.passion.main

«module name»
controller

«required modules»
model
view

«exported packages»
com.passion.controller

«internal packages»
None

«module name»
view

«required modules»
model

«exported packages»
com.passion.view

«internal packages»
None

«module name»
model

«required modules»
None

«exported packages»
com.passion.model

«internal packages»
None

Module declarations

```
// File path: src/main/module-info.java
module main {
    requires controller;
}
```
                    (a)

```
// File path: src/controller/module-info.java
module controller {
    requires model;
    requires view;
    exports com.passion.controller;
}
```
                    (b)

```
// File path: src/view/module-info.java
module view {
    requires model;
    exports com.passion.view;
}
```
                    (c)

```
// File path: src/model/module-info.java
module model {
    exports com.passion.model;
}
```
                    (d)

declaration is in a source file named module-info.java, and is placed in its corresponding exploded module directory, as shown in Figure 19.12.

Figure 19.12(a) shows the contents of the src directory where each module is mapped to its corresponding exploded module. Each module has one package that contains one source file. This package is mapped to its directory hierarchy under the root directory of its module.

Figure 19.12 *Compiling Exploded Modules Containing Source Code*

```
src/
├── controller/                                (3)
│   ├── com/                                  >javac --module-path mods \
│   │   └── passion/                              -d mods/controller \
│   │       └── controller/                       src/controller/module-info.java \
│   │           └── AdviceController.java         src/controller/com/passion/ \
│   └── module-info.java                             controller/AdviceController.java
├── main/                                      (4)
│   ├── com/                                  >javac --module-path mods \
│   │   └── passion/                              -d mods/main \
│   │       └── main/                             src/main/module-info.java \
│   │           └── Main.java                     src/main/com/passion/main/ \
│   └── module-info.java                                  Main.java
├── model/                                     (1)
│   ├── com/                                  >javac --module-path mods \
│   │   └── passion/                              -d mods/model \
│   │       └── model/                            src/model/module-info.java \
│   │           └── AdviceModel.java              src/model/com/passion/model/ \
│   └── module-info.java                                  AdviceModel.java
└── view/                                      (2)
    ├── com/                                  >javac --module-path mods \
    │   └── passion/                              -d mods/view \
    │       └── view/                             src/view/module-info.java \
    │           └── AdviceView.java               src/view/com/passion/view/ \
    └── module-info.java                                  AdviceView.java
```

(a) Exploded modules containing source code   *(b) Order of compiling exploded modules individually*

Creating the Source Files in the Exploded Modules

The classes that are in packages included in the modules are declared in their respective source files. Example 19.1 shows the source files for the adviceApp application.

The source code of the AdviceModel.java file in the model module is shown at (1) in Example 19.1. This source file should reside in the package com.passion.model in the model module. Its file path src/model/com/passion/model/AdviceModel.java in the exploded module is shown as a comment at (1). The class AdviceModel is declared to be in package com.passion.model. It keeps track of the current advice (the String field currentAdvice). Its constructor creates an AdviceModel with the field current-Advice initialized to the string "No advice." The method setCurrentAdvice() sets the field currentAdvice to the advice corresponding to its int parameter value. The method getCurrentAdvice() returns the value of the field currentAdvice.

The source code of the `AdviceView.java` file in the `view` module is shown at (2) in Example 19.1. This source file should reside in the package `com.passion.view` in the view module. Its file path `src/view/com/passion/view/AdviceView.java` in the exploded module is shown as a comment at (2). The class `AdviceView` is declared to be in package `com.passion.view`. It uses an `AdviceModel`. This model is passed to an `AdviceView` in the constructor. The method `updateAdviceDisplay()` accesses its model for the current advice and prints it.

Analogously, the source code of the `AdviceController.java` file in the `controller` module is shown at (3) in Example 19.1. An `AdviceController` uses an `AdviceModel` and an `AdviceView`, both of which are created in the constructor, where the Advice-Model is injected into the `AdviceView`. The method `showAdvice()` calls the `AdviceModel` to set the current advice based on its `int` parameter value, followed by a call to the `AdviceView` to update the advice display.

Finally, the source code of the `Main.java` file in the `main` module is shown at (4) in Example 19.1. The `Main` class is the entry point of the application. It simulates a user by calling an `AdviceController` several times to show different advice.

Note that all source code should be explicitly contained in packages, except for the module declaration—that is, the `module-info.java` file, which is always located immediately under the module root directory. The name of the module in the module declaration must match the name of the module root directory.

Example 19.1 *Source Code Files for the* `adviceApp` *Application*

```
// File path: src/model/com/passion/model/AdviceModel.java        (1)
package com.passion.model;

public class AdviceModel {

  private String currentAdvice;

  public AdviceModel() { this.setCurrentAdvice(0); }

  public void setCurrentAdvice(int i) {
    String advice;
    switch(i) {
      case 1 : advice = "See no evil."; break;
      case 2 : advice = "Speak no evil."; break;
      case 3 : advice = "Hear no evil."; break;
      default: advice = "No advice.";
    }
    currentAdvice = advice;
  }

  public String getCurrentAdvice() { return currentAdvice; }
}
```

```java
// File path: src/view/com/passion/view/AdviceView.java                (2)
package com.passion.view;
import com.passion.model.AdviceModel;               // From model module.

public class AdviceView {

  private AdviceModel model;

  public AdviceView(AdviceModel model) { this.model = model; }

  public void updateAdviceDisplay(){
    System.out.println(model.getCurrentAdvice());
  }
}
```

```java
// File path: src/controller/com/passion/controller/AdviceController.java   (3)
package com.passion.controller;
import com.passion.model.AdviceModel;               // From model module.
import com.passion.view.AdviceView;                 // From view module.

public class AdviceController {

  private AdviceModel model;
  private AdviceView view;

  public AdviceController() {
    model = new AdviceModel();
    view = new AdviceView(model);                   // Inject the model.
  }

  public void showAdvice(int adviceNumber) {
    model.setCurrentAdvice(adviceNumber);
    view.updateAdviceDisplay();
  }
}
```

```java
// File path: src/main/com/passion/main/Main.java                       (4)
package com.passion.main;
import com.passion.controller.AdviceController;     // From controller module.

public class Main {
  public static void main(String... args) {
    AdviceController controller = new AdviceController();
    controller.showAdvice(1);
    controller.showAdvice(2);
    controller.showAdvice(3);
    controller.showAdvice(0);
  }
}
```

19.6   Compiling and Running a Modular Application

Both the javac tool to compile Java source code and the java tool to launch an application include new command-line options to specifically support building of modular applications.

When the javac tool or the java tool is called, initially a *module resolution* is performed on the application's structure. This process checks that dependencies among the modules are resolved in the application, thus ensuring a reliable configuration, by catching any problems as early as possible.

The astute reader will soon notice that the tool commands in this chapter are run on a Unix-based platform. Platform-dependent idiosyncrasies are pointed out where appropriate. The first one to note is the line-continuation character to break up a command line over several lines. This is to make the command and its options easier to read. The *line-continuation character* is a \ (backslash) on the Unix-based platform and a ∧ (caret) on the Windows platform. Below, the command on a single line and the command that spans over two lines are equivalent.

```
>javac One.java Two.java

>javac One.java\
 Two.java
```

Individual Module Compilation

We first look at how to compile the modules of the adviceApp application individually. Typically, in order to compile a module, the compiler needs to know the source directory to find the source code of the module, the destination directory to place the Java bytecode class files for the module, and any additional modules that the module requires.

The modules in an application can only be compiled in an order that respects the module dependencies—that is, all modules a module requires have already been compiled—or if it does not depend on any other modules. In the case of the advice-App application, there is only one such order, shown in Figure 19.12(b). We can compile the model module first since it does not require any other modules (apart from the java.base module that is readily accessible by default). Figure 19.13 shows how the model module is compiled. The javac command in Figure 19.13(c) shows how the source code of the model module under the src/model directory is compiled to the mods/model directory where the necessary package is created and the class files are placed. Note how the mods/model directory mirrors the src/model directory.

```
>javac --module-path mods \
       -d mods/model \
       src/model/module-info.java \
       src/model/com/passion/model/AdviceModel.java
```

The --module-path option (*short form*: -p) is used to specify where to find the modules required to compile the source code files specified in the command line. In the case of the `model` module, this option is superfluous as this module does not depend on any other module. However, the other modules in the `adviceApp` application do so. As modules are compiled, their exploded modules containing the class files will be readily found in the `mods` directory specified by this option. This option can also specify a colon-separated (:) list of directories (semicolon (;) separated in Windows) to look up required modules in different directories.

The `-d` option (*no long form*) specifies the *destination directory* (also called *target directory*) for placing the Java bytecode class files. In this case they will be placed under the `mods/model` directory, which is created by the compiler if necessary.

The source files in the module are specified *last* in the command line with their full pathname. The compiler creates the necessary directory hierarchy under the destination directory `mods/model` specified by the `-d` option. The module declaration in the `module-info.java` file is also compiled to a class file, as any other Java source file. This class file is called the *module descriptor*. It resides immediately under the module root directory, which in this case is `mods/model`.

After the `model` module is compiled, the next candidate to compile is the `view` model, as its required module `model` has now been compiled to the `mods/model` directory. Figure 19.14(a) shows the final result of compiling the modules in the `adviceApp` application by executing the javac commands in the order shown in Figure 19.12(b).

Figure 19.13   *Compiling the* `model` *Module*

```
src/                              mods/
└── model/                        └── model/
    ├── com/                          ├── com/
    │   └── passion/                  │   └── passion/
    │       └── model/                │       └── model/
    │           └── AdviceModel.java  │           └── AdviceModel.class
    └── module-info.java              └── module-info.class
```

(a) Exploded module with source files   (b) Exploded module with Java bytecode classes

```
>javac --module-path mods \
  -d mods/model \
  src/model/module-info.java \
  src/model/com/passion/model/AdviceModel.java
```

(c) Command to compile the `model` module

Multi-Module Compilation

It is tedious compiling modules individually. It is more convenient to use the following command:

```
>javac --module-source-path src -d mods --module main
```

The `--module-source-path` option (*no short form*), as the name suggests, indicates the `src` directory where the exploded modules with the source files for the modules can be found.

The -d option (*no short form*) indicates the directory mods for the exploded modules with the class files. The compiler creates the module root directories and the package hierarchies as necessary under the mods directory.

The --module option (*short form*: -m) can be used to specify the name of a single module or a list of module names separated by a comma (,) with no intervening space characters. For each module specified, the compiler will only compile those modules that this module depends on. The compiler does the necessary module dependency analysis and compiles all the modules in the right order. If only the model module had been specified, only it will be compiled, as it does not depend on any other module.

The result of the above command is the same as before, shown in Figure 19.14(a).

Figure 19.14 *Creating Modular JARs*

```
mods/
├── controller/
│   ├── com/
│   │   └── passion/
│   │       └── controller/
│   │           └── AdviceController.class
│   └── module-info.class
├── main/
│   ├── com/
│   │   └── passion/
│   │       └── main/
│   │           └── Main.class
│   └── module-info.class
├── model/
│   ├── com/
│   │   └── passion/
│   │       └── model/
│   │           └── AdviceModel.class
│   └── module-info.class
└── view/
    ├── com/
    │   └── passion/
    │       └── view/
    │           └── AdviceView.class
    └── module-info.class
```

```
>jar --verbose \
     --create \
     --file mlib/controller.jar \
     -C mods/controller .
```

```
>jar --verbose \
     --create \
     --file mlib/main.jar \
     --main-class com.passion.main.Main \
     -C mods/main .
```

```
>jar --verbose \
     --create \
     --file mlib/model.jar \
     -C mods/model .
```

```
>jar --verbose \
     --create \
     --file mlib/view.jar \
     -C mods/view .
```

(a) Exploded modules with Java bytecode classes　　　　　　(b) Creating JAR files

```
mlib/
├── controller.jar
├── main.jar
├── model.jar
└── view.jar
```

(c) JAR file directory

Running a Modular Application from Exploded Modules

Typically, the java command needs to know where to find the modules needed to run the application and also the entry point of the application, meaning the class whose main() method should be executed to launch the application.

```
>java --module-path mods --module main/com.passion.main.Main
See no evil.
Speak no evil.
Hear no evil.
No advice.
```

The --module-path option (*short form*: -p) is used to specify where to find the modules needed to run the application. In this case it is the mods directory containing the exploded modules with the class files. This option can also specify a colon-separated (:) list of directories (semicolon (;) separated in Windows) to look up the required modules.

The --module option (*short form*: -m) in the command explicitly specifies the *entry point* of the application. In this case, it is the class Main in the com.passion.main package of the main module that provides the main() method. This requires the *fully qualified name* of the class (com.passion.main.Main) and the *full name* of the module (main). Note the *directory-level separator* (/) in the specification of the entry point.

19.7 Creating JAR Files

A *JAR* (Java Archive) file is a convenient way of bundling and deploying Java executable code and any other resources that are required (e.g., image or audio files). A JAR file is created by using the jar tool. The jar command has many options, akin to the Unix tar command (p. 1221).

In addition to creating *plain JARs* (also referred to as *non-modular JARs*), the jar tool of the JDK has been enhanced to create and manipulate *modular JARs*, making it convenient to bundle and deploy modules. The procedure for creating a plain or a modular JAR is the same; the main difference being that a modular JAR always contains the module descriptor—that is, the module-info.class file.

Creating Modular JARs

Figure 19.14(b) shows the jar commands that can be used to create a modular JAR for each of the modules in the adviceApp application. The resulting modular JARs are placed under the mlib directory, as shown in Figure 19.14(c). We take a closer look at the jar command to create a modular JAR for the model module:

```
>jar --verbose \
    --create \
    --file mlib/model.jar \
    -C mods/model .
```

Possible output to the terminal:

```
added manifest
added module-info: module-info.class
adding: com/(in = 0) (mods= 0)(stored 0%)
adding: com/passion/(in = 0) (mods= 0)(stored 0%)
adding: com/passion/model/(in = 0) (mods= 0)(stored 0%)
adding: com/passion/model/AdviceModel.class(in = 641) (mods= 415)(deflated 35%)
```

The --verbose option (*short form*: -v) instructs the jar tool to print information about its operation on the terminal, as evident from the output on the terminal.

The --create option (*short form*: -c) results in a modular JAR to be created, as the module descriptor will be included in the JAR file (see below).

The --file option (*short form*: -f) specifies the file name of the modular JAR. In this case, it is model.jar that will be created and located under the mlib directory. Note there are no restrictions on the file name of the modular JAR, as long as it is a legal file name. Of course, having a descriptive file name that reflects what the module in the modular JAR stands for can aid readability.

The -C option instructs the jar tool to change to the mods/model directory and include the contents of this directory which is designated by the dot (.) special notation. From the output on the terminal we can see what is added to the JAR file. Note that the modular JAR does not include information about the module root directory (in the above case, mods/model) in the modular JAR because the module descriptor already has information about the name of the module. The contents included in the modular JARs are shown by the dashed boxes in Figure 19.14(a).

The observant reader will notice that the jar command in Figure 19.14(b) to create the main.jar has an extra option to specify the application entry point:

```
>jar --verbose \
    --create \
    --file mlib/main.jar \
    --main-class com.passion.main.Main \
    -C mods/main .
```

Since the entry point of the application is in the model module, the --main-class option (*short form*: -e) specifies the fully qualified name of the class containing the main() method—that is, com.passion.main.Main. The module name is *not* specified.

Using the short form of the first four options in the above jar command, respectively (see Table 19.6), the command can be written as follows:

```
>jar -vcfe mlib/main.jar com.passion.main.Main -C mods/main .
```

Note that if the files named module-info.class are deleted in Figure 19.14(a), the jar commands in Figure 19.14(b) will still create JAR files, but these will be plain JARs, and not modular JARs.

Running an Application from a Modular JAR

The adviceApp application can be run from the modular JARs in the mlib directory by any of the following java commands, giving the same output as before:

```
>java --module-path mlib --module main
```

or

```
>java --module-path mlib --module main/com.passion.main.Main
```

The --module-path option (*short form*: -p) specifies the mlib directory in which to find the modular JARs to run the application. Previously the exploded module directory mods containing the class files for each module was specified.

As seen previously, the --module option (*short form*: -m) specifies the entry point of the application in the java command. In the first java command, only the module name main is specified. The main module can be found in the main.jar file under the mlib directory by examining the module descriptor in each module on the module path. The main.jar file contains the information about the class with the main() method, as it was specified when the modular JAR for the main module was created—that is, com.passion.main.Main. In the second java command, the entry point is explicitly given, with the module name and the fully qualified class name. Specifying the entry point explicitly overrides the entry point in any modular JAR. However, it makes no difference which command we use in the example above, as there is only one entry point for the application.

We have seen how to create, compile, bundle, and run a modular application. Now we take up the discussion about the remaining directives that can be declared in a module declaration: opening code for reflection (p. 1191) and providing services (p. 1196).

19.8 Open Modules and the opens Directive

Reflection is a powerful feature in Java that enables inspection and modification of runtime behavior of Java programs. The Reflection API is primarily in the java.lang.reflect package. Reference types (classes, interfaces, and enums) can be inspected at runtime to access information about the declarations contained in them (e.g., fields, methods, and constructors)—often referred to as *reflective access*. In fact, classes can be programmatically instantiated and methods can be invoked and values of fields can be changed. An example of using reflection to process annotations in Java programs is provided in §25.6, p. 1587.

Some frameworks, such as Spring and Hibernate, make heavy use of reflection in the services they provide. They rely on *deep reflection*: being able to use reflection, not only on public classes and their public members, but also on non-public classes and non-public members. Note that these frameworks require access for reflection at runtime, and not at compile time.

However, things changed with the introduction of modules in Java, where encapsulation is in the front seat. Reflection is now only allowed on public members of public types in *exported* packages from a module. In other words, the exports directive does not permit reflection on non-public types and non-public members from exported packages.

The opens directive in a module declaration addresses this issue of reflection at runtime, allowing deep reflection on *all* classes and *all* members contained in an *open package*.

```
module org.liberal {
    opens org.liberal.sesame;      // An open package
}
```

The adviceApp application (Example 19.1, Figure 19.12) is now modified to illustrate the opens directive. We will refer to the modified application as adviceOpen. The module controller opens the com.passion.controller package to enable clients to inspect its class AdviceController at runtime, and elicit advice by invoking the method showAdvice(). The declaration of the module controller specifies this vital information using an opens directive, as shown below in the module declaration at (1).

The idea is that module main will use reflective access on the controller module to elicit advice. Therefore, the main module does not *require* the controller module, as we can see from the module declaration below at (2).

It is not necessary for a module to explicitly require a module that has open packages for the purposes of reflection. As long as the module with the open packages is available at runtime, reflection can be used to access the contents of the open packages. The emphasis here is on use of the opens directive rather than a full-blown treatise on reflection.

```
// Filepath: src/controller/module-info.java
module controller {                                // (1)
    requires model;
    requires view;
    opens com.passion.controller;                  // Open package
}
```

```
// Filepath: src/main/module-info.java
module main {}                                      // (2)
```

In Example 19.2, the main() method at (1) in the class Main of the package com.passion.main in the module main uses reflection to invoke the showAdvice() method of the AdviceController class in the com.passion.controller open package.

The comments in the main() method are self-explanatory, but a few things should be noted.

The forName() static method of the Class class at (2) loads the specified class and returns the Class object associated with the class whose name is com.passion .controller.AdviceController. Note that module controller is not specified. We will make it available when we run the application with the java command.

The Class object from (2) is used at (3) to obtain the object representing the no-argument constructor of the AdviceController class. The newInstance() method is invoked at (4) on the constructor object to create an instance of the AdviceController class.

The class object from (2) is used at (5) to obtain all Method objects that represent methods in the AdviceController class. The method getDeclaredMethods() returns an array containing Method objects reflecting *all* declared methods of the Advice-Controller class represented by the Class object cObj, including public, protected, default access, and private methods in the class. As this class only has one private method—showAdvice()—index 0 designates this method in the array of Method objects, as shown at (6).

The if statement at (7) ensures that the method reference indeed designates the private method showAdvice().

However, before a non-public method is invoked via reflection, it is necessary to explicitly suppress checks for language access control at runtime by calling the setAccessible() method of the Method class with the value true, as shown at (8).

At (9) through (12), the private method showAdvice() designated by the method reference is invoked on the AdviceController instance specified in the argument to the invoke() method, together with an int parameter required by the showAdvice() method for specific advice.

The code in the main() method is enclosed in a try-catch construct to catch the checked exceptions that can be thrown by the various methods.

Example 19.2 *Selected Source Code Files in the* adviceOpen *Application*

```java
// File path: src/main/com/passion/main/Main.java
package com.passion.main;
import java.lang.reflect.*;                            // Types for reflection

public class Main {
  public static void main(String... args) {                          // (1)
    try {
      // Get the runtime object representing the class.
      Class<?> cObj
          = Class.forName("com.passion.controller.AdviceController");  // (2)

      // Get the no-argument constructor of the class.
      Constructor<?> constructor = cObj.getDeclaredConstructor();      // (3)

      // Create an instance of the class.
      Object instance = constructor.newInstance();                     // (4)

      // Get all declared methods, including those that are non-public.
      Method[] methods = cObj.getDeclaredMethods();                    // (5)
      // Class has only one method.
      Method method = methods[0];                                      // (6)
```

```java
      // Check if it is the right method.
      if (!method.getName().equals("showAdvice")) {                    // (7)
        System.out.printf("Method showAdvice() not found in %s.%n",
                          cObj.getName());
        return;
      }

      // Disable access control checks on the method as it is a private method.
      method.setAccessible(true);                                      // (8)

      // Invoke the method on the instance, passing any arguments.
      method.invoke(instance, 1);                                      // (9)
      method.invoke(instance, 2);                                      // (10)
      method.invoke(instance, 3);                                      // (11)
      method.invoke(instance, 0);                                      // (12)

    } catch (ClassNotFoundException | NoSuchMethodException |
             InstantiationException | IllegalAccessException |
             IllegalArgumentException | InvocationTargetException ex) {
      ex.printStackTrace();
    }
  }
}
```

```java
// File path: src/controller/com/passion/controller/AdviceController.java
package com.passion.controller;

import com.passion.model.AdviceModel;              // From model module.
import com.passion.view.AdviceView;                // From view module.

public class AdviceController {

  private AdviceModel model;
  private AdviceView view;

  public AdviceController() {
    model = new AdviceModel();
    view = new AdviceView(model);
  }

  private void showAdvice(int adviceNumber) {       // (13)
    model.setCurrentAdvice(adviceNumber);
    view.updateAdviceDisplay();
  }
}
```

The accessibility of the showAdvice() method at (13) in class AdviceController is changed to private in Example 19.2 to illustrate that an open package allows reflection on private members.

The other two modules, model and view, are the same as in the adviceApp application (Example 19.1, Figure 19.12).

We can compile all modules in the adviceOpen application, as we did for the adviceApp:

```
>javac -d mods --module-source-path src --module model,view,controller,main
```

However, trying to run the application throws an exception:

```
>java --module-path mods --module main/com.passion.main.Main
java.lang.ClassNotFoundException: com.passion.controller.AdviceController
...
```

The reason for the exception is that the controller module has not been resolved at runtime, since it is not required by any module in the application. We can include modules needed by the application using the --add-modules option:

```
>java --add-modules controller --module-path mods \
      --module main/com.passion.main.Main
See no evil.
Speak no evil.
Hear no evil.
No advice.
```

Qualified Opens Directive

Sometimes it is necessary that only certain modules can access an open package for reflection. This can be achieved by using the opens-to directive, as shown below at (1), where package org.liberal.sesame in module org.liberal is *only* open to modules com.aladdin and forty.thieves. This is known as a *qualified opens* directive. The to clause can be used to specify a comma-separated list of modules that can inspect the open package.

```
module org.liberal {
    opens org.liberal.sesame to com.aladdin, forty.thieves; // (1) Qualified opens
    opens org.liberal.pandorasbox;                          // (2) Unqualified opens
}
```

Apart from modules com.aladdin and forty.thieves, no other module can inspect package org.liberal.sesame in module org.liberal. Any attempt made by other modules to inspect package org.liberal.sesame will result in a java.lang.Illegal-AccessException. Unqualified open package org.liberal.pandorasbox, shown at (2), allows *any* module to inspect this package.

The declaration of module controller can be modified to use the qualified opens directive, as shown below. The application adviceOpen can be compiled and run as before.

```
module controller {
    requires model;
    requires view;
    opens com.passion.controller to main;    // Package is only open to main module.
}
```

Open Modules

An *open module* can be declared with the restricted keyword open in its declaration file module-info.java:

```
open module module_name {
    // Any number of module directives, except the opens directive.
}
```

An open module does not declare any open packages, since its declaration implies that all its packages are open. However, note that making a module open also means that it would be possible to use reflection on *all types and their members in all packages* in the module. Making a module open should be done judiciously, and in a way that does not weaken the principle of encapsulation.

The declaration of module controller can be modified so that the module is open for other modules, as shown below. The application adviceOpen can be compiled and run as before.

```
open module controller {                    // An open module
    requires model;
    requires view;
}
```

19.9 Services

Programming to interfaces is a powerful design paradigm that advocates writing code using interfaces and abstract classes—that is, using abstract types and not concrete types. This allows new implementations of abstract types to be used by the code if and when necessary. This strategy results in the code being loosely coupled.

The requires directives in module declarations create explicit dependencies between concrete modules, requiring explicit naming of modules with heavy reliance on concrete types, thus making the modules tightly coupled. As we shall see, services allow programming to interfaces, but at a higher level of abstraction, resulting in the modules being loosely coupled, as direct dependencies between them are removed.

The main advantage of services is application *extensibility*: adding functionality by providing new services without having to recompile the whole application. This is feasible as services are discoverable at runtime. This design strategy is typically employed in implementing *plugins* which can extend the capabilities of an application.

A *service* is a specific abstract type, typically an interface, but it can be an abstract class as well, that specifies some specific functionality. The following artifacts are typically required to create a service:

- *The service interface*

    The service interface specifies the abstract type that represents the service. It is also known as a *service provider interface*.

- *The service provider*

  A service provider implements the service. There can be zero or more service providers of a service. A service provider advertises the implementation of a specific service with the provides-with directive.

- *The service locator*

  The service locator discovers service providers at runtime through a *service loader* which is an instance of the java.util.ServiceLoader<S> class, where type parameter S designates the type of service to be loaded. A service loader locates and loads service providers at runtime. A service locator announces the services it is interested in with the uses directive.

- *The service consumer*

  A service consumer utilizes the service. The service consumer accesses a particular implementation of the service via the *service locator,* and does not communicate directly with a service provider. It can choose which implementation of the service to consume from the ones provided by the service locator.

We illustrate the setup necessary to use services by implementing a variant of the adviceApp we have seen earlier (Example 19.1, Figure 19.12). Each artifact required to set up a service will be implemented as a module in our example below, although other configurations are possible, typically where the service locator is merged with either the service interface or the service consumer. The service providers, being autonomous modules, can be added or removed as necessary.

Figure 19.15, p. 1198 shows the module diagram and the module declarations of the adviceService application, and Example 19.3 to Example 19.6 show the source code in each module of the application.

Specifying the Service Interface

The service is represented by the interface IAdvice that is declared in package org.advice.si of the serviceinterface module (Example 19.3). It specifies the functionality that the service will provide: two abstract methods getContent() and get-Locale() that return the advice (as a string) and the associated locale at (1) and (2), respectively. In other words, the advice service is locale-specific. Since the two methods have no accessibility modifier in their declaration, they are implicitly public, and as they do not provide an implementation, they are implicitly abstract.

Example 19.3 *Specifying the* Advice *Service Interface*

```
// File: ./src/serviceinterface/org/advice/si/IAdvice.java
package org.advice.si;
import java.util.Locale;

// Service interface
public interface IAdvice {
```

```
       String getContent();             // (1) Returns the content of the advice.
       Locale getLocale();              // (2) Returns the associated locale.
   }
```

Figure 19.15 *Module Graph and Module Declarations for Services*

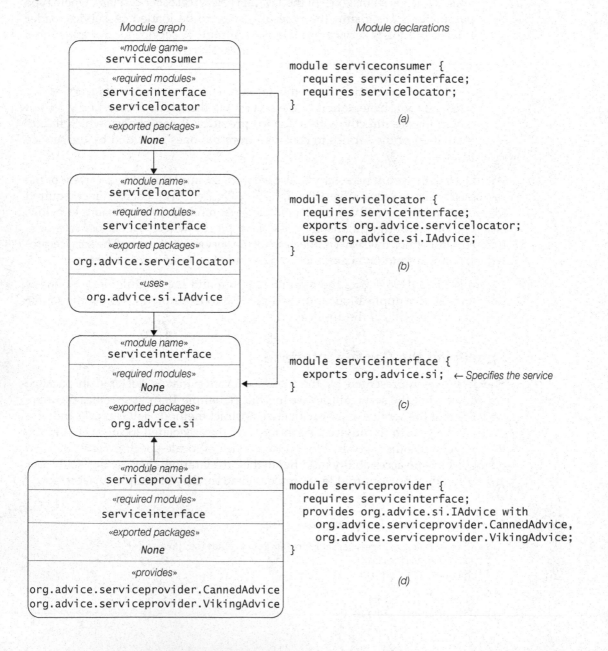

Module graph

«module game»
serviceconsumer

«required modules»
serviceinterface
servicelocator

«exported packages»
None

«module name»
servicelocator

«required modules»
serviceinterface

«exported packages»
org.advice.servicelocator

«uses»
org.advice.si.IAdvice

«module name»
serviceinterface

«required modules»
None

«exported packages»
org.advice.si

«module name»
serviceprovider

«required modules»
serviceinterface

«exported packages»
None

«provides»
org.advice.serviceprovider.CannedAdvice
org.advice.serviceprovider.VikingAdvice

Module declarations

```
module serviceconsumer {
  requires serviceinterface;
  requires servicelocator;
}
```
         (a)

```
module servicelocator {
  requires serviceinterface;
  exports org.advice.servicelocator;
  uses org.advice.si.IAdvice;
}
```
             (b)

```
module serviceinterface {
  exports org.advice.si;   ← Specifies the service
}
```
             (c)

```
module serviceprovider {
  requires serviceinterface;
  provides org.advice.si.IAdvice with
    org.advice.serviceprovider.CannedAdvice,
    org.advice.serviceprovider.VikingAdvice;
}
```
             (d)

The declaration of the serviceinterface module in Figure 19.15(c) exports the package org.advice.si containing the service interface IAdvice so that service providers can implement it.

```
// File: ./src/serviceinterface/module-info.java
module serviceinterface {
    exports org.advice.si;
}
```

Implementing Service Providers

Two service providers are implemented in the serviceprovider module (Example 19.4). The package org.advice.serviceprovider contains the class Canned-Advice that implements the service interface IAdvice. The getContent() and the getLocale() methods return the canned advice and the associated UK locale at (1) and (2), respectively.

Example 19.4 *Implementing the Advice Service Providers*

```
// File:./src/serviceprovider/org/advice/serviceprovider/CannedAdvice.java
package org.advice.serviceprovider;

import org.advice.si.IAdvice;
import java.util.Locale;

public class CannedAdvice implements IAdvice {
  public String getContent() {                          // (1)
    return "Keep calm and service on!";
  }
  public Locale getLocale() { return Locale.UK; }       // (2)
}
```

```
// File:./src/serviceprovider/org/advice/serviceprovider/VikingAdvice.java
package org.advice.serviceprovider;

import org.advice.si.IAdvice;
import java.util.Locale;

public class VikingAdvice implements IAdvice {
  public String getContent() {                                    // (3)
    return "Gi aldri opp!";     // Never give up!
  }
  public Locale getLocale() { return new Locale("no", "Norway"); } // (4)
}
```

The package org.advice.serviceprovider also contains the class VikingAdvice that implements the service interface IAdvice. The getContent() and the getLocale() methods return the Viking advice and the associated Norwegian locale at (3) and (4), respectively.

The serviceprovider module in Figure 19.15(d) requires the module serviceinterface in order to implement the service. The module advertizes that it implements the service in a provides-with directive at (1) below. In the directive, the service interface that is implemented is specified first, and the with clause specifies a comma-separated list of *classes* in this module that implement the service. This information is used by the service loader at runtime to locate and load the classes that implement this service in this module. Note that the package implementing the service is not exported, avoiding any service consumers having explicit dependency on service providers.

```
// File: ./src/serviceprovider/module-info.java
module serviceprovider {
  requires serviceinterface;
  provides org.advice.si.IAdvice with               // (1)
    org.advice.serviceprovider.CannedAdvice,
    org.advice.serviceprovider.VikingAdvice;
}
```

Implementing the Service Locator

The class java.util.ServiceLoader<S>, where the type parameter S designates the type of service, is at the core of finding and loading service providers for the service S. A service loader for a specific service is created by calling the static method load() of the ServiceLoader class, passing the runtime Class object of the service interface, as shown below. Typically, a stream is then created by calling the stream() method on the service loader. This stream can be used to lazily load the available service providers for the specified service S. The type of an element in this stream is the static member interface ServiceProvider.Provider<S>.

```
ServiceLoader<IAdvice> loader = ServiceLoader.load(IAdvice.class);
Stream<ServiceLoader.Provider<IAdvice>> spStream = loader.stream();
```

The procedure above allows processing of stream elements as type Provider<S> without instantiating the service provider. The get() method of the Provider<S> interface must be invoked on a stream element of type Provider<S> to obtain an instance of the service provider—that is, the class that implements the service interface S. Given the service provider, the service implemented by the provider can be utilized.

static <S> ServiceLoader<S> load(Class<S> service)

This static method creates a service loader for the given service type specified by its runtime object, using the current thread's context class loader.

Stream<ServiceLoader.Provider<S>> stream()

Returns a stream that lazily loads available providers of this loader's service (designated by type parameter S). The stream elements are of type Service-Loader.Provider<S>.

The interface `Provider<S>` is a static member interface of the class `Service-Loader<S>` that extends the `java.util.function.Supplier<S>` functional interface. The `get()` method of the `Provider<S>` interface must be invoked to get or instantiate the service provider for the service S.

A service locator for the advice service is implemented by the class `org.advice` `.servicelocator.AdviceLocator` in the `servicelocator` module (Example 19.5). The class provides two static methods, `getAdvice()` and `getAllAdvice()`, which return a service provider that implements the `IAdvice` service interface for a particular locale or *all* service providers that implement the `IAdvice` service interface, as shown at (1) and (8), respectively. In other words, the former returns a service provider for a particular locale and the latter returns all service providers that implement the `IAdvice` service interface.

The method `getAdvice()` at (1) is passed the desired locale. Its return type is `Optional<IAdvice>`, as there might not be any service provider for this service for the desired locale. At (2), a service loader is created for the `IAdvice` service interface. A stream is built with the service loader as the source at (3). This stream of element type `Provider<IAdvice>` is processed to find a service provider for the desired locale. Note how at (5), the stream is converted from type `Stream<ServiceLoader.Provider<IAdvice>>` to `Stream<IAdvice>` by the `map()` intermediate operation that applies the `get()` method of the `Provider<S>` interface to each element. The resulting stream is filtered at (6) for a service provider with the desired locale. The first service provider that has the desired locale is selected by the `findFirst()` terminal operation at (7). This operation returns an `Optional<IAdvice>` as there might not be such a service provider in the stream.

Analogously, the method `getAllAdvice()` at (8) collects all service providers for the `IAdvice` service interface in a list and returns them. In this case, an empty list will indicate that no service providers were found.

Example 19.5 *Implementing the Advice Service Locator*

```
// File:./src/servicelocator/org/advice/servicelocator/AdviceLocator.java
package org.advice.servicelocator;

import java.util.*;
import java.util.stream.*;
import org.advice.si.*;

public class AdviceLocator {

  /** Get advice for a particular locale. */
  public static Optional<IAdvice> getAdvice(Locale desiredLocale) {      // (1)
    ServiceLoader<IAdvice> loader = ServiceLoader.load(IAdvice.class);   // (2)
    Stream<ServiceLoader.Provider<IAdvice>> spStream = loader.stream(); // (3)
    Optional<IAdvice> optAdvice = spStream                               // (4)
      .map(ServiceLoader.Provider::get)                          // (5) Stream<IAdvice>
```

```
        .filter(a -> desiredLocale.equals(a.getLocale()))    // (6)
        .findFirst();                                        // (7)
      return optAdvice;
    }

    /** Get all advice implemented by all providers. */
    public static List<IAdvice> getAllAdvice() {             // (8)
      ServiceLoader<IAdvice> loader = ServiceLoader.load(IAdvice.class);
      List<IAdvice> allAdvice = loader
        .stream()
        .map(p -> p.get())                      // (9) map(ServiceLoader.Provider::get)
        .collect(Collectors.toList());          // (10) List<IAdvice>
      return allAdvice;
    }
}
```

At (1) below, the servicelocator module (Figure 19.15(b)) requires the serviceinterface module in order to locate its service providers, and it exports the package org.advice.servicelocator at (2) so that service consumers can locate service providers. The uses directive at (3) declares which service (org.advice.si.IAdvice) is used by this module, allowing it to look up this particular service at runtime.

```
// File: ./src/servicelocator/module-info.java
module servicelocator {
  requires serviceinterface;          // (1)
  exports org.advice.servicelocator;  // (2)
  uses org.advice.si.IAdvice;         // (3) In module serviceinterface.
}
```

Implementing the Service Consumer

The class AdviceConsumer implements a simple service consumer for the IAdvice service in the package org.advice.serviceconsumer of the serviceconsumer module (Example 19.6).

The code at (1) shows how advice for the UK locale is obtained via the org.advice .servicelocator.AdviceLocator class in the servicelocator module. The static method getAdvice() of the AdviceLocator class at (2) returns an Optional<IAdvice> object. This object can be queried to extract the advice at (3) with the getContent() method, if there is one. Otherwise, the orElse() method at (4) provides an appropriate message.

The code at (5) shows how all advice providers for the IAdvice service can be obtained via the AdviceLocator class. The static method getAllAdvice() of the AdviceLocator class at (6) returns a List<IAdvice> object with all providers for this service. A stream on this list is used at (7) to print the advice from each provider by extracting the advice with the getContent() method.

Example 19.6 *Implementing of the Advice Service Consumer*

```java
// File: ./src/serviceconsumer/org/advice/serviceconsumer/AdviceConsumer.java
package org.advice.serviceconsumer;

import java.util.*;
import org.advice.servicelocator.*;
import org.advice.si.*;

public class AdviceConsumer {
  public static void main(String[] args) {

    // Get advice for the UK locale.                                  // (1)
    Optional<IAdvice> optAdvice = AdviceLocator.getAdvice(Locale.UK); // (2)
    String adviceStr = optAdvice.map(IAdvice::getContent)             // (3)
                               .orElse("Sorry. No Advice!");          // (4)
    System.out.println("Advice for UK locale: " + adviceStr);

    // Get all implemented advice.                                    // (5)
    System.out.println("Printing all advice:");
    List<IAdvice> allAdvice = AdviceLocator.getAllAdvice();           // (6)
    allAdvice.stream()                                                // (7)
      .forEach(a -> System.out.println(a.getContent()));
  }
}
```

The serviceconsumer module (Figure 19.15(a)) only requires the module that declares the service, as shown at (1), and the module that can locate service providers for this service as at (2). Note that the consumer module does not directly depend on any service providers.

```java
// File: ./src/serviceconsumer/module-info.java
module serviceconsumer {
  requires serviceinterface;   // (1)
  requires servicelocator;     // (2)
}
```

Compiling and Running a Service

The directory structure of the adviceService application is analogous to that of the adviceApp (Figure 19.9, p. 1181).

We can compile all modules in the adviceService application as before. However, note that compilation of the serviceprovider module does not require any other modules except the serviceinterface module.

```
>javac -d mods \
  --module-source-path src \
  --module serviceprovider,serviceconsumer,servicelocator,serviceinterface
```

We can run the application as before:

```
>java --module-path mods \
      --module serviceconsumer/org.advice.serviceconsumer.AdviceConsumer
Advice for UK locale: Keep calm and service on!
Printing all advice:
Keep calm and service on!
Gi aldri opp!
```

We leave it as an exercise to experiment other configurations of implementing services. In particular, merging the service locator with the service consumer is highly recommended.

19.10 Creating Runtime Images

The *Java Linker* tool, jlink, can be used to assemble a customized *runtime image* of a modular application. This image only includes the modules in the application and their dependencies, together with a minimal JRE (Java Runtime Environment) to run the application.

We only present the basic use of the jlink tool, and strongly encourage consulting the documentation for the JDK tools for more in-depth coverage.

At a minimum, the jlink tool requires the following information to create a runtime image:

- The *module path* given by the --module-path option (*short form*: -p) to find modules that are to be included in the runtime image.
- The *names of the modules* that should be included in the runtime image. These modules are specified using the --add-modules option, and are looked up in the module path. If any standard or JDK modules required by the application are not specified, they are automatically included by the tool. The dependencies between the modules are automatically resolved.
- The *output directory* in which to create the runtime image, specified with the --output option.

The following command creates a runtime image of the adviceApp in the advice directory, assuming that the JAR files for the application modules can be found in the directory mlib:

```
jlink --module-path mlib --add-modules model,view,controller,main,java.base \
      --output advice
```

The standard module java.base is explicitly specified. If omitted, it will be automatically included by the jlink tool.

The output directory advice containing the runtime image has the following structure, shown below with some of the files in the runtime image. The size of this particular runtime image is approximately 39 MB. Note the java command to launch the application under the directory advice/bin.

```
advice/
├── bin/
│   ├── java          <=== Java command to launch the application
│   └── ...
│
├── conf/
│
├── include/
│
├── legal/
│
├── lib/
│   ├── jrt-fs.jar    <=== Java runtime file system
│   ├── modules       <=== Container for application modules
│   └── ...
│
└── release
```

The modules in the runtime image advice can be listed by the following command:

```
>advice/bin/java --list-modules
controller
java.base@17.0.2
main
model
view
```

The application can be run from the runtime image by the following command, as the entry point of the application is specified in the main modular JAR included in the runtime image:

```
>advice/bin/java --module main
See no evil.
Speak no evil.
Hear no evil.
No advice.
```

A runtime image is platform specific, and thus meant to be run on the platform it was created for. As the runtime image contains platform-specific files, it will most likely not run on other platforms.

It is not possible to automatically update a runtime image with a newer version of Java. The runtime image must be rebuilt with the appropriate version of Java.

Runtime images are beneficial in many ways: They have a smaller memory footprint, can boost performance, are more secure, and are easier to maintain. Not surprisingly, runtime images are ideal for running on smaller devices.

19.11 Categories of Modules

The Java Module System is designed to allow both non-modular and modular code to work together. Types are usually bundled in JAR files. Regardless of whether it a plain JAR or a modular JAR, how its content is handled by the module system depends on the path on which it is placed when using the JDK tools: *the class path* (§6.4, p. 337) or *the module path* (p. 1186). Many JDK tools, like javac and java commands, allow both paths to be specified on the command line in order to mix non-modular and modular code. Interpretation of JARs placed on either of these two paths is shown in Table 19.4, and is the subject of this section. Understanding this distinction is also essential for migrating code into modules (p. 1209).

Table 19.4   *How JARs Are Handled Depends on the Path*

Path	Plain JAR	Modular JAR
On the class path: -cp	Included in the *unnamed module*	Included in the *unnamed module*
On the module path: -p	Treated as an *automatic module*	Treated as an *explicit module*

Searching for types on the class path is different from searching for types on the module path. Class path search is a linear search on the entire class path, finding the first occurrence of a type and terminating if the type is found. Module path search is according to the module dependencies and therefore more efficient.

The Unnamed Module

Types from any JAR that is placed on the class path are included in *the unnamed module*, regardless of whether it is a plain or a modular JAR. If it is a modular JAR, its module descriptor is ignored. However, note that a unique unnamed module is associated with each class loader. Classes loaded by a class loader via the classpath are members of the unnamed module associated with that class loader. Colloquially we refer to *the unnamed module* as the one associated with the application class loader.

The unnamed module is a catchall solution to capture code that is on the class path. It is analogous to code not declared in packages being part of the unnamed package. It is a compatibility feature that allows code on the class path to work with modules on the module path.

Types in the unnamed module can access code from both the class path and the module path—that is, the unnamed module can read *all* modules.

All packages in the unnamed module are exported and open for reflection. Types in the unnamed module are accessible to other types in the unnamed module, and also accessible to *automatic* modules, but only by reflection to explicit modules. An explicit module on the module path cannot access code in the unnamed module, as the unnamed module cannot be specified in a requires directive because it has no name. Access to types in the unnamed module is governed by accessibility rules for types in packages—that is, only `public` types in a package are accessible to other packages in the unnamed module and in any automatic modules.

Automatic Modules

A plain JAR—that is, a JAR that does not have a `module-info.class` file in its top-level directory—defines an *automatic module* when placed on the module path. An automatic module has a module name which is determined according to the scheme described below.

An automatic module can read all other modules, including the unnamed module. This means that if an explicit module reads a single automatic module, all other automatic modules can be implicitly read by the explicit module. This avoids having a `requires` directive to every automatic module required by a named module.

All packages in the automatic module are exported and open for reflection. Access to its types is solely determined by the accessibility rules for types in packages. Explicit modules can read automatic modules by specifying them in the `requires` directives, as they have a name.

An automatic module is a migration feature. Resorting to an automatic module should be a temporary measure. As such, a module should be migrated to an explicit module by defining an appropriate module descriptor.

Scheme for Naming Automatic Modules

If the JAR file has the attribute `Automatic-Module-Name` defined in its `META-INF/MANIFEST.MF` file (p. 1212), its value is used as the module name. This is the recommended practice, as it avoids issues like name clashes.

If the JAR file does not have the attribute `Automatic-Module-Name` defined in its `META-INF/MANIFEST.MF` file, its name is derived from the *file name* of the JAR file according to the following algorithm:

- Remove the `.jar` suffix from the name.
- Remove any version information at the end of the name, which is usually specified in the version number format after a hyphen (-); for example, `-1.2.3-ERC`.
- All non-alphanumeric characters are replaced with a dot (.), any sequence of dots is replaced with a single dot, and all leading and trailing dots are removed. This step avoids constructing a module name with illegal characters.

As an example, the JAR file name `ying-yang.jar` of an automatic module will derive the module name `ying.yang`, as will the JAR file name `ying-yang-1.2.3-ERC.jar`. File names for plain JARs acting as automatic modules should be chosen with care so as to avoid name clashes when such JARs do not specify a unique module name in their manifest file.

Explicit Modules

As the name implies, an explicit module is described by its module descriptor that explicitly specifies its name and the modules it reads (i.e., its dependencies), including any packages it exports or opens, or any services it provides or uses. A modular JAR is treated as an explicit module when specified on the module path.

Access to types in an explicit module is determined by the accessibility rules for types in packages *exported* or *opened* by the explicit module.

An explicit module *cannot* access code in the unnamed module as it cannot refer to the unnamed module in its module declaration.

Named Modules

Explicit modules and automatic modules are characterized as *named modules*. In the case of the explicit module, the name is specified in the module declaration. For the automatic modules, the name is either in the manifest file of its JAR or generated from its file name. A plain JAR or a modular JAR is treated as a named module when specified on the module path. Comparison of modules is shown in Table 19.5.

Table 19.5   *Module Comparison*

| | | Named modules | |
Criteria	Unnamed module	Automatic module	Explicit module
JAR	Plain or modular JAR	Plain JAR	Modular JAR
Path	On class path	On module path	On module path
Name	Not applicable	Either in manifest file or from file name	Specified in module descriptor
Module descriptor	Not applicable	Not applicable	Mandatory
Reads	All modules	All modules	Only named modules that are required
Exports/Opens	All packages	All packages	Only exported/open packages

19.12 Migrating to Modules

The module system allows incremental migration of non-modular code to modules. Knowledge of dependencies between types in the plain JARs is crucial to drive this migration. This is probably easier with an application whose code one has control over than it is with libraries and frameworks from third parties. Regardless, having a better handle on dependencies makes the process easier. The jar tool (p. 1211) is useful to obtain information about the contents of a JAR and the jdeps tool (p. 1214) is a great tool to discover dependencies in the code.

The scenarios presented below are very much idealized, and deal with code in plain and modular JARs. The basic idea is to move code from the class path to the module path, either converting plain JARs to explicit modules directly or via automatic modules.

Bottom-Up Strategy for Code Migration

If all *direct* dependencies of a plain JAR are known to be modules, the plain JAR can be directly converted to an explicit module by declaring their dependencies and exports in a module declaration. This idea is embodied in the following algorithm, based on the graph of dependencies between the plain JARs (see Figure 19.16).

(1) Place all plain JARs on the *class path* such that they are in the unnamed module.

(2) Choose *leaf* JARs from the class path—that is, JARs that do not have any dependencies. Turn them into explicit modules by adding appropriate exports directives in their module descriptors and move them from the class path to the module path.

(3) From the class path, choose plain JARs from the next higher level, that have direct module dependencies. Turn them into explicit modules. Their module declarations must specify requires directives on their dependencies and appropriate exports directives for packages they export. Move the newly created explicit modules from the class path to the *module path*.

(4) Repeat step (3) until the unnamed module is empty.

There are variations on the bottom-up strategy, but the gist is represented by the algorithm above. Note that when applying the bottom-up strategy for migration, the explicit module on the module path never accesses code in any plain JAR on the class path.

Figure 19.16 shows the bottom-up strategy applied to the plain JARs: main.jar, controller.jar, view.jar, and model.jar, that are converted to modular JARs—that is, explicit modules—as they are moved from the class path to the module path.

Figure 19.16 *Bottom-Up Strategy for Code Migration*

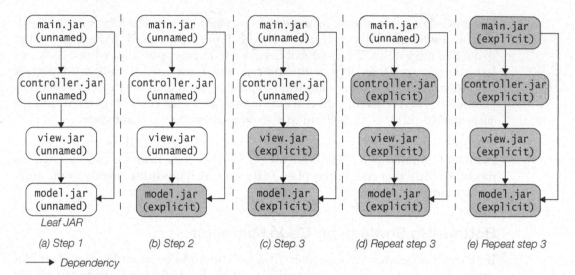

(a) Step 1   (b) Step 2   (c) Step 3   (d) Repeat step 3   (e) Repeat step 3

⟶ Dependency

Top-Down Strategy for Code Migration

Migrating to modular code via *automatic* modules is convenient when it will take too long to wait for all dependencies to be available. The algorithm below migrates the code into explicit modules via automatic modules, based on the graph of known dependencies between the plain JARs (see Figure 19.17).

(1) Place all plain JARs on the module path. All plain JARs are now automatic modules.

(2) Choose *root* JARs that are automatic modules. A root JAR is one that no other JAR depends on. Turn these automatic modules into explicit modules by adding module declarations. Add `requires` directives using names of the automatic modules that a root JAR depends on.

(3) Choose automatic modules at the next lower level that are directly required by their parent modular JARs. Turn these automatic modules into explicit modules. Add `requires` directives using names of the automatic modules that these JARs depend on. Add appropriate `exports` directives for any packages exported.

(4) Repeat step (3) until all automatic modules have been converted to explicit modules.

Again, there are variations to the top-down strategy, but the algorithm embodies the main idea of this strategy. Note that in real life, both strategies will most likely be applied to complete the migration.

Figure 19.17 shows the top-down strategy applied to the plain JARs: `main.jar`, `controller.jar`, `view.jar`, and `model.jar`, which are first placed on the module path as automatic modules and then are converted to modular JARs—that is, explicit modules.

Figure 19.17 *Top-Down Strategy for Code Migration*

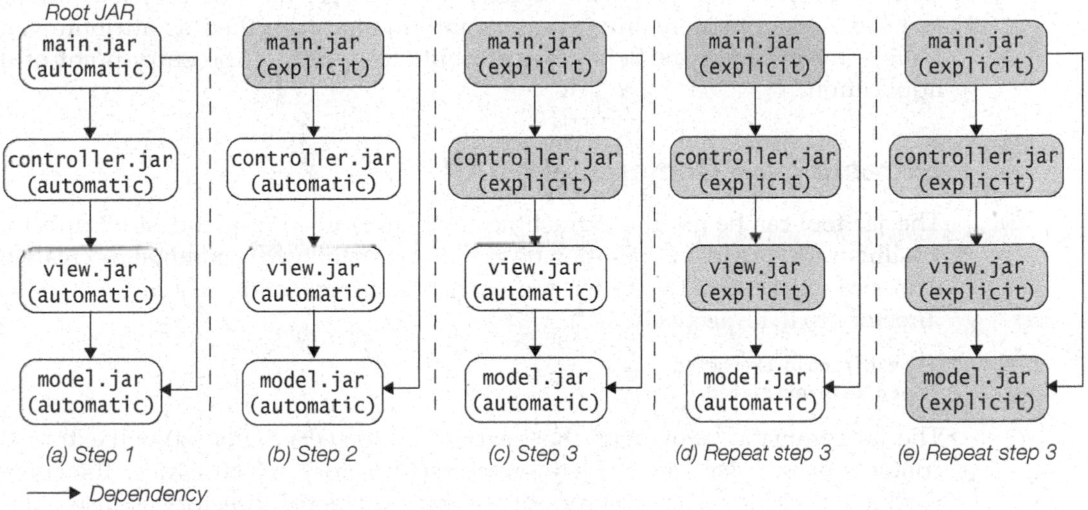

19.13 Exploring Modules

This section provides an introduction to using the JDK tools to discover, explore, and analyze modular applications.

Given the JARs main.jar, control.jar, view.jar, and model.jar for the adviceApp application in the mlib directory in Figure 19.14(c), p. 1188, we will use JDK tools to explore these archives for miscellaneous information about this application.

Listing the Contents of a JAR

We can list the contents of a JAR using the --list option (*short form*: -t) of the jar tool. The JAR file is specified with the --file option (*short form*: -f). The contents of main.jar are printed by the following jar command:

```
>jar --list --file mlib/main.jar
META-INF/
META-INF/MANIFEST.MF
module-info.class
com/
com/passion/
com/passion/main/
com/passion/main/Main.class
```

From the output on the terminal, we can see that there is a META-INF directory listed, in addition to the module descriptor file (module-info.class), the directory hierarchy of the package com.passion.main, and the file Main.class contained in it.

The META-INF directory is used internally to record any metadata in the JAR archive. In the listing above, the META-INF directory contains the file MANIFEST.MF. This manifest file is used to store any necessary information (specified as attribute-value pairs)—for example, the Main-Class attribute to designate the entry point of the application.

Extracting the Contents of a JAR

The jar tool can be used to extract the contents of a JAR into a desired directory. We illustrate the extract operation on main.jar. The following commands create the main-extracted directory under the current directory and change the working directory to it, respectively.

```
>mkdir main-extracted
>cd main-extracted
```

The jar command below with the --extract option (*short form*: -x) will extract the contents of main.jar into the main-extracted directory, which is now the current working directory. The structure of the main-extracted directory is also shown below after the extraction (printed using the tree command), showing the exploded module structure and the META-INF directory from main.jar.

```
>jar --extract --file ../mlib/main.jar
>tree -F --dirsfirst --noreport main-extracted
main-extracted
├── META-INF/
│   └── MANIFEST.MF
├── com/
│   └── passion/
│       └── main/
│           └── Main.class
└── module-info.class
```

The contents of the MANIFEST.MF file, listed below using the more command, show that the entry point of the application is given by the value of Main-Class—that is, the class com.passion.main.Main.

```
>more main-extracted/META-INF/MANIFEST.MF
Manifest-Version: 1.0
Created-By: 17.0.2 (Oracle Corporation)
Main-Class: com.passion.main.Main
```

Listing All Observable Modules

The java command with the --list-modules option (*no short form*) lists the *system modules* that are installed in the JDK, and then exits. These modules are available to every application. This lengthy list gives an idea of how the JDK has been modularized. The java command lists each module with its version; in this case, it is Java 17.0.2. Module names starting with the prefix java implement the Java SE Language Specification, whereas those starting with jdk are JDK specific. The reader will no doubt recognize some names, specially java.base.

The system modules are found in the jmods directory under the installation directory of the JDK. These are *JMOD files* having a module name with the extension ".jmod". JMOD files have a special non-executable format that allows native binary libraries and other configuration files to be packaged with bytecode artifacts that can then be linked to create runtime images with the jlink tool (p. 1222).

```
>java --list-modules
java.base@17.0.2
...
java.se@17.0.2
...
jdk.compiler@17.0.2
...
jdk.jartool@17.0.2
...
```

Specifying a module path in the java command below not only lists the system modules, but also the modular JARs found in the specified module path—in other words, all *observable modules*. In the java command below, the absolute path of all JARs found in the mlib directory is listed last in the output.

```
>java --module-path mlib --list-modules
java.base@17.0.2
...
jdk.javadoc@17.0.2
...
jdk.jdeps@17.0.2
...
controller file:.../adviceApp/mlib/controller.jar
main file:.../adviceApp/mlib/main.jar
model file:.../adviceApp/mlib/model.jar
view file:.../adviceApp/mlib/view.jar
```

Describing the Module Descriptor of a JAR

Both the java tool and the jar tool have the --describe-module option (*short form:* -d) to show the information contained in the module descriptor of a JAR. Both commands are used respectively below.

```
>java --module-path mlib --describe-module main
main file:.../adviceApp/mlib/main.jar
requires java.base mandated
requires controller
contains com.passion.main
```

```
>jar --file mlib/main.jar --describe-module
main jar:file:.../adviceApp/mlib/main.jar/!module-info.class
requires controller
requires java.base mandated
contains com.passion.main
main-class com.passion.main.Main
```

Note that in the java command, the --describe-module option requires a module name, whereas that is not the case in the jar command, where the --file option specifies the modular JAR.

Since the module descriptor is a Java bytecode class file, it must be disassembled to display its information. In both cases, first the module name is printed, followed by the path of the JAR. In the case of the jar command, the name module-info.class is appended to the path of the JAR. In both cases, the names of modules required (java.base and controller) are reported. The main module also *contains* an *internal* package (com.passion.main). Not surprisingly, the java.base module is mandated. However, only the jar command reports that the main-class is com.passion.main.Main. The jar command is useful to find the entry point of an application.

The --describe-module option (*short form*: -d) can also be used on a system module. The following java command describes the module descriptor of the java.base system module. The command lists all modules the java.base module *exports*, *uses*, *exports qualified*, and *contains* (p. 1177). As can be expected from its status as a mandated module for all other modules, it does *not require* any module.

```
>java --describe-module java.base
java.base@17.0.2
exports java.io
exports java.lang
...
uses java.util.spi.CurrencyNameProvider
uses java.util.spi.TimeZoneNameProvider
...
qualified exports jdk.internal to jdk.jfr
qualified exports sun.net.www to java.desktop java.net.http jdk.jartool
...
contains com.sun.crypto.provider
contains com.sun.java.util.jar.pack
...
```

Viewing Dependencies

The *Java Dependency Analysis tool*, jdeps, is a versatile command-line tool for static analysis of dependencies between Java artifacts like class files and JARs. It can analyze dependencies at all levels: module, package, and class. It allows the results to be filtered and aggregated in various ways, even generating various graphs to illustrate its findings. It is an indispensable tool when migrating non-modular code to make use of the module system.

In this section, we confine our discussion to modular code—that is, either an exploded module directory with the compiled module code (e.g., mods/main) or a modular JAR (e.g., mlib/main.jar).

In this section, the results from some of the jdeps commands have been edited to fit the width of the page without any loss of information, or elided to shorten repetitious outputs.

Viewing Package-Level Dependencies

The jdeps command with no options, shown below, illustrates the *default behavior* of the tool. Line numbers have been added for illustrative purposes.

When presented with the root module directory mods/model (1), the default behavior of jdeps is to print the name of the module (2), the path to its location (3), its module descriptor (4), followed by its module dependencies (5), and lastly the *package-level* dependencies (6). The package-level dependency at (6) shows that the package com.passion.model in the model module depends on the java.lang package in the proverbial java.base module.

```
(1)  >jdeps mods/model
(2)  model
(3)  [file:.../adviceApp/mods/model/]
(4)     requires mandated java.base (@17.0.2)
(5)  model -> java.base
(6)     com.passion.model          -> java.lang        java.base
```

The following jdeps command if let loose on the model.jar archive will print the same information for the model module, barring the difference in the file location:

```
>jdeps mlib/model.jar
```

However, the following jdeps command with the main.jar archive gives an error:

```
>jdeps mlib/main.jar
Exception in thread "main" java.lang.module.FindException: Module controller
not found, required by main
        at java.base/...
```

Dependency analysis cannot be performed on the main module by the jdeps tool because the modules the main module depends on cannot be found. In the case of the model module, which does not depend on any other user-defined module, the dependency analysis can readily be performed.

The two options --module-path (*no short form*) and --module (*short form*: -m) in the jdeps command below unambiguously specify the location of other modular JARs and the module to analyze, respectively. The format of the output is the same as before, and can be verified easily.

```
>jdeps --module-path mlib --module main
main
 [file:.../adviceApp/mlib/main.jar]
   requires controller
   requires mandated java.base (@17.0.2)
main -> controller
main -> java.base
   com.passion.main       -> com.passion.controller    controller
   com.passion.main       -> java.lang                 java.base
```

However, if one wishes to analyze all modules that the specified module depends on recursively, the --recursive option (*short form*: -R) can be specified. The output will be in the same format as before, showing the package-level dependencies for each module. The output from the jdeps command for each module is elided below, but has the same format we have seen previously.

```
>jdeps --module-path mlib --module main --recursive
controller
...
```

```
main
...
model
...
view
...
```

Viewing Module Dependencies

If the default output from the jdeps command is overwhelming, it can be filtered. The -summary option (*short form*: -s) will only print the *module dependencies*, as shown by the jdeps command below. Only the module dependencies of the main module will be shown in the output.

```
>jdeps --module-path mlib --module main -summary
main -> controller
main -> java.base
```

If we use the --recursive option (*short form*: -R) with the -summary option (*short form*: -s), then the module dependencies of each module will be printed recursively, starting with the specified module.

```
>jdeps --module-path mlib --module main -summary --recursive          (1)
controller -> java.base
controller -> model
controller -> view
main -> controller
main -> java.base
model -> java.base
view -> java.base
view -> model
```

Finally, we illustrate the graph-generating capabilities of the jdeps tool. The jdeps command takes all JARs of the adviceApp application from the mlib directory and creates a module graph (options -summary and --recursive) in the DOT format (option -dotoutput) under the current directory. The DOT file summary.dot containing the graph will be created. Using the dot command, this graph can be converted to a pdf file (summary.pdf) as shown in Figure 19.18.

```
>jdeps -dotoutput . -summary --recursive  mlib/*
>dot -Tpdf summary.dot >summary.pdf
```

The module graph in Figure 19.18 shows the same module dependencies printed by the jdeps command above at (1). Comparing the module graph in Figure 19.18 with the one in Figure 19.8, we see that jdeps has added the *implicit dependency* of each module on the java.base module.

Viewing Class-Level Dependencies

It is possible to dive deeper into dependencies with the jdeps tool. The -verbose option (*short form*: -v) will elicit the *class dependencies* of the specified module. Instead of package dependencies to round off the output, class dependencies are

Figure 19.18 *Module Graph Using the* jdeps *Tool*

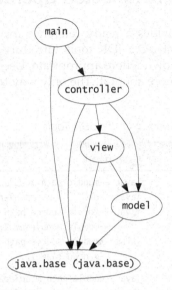

listed. The last line in the output shows that the class com.passion.main.Main in the main module depends on the java.lang.String class in the java.base module.

```
>jdeps --module-path mlib --module main -verbose
main
 [file:.../adviceApp/mlib/main.jar]
   requires controller
   requires mandated java.base (@17.0.2)
main -> controller
main -> java.base
   com.passion.main.Main  -> com.passion.controller.AdviceController  controller
   com.passion.main.Main  -> java.lang.Object                         java.base
   com.passion.main.Main  -> java.lang.String                         java.base
```

If we use the --recursive option (*short form*: -R) with the -verbose option (*short form*: -v), then the class dependencies of each module will be printed recursively, starting with the specified module.

```
>jdeps --module-path mlib --module main -verbose --recursive
controller
...
main
...
model
...
view
...
```

19.14 Summary of Selected Operations with the JDK Tools

Table 19.6 provides a ready reference for commands to perform miscellaneous operations using the JDK tools introduced in this chapter. Short forms for the options are shown where appropriate. Use the indicated reference for each operation to learn more about it. The only way to become familiar with these tools is to use them.

Table 19.6 *Selected Operations with the JDK Tools*

Operation	Command

Compiling modular code (p. 1186)	`javac --module-path modulepath -d directory sourceAndModuleInfoFiles`
	`javac -p          modulepath -d directory sourceAndModuleInfoFiles`
	`javac --module-source-path modulepath -d directory \`
	`       --module moduleName1,...`
	`javac --module-source-path modulepath -d directory \`
	`        -m moduleName1,...`

Launching modular application (p. 1189)	`java --module-path modulepath --module moduleName/qualifiedClassName`
	`java -p          modulepath -m          moduleName/qualifiedClassName`
	`java --module-path modulepath -module moduleName`
	`java -p          modulepath -m       moduleName`

Creating and listing a modular JAR archive (p. 1189)	`jar --verbose --create --file jarfile -C directory files`
	`jar -vcf jarfile -C directory .`
	`jar -vcf jarfile --main-class qualifiedMainClassName -C directory .`
	`jar -vcfe jarfile qualifiedMainClassName -C directory .`
	
	`jar --list --file jarfile`
	`jar -tf jarfile`

Listing available modules (p. 1212)	`java --list-modules`
	`java --module-path modulepath --list-modules`
	`java -p          modulepath --list-modules`

Describing a module—that is, printing the module descriptor (p. 1213)	`java --module-path modulepath --describe-module moduleName`
	`java -p          modulepath -d              moduleName`
	
	`jar --file jarFile --describe-module`
	`jar -f    jarFile -d`

Viewing package-level dependencies (p. 1214)	`jdeps --module-path modulepath -m moduleName`
	`jdeps --module-path modulepath -m moduleName --recursive`
	`jdeps --module-path modulepath -m moduleName -R`

Viewing module dependencies (p. 1216)	`jdeps --module-path modulepath -m moduleName -summary`
	`jdeps --module-path modulepath -m moduleName -summary --recursive`
	`jdeps --module-path modulepath -m moduleName -s -R`

Table 19.6   *Selected Operations with the JDK Tools (Continued)*

Operation	Command

Viewing class-level dependencies (p. 1216)	`jdeps --module-path` *modulepath* `-m` *moduleName* `-verbose`
	`jdeps --module-path` *modulepath* `-m` *moduleName* `-verbose --recursive`
	`jdeps --module-path` *modulepath* `-m` *moduleName* `-v -R`

Selected Options for the `javac` Tool

The Java language compiler, javac, compiles Java source code into Java bytecode. The general form of the javac command is:

`javac [options] [sourcefiles]`

Table 19.7 shows some selected options that can be used when compiling modules. The optional *sourcefiles* is an itemized list of source files, often omitted in favor of using module-related options.

Table 19.7   *Selected Options for the* javac *Tool*

Option	Description
`--module-source-path` *moduleSourcePath*	The *moduleSourcePath* specifies the *source directory* where the exploded modules with the *source code files* can be found.
`--module-path` *modulepath* `-p` *modulepath*	The *modulepath* specifies where the modules needed by the application can be found. This can be a root directory of the exploded modules with the *class files* or a root directory where the modular JARs can be found. Multiple directories of modules can be specified, separated by a colon (:) on a Unix-based platform and semicolon (;) on the Windows platform.
`--module` *moduleName* `-m` *moduleName*	Specifies the module(s) to be compiled. Can be a single module name or a comma-separated (,) list of module names. For each module specified, all modules it depends on are also compiled, according to the module dependencies.
`-d` *classesDirectory*	Specifies the *destination directory* for the class files. Mandatory when compiling modules. For classes in a package, their class files are put in a directory hierarchy that reflects the package name, with directories being created as needed. Without the -d option, the class files are put in the same directory as their respective source files. Specifying the directory path is platform dependent: slash (/) on Unix-based platforms and backslash (\) on Windows platforms being used when specifying the directory path.

Table 19.7 *Selected Options for the* javac *Tool (Continued)*

Option	Description
--add-modules module,...	Specifies root modules to resolve in addition to the initial modules. These modules can be modular JAR files, JMOD files, or even exploded modules.

Selected Options for the java **Tool**

The java tool launches an application—that is, it creates an instance of the JVM in which to run the application. A typical command to launch a modular application is by specifying the location of its modules (*path*) and the entry point of the application (as *module* or *module/mainclass*):

```
java --module-path path --module module[/mainclass]
```

Table 19.8 shows some selected options that can be used for launching and exploring modular applications.

Table 19.8 *Selected Options for the* java *Tool*

Option	Description
--module-path *modulepath*... -p *modulepath*	The *modulepath* specifies the location where the modules needed to run the application can be found. This can be a root directory for the exploded modules with the *class files* or a directory where the modular JARs can be found. Multiple directories of modules can be specified, separated by a colon (:) on a Unix-based platform and semicolon (;) on Windows platforms.
--module *module[/mainclass]* -m *module[/mainclass]*	When *module/mainclass* is specified, it explicitly states the *module name* and the *fully qualified name of the class* with the main() method, thereby overriding any other entry point in the application. Without the *mainclass*, the entry point of the application is given by the *module* which must necessarily contain the main-class.
--add-modules *module*,...	Specifies root modules to resolve in addition to the initial modules.
--list-modules	Only lists the observable modules, and does not launch the application. That is, it lists the modules that the JVM can use when the application is run.
--describe-module *moduleName* -d *moduleName*	Describes a specified module, in particular its module descriptor, but does not launch the application.
--validate-modules	Validates all modules on the module path to find conflicts and errors within modules.

Selected Options for the `jar` Tool

The jar tool is an archiving and compression tool that can be used to bundle Java artifacts and any other resources that comprise the application. The archive file names have the `.jar` extension. A typical command to create a modular JAR (*jarfile*) with an application entry point (*qualifiedMainClassName*), based on the contents of a specific directory (*DIR*), is shown below. Note the obligatory dot (.) at the end of the command.

```
jar --create --file jarfile --main-class qualifiedMainClassName -C DIR .
```

Table 19.9 gives an overview of some selected options that can be used for working with JARs.

Table 19.9 *Selected Options for the* jar *Tool*

Option	Description
`--create` *or* `-c`	Creates a new archive.
`--extract` *or* `-x`	Extracts specified or all files in the archive.
`--list` *or* `-t`	Lists the contents of the archive.
`--update` *or* `-u`	Updates an existing archive with specified files.
`--describe-module` *or* `-d`	Prints the module descriptor of the archive and the main-class, if one is specified in the manifest.
`--verbose` *or* `-v`	Prints extra information about the operation.

`--file jarfile`
`--file=jarfile`
`-f jarfile`
`-f=jarfile`
	Specifies the name of the archive.

`-C DIR files`	Changes to the specified directory and includes the contents of the specified *files* from this directory. If *files* is a dot (.), the contents under the specified directory *DIR* are included.

`--main-class qualifiedMainClassName`
`--main-class=qualifiedMainClassName`
`-e qualifiedMainClassName`
`-e=qualifiedMainClassName`
	Specifies the entry point of the application.

`--manifest TXTFILE`
`--manifest=TXTFILE`
`-m TXTFILE`
`-m=TXTFILE`
	Reads the manifest information for the archive from the specified *TXTFILE* and incorporates it in the archive—for example, the value of the Main-Class attribute that specifies the entry point of the application.

`--module-path modulepath` `-p        modulepath`	Specifies the location of the modules for recording hashes.

Selected Options for the jdeps Tool

The Java Class Dependency Analyzer, jdeps, is the tool of choice when working with modules, as it is module savvy and highly versatile. Among its extensive module analyzing capabilities, it can be used to explore dependencies at different levels: module level, package level, and class level.

Table 19.10 gives an overview of some selected options for the jdeps tool that can be used for analyzing modules.

Table 19.10   *Selected Options for the* jdeps *Tool*

Option	Description
--module-path *modulepath*	Specifies where to find the module JARs needed by the application. No short form, as -p is already reserved for --package.
--module-name *moduleName* -m *moduleName*	Specifies the root module for module dependency analysis.
-summary *or* -s	Presents only a summary of the module dependencies.
--recursive *or* -R	Forces jdeps to recursively iterate over the module dependencies. When used alone, also prints the package-level dependencies.
-verbose *or* -v -verbose:package -verbose:class	Also includes all class-level dependencies in the printout. Includes package-level dependencies in the printout, excluding, by default, dependencies within the same package. Includes class-level dependencies in the printout, excluding, by default, dependencies within the same JAR.

Selected Options for the jlink Tool

The jlink tool creates a runtime image of an application. A typical command to create a runtime image of an application requires the location of its modules (*path*), names of modules to include (*module_names*), and output directory to store the runtime image (*output_dir*):

```
jlink --module-path path --add-modules module_names --output output_dir
```

The runtime image can be executed by the *output_dir*/java command.

Selected options for the jlink tool are summarized in Table 19.11.

Table 19.11   *Selected Options for the* jlink *Tool*

Option	Description
--module-path *modulepath*... -p *modulepath*	Specifies the location where the modules for the application can be found. This can be a root directory for the exploded modules with the *class files* or a directory where the modular JARs can be found. Multiple directories of modules can be specified, separated by a colon (:) on Unix-based platforms and semicolon (;) on Windows platforms.
--add-modules *module*,...	Specifies the modules to include in the generated runtime image. All application modules must be listed. Any standard or JDK modules needed will be automatically included.
--output *path*	Specifies the location of the generated runtime image.

Final Remarks on Options for the JDK Tools

It is worth taking a note of how the command options having the short form -p, -m, and -d are specified in different JDK tools. Table 19.12 gives an overview of which long form they represent in which tool and how they are specified.

Table 19.12   *Selected Common Shorthand Options for JDK Tools*

javac	java	jar	jdeps
--module-path *path* -p *path*	--module-path *path* -p *path*	--module-path *path* -p *path*	--module-path *path* *(no short form as -p is reserved for* --package*)*
--module *module* -m *module*	--module *module[/mainclass]* -m *module[/mainclass]*	--manifest *TXTFILE* -m *TXTFILE*	--module *module* -m *module*
(no long form) -d *classesDirectory*	--describe-module *module* -d *module*	--describe-module -d	*(no -d option)*

 Review Questions

19.1   Given the following code:

```
module store {
   requires transitive product;
   exports store.frontend to ui;
   exports store.backend;
}
```

```
module product {
  exports product.data;
}

module ui {
  requires store;
}

module customer {
  requires ui;
  exports customer.data;
}
```

Which statement is true?
Select the one correct answer.

(a) The code in module ui can access public types from packages store.frontend, store.backend, customer.data, and product.data.

(b) The code in module ui can access public types from packages store.frontend, store.backend, and product.data.

(c) The code in module customer can access public types from package store.frontend, store.backend, and product.data.

(d) The code in module customer can access public types from package product.data.

(e) The code in module product can access public types from package customer.data.

19.2   Which statement is true about the requires directive?
Select the one correct answer.

(a) It allows access to any public types in the module specified in the requires directive.

(b) It allows access to non-public types using reflection in the module specified in the requires directive.

(c) It allows access to protected types in the module specified in the requires directive.

(d) It allows access to all types except protected types in the module specified in the requires directive.

(e) It allows access to public types in the exported packages of the module specified in the requires directive.

19.3   Place the following modules in order, based on the number of dependencies they have, starting from the module that has the most dependencies.
Select the one correct answer.

(a) java.base java.se java.logging
(b) java.logging java.se java.base
(c) java.base java.logging java.se
(d) java.logging java.base java.se
(e) java.se java.logging java.base
(f) java.se java.base java.logging

19.4 Given the following code:

```
module zoo {
  requires animals;
}

module animals {
  exports animals.primates;
}
```

Which type declarations from the module `animals` can be accessed by code in the module zoo?
Select the two correct answers.

(a) `package animals.primates;`
    `class Ape { }`

(b) `package animals.primates;`
    `protected class Gorilla { }`

(c) `package animals.primates;`
    `public interface Toolmaker { }`

(d) `package animals.primates.fossil;`
    `public class JavaMan { }`

(e) `package animals;`
    `public class Hybrid { }`

(f) `package animals.primates;`
    `public class Chimpanzee extends Ape { }`

19.5 The code in the `music` module needs to access types from package `production.company` contained in the `production` module.
Which module definitions implement this requirement?
Select the two correct answers.

(a) `module music {`
    `    requires production;`
    `}`

(b) `module music {`
    `    requires production.company;`
    `}`

(c) `module music {`
    `    requires production.company.*;`
    `}`

(d) `module production {`
    `    exports production.company;`
    `}`

(e) `module production {`
    `    exports production.*;`
    `}`

(f) `module production {`
    `    exports production.company.*;`
    `}`

19.6   Which of the following statements are true?
Select the two correct answers.

(a) An automatic module is a plain JAR loaded from the class path.
(b) Plain JARs loaded from the module path are included in the unnamed module.
(c) An automatic module is a plain JAR loaded from the module path.
(d) Plain JARs loaded from the class path are included in the unnamed module.

19.7   Given the following code:

```
module store {
  requires product;
  exports store.frontend;
}

module marketing {
  requires store;
  opens marketing.offers;
}

module product {
  exports product.data;
  exports product.pricing to marketing;
}
```

Which statement is true?
Select the one correct answer.

(a) The code in module store can access types defined in package product.data, but only by reflection in package marketing.offers.
(b) The code in module marketing can access types defined in packages product.data and product.pricing.
(c) The code in module marketing can access types defined in packages product.data and store.frontend.
(d) The code in module store can access types defined in packages product.data and product.pricing.
(e) The code in module product can access types defined in package store.front-end, and those in package marketing.offers by reflection.

19.8   The code contained in module music needs to access types from the production.recording package through reflection. It also needs to access public types from the packages production.mix and artist.recording.

Which module definitions implement these requirements?
Select the one correct answer.

(a) ```
module music {
    requires artist.recording;
    requires production.mix;
}
module production {
  opens production.mix;
  exports production.recording;
}
```
```

```
        module artist {
          exports artist.recording;
        }
```

(b) module music {
```
          requires production;
        }
        module production {
          requires transitive artist;
          opens production.recording;
          exports production.mix;
        }
        module artist {
          exports artist.recording;
        }
```

(c) module music {
```
          requires production;
        }
        module production {
          opens production.mix;
          exports recording;
        }
        module artist {
          requires transitive production;
          exports artist.recording;
        }
```

(d) module music {
```
          requires production.recording;
        }
        module production {
          opens music;
          exports production.mix;
        }
        module artist {
          requires transitive production.recording;
          exports artist.recording;
        }
```

19.9 Given the following code:

```
        module music {
          exports music.sound;
        }

        module brass {
          requires music;
          provides music.sound.Instrument with brass.sound.Trumpet;
        }
```

What is the correct definition for module player that wants to utilize the music.sound.Instrument service?

Select the one correct answer.

(a) ```
module player {
    requires brass;
    uses music.sound.Instrument;
}
```

(b) ```
module player {
    requires music;
    uses music.sound.Instrument;
}
```

(c) ```
module player {
    requires brass;
    uses brass.sound.Trumpet;
}
```

(d) ```
module player {
    requires music;
    uses brass.sound.Trumpet;
}
```

19.10   Which of the following statements are true about the jlink tool and runtime images?

Select the two correct answers.

(a) The jlink tool can create platform-independent runtime images.
(b) The jlink tool can create platform-specific runtime images.
(c) Runtime images only contain application code.
(d) Runtime images are automatically updated when a new Java version is installed.
(e) The runtime image of an application can be executed on a system that has no JVM installed.

19.11   Given the following code:

```
module music {
    requires artist;
    requires instrument;
    exports preferences.style to catalog;
}

module instrument {
    requires transitive music;
    opens instrument.data;
}

module artist {
    exports preferences.style;
}

module catalog {
}
```

What are the reasons why the module declarations will fail to compile?

Select the two correct answers.

(a) There is a cyclic dependency between modules.
(b) There is a split package deployment.
(c) There is an opens directive in a non-open module.
(d) There is a qualified export referring to a module that does not require this export.

19.12   Which statement is true?
Select the one correct answer.

(a) A modular JAR is not backward compatible and thus cannot be used in the context of a class path.
(b) A plain JAR is not forward compatible and thus cannot be used in the context of a module path.
(c) The --list-modules option of the java command includes the unnamed module.
(d) The --list-modules option of the java command does not include automatic modules.
(e) By default, an automatic module is referred to by its JAR file name.
(f) By default, the unnamed module is referred to by its JAR file name.

19.13   Which of the following statements are true?
Select the two correct answers.

(a) An automatic module implicitly requires all explicit modules, but not other automatic modules or the unnamed module.
(b) An automatic module implicitly requires all explicit modules and other automatic modules, but not the unnamed module.
(c) An automatic module implicitly requires all other modules, including explicit and automatic modules, and the unnamed module.
(d) An explicit module must use the requires directive to access types in an automatic module.
(e) An explicit module must use the requires directive to access types in the unnamed module.

Java I/O: Part I   20

 Chapter Topics

- Understanding the concept of I/O streams to read data from an input source and write data to an output destination

- Understanding the hierarchy of byte streams, as represented by the `InputStream` and `OutputStream` abstract classes, to handle data as bytes

- Reading and writing bytes using file streams, as represented by the `FileInputStream` and `FileOutputStream` classes

- Reading and writing binary files using the `DataInputStream` and `DataOutputStream` classes

- Understanding the hierarchy of character streams, as represented by the `Reader` and `Writer` abstract classes

- Using character encodings, including Unicode and UTF-8, with the `InputStreamReader` and `OutputStreamWriter` classes

- Reading and writing text files using the `FileReader` and `PrintWriter` classes

- Using buffered character streams for efficient reading and writing of characters, as represented by the `BufferedReader` and `BufferedWriter` classes

- Understanding the standard input, output, and error streams, as represented by the fields `System.in`, `System.out`, and `System.err`, respectively

- Using the `Console` class that allows character-based input and output from a console

- Performing object serialization/de-serialization—that is, writing and reading binary representation of objects, using the `ObjectOutputStream` and `ObjectInputStream` classes

- Applying selective serialization, exploiting customized serialization, using class versioning, and understanding how the inheritance relationship can affect serialization

Java SE 17 Developer Exam Objectives	
[9.1] Read and write console and file data using I/O Streams	*§20.1, p. 1233 to §20.4, p. 1256*
[9.2] Serialize and de-serialize Java objects	*§20.5, p. 1261*
Java SE 11 Developer Exam Objectives	
[9.1] Read and write console and file data using I/O Streams	*§20.1, p. 1233 to §20.4, p. 1256*
[9.2] Implement serialization and deserialization techniques on Java objects	*§20.5, p. 1261*

The java.io package provides an extensive library of classes for dealing with input and output of data. Although data can be read from various sources and written to various destinations, the emphasis in this chapter is on using the standard I/O API provided by the java.io package for reading and writing various kinds of data to *files*: bytes, characters, binary files, text files, buffered I/O, and object serialization.

The java.io package also provides a general interface to interact with the file system of the host platform, but we will use the newer and enhanced I/O API in the java.nio.file package that provides access to files, file attributes, and file systems (Chapter 21, p. 1285).

In this chapter, we assume a basic understanding of a *hierarchical file system* in which files and directories are referenced by a *string* that specifies the *path* of an entity in the file system. The idiosyncrasies of file systems on different platforms are explored in Chapter 21, p. 1285.

It is important to note that the term *stream* in this chapter refers to *I/O streams*. Streams that provide functional-style operations on sequences of elements are discussed in Chapter 16, p. 879.

20.1 Input and Output

Java provides *I/O streams* as a general mechanism for dealing with data input and output. I/O streams implement *sequential processing* of data. An *input stream* allows an application to read a sequence of data, and an *output stream* allows an application to write a sequence of data. An *input stream* acts as a *source* of data, and an *output stream* acts as a *destination* of data. The following entities can act as both input and output streams:

- A file—which is the focus in this chapter
- An array of bytes or characters
- A network connection

There are two categories of I/O streams:

- *Byte streams* that process *bytes* as a unit of data
- *Character streams* that process *characters* as a unit of data

A *low-level I/O stream* operates directly on the data source (e.g., a file or an array of bytes), and processes the data primarily as *bytes*.

A *high-level I/O stream* is *chained* to an underlying stream, and provides additional capabilities for processing data managed by the underlying stream—for example, processing bytes from the underlying stream as Java primitive values or objects. In other words, a high-level I/O stream acts as a *wrapper* for the underlying stream.

In the rest of this chapter we primarily explore how to use I/O streams of the standard I/O API provided by the java.io package to read and write various kinds of data that is stored in files.

20.2 Byte Streams: Input Streams and Output Streams

The abstract classes InputStream and OutputStream in the java.io package are the root of the inheritance hierarchies for handling the reading and writing of data as *bytes* (Figure 20.1). Their subclasses, implementing different kinds of input and output (I/O) streams, override the following methods from the InputStream and OutputStream classes to customize the reading and writing of bytes, respectively:

From the InputStream abstract class:

```
int read() throws IOException
int read(byte[] b) throws IOException
int read(byte[] b, int off, int len) throws IOException
```

Note that the first read() method reads a *byte*, but returns an int value. The byte read resides in the eight least significant bits of the int value, while the remaining bits in the int value are zeroed out. The read() methods return the value −1 when the end of the input stream is reached.

```
long transferTo(OutputStream out) throws IOException
```

Reads bytes from this input stream and writes to the specified output stream in the order they are read. The I/O streams are *not closed* after the operation (see below).

From the OutputStream abstract class:

```
void write(int b) throws IOException
void write(byte[] b) throws IOException
void write(byte[] b, int off, int len) throws IOException
```

The first write() method takes an int as an argument, but truncates it to the eight least significant bits before writing it out as a byte to the output stream.

```
void close() throws IOException          Both InputStream and OutputStream
void flush() throws IOException          Only for OutputStream
```

A I/O stream should be *closed* when no longer needed, to free system resources. Closing an output stream automatically *flushes* the output stream, meaning that any data in its internal buffer is written out.

Since byte streams also implement the AutoCloseable interface, they can be declared in a try-with-resources statement (§7.7, p. 407) that will ensure they are properly closed after use at runtime.

An output stream can also be manually flushed by calling the second method.

Read and write operations on streams are *blocking* operations—that is, a call to a read or write method does not return before a byte has been read or written.

Many methods in the classes contained in the java.io package throw the checked IOException. A calling method must therefore either catch the exception explicitly, or specify it in a throws clause.

Figure 20.1 *Partial Byte Stream Inheritance Hierarchies in the* `java.io` *Package*

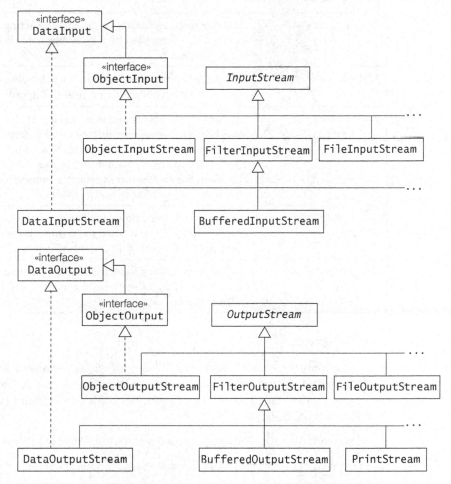

Table 20.1 and Table 20.2 give an overview of selected byte streams. Usually an output stream has a corresponding input stream of the same type.

Table 20.1 *Selected Input Streams*

`FileInputStream`	Data is read as bytes from a file. The file acting as the input stream can be specified by a `File` object, a `FileDescriptor`, or a `String` file name.
`FilterInputStream`	The superclass of all *input filter streams*. An input filter stream must be chained to an underlying input stream.
`DataInputStream`	A filter stream that allows the *binary representation of Java primitive values* to be read from an underlying input stream. The underlying input stream must be specified.
`ObjectInputStream`	A filter stream that allows *binary representations of Java objects and Java primitive values* to be read from a specified input stream.

Table 20.2 *Selected Output Streams*

FileOutputStream	Data is written as *bytes* to a file. The file acting as the output stream can be specified by a File object, a FileDescriptor, or a String file name.
FilterOutputStream	The superclass of all *output filter streams*. An output filter stream must be chained to an underlying output stream.
PrintStream	A filter output stream that converts a *text representation of Java objects and Java primitive values* to bytes before writing them to an underlying output stream, which must be specified. This is the type of System.out and System.err (p. 1255). However, the PrintWriter class is recommended when writing characters rather than bytes (p. 1247).
DataOutputStream	A filter stream that allows the *binary representation of Java primitive values* to be written to an underlying output stream. The underlying output stream must be specified.
ObjectOutputStream	A filter stream that allows the *binary representation of Java objects and Java primitive values* to be written to a specified underlying output stream.

File Streams

The subclasses FileInputStream and FileOutputStream represent low-level streams that define byte input and output streams that are connected to files. Data can only be read or written as a sequence of *bytes*. Such file streams are typically used for handling image data.

A FileInputStream for reading bytes can be created using the following constructor:

> FileInputStream(String name) throws FileNotFoundException

The file designated by the file name is assigned to a new file input stream.

If the file does not exist, a FileNotFoundException is thrown. If it exists, it is set to be read from the beginning. A SecurityException is thrown if the file does not have read access.

A FileOutputStream for writing bytes can be created using the following constructor:

> FileOutputStream(String name) throws FileNotFoundException
> FileOutputStream(String name, boolean append) throws FileNotFoundException

The file designated by the file name is assigned to a new file output stream.

If the file does not exist, it is created. If it exists, its contents are reset, unless the appropriate constructor is used to indicate that output should be appended to the file. A SecurityException is thrown if the file does not have write access or it cannot be created. A FileNotFoundException is thrown if it is not possible to open the file for any other reasons.

The `FileInputStream` class provides an implementation for the `read()` methods in its superclass `InputStream`. Similarly, the `FileOutputStream` class provides an implementation for the `write()` methods in its superclass `OutputStream`.

Example 20.1 demonstrates using a buffer to read bytes from and write bytes to file streams. The input and the output file names are specified on the command line. The streams are created at (1) and (2).

The bytes are read into a buffer by the `read()` method that returns the number of bytes read. The same number of bytes from the buffer are written to the output file by the `write()` method, regardless of whether the buffer is full or not after every read operation.

The end of file is reached when the `read()` method returns the value -1. The code at (3a) using a buffer can be replaced by a call to the `transferTo()` method at (3b) to do the same operation. The streams are closed by the try-with-resources statement. Note that most of the code consists of a try-with-resources statement with catch clauses to handle the various exceptions.

Example 20.1   *Copying a File Using a Byte Buffer*

```java
/* Copy a file using a byte buffer.
   Command syntax: java CopyFile <from_file> <to_file> */
import java.io.*;

class CopyFile {
  public static void main(String[] args) {

    try (// Assign the files:
       FileInputStream fromFile = new FileInputStream(args[0]);      // (1)
       FileOutputStream toFile = new FileOutputStream(args[1])) {    // (2)

       // Copy bytes using buffer:                                   // (3a)
       byte[] buffer = new byte[1024];
       int length = 0;
       while((length = fromFile.read(buffer)) != -1) {
         toFile.write(buffer, 0, length);
       }

       // Transfer bytes:
//       fromFile.transferTo(toFile);                               // (3b)

    } catch(ArrayIndexOutOfBoundsException e) {
       System.err.println("Usage: java CopyFile <from_file> <to_file>");
    } catch(FileNotFoundException e) {
       System.err.println("File could not be copied: " + e);
    } catch(IOException e) {
       System.err.println("I/O error.");
    }
  }
}
```

I/O Filter Streams

An *I/O filter stream* is a high-level I/O stream that provides additional functionality to an underlying stream to which it is chained. The data from the underlying stream is manipulated in some way by the filter stream. The FilterInputStream and FilterOutputStream classes, together with their subclasses, define input and output filter streams. The subclasses BufferedInputStream and BufferedOutputStream implement filter streams that buffer input from and output to the underlying stream, respectively. The subclasses DataInputStream and DataOutputStream implement filter streams that allow binary representation of Java primitive values to be read and written, respectively, from and to an underlying stream.

Reading and Writing Binary Values

The java.io package contains the two interfaces DataInput and DataOutput, which streams can implement to allow reading and writing of *binary representation of Java primitive values* (boolean, char, byte, short, int, long, float, double). The methods for writing binary representations of Java primitive values are named write*X*, where *X* is any Java primitive data type. The methods for reading binary representations of Java primitive values are similarly named read*X*. Table 20.3 gives an overview of the read*X*() and write*X*() methods found in these two interfaces. A file containing *binary values* (i.e., binary representation of Java primitive values) is usually called a *binary file*.

Note the methods provided for reading and writing strings. However, the recommended practice for reading and writing characters is to use *character streams*, called *readers* and *writers*, which are discussed in §20.3.

The filter streams DataOutputStream and DataInputStream implement the DataOutput and DataInput interfaces, respectively, and can be used to read and write binary representation of Java primitive values from and to an underlying stream. Both the write*X*() and read*X*() methods throw an IOException in the event of an I/O error. In particular, the read*X*() methods throw an EOFException (a subclass of IOException) if the input stream does not contain the correct number of bytes to read. Bytes can also be skipped from a DataInput stream, using the skipBytes(int n) method which skips n bytes.

```
DataInputStream(InputStream in)
DataOutputStream(OutputStream out)
```

These constructors can be used to set up filter streams from an underlying stream for reading and writing Java primitive values, respectively.

Table 20.3 *The* DataInput *and* DataOutput *Interfaces*

Type	Methods in the DataInput interface	Methods in the DataOutput interface
boolean	readBoolean()	writeBoolean(boolean b)
char	readChar()	writeChar(int c)

Table 20.3 *The `DataInput` and `DataOutput` Interfaces (Continued)*

Type	Methods in the `DataInput` interface	Methods in the `DataOutput` interface
byte	readByte()	writeByte(int b)
short	readShort()	writeShort(int s)
int	readInt()	writeInt(int i)
long	readLong()	writeLong(long l)
float	readFloat()	writeFloat(float f)
double	readDouble()	writeDouble(double d)
String	readLine()	writeChars(String str)
String	readUTF()	writeUTF(String str)

Writing Binary Values to a File

To write the binary representation of Java primitive values to a *binary file*, the following procedure can be used, which is also depicted in Figure 20.2.

1. Use a try-with-resources statement for declaring and creating the necessary streams, which guarantees closing of the filter stream and any underlying stream.

2. Create a `FileOutputStream`:

    ```
    FileOutputStream outputFile = new FileOutputStream("primitives.data");
    ```

3. Create a `DataOutputStream` which is chained to the `FileOutputStream`:

    ```
    DataOutputStream outputStream = new DataOutputStream(outputFile);
    ```

4. Write Java primitive values using relevant `writeX()` methods:

    Note that in the case of char, byte, and short data types, the int argument to the `writeX()` method is converted to the corresponding type, before it is written (see Table 20.3).

See also the numbered lines in Example 20.2 corresponding to the steps above.

Figure 20.2 *Stream Chaining for Reading and Writing Binary Values to a File*

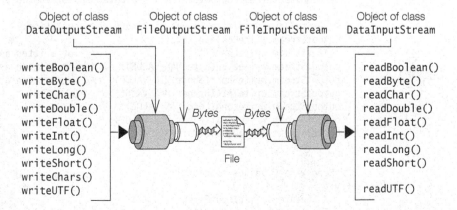

Object of class `DataOutputStream`	Object of class `FileOutputStream`	Object of class `FileInputStream`	Object of class `DataInputStream`

```
writeBoolean()
writeByte()
writeChar()
writeDouble()
writeFloat()
writeInt()
writeLong()
writeShort()
writeChars()
writeUTF()
```

Bytes   *Bytes*

File

```
readBoolean()
readByte()
readChar()
readDouble()
readFloat()
readInt()
readLong()
readShort()

readUTF()
```

Reading Binary Values from a File

To read the binary representation of Java primitive values from a *binary file*, the following procedure can be used, which is also depicted in Figure 20.2.

1. Use a try-with-resources statement for declaring and creating the necessary streams, which guarantees closing of the filter stream and any underlying stream.

2. Create a `FileInputStream`:

   ```
   FileInputStream inputFile = new FileInputStream("primitives.data");
   ```

3. Create a `DataInputStream` which is chained to the `FileInputStream`:

   ```
   DataInputStream inputStream = new DataInputStream(inputFile);
   ```

4. Read the (exact number of) Java primitive values in the *same order* they were written out to the file, using relevant read*X*() methods. Not doing so will unleash the wrath of the `IOException`.

See also the numbered lines in Example 20.2 corresponding to the steps above. Example 20.2 uses both procedures described above: first to write and then to read some Java primitive values to and from a file. It also checks to see if the end of the stream has been reached, signaled by an `EOFException`. The values are also written to the standard output stream.

. . . .

Example 20.2 *Reading and Writing Binary Values*

```java
import java.io.*;

public class BinaryValuesIO {
  public static void main(String[] args) throws IOException {

    // Write binary values to a file:
    try(                                                            // (1)
        // Create a FileOutputStream.                                  (2)
        FileOutputStream outputFile = new FileOutputStream("primitives.data");
        // Create a DataOutputStream which is chained to the FileOutputStream.(3)
        DataOutputStream outputStream = new DataOutputStream(outputFile)) {

      // Write Java primitive values in binary representation:           (4)
      outputStream.writeBoolean(true);
      outputStream.writeChar('A');              // int written as Unicode char
      outputStream.writeByte(Byte.MAX_VALUE);   // int written as 8-bits byte
      outputStream.writeShort(Short.MIN_VALUE); // int written as 16-bits short
      outputStream.writeInt(Integer.MAX_VALUE);
      outputStream.writeLong(Long.MIN_VALUE);
      outputStream.writeFloat(Float.MAX_VALUE);
      outputStream.writeDouble(Math.PI);
    }

    // Read binary values from a file:
    try (                                                           // (1)
        // Create a FileInputStream.                                   (2)
        FileInputStream inputFile = new FileInputStream("primitives.data");
```

```
                    // Create a DataInputStream which is chained to the FileInputStream.  (3)
                    DataInputStream inputStream = new DataInputStream(inputFile)) {

                    // Read the binary representation of Java primitive values
                    // in the same order they were written out:                           (4)
                    System.out.println(inputStream.readBoolean());
                    System.out.println(inputStream.readChar());
                    System.out.println(inputStream.readByte());
                    System.out.println(inputStream.readShort());
                    System.out.println(inputStream.readInt());
                    System.out.println(inputStream.readLong());
                    System.out.println(inputStream.readFloat());
                    System.out.println(inputStream.readDouble());

                    // Check for end of stream:
                    int value = inputStream.readByte();
                    System.out.println("More input: " + value);
                } catch (FileNotFoundException fnf) {
                    System.out.println("File not found.");
                } catch (EOFException eof) {
                    System.out.println("End of input stream.");
                }
            }
        }
```

Output from the program:

```
true
A
127
-32768
2147483647
-9223372036854775808
3.4028235E38
3.141592653589793
End of input stream.
```

20.3 Character Streams: Readers and Writers

A *character encoding* is a scheme for representing characters. Java programs represent values of the char type internally in the 16-bit Unicode character encoding, but the host platform might use another character encoding to represent and store characters externally. For example, the ASCII (American Standard Code for Information Interchange) character encoding is widely used to represent characters on many platforms. However, it is only one small subset of the Unicode standard.

The abstract classes Reader and Writer are the roots of the inheritance hierarchies for streams that read and write *Unicode characters* using a specific character encoding (Figure 20.3). A *reader* is an input character stream that implements the Readable interface and reads a sequence of Unicode characters, and a *writer* is an output character stream that implements the Writer interface and writes a sequence of

Figure 20.3 *Selected Character Streams in the* `java.io` *Package*

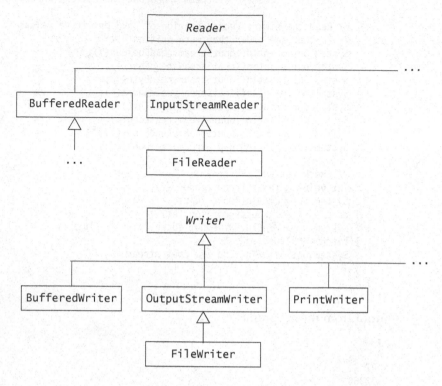

Unicode characters. Character encodings (usually called *charsets*) are used by readers and writers to convert between external bytes and internal Unicode characters. The same character encoding that was used to write the characters must be used to read those characters. The `java.nio.charset.Charset` class represents charsets. Kindly refer to the `Charset` class API documentation for more details.

```
static Charset forName(String charsetName)
```
Returns a charset object for the named charset. Selected common charset names are "UTF-8", "UTF-16", "US-ASCII", and "ISO-8859-1".

```
static Charset defaultCharset()
```
Returns the default charset of this Java virtual machine.

Table 20.4 and Table 20.5 give an overview of some selected character streams found in the `java.io` package.

Table 20.4 *Selected Readers*

Reader	Description
BufferedReader	A reader is a high-level input stream that buffers the characters read from an underlying stream. The underlying stream must be specified and an optional buffer size can be given.

Table 20.4 *Selected Readers (Continued)*

Reader	Description
InputStreamReader	Characters are read from a byte input stream which must be specified. The default character encoding is used if no character encoding is explicitly specified in the constructor. This class provides the bridge from byte streams to character streams.
FileReader	Characters are read from a file, using the default character encoding, unless an encoding is explicitly specified in the constructor. The file can be specified by a String file name. It automatically creates a FileInputStream that is associated with the file.

Readers use the following methods for reading Unicode characters:

```
int read() throws IOException
int read(char cbuf[]) throws IOException
int read(char cbuf[], int off, int len) throws IOException
```

Note that the read() methods read the character as an int in the range 0 to 65,535 (0x0000–0xFFFF).

The first method returns the character as an int value. The last two methods store the characters in the specified array and return the number of characters read. The value -1 is returned if the end of the stream has been reached.

```
long skip(long n) throws IOException
```

A reader can skip over characters using the skip() method.

```
void close() throws IOException
```

Like byte streams, a character stream should be closed when no longer needed in order to free system resources.

```
boolean ready() throws IOException
```

When called, this method returns true if the next read operation is guaranteed not to block. Returning false does *not* guarantee that the next read operation will block.

```
long transferTo(Writer out) throws IOException
```

Reads all characters from this reader and writes the characters to the specified writer in the order they are read. The I/O streams are not *closed* after the operation.

Table 20.5 *Selected Writers*

Writers	Description
BufferedWriter	A writer is a high-level output stream that buffers the characters before writing them to an underlying stream. The underlying stream must be specified, and an optional buffer size can be specified.

Table 20.5   *Selected Writers (Continued)*

Writers	Description
OutputStreamWriter	Characters are written to a byte output stream that must be specified. The default character encoding is used if no explicit character encoding is specified in the constructor. This class provides the bridge from character streams to byte streams.
FileWriter	Characters are written to a file, using the default character encoding, unless an encoding is explicitly specified in the constructor. The file can be specified by a String file name. It automatically creates a FileOutputStream that is associated with the file. A boolean parameter can be specified to indicate whether the file should be overwritten or appended with new content.
PrintWriter	A print writer is a high-level output stream that allows *text representation of Java objects and Java primitive values* to be written to an underlying output stream or writer. The underlying output stream or writer must be specified. An explicit encoding can be specified in the constructor, and also whether the print writer should do automatic line flushing.

Writers use the following methods for writing Unicode characters:

```
void write(int c) throws IOException
```

The write() method takes an int as an argument, but writes only the least significant 16 bits.

```
void write(char[] cbuf) throws IOException
void write(String str) throws IOException
void write(char[] cbuf, int off, int length) throws IOException
void write(String str, int off, int length) throws IOException
```

Write the characters from an array of characters or a string.

```
void close() throws IOException
void flush() throws IOException
```

Like byte streams, a character stream should be closed when no longer needed in order to free system resources. Closing a character output stream automatically *flushes* the stream. A character output stream can also be manually flushed.

Like byte streams, many methods of the character stream classes throw a checked IOException that a calling method must either catch explicitly or specify in a throws clause. They also implement the AutoCloseable interface, and can thus be declared in a try-with-resources statement (§7.7, p. 407) that will ensure they are automatically closed after use at runtime.

Analogous to Example 20.1 that demonstrates usage of a byte buffer for writing and reading bytes to and from file streams, Example 20.3 demonstrates using a character buffer for writing and reading characters to and from file streams. Later in this section, we will use buffered readers (p. 1251) and buffered writers (p. 1250) for reading and writing characters from files, respectively.

Example 20.3 *Copying a File Using a Character Buffer*

```java
/* Copy a file using a character buffer.
   Command syntax: java CopyCharacterFile <from_file> <to_file> */
import java.io.*;

class CopyCharacterFile {
  public static void main(String[] args) {

    try (// Assign the files:
        FileReader fromFile = new FileReader(args[0]);          // (1)
        FileWriter toFile = new FileWriter(args[1])) {          // (2)

      // Copy characters using buffer:                          // (3a)
      char[] buffer = new char[1024];
      int length = 0;
      while((length = fromFile.read(buffer)) != -1) {
        toFile.write(buffer, 0, length);
      }

      // Transfer characters:
//      fromFile.transferTo(toFile);                            // (3b)

    } catch(ArrayIndexOutOfBoundsException e) {
      System.err.println("Usage: java CopyCharacterFile <from_file> <to_file>");
    } catch(FileNotFoundException e) {
      System.err.println("File could not be copied: " + e);
    } catch(IOException e) {
      System.err.println("I/O error.");
    }
  }
}
```

Print Writers

The capabilities of the OutputStreamWriter and the InputStreamReader classes are limited, as they primarily write and read characters.

In order to write a *text representation* of Java primitive values and objects, a Print-Writer should be chained to either a writer, or a byte output stream, or accept a String file name, using one of the following constructors:

```java
PrintWriter(Writer out)
PrintWriter(Writer out, boolean autoFlush)
PrintWriter(OutputStream out)
PrintWriter(OutputStream out, boolean autoFlush)
PrintWriter(String fileName) throws FileNotFoundException
PrintWriter(String fileName, Charset charset)
          throws FileNotFoundException
PrintWriter(String fileName, String charsetName)
          throws FileNotFoundException, UnsupportedEncodingException
```

The boolean autoFlush argument specifies whether the PrintWriter should do automatic line flushing.

When the underlying writer is specified, the character encoding supplied by the underlying writer is used. However, an OutputStream has no notion of any character encoding, so the necessary intermediate OutputStreamWriter is automatically created, which will convert characters into bytes, using the default character encoding.

```
boolean checkError()
protected void clearError()
```

The first method flushes the output stream if it's not closed and checks its error state.

The second method clears the error state of this output stream.

Table 20.6 *Print Methods of the* PrintWriter *Class*

The print() methods	The println() methods
–	println()
print(boolean b)	println(boolean b)
print(char c)	println(char c)
print(int i)	println(int i)
print(long l)	println(long l)
print(float f)	println(float f)
print(double d)	println(double d)
print(char[] s)	println(char[] ca)
print(String s)	println(String str)
print(Object obj)	println(Object obj)

Writing Text Representation of Primitive Values and Objects

In addition to overriding the write() methods from its super class Writer, the PrintWriter class provides methods for writing text representation of Java primitive values and of objects (see Table 20.6). The println() methods write the text representation of their argument to the underlying stream, and then append a *line separator*. The println() methods use the correct platform-dependent line separator. For example, on Unix-based platforms the line separator is '\n' (newline), while on Windows-based platforms it is "\r\n" (carriage return + newline) and on Mac-based platforms it is '\r' (carriage return).

The print methods create a text representation of an object by calling the toString() method on the object. The print methods do not throw any IOException. Instead, the checkError() method of the PrintWriter class must be called to check for errors.

Writing Formatted Values

Although formatting of values is covered extensively in Chapter 18, p. 1095, here we mention the support for formatting values provided by I/O streams. The PrintWriter class provides the format() methods and the printf() convenient methods to write *formatted* values. The printf() methods are functionally equivalent to the format() methods. As the methods return a PrintWriter, calls to these methods can be chained.

The printf() and the format() methods for printing formatted values are also provided by the PrintStream and the Console classes (p. 1256). The format() method is also provided by the String class (§8.4, p. 457). We assume familiarity with printing formatted values on the standard output stream by calling the printf() method on the System.out field which is an object of the PrintStream class (§1.9, p. 24).

```
PrintWriter format(String format, Object... args)
PrintWriter format(Locale loc, String format, Object... args)

PrintWriter printf(String format, Object... args)
PrintWriter printf(Locale loc, String format, Object... args)
```

The String parameter format specifies how formatting will be done. It contains *format specifiers* that determine how each subsequent value in the variable arity parameter args will be formatted and printed. The resulting string from the formatting will be written to the current writer.

If the locale is specified, it is taken into consideration to format the args.

Any error in the format string will result in a runtime exception.

Writing Text Files

When writing text representation of values to a file using the default character encoding, any one of the following four procedures for setting up a PrintWriter can be used.

Setting up a PrintWriter based on an OutputStreamWriter which is chained to a FileOutputStream (Figure 20.4(a)):

1. Create a FileOutputStream:

   ```
   FileOutputStream outputFile = new FileOutputStream("info.txt");
   ```

2. Create an OutputStreamWriter which is chained to the FileOutputStream:

   ```
   OutputStreamWriter outputStream = new OutputStreamWriter(outputFile);
   ```

   The OutputStreamWriter uses the default character encoding for writing the characters to the file.

3. Create a PrintWriter which is chained to the OutputStreamWriter:

   ```
   PrintWriter printWriter1 = new PrintWriter(outputStream, true);
   ```

   The value true for the second parameter in the constructor will result in the output buffer being flushed by the println() and printf() methods.

Figure 20.4 *Setting Up a* `PrintWriter` *to Write to a File*

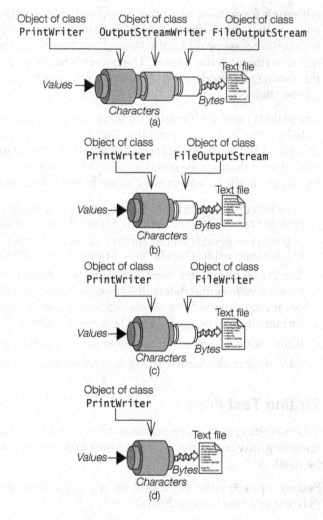

Setting up a `PrintWriter` based on a `FileOutputStream` (Figure 20.4(b)):

1. Create a `FileOutputStream`:

    ```
    FileOutputStream outputFile = new FileOutputStream("info.txt");
    ```

2. Create a `PrintWriter` which is chained to the `FileOutputStream`:

    ```
    PrintWriter printWriter2 = new PrintWriter(outputFile, true);
    ```

    The intermediate `OutputStreamWriter` to convert the characters using the default encoding is automatically supplied. The output buffer will also perform automatic line flushing.

Setting up a `PrintWriter` based on a `FileWriter` (Figure 20.4(c)):

1. Create a `FileWriter` which is a subclass of `OutputStreamWriter`:

    ```
    FileWriter fileWriter = new FileWriter("info.txt");
    ```

This is equivalent to having an `OutputStreamWriter` chained to a `FileOutput-Stream` for writing the characters to the file, as shown in Figure 20.4(a).

2. Create a `PrintWriter` which is chained to the `FileWriter`:

    ```
    PrintWriter printWriter3 = new PrintWriter(fileWriter, true);
    ```

    The output buffer will be flushed by the `println()` and `printf()` methods.

Setting up a `PrintWriter`, given the file name (Figure 20.4(d)):

1. Create a `PrintWriter`, supplying the file name:

    ```
    PrintWriter printWriter4 = new PrintWriter("info.txt");
    ```

    The underlying `OutputStreamWriter` is created to write the characters to the file in the default encoding, as shown in Figure 20.4(d). In this case, there is no automatic flushing by the `println()` and `printf()` methods.

If a specific character encoding is desired for the writer, the third procedure (Figure 20.4(c)) can be used, with the encoding being specified for the `FileWriter`:

```
Charset utf8 = Charset.forName("UTF-8");
FileWriter fileWriter = new FileWriter("info.txt", utf8);
PrintWriter printWriter5 = new PrintWriter(fileWriter, true);
```

This writer will use the UTF-8 character encoding to write the characters to the file. Alternatively, we can use a `PrintWriter` constructor that accepts a character encoding:

```
Charset utf8 = Charset.forName("UTF-8");
PrintWriter printWriter6 = new PrintWriter("info.txt", utf8);
```

A `BufferedWriter` can also be used to improve the efficiency of writing characters to the underlying stream, as explained later in this section.

Reading Text Files

When reading *characters* from a file using the default character encoding, the following two procedures for setting up an `InputStreamReader` can be used.

Setting up an `InputStreamReader` which is chained to a `FileInputStream` (Figure 20.5(a)):

1. Create a `FileInputStream`:

    ```
    FileInputStream inputFile = new FileInputStream("info.txt");
    ```

2. Create an `InputStreamReader` which is chained to the `FileInputStream`:

    ```
    InputStreamReader reader = new InputStreamReader(inputFile);
    ```

    The `InputStreamReader` uses the default character encoding for reading the characters from the file.

Setting up a `FileReader` which is a subclass of `InputStreamReader` (Figure 20.5(b)):

1. Create a `FileReader`:

    ```
    FileReader fileReader = new FileReader("info.txt");
    ```

Figure 20.5 *Setting Up Readers to Read Characters*

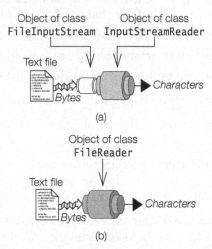

(a)

(b)

This is equivalent to having an InputStreamReader chained to a FileInputStream for reading the characters from the file, using the default character encoding.

If a specific character encoding is desired for the reader, the first procedure can be used (Figure 20.5(a)), with the encoding being specified for the InputStreamReader:

```
Charset utf8 = Charset.forName("UTF-8");
FileInputStream inputFile = new FileInputStream("info.txt");
InputStreamReader reader = new InputStreamReader(inputFile, utf8);
```

This reader will use the UTF-8 character encoding to read the characters from the file. Alternatively, we can use one of the FileReader constructors that accept a character encoding:

```
Charset utf8 = Charset.forName("UTF-8");
FileReader reader = new FileReader("info.txt", utf8);
```

A BufferedReader can also be used to improve the efficiency of reading characters from the underlying stream, as explained later in this section (p. 1251).

Using Buffered Writers

A BufferedWriter can be chained to the underlying writer by using one of the following constructors:

```
BufferedWriter(Writer out)
BufferedWriter(Writer out, int size)
```

The default buffer size is used, unless the buffer size is explicitly specified.

Characters, strings, and arrays of characters can be written using the methods for a Writer, but these now use buffering to provide efficient writing of characters. In addition, the BufferedWriter class provides the method newLine() for writing the platform-dependent line separator.

The following code creates a PrintWriter whose output is buffered, and the characters are written using the UTF-8 character encoding (Figure 20.6(a)):

```
Charset utf8 = Charset.forName("UTF-8");
FileOutputStream   outputFile     = new FileOutputStream("info.txt");
OutputStreamWriter outputStream   = new OutputStreamWriter(outputFile, utf8);
BufferedWriter     bufferedWriter1 = new BufferedWriter(outputStream);
PrintWriter        printWriter1   = new PrintWriter(bufferedWriter1, true);
```

Figure 20.6 *Buffered Writers*

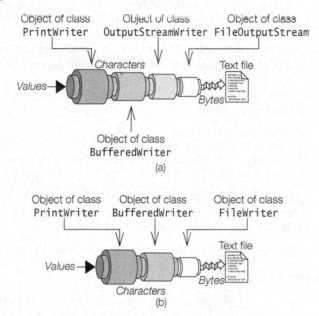

The following code creates a PrintWriter whose output is buffered, and the characters are written using the default character encoding (Figure 20.6(b)):

```
FileWriter     fileWriter     = new FileWriter("info.txt");
BufferedWriter bufferedWriter2 = new BufferedWriter(fileWriter);
PrintWriter    printWriter2   = new PrintWriter(bufferedWriter2, true);
```

Note that in both cases, the PrintWriter is used to write the characters. The Buffered-Writer is sandwiched between the PrintWriter and the underlying OutputStreamWriter (which is the superclass of the FileWriter class).

Using Buffered Readers

A BufferedReader can be chained to the underlying reader by using one of the following constructors:

```
BufferedReader(Reader in)
BufferedReader(Reader in, int size)
```

The default buffer size is used, unless the buffer size is explicitly specified.

In addition to the methods of the Reader class, the BufferedReader class provides the method readLine() to read a line of text from the underlying reader.

```
String readLine() throws IOException
```
The null value is returned when the end of the stream is reached. The returned string must explicitly be converted to other values.

The BufferedReader class also provides the lines() method to create a *stream of text lines* with a buffered reader as the data source (§16.4, p. 902).

```
Stream<String> lines()
```
Returns a *finite sequential ordered* Stream of element type String, where the elements are text lines read by this BufferedReader.

The following code creates a BufferedReader that can be used to read text lines from a file (Figure 20.7(b)):

```
// Using the UTF-8 character encoding:
Charset utf8 = Charset.forName("UTF-8");
FileReader      fileReader      = new FileReader("lines.txt", utf8);
BufferedReader bufferedReader1 = new BufferedReader(reader)

// Use the default encoding:
FileReader      fileReader      = new FileReader("lines.txt");
BufferedReader bufferedReader2 = new BufferedReader(fileReader);
```

Note that in both cases the BufferedReader object is used to read the text lines.

Figure 20.7 *Buffered Readers*

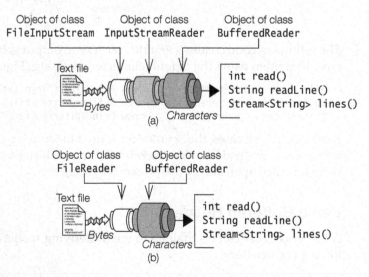

```
Object of class      Object of class      Object of class
FileInputStream   InputStreamReader   BufferedReader
```
```
Text file                                              int read()
                                                       String readLine()
          Bytes                                        Stream<String> lines()
                       (a)   Characters
```

```
Object of class      Object of class
FileReader          BufferedReader
```
```
Text file                                 int read()
                                          String readLine()
          Bytes                           Stream<String> lines()
                    Characters
                       (b)
```

Java primitive values and objects cannot be read directly from their text representation in a file. Characters must be read and converted to the relevant values explicitly. If the text representation of the values is written as *lines of text*, each line can be read and *tokenized* first—that is, grouping characters into *tokens* that meaningfully represent a value. For example, the line "Potatoes 2.50" contains two tokens: the item token "Potatoes" and the price token "2.50". Once a line is tokenized, the tokens can be parsed to obtain the appropriate type of value. The item token is already of type String, but the price token "2.50" needs to be parsed to a double value using the Double.parseDouble() method. A *scanner* provided by the java.io.Scanner class or the String.split() method called on each line can be used to tokenize the character input—both of which are beyond the scope of this book.

In contrast to Example 20.2, which demonstrated the reading and writing of binary representations of primitive data values, Example 20.4 illustrates the reading and writing of text representations of values using I/O streams that are readers and writers.

The CharEncodingDemo class in Example 20.4 writes text representations of values using the UTF-8 character encoding specified at (1). It uses a try-with-resources statement for handling the closing of I/O streams, as shown at (2) and (4). The PrintWriter is buffered (Figure 20.6(b)). Its underlying writer uses the specified encoding, as shown at (2). Values are written out with the text representation of one value on each line, as shown at (3). The example uses the same character encoding to read the text file. A BufferedReader is created (Figure 20.7(b)). Its underlying reader uses the specified encoding, as shown at (4). The text representation of the values is read as one value per line, and parsed accordingly. Each text line in the file is read by calling the readLine() method. The characters in the line are explicitly converted to an appropriate type of value, as shown at (5).

The values are printed on the standard output stream, as shown at (6). We check for the end of the stream at (7), which is signaled by the null value returned by the readLine() method of the BufferedReader class. Note the exceptions that are specified in the throws clause of the main() method.

Although buffering might seem like overkill in this simple example, for efficiency reasons, it should be considered when reading and writing characters from external storage.

It is a useful exercise to modify Example 20.4 to use the various setups for chaining streams for reading and writing characters, as outlined in this section.

Example 20.4 *Demonstrating Readers and Writers, and Character Encoding*

```java
import java.io.*;
import java.nio.charset.Charset;
import java.time.LocalDate;

public class CharEncodingDemo {
  public static void main(String[] args)
        throws FileNotFoundException, IOException, NumberFormatException {

    // UTF-8 character encoding.
    Charset utf8 = Charset.forName("UTF-8");                        // (1)
```

```
try(// Create a BufferedWriter that uses UTF-8 character encoding      (2)
    FileWriter writer = new FileWriter("info.txt", utf8);
    BufferedWriter bufferedWriter1 = new BufferedWriter(writer);
    PrintWriter printWriter = new PrintWriter(bufferedWriter1, true);) {

    System.out.println("Writing using encoding: " + writer.getEncoding());
    // Print some values, one on each line.                            (3)
    printWriter.println(LocalDate.now());
    printWriter.println(Integer.MAX_VALUE);
    printWriter.println(Long.MIN_VALUE);
    printWriter.println(Math.PI);
}

try(// Create a BufferedReader that uses UTF-8 character encoding      (4)
    FileReader reader = new FileReader("info.txt", utf8);
    BufferedReader bufferedReader = new BufferedReader(reader);) {

    System.out.println("Reading using encoding: " + reader.getEncoding());
    // Read the character input and parse accordingly.                 (5)
    LocalDate ld = LocalDate.parse(bufferedReader.readLine());
    int iMax = Integer.parseInt(bufferedReader.readLine());
    long lMin = Long.parseLong(bufferedReader.readLine());
    double pi = Double.parseDouble(bufferedReader.readLine());

    // Write the values read on the terminal                           (6)
    System.out.println("Values read:");
    System.out.println(ld);
    System.out.println(iMax);
    System.out.println(lMin);
    System.out.println(pi);

    // Check for end of stream:                                        (7)
    String line = bufferedReader.readLine();
    if (line != null ) {
      System.out.println("More input: " + line);
    } else {
      System.out.println("End of input stream");
    }
  }
 }
}
```

Output from the program:

```
Writing using encoding: UTF8
Reading using encoding: UTF8
Values read:
2021-06-22
2147483647
-9223372036854775808
3.141592653589793
End of input stream
```

The Standard Input, Output, and Error Streams

The *standard output* stream (usually the display) is represented by the PrintStream object System.out. The *standard input* stream (usually the keyboard) is represented by the InputStream object System.in. In other words, it is a byte input stream. The *standard error* stream (also usually the display) is represented by System.err, which is another object of the PrintStream class. The PrintStream class offers print() methods that act as corresponding print() methods from the PrintWriter class. The print() methods can be used to write output to System.out and System.err. In other words, both System.out and System.err act like PrintWriter, but in addition they have write() methods for writing bytes.

The System class provides the methods setIn(InputStream), setOut(PrintStream), and setErr(PrintStream) that can be passed an I/O stream to reassign the standard streams.

In order to read *characters* typed by the user, the Console class is recommended (p. 1256).

Comparison of Byte Streams and Character Streams

It is instructive to see which byte streams correspond to which character streams. Table 20.7 shows the correspondence between byte and character streams. Note that not all classes have a corresponding counterpart.

Table 20.7 *Correspondence between Selected Byte and Character Streams*

Byte streams	Character streams
OutputStream	Writer
InputStream	Reader
No counterpart	OutputStreamWriter
No counterpart	InputStreamReader
FileOutputStream	FileWriter
FileInputStream	FileReader
BufferedOutputStream	BufferedWriter
BufferedInputStream	BufferedReader
PrintStream	PrintWriter
DataOutputStream	*No counterpart*
DataInputStream	*No counterpart*
ObjectOutputStream	*No counterpart*
ObjectInputStream	*No counterpart*

20.4 The Console Class

A *console* is a unique *character-based* device associated with a JVM. Whether a JVM has a console depends on the platform, and also on the manner in which the JVM is invoked. When the JVM is started from a command line, and the standard input and output streams have not been redirected, the console will normally correspond to the keyboard and the display (Figure 20.8). In any case, the console will be represented by an instance of the class java.io.Console. This Console instance is a *singleton*, and can only be obtained by calling the static method console() of the System class. If there is no console associated with the JVM, the null value is returned by this method.

```
// Obtaining the console:
Console console = System.console();
if (console == null) {
  System.err.println("No console available.");
  return;
}
// Continue ...
```

Figure 20.8 *Keyboard and Display as Console*

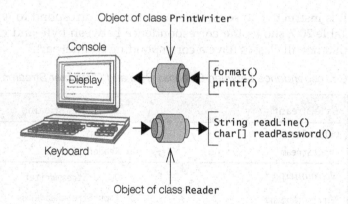

For creating dialogue for console-based applications, the Console class provides the following functionality:

• Prompt and read a line of character-based response.

```
String username = console.readLine("Enter the username (%d chars): ", 4);
```

The readLine() method first prints the formatted prompt on the console, and then returns the characters typed at the console when the line is terminated by the ENTER key.

• Prompt and read passwords without echoing the characters on the console.

```
char[] password;
do {
    password = console.readPassword("Enter password (min. %d chars): ", 6);
} while (password.length < 6);
```

The readPassword() method first prints the formatted prompt, and returns the password characters typed by the user in an array of char when the line is terminated by the ENTER key. The password characters are not echoed on the display.

Since a password is sensitive data, one recommended practice is to have it stored in memory for only as long as it is necessary and to zero-fill the char array as soon as possible in order to overwrite the password characters.

* Print formatted values to the console.

  Similar to the PrintWriter and the PrintStream classes, the Console class also provides the format() and the printf() methods for printing formatted values, but its methods do *not* allow a locale to be specified.

Note that the console only returns character-based input. For reading other types of values from the standard input stream, the java.util.Scanner class can be considered.

The Console class provides methods for *formatted prompting* and *reading* from the console, and obtaining the reader associated with it.

```
String readLine()
String readLine(String format, Object... args)
```

The first method reads a single line of text from the console. The second method prints a formatted prompt first, then reads a single line of text from the console. The prompt is constructed by formatting the specified args according to the specified format.

```
char[] readPassword()
char[] readPassword(String format, Object... args)
```

The first method reads a password or a password phrase from the console with echoing disabled. The second method does the same, but first prints a formatted prompt.

```
Reader reader()
```

This retrieves the unique Reader object associated with this console.

The Console class provides the following methods for *writing* formatted strings to the console, and obtaining the writer associated with it:

```
Console format(String format, Object... args)
Console printf(String format, Object... args)
```

Write a formatted string to this console's output stream using the specified format string and arguments, according to the default locale. See the PrintWriter class with analogous methods (p. 1245).

```
PrintWriter writer()
```

Retrieves the unique PrintWriter object associated with this console.

```
void flush()
```

Flushes the console and forces any buffered output to be written immediately.

Example 20.5 illustrates using the Console class to change a password. The example illustrates the capability of the Console class, and in no way should be construed to provide the ultimate secure implementation to change a password.

The console is obtained at (1). The code at (2) implements the procedure for changing the password. The user is asked to submit the new password, and then asked to confirm it. Note that the password characters are not echoed. The respective char arrays returned with this input are compared for equality by the static method equals() in the java.util.Arrays class, which compares two arrays.

Example 20.5 *Changing Passwords*

```java
import java.io.Console;
import java.io.IOException;
import java.util.Arrays;

/** Class to change the password of a user */
public class ChangePassword {
  public static void main (String[] args) throws IOException  {

    // Obtain the console:                                         (1)
    Console console = System.console();
    if (console == null) {
      System.err.println("No console available.");
      return;
    }

    // Changing the password:                                      (2)
    boolean noMatch = false;
    do {
      // Read the new password and its confirmation:
      char[] newPasswordSelected
          = console.readPassword("Enter your new password: ");
      char[] newPasswordConfirmed
          = console.readPassword("Confirm your new password: ");

      // Compare the supplied passwords:
      noMatch = newPasswordSelected.length == 0  ||
                newPasswordConfirmed.length == 0 ||
                !Arrays.equals(newPasswordSelected, newPasswordConfirmed);
      if (noMatch) {
        console.format("Passwords don't match. Please try again.%n");
      } else {
        // Necessary code to change the password.
        console.format("Password changed.");
      }
    } while (noMatch);
  }
}
```

Running the program:

```
>java ChangePassword
Enter your new password:
```

```
Confirm your new password:
Password changed.
```

Review Questions

20.1 Given the following code, under which circumstance will the method return false?

```
public static boolean test(InputStream is) throws IOException {
  int value = is.read();
  return value >= 0;
}
```

Select the one correct answer.

(a) A character of more than 8 bits was read from the input stream.

(b) An I/O error occurred.

(c) This method will never return false.

(d) The end of the stream was reached in the input stream.

20.2 How can we programmatically check whether a call to a print() method of the PrintWriter class was successful or not?

Select the one correct answer.

(a) Check if the return value from the call is -1.

(b) Check if the return value from the call is null.

(c) Catch the IOException that is thrown when an I/O error occurs.

(d) Call the checkError() method of the PrintWriter class immediately after the print() method call returns to see if an IOException was thrown.

20.3 Given the following program:

```
import java.io.*;
public class MoreEndings {
  public static void main(String[] args) {
    try (FileInputStream fis = new FileInputStream("seq.txt");
        InputStreamReader isr = new InputStreamReader(fis);) {
      int i = isr.read();
      while (i != -1) {
        System.out.print((char)i + "|");
        i = isr.read();
      }
    } catch (FileNotFoundException fnf) {
      System.out.println("File not found");
    } catch (EOFException eofe) {
      System.out.println("End of stream");
    } catch (IOException ioe) {
      System.out.println("Input error");
    }
  }
}
```

Assume that the file seq.txt exists in the current directory, has the required access permissions, and contains the string "Hello".

Which statement about the program is true?
Select the one correct answer.

(a) The program will fail to compile because a certain unchecked exception is not caught.
(b) The program will compile and print H|e|1|1|o|Input error.
(c) The program will compile and print H|e|1|1|o|End of stream.
(d) The program will compile, print H|e|1|1|o|, and then terminate normally.
(e) The program will compile, print H|e|1|1|o|, and then block in order to read from the file.
(f) The program will compile, print H|e|1|1|o|, and terminate because of an uncaught exception.

20.4   Given the following program:

```
import java.io.*;

public class NoEndings {
  public static void main(String[] args) {
    try (FileReader fr = new FileReader("greetings.txt");
        BufferedReader br = new BufferedReader(fr)) {
      System.out.print(br.readLine() + "|");
      System.out.print(br.readLine() + "|");
      System.out.print(br.readLine() + "|");
    } catch (EOFException eofe) {
      System.out.println("End of stream");
    } catch (IOException ioe) {
      System.out.println("Input error");
    }
  }
}
```

Assume that the file greeting.txt exists in the current directory, has the required access permissions, and contains the following two text lines:

```
Hello
Howdy
```

Which statement is true about the program?
Select the one correct answer.

(a) The program will fail to compile because the FileNotFoundException is not caught.
(b) The program will compile, print Hello|Howdy|null|, and then terminate normally.
(c) The program will compile and print Hello|Howdy|Input error.
(d) The program will compile and print Hello|Howdy|End of stream.
(e) The program will compile, print Hello|Howdy|, and then block in order to read from the file.
(f) The program will compile, print Hello|Howdy|, and terminate because of an uncaught exception.

20.5 Object Serialization

Object serialization allows the state of an object to be transformed into a sequence of bytes that can be converted back into a copy of the object (called *deserialization*). After deserialization, the object has the same state as it had when it was serialized, barring any data members that were not serializable. This mechanism is generally known as *persistence*—the serialized result of an object can be stored in a repository from which it can be later retrieved.

Java provides the object serialization facility through the ObjectInput and Object-Output interfaces, which allow the writing and reading of objects to and from I/O streams. These two interfaces extend the DataInput and DataOutput interfaces, respectively (Figure 20.1, p. 1235).

The ObjectOutputStream class and the ObjectInputStream class implement the Object-Output interface and the ObjectInput interface, respectively, providing methods to write and read binary representation of both objects as well as Java primitive values. Figure 20.9 gives an overview of how these classes can be chained to underlying streams and some selected methods they provide. The figure does not show the methods inherited from the abstract OutputStream and InputStream superclasses.

The read and write methods in the two classes can throw an IOException, and the read methods will throw an EOFException if an attempt is made to read past the end of the stream.

Figure 20.9 *Object Stream Chaining*

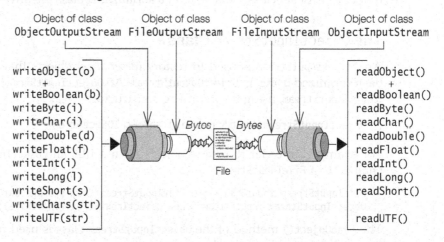

The ObjectOutputStream Class

The class ObjectOutputStream can write objects to any stream that is a subclass of the OutputStream—for example, to a file or a network connection (socket). An Object-OutputStream must be chained to an OutputStream using the following constructor:

```
ObjectOutputStream(OutputStream out) throws IOException
```

For example, in order to store objects in a file and thus provide persistent storage for objects, an `ObjectOutputStream` can be chained to a `FileOutputStream`:

```
FileOutputStream outputFile = new FileOutputStream("obj-storage.dat");
ObjectOutputStream outputStream = new ObjectOutputStream(outputFile);
```

Objects can be written to the stream using the `writeObject()` method of the `ObjectOutputStream` class:

```
final void writeObject(Object obj) throws IOException
```

The `writeObject()` method can be used to write *any* object to a stream, including strings and arrays, as long as the object implements the `java.io.Serializable` interface, which is a *marker interface* with no methods. The `String` class, the primitive wrapper classes, and all array types implement the `Serializable` interface. A serializable object can be any compound object containing references to other objects, and all constituent objects that are serializable are serialized recursively when the compound object is written out. This is true even if there are cyclic references between the objects. Each object is written out only once during serialization. The following information is included when an object is serialized:

- The class information needed to reconstruct the object
- The values of all serializable non-transient and non-static members, including those that are inherited

A checked exception of the type `java.io.NotSerializableException` is thrown if a non-serializable object is encountered during the serialization process. Note also that objects of subclasses that extend a serializable class are always serializable.

The `ObjectInputStream` Class

An `ObjectInputStream` is used to restore (*deserialize*) objects that have previously been serialized using an `ObjectOutputStream`. An `ObjectInputStream` must be chained to an `InputStream`, using the following constructor:

```
ObjectInputStream(InputStream in) throws IOException
```

For example, in order to restore objects from a file, an `ObjectInputStream` can be chained to a `FileInputStream`:

```
FileInputStream inputFile = new FileInputStream("obj-storage.dat");
ObjectInputStream inputStream = new ObjectInputStream(inputFile);
```

The `readObject()` method of the `ObjectInputStream` class is used to read the serialized state of an object from the stream:

```
final Object readObject() throws ClassNotFoundException, IOException
```

Note that the reference type of the returned object is `Object`, regardless of the actual type of the retrieved object, and can be cast to the desired type. Objects and values must be read in the same order as when they were serialized.

Serializable, non-transient data members of an object, including those data members that are inherited, are restored to the values they had at the time of serialization. For compound objects containing references to other objects, the constituent objects are read to re-create the whole object structure. In order to deserialize objects, the appropriate classes must be available at runtime. Note that new objects are created during deserialization, so that no existing objects are overwritten.

The class `ObjectSerializationDemo` in Example 20.6 serializes some objects in the `writeData()` method at (1), and then deserializes them in the `readData()` method at (2). The `readData()` method also writes the data to the standard output stream.

The `writeData()` method at (1) writes the following values to the output stream: an array of strings (`strArray`), a long value (`num`), an array of int values (`intArray`), a `String` object (`commonStr`) which is shared with the array `strArray` of strings, and an instance (`oneCD`) of the record class `CD` whose component fields are all serializable.

Duplication is automatically avoided when the same object is serialized several times. The shared `String` object (`commonStr`) is actually only serialized once. Note that the array elements and the characters in a `String` object are not written out explicitly one by one. It is enough to pass the object reference in the `writeObject()` method call. The method also recursively goes through the array of strings, `strArray`, serializing each `String` object in the array. The current state of the `oneCD` instance is also serialized.

The method `readData()` at (2) deserializes the data in the order in which it was written. An explicit cast is needed to convert the reference of a deserialized object to a subtype. Applying the right cast is of course the responsibility of the application. Note that new objects are created by the `readObject()` method, and that an object created during the deserialization process has the same state as the object that was serialized.

Efficient Record Serialization

Example 20.6 shows an example of serializing and deserializing an instance of a record class (§5.14, p. 299). It is worth noting that both processes on records are very efficient as the state components of a record entirely describe the state values to serialize, and as the canonical constructor of a record class is always used to create the complete state of a record, the canonical constructor is also always used during deserialization. By design, selective and customized serialization, discussed later in this section, are not allowed for records.

Example 20.6   *Object Serialization*

```
import java.io.Serializable;
import java.time.Year;
/** A record class that represents a CD. */
public record CD(String artist, String title, int noOfTracks,
                 Year year, Genre genre) implements Serializable {
```

```java
        public enum Genre implements Serializable {POP, JAZZ, OTHER}
    }
```

```java
//Reading and Writing Objects
import java.io.*;
import java.time.Year;
import java.util.Arrays;

public class ObjectSerializationDemo {
    void writeData() {                                          // (1)
        try (// Set up the output stream:
            FileOutputStream outputFile = new FileOutputStream("obj-storage.dat");
            ObjectOutputStream outputStream = new ObjectOutputStream(outputFile)) {

            // Write data:
            String[] strArray = {"Seven", "Eight", "Six"};
            long num = 2014;
            int[] intArray = {1, 3, 1949};
            String commonStr = strArray[2];                    // "Six"
            CD oneCD = new CD("Jaav", "Java Jive", 8, Year.of(2017), CD.Genre.POP);
            outputStream.writeObject(strArray);
            outputStream.writeLong(num);
            outputStream.writeObject(intArray);
            outputStream.writeObject(commonStr);
            outputStream.writeObject(oneCD);

        } catch (FileNotFoundException e) {
            System.err.println("File not found: " + e);
        } catch (IOException e) {
            System.err.println("Write error: " + e);
        }
    }

    void readData() {                                           // (2)
        try (// Set up the input stream:
            FileInputStream inputFile = new FileInputStream("obj-storage.dat");
            ObjectInputStream inputStream = new ObjectInputStream(inputFile)) {

            // Read the data:
            String[] strArray = (String[]) inputStream.readObject();
            long num = inputStream.readLong();
            int[] intArray = (int[]) inputStream.readObject();
            String commonStr = (String) inputStream.readObject();
            CD oneCD = (CD) inputStream.readObject();

            // Write data to the standard output stream:
            System.out.println(Arrays.toString(strArray));
            System.out.println(num);
            System.out.println(Arrays.toString(intArray));
            System.out.println(commonStr);
            System.out.println(oneCD);

        } catch (FileNotFoundException e) {
            System.err.println("File not found: " + e);
```

```
        } catch (EOFException e) {
          System.err.println("End of stream: " + e);
        } catch (IOException e) {
          System.err.println("Read error: " + e);
        } catch (ClassNotFoundException e) {
          System.err.println("Class not found: " + e);
        }
    }

    public static void main(String[] args) {
      ObjectSerializationDemo demo = new ObjectSerializationDemo();
      demo.writeData();
      demo.readData();
    }
}
```

Output from the program:

```
[Seven, Eight, Six]
2014
[1, 3, 1949]
Six
CD[artist=Jaav, title=Java Jive, noOfTracks=8, year=2017, genre=POP]
```

Selective Serialization

As noted earlier, static fields are not serialized, as these are not part of the state of an object. An instance field of an object can be omitted from being serialized by specifying the transient modifier in the declaration of the field—typically used for sensitive data in a field. Selective serialization discussed here is *not* applicable to record classes.

Example 20.7 illustrates some salient aspects of serialization. The setup comprises the classes Wheel and Unicycle, and their client class SerialClient. The class Unicycle has a field of type Wheel, and the class Wheel has a field of type int. The class Unicycle is a compound object with a Wheel object as a constituent object. The class Serial-Client serializes and deserializes a unicycle in the try-with-resources statements at (4) and (5), respectively. The state of the objects is printed to the standard output stream before serialization, and so is the state of the object created by deserialization.

Both the Compound Object and Its Constituents Are Serializable

If we run the program with the following declarations for the Wheel and the Unicycle classes, where a compound object of the serializable class Unicycle uses an object of the serializable class Wheel as a constituent object:

```
class Wheel implements Serializable {                          // (1a)
  private int wheelSize;
    ...
}
```

```
class Unicycle implements Serializable {                            // (2)
  private Wheel wheel;                                              // (3a)
  ...
}
```

we get the following output, showing that both serialization and deserialization
were successful:

```
Before writing: Unicycle with wheel size: 65
After reading: Unicycle with wheel size: 65
```

A compound object with its constituent objects is often referred to as an *object
graph*. Serializing a compound object serializes its complete object graph—that is,
the compound object and its constituent objects are recursively serialized.

Example 20.7 *Non-Serializable Objects*

```
import java.io.Serializable;

// public class Wheel implements Serializable {                    // (1a)
public class Wheel {                                                // (1b)
  private int wheelSize;

  public Wheel(int ws) { wheelSize = ws; }

  @Override
  public String toString() { return "wheel size: " + wheelSize; }
}
```

```
import java.io.Serializable;

public class Unicycle implements Serializable {                    // (2)
  private Wheel wheel;                                             // (3a)
//transient private Wheel wheel;                                   // (3b)

  public Unicycle (Wheel wheel) { this.wheel = wheel; }

  @Override
  public String toString() { return "Unicycle with " + wheel; }
}
```

```
import java.io.*;

public class SerialClient {

  public static void main(String args[])
      throws IOException, ClassNotFoundException {

    try (// Set up the output stream:                              // (4)
        FileOutputStream outputFile = new FileOutputStream("storage.dat");
        ObjectOutputStream outputStream = new ObjectOutputStream(outputFile)) {
```

```
                // Write the data:
                Wheel wheel = new Wheel(65);
                Unicycle uc = new Unicycle(wheel);
                System.out.println("Before writing: " + uc);
                outputStream.writeObject(uc);
            }

        try (// Set up the input streams:                                    // (5)
            FileInputStream inputFile = new FileInputStream("storage.dat");
            ObjectInputStream inputStream = new ObjectInputStream(inputFile)) {

            // Read data.
            Unicycle uc = (Unicycle) inputStream.readObject();

            // Write data on standard output stream.
            System.out.println("After reading: " + uc);
        }
    }
}
```

Transient Fields Are Not Serializable

If we declare the wheel field of the Unicycle class in Example 20.7 to be transient for the sake of demonstrating how such fields are handled at serialization, (3b):

```
class Wheel implements Serializable {                                        // (1a)
    private int wheelSize;
    ...
}

class Unicycle implements Serializable {                                     // (2)
    transient private Wheel wheel;                                          // (3b)
    ...
}
```

we get the following output, showing that the wheel field of the Unicycle object was not serialized:

```
Before writing: Unicycle with wheel size: 65
After reading: Unicycle with null
```

Serializable Compound Object with Non-Serializable Constituents

In order for a compound object to be serialized, its constituent objects must be serializable; otherwise, serialization will not succeed. If the class Wheel in Example 20.7 is *not* serializable, (1b):

```
class Wheel {                                                                // (1b)
    private int wheelSize;
    ...
}
```

```
class Unicycle implements Serializable {                      // (2)
  private Wheel wheel;                                        // (3a)
  ...
}
```

we get the following output when we run the program—that is, a Unicycle object *cannot* be serialized because its constituent Wheel object is not serializable:

```
>java SerialClient
Before writing: Unicycle with wheel size: 65
Exception in thread "main" java.io.NotSerializableException: Wheel
  ...
  at SerialClient.main(SerialClient.java:20)
```

Customizing Object Serialization

As we have seen, the class of the object must implement the Serializable interface if we want the object to be serialized. If this object is a compound object, then all its constituent objects must also be serializable, and so on.

It is not always possible for a client to declare that a class is Serializable. It might be declared final, and therefore not extendable. The client might not have access to the code, or extending this class with a serializable subclass might not be an option. Java provides a customizable solution for serializing objects in such cases.

Customized serialization discussed here is *not* applicable to record classes.

The basic idea behind the scheme is to use default serialization as much as possible, and to provide *hooks* in the code for the serialization mechanism to call specific methods to deal with objects or values that should not or cannot be serialized by the default methods of the object streams.

Customizing serialization is illustrated in Example 20.8, using the Wheel and Unicycle classes from Example 20.7. The serializable class Unicycle would like to use the Wheel class, but this class is not serializable. If the wheel field in the Unicycle class is declared to be transient, it will be ignored by the default serialization procedure. This is not a viable option, as the unicycle will be missing the wheel size when a serialized unicycle is deserialized, as was illustrated in Example 20.7.

Any serializable object has the option of customizing its own serialization if it implements the following pair of methods:

```
private void writeObject(ObjectOutputStream) throws IOException;
private void readObject(ObjectInputStream)
                    throws IOException, ClassNotFoundException;
```

These methods are *not* part of any interface. Although private, these methods can be called by the JVM. The first method above is called on the object when its serialization starts. The serialization procedure uses the reference value of the object to be serialized that is passed in the call to the ObjectOutputStream.writeObject() method, which in turn calls the first method above on this object. The second method above is called on the object created when the deserialization procedure is initiated by the call to the ObjectInputStream.readObject() method.

Customizing serialization for objects of the class `Unicycle` in Example 20.8 is achieved by the private methods at (3c) and (3d). Note that the field `wheel` is declared `transient` at (3b) and excluded by the normal serialization process.

In the private method `writeObject()` at (3c) in Example 20.8, the pertinent lines of code are the following:

```
oos.defaultWriteObject();              // Method in the ObjectOutputStream class
oos.writeInt(wheel.getWheelSize());    // Method in the ObjectOutputStream class
```

The call to the `defaultWriteObject()` method of the `ObjectOutputStream` does what its name implies: normal serialization of the current object. The second line of code does the customization: It writes the binary `int` value of the wheel size to the `ObjectOutputStream`. The code for customization can be called both before and after the call to the `defaultWriteObject()` method, as long as the same order is used during deserialization.

In the private method `readObject()` at (3d), the pertinent lines of code are the following:

```
ois.defaultReadObject();               // Method in the ObjectInputStream class
int wheelSize = ois.readInt();         // Method in the ObjectInputStream class
this.wheel = new Wheel(wheelSize);
```

The call to the `defaultReadObject()` method of the `ObjectInputStream` does what its name implies: normal deserialization of the current object. The second line of code reads the binary `int` value of the wheel size from the `ObjectInputStream`. The third line of code creates a `Wheel` object, passes this value in the constructor call, and assigns its reference value to the `wheel` field of the current object. Again, code for customization can be called both before and after the call to the `defaultReadObject()` method, as long as it is in correspondence with the customization code in the `writeObject()` method.

The client class `SerialClient` in Example 20.8 is the same as the one in Example 20.7. The output from the program confirms that the object state prior to serialization is identical to the object state after deserialization.

Example 20.8 *Customized Serialization*

```
public class Wheel {                                                // (1b)
    private int wheelSize;

    public Wheel(int ws) { wheelSize = ws; }

    public int getWheelSize() { return wheelSize; }

    @Override
    public String toString() { return "wheel size: " + wheelSize; }
}
```

```java
import java.io.*;

public class Unicycle implements Serializable {           // (2)
  transient private Wheel wheel;                          // (3b)

  public Unicycle(Wheel wheel) { this.wheel = wheel; }

  @Override
  public String toString() { return "Unicycle with " + wheel; }

  private void writeObject(ObjectOutputStream oos) {      // (3c)
    try {
      oos.defaultWriteObject();
      oos.writeInt(wheel.getWheelSize());
    } catch (IOException e) {
      e.printStackTrace();
    }
  }

  private void readObject(ObjectInputStream ois) {        // (3d)
    try {
      ois.defaultReadObject();
      int wheelSize = ois.readInt();
      this.wheel = new Wheel(wheelSize);
    } catch (IOException e) {
      e.printStackTrace();
    } catch (ClassNotFoundException e) {
      e.printStackTrace();
    }
  }
}
```

```java
public class SerialClient { // Same as in Example 20.7 }
```

Output from the program:

```
Before writing: Unicycle with wheel size: 65
After reading: Unicycle with wheel size: 65
```

Serialization and Inheritance

The inheritance hierarchy of an object also determines what its state will be after it is deserialized. An object will have the same state at deserialization as it had at the time it was serialized if *all* its superclasses are also serializable. This is because the normal object creation and initialization procedure using constructors is *not* run during deserialization.

However, if any superclass of an object is *not* serializable, then the normal creation procedure using *no-argument* or *default* constructors *is* run, starting at the first non-serializable superclass, all the way up to the Object class. This means that the state at deserialization might not be the same as at the time the object was serialized because superconstructors run during deserialization may have initialized the state of the object. If the non-serializable superclass does not provide a non-argument constructor or the default constructor, a `java.io.InvalidClassException` is thrown during deserialization.

Example 20.9 illustrates how inheritance affects serialization. The Student class is a subclass of the Person class. Whether the superclass Person is serializable or not has implications for serializing objects of the Student subclass, in particular, when their byte representation is deserialized.

Superclass Is Serializable

If the superclass is serializable, then any object of a subclass is also serializable. In Example 20.9, the code at (4) in the class SerialInheritance serializes a Student object:

```
Student student = new Student("Pendu", 1007);
System.out.println("Before writing: " + student);
outputStream.writeObject(student);
```

The corresponding code for deserialization of the streamed object is at (5) in the class SerialInheritance:

```
Student student = (Student) inputStream.readObject();
System.out.println("After reading: " + student);
```

We get the following output from the program in Example 20.9 when it is run with (1a) and (3a) in the Person class and the Student class, respectively—that is, when the superclass is serializable and so is the subclass, by virtue of inheritance.

The results show that the object state prior to serialization is identical to the object state after deserialization. In this case, no superclass constructors were run during deserialization.

```
Before writing: Student state(Pendu, 1007)
After reading: Student state(Pendu, 1007)
```

Superclass Is Not Serializable

However, the result of deserialization is not the same when the superclass Person is not serializable, but the subclass Student is. We get the following output from the program in Example 20.9 when it is run with (1b) and (3b) in the Person class and the Student class, respectively—that is, when only the subclass is serializable, but not the superclass. The output shows that the object state prior to serialization is not identical to the object state after deserialization.

```
Before writing: Student state(Pendu, 1007)
No-argument constructor executed.
After reading: Student state(null, 1007)
```

During deserialization, the *zero-argument* constructor of the Person superclass at (2) is run. As we can see from the declaration of the Person class in Example 20.9, this zero-argument constructor does not initialize the name field, which remains initialized with the default value for reference types (null).

If the superclass Person does not provide the no-argument constructor or the default constructor, as in the declaration below, the call to the readObject() method to perform deserialization throws an InvalidClassException.

```java
public class Person {                                    // (1b)
  private String name;

  public Person(String name) { this.name = name; }

  public String getName() { return name; }
}
```

Output from the program (*edited to fit on the page*):
```
Before writing: Student state(Pendu, 1007)
Exception in thread "main" java.io.InvalidClassException:
        Student; no valid constructor
        ...
        at SerialInheritance.main(SerialInheritance.java:28)
```

The upshot of serializing objects of subclasses is that the superclass should be serializable, unless there are compelling reasons for why it is not. And if the superclass is not serializable, it should at least provide either the default constructor or the no-argument constructor to avoid an exception during deserialization.

Although a superclass might be serializable, its subclasses can prevent their objects from being serialized by implementing the private method writeObject (ObjectOutputStream) that throws a java.io.NotSerializableException.

Example 20.9 *Serialization and Inheritance*

```java
import java.io.Serializable;

// A superclass
public class Person implements Serializable {            // (1a)
//public class Person {                                  // (1b)
  private String name;

  public Person() {                                      // (2)
    System.out.println("No-argument constructor executed.");
  }
  public Person(String name) { this.name = name; }

  public String getName() { return name; }
}
```

```java
import java.io.Serializable;

public class Student extends Person {                             // (3a)
//public class Student extends Person implements Serializable {   // (3b)

  private long studNum;

  public Student(String name, long studNum) {
    super(name);
```

```
        this.studNum = studNum;
    }

    @Override
    public String toString() {
        return "Student state(" + getName() + ", " + studNum + ")";
    }
}
```

```
import java.io.*;

public class SerialInheritance {
    public static void main(String[] args)
            throws IOException, ClassNotFoundException {

        // Serialization:
        try (// Set up the output stream:                                    (4)
            FileOutputStream outputFile = new FileOutputStream("storage.dat");
            ObjectOutputStream outputStream = new ObjectOutputStream(outputFile)) {

            // Write data:
            Student student = new Student("Pendu", 1007);
            System.out.println("Before writing: " + student);
            outputStream.writeObject(student);
        }

        // Deserialization:
        try (// Set up the input stream:                                     (5)
            FileInputStream inputFile = new FileInputStream("storage.dat");
            ObjectInputStream inputStream = new ObjectInputStream(inputFile)) {

            // Read data.
            Student student = (Student) inputStream.readObject();

            // Write data on standard output stream.
            System.out.println("After reading: " + student);
        }
    }
}
```

Serialization and Versioning

Class versioning comes into play when we serialize an object with one definition of a class, but deserialize the streamed object with a different class definition. By streamed object, we mean the serialized representation of an object. Between serialization and deserialization of an object, the class definition can change.

Note that at serialization and at deserialization, the definition of the class (i.e., its bytecode file) should be accessible. In the examples so far, the class definition has been the same at both serialization and deserialization. Example 20.10 illustrates the problem of class definition mismatch at deserialization and the solution provided by Java.

Example 20.10 makes use of the following classes (numbering refers to code lines in the example):

(1) The original version of the serializable class Item. It has one field named price. An object of this class will be serialized and read using different versions of this class.

(2) A newer version of the class Item that has been augmented with a field for the weight of an item. This class will only be used for deserialization of objects that have been serialized with the original version of the class.

(3) The class Serializer serializes an object of the original version of the class Item.

(4) The class DeSerializer deserializes a streamed object of the class Item. In the example, deserialization is based on a different version of the Item class than the one used at serialization.

There are no surprises if we use the original class Item to serialize and deserialize an object of the Item class.

```
// Original version of the Item class.
public class Item implements Serializable {                           // (1)
  private double price;
  //...
}
```

Result:

```
Before writing: Price: 100.00
After reading: Price: 100.00
```

If we deserialize a streamed object of the original class Item at (1) based on the byte-code file of the augmented version of the Item class at (2), an InvalidClassException is thrown at runtime.

```
// New version of the Item class.
public class Item implements Serializable {                           // (2)
  private double price;
  private double weight;                                    // Additional field
  //...
}
```

Result (*edited to fit on the page*):

```
Exception in thread "main" java.io.InvalidClassException: Item;
local class incompatible:
  stream classdesc serialVersionUID = -4194294879924868414,
  local class serialVersionUID = -1186964199368835959
    ...
      at DeSerializer.main(DeSerializer.java:14)
```

The question is, how was the class definition mismatch discovered at runtime? The answer lies in the stack trace of the exception thrown. The local class was incompatible, meaning the class we are using to deserialize is not compatible with the class that was used when the object was serialized. In addition, two long numbers are printed, representing the serialVersionUID of the respective class definitions. The first serialVersionUID is generated by the serialization process based on the class definition and becomes part of the streamed object. The second serialVersionUID is generated based on the local class definition that is accessible at deserialization. The two are not equal, and deserialization fails.

A serializable class can provide its serialVersionUID by declaring it in its class declaration, exactly as shown below, except for the initial value which of course can be different:

```
static final long serialVersionUID = 100l ;                // Appropriate value.
```

As we saw in the example above, if a serializable class does not provide a serialVersionUID, one is implicitly generated. By providing an explicit serialVersionUID, it is possible to control what happens at deserialization. As newer versions of the class are created, the serialVersionUID can be kept the same until it is deemed that older streamed objects are no longer compatible for deserialization. After the change to the serialVersionUID, it will not be possible to deserialize older streamed objects of the class based on newer versions of the class. Although static members of a class are not serialized, the only exception is the value of the static final long serialVersionUID field.

In the scenario below, the original version and the newer version of the class Item both declare a serialVersionUID at (1a) and at (2a), respectively, that has the same value. An Item object is serialized using the original version, but deserialized based on the newer version. We see that serialization succeeds, and the weight field is initialized to the default value 0.0. In other words, the object created is of the newer version of the class.

```
// Original version of the Item class.
public class Item implements Serializable {     // (1)
  static final long serialVersionUID = 1000L;   // (1a)
  private double price;
//...
}

// New version of the Item class.
public class Item implements Serializable {     // (2)
  static final long serialVersionUID = 1000L;   // (2a) Same serialVersionUID
  private double price;
  private double weight;                        // Additional field
//...
}
```

Result:

```
Before writing: Price: 100.00
After reading: Price: 100.00, Weight: 0.00
```

However, if we now deserialize the streamed object of the original class having 1000L as the serialVersionUID, based on the newer version of the class having the serialVersionUID equal to 1001L, deserialization fails as we would expect because the serialVersionUIDs are different.

```
// New version of the Item class.
public class Item implements Serializable {      // (2)
  static final long serialVersionUID = 1001L;   // (2b) Different serialVersionUID
  private double price;
  private double weight;
//...
}
```

Result (*edited to fit on the page*):

```
Exception in thread "main" java.io.InvalidClassException: Item;
local class incompatible:
  stream classdesc serialVersionUID = 1000,
  local class serialVersionUID = 1001
    ...
      at DeSerializer.main(DeSerializer.java:14)
```

Best practices advocate that serializable classes should use the serialVersionUID
solution for better control of what happens at deserialization as classes evolve.

Example 20.10 *Class Versioning*

```
import java.io.Serializable;

// Original version of the Item class.
public class Item implements Serializable {                    // (1)
//static final long serialVersionUID = 1000L;                  // (1a)

  private double price;

  public Item(double price) {
    this.price = price;
  }

  @Override
  public String toString() {
    return String.format("Price: %.2f%n", this.price);
  }
}
```

```
import java.io.Serializable;

// New version of the Item class.
public class Item implements Serializable {                    // (2)
//static final long serialVersionUID = 1000L;                  // (2a)
//static final long serialVersionUID = 1001L;                  // (2b)

  private double price;
  private double weight;
  public Item(double price, double weight) {
    this.price = price;
    this.weight = weight;
  }
```

```
        @Override
        public String toString() {
          return String.format("Price: %.2f, Weight: %.2f", this.price, this.weight);
        }
      }
```

```
// Serializer for objects of class Item.
import java.io.*;

public class Serializer {                                              // (3)
  public static void main(String args[])
      throws IOException, ClassNotFoundException {
    try (// Set up the output stream:
        FileOutputStream outputFile = new FileOutputStream("item_storage.dat");
        ObjectOutputStream outputStream = new ObjectOutputStream(outputFile)) {

      // Serialize an object of the original class:
      Item item = new Item(100.00);
      System.out.println("Before writing: " + item);
      outputStream.writeObject(item);
    }
  }
}
```

```
// Deserializer for objects of class Item.
import java.io.*;

public class DeSerializer{                                             // (4)
  public static void main(String args[])
      throws IOException, ClassNotFoundException {
    try (// Set up the input streams:
        FileInputStream inputFile = new FileInputStream("item_storage.dat");
        ObjectInputStream inputStream = new ObjectInputStream(inputFile)) {

      // Read a serialized object of the Item class.
      Item item = (Item) inputStream.readObject();

      // Write data on standard output stream.
      System.out.println("After reading: " + item);
    }
  }
}
```

 Review Questions

20.5　Which of the following best describes the data written by an ObjectOutputStream? Select the one correct answer.

(a) Bytes and other Java primitive types

(b) Object graphs

(c) Object graphs and Java primitive types

(d) Single objects

(e) Single objects and Java primitive types

20.6   Which of the following statements are true about serialization?
Select the four correct answers.

(a) All static fields of a class are treated the same way as `transient` instance fields
of the class when it comes to serialization.

(b) All instance fields of a serializable class must also be serializable or be specified with the `transient` modifier.

(c) Any `private` instance field of a class is not serialized.

(d) A serializable class must implement the `Serializable` interface.

(e) A serializable class must extend the `Serializable` class.

(f) Subclasses of a serializable class must explicitly extend the `Serializable` class
in order to serialize subclass objects.

(g) Subclasses of a serializable class must explicitly implement the `Serializable`
interface in order to serialize subclass objects.

(h) A serializable class must be specified with the `final` modifier.

(i) A `serialVersionUID` is always stored in the streamed object of a serializable
class.

20.7   Which of the following statements is true?
Select the one correct answer.

(a) All versions of a serializable class must provide a declaration of a `serialVer-
sionUID`.

(b) Even if two versions of a serializable class have the same `serialVersionUID`,
there is no guarantee that an object serialized based on one version can be
deserialized to an object of the other.

(c) The `serialVersionUID` of any two unrelated serializable classes must be
unique.

(d) The `serialVersionUID` of a serializable class must be incremented every time a
new version of the class is created.

(e) Only a serializable class can declare a `static final` field of type `long` having
the name `serialVersionUID`.

20.8   Given the following code:

```
public class Person  {
  protected String name;
  public Person() {this.name = "NoName"; }
  public Person(String name) { this.name = name; }
}
```

```
import java.io.Serializable;
public class Student extends Person implements Serializable {
  private long studNum;
  public Student(String name, long studNum) {
    super(name);
```

```
      this.studNum = studNum;
    }
    public String toString() { return "(" + name + ", " + studNum + ")"; }
}
```

```
import java.io.*;
public class RQ800_10 {

    public static void main(String args[])
        throws IOException, ClassNotFoundException {
      try (FileOutputStream outputFile = new FileOutputStream("storage.dat");
          ObjectOutputStream outputStream = new ObjectOutputStream(outputFile)) {
        Student stud1 = new Student("Aesop", 100);
        System.out.print(stud1);
        outputStream.writeObject(stud1);
      }

      try (FileInputStream inputFile = new FileInputStream("storage.dat");
          ObjectInputStream inputStream = new ObjectInputStream(inputFile)) {
        Student stud2 = (Student) inputStream.readObject();
        System.out.println(stud2);
      }
    }
}
```

Which statement about the program is true?
Select the one correct answer.

(a) It will fail to compile.
(b) It will compile, but it will throw an exception at runtime.
(c) It will print (Aesop, 100)(Aesop, 100).
(d) It will print (Aesop, 100)(null, 100).
(e) It will print (Aesop, 100)(NoName, 100).

20.9   Given the following code:

```
import java.io.Serializable;
public class Person implements Serializable {
  protected String name;
  public Person() { this.name = "NoName"; }
  public Person(String name) { this.name = name; }
}
```

```
public class Student extends Person {
  private long studNum;
  public Student(String name, long studNum) {
    super(name);
    this.studNum = studNum;
  }
  public String toString() { return "(" + name + ", " + studNum + ")"; }
}
```

```
import java.io.*;
public class RQ800_30 {
```

```
        public static void main(String args[])
            throws IOException, ClassNotFoundException {
          try (FileOutputStream outputFile = new FileOutputStream("storage.dat");
              ObjectOutputStream outputStream = new ObjectOutputStream(outputFile)) {
            Student stud1 = new Student("Aesop", 100);
            System.out.print(stud1);
            outputStream.writeObject(stud1);
          }

          try (FileInputStream inputFile = new FileInputStream("storage.dat");
              ObjectInputStream inputStream = new ObjectInputStream(inputFile)) {
            Student stud2 = (Student) inputStream.readObject();
            System.out.println(stud2);
          }
        }
      }
```

Which statement about the program is true?
Select the one correct answer.

(a) It will fail to compile.
(b) It will compile, but it will throw an exception at runtime.
(c) It will print (Aesop, 100)(Aesop, 100).
(d) It will print (Aesop, 100)(null, 100).
(e) It will print (Aesop, 100)(NoName, 100).

20.10   Given the following code:

```
      public class Person {
        protected transient String name;
        public Person() { this.name = "NoName"; }
        public Person(String name) { this.name = name; }
      }
```

```
      public class Student extends Person {
        protected long studNum;
        public Student() { }
        public Student(String name, long studNum) {
          super(name);
          this.studNum = studNum;
        }
      }
```

```
      import java.io.IOException;
      import java.io.ObjectInputStream;
      import java.io.Serializable;

      public class GraduateStudent extends Student implements Serializable {
        private int year;
        public GraduateStudent(String name, long studNum, int year) {
          super(name, studNum);
          this.year = year;
        }
```

```
        public String toString() {
          return "(" + name + ", " + studNum + ", " + year + ")";
        }

        private void readObject(ObjectInputStream ois)
            throws IOException, ClassNotFoundException {
          ois.defaultReadObject();
          this.name = "NewName";
          this.studNum = 200;
          this.year = 2;
        }
      }
```

```
import java.io.*;
public class RQ800_70 {

  public static void main(String args[])
      throws IOException, ClassNotFoundException {
    try (FileOutputStream outputFile = new FileOutputStream("storage.dat");
        ObjectOutputStream outputStream = new ObjectOutputStream(outputFile)) {
      GraduateStudent stud1 = new GraduateStudent("Aesop", 100, 1);
      System.out.print(stud1);
      outputStream.writeObject(stud1);
    }

    try (FileInputStream inputFile = new FileInputStream("storage.dat");
        ObjectInputStream inputStream = new ObjectInputStream(inputFile)) {
      GraduateStudent stud2 = (GraduateStudent) inputStream.readObject();
      System.out.println(stud2);
    }
  }
}
```

Which statement about the program is true?
Select the one correct answer.

(a) It will fail to compile.
(b) It will compile, but it will throw an exception at runtime.
(c) It will print (Aesop, 100, 1)(Aesop, 100, 1).
(d) It will print (Aesop, 100, 1)(NoName, 0, 1).
(e) It will print (Aesop, 100, 1)(NewName, 200, 2).

20.11 Given the following code:

```
import java.io.Serializable;
public class Product implements Serializable {
  private String name;

  public Product(String name) {
    this.name = name;
    System.out.print("product ");
  }

  @Override
  public String toString() {
```

```
      return name;
  }
}
```

```
public class Food extends Product {
  private int calories;

  public Food(String name, int calories) {
    super(name);
    this.calories = calories;
    System.out.print("food ");
  }

  @Override
  public String toString() {
    return super.toString()+" "+calories;
  }
}
```

```
import java.io.*;
public class RQ20 {
  public static void main(String[] args) {
    Product p = new Food("cookie", 300);
    try(ObjectOutputStream out =
            new ObjectOutputStream(new FileOutputStream("prod.dat"))) {
      out.writeObject(p);
    } catch (Exception ex) {
      System.out.println("error serializing product");
    }
    try(ObjectInputStream in =
            new ObjectInputStream(new FileInputStream("prod.dat"))) {
      p = (Food)in.readObject();
    } catch (Exception ex) {
      System.out.println("error deserializing product");
    }
    System.out.println(p);
  }
}
```

What is the result?

Select the one correct answer.

(a) product food cookie 300
(b) product food product food cookie 300
(c) product food cookie 0
(d) product food product food cookie 0
(e) product food error serializing product
(f) product food error deserializing product

20.12   Given the following code:

```
import java.io.*;
public class RQ21 {
  public static void main(String[] args) {
    char[] buffer = new char[4];
```

```
      int count = 0;
      try(FileReader in = new FileReader("test1.txt");
          FileWriter out = new FileWriter("test2.txt")) {
        while((count = in.read(buffer)) != -1) {
          out.write(buffer);
        }
      } catch (Exception ex) {
        System.out.println("error");
      }
    }
  }
```

Assume that the text1.txt file only contains the line "abcdefg".
What is the content of the text2.txt file after the program is run?
Select the one correct answer.

(a) abcdefg
(b) abcd
(c) abcdefgd
(d) abcdef

20.13 Given the following code:

```
import java.io.*;
public class Album implements Serializable {
  private static int numberOfTracks = 5;
  private String title;
  private transient int currentTrack;

  public Album(String title, int currentTrack) {
    this.title = title;
    this.currentTrack = currentTrack;
  }

  public void readObject(ObjectInputStream in)
                    throws IOException, ClassNotFoundException {
    in.defaultReadObject();
    currentTrack = 3;
  }

  @Override
  public String toString() {
    return title+" "+numberOfTracks +" "+currentTrack;
  }
}
```

```
import java.io.*;
public class RQ22 {
  public static void main(String[] args) {
    Album a = new Album("Songs", 2);
    try (ObjectOutputStream out =
            new ObjectOutputStream(new FileOutputStream("song.dat"))) {
      out.writeObject(a);
    } catch (Exception ex) {
      System.out.println("error serializing product");
    }
```

```
      try (ObjectInputStream in =
              new ObjectInputStream(new FileInputStream("song.dat"))) {
        a = (Album)in.readObject();
      } catch (Exception ex) {
        ex.printStackTrace();
      }
      System.out.println(a);
    }
  }
```

What is the result?

Select the one correct answer.

(a) Songs 5 3

(b) Songs 5 2

(c) Songs 5 0

(d) Songs 0 3

(e) Songs 0 2

(f) Songs 0 0

Java I/O: Part II

21

 Chapter Topics

- Understanding the characteristics of a hierarchical file system
- Creating Path objects with the of() method of the Path interface, the getPath() method of the default file system, and the get() method of the Paths class
- Interoperability of Path objects with the java.io.File legacy class and the java.net.URI class
- Querying Path objects: converting, normalizing, resolving, relativizing, and comparing
- Using methods of the Path interface to perform operations on directory entries: Existence, uniqueness, copying, moving, and renaming directory entries
- Reading and writing byte and character data to files using Path objects and buffered I/O streams
- Understanding the purpose of specifying a variable arity parameter to customize the behavior of file operations with constants defined by the LinkOption, StandardCopyOption, OpenOption, and FileVisitOption enum types in the java.nio.file package
- Using methods of the Files class for accessing specific file attributes: size, kind of entry, file accessibility, last modified timestamp, owner, file permissions, and access by attribute name
- Retrieving read-only file attributes in a bulk operation provided by the Files.readAttributes() method, and accessing them using the interfaces BasicFileAttributes, PosixFileAttributes, and DosFileAttributes
- Retrieving readable and updatable file attributes in a bulk operation provided by the Files.getFileAttributeView() method that creates *views* represented by the interfaces BasicFileAttributeView, PosixFileAttributeView, and DosFileAttributeView

- Creating directory entries with methods provided by the Files class: regular and temporary files, regular and temporary directories, and symbolic links
- Using a stream to read text files (Files.lines())
- Using streams for listing entries in a directory (Files.list()), for walking the directory hierarchy (Files.walk()), and for finding directory entries (Files.find())

Java SE 17 Developer Exam Objectives	
[9.3] Create, traverse, read, and write Path objects and their properties using java.nio.file API	*§21.1, p. 1287* *to* *§21.8, p. 1345*
Java SE 11 Developer Exam Objectives	
[9.3] Handle file system objects using java.nio.file API	*§21.1, p. 1287* *to* *§21.8, p. 1345*

The standard I/O API in the java.io package provides the capabilities for reading and writing various kinds of data using the concept of I/O streams (Chapter 20, p. 1231). However, its support for *managing* files and directories in a file system has been superceded by the newer and enhanced I/O API called *NIO.2* (*Non-blocking I/O*, version 2) in the java.nio package.

The primary focus in this chapter is on the support provided by the NIO.2 API for programmatically interacting with a file system for accessing files, managing file attributes, and traversing the file system. Primary support for file I/O and accessing files and directories in a file system is provided by the java.nio.file package.

The java.nio.file.Path interface allows paths in the file system to be represented programmatically. It provides extensive support for constructing and querying paths, and for how paths can be used to manipulate files and directories in the file system.

The java.nio.file.Files utility class provides comprehensive support for file operations, such as querying, creating, deleting, copying, and moving files. In addition, it provides methods for creating streams on files and directories, making it possible to write powerful file operations.

Support for interoperability between the two I/O APIs is also covered, and other auxiliary classes are introduced where they are needed in the chapter.

21.1 Characteristics of a Hierarchical File System

We first look at some characteristics of a hierarchical file system, and introduce the terminology used in this chapter.

Hierarchical File Systems

A *file system* allows persistent storage and organization of data as a *hierarchical* (or *tree*) structure on some external media. A tree structure has a *root component* (also called *root node*) at the top, under which other tree nodes represent files and directories. Each directory can have files and nested directories (often called *subdirectories*). An operative system can have multiple file systems, each of which is identifiable by its root component.

Below is an example of a file system, where the root component is platform dependent. On Unix-based platforms, the root component of the file system is denoted by the slash character (/). The root component for Windows-based platforms is a combination of a *volume* name (i.e., file system name), a colon (:), and a backslash character (\). For example, C:\ designates the root component of the ubiquitous volume named C on a Windows-based platform.

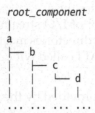

When it is not necessary to distinguish between a file and a directory in the file system, we will use the term *directory entry* to mean both. Each directory entry in a hierarchical file system is uniquely identifiable by a *path* from the root component to the node representing the directory entry. The path of a directory entry in a file system is specified using the naming conventions of the host system, where *name elements* that comprise the path are separated by a platform-specific *name separator character* or *delimiter*. The name separator character for name elements on Unix-based platforms is the slash character (/), whereas on Windows-based platforms, it is the backslash character (\). For the most part, we will use conventions for Unix-based platforms.

Two examples of paths are given below, where each path has three name elements.

```
/a/b/c          on Unix-based platforms
C:\a\b\c        on Windows-based platforms
```

Absolute and Relative Paths

Directory entries can be referenced using both *absolute* and *relative* paths, but the path naming must follow the conventions of the host platform.

An absolute path starts with the platform-dependent root component of the file system, as in the examples above. All information is contained in an absolute path to reference the directory entry—that is, an absolute path uniquely identifies a directory entry in the file system.

A relative path is without designation of the root component and therefore requires additional path information to locate its directory entry in the file system. Typically, a relative path is interpreted in relation to the *current directory* (see the next subsection). Some examples of relative paths are given below, but they alone are not enough to uniquely identify a directory entry.

```
c/d             on Unix-based platforms
c\d             on Windows-based platforms
```

Note that in a path, the name elements are all parent directory names, except for the last name element, which can be either a file name or a directory name. The name of a directory entry does not distinguish whether it is a file or a directory in the file system. Although *file extensions* can be used in a file name for readability, it is immaterial for the file system. Care must also be exercised when choosing name elements, as characters allowed are usually platform dependent.

Java programs should not rely on system-specific path conventions. In the next section we will construct paths in a platform-independent way.

Current and Parent Directory Designators

A file system has a notion of a current directory which changes while traversing in the file system. The *current directory* is designated by the period character (.) and its *parent directory* by two periods (..). These designators can be used in constructing paths. Given that the current directory is /a/b in the directory tree shown earlier, Table 21.1 illustrates relative paths constructed using the current and the parent directory designators, and their corresponding absolute paths.

Table 21.1   *Using Current and Parent Directory Designators*

Relative path (Current directory: /a/b)	Absolute path
./c/d	/a/b/c/d
.	/a/b
./..	/a
./../..	/ (i.e., the root component)

Symbolic Links

Apart from regular files, a file system may allow symbolic links to be created. A *symbolic link* (also called *a hard link*, *a shortcut*, or *an alias*) is a special file that acts as a reference to a directory entry, called the *target* of the symbolic link. Creating an *alias* of a directory entry in the file system is similar to creating a symbolic link. Using symbolic links is transparent to the user, as the file system takes care of using the target when a symbolic link is used in a file operation, with one caveat: Deleting the symbolic link does *not* delete the target. In many file operations, it is possible to indicate whether symbolic links should be followed or not.

21.2 Creating Path Objects

File operations that a Java program invokes are performed on a file system. Unless the program utilizes a specific file system constructed by the factory methods of the java.nio.file.FileSystems utility class, file operations are performed on a file system called the *default file system* that is accessible to the JVM. We can think of the default file system as the *local* file system. The default file system is platform specific and can be obtained as an instance of the java.nio.file.FileSystem abstract class by invoking the getDefault() factory method of the FileSystems utility class.

```
FileSystem dfs = FileSystems.getDefault();     // The default file system
```

File operations can access the default file system directly to perform their operations. The default file system can be queried for various file system properties.

static FileSystem getDefault()   Declared in java.nio.file.FileSystems

Returns the platform-specific default file system. If the method is called several times, it returns the same FileSystem instance for the default file system.

abstract String getSeparator()   Declared in java.nio.file.FileSystem

Returns the platform-specific name separator for name elements in a path, represented as a string.

Paths in the file system are programmatically represented by objects that implement the Path interface. The Path interface and various other classes provide factory methods that create Path objects (see below). A Path object is also platform specific.

A Path object implements the Iterable<Path> interface, meaning it is possible to traverse over its name elements from the first name element to the last. It is also immutable and therefore thread-safe.

In this section, we look at how to create Path objects. A Path object can be queried and manipulated in various ways, and may not represent an existing directory entry in the file system (p. 1294). A Path object can be used in file operations to access and manipulate the directory entry it denotes in the file system (p. 1304).

The methods below can be used to create Path objects. The methods are also shown in Figure 21.1, together with the relationship between the different classes of these methods. Note in particular the interoperability between the java.nio.file.Path interface that represents a path and the two classes java.io.File and java.net.URI. The class java.io.File represents a pathname in the standard I/O API and the class java.net.URI represents a *Uniform Resource Identifier* (*URI*) that identifies a resource (e.g., a file or a website).

static Path of(String first, String... more)
static Path of(URI uri)

These methods are declared in the java.nio.file.Path interface.

abstract Path getPath(String first, String... more)

This method is declared in the java.nio.file.FileSystem class.

static Path get(String first, String... more)
static Path get(URI uri)

These static methods are declared in the java.nio.file.Paths class.

Path toPath()

This method is declared in the java.io.File class.

Figure 21.1 *Creating* Path *Objects*

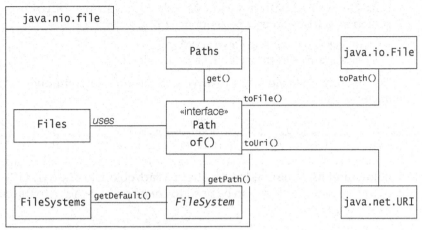

Any parameters for a method are not shown.

Creating Path **Objects with the** Path.of() **Method**

The simplest way to create a Path is to use the static factory method Path.of(String first, String... more). It joins the first string with any strings in the variable arity parameter more to create a path string that is the basis of constructing a Path object. This method creates a Path object in accordance with the default file system.

For instance, the default file system can be queried for the platform-specific name separator for name elements in a path.

The three absolute paths below are equivalent on a Unix platform, as they create a Path object based on the same path string. The nameSeparator string is the platform-specific name separator obtained from the default file system. At (1) and (2) below, only the first string parameter is specified in the Path.of() method, and it is the basis for constructing a Path object. However, specifying the variable arity parameter where possible is recommended when a Path object is constructed as shown at (3), as joining of the name elements is implicitly done using the platform-specific name separator. The equals() methods simply checks for equality on the path string, not on any directory entry denoted by the Path objects.

```
FileSystem dfs = FileSystems.getDefault();      // Obtain the default file system.
String nameSeparator = dfs.getSeparator();      // The name separator for a path.

Path absPath1 = Path.of("/a/b/c");                          // (1) /a/b/c
Path absPath2 = Path.of(nameSeparator + "a" +              // (2) /a/b/c
                        nameSeparator + "b" +
                        nameSeparator + "c");
Path absPath3 = Path.of(nameSeparator, "a", "b", "c");     // (3) /a/b/c
System.out.println(absPath1.equals(absPath2) &&
                   absPath2.equals(absPath3));             // true
```

The two absolute paths below are equivalent on a Windows platform, as they create Path objects based on the same path string. Note that the backslash character must be escaped with a second backslash in a string. Otherwise, it will be interpreted as starting an escape sequence (§2.1, p. 38).

```
Path absPath4 = Path.of("C:\\a\\b\\c");                    // (4) C:\a\b\c
Path absPath5 = Path.of("C:", "a", "b", "c");              // (5) C:\a\b\c
```

The Path created below is a relative path, as no root component is specified in the arguments.

```
Path relPath1 = Path.of("c", "d");                         //   c/d
```

Often we need to create a Path object to denote the current directory. This can be done via a *system property* named "user.dir" that can be looked up, as shown at (1) below, and its value used to construct a Path object, as shown at (2). The path string of the current directory can be used to create paths relative to the current directory, as shown at (3).

```
String pathOfCurrDir = System.getProperty("user.dir");  // (1)
Path currDir = Path.of(pathOfCurrDir);                  // (2)
Path relPath = Path.of(pathOfCurrDir, "d");             // (3) <curr-dir-path>/d
```

Creating Path Objects with the Paths.get() Method

The Paths utility class provides the get(String first, String... more) static factory method to construct Path objects. In fact, this method invokes the Path.of(String first, String... more) convenience method to obtain a Path.

```
Path absPath7 = Paths.get(nameSeparator, "a", "b", "c");
Path relPath3 = Paths.get("c", "d");
```

Creating Path Objects Using the Default File System

We have seen how to obtain the default file system that is accessible to the JVM:

```
FileSystem dfs = FileSystems.getDefault();      // The default file system
```

The default file system provides the getPath(String first, String... more) method to construct Path objects. In fact, the Path.of(String first, String... more) method is a convenience method that invokes the FileSystem.getPath() method to obtain a Path object.

```
Path absPath6 = dfs.getPath(nameSeparator, "a", "b", "c");
Path relPath2 = dfs.getPath("c", "d");
```

Interoperability with the java.io.File Legacy Class

An object of the legacy class java.io.File can be used to query the file system for information about a file or a directory. The class also provides methods to create, rename, and delete directory entries in the file system. Although there is an overlap of functionality between the Path interface and the File class, the Path interface is recommended over the File class for new code. The interoperability between a File object and a Path object allows the limitations of the legacy class java.io.File to be addressed.

```
File(String pathname)
Path toPath()
```

This constructor and this method of the java.io.File class can be used to create a File object from a pathname and to convert a File object to a Path object, respectively.

```
default File toFile()
```

This method of the java.nio.file.Path interface can be used to convert a Path object to a File object.

The code below illustrates the round trip between a File object and a Path object:

```
File file = new File(File.separator + "a" +
                     File.separator + "b" +
                     File.separator + "c");        // /a/b/c

// File --> Path, using the java.io.File.toPath() instance method
Path fileToPath = file.toPath();                   // /a/b/c

// Path --> File, using the java.nio.file.Path.toFile() default method.
File pathToFile = fileToPath.toFile();             // /a/b/c
```

Interoperability with the java.net.URI **Class**

A URI consists of a string that identifies a resource, which can be a local resource or a remote resource. Among other pertinent information, a URI specifies a *scheme* (e.g., file, ftp, http, and https) that indicates what protocol to use to handle the resource. The examples of URIs below show two *schema*: file and http. We will not elaborate on the syntax of URIs, or different schema, as it is beyond the scope of this book.

```
file:///a/b/c/d                 // Scheme: file, to access a local file.
http://www.whatever.com         // Scheme: http, to access a remote website.
```

```
URI(String str) throws URISyntaxException
static URI create(String str)
```

This constructor and this static method in the java.net.URI class create a URL object based on the specified string. The second method is preferred when it is known that the URI string is well formed.

```
// Create a URI object, using the URL.create(String str) static factory method.
URI uri1 = URI.create("file:///a/b/c/d");  // Local file.
```

The following methods can be used to convert a URI object to a Path object. The Paths.get(URI uri) static factory method actually invokes the Path.of(URI uri) static factory method.

```
// URI --> Path, using the Path.of(URI uri) static factory method.
Path uriToPath1 = Path.of(uri1);        // /a/b/c/d

// URI --> Path, using the Paths.get(URI uri) static factory method.
Path uriToPath2 = Paths.get(uri1);      // /a/b/c/d
```

The following method in the Path interface can be used to convert a Path object to a URI object:

```
// Path --> URI, using the Path.toUri() instance method.
URI pathToUri = uriToPath1.toUri();      // file:///a/b/c/d
```

Interoperability between a Path object and a URI object allows an application to leverage both the NIO.2 API and the network API.

21.3 Working with Path Objects

The java.nio.file.Path interface provides a myriad of methods to query and manipulate Path objects. In this section, selected methods from the Path interface are presented for working on Path objects. A majority of these methods perform syntactic operations on the path string contained in a Path object. As Path objects are immutable, the methods return a new Path object, making it possible to use this distinctive style of method chaining. There is also no requirement that the path string in a Path object must refer to an existing resource. Very few methods enforce this requirement, and if they do, they will throw a checked IOException if that it is not the case.

Querying Path Objects

The following methods of the java.nio.file.Path interface can be used for querying a Path object for its various properties. The names of most methods reflect their operation. The description in the API of these methods and Example 21.1 below should aid in understanding their functionality.

String toString()
Returns the text representation of this path.

boolean isAbsolute()
Determines whether this path is an absolute path or not.

FileSystem getFileSystem()
Returns the file system that created this object. Each Path object is created with respect to a file system.

Path getFileName()
Returns the name of the directory entry denoted by this path as a Path object— that is, the *last* name element in this path which denotes either a file or a directory.

Path getParent()

Returns the parent path, or null if this path does not have a parent—that is, logically going up one level in the directory hierarchy from the current position given by this path. It returns null if this Path does not have a parent—for example, if the path denotes the root component or it is a relative path that comprises a single name element, as there is no parent in these cases.

Path getRoot()

Returns the root component of this path as a Path object, or null if this path does not have a root component.

int getNameCount()

Returns the number of name elements in the path. It returns the value n, where $n-1$ is the index of the last name element and the first name element has index 0. Note that the root component is not included in the count of the name elements.

Path getName(int index)

Returns a name element of this path as a Path object, where the name element closest to the root component has index 0.

Path subpath(int beginIndex, int endIndex)

Returns a relative Path that is a subsequence of the name elements of this path, where beginIndex is inclusive but endIndex is exclusive (i.e., name elements in the range [beginIndex, endIndex)). Illegal indices will result in an IllegalArgumentException.

boolean startsWith(Path other)
default boolean startsWith(String other)

Determine whether this path starts with either the given path or a Path object constructed from the given other string. The methods can be used for conditional handing of paths.

boolean endsWith(Path other)
default boolean endsWith(String other)

Determine whether this path ends with either the given path or a Path object constructed from the given other string. These methods can be used for conditional handing of paths.

Example 21.1 illustrates methods for querying a Path object. An absolute path is created at (1). The output from the program shows the result of executing methods for text representation at (2), determining whether a path is absolute at (3), which file system created the path at (4), accessing name elements at (5), and testing the prefix and the suffix of a path at (6).

Example 21.1 *Querying* Path *Objects*

```java
import java.nio.file.FileSystem;
import java.nio.file.FileSystems;
import java.nio.file.Path;
import java.util.ArrayList;
import java.util.List;

public class QueryingPaths {

  public static void main(String[] args) {
    FileSystem dfs = FileSystems.getDefault();        // The default file system
    String nameSeparator = dfs.getSeparator();        // The name separator

    Path absPath = Path.of(nameSeparator, "a", "b", "c");              // (1)

    System.out.printf("toString(): %s%n",    absPath);                 // (2)
    System.out.printf("isAbsolute(): %s%n", absPath.isAbsolute());     // (3)
    System.out.printf("getFileSystem(): %s%n",
                      absPath.getFileSystem().getClass().getName());   // (4)

    System.out.println("\n***Accessing Name Elements:");               // (5)
    System.out.printf("getFileName(): %s%n",  absPath.getFileName());
    System.out.printf("getParent(): %s%n",    absPath.getParent());
    System.out.printf("getRoot(): %s%n",      absPath.getRoot());
    System.out.printf("getNameCount(): %d%n", absPath.getNameCount());

    List<Path> pl = new ArrayList<>();
    absPath.forEach(p -> pl.add(p));
    System.out.printf("List of name elements: %s%n",  pl);

    System.out.printf("getName(0): %s%n",      absPath.getName(0));
    System.out.printf("subpath(0,2): %s%n",    absPath.subpath(0,2));

    System.out.println("\n***Path Prefix and Suffix:");                // (6)
    System.out.printf("startsWith(\"%s\"): %s%n",
                      nameSeparator + "a",
                      absPath.startsWith(nameSeparator + "a"));
    System.out.printf("endsWith(\"b/c\"): %s%n",
                      absPath.endsWith("b/c"));
  }
}
```

Possible output from the program:

```
toString(): /a/b/c
isAbsolute(): true
getFileSystem(): sun.nio.fs.MacOSXFileSystem

***Accessing Name Elements:
getFileName(): c
getParent(): /a/b
getRoot(): /
getNameCount(): 3
List of name elements: [a, b, c]
```

```
getName(0): a
subpath(0,2): a/b

***Path Prefix and Suffix:
startsWith("/a"): true
endsWith("b/c"): true
```

Converting Path **Objects**

The Path interface provides many methods for converting paths. A majority of these methods manipulate the path strings syntactically and do not assume that the path strings of the Path objects denote actual directory entries in the file system.

Path toAbsolutePath()

Returns a Path object representing the absolute path of this Path object. If this Path object represents a relative path, an absolute path is constructed by appending it to the absolute path of the current directory. If this Path is an absolute path, it just returns this Path object.

Path normalize()

Returns a Path object that is created from this Path object with redundant name elements eliminated. This typically involves eliminating the "." and "*dir/..*" strings in this Path object, as these do not change the hierarchy of a path. The method applies the elimination procedure repeatedly until all such redundancies are eliminated.

Path resolve(Path other)
default Path resolve(String other)

These method resolve the given Path object (either specified or created from the specified string) against this Path object.

If the other Path object represents an absolute path, the other Path object is returned as the result, regardless of whether this Path object represents an absolute or a relative path. Otherwise, the method creates a result Path object by *joining* the other Path object to this Path object.

default Path resolveSibling(Path other)
default Path resolveSibling(String other)

Resolve the given Path object (either specified or created from the specified string) against this Path object's *parent* path. That is, they resolve the given Path object by calling the resolve(other) method on this Path object's parent path.

Path relativize(Path other)

Constructs a relative Path object between this Path object and the given other Path object. The constructed relative Path object when resolved against this Path object should yield a path that represents the same directory entry as the given other Path object.

A relative `Path` object can only be constructed when this `Path` object and the given `Path` object *both* represent either absolute paths or relative paths.

If this path is `/w/x` and the given path is `/w/x/y/z`, the resulting relative path is `y/z`. That is, the given path `/w/x/y/z` and the resulting relative path `y/z` represent the same directory entry.

For two `Path` objects that are equal, the empty path is returned.

The `relativize()` method is the inverse of the `resolve()` method.

`Path toRealPath(LinkOption... options) throws IOException`

Returns a `Path` object that represents the *real* path of an existing directory entry. Note that this method throws an `IOException` if the path does not exist in the file system. It converts the path to an absolute path and removes any redundant elements, and does not follow symbolic links if the enum constant `LinkOption.NOFOLLOW_LINKS` is specified (p. 1301).

Converting a Path to an Absolute Path

The method `toAbsolutePath()` of the `Path` interface converts a path to an absolute path. Table 21.2 illustrates how this method works for `Path` objects declared in the second column. A print statement that calls the method on each path declaration, analogous to the one below, creates the text representation of the resulting absolute path shown in the rightmost column. The current directory has the absolute path `/a/b`.

```
System.out.println(absPath1.toAbsolutePath());        // (1) /a
```

In Table 21.2, (1) and (2) show that if the `Path` object already represents an absolute path, the same `Path` object is returned. If the `Path` object represents a relative path, as shown at (3), (4), and (5), the resulting absolute path is created by appending the relative path to the absolute path of the current directory. The path need not exist in the file system, and the method does not attempt to clean up the path string of the resulting `Path` object—in contrast to the `normalize()` method (p. 1299).

Table 21.2 *Converting to an Absolute Path*

	Absolute path of the current directory: /a/b Path	Text representation of the absolute path returned by the toAbsolutePath() method
(1)	`Path absPath1 = Path.of("/a");`	`/a`
(2)	`Path absPath2 = Path.of("/a/b/c");`	`/a/b/c`
(3)	`Path relPath1 = Path.of("d");`	`/a/b/d`
(4)	`Path relPath2 = Path.of("../f");`	`/a/b/../f`
(5)	`Path relPath3 = Path.of("./../g");`	`/a/b/./../g`

Normalizing a Path

The normalize() method of the Path interface removes redundancies in a Path object. For example, the current directory designator "." is redundant in a Path object, as it does not add any new level to the path hierarchy. Also the string "*dir/..*" in a path is redundant, as it implies going one level down in the path hierarchy and then one level up again—not changing the hierarchy represented by the path.

Table 21.3 illustrates how the normalize() method converts the Path objects declared in the second column. A print statement that calls the method on each path declaration, analogous to the one below, creates the text representation of the resulting path shown in the rightmost column.

```
System.out.println(path1.normalize());        // (1) a/b/c
```

The numbers below refer to the rows in Table 21.3.

(1) All occurrences of the current directory designator "." are redundant and are eliminated from the path.

(2) The occurrences of the redundant string "a/.." are eliminated from the path.

(3) The occurrences of the parent directory designator ".." are significant in this case, as each occurrence implies traversing one level up the path hierarchy.

(4) All occurrences of the current directory designator "." are eliminated from the path, but occurrences of the parent directory designator ".." are significant.

(5) The occurrence of the redundant current directory designator "." is eliminated from the path, resulting in an empty path whose text representation is the empty string.

Because of redundancies in a path, comparison on paths is best performed on normalized paths (p. 1303).

Table 21.3 *Normalizing Paths*

	Path	Text representation of the path returned by the normalize() method
(1)	Path path1 = Path.of("./a/./b/c/.");	a/b/c
(2)	Path path2 = Path.of("a/../a/../b");	b
(3)	Path path3 = Path.of("../../d");	../../d
(4)	Path path4 = Path.of("./../../.");	../..
(5)	Path path5 = Path.of(".");	*empty string*

Resolving Two Paths

Table 21.4 illustrates how the resolve() method of the Path interface performs resolution between two paths. The four combinations of mixing absolute and relative paths when calling the resolve() method are represented by the rows (R1 and R2) and the columns (C1 and C2) in Table 21.4. The results shown are obtained by executing a print statement that calls the resolve() method, analogous to the one below, for each combination.

```
System.out.println(absPath1.resolve(absPath2));        // (R1, C1)
```

If the given path is an absolute path, it is returned as the result, as in column C1, regardless of whether the path on which the method is invoked is an absolute or a relative path. Otherwise, the method creates a result path by appending the given path to the path on which the method is invoked, as in column C2.

In the special case when the given path is an empty path, the method returns the path on which it was invoked:

```
Path anyPath = Path.of("/a/n/y");
Path emptyPath = Path.of("");
System.out.println(anyPath.resolve(emptyPath));        // /a/n/y
```

Note that the paths need not exist to use this method, and the resulting path after resolution is not normalized.

Table 21.4 *Resolving Paths*

`p1.resolve(p2)`, where *p1* can be absPath1 or relPath1, and where *p2* can be absPath2 or relPath2	C1	C2
	Path absPath2 = Path.of("/c");	Path relPath2 = Path.of("../e/f");
R1 Path absPath1 = Path.of("/a/b");	/c	/a/b/../e/f
R2 Path relPath1 = Path.of("d");	/c	d/../e/f

Constructing the Relative Path between Two Paths

Table 21.5 illustrates how the relativize() method of the Path interface constructs a relative path between this path and the given path, so that the resulting relative path denotes the same directory entry as the given path.

The four combinations of mixing absolute and relative paths when calling the relativize() method are represented by the rows (R1 and R2) and the columns (C1 and C2) in Table 21.5. The results shown are obtained by executing a print statement that calls the relativize() method, analogous to the one below, for each combination.

```
System.out.println(absPath1.revitalize(absPath2));      // (R1, C1)
```

For the case (R1, C1) where both paths are absolute paths in Table 21.5, the resulting relative path is constructed relative to the root of the directory hierarchy. The relative path between the absolute path /a/b and the given absolute path /c is ../../c, indicating traversing two levels up from the path /a/b to the root and joining with the given path /c. Both the resulting relative path ../../c and the given path /c denote the same directory entry.

For the case (R2, C2) where both paths are relative paths in Table 21.5, the resulting relative path is constructed relative to the *current directory*. The relative path between the relative path d and the given relative path e/f is ../e/f, indicating traversing one level up from the path d to the current directory and joining with the given path e/f. Both the resulting relative path ../e/f and the given path e/f denote the same directory entry.

From Table 21.5, we see that an IllegalArgumentException is thrown when both paths are neither absolute paths nor relative paths, as it is not possible to create a relative path between paths that do not satisfy this criteria.

The code below shows the relationship between the relativize() and the resolve() methods:

```
Path p = Path.of("/a/b");
Path other = Path.of("/a/b/c/d");
Path q = p.relativize(other);                                    // c/d
System.out.println(p.relativize(p.resolve(q)).equals(q));        // true
System.out.println(p.resolve(q).equals(other));                  // true
```

Note that the paths need not exist to use this method, as it operates syntactically on the path strings.

Table 21.5 *Constructing a Relative Path between Two Paths*

p1.relativize(p2), where p1 can be absPath1 or relPath1, and where p2 can be absPath2 or relPath2	C1 Path absPath2 = Path.of("/c");	C2 Path relPath2 = Path.of("e/f");
R1 Path absPath1 = Path.of("/a/b");	../../c	IllegalArgumentException
R2 Path relPath1 = Path.of("d");	IllegalArgumentException	../e/f

Link Option

The enum type LinkOption defines how symbolic links should be handled by a file operation. This enum type defines only one constant, shown in Table 21.6. If the constant NOFOLLOW_LINKS is specified in a method call, symbolic links are not followed by the method.

The enum type LinkOption implements both the CopyOption interface (p. 1308) and the OpenOption interface (p. 1314). Many file operations declare a variable arity parameter of one of these interface types or just the enum type LinkOption, making it possible to configure their operation.

Table 21.6 *Link Option*

Enum java.nio.file.LinkOption implements the java.nio.file.CopyOption and the java.nio.file.OpenOption interfaces	Description
NOFOLLOW_LINKS	Do not follow symbolic links.

Converting a Path to a Real Path

The toRealPath() method of the Path interface converts this path to an absolute path that denotes the same directory entry as this path. The name elements in the path must represent actual directories in the file system or the method throws an IOException. It accepts a variable arity parameter of the enum type java.nio.file.LinkOption (Table 21.6). If the variable arity parameter is not specified, symbolic links are followed to their final target.

The toRealPath() method performs several operations to construct the real path:

- If this path is a relative path, it is first converted to an absolute path.

- Any redundant name elements are removed to create a new path. In other words, it normalizes the result path.

- If LinkOption.NOFOLLOW_LINKS is specified, any symbolic links are not followed.

Table 21.7 show the results of calling the toRealPath() method on selected paths. Since the method throws an IOException, it should typically be called in a try-catch construct.

```
try {
  Path somePath = Path.of("some/path");
  Path realPath = somePath.toRealPath(LinkOption.NOFOLLOW_LINKS);
  System.out.println(realPath);
} catch (NoSuchFileException nsfe) {
  nsfe.printStackTrace();
} catch (IOException ioe) {
  ioe.printStackTrace();
}
```

Table 21.7 *Converting to a Real Path*

	Current directory: /book/chap01 The symbolic link ./alias_appendixA has the target /book/appendixA.	Text representation of the Path returned by the toRealPath() method
(1)	Path currDir = Path.of(".");	/book/chap01
(2)	Path parentDir = Path.of("..");	/book
(3)	Path path3 = Path.of("./examples/../../examples/D.java");	/book/chap01/examples/D.java

Table 21.7 *Converting to a Real Path (Continued)*

	Current directory: /book/chap01 The symbolic link ./alias_appendixA has the target /book/appendixA.	Text representation of the Path returned by the toRealPath() method
(4)	`Path path4 = Path.of("./alias_appendixA");`	`path4.toRealPath()` returns `/book/appendixA.` `path4.toRealPath(LinkOption. NOFOLLOW_LINKS)` returns `/book/chap01/alias_appendixA.`

Comparing Path Objects

The methods in the Path interface for comparing two paths only consult the path strings, and do not access the file system or require that the paths exist in the file system.

```
boolean equals(Object other)
```

Determines whether this path is equal to the given object by comparing their path strings. It does *not* eliminate any redundancies from the paths before testing for equality. See also the Files.isSameFile() method (p. 1306).

```
int compareTo(Path other)
```

A Path object implements the Comparable<Path> interface. This method compares two path strings lexicographically according to the established contract of this method. It means paths can be compared, searched, and sorted.

The code below illustrates sorting paths according to their natural order. Comparison of the paths is based purely on comparison of their path strings, as is the equality comparison.

```
Path p1 = Path.of("/", "a", "b", "c", "d");
Path p2 = Path.of("/", "a", "b");
Path p3 = Path.of("/", "a", "b", "c");
Path p4 = Path.of("a", "b");

// Sorting paths according to natural order:
List<Path> sortedPaths = Stream.of(p1, p2, p3, p4)
                               .sorted()
                               .toList();
System.out.println(sortedPaths);
// [/a/b, /a/b/c, /a/b/c/d, a/b]

// Comparing for lexicographical equality:
System.out.println(p2);                         // Absolute path: /a/b
System.out.println(p3.subpath(0, 2));           // Relative path: a/b
System.out.println(p2.equals(p3.subpath(0, 2))); // false
```

21.4   Operations on Directory Entries

The static methods of the Files class interact with the file system to access directory entries in the file system. The methods make heavy use of Path objects that denote directory entries.

Characteristics of Methods in the Files Class

It is worth noting certain aspects of the static methods in the Files class, as this will aid in using and understanding the operations they perform.

Handling System Resources

The NIO.2 API uses many resources, such as files and streams, that should be closed after use to avoid any degradation of performance due to lack of system resources. As these resources implement the java.io.Closeable interface, they are best handled in a try-with-resources statement that guarantees to close them after its execution.

Handling Exceptions

Errors are bound to occur when interacting with the file system. Numerous errors can occur, and among the most common errors are the following:

- A required file or directory does not exist in the file system.
- Permissions to access a file are incorrect.

A majority of the static methods in the Files class throw a java.io.IOException that acts as the catchall for various I/O errors. Its subclass, java.nio.file.NoSuchFile-Exception, unequivocally makes clear the cause of the exception. As these exceptions are checked exceptions, code using these methods should diligently handle these exceptions with either a try-catch-finally construct or a throws clause.

For brevity, the exception handling may be omitted in some code presented in this chapter.

Handling Symbolic Links

The methods of the Files class are savvy with regard to symbolic links. Following of symbolic links is typically indicated by specifying or omitting the constant LinkOption.NOFOLLOW_LINKS for the variable arity parameter of the method (see below).

Specifying Variable Arity Parameters

Many static methods in the Files class have a variable arity parameter. Such a parameter allows zero or more options to customize the operation implemented by the method. For example, the following method takes into consideration symbolic links depending on whether or not the variable arity parameter options is specified:

```
// Method header:
static boolean exists(Path path, LinkOption... options)  // Variable arity param.

// Method calls:
Path path = Path.of("alias");
boolean result1 = Files.exists(path);           // Follow symbolic links.
boolean result2 = Files.exists(path,
                  LinkOption.NOFOLLOW_LINKS);   // Do not follow symbolic links.
```

Executing Atomic Operations

Certain file operations can be performed as *atomic operations*. Such an operation guarantees the integrity of any resource it uses. It runs independently and cannot be interrupted by other operations that might be running concurrently. See the *atomic move* operation (p. 1305).

Determining the Existence of a Directory Entry

The following static methods of the Files class test the existence or nonexistence of a directory entry denoted by a path.

```
static boolean exists(Path path, LinkOption... options)
static boolean notExists(Path path, LinkOption... options)
```

The first method tests whether a directory entry exists. The second method tests whether the directory entry denoted by this path does not exist.

These methods normalize the path, and do not follow symbolic links if the enum constant LinkOption.NOFOLLOW_LINKS is specified for the options variable arity parameter.

These methods are *not* complements of each other. Both return false if they are not able to determine whether a directory entry exists or not. This can occur due to lack of access permissions.

Note that the result returned by these methods is immediately outdated. The outcome of subsequent access of the directory entry is unpredictable, as concurrently running threads might change the conditions after the method returns.

Although a Path object can represent a hypothetical path, ultimately the existence of the directory entry it denotes must be verified by interacting with the file system.

Given the following directory hierarchy, the code below demonstrates what result is returned by the exists() and notExists() methods of the Files class.

```
Current directory
└── project/
    ├── src/
    │   ├── pkg
    │   │   └── Main.java
    │   │
    │   └── manifest.txt ◄---┐
    │                        ┊ Symbolic link
    └── manifest_link --------┘
```

```java
Path path1 = Path.of("project", "src", "pkg", "Main.java");
System.out.println(Files.exists(path1));                          // true
System.out.println(Files.notExists(path1));                       // false

Path path2 = Path.of("project", "..", "project", ".", "src", "pkg", "Main.java");
System.out.println(Files.exists(path2));                          // true
System.out.println(Files.notExists(path2));                       // false

Path path3 = Path.of("project", "readme.txt");
System.out.println(Files.exists(path3));                          // false
System.out.println(Files.notExists(path3));                       // true
```

Given that the path ./project/manifest_link is a symbolic link to the path ./project/src/manifest.txt, the code below demonstrates following symbolic links in the exists() method.

```java
Path target   = Path.of("project", "src", "manifest.txt");
Path symLink = Path.of("project", "manifest_link");

boolean result4 = Files.exists(target);                                // (1)
boolean result5 = Files.exists(symLink);                               // (2)
boolean result6 = Files.exists(symLink, LinkOption.NOFOLLOW_LINKS);    // (3)

System.out.println("target: " + result4);                         // (1a) true
System.out.println("symLink->target: " + result5);               // (2a) true
System.out.println("symLink_NOFOLLOW_LINKS: " + result6);        // (3a) true
```

Note that (1) and (2) above are equivalent. The existence of the target is tested at (2) as the symbolic link is followed by default. Whereas at (3), the existence of the symbolic link itself is tested, since the enum constant LinkOption.NOFOLLOW_LINKS is specified.

Uniqueness of a Directory Entry

The method isSameFile() in the Files class can be used to check whether two paths denote the *same* directory entry. It does not take into consideration other aspects of the directory entry, like its file name or contents.

> static boolean isSameFile(Path path1, Path path2) throws IOException
>
> Determines whether the two paths denote the same directory entry. If the paths are equal, it returns true and does not check whether the paths exist.
>
> This method normalizes the paths and follows symbolic links.
>
> It implements an *equivalence relation* (which is *reflexive*, *symmetric*, and *transitive*) for non-null paths, if the file system and the directory entries do not change.

The numbers below refer to corresponding lines in the code to illustrate the workings of the isSameFile() method:

(1) Paths are always normalized, as in the case of path2.

(2) Symbolic links are always followed, as in the case of symLink.

(3) Only paths are compared. Paths passed to the method are not equal.

(4) Equal paths return true, and their existence is not checked. The path ./Main.java does not exist.

(5) The paths must exist in the file system, if they are not equal. The path ./Main.java does not exist, resulting in a java.nio.file.NoSuchFileException.

```java
Path path1 = Path.of("project", "src", "pkg", "Main.java");
Path path2 = Path.of("project", "..", "project", ".", "src", "pkg", "Main.java");

Path target  = Path.of("project", "src", "manifest.txt");
Path symLink = Path.of("project", "manifest_link");

System.out.println(Files.isSameFile(path1, path2));          // (1) true
System.out.println(Files.isSameFile(symLink, target));       // (2) true
System.out.println(Files.isSameFile(path1, target));         // (3) false
System.out.println(Files.isSameFile(Path.of("Main.java"),
                                    Path.of("Main.java")));   // (4) true
System.out.println(Files.isSameFile(path1,
                          Path.of("Main.java")));  // (5) NoSuchFileException
```

Deleting Directory Entries

The methods delete() and deleteIfExists() in the Files class can be used for deleting directory entries.

```java
static void delete(Path path) throws IOException
static boolean deleteIfExists(Path path) throws IOException
```

Delete a directory entry denoted by the path.

If the path does not exist, the first method throws a NoSuchFileException, but the second method does not.

Deleting a symbolic link only deletes the link, and not the target of the link.

To delete a directory, it must be empty or a java.nio.file.DirectoryNotEmpty-Exception is thrown.

Consider the following paths that exist:
```java
Path projDir  = Path.of("project");
Path target   = Path.of("project", "src", "manifest.txt");
Path symLink  = Path.of("project", "manifest_link");
```

The delete() method throws a NoSuchFileException, if the path does not exist.

```java
Files.delete(symLink);                    // Exists. Link deleted, not target.
Files.delete(Path.of("Main.java"));       // Does not exist: NoSuchFileException
```

The deleteIfExists() method does not throw a NoSuchFileException. It indicates the result by the boolean return value.

```java
System.out.println(Files.deleteIfExists(target));            // Exists.
                                                             //   Deleted: true
System.out.println(Files.deleteIfExists(Path.of("Main.java"))); // Does not
                                                             //   exist: false
```

In order to delete a directory, it must be empty. The directory ./project is not empty. Both methods throw a DirectoryNotEmptyException.

```
Files.delete(projDir);                                      // DirectoryNotEmptyException
System.out.println(Files.deleteIfExists(projDir)); // DirectoryNotEmptyException
```

Also keep in mind that deleting a directory entry might not be possible, if another program is using it.

Copy Options

The enum types LinkOption (Table 21.6) and StandardCopyOption (Table 21.8) implement the CopyOption interface. These options can be used to configure copying and moving of directory entries. A variable arity parameter of type CopyOption... is declared by the copy() and move() methods of the Files class that support specific constants of the LinkOption and StandardCopyOption enum types.

Table 21.8   *Standard Copy Options*

Enum java.nio.file.StandardCopyOption implements the java.nio.file.CopyOption interface	Description
REPLACE_EXISTING	Replace a file if it exists.
COPY_ATTRIBUTES	Copy file attributes to the new file (p. 1321).
ATOMIC_MOVE	Move the file as an atomic file system operation—that is, an operation that is either performed uninterrupted in its entirety, or it fails.

Copying Directory Entries

The overloaded copy() methods of the Files class implement copying contents of files. Two of the copy() methods can be configured by specifying *copy options*.

```
static Path copy(Path source, Path destination, CopyOption... options)
                throws IOException
```

Copies a source directory entry to the destination directory entry. It returns the path to the destination directory entry. The default behavior is outlined below, but can be configured by copy options:

- If destination already exists or is a symbolic link, copying *fails*.
- If source and destination are the same, the method completes without any copying.
- If source is a symbolic link, the target of the link is copied.
- If source is a directory, just an *empty* destination directory is created.

The following copy options can be specified to configure the default copying behavior:

- `StandardCopyOption.REPLACE_EXISTING`: If the destination exists, this option indicates to replace the destination if it is a file or an empty directory. If the destination exists and is a symbolic link, it indicates to replace the symbolic link and not its target.
- `StandardCopyOption.COPY_ATTRIBUTES`: This option indicates to copy the file attributes of the source to the destination. However, copying of attributes is platform dependent.
- `LinkOption.NOFOLLOW_LINKS`: This option indicates not to follow symbolic links. If the source is a symbolic link, then the symbolic link is copied and not its target.

```
static long copy(InputStream in, Path destination, CopyOption... options)
            throws IOException
```

Copies all bytes from an input stream to a `destination` path, and returns the number of bytes copied. The input stream will be at the end of the stream after copying, but may not be because of I/O errors.

By default, if the `destination` path already exists or is a symbolic link, copying *fails*.

It can be configured by the following copy option:

- `StandardCopyOption.REPLACE_EXISTING`: If the `destination` path exists and is a file or an empty directory, this option indicates to replace the `destination`. If the `destination` exists and is a symbolic link, this option indicates to replace the symbolic link and not its target.

```
static long copy(Path source, OutputStream output) throws IOException
```

Copies all bytes from the `source` to the output stream, and returns the number of bytes copied. It may be necessary to flush the output stream.

Note that this `copy()` method cannot be configured.

The output stream may be in an inconsistent state because of I/O errors.

The first thing to keep in mind is that the copy methods do *not* create the intermediate directories that are in the destination path. Given the destination path `./project/archive/destFile`, the parent path `./project/archive` must exist. Otherwise, a `NoSuchFileException` is thrown.

Note also that copying fails if the destination path already exists—a `FileAlreadyExistsException` is thrown, unless the method is qualified by the enum constant `StandardCopyOption.REPLACE_EXISTING`.

Copy and Replace Directory Entries

Consider copying the source file:

```
./project/src/pkg/Main.java
```

to the destination file:

```
./project/archive/src/pkg/Main.java
```

The numbers below refer to corresponding lines in the code below to illustrate copying of files:

(1) Creates the Path object that denotes the source file.

(2) Creates the Path object for the *parent* path of the destination file. This parent path must exist.

(3) Resolves the parent path with the source pathname, so that if the destination file is to have the same name as the source file, its Path object can be constructed from the parent path and the file name of the source file.

Items (4) through (6) illustrate the scenario when calling the copy() method successively.

(4) Creates the destination file and copies the contents of the source file to the destination file.

(5) Overwrites the contents of the destination file with the contents of the source file.

(6) Fails, as the destination file already exists.

```
Path source = Path.of("project", "src", "pkg", "Main.java");           // (1)
Path parentDestinationPath = Path.of("project", "archive", "src", "pkg"); // (2)
Path destination = parentDestinationPath.resolve(source.getFileName()); // (3)

Files.copy(source, destination);      // (4) OK. Destination file does not exist.
Files.copy(source, destination,       // (5) OK. Destination file replaced.
        StandardCopyOption.REPLACE_EXISTING);
Files.copy(source, destination);      // (6) FileAlreadyExistsException
```

The copy() method does *not* copy the entries in a source directory to a destination directory. The code below attempts to copy the source directory:

```
./project/src
```

to the destination directory:

```
./project/backup
```

Possible outcomes of the following copying operation can be any of the bulleted options listed below:

```
Path srcDir  = Path.of("project", "src");
Path destDir = Path.of("project", "backup");
Files.copy(srcDir, destDir, StandardCopyOption.REPLACE_EXISTING);
```

- If an entry named backup does not exist in the project directory, an empty directory named backup is created.

- If an entry named backup exists in the project directory and it is an empty directory, a new empty directory named backup is created.

- If an entry named backup exists in the project directory and it is a file, the file is deleted and an empty directory named backup is created.

- If an entry named backup exists in the project directory and it is a non-empty directory, the copying operation fails with a DirectoryNotEmptyException.

Another special case to consider is copying a file to a directory. Consider the scenario when copying the source file:

```
./project/src/pkg/Main.java
```

to the destination directory:

```
./project/classes
```

The code and possible outcomes are outlined below.

```
Path srcFile = Path.of("project", "src", "pkg", "Main.java");
Path destDir = Path.of("project", "classes");
Files.copy(srcFile, destDir, StandardCopyOption.REPLACE_EXISTING);
```

- If an entry named classes does not exist in the project directory, a file named classes is created and the contents of the source file are copied to the file classes.

- If an entry named classes exists in the project directory and it is a file, the file is deleted, a new file named classes is created, and the contents of the source file are copied to the file classes.

- If an entry named classes exists in the project directory and it is an empty directory, the directory is deleted, a file named classes is created, and the contents of the source file are copied to the file classes.

- If an entry named classes exists in the project directory and it is a non-empty directory, the copying operation fails with a DirectoryNotEmptyException.

Copy Files Using I/O Streams

The Files class provides methods to copy files using byte I/O streams from the java.io package (§20.2, p. 1234). Bytes can be copied from a source file to an InputStream and from an OutputStream to a destination file. We demonstrate copying where input streams and output streams are assigned to files. See also reading and writing files using paths (p. 1314).

The code below reads bytes from the input file project/src/pkg/Util.java using a BufferedInputStream and writes the bytes to the output file path project/backup/Util.java.

```
String inputFileName  = "project/src/pkg/Util.java";
Path outputFilePath = Path.of("project", "backup", "Util.java");
```

```
try (var fis = new FileInputStream(inputFileName);
     var bis = new BufferedInputStream(fis)) {
  long bytesCopied = Files.copy(bis, outputFilePath,
                                  StandardCopyOption.REPLACE_EXISTING);
  System.out.println("Bytes copied: " + bytesCopied);       // Bytes copied: 103
}
```

The code below copies bytes from the input file path project/backup/Util.java to the output file project/archive/src/pkg/Util.java using a BufferedOutputStream.

```
Path inputFilePath  = Path.of("project", "backup", "Util.java");
String outputFileName = "project/archive/src/pkg/Util.java";
try (var fos = new FileOutputStream(outputFileName);
     var bos = new BufferedOutputStream(fos)) {
  long bytesCopied = Files.copy(inputFilePath, bos);
  System.out.println("Bytes copied: " + bytesCopied);       // Bytes copied: 103
}
```

The following statement can be used to print the contents of a file to the standard output:

```
Files.copy(inputFilePath, System.out);      // Prints file content to standard out.
```

In general, any InputStream or OutputStream can be used in the respective copy() methods.

Moving and Renaming Directory Entries

The move() method of the Files class implements moving and renaming directory entries. The method can be configured by specifying *copy options*.

The move() method emulates the copying behavior of the copy() method. But in contrast to the copy() method, the move() method deletes the source if the operation succeeds. Both methods allow the destination to be overwritten, if the constant StandardCopyOption.REPLACE_EXISTING is specified.

```
static Path move(Path source, Path destination, CopyOption... options)
          throws IOException
```

Moves or renames the source to the destination. After moving, the source is deleted. The method returns the path to the destination. The default behavior is outlined below, but can be configured by copy options:

- If destination already exists, the move *fails*.
- If source and destination are the same, the method has no effect.
- If source is a symbolic link, the target of the link is moved.
- If source is an empty directory, the empty directory is moved to the destination.

The following copy options can be specified to configure the default moving behavior:

- StandardCopyOption.REPLACE_EXISTING: If the destination exists, this option indicates to replace the destination if it is a file or an empty directory. If the destination exists and is a symbolic link, this option indicates to replace the symbolic link and not its target.

- StandardCopyOption.ATOMIC_MOVE: The move is performed as an *atomic file system operation*. It is implementation specific whether the move is performed if the destination exists or whether an IOException is thrown. If the move cannot be performed, the method throws an AtomicMoveNotSupportedException.

Moving Directory Entries

The code below illustrates moving a file (./project/src/manifest.txt) to a new location (./project/bkup/manifest.txt). If the file exists at the new location, it is replaced by the source file.

```
Path srcFile  = Path.of("project", "src",  "manifest.txt");
Path destFile = Path.of("project", "bkup", "manifest.txt");
Files.move(srcFile, destFile, StandardCopyOption.REPLACE_EXISTING);
```

We can move a directory *and* its hierarchy (./project/bkup) to a new location (./project/archive/backup). The directory (and its contents) are moved to the new location and renamed (backup).

```
Path srcDir = Path.of("project", "bkup");
Path destDir = Path.of("project", "archive", "backup");  // Parent path exists.
Files.move(srcDir, destDir);
```

Renaming Directory Entries

The move() method can be used to rename a directory entry. The code below illustrates renaming an existing file (Util.java). Its name is changed (UX.java), but not its contents.

```
Path oldFileName  = Path.of("project", "backup", "Util.java");
Path newFileName  = Path.of("project", "backup", "UX.java");
Files.move(oldFileName, newFileName);
```

Analogously, the code below illustrates renaming an existing directory (backup). Its name is changed (bkup), but not its hierarchy.

```
Path oldDirName  = Path.of("project", "backup");
Path newDirName  = Path.of("project", "bkup");
Files.move(oldDirName, newDirName);
```

Atomic Move

The enum constant StandardCopyOption.ATOMIC_MOVE can be specified in the move() method to indicate an *atomic move*—that is, an operation that is indivisible. It either completes in its entirety or it fails. The upshot of an atomic operation is that other threads will never see incomplete or partial results. An AtomicMoveNotSupportedException will be thrown if the file system does not support this feature.

In the following code, the file `Util.java` in the directory `./project/src/pkg` is moved in an atomic operation to its new location `./project/archive/src/pkg`.

```
Path srcFile = Path.of("project", "src", "pkg", "Util.java");
Path destFile = Path.of("project", "archive", "src", "pkg", "Util.java");
Files.move(srcFile, destFile, StandardCopyOption.REPLACE_EXISTING,
                              StandardCopyOption.ATOMIC_MOVE);
```

21.5 Reading and Writing Files Using Paths

The `Files` class provides methods for reading and writing bytes and characters using I/O streams and `Path` objects.

Methods provided for reading and writing files typically close the file after use.

Open Options

The `java.nio.file.OpenOption` interface is implemented by objects that can be specified as options to configure how a file operation should open or create a file. Methods for writing to files can be configured for this purpose by specifying constants defined by the enum type `java.nio.file.StandardOpenOption` that implements the `OpenOption` interface.

Table 21.9 shows the options defined by constants of the `StandardOpenOption` enum type. Such options are specified as values for the variable arity parameter of type `OpenOption` in methods such as `newBufferedWriter()`, `write()`, `writeString()`, `newOutputStream()`, and `newInputStream()` of the `Files` class.

For write operations, if no options are supplied, it implies that the following options for opening and creating a file are present: `CREATE`, `TRUNCATE_EXISTING`, and `WRITE`—meaning the file is opened for writing, created if it does not exist, and truncated to size 0.

Table 21.9   *Selected Standard Open Options*

Enum `java.nio.file.StandardOpenOption` implements the `java.nio.file.OpenOption` interface	Description
READ	Open the file for read access.
WRITE	Open the file for write access.
APPEND	If the file is opened for WRITE access, write bytes to the end of the file. That is, its previous content is not overwritten.
TRUNCATE_EXISTING	If the file already exists and it is opened for WRITE access, truncate its length to 0 so that bytes are written from the beginning of the file.

Table 21.9 *Selected Standard Open Options (Continued)*

Enum java.nio.file.StandardOpenOption implements the java.nio.file.OpenOption interface	Description
CREATE	Open the file if it exists; otherwise, create a new file.
CREATE_NEW	Fail if the file already exists; otherwise, create a new file.
DELETE_ON_CLOSE	Delete the file when the stream is closed. Typically used for temporary files.

Reading and Writing Character Data

The Files class provides methods for reading and writing *character data* to files. These methods can be categorized as follows:

* Methods that create character I/O streams (BufferedReader, BufferedWriter) chained to a Path object that denotes a file. The methods of the buffered reader and writer can then be used to read and write characters to the file, respectively.

* Methods that directly use a Path object, and read and write characters to the file denoted by the Path object.

Reading and Writing Character Data Using Buffered I/O Streams

The newBufferedReader() and newBufferedWriter() methods of the Files class create buffered readers and writers, respectively, that are chained to a Path object denoting a file. Interoperability between character I/O streams in the java.io package can then be leveraged to chain appropriate I/O streams for reading and writing character data to a file (§20.3, p. 1241).

Previously we have used constructors of the BufferedReader class (§20.3, p. 1251) and the BufferedWriter class (§20.3, p. 1250) in the java.io package to instantiate buffered readers and writers that are chained to a Reader or a Writer, respectively. Using the methods of the Files class is the recommended practice for creating buffered readers and writers when dealing with text files.

```
static BufferedReader newBufferedReader(Path path) throws IOException
static BufferedReader newBufferedReader(Path path, Charset cs)
                                        throws IOException
```

Opens the file denoted by the specified path for reading, and returns a BufferedReader of a default size to read text efficiently from the file, using either the UTF-8 charset or the specified charset to decode the bytes, respectively. Contrast these methods with the constructors of the java.io.BufferReader class (§20.3, p. 1251).

```
static BufferedWriter newBufferedWriter(Path path, OpenOption... options)
                                  throws IOException
static BufferedWriter newBufferedWriter(Path path, Charset cs,
                  OpenOption... options) throws IOException
```

Opens or creates a file denoted by the specified path for writing, returning a
BufferedWriter of a default size that can be used to write text efficiently to the
file, using either the UTF-8 charset or the specified charset to encode the characters, respectively. See also constructors of the java.io.BufferWriter class
(§20.3, p. 1250).

The code at (1) and at (3) in Example 21.2 illustrates writing lines to a text file using
a buffered writer and reading lines from a text file using a buffered reader, respectively. The methods newBufferedWriter() and newBufferedReader() create the necessary buffered writer and reader at (2) and (4), respectively, whose methods are
used to write and read the lines from the file.

Example 21.2 *Reading and Writing Text Files*

```java
import java.io.*;
import java.nio.file.*;
import java.util.*;

public class ReadingWritingTextFiles {

  public static void main(String[] args) throws IOException {
    // List of strings:
    List<String> lines = List.of("Guess who got caught?", "Who?",
                                 "NullPointerException.",
                                 "Seriously?", "No. Finally.");
    // Text file:
    String filename = "project/linesOnly.txt";
    Path path = Path.of(filename);

    // Writing lines using buffered writer:                         (1)
    try (BufferedWriter writer = Files.newBufferedWriter(path)) {   // (2)
      for(String str : lines) {
        writer.write(str);                  // Write a string.
        writer.newLine();                   // Terminate with a newline.
      }
    } catch (IOException ioe) {
      ioe.printStackTrace();
    }

    // Read lines using buffered reader:                            (3)
    lines = new ArrayList<>();
    try(BufferedReader reader= Files.newBufferedReader(path)) {        // (4)
      String line = null;
      while ((line = reader.readLine()) != null) {  // EOF when null is returned.
        lines.add(line);
      }
    } catch (IOException ioe) {
      ioe.printStackTrace();
    }
    System.out.printf("Lines read from file \"%s\":%n%s%n", path, lines);
```

```
        // Write the list of strings in one operation:
        Files.write(path, lines);                                      // (5)

        // Write the joined lines in one operation:
        String joinedLines = String.join(System.lineSeparator(), lines);
        Files.writeString(path, joinedLines);                          // (6)

        // Read all contents into a String, including line separators:
        String allContent = Files.readString(path);                    // (7)
        System.out.printf("All lines read from file \"%s\":%n%s%n", path, allContent);

        // Read all lines into a list of String:
        lines = Files.readAllLines(path);                              // (8)
        System.out.printf("List of lines read from file \"%s\":%n%s%n", path, lines);
    }
}
```

Output from the program:

```
Lines read from file "project/linesOnly.txt":
[Guess who got caught?, Who?, NullPointerException., Seriously?, No. Finally.]
All lines read from file "project/linesOnly.txt":
Guess who got caught?
Who?
NullPointerException.
Seriously?
No. Finally.
List of lines read from file "project/linesOnly.txt":
[Guess who got caught?, Who?, NullPointerException., Seriously?, No. Finally.]
```

Reading and Writing Character Data Using *Path* Objects

The Files class provides methods that directly use a Path object, and read and write characters to the file denoted by the Path object, without the need to specify an I/O stream. These methods also close the file when done.

```
static Path write(Path path, Iterable<? extends CharSequence> lines,
                  OpenOption... options) throws IOException
static Path write(Path path, Iterable<? extends CharSequence> lines,
                  Charset cs, OpenOption... options) throws IOException
```

Open or create a file denoted by the specified path, and writes text lines to the file, using either the UTF-8 charset or the specified charset, respectively.

No options implies the following options: CREATE, TRUNCATE_EXISTING, and WRITE.

```
static Path writeString(Path path, CharSequence csq, OpenOption... options)
            throws IOException
static Path writeString(Path path, CharSequence csq, Charset cs,
                        OpenOption... options) throws IOException
```

Open or create a file denoted by the specified path, and writes characters in the CharSequence csq verbatim to the file, using either the UTF-8 charset or the specified charset, respectively.

No options implies the following options: CREATE, TRUNCATE_EXISTING, and WRITE.

```
static String readString(Path path) throws IOException
static String readString(Path path, Charset cs) throws IOException
```

Read all content from a file denoted by the specified path into a string, decoding the bytes to characters using the UTF-8 charset or the specified charset, respectively. The string returned will contain all characters, including line separators. These methods are not recommended for reading large files.

```
static List<String> readAllLines(Path path) throws IOException
static List<String> readAllLines(Path path, Charset cs) throws IOException
```

Read all *lines* from the file denoted by the specified path, decoding the bytes to characters using the UTF-8 charset or the specified charset, respectively. These methods are not recommended for reading large files, as these can result in a lethal java.lang.OutOfMemoryError.

The code at (5) to (8) in Example 21.2 illustrates methods of the Files class that directly write and read character data to a file denoted by a Path object.

The write() method at (5) writes an Iterable (in this case, the List of String) to the file in one operation. It automatically terminates each string written with a newline.

```
Files.write(path, lines);                                              // (5)
```

The writeString() method at (6) writes the contents of a single CharSequence (in this case, the string joinedLines) to the file. The strings in the lines list are joined with an appropriate line separator by the String.join() method. The end result written to the file is again lines of text.

```
String joinedLines = String.join(System.lineSeparator(), lines);
Files.writeString(path, joinedLines);                                  // (6)
```

The readString() method at (7) reads the *whole* file in one operation. It returns all characters read in a string, *including any line separators*.

```
String allContent = Files.readString(path);                            // (7)
```

The readAllLines() method at (8) reads all *text lines* in the file in one operation, returning the lines read in a List of String.

```
lines = Files.readAllLines(path);                                      // (8)
```

The methods in the Files class for writing and reading directly from a file denoted by a Path object should be used with care, as they might not scale up when handling large files. This is especially the case regarding the readString() and readAllLines() methods that read the whole file in one fell swoop. A better solution for reading text files using streams is provided later in the chapter (p. 1345).

Reading and Writing Bytes

The Files class also provides methods for reading and writing *bytes* to files. These methods that can be categorized as follows:

- Methods that create low-level *byte* I/O streams (InputStream, OutputStream) chained to a Path object that denotes a file. The methods of the I/O streams can then be used to read and write bytes to the file.

- Methods that directly use a Path object, and read and write bytes to the file denoted by the Path object.

Reading and Writing Bytes Using I/O Streams

The newInputStream() and newOutputStream() methods of the Files class create an input stream and an output stream, respectively, that are chained to a Path object denoting a file. Interoperability between I/O streams in the java.io package can then be leveraged to chain appropriate I/O streams for reading and writing data to a file (§20.2, p. 1234).

```
static InputStream newInputStream(Path path, OpenOption... options)
                              throws IOException
```

Opens a file denoted by the specified path, and returns an input stream to read from the file. No options implies the READ option.

```
static OutputStream newOutputStream(Path path, OpenOption... options)
                              throws IOException
```

Opens or creates a file denoted by the specified path, and returns an output stream that can be used to write bytes to the file. No options implies the following options: CREATE, TRUNCATE_EXISTING, and WRITE.

Previously we have seen how the copy() methods of the Files class use byte I/O streams for reading and writing bytes to files (p. 1311).

The code at (1) in Example 21.3 is a reworking of Example 20.1, p. 1237, to copy bytes from a source file to a destination file using an explicit byte buffer. The main difference is that the input stream and the output stream on the respective files are created by the newInputStream() and newOutputStream() methods of the Files class, based on Path objects that denote the files, rather than on file I/O streams. As before, the methods read() and write() of the InputStream and OutputStream classes, respectively, are used to read and write the bytes from the source file to the destination file using a byte buffer.

- -

Example 21.3 *Reading and Writing Bytes*

```
import java.io.*;
import java.nio.file.*;

public class ReadingWritingBytes {
  public static void main(String[] args) {
    // Source and destination files:
    Path srcPath  = Path.of("project", "source.dat");
    Path destPath = Path.of("project", "destination.dat");

    try (InputStream is = Files.newInputStream(srcPath);               // (1)
         OutputStream os = Files.newOutputStream(destPath))  {
      byte[] buffer = new byte[1024];
      int length = 0;
```

```
        while((length = is.read(buffer, 0, buffer.length)) != -1) {
          os.write(buffer, 0, length);
        }
    } catch (IOException ioe) {
      ioe.printStackTrace();
    }

    try {
      // Reads the file contents into an array of bytes:
      byte[] allBytes = Files.readAllBytes(srcPath);                    // (2)

      // Writes an array of bytes to a file:
      Files.write(destPath, allBytes);                                 // (3)
    } catch (IOException ioe) {
      ioe.printStackTrace();
    }
  }
}
```

Reading and Writing Bytes Using *Path* Objects

The Files class provides methods that directly use a Path object, and read and write bytes to the file denoted by the Path object, without the need to specify a file I/O stream. The method readAllBytes() reads all bytes from a file into a byte array in one operation, and the method write() writes the bytes in a byte array to a file. These methods also close the file when done.

static byte[] readAllBytes(Path path) throws IOException

Reads all the bytes from the file denoted by the specified path. The bytes are returned in a byte array.

static Path write(Path path, byte[] bytes, OpenOption... options)
            throws IOException

Writes bytes in a byte array to the file denoted by the specified path. No options implies the following options: CREATE, TRUNCATE_EXISTING, and WRITE.

The code at (2) and (3) in Example 21.3 shows yet another example of copying the contents of a source file to a destination file. The readAllBytes() and write() methods accomplish the task in a single call to each method.

```
byte[] allBytes = Files.readAllBytes(srcPath);                       // (2)
...
Files.write(destPath, allBytes);                                     // (3)
```

Note that these methods are meant for simple cases, and not for handling large files, as data is handled using an array of bytes.

21.6   Managing File Attributes

Useful metadata is associated with directory entries in a file system—for example, the file permissions that indicate whether the entry is readable or writable, or whether it is a symbolic link, and its size. Such metadata in the file system is often referred to as *file attributes*. Managing file attributes is a separate concern from the data that is stored in files.

There are basically two approaches provided by the NIO.2 API for managing file attributes:

- Accessing *individual file attributes* associated with a directory entry in the file system (p. 1321)
- Accessing a *set of file attributes* associated with a directory entry in the file system as a *bulk operation* (p. 1328)

Accessing Individual File Attributes

The Files class provides a myriad of static methods to access individual file attributes of a directory entry. It is a good idea to consult the code in Example 21.4 as we take a closer look at the relevant methods in this subsection. Since methods in the Files class can throw an IOException, the main() method specifies a throws clause with this exception.

Example 21.4   Accessing Individual Attributes

```
import java.io.IOException;
import java.nio.file.*;
import java.nio.file.attribute.*;
import java.util.*;

import static java.lang.System.out;
import static java.nio.file.attribute.PosixFilePermission.*;

public class IndividualFileAttributes {

  public static void main(String[] args) throws IOException {

    Path fPath = Path.of("project", "src", "pkg", "Main.java");
    out.println("File: " + fPath);

    out.println("Accessing Individual File Attributes:");
    out.println("size file (bytes): " + Files.size(fPath));          // (1)
    out.println("isDirectory:       " + Files.isDirectory(fPath));   // (2)
    out.println("isRegularFile:     " + Files.isRegularFile(fPath)); // (3)
    out.println("isSymbolicLink:    " + Files.isSymbolicLink(fPath));// (4)
    out.println();

    out.println("isReadable:        " + Files.isReadable(fPath));    // (5)
    out.println("isWritable:        " + Files.isWritable(fPath));    // (6)
```

```
        out.println("isExecutable:      " + Files.isExecutable(fPath));        // (7)
        out.println("isHidden:          " + Files.isHidden(fPath));            // (8)
        out.println();

        out.println("getLastModifiedTime: " + Files.getLastModifiedTime(fPath));// (9)
        out.println("getOwner:          " + Files.getOwner(fPath));            // (10)
        out.println();

        // Get the POSIX file permissions for the directory entry:
        Set<PosixFilePermission> filePermissions
            = Files.getPosixFilePermissions(fPath);                           // (11)
        out.println("getPosixFilePermissions (set): " + filePermissions);     // (12)
        out.println("getPosixFilePermissions (string): "
                + PosixFilePermissions.toString(filePermissions));            // (13)

        // Get the group of the directory entry:
        out.println("getAttribute-group:  " + Files.getAttribute(fPath,       // (14)
                                                    "posix:group"));
        out.println();

        // Update last modified time for the directory entry.               (15)
        long currentTime = System.currentTimeMillis();
        FileTime timestamp = FileTime.fromMillis(currentTime);
        Files.setLastModifiedTime(fPath, timestamp);

        // Set new owner for the directory entry.                           (16)
        FileSystem fs = fPath.getFileSystem();   // File system that created the path.
        UserPrincipalLookupService upls
            = fs.getUserPrincipalLookupService();// Obtain service to look up user.
        UserPrincipal user = upls.lookupPrincipalByName("khalid"); // User lookup.
        Files.setOwner(fPath, user);                             // Set user.

        // Set POSIX file permissions for the directory entry:              (17)
        Set<PosixFilePermission> newfilePermissions
            = EnumSet.of(OWNER_READ, OWNER_WRITE, GROUP_READ, GROUP_WRITE);  // (18a)
        //Set<PosixFilePermission> newfilePermissions
        //  = PosixFilePermissions.fromString("rw-rw----");                 // (18b)
        Files.setPosixFilePermissions(fPath, newfilePermissions);           // (19)
        filePermissions = Files.getPosixFilePermissions(fPath);
        out.println("getPosixFilePermissions (set): " + filePermissions);
        out.println("getPosixFilePermissions (string): "
                + PosixFilePermissions.toString(filePermissions));

        // Setting the value of a file attribute by its attribute name.
        Files.setAttribute(fPath, "lastAccessTime", timestamp);             // (20)
    }
}
```

Possible output from the program:

```
File: project/src/pkg/Main.java
Accessing Individual File Attributes:
size file (bytes): 13
```

```
isDirectory:        false
isRegularFile:      true
isSymbolicLink:     false

isReadable:         true
isWritable:         true
isExecutable:       false
isHidden:           false

getLastModifiedTime: 2021-08-06T10:28:47.416033Z
getOwner:            khalid

getPosixFilePermissions (set): [OTHERS_READ, OWNER_WRITE, OWNER_READ, GROUP_READ]
getPosixFilePermissions (string): rw-r--r--
getAttribute-group:  admin

getPosixFilePermissions (set): [GROUP_WRITE, OWNER_WRITE, OWNER_READ, GROUP_READ]
getPosixFilePermissions (string): rw-rw----
```

Determining the File Size

The method `size()` in the `Files` class is called at (1) in Example 21.4 to determine the size of the file denoted by the `Path` object. If the `Path` object denotes a directory, the method returns the size of the directory file and *not* the size of the entries in the directory.

> `static long size(Path path) throws IOException`
>
> Returns the size of a file (in bytes). The size of files that are not regular files is unspecified, as it is implementation specific.

Determining the Kind of Directory Entry

The following methods in the `Files` class are called at (2), (3), and (4) in Example 21.4 to determine what kind of directory entry is denoted by the `Path` object.

> `static boolean isDirectory(Path path, LinkOption... options)`
> `static boolean isRegularFile(Path path, LinkOption... options)`
> `static boolean isSymbolicLink(Path path)`
>
> Return `true` if the directory entry is a directory, a regular file, or a symbolic link, respectively. They return `false` if the directory entry does not exist, or is not of the expected kind, or it is not possible to determine what kind of directory entry it is. In the first two methods, symbolic links are followed by default, unless the constant `LinkOption.NOFOLLOW_LINKS` is specified.

Determining File Accessibility

The methods in the `Files` class shown below are called at (5), (6), (7), and (8) in Example 21.4, respectively, to determine accessibility of the directory entry denoted by the `Path` object.

```
static boolean isReadable(Path path)
static boolean isWritable(Path path)
static boolean isExecutable(Path path)
```

Test whether a file is readable, writable, or executable, respectively. The file must exist and the JVM must have the appropriate privileges to access the file.

Note that the result returned by these method is immediately outdated. The outcome of subsequent attempts to access the file is not guaranteed, as concurrently running threads might change the conditions after the method returns.

```
static boolean isHidden(Path path) throws IOException
```

Determines whether or not a file is considered *hidden*. The exact definition of a hidden file is platform specific. On Unix platforms, files whose name begins with a period character (.) are considered to be hidden.

Timestamp for Last Modification Time

Three different timestamps are associated with a directory entry, whose purpose is evident from their names: *last modified time, last access time*, and *creation time*. The timestamps are represented by the `java.nio.file.attribute.FileTime` class that provides the following methods for interoperability with `Instant` objects and with `long` values in milliseconds.

```
class java.nio.file.attribute.FileTime
```

```
static FileTime from(Instant instant)
static FileTime fromMillis(long value)
```

These static methods create a `FileTime` object representing the same point of time value on the timeline as the specified `Instant` object, or a `FileTime` object from the `long` value that specifies the number of milliseconds since the epoch (1970-01-01T00:00:00Z), respectively.

```
Instant toInstant()
long toMillis()
```

These instance methods convert this `FileTime` object to an `Instant` or to a `long` value in milliseconds from the epoch, respectively.

The `Files` class only provides static methods to read and update the last modified time of a directory entry. In Example 21.4, the statement at (9) prints the last modified time of the directory entry. The code at (15) sets the last modified time of the directory entry to the current time.

```
static FileTime getLastModifiedTime(Path path, LinkOption... options)
                                     throws IOException
static Path     setLastModifiedTime(Path path, FileTime time)
                                     throws IOException
```

Return or update the timestamp for the last modified time attribute of a directory entry, respectively. The timestamp is represented by the class java.nio .file.attribute.FileTime.

The first method follows symbolic links by default, unless the constant Link-Option.NOFOLLOW_LINKS is specified.

Accessing the Owner

The Files class only provides static methods to get and set the *owner* of a directory entry (i.e., one with a user account and appropriate access permissions). In Example 21.4, the statement at (10) prints the name of the owner of the directory entry. The code at (16) executes the necessary steps to obtain a user that can be set as the owner of the directory entry. This involves querying the file system to obtain the user look service and using the service to look up the user by name. We leave it to the reader to discover the exciting details from the API of the classes involved.

```
static UserPrincipal getOwner(Path path, LinkOption... options)
static Path setOwner(Path path, UserPrincipal owner)
```

Return or update the owner of a file, respectively.

Handling File Permissions

For a directory entry, POSIX-based file systems (*Portable Operating System Interface*) typically define *read*, *write*, and *execute* permissions for the *owner*, the *group* that the owner belongs to, and for *others*. In Java, these nine permissions are represented by the enum type PosixFilePermission (Table 21.10).

A human-readable form of file permissions affords interoperability with the enum type PosixFilePermission. This form is specified as a string of nine characters, where characters are interpreted as three permission groups of three characters. From the start of the string, the first permission group, the second permission group, and the third permission group specify the permissions for the owner, the group, and others, respectively. Each permission group is defined by the following pattern:

(r|-)(w|-)(x|-)

that is comprised of three groupings, where each grouping (a|b) is interpreted as either a or b. For example, rwx and --- are valid permissions groups, but w_w and xwr are not. The characters r, w, and x stand for read, write, and execute permissions, respectively, and the character - indicates that the permission corresponding to the position of the character - is not set.

The set of file permissions created by the following statement:

```
Set<PosixFilePermission> permSet1
    = EnumSet.of(OWNER_READ, OWNER_WRITE, GROUP_READ, OTHERS_READ);
```

is equivalent to the permissions in the string "rw-r--r--".

The utility class PosixFilePermissions provides methods for converting between the two forms of specifying file permissions.

Table 21.10 *POSIX File Permissions*

Enum type java.nio.file.attribute.PosixFilePermission	Description
OWNER_EXECUTE	Execute/search permission, owner
OWNER_READ	Read permission, owner
OWNER_WRITE	Write permission, owner
GROUP_EXECUTE	Execute/search permission, group
GROUP_READ	Read permission, group
GROUP_WRITE	Write permission, group
OTHERS_EXECUTE	Execute/search permission, others
OTHERS_READ	Read permission, others
OTHERS_WRITE	Write permission, others

Following are methods from the utility class java.nio.file.attribute.Posix-FilePermissions:

static Set<PosixFilePermission> fromString(String permStr)

Returns the set of permissions corresponding to a given String representation. The permStr parameter is a String representing the permissions, as explained earlier.

static String toString(Set<PosixFilePermission> perms)

Returns the String representation of a set of permissions.

static FileAttribute<Set<PosixFilePermission>>
        asFileAttribute(Set<PosixFilePermission> perms)

Creates a FileAttribute, encapsulating a copy of the given file permissions, suitable for passing to methods that create files and directories (p. 1339).

The getPosixFilePermissions() and setPosixFilePermissions() methods of the Files class can be used to retrieve and update file permissions of a directory entry, as shown at (11) and (19), respectively. The methods toString() and fromString() of the PosixFilePermissions class at (13) and (18b) convert between a set of Posix-FilePermission and a string representation of file permissions, respectively. Note that (18a) and (18b) define the same set of file permissions.

```
// Get the POSIX file permissions for the directory entry:
Set<PosixFilePermission> filePermissions
    = Files.getPosixFilePermissions(fPath);                                  // (11)
out.println("getPosixFilePermissions (set):    " + filePermissions);         // (12)
out.println("getPosixFilePermissions (string): "
            + PosixFilePermissions.toString(filePermissions));               // (13)
...
// Set POSIX file permissions for the directory entry:                       (17)
Set<PosixFilePermission> newfilePermissions
        = EnumSet.of(OWNER_READ, OWNER_WRITE, GROUP_READ, OTHERS_READ);//    (18a)
//Set<PosixFilePermission> newfilePermissions
//       = PosixFilePermissions.fromString("rw-r--r--");                     // (18b)
Files.setPosixFilePermissions(fPath, newfilePermissions);                    // (19)
```

The following methods from the utility class java.nio.file.Files can be used for retrieving and updating the POSIX-specific file permissions of a directory entry:

```
static Set<PosixFilePermission>
        getPosixFilePermissions(Path path, LinkOption... options)
                                 throws IOException
```

Returns POSIX permissions of a directory entry as a set of enum type Posix-FilePermission. By default, symbolic links are followed, unless the constant LinkOption.NOFOLLOW_LINKS is specified.

```
static Path setPosixFilePermissions(Path path,
                                   Set<PosixFilePermission> perms)
                                   throws IOException
```

Sets the POSIX permissions of a directory entry, given by the parameter perms.

Accessing File Attributes through View and Attribute Names

The getAttribute() and setAttribute() methods of the Files class are general methods that can be used to read and update any file attribute by its name. These methods are useful when the Files class does not provide a specialized method for a particular file attribute.

The statement at (14) in Example 21.4 prints the group of the directory entry. The full attribute name of the group attribute is specified as "posix:group", as the group attribute can be accessed via the POSIX file attribute view (p. 1336).

The statement at (20) in Example 21.4 sets the last access time of the directory entry to the current time. The attribute named "lastAccessTime" can be accessed via the basic file attribute view that is implied by default (p. 1334). The value of this file attribute is the FileTime object denoted by the timestamp reference.

```
static Object getAttribute(Path path, String attribute,
                           LinkOption... options) throws IOException
static Path   setAttribute(Path path, String attribute, Object value,
                           LinkOption... options) throws IOException
```

Read and set, respectively, the value of a file attribute of a directory entry denoted by the given Path object. By default, symbolic links are followed, unless the constant LinkOption.NOFOLLOW_LINKS is specified.

The attribute parameter has the general format:

   view-name:attribute-name

where the *view-name* can be omitted. Typical view names are "basic", "posix", and "dos". Omitting the *view-name* defaults to "basic". The *attribute-name* is the name of the file attribute—for example, "lastModifiedTime" or "lastAccess-Time". Attribute views are discussed in detail later (p. 1328).

The second method sets the file attribute to the value parameter.

Bulk Operations to Retrieve File Attributes

Accessing file attributes individually raises two concerns:

- Accessing an individual file attribute incurs a cost, and frequent such accesses can adversely impact performance.
- File attributes are very much file-system-specific, and therefore not conducive to generalizing over different file systems.

To address these concerns, the NIO.2 API provides *bulk operations* to retrieve file attributes—thus avoiding retrieval of individual file attributes and only handling file-system-specific attributes.

The following three approaches can be used to access file attributes of a directory entry in a file system:

- The methods of the Files class can be used to access individual file attributes of a directory entry denoted by a Path, as discussed earlier (p. 1321).
- A *bulk operation* using the readAttributes() method of the Files class can be used to retrieve a *set of file attributes* into a *read-only object* that implements *a file attributes interface*. This read-only object acts as a repository for file attribute values pertaining to the directory entry whose Path object was specified in the call to the readAttributes() method. The interface BasicFileAttributes, and its subinterfaces PosixFileAttributes and DosFileAttributes, define methods to read the retrieved file attribute values (Table 21.11, p. 1330).

In the code below at (1), the set of file attributes to read for the directory entry denoted by the path parameter is determined by the runtime object BasicFile-Attributes.class.

```
BasicFileAttributes bfa = Files.readAttributes(path,              // (1)
                                      BasicFileAttributes.class);
```

The retrieved values of the file attributes are accessible by querying the `BasicFileAttributes` object that is returned by the `readAttributes()` method (p. 1330).

- A *bulk operation* using the `getFileAttributeView()` method of the `Files` class can be used to retrieve *a set of file attributes* into an *updatable file attribute view* that acts as a repository object. This object can be used to read or update selected file attributes pertaining to the directory entry whose `Path` object was specified in the call to the `getFileAttributeView()` method. The interface `BasicFileAttributeView`, and its subinterfaces `PosixFileAttributeView` and `DosFileAttributeView`, define methods to read and update the retrieved file attributes (Table 21.12, p. 1334).

In the code below at (6), the set of file attributes to retrieve for the directory entry denoted by the path parameter is determined by the runtime object `Basic-FileAttributeView.class`.

```
BasicFileAttributeView bfaView = Files.getFileAttributeView(path,        // (6)
                                      BasicFileAttributeView.class);
```

The retrieved file attributes can be read and updated by querying the `Basic-FileAttributeView` object that is returned by the `getFileAttributeView()` method (p. 1334).

Details of the API for the `readAttributes()` and the `getFileAttributeView()` methods in the `Files` class are given below. By default, these methods follow symbolic links, unless the constant `LinkOption.NOFOLLOW_LINKS` is specified.

```
static <A extends BasicFileAttributes> A
       readAttributes(Path path, Class<A> type, LinkOption... options)
       throws IOException
```

Reads a *set of read-only file attributes* as a *bulk operation* for the directory entry denoted by the path parameter. The file attributes to retrieve are determined by the type parameter A. The parameter type is the `Class<A>` of the file attributes required to retrieve. The type parameter A is typically the interface `BasicFile-Attributes`, or one of its subinterfaces `PosixFileAttributes` or `DosFileAttributes` (Table 21.11, p. 1330).

```
static <V extends FileAttributeView> V
       getFileAttributeView(Path path, Class<V> type, LinkOption... options)
```

Reads a *set of file attributes* of a file as a *bulk operation*. It returns a *file attribute view* of a given type, which can be used to *read or update* the retrieved file attribute values. The file attributes to retrieve are determined by the type parameter V. The parameter type is the `Class<V>` of the file attributes required to retrieve. The type parameter V is typically the interface `BasicFileAttributeView`, or one of its subinterfaces `PosixFileAttributeView` or `DosFileAttributeView`— that are all subinterfaces of the `FileAttributeView` interface (Table 21.12, p. 1334).

```
static Map<String,Object> readAttributes(Path path, String attributes,
                                           LinkOption... options)
                           throws IOException
```

Reads a *set of file attributes* as a *bulk operation* for the directory entry denoted by the path parameter. It returns a map of file attribute names and their values.

The attributes parameter of type String has the general format:

   view-name:attribute-list

where the *view-name* can be omitted, and *attribute-list* is a comma-separated list of attribute names. Omitting the *view-name* defaults to "basic". For example, "*" will read all BasicFileAttributes, and "lastModifiedTime,lastAccessTime" will read only last modified time and last access time attributes.

Table 21.11 summarizes the interfaces that provide read-only access to file attribute values. The BasicFileAttributes interface defines the basic set of file attributes that are common to many file systems. Its two subinterfaces PosixFileAttributes and DosFileAttributes define *additional* file attributes associated with POSIX-based and DOS-based file systems, respectively. An object of the appropriate file attributes interface pertaining to a specific directory entry is returned by the Files.read-Attributes() method.

Table 21.11   *Interfaces for Read-Only Access to File Attributes*

Read-only file attributes interfaces in the java.nio.file.attribute package.	Note that when an object of the read-only file attributes interface is created, it is opened on a specific directory entry in the file system. The object provides information about file attributes associated with this directory entry. The methods in these interfaces do not throw a checked exception.
BasicFileAttributes	Provides *read-only* access to a basic set of file attributes that are common to many file systems (p. 1330).
PosixFileAttributes extends BasicFileAttributes	In addition to the basic set of file attributes, provides *read-only* access to file attributes associated with POSIX-based file systems (p. 1332).
DosFileAttributes extends BasicFileAttributes	In addition to the basic set of file attributes, provides *read-only* access to file attributes associated with DOS/ Windows-based file systems (p. 1333).

The BasicFileAttributes Interface

The methods of the java.nio.file.attribute.BasicFileAttributes interface reflect the basic set of file attributes that are common to most file systems.

```
interface java.nio.file.attribute.BasicFileAttributes
```

```
long size()
```
Returns the size of the directory entry (in bytes).

```
boolean isDirectory()
boolean isRegularFile()
boolean isSymbolicLink()
boolean isOther()
```
Determine whether the directory entry is of a specific kind.

```
FileTime lastModifiedTime()
FileTime lastAccessTime()
FileTime creationTime()
```
Return the appropriate timestamp for the directory entry.

The method printBasicFileAttributes() of the utility class FileUtils, shown below, prints the values of the basic file attributes by calling the relevant methods on the BasicFileAttributes object that is passed as a parameter.

```
// Declared in utility class FileUtils.
public static void printBasicFileAttributes(BasicFileAttributes bfa) {
  out.println("Printing basic file attributes:");
  out.println("lastModifiedTime: " + bfa.lastModifiedTime());
  out.println("lastAccessTime:   " + bfa.lastAccessTime());
  out.println("creationTime:     " + bfa.creationTime());

  out.println("size:             " + bfa.size());
  out.println("isDirectory:      " + bfa.isDirectory());
  out.println("isRegularFile:    " + bfa.isRegularFile());
  out.println("isSymbolicLink:   " + bfa.isSymbolicLink());
  out.println("isOther:          " + bfa.isOther());
  out.println();
}
```

The code below obtains a BasicFileAttributes object at (1) that pertains to the file denoted by the path reference. The printBasicFileAttributes() method is called at (2) with this BasicFileAttributes object as the parameter.

```
Path path = Path.of("project", "src", "pkg", "Main.java");
out.println("File: " + path);
BasicFileAttributes bfa = Files.readAttributes(path,             // (1)
                                    BasicFileAttributes.class);
FileUtils.printBasicFileAttributes(bfa);                         // (2)
```

Possible output from the code:

```
File: project/src/pkg/Main.java
Printing basic file attributes:
lastModifiedTime: 2021-07-23T10:15:34.854Z
lastAccessTime:   2021-07-23T10:16:33.166281Z
creationTime:     2021-07-20T23:03:58Z
size:             116
isDirectory:      false
```

```
isRegularFile:    true
isSymbolicLink:   false
isOther:          false
```

Note that the basic file attributes in the `BasicFileAttributes` object are read-only, as the `BasicFileAttributes` interface does not provide any set methods. However, values of updatable file attributes can be changed by appropriate set methods of the `Files` class (p. 1321).

The `PosixFileAttributes` Interface

As the `PosixFileAttributes` interface is a subinterface of the `BasicFileAttributes` interface, a `PosixFileAttributes` object has both the basic set of file attributes and the POSIX-specific file attributes.

```
interface java.nio.file.attribute.PosixFileAttributes
            extends BasicFileAttributes
```

```
UserPrincipal owner()
GroupPrincipal group()
```

Return the owner or the group of the directory entry, represented by the interface `java.nio.file.attribute.UserPrincipal` and its subinterface `java.nio.file.attribute.GroupPrincipal`, respectively.

```
Set<PosixFilePermission> permissions()
```

Returns a set with a copy of the POSIX permissions for the directory entry. Permissions are defined by the enum type `PosixFilePermission` discussed earlier in this chapter (Table 21.10, p. 1326).

The methods of the subinterface `PosixFileAttributes` augment the basic set of file attributes with the following POSIX-specific attributes: owner, group, and file permissions. The method `printPosixFileAttributes()` in the utility class `FileUtils`, shown below, prints the values of the POSIX-specific file attributes by calling the relevant methods on the `PosixFileAttributes` object that is passed as a parameter.

```
// Declared in the utility class FileUtils.
public static void printPosixFileAttributes(PosixFileAttributes pfa) {
  out.println("Printing POSIX-specific file attributes:");
  UserPrincipal user = pfa.owner();
  GroupPrincipal group = pfa.group();
  Set<PosixFilePermission> permissions = pfa.permissions();
  String perms = PosixFilePermissions.toString(permissions);

  out.println("owner:          " + user);
  out.println("group:          " + group);
  out.println("permissions:    " + perms);
  out.println();
}
```

The code below obtains a `PosixFileAttributes` object at (3) that pertains to the file denoted by the path reference. Both the `printBasicFileAttributes()` method and the `printPosixFileAttributes()` method are called at (4) and (5), respectively, with this `PosixFileAttributes` object as the parameter. The call to the `printBasicFile-Attributes()` method at (4) will print the basic file attributes in the `PosixFileAttributes` object.

```
Path path = Path.of("project", "src", "pkg", "Main.java");
out.println("File: " + path);
PosixFileAttributes pfa = Files.readAttributes(path,                  // (3)
                                      PosixFileAttributes.class);
FileUtils.printBasicFileAttributes(pfa);                             // (4)
FileUtils.printPosixFileAttributes(pfa);                            // (5)
```

Possible output from the code:

```
File: project/src/pkg/Main.java
Printing basic file attributes:
...
Printing POSIX-specific file attributes:
owner:         javadude
group:         admin
permissions:   rw-r--r--
```

Note that both the basic and the POSIX-specific file attributes in the `PosixFileAttributes` object are read-only, as the `PosixFileAttributes` interface does not provide any set methods. However, values of updatable file attributes can be changed by appropriate set methods of the `Files` class (p. 1321).

The `DosFileAttributes` Interface

As the `DosFileAttributes` interface is a subinterface of the `BasicFileAttributes` interface, a `DosFileAttributes` object has both the basic set of file attributes and the DOS-specific file attributes. Its usage is analogous to the `PosixFileAttributes` interface discussed earlier (p. 1332).

```
interface java.nio.file.attribute.DosFileAttributes
        extends BasicFileAttributes

boolean isReadOnly()
boolean isSystem()
boolean isArchive()
boolean isHidden()
```

Determine whether the file entry is of a specific kind.

File Attribute Views

Table 21.12 summarizes the *file attribute views* that different interfaces provide for *readable or updatable* access to file attributes, in contrast to the file attributes interfaces in Table 21.11, p. 1330, that allow read-only access. The `BasicFileAttributeView` interface allows access to the basic set of file attributes that are common to many file systems. Its two subinterfaces, `PosixFileAttributeView` and `DosFileAttributeView`, additionally allow access to file attributes associated with POSIX-based and DOS-based file systems, respectively.

An object of the appropriate view interface pertaining to a specific directory entry is returned by the `Files.getFileAttributeView()` method. All file interface views provide a `readAttributes()` method that returns the read-only file attributes object associated with the view.

Table 21.12   *Selected File Attribute Views*

Updatable file attribute view interfaces in the java.nio.file.attribute package.	Note that when the view is created, it is opened on a specific directory entry in the file system. The view provides information about file attributes associated with this directory entry.
`AttributeView`	Can read or update non-opaque values associated with directory entries in a file system.
`FileAttributeView` extends `AttributeView`	Can read or update file attributes.
`FileOwnerAttributeView` extends `FileAttributeView`	Can read or update the owner.

`BasicFileAttributeView`
extends `FileAttributeView`
 	
Corresponding read-only file attributes interface:
`BasicFileAttributes`
	Can read or update a basic set of file attributes. Can obtain a read-only `BasicFileAttributes` object via the view. Can set a timestamp for when the directory entry was last modified, last accessed, and created. (p. 1334)

`PosixFileAttributeView`
extends `BasicFileAttributeView`,
`FileOwnerAttributeView`
 	
Corresponding read-only file attributes interface:
`PosixFileAttributes`
	Can read or update POSIX file attributes. Can obtain a read-only `PosixFileAttributes` object via the view. Can set group and file permissions, and update the owner. (p. 1336)

`DosFileAttributeView`
extends `BasicFileAttributeView`
 	
Corresponding read-only file attributes interface:
`DosFileAttributes`
	Can read or update DOS file attributes. Can obtain a read-only `DosFileAttributes` object via the view. Can set archive, hidden, read-only, and system attributes. (p. 1338)

The `BasicFileAttributeView` Interface

The `java.nio.file.attribute.BasicFileAttributeView` interface defines a file attribute view for the basic set of file attributes.

```
interface BasicFileAttributeView extends FileAttributeView
```

```
String name()
```

Returns the name of the attribute view, which in this case is the string "basic".

```
BasicFileAttributes readAttributes()
```

Reads the basic file attributes as a bulk operation. The `BasicFileAttributes` object can be used to read the values of the basic file attributes (p. 1330). This method is analogous to the `readAttributes()` method of the `Files` class (p. 1328).

```
void setTimes(FileTime lastModifiedTime,
              FileTime lastAccessTime,
              FileTime createTime)
```

Updates any or all timestamps for the file's last modified time, last access time, and creation time attributes. If any parameter has the value `null`, the corresponding timestamp is not changed. Note that apart from the `Files.setLast-Modified()` method, there are no methods in the `Files` class for the last access and creation times for a directory entry.

The code below obtains a `BasicFileAttributeView` object at (6) that pertains to the file denoted by the path reference. A `BasicFileAttributes` object is obtained at (7), providing read-only access to the basic file attributes, whose values are printed by calling the `printBasicFileAttributes()` method. The last modified time of the directory entry is explicitly read by calling the `lastModifiedTime()` method of the `Basic-FileAttributes` object.

```
Path path = Path.of("project", "src", "pkg", "Main.java");
out.println("File: " + path);

BasicFileAttributeView bfaView = Files.getFileAttributeView(path,        // (6)
                                        BasicFileAttributeView.class);
System.out.printf("Using view: %s%n", bfaView.name());


// Reading the basic set of file attributes:                            (7)
BasicFileAttributes bfa2 = bfaView.readAttributes();
FileUtils.printBasicFileAttributes(bfa2);
FileTime currentLastModifiedTime = bfa2.lastModifiedTime();


// Updating timestamp for last modified time using view:               (8)
long newLMTinMillis = currentLastModifiedTime.toMillis() + 15*60*1000L;
FileTime newLastModifiedTime = FileTime.fromMillis(newLMTinMillis);
bfaView.setTimes(newLastModifiedTime, null, null);


// Reading the updated last modified time:                             (9)
out.println("updated lastModifiedTime (incorrect): "
                              + bfa2.lastModifiedTime());    // (10)
out.println("updated lastModifiedTime: "
                              + Files.getLastModifiedTime(path)); // (11)
out.println("updated lastModifiedTime: " + Files.getAttribute(path,    // (12)
                              "basic:lastModifiedTime"));
```

Possible output from the code:

```
File: project/src/pkg/Main.java
Using view: basic
Printing basic file attributes:
...
lastModifiedTime: 2021-07-26T15:15:46.813Z
...
updated lastModifiedTime (incorrect): 2021-07-26T15:15:46.813Z
updated lastModifiedTime: 2021-07-26T15:30:46.813Z
updated lastModifiedTime: 2021-07-26T15:30:46.813Z
```

The BasicFileAttributeView object allows the last modified, last access, and creation times of the directory entry to be updated by calling the setTimes() method. The code at (9) shows how the last modified time of the directory entry can be updated to a new value via the view. A FileTime object is created representing the new last modified time by first converting the current last modified time to milliseconds and incrementing it by 15 minutes. In the call to the setTimes() method, only the last modified time is specified. The other timestamps are specified as null, indicating that they should not be changed.

In order to verify the new last modified time, we might be tempted to use the current BasicFileAttributes object associated with the view, but its copies of the file attribute values are not updatable. We can create a new BasicFileAttributes object that reflects the new values of the file attributes, or alternately use the getLastModifiedTime() or the getAttribute() methods of the Files class, as shown at (11) and (12), respectively.

The PosixFileAttributeView Interface

As the PosixFileAttributeView interface is a subinterface of the BasicFileAttributeView interface, it allows both the basic set of file attributes and the POSIX-specific file attributes to be read and updated.

```
interface PosixFileAttributeView
        extends BasicFileAttributeView, FileOwnerAttributeView
```

String name()
Returns the name of the attribute view, which in this case is the string "posix".

PosixFileAttributes readAttributes()
Retrieves the basic and POSIX-specific file attributes as a bulk operation into a PosixFileAttributes object whose methods can be used to read the values of these file attributes (p. 1332). This method is analogous to the readAttributes() method of the Files class (p. 1328).

void setGroup(GroupPrincipal group) throws IOException
Updates the group of the directory entry. Note that there is no analogous method in the Files class for handling the group.

```
void setPermissions(Set<PosixFilePermission> perms)
```

Updates the file permissions. This method is analogous to the `Files.setPosix-FilePermissions()` method (p. 1325).

The `PosixFileAttributeView` interface extends the `java.nio.file.attribute.File-OwnerAttributeView` interface that defines the methods for reading and updating the owner of the directory entry. See also analogous methods relating to ownership in the `Files` class (p. 1325).

```
interface java.nio.file.attribute.FileOwnerAttributeView
        extends FileAttributeView
```

```
UserPrincipal getOwner() throws IOException
void           setOwner(UserPrincipal owner) throws IOException
```

Return or update the owner of a directory entry, respectively. These methods are analogous to the methods in the `Files` class (p. 1325).

A `PosixFileAttributeView` object can thus read both the basic set of file attributes and the POSIX-specific file attributes, and can update the owner, group, file permissions, and timestamps for the last modified, last access, and creation times for a directory entry.

The code below obtains a `PosixFileAttributeView` object at (13) that pertains to the file denoted by the `path` reference. The associated `PosixFileAttributes` object is obtained at (14), providing read-only access to the basic file attributes and the POSIX-specific file attributes, whose values are printed by calling the methods `printBasicFileAttributes()` and `printPosixFileAttributes()` in the utility class `FileUtils`, respectively.

```
Path path = Path.of("project", "src", "pkg", "Main.java");
out.println("File: " + path);

PosixFileAttributeView pfaView = Files.getFileAttributeView(path,      // (13)
                                        PosixFileAttributeView.class);
System.out.printf("Using view: %s%n", pfaView.name());

// Reading the basic + POSIX set of file attributes:                   // (14)
PosixFileAttributes pfa2 = pfaView.readAttributes();
FileUtils.printBasicFileAttributes(pfa2);
FileUtils.printPosixFileAttributes(pfa2);

// Updating owner and group file attributes using view.                // (15)
FileSystem fs = path.getFileSystem();
UserPrincipalLookupService upls = fs.getUserPrincipalLookupService();
UserPrincipal newUser = upls.lookupPrincipalByName("javadude");
GroupPrincipal newGroup = upls.lookupPrincipalByGroupName("admin");
pfaView.setOwner(newUser);
pfaView.setGroup(newGroup);

//Updating file permissions using view.                                // (16)
Set<PosixFilePermission> newPerms = PosixFilePermissions.fromString("r--r--r--");
pfaView.setPermissions(newPerms);
```

```
//Updating last access time using view.                                // (17)
FileTime currentAccessTime = pfa2.lastAccessTime();
long newLATinMillis = currentAccessTime.toMillis() + 10*60*1000L;
FileTime newLastAccessTime = FileTime.fromMillis(newLATinMillis);
pfaView.setTimes(null, newLastAccessTime, null);

// Reading the updated file attributes:                                 // (18)
pfa2 = pfaView.readAttributes();
FileUtils.printBasicFileAttributes(pfa2);
FileUtils.printPosixFileAttributes(pfa2);
```

The code from (15) to (17) shows how the PosixFileAttributeView object can be used to update various file attributes. Keep in mind that this view inherits from the BasicFileAttributeView and the FileOwnerAttributeView interfaces.

The code at (15) updates the owner and the group of the directory entry via the view. An owner and a group are looked up in the appropriate lookup services, and updated by the setOwner() and setGroup() methods of the PosixFileAttributeView interface. See also corresponding methods in the Files class (p. 1325).

The code at (16) updates the file permissions of the directory entry via the view, analogous to the Files.setPosixFilePermissions() method (p. 1325). File permissions are set to read-only for the owner, the group, and other users.

The code at (17) updates only the last access time of the directory entry via the view, analogous to updating the last modified time via the BasicFileAttributeView object (p. 1334).

Updated file attribute values can be read using the appropriate methods of the Files class, or by obtaining a new PosixFileAttributes object, as shown at (18).

The DosFileAttributeView Interface

As the DosFileAttributeView interface is a subinterface of the BasicFileAttributeView interface, it allows both the basic set of file attributes and the DOS-specific file attributes to be read and updated. Its usage is analogous to the PosixFileAttributeView interface discussed earlier (p. 1336).

```
interface DosFileAttributeView extends BasicFileAttributeView
```

```
String name()
```
Returns the name of the attribute view, which in this case is the string "dos".

```
DosFileAttributes readAttributes()
```
Reads the basic file attributes as a bulk operation. The DosFileAttributes object can be used to read the values of the basic and DOS-specific file attributes (p. 1333). This method is analogous to the readAttributes() method of the Files class (p. 1328)

```
void setReadOnly(boolean value)
void setSystem(boolean value)
void setArchive(boolean value)
void setHidden(boolean value)
```

Update the value of the appropriate attribute. These methods are all implementation specific.

21.7 Creating Directory Entries

The Files class provides methods for creating files and directories. These methods can accept a variable arity parameter of type FileAttribute<?>. The interface java.nio .file.attribute.FileAttribute<T> defines an object that encapsulates the value of a file attribute that can be set when a file or a directory is created by these methods. For a POSIX-based file system, the PosixFilePermissions.asFileAttribute() method creates a FileAttribute that encapsulates a set of type PosixFilePermission (p. 1325).

The methods for creating regular files and directories throw a FileAlreadyExists-Exception if the directory entry with that name already exists. All methods for creating directory entries can throw an IOException, and should be called in a try block or the exception should be specified in a throws clause.

The steps to check whether the directory entry exists and to create the new directory entry if it does not exist are performed as a single *atomic operation*.

The following code calls the printDirEntryInfo() method in the utility class FileUtils on a path to print what kind of directory entry it denotes and its file permissions.

```
public static void printDirEntryInfo(Path path) throws IOException {
    String fmt = Files.isSymbolicLink(path)? "Symbolic link: %s%n":
        Files.isRegularFile(path)? "File: %s%n":
            Files.isDirectory(path)? "Directory: %s%n":
                "Directory entry: %s%n";
    out.printf(fmt, path);
    Set<PosixFilePermission> perms = Files.getPosixFilePermissions(path);
    String permStr = PosixFilePermissions.toString(perms);
    out.println(permStr);
}
```

Creating Regular and Temporary Files

The following methods of the Files class can be used to create regular and temporary files, and symbolic links.

```
static Path createFile(Path path, FileAttribute<?>... attrs)
                       throws IOException
```

Creates an empty file that is denoted by the path parameter, but fails by throwing a FileAlreadyExistsException if the file already exists. It does *not* create nonexistent parent directories, and throws a NoSuchFileException if any parent directory does not exist.

```
static Path createTempFile(String prefix, String suffix,
                           FileAttribute<?>... attrs) throws IOException
static Path createTempFile(Path dir, String prefix, String suffix,
                           FileAttribute<?>... attrs) throws IOException
```

Create an empty file in the *default temporary-file directory* or in the *specified directory* denoted by the Path object, respectively, using the specified prefix and suffix to generate its name. The default temporary-file directory and naming of temporary files is file-system-specific.

```
static Path createSymbolicLink(Path symLink, Path target,
                               FileAttribute<?>... attrs) throws IOException
```

Creates a symbolic link to a target (*optional operation*). When the target is a *relative path* then file system operations on the target are relative to the path of the symbolic link. The target of the symbolic link need not exist. Throws a File-AlreadyExistsException if a directory entry with the same name as the symbolic link already exists.

```
static Path readSymbolicLink(Path symLink) throws IOException
```

Returns a Path object that denoted the target of a symbolic link (*optional operation*). The target of the symbolic link need not exist.

For creating files, we will use the following FileAttribute object denoted by the fileAttr reference (p. 1325). It specifies read and write permissions for the owner, but only read access for the group and others.

```
Set<PosixFilePermission> filePerms = PosixFilePermissions.fromString("rw-r--r--");
FileAttribute<Set<PosixFilePermission>> fileAttr =
        PosixFilePermissions.asFileAttribute(perms);
```

Creating Regular Files

The createFile() method of the Files class fails to create a regular file if the file already exists, or the parent directories on the path do not exist. The code below at (1) creates a file with the path project/docs/readme.txt relative to the current directory under the assumption that the file name does not exist and the parent directories exist on the path. However, running this code repeatedly will result in a FileAlreadyExistsException, unless the file is deleted (e.g., calling Files.deleteIf-Exists(regularFile)) before rerunning the code.

```
try {
  Path regularFile  = Path.of("project", "docs", "readme.txt");
  Path createdFile1 = Files.createFile(regularFile, fileAttr);        // (1)
  FileUtils.printDirEntryInfo(createdFile1);
} catch (NoSuchFileException | FileAlreadyExistsException fe) {
  fe.printStackTrace();
} catch (IOException ioe) {
  ioe.printStackTrace();
}
```

Possible output from the code:

```
File: project/docs/readme.txt
rw-r--r--
```

Creating Temporary Files

Programs usually create temporary files during execution, and delete such files when done in the interest of good housekeeping. The JVM defines a system property for the default temporary-file directory where temporary files are created, if a specific location is not specified. This location is printed by the code below at (1).

How the name of the temporary file is generated is file-system specific. The code at (2) creates a temporary file under the default temporary-file directory, that has default file permissions.

The code at (3) creates temporary files under a specific directory. How the specification of file name prefix and suffix affect the generated file name can be seen in the output, where the null value as the prefix omits the prefix, and the null value as the suffix appends the default file name extension ".tmp".

The NIO.2 API does not define a method to request that a file be deleted when the JVM terminates.

```java
try {
    // System property that defines the default temporary-file directory.       (1)
    String tmpdir = System.getProperty("java.io.tmpdir");
    System.out.println("Default temporary directory: " + tmpdir);

    // Create under the default temporary-file directory.                       (2)
    Path tmpFile1 = Files.createTempFile("events", ".log");
    FileUtils.printDirEntryInfo(tmpFile1);

    // Create under a specific directory:                                        (3)
    Path tmpFileDir = Path.of("project");
    Path tmpFile2 = Files.createTempFile(tmpFileDir, "proj_", ".dat", fileAttr);
    Path tmpFile3 = Files.createTempFile(tmpFileDir, "proj_", null,   fileAttr);
    Path tmpFile4 = Files.createTempFile(tmpFileDir, null,    ".dat", fileAttr);
    Path tmpFile5 = Files.createTempFile(tmpFileDir, null,    null,   fileAttr);
    FileUtils.printDirEntryInfo(tmpFile2);
    FileUtils.printDirEntryInfo(tmpFile3);
    FileUtils.printDirEntryInfo(tmpFile4);
    FileUtils.printDirEntryInfo(tmpFile5);
} catch (IOException ioe) {
    ioe.printStackTrace();
}
```

Possible output from the code (*edited to fit on the page*):

```
Default temporary directory: /var/folders/cr/wk7fqcjx07z95d9vxcgjnrtc0000gr/T/
File:
/var/folders/cr/wk7fqcjx07z95d9vxcgjnrtc0000gr/T/events4720093907665196131.log
rw-------
File: project/proj_6062790522710209175.dat
rw-r--r--
File: project/proj_9570151255593453845.tmp
rw-r--r--
File: project/3032983609251590109.dat
rw-r--r--
File: project/8205471872222375044.tmp
rw-r--r--
```

Creating Symbolic Links

The code below illustrates creating symbolic links to directory entries. We assume that the symbolic link at (1) below does not exist; otherwise, a resounding `File-AlreadyExistsException` will be thrown by the `createSymbolicLink()` method of the `Files` class. However, the target path need *not* exists, but that might limit the file operations that can be performed using the symbolic link. We assume that the target path at (2) exists when the code below is run.

The `createSymbolicLink()` method can be called with a relative path or the absolute path of the target, as shown at (3a) and (3b), respectively. In both cases, the symbolic link will be created with the default file permissions, as we have not specified the optional `FileAttribute` variable arity parameter. Note that the symbolic link is created to a file or a directory, depending on the kind of the target.

The method `readSymbolicLink()` method of the `Files` class returns the path of the target denoted by the symbolic link.

```
try {
  Path symbLinkPath  = Path.of(".", "readme_link");                      // (1)
  Path targetPath     = Path.of(".", "project", "backup", "readme.txt"); // (2)

  Path symbLink = Files.createSymbolicLink(symbLinkPath, targetPath);    // (3a)
//Path symbLink = Files.createSymbolicLink(symbLinkPath,
//                                          targetPath.toAbsolutePath());// (3b)
  Path target = Files.readSymbolicLink(symbLink);                        // (4)

  FileUtils.printDirEntryInfo(symbLink);
  FileUtils.printDirEntryInfo(target);
} catch (FileAlreadyExistsException fe) {
  fe.printStackTrace();
} catch (IOException ioe) {
  ioe.printStackTrace();
}
```

Possible output from the code:

```
Symbolic link: ./readme_link
rw-r--r--
File: ./project/backup/readme.txt
rw-r--r--
```

Creating Regular and Temporary Directories

The `Files` class provides methods to create regular and temporary directories.

```
static Path createDirectory(Path dir, FileAttribute<?>... attrs)
                    throws IOException
```

Creates a new directory denoted by the `Path` object. It does *not* create nonexistent parent directories, and throws a `NoSuchFileException` if any parent directory does not exist. It also throws a `FileAlreadyExistsException` if the directory entry with that name already exists.

```
static Path createDirectories(Path dir, FileAttribute<?>... attrs)
              throws IOException
```

Creates a directory by creating all nonexistent parent directories first. It does not throw an exception if any of the directories already exist. If the method fails, some directories may have been created.

```
static Path createTempDirectory(String prefix, FileAttribute<?>... attrs)
                                 throws IOException
static Path createTempDirectory(Path dir, String prefix,
                                FileAttribute<?>... attrs)
                                 throws IOException
```

Create a new directory in the *default temporary-file directory* or in the *specified directory* denoted by the Path object, using the mandatory non-null prefix to append to its generated name. A NoSuchFileException is thrown by the second method if the specified location does not exist.

For creating directories, we will use the following FileAttribute object denoted by the dirFileAttr reference (p. 1325). It specifies read, write, and execute permissions for all users: the owner, the group, and others—often called *full permissions*.

```
Set<PosixFilePermission> dPerms = PosixFilePermissions.fromString("rwxrwxrwx");
FileAttribute<Set<PosixFilePermission>> dirFileAttr =
        PosixFilePermissions.asFileAttribute(dPerms);
```

Creating Regular Directories

The Files class provides two methods to create regular directories. The create-Directory() method fails to create a regular directory if the directory already exists, or if the parent directories on the path do not exist. The code below creates a directory with the path project/bin relative to the current directory, under the assumption that the directory name bin does not exist and the parent directory ./project exists on the path. The directory is first created with the default file permissions at (1), then deleted at (2) and created again at (3) with specific file permissions. The second call to the createDirectory() method at (3) would throw a FileAlready-ExistsException if we did not delete the directory before creating it with specific file permissions.

The astute reader will have noticed from the output that the *write* permission for the group and others is not set at creation time by the createDirectory() method, regardless of the file permissions specified. This can be remedied by setting the file permissions explicitly after the directory has been created, as at (4).

```
try {
  Path regularDir  = Path.of("project", "bin");
  Path createdDir = Files.createDirectory(regularDir);              // (1)
  FileUtils.printDirEntryInfo(createdDir);

  if (Files.deleteIfExists(regularDir)) {                           // (2)
    System.out.printf("Directory deleted: %s%n", regularDir);
  }
  Path newDir = Files.createDirectory(regularDir, dirFileAttr);     // (3)
  FileUtils.printDirEntryInfo(newDir);
```

```
    Files.setPosixFilePermissions(newDir, dPerms);                    // (4)
    FileUtils.printDirEntryInfo(newDir);
} catch (NoSuchFileException | FileAlreadyExistsException fe) {
    fe.printStackTrace();
} catch (IOException ioe) {
    ioe.printStackTrace();
}
```

Possible output from the code:

```
Directory: project/bin
rwxr-xr-
Directory deleted: project/bin
Directory: project/bin
rwxr-xr-x
Directory: project/bin
rwxrwxrwx
```

The method createDirectories() first creates all nonexistent parent directories in the path if necessary, and only creates the directory if it does not exist—a convenient way to ensure that a directory always exists. In the code below at (5), the parent directories (in the path project/branches/maintenance) are created from top to bottom, relative to the current directory if necessary, and the directory versions is only created if it does not exist from before. A FileAlreadyExistsException at (6) is thrown if a directory entry named versions exists, but is not a directory.

```
try {
    Path regularDir2 = Path.of("project", "branches", "maintenance", "versions");
    Path createdDir2 = Files.createDirectories(regularDir2, dirFileAttr);  // (5)
    FileUtils.printDirEntryInfo(createdDir2);
} catch (FileAlreadyExistsException fe) {                              // (6)
    fe.printStackTrace();
} catch (IOException ioe) {
    ioe.printStackTrace();
}
```

Output from the code:

```
Directory: project/branches/maintenance/versions
rwxrwxrwx
```

Creating Temporary Directories

Analogous to temporary files, temporary directories can be created by the create-TempDirectory() methods of the Files class. Again, these directories can be created in the default temporary-file directory, or in a specific location if one is specified in the method call, with either the default file permissions or specific permissions.

The code at (7) creates a temporary directory named "log_dir" under the default temporary-file directory. A temporary directory with the same name is also created under a specific location (the ./project directory) at (8). A NoSuchFileException is thrown if the specified location does not exist. A prefix can be specified for the directory name or it can be null.

```
try {
    // Create under the default temporary-file directory.                (7)
    Path tmpDirPath1 = Files.createTempDirectory("log_dir", dirFileAttr);
    FileUtils.printDirEntryInfo(tmpDirPath1);

    // Create under a specific location:                                 (8)
    Path tmpDirLoc = Path.of("project");
    Path tmpDirPath2 = Files.createTempDirectory(tmpDirLoc, "log_dir", dirFileAttr);
    Path tmpDirPath3 = Files.createTempDirectory(tmpDirLoc, null, dirFileAttr);
    FileUtils.printDirEntryInfo(tmpDirPath2);
    FileUtils.printDirEntryInfo(tmpDirPath3);

    Files.setPosixFilePermissions(tmpDirPath3, dPerms);                  // (9)
    FileUtils.printDirEntryInfo(tmpDirPath3);
} catch (NoSuchFileException nsfe) {
    nsfe.printStackTrace();
} catch (IOException ioe) {
    ioe.printStackTrace();
}
```

Possible output from the code (*edited to fit the page*):

```
Directory:
/var/folders/cr/wk7fqcjx07z95d9vxcgjnrtc0000gr/T/log_dir18136008118052819366
rwxr-xr-x
Directory: project/log_dir14908011762674796217
rwxr-xr-x
Directory: project/18428782809319921018
rwxr-xr-x
Directory: project/18428782809319921018
rwxrwxrwx
```

We notice from the output that the *write* permission for the group and others is not set at creation time by the `createTempDirectory()` method, regardless of the file permissions specified. Again, this can be remedied by setting the file permissions explicitly after the temporary directory has been created, as at (9).

21.8 Stream Operations on Directory Entries

The `Files` class provides static methods that create specialized streams to implement complex file operations on directory entries, which are concise and powerful, taking full advantage of the Stream API. They are also efficient as the lazy execution of the streams ensures that an element is only made available for processing when needed by the terminal stream operation.

Streams we have seen earlier do not use any system resources, as they are backed by data structures and generator functions. Such streams need not be closed, as they are handled as any other objects by the runtime environment with regard to memory management. In contrast, the streams that are backed by *file system resources* must be closed in order to avoid resource leakage—analogous to using I/O streams. As streams implement the AutoCloseable interface, the recommended practice is to use the try-with-resources statement, ensuring proper and prompt closing of file system resources after the stream operations complete.

Methods that create streams on directory entries throw a checked IOException, and in particular, they throw a NoSuchFileException if the directory entry does not exist. Any code using these methods is forced to handle these exceptions with either a try-catch-finally construct or a throws clause.

The examples in this section illustrate both closing of streams and handling of exceptions.

Reading Text Lines Using a Functional Stream

The lines() method of the Files class creates a stream that can be used to read the lines in a text file. It is efficient as it does not read the whole file into memory, making available only one line at a time for processing. Whereas the BufferedReader class provides an analogous method that uses a BufferedReader, the stream created by the Files.lines() method is backed by a more efficient FileChannel.

```
static Stream<String> lines(Path path) throws IOException
static Stream<String> lines(Path path, Charset cs) throws IOException
```

Return a Stream of type String, where the elements are text lines read from a file denoted by the specified path. The first method decodes the bytes into characters using the UTF-8 charset. The charset to use can be explicitly specified, as in the second method.

As an example of using the lines() method, we implement the solution to finding palindromes (§13.3, p. 688), where the words are read from a file.

```
Path wordFile = Path.of(".", "project", "wordlist.txt");
System.out.println("Find palindromes, greater than length 2.");
try (Stream<String> stream = Files.lines(wordFile)){
  List<String> palindromes = stream
      .filter(str -> str.length() > 2)
      .filter(str -> str.equals(new StringBuilder(str).reverse().toString()))
      .toList();
  System.out.printf("List of palindromes:   %s%n", palindromes);
  System.out.printf("Number of palindromes: %s%n", palindromes.size());
} catch (IOException e) {
  e.printStackTrace();
}
```

Possible output from the code (*edited to fit on the page*):

```
Find palindromes, greater than length 2.
List of palindromes:   [aba, abba, aga, aha, ...]
Number of palindromes: 90
```

The following code creates a map to count the number of lines with different lengths:

```
Path textFile = Path.of(".", "project", "linesOnly.txt");
try (Stream<String> stream = Files.lines(textFile)) {
  Map<Integer, Long> grpMap =
      stream.collect(Collectors.groupingBy(String::length,
                                           Collectors.counting()));
  System.out.println(grpMap);
} catch (IOException e) {
  e.printStackTrace();
}
```

Possible output from the code:

```
{4=1, 21=2, 10=1, 12=1}
```

Directory Hierarchy Traversal

Tree traversal is an important topic in computer science. Other synonyms used in the literature for traversing such structures are *walking*, *navigating*, and *visiting* a tree.

Note that in order to traverse a directory hierarchy and access its entries, the directory must have *execute* permission.

The Files class provides methods to traverse a directory hierarchy which has a tree structure. We will use the directory hierarchy shown below to illustrate these traversal methods. The directory hierarchy below is rooted at directory a—that is, this directory is the *start* or the *root* of the directory hierarchy. Traversal of the directory hierarchy starts by visiting directory a and is considered to be at *depth* 0. Dropping down each level of directories in the hierarchy increases the depth. The directory a/b and the file a/x.txt are at depth 1 in relation to the directory a, and are said to be *siblings* at depth 1. The directory hierarchy below has a maximum depth of 3, as there are no directories below this depth. Note that the file a/b/c/dir_link is a symbolic link to the directory a/b, and as we shall see, it can influence the traversal if symbolic links are to be followed.

```
a/
├── b/ ◄--------------------------------
│    ├── c/                            │
│    │    ├── dir_link----------------─┘
│    │    └── z.txt
│    └── d/
│         └── y.txt
└── x.txt

0    1    2    3 ---> Increasing depth
```

Traversal Strategies

There are primarily two main strategies for traversing a tree structure, or as in our case, a directory hierarchy. Both strategies start at the root of the directory hierarchy.

- *Depth-first traversal*

  Any subdirectory encountered at a particular depth level is traversed to its maximum depth before continuing with any sibling of this subdirectory at this depth level. The depth-first traversal of the hierarchy rooted at directory a is shown below. Note how at depth level 2, the directory a/b/c is traversed completely before traversing its sibling directory a/b/d. The traversal methods of the Files class use the depth-first traversal strategy.

```
Visited entry          Depth
./a                    0
./a/x.txt              1
./a/b                  1
./a/b/c                2
./a/b/c/z.txt          3
./a/b/c/dir_link       3
./a/b/d                2
./a/b/d/y.txt          3
```

- *Breadth-first traversal*

  The siblings at each depth level are traversed before moving on to the next depth level—in other words, the traversal is by depth level. The breadth-first traversal of the hierarchy rooted at directory a is shown below. Note how entries at each depth are traversed before traversing the entries at the next depth level.

```
Visited entry          Depth
./a                    0
./a/x.txt              1
./a/b                  1
./a/b/d                2
./a/b/c                2
./a/b/c/z.txt          3
./a/b/c/dir_link       3
./a/b/d/y.txt          3
```

Both strategies have their pros and cons, and each excels at solving particular traversal problems. For example, finding a search goal that is closest to the root is best found by the breadth-first strategy in the shortest amount of time, whereas a goal that is farthest from the root is best found by the depth-first strategy in the shortest amount of time. Depth-first search may need to backtrack when trying to find a solution, whereas breadth-first search is more predictive. Breath-first search requires more memory as entries at previous levels must be maintained. The interested reader should consult the ample body of literature readily available on this important subject of trees and graph algorithms.

Listing the Immediate Entries in a Directory

A common file operation is to list the entries in a directory, similar to basic usage of the DOS command dir or the Unix command ls. The list() method of the Files class creates a stream whose elements are Path objects that denote the entries in a directory.

> static Stream<Path> list(Path dir) throws IOException
>
> Creates a lazily populated Stream whose elements are the entries in the directory—it does *not* recurse on the entries of the directory. The stream does not include the directory itself or its parent. It throws a java.nio.file.NotDirectoryException if it is not a directory (*optional specific exception*). Also, it does not follow symbolic links.

The following code lists the entries under the directory a. Note that the stream only contains the *immediate* entries in the directory. Any subdirectories under the specified directory are *not* traversed. The Path object passed a parameter must denote a directory, or a disgruntled NotDirectoryException is thrown.

```
Path dir = Path.of(".", "a");
System.out.printf("Immediate entries under directory \"%s\":%n", dir);
try(Stream<Path> stream = Files.list(dir)) {
   stream.forEach(System.out::println);
} catch (NotDirectoryException nde) {
nde.printStackTrace();
} catch (IOException ioe) {
ioe.printStackTrace();
}
```

Output from the code:

```
Immediate entries under directory "./a":
./a/x.txt
./a/b
```

File Visit Option

In the file operations we have seen so far, the default behavior was to follow symbolic links. Not so in the case of the traversal methods find() and walk() of the Files class—these methods do *not* follow symbolic links, unless instructed explicitly to do so. The FileVisitOption enum type defines the constant FOLLOW_LINKS (Table 21.13) that can be specified to indicate that symbolic links should be followed when using these methods.

Table 21.13 *File Visit Option*

Enum java.nio.file.FileVisitOption constant	Description
FOLLOW_LINKS	Indicates that symbolic links should be followed.

Walking the Directory Hierarchy

The walk() method of the Files class creates a stream to walk or traverse the directory hierarchy rooted at a specific directory entry.

```
static Stream<Path> walk(Path start, FileVisitOption... options)
                         throws IOException
static Stream<Path> walk(Path start, int depth,
                         FileVisitOption... options)
                         throws IOException
```

Return a Stream that is lazily populated with Path objects by walking the directory hierarchy rooted at the entry specified by the start parameter. The start parameter can be a directory or a file.

The first method is equivalent to calling the second method with a depth of Integer.MAX_VALUE. The methods traverse the entries *depth-first* to a depth limit that is the minimum of the maximum depth of the directory hierarchy rooted at the start entry and any depth that is specified or implied.

These methods do *not* follow symbolic links, unless the constant FileVisit-Option.FOLLOW_LINKS is specified.

Example 21.5 illustrates using the walk() method. The hierarchy of directory a (p. 1347) is traversed to illustrate different scenarios. The code at (1) creates the symbolic link a/b/c/dir_link to the directory a/b, if necessary.

Example 21.5   *Traversing the Directory Hierarchy*

```
import java.io.IOException;
import java.nio.file.*;
import java.util.stream.Stream;

public class WalkTheWalk {

  public static void main(String[] args) throws IOException {

    // Creating symbolic link.                                    // (1)
    try {
      Path targetPath = Path.of(".", "a", "b");
      Path symbLinkPath  = Path.of(".", "a", "b", "c", "dir_link");
      if (Files.notExists(symbLinkPath, LinkOption.NOFOLLOW_LINKS)) {
        Files.createSymbolicLink(symbLinkPath, targetPath.toAbsolutePath());
      }
    } catch (IOException ioe) {
      ioe.printStackTrace();
      return;
    }

    // Do the walk.                                               // (2)
    Path start = Path.of(".", "a");
    int MAX_DEPTH = 4;
```

```
        for (int depth = 0; depth <= MAX_DEPTH; ++depth) {              // (3)
          try(Stream<Path> stream = Files.walk(start, depth,            // (4)
                                       FileVisitOption.FOLLOW_LINKS)) {
            System.out.println("Depth limit: " + depth);
            stream.forEach(System.out::println);
          } catch (IOException ioe) {
            ioe.printStackTrace();
          }
        }
      }
    }
```

Output from the program (*edited to fit on the page*):

```
Depth: 0
./a
Depth: 1
./a
./a/x.txt
./a/b
Depth: 2
./a
./a/x.txt
./a/b
./a/b/c
./a/b/d
Depth: 3
./a
./a/x.txt
./a/b
./a/b/c
./a/b/c/z.txt
./a/b/c/dir_link
./a/b/d
./a/b/d/y.txt
Depth: 4
./a
./a/x.txt
./a/b
./a/b/c
./a/b/c/z.txt
Exception in thread "main" java.io.UncheckedIOException:
    java.nio.file.FileSystemLoopException: ./a/b/c/dir_link
  ...
```

Limiting Traversal by Depth Specification

The walk() method at (4) in Example 21.5 is called multiple times in the for(;;) loop at (3). From the output, we can see that, for each value of the loop variable depth, the walk() method starts the traversal at the directory a and descends to the depth level given by the loop variable depth. For example, when the value of the depth variable is 3, traversal descends from depth level 0 to depth level 3.

If the constant FileVisitOption.FOLLOW_LINKS is *not* specified, so that symbolic links are not followed, the traversal will only go as far as the minimum of the maximum depth of the hierarchy and any specified depth level.

Specifying the depth level can result in a more efficient search if it is known that the result is at an approximate depth level, thus avoiding useless searching farther down in the hierarchy.

Handling Symbolic Links

Specifying the constant FileVisitOption.FOLLOW_LINKS in the walk() method call results in symbolic links being followed.

A symbolic link to a file is not a problem, as after visiting the target file, the traversal can continue with the next sibling of the symbolic link.

A symbolic link to a directory that is *not* a *parent directory* of the symbolic link is also not a problem, as traversal can continue with the next sibling of the symbolic link, after visiting the target directory.

The problem arises when a symbolic link is to a directory that is a *parent directory* of the symbolic link. That creates a *cyclic path dependency*. An example of such a cyclic path dependency is introduced by the symbolic link a/b/c/dir_link to one of its parent directories, a/b, as can be seen in the figure of the directory hierarchy (p. 1347).

When the constant FileVisitOption.FOLLOW_LINKS is specified in the walk() method call, the method detects such cyclic path dependencies by monitoring which entries have been visited. Example 21.5 illustrates this scenario when the constant FileVisitOption.FOLLOW_LINKS is specified and the specified depth is greater than 3. From the output, we can see that, at depth level 4, the method detects that the symbolic link a/b/c/dir_link to its parent directory a/b creates a cyclic path dependency, as the target directory lies on the path to the symbolic link and has been visited before. The method throws a hefty FileSystemLoopException to announce the outcome.

Copying an Entire Directory

The Files.copy() method only copies a single file or creates an empty directory at its destination, depending on whether the source is a file or a directory, respectively. Shown below is the copyEntireDirectory() method that copies an *entire* directory.

```
/** Declared in FileUtils class.
 * Copy an entire directory.
 * @param sourceDir        Directory to copy.
 * @param destinationDir   Directory to which the source directory is copied.
 * @param options          Copy options for all entries.
 */
public static void copyEntireDirectory(Path sourceDir,
                                       Path destinationDir,
                                       CopyOption... options) {
```

```
try (Stream<Path> stream = Files.walk(sourceDir)) {              // (1)
    stream.forEach(entry -> {
        Path relativeEntryPath = sourceDir.relativize(entry);        // (2)
        Path destination = destinationDir.resolve(relativeEntryPath); // (3)
        try {
            Files.copy(entry, destination, options);               // (4)
        } catch (DirectoryNotEmptyException e) {
            e.printStackTrace();
        } catch (IOException e) {
            e.printStackTrace();
        }
    });
} catch (IOException e) {
    e.printStackTrace();
}
}
```

The method copyEntireDirectory() copies each entry with the Files.copy() method at (4) as the directory hierarchy is traversed in the stream created by the Files.walk() method at (1). For each entry, the destination where the entry should be copied is determined by the code at (2) and (3).

First, the *relative* path between the source directory path and the current entry path is determined by the relativize() method at (2):

```
Source directory:      ./a/b
Current entry:         ./a/b/c/d
Relative entry path:   c/d
```

The *destination* path to copy the current entry is determined by joining the destination directory path with the relative entry path by calling the resolve() method at (3):

```
Destination directory:    ./x/y
Relative entry path:      c/d
Destination entry paths: ./x/y/c/d
```

In the scenario above, the entry ./a/b/c/d is copied to the destination path ./x/y/c/d during the copying of source directory ./a/b to the destination directory ./x/y.

```
CopyOption[] options = new CopyOption[] {
    StandardCopyOption.REPLACE_EXISTING, StandardCopyOption.COPY_ATTRIBUTES,
    LinkOption.NOFOLLOW_LINKS};
Path sourceDirectory      = Path.of(".", "a", "b");         //        ./a/b
Path destinationDirectory = Path.of(".", "x", "y");         // (5a) ./x/y
// Path destinationDirectory = Path.of(".", "x")
//                 .resolve(sourceDirectory.getFileName()); // (5b) ./x/b
FileUtils.copyEntireDirectory(sourceDirectory, destinationDirectory, options);
```

If the destination directory should have the same name as the source directory, we can use the code at (5b) rather than the code at (5a).

A few things should be noted about the declaration of the copyEntireDirectory() method. It can be customized to copy the entries by specifying copy options. It closes the stream created by the walk() method in a try-with-resources statement. Calling the method copy() in the body of the lambda expression requires handling

any IOException inside the lambda body. Any IOException from calling the walk()
method is also explicitly handled.

Searching for Directory Entries

The find() method of the Files class can be used for searching or finding directory
entries in the file system.

```
static Stream<Path> find(Path start, int depth,
                         BiPredicate<Path,BasicFileAttributes> matcher,
                         FileVisitOption... options) throws IOException
```

Returns a Stream that is lazily populated with Path objects by searching for
entries in a directory hierarchy rooted at the Path object denoted by the start
parameter. The start parameter can be a directory or a file.

The method walks the directory hierarchy in exactly the same manner as the
walk() method. The methods traverse the entries *depth-first* to a depth limit that
is the minimum of the actual depth of the directory hierarchy rooted at the
start entry and the depth that is specified.

The matcher parameter defines a BiPredicate that is used to decide whether a
directory entry should be included in the stream. For each directory entry in
the stream, the BiPredicate is invoked on its Path and its BasicFileAttributes—
making it possible to define a customized filter.

This method does *not* follow symbolic links, unless the constant FileVisit-
Option.FOLLOW_LINKS is specified.

The find() method is analogous to the walk() method in many respects: It traverses
the directory hierarchy in the same way, does not follow symbolic links by default,
follows symbolic links only if the constant FileVisitOption.FOLLOW_LINKS is specified, and monitors visiting entries to detect cyclic path dependencies since the
depth limit is always specified.

Whereas both walk() and find() methods create a stream of Path objects, the find()
method also allows a matcher for the search to be defined by a lambda expression
that implements the BiPredicate<Path, BasicFileAttributes> functional interface.
This matcher is applied by the method and determines whether an entry is allowed
in the stream. This is in contrast to an explicit intermediate filter operation on the
stream, as in the case of a stream created by the walk() method. The find() method
supplies the BasicFileAttributes object associated with a Path—analogous to using
the readAttributes() method of the Files class (p. 1328). Given the Path object and
its associated BasicFileAttributes object with the basic set of read-only file attributes, it is possible to write complex search criteria on a directory entry. The methods of the BasicFileAttributes interface also do not throw checked exceptions, and
are therefore convenient to call in a lambda expression, as opposed to corresponding methods of the Files class.

In the following code, we use the `find()` method to find regular files whose name ends with ".txt" and whose size is greater than 0 bytes. The `BiPredicate` at (1) defines the filtering criteria based on querying the `Path` object in the stream for its file extension and its associated `BasicFileAttributes` object with read-only file attributes for whether it is a regular file and for its size.

```
System.out.println("Find regular files whose name ends with \".txt\""
                    + " and whose size is > 0:");
Path startEntry = Path.of(".", "a");
int depth = 5;
try (var pStream = Files.find(startEntry, depth,
                              (path, attrs) -> attrs.isRegularFile()       // (1)
                              && attrs.size() > 0
                              && path.toString().endsWith(".txt"))) {
  List<Path> pList = pStream.toList();
  System.out.println(pList);
} catch (IOException ioe) {
  ioe.printStackTrace();
}
```

Output from the code:

```
Find regular files whose name ends with ".txt" and whose size is > 0:
[./a/x.txt, ./a/b/c/z.txt, ./a/b/d/y.txt]
```

Note that the method `find()` requires the depth of the search to be specified. However, the actual depth traversed is always the minimum of the maximum depth of the directory hierarchy and the depth specified. The maximum depth of the hierarchy rooted at directory a is 3 and the specified depth is 5. The actual depth traversed in the directory hierarchy is thus 3. In the code above, different values for the depth can give different results.

If the constant `FileVisitOption.FOLLOW_LINKS` is specified in the `find()` method, its behavior is analogous to the behavior of the `walk()` method. It will keep track of the directories visited, and any cyclic path dependency encountered will unceremoniously result in a `FileSystemLoopException`. The curious reader is encouraged to experiment with the code above by specifying the constant `FileVisit-Option.FOLLOW_LINKS` and passing different values for the depth in the `find()` method call.

 ## Review Questions

21.1   Assume that the current directory has the absolute path /wrk.
         Which of the following statements are true about the following program?

```
import java.io.IOException;
import java.nio.file.Path;

public final class Filing {
  public static void main (String[] args) throws IOException {
    Path file = Path.of("./document", "../book/../chapter1");
```

```
        System.out.println(file.toAbsolutePath());   // (1)
        System.out.println(file.toRealPath());        // (2)
        System.out.println(file.normalize());         // (3)
        System.out.println(file.toString());          // (4)
        System.out.println(file.getParent());         // (5)
      }
    }
```

Select the two correct answers.

(a) The line at (1) will print /wrk/document/book/chapter1.

(b) The line at (2) will print /wrk/chapter1.

(c) The line at (3) will print chapter1.

(d) The line at (4) will print ./document/book/chapter1.

(e) The line at (5) will print ./document/book/.

21.2   Given the following program:

```
    import java.io.IOException;
    import java.nio.file.*;
    import java.util.stream.Stream;

    public class ListingFiles {
      public static void main(String[] args) throws IOException {
        Path dirPath = Path.of(".", "wrk");
        printFiles1(dirPath);
        printFiles2(dirPath);
        printFiles3(dirPath);
      }

      public static void printFiles1(Path dirPath) throws IOException {
        try (Stream<Path> paths = Files.list(dirPath)) {
          paths.forEach(System.out::println);
        }
        System.out.println();
      }

      public static void printFiles2(Path dirPath) throws IOException {
        try (Stream<Path> paths = Files.walk(dirPath)) {
          paths.forEach(System.out::println);
        }
        System.out.println();
      }

      public static void printFiles3(Path dirPath) throws IOException {
        try (Stream<Path> paths = Files.find(dirPath, Integer.MAX_VALUE,
                                             (p, a) -> true)) {
          paths.forEach(System.out::println);
        }
        System.out.println();
      }
    }
```

Assume that the directory ./wrk has the following directory hierarchy:

```
./wrk
└── src
    └── readme.txt
```

Which statement is true about the program?
Select the one correct answer.

(a) All three methods printFiles1(), printFiles2(), and printFiles3() will produce the same output.

(b) Only the methods printFiles1() and printFiles2() will produce the same output.

(c) Only the methods printFiles2() and printFiles3() will produce the same output.

(d) Only the methods printFiles1() and printFiles3() will produce the same output.

(e) The program will fail to compile because the list() method does not exist in the Files class.

21.3   Given the following code:

```
import java.nio.file.*;
public class RQ1 {
  public static void main(String[] args) {
    Path earth = Path.of("/", "planets", "earth");
    Path moonOrbit = earth.resolve(Path.of("moon", "orbit.param"));
    Path mars = earth.resolveSibling("mars");
    Path fromMarsToMoon = mars.relativize(moonOrbit);
    System.out.println(fromMarsToMoon);
  }
}
```

What is the result?
Select the one correct answer.

(a) ../earth/moon/orbit.param

(b) /planets/mars/../earth/moon/orbit.param

(c) /planets/earth/moon/orbit.param

(d) ./mars/../earth/moon/orbit.param

(e) The program will throw an exception at runtime.

21.4   Given the following code:

```
import java.nio.file.*;
public class RQ2 {
  public static void main(String[] args) {
    /* Assume current directory path is /planets. */
    Path path = Path.of("./mars/../earth").normalize().toAbsolutePath();
    System.out.println(path.getNameCount());
  }
}
```

What is the result?
Select the one correct answer.

(a) 1

(b) 2

(c) 5

(d) The program will throw an exception at runtime.

21.5 Given the following code:

```
import java.io.*;
import java.nio.file.*;
public class RQ3 {
  public static void main(String[] args) {
      try (var stream = Files.list(Path.of("/test")
                              .toRealPath(LinkOption.NOFOLLOW_LINKS))) {
          stream.filter(p -> p.getFileName().toString().endsWith("txt"))
                  .forEach(p -> System.out.println(p));
      } catch (IOException ex) {
        ex.printStackTrace();
      }
    }
  }
}
```

and the following hierarchy for the /test directory:

```
/test
├── a.txt
│   └── b.txt
├── c
│   └── d.txt
├── e.txt
└── f.txt
```

What is the result?
Select the one correct answer.

(a) /test/a.txt
     /test/a.txt/b.txt
     /test/c/d.txt
     /test/e.txt
     /test/f.txt

(b) /test/a.txt/b.txt
     /test/c/d.txt
     /test/e.txt
     /test/f.txt

(c) /test/a.txt/b.txt
     /test/e.txt
     /test/f.txt

(d) /test/a.txt
     /test/e.txt
     /test/f.txt

(e) a.txt/b.txt
     c/d.txt
     e.txt
     f.txt

(f) b.txt
     d.txt
     e.txt
     f.txt

(g) a.txt/b.txt
   e.txt
   f.txt

(h) a.txt
   b.txt
   d.txt
   e.txt
   f.txt

21.6 Given the following code:

```
import java.io.*;
import java.nio.file.*;
public class RQ4 {
  public static void main(String[] args) {
    try (var stream = Files.walk(Path.of("/test")
                                .toRealPath(LinkOption.NOFOLLOW_LINKS))) {
      stream.map(p -> p.getFileName().toString())
            .filter(p -> p.endsWith("txt"))
            .sorted()
            .forEach(System.out::println);
    } catch (IOException ex) {
      ex.printStackTrace();
    }
  }
}
```

and the following hierarchy for the /test directory:

```
/test
├── a.txt
│   └── b.txt
├── c
│   └── d.txt
├── e.txt
└── f.txt
```

What is the result?
Select the one correct answer.

(a) /test/a.txt
   /test/a.txt/b.txt
   /test/c/d.txt
   /test/e.txt
   /test/f.txt

(b) /test/a.txt/b.txt
   /test/c/d.txt
   /test/e.txt
   /test/f.txt

(c) /test/a.txt/b.txt
   /test/e.txt
   /test/f.txt

(d) /test/a.txt
    /test/e.txt
    /test/f.txt

(e) b.txt
    d.txt
    e.txt
    f.txt

(f) b.txt
    e.txt
    f.txt

(g) a.txt
    b.txt
    d.txt
    e.txt
    f.txt

21.7 Which of the following statements is true?
      Select the one correct answer.

(a) The Files.createDirectories() method throws an exception when the directory to create already exists.
(b) The Files.delete() method throws an exception when trying to delete a non-existent path.
(c) The Files.move() method throws an exception when attempting to move a non-empty directory in the same file system.
(d) The Files.exists() method throws an exception when a path does not exist in the file system.

21.8 Given the following code:

```
import java.io.*;
import java.nio.file.*;
public class RQ6 {
  public static void main(String[] args) {
    try {
      Path p1 = Path.of("/users/joe/test/a.jpg");
      Path p2 = Path.of("/users").resolve(p1.getName(1).resolve("test/a.jpg"));
      Files.move(p1, p2);
    } catch (IOException ex) {
      ex.printStackTrace();
    }
  }
}
```

Assuming that the relevant paths exist, what is the result?
Select the one correct answer.

(a) The file a.jpg is moved to the /users directory.
(b) The file a.jpg is moved to the /users/joe/test directory.
(c) No action is taken when trying to move the file a.jpg.
(d) An IOException is thrown when trying to move the file a.jpg.

21.9 Given the following code:

```
import java.nio.file.*;
public class RQ7 {
  public static void main(String[] args) {
    Path p1 = Path.of("/test");
    Path p2 = Path.of("store");
    System.out.println(p1.resolve(p2));
    System.out.println(p2.resolve(p1));
  }
}
```

What is the result?
Select the one correct answer.

(a) /test/store
    /store/test

(b) /test
    /store

(c) /test/store
    /test

(d) /test/store
    /test/store

21.10 Given the following code:

```
import java.io.IOException;
import java.nio.file.*;
public class RQ8 {
  public static void main(String[] args) {
    try {
      Path source = Path.of("/test/readme.txt");
      Path destination = Path.of("/backup/readme_save.txt");
      Files.copy(source, destination);
    } catch (IOException ex) {
      ex.printStackTrace();
    }
  }
}
```

Assuming that both source and destination files exist and are accessible, what is the result?
Select the one correct answer.

(a) The destination file will be overwritten with the content of the source file.
(b) The content of the source file will be appended to the end of the destination file.
(c) The content of the source file will be inserted at the beginning of the destination file.
(d) The program will throw an exception at runtime.

21.11   Given the following code:

```
import java.io.IOException;
import java.nio.file.*;
public class RQ9 {
  public static void main(String[] args) {
    Path p = Path.of("/test/test.html");
    try (var stream = Files.lines(p)){
      String result = stream.filter(s->s.startsWith("<"))
                            .map(s->s.substring(s.indexOf(">"), s.indexOf(">")+1))
                            .reduce("", (s1,s2) -> s1+s2);
      System.out.println(result);
    } catch (IOException ex) {
      ex.printStackTrace();
    }
  }
}
```

and that the /test/test.html file contains the following lines:

```
<!DOCTYPE html>
<html>
<body>
Hello World
</body>
</html>
```

What is the result?
Select the one correct answer.

(a) An empty string
(b) <<<<<
(c) <><><><><>
(d) >>>>>
(e) The program will throw an exception at runtime.

21.12   Given the following code:

```
import java.io.IOException;
import java.nio.file.*;
import java.nio.file.attribute.*;
import java.util.*;

public class RQ10 {
  public static void main(String[] args) {
    Path directory = Path.of("/test/data");
    Path file = Path.of("/test/data/info.txt");
    try {
      Set<PosixFilePermission> permissions = new HashSet<>();
      permissions.add(PosixFilePermission.OWNER_READ);
      Files.setPosixFilePermissions(directory, permissions);

      permissions.add(PosixFilePermission.OWNER_WRITE);
      Files.setPosixFilePermissions(file, permissions);
```

```
                    try (var stream = Files.walk(directory)) {
                      stream.forEach(System.out::println);
                    }
                 } catch(IOException e) {
                    System.out.println(e);
                 }
              }
           }
```

assume that the directory /test/data exists and only contains the info.txt file, and that full permissions are set for both the directory and the file prior to program execution.

What is the result?
Select the one correct answer.

(a) /test/data
(b) /test/data/info.txt
(c) java.nio.file.AccessDeniedException:/test/data/info.txt
(d) java.nio.file.AccessDeniedException:/test/data

21.13   Given the following code:

```
import static java.nio.file.attribute.PosixFilePermission.*;
import java.io.IOException;
import java.nio.file.*;
import java.nio.file.attribute.*;
import java.util.Set;

public class RQ11 {
  public static void main(String[] args) {
    try {
      Path file = Path.of("/test/data/info.txt");
      Set<PosixFilePermission> perms
              = PosixFilePermissions.fromString("---------");
      Files.setPosixFilePermissions(file, perms);

      PosixFileAttributeView pfaView = Files.getFileAttributeView(file,
          PosixFileAttributeView.class);
      PosixFileAttributes pfa = pfaView.readAttributes();

      perms = Set.of(OWNER_READ, GROUP_WRITE, OTHERS_READ);
      pfaView.setPermissions(perms);

      perms = pfa.permissions();
      perms.add(OWNER_WRITE);
      pfaView.setPermissions(perms);

      perms = pfa.permissions();
      perms.remove(GROUP_WRITE);
      pfaView.setPermissions(perms);

      perms = pfa.permissions();
      System.out.println(perms);
```

```
        } catch (IOException e) {
          System.out.println(e);
        }
      }
    }
```

What is the result?

Select the one correct answer.

(a) [OWNER_READ, OWNER_WRITE, GROUP_WRITE, OTHERS_READ]

(b) [OWNER_READ, OWNER_WRITE, OTHERS_READ]

(c) [OWNER_WRITE]

(d) []

(e) The program will throw an exception at runtime.

21.14   Given the following code:

```
import java.io.*;
import java.net.*;
import java.nio.file.*;
public class RQ12 {
  public static void main(String[] args) {
    try {
      URI uri = URI.create("file:///test/ora.html");
      Path p1 = Path.of(uri);
      Path p2 = Path.of("/test/ora.html");
      Files.copy(p1, p2);
      File file = p2.toFile();
    } catch (IOException ex) {
      ex.printStackTrace();
    }
  }
}
```

Assume that the file /test/ora.html exists.

What is the result?

Select the one correct answer.

(a) No output is produced.

(b) An exception is thrown when converting a URI object to a Path object.

(c) An exception is thrown when copying path p1 to path p2.

(d) An exception is thrown when converting a Path object to a File object.

Concurrency: Part I 22

 Chapter Topics

- Distinguishing between concurrency and parallelism
- Understanding runtime organization for thread execution: what is shared memory and what is private to a thread
- Creating threads by extending the Thread class or by implementing the Runnable interface
- Writing synchronized code using synchronized methods and synchronized statements to achieve mutually exclusive access to shared resources
- Managing the thread lifecycle: thread states, the transitions between them, and thread coordination
- Understanding threading problems: liveness, fairness, deadlock, starvation, livelock, and memory consistency errors
- Understanding which thread behavior a program can take as guaranteed, and which behavior is not guaranteed, including the happens-before relationship

Java SE 17 Developer Exam Objectives	
[8.1] Create worker threads using Runnable and Callable, manage the thread lifecycle, including automations provided by different Executor services and concurrent API	§22.1, p. 1367, to §22.5, p. 1408
○ Creating threads with the Runnable functional interface and managing the thread lifecycle are covered in this chapter.	
○ Creating worker threads with the Callable functional interface, and managing concurrency using executor services of the Concurrency API are covered in §23.2, p. 1423.	

Java SE 11 Developer Exam Objectives	
[8.1] Create worker threads using Runnable and Callable, and manage concurrency using an ExecutorService and java.util.concurrent API ○ *Creating threads with the* Runnable *functional interface is covered in this chapter.* ○ *Creating worker threads with the* Callable *functional interface, and managing concurrency using executor services of the Concurrency API are covered in §23.2, p. 1423.*	*§22.3, p. 1371*

Support for multithreaded programming (also called *concurrent programming*) is an integral feature of the Java ecosystem to harness the computing power of multi-processor and multicore architectures. The programming language, the tools (particularly the JVM), and the APIs have all evolved to meet this challenge.

This chapter focuses on *low-level* support for multithreaded programming. This includes creating threads to execute tasks, understanding the thread lifecycle, how threads cooperate, and thread issues that are common in concurrent programming.

Chapter 23, p. 1419, deals with *high-level* support for building massively concurrent applications. This support is primarily provided by the frameworks in the java.util.concurrent package. High-level mechanisms allow the programmer to concentrate on *task management* in concurrent applications, while taking care of low-level *thread management*.

22.1 Threads and Concurrency

We first look at some basic concepts before diving into multithreaded programming in Java.

Multitasking

Multitasking allows several activities to occur concurrently on the computer. A distinction is usually made between:

- Process-based multitasking
- Thread-based multitasking (associated synonymously with *concurrency* in Java)

At the coarse-grain level there is *process-based* multitasking, which allows processes (i.e., programs) to run concurrently on the computer. A familiar example is running a spreadsheet program while also working with a word processor. At the fine-grain level there is *thread-based* multitasking, which allows parts of the *same* program to run concurrently on the computer. A familiar example is a word processor that is formatting text as it is typed and is spell-checking at the same time. This is only feasible if the two tasks are performed by two independent paths of execution at runtime. The two tasks would correspond to executing parts of the program code concurrently.

The sequence of code executed for each task defines an *independent sequential path of execution* within the program, and is called a *thread (of execution)*. Many threads can run concurrently within a program, doing different tasks. At runtime, threads in a program exist in a common memory space, and can therefore share both data and code (i.e., they are *lightweight* compared to processes). They also share the process running the program.

In a single-threaded environment only one task at a time can be performed. CPU cycles are wasted—for example, when waiting for user input. Multitasking allows idle CPU time to be put to good use.

Some advantages of thread-based multitasking as compared to process-based multitasking are:

- Threads share the same address space—that is, global data is accessible to all threads.
- Context switching between threads—that is, switching of execution from one thread to another—is usually less expensive than between processes.
- The cost of coordination between threads is relatively low.

Java supports thread-based multitasking—that is, concurrency—and provides support for multithreaded programming. *Thread-safety* is the term used to describe the design of classes that ensure that the state of their objects is always consistent, even when the objects are used concurrently by multiple threads.

Understanding Concurrency and Parallelism

There is an important distinction between the concept of *parallelism* and *concurrency* when it comes to code execution.

Parallel code execution implies *simultaneous* execution of instructions on different CPU cores. Concurrent execution is a more general idea that does not necessarily imply that the code of different threads is actually executed in parallel. It is possible to create more threads than the CPU cores can execute in parallel, which will cause threads to take turns at sharing time slices on the CPU cores. This means that sometimes the threads are running in parallel and sometimes it only feels like they are because they compete for time slices to execute on a limited number of CPU cores. In other words, concurrent execution gives an illusion of parallel execution.

The JVM is not the only process on the computer that requires CPU time. The operating system and other tasks also share CPU time, making it impossible to predict how much CPU time is allocated and when a thread will get to run, or if any given set of code will be executed in parallel at all. These factors have very important consequences:

1. Execution of code in different threads is unpredictable.

2. A thread that started earlier may or may not complete its work sooner than the thread that started later, even if it has less work to do.

3. Any attempt to control exact execution order will very likely impact performance and may result in all sorts of unwanted side effects, which will be discussed later in this chapter.

The following analogy can be helpful in understanding concurrent code execution:

Imagine that a CPU core is a road and a thread is a car. It would be rather inefficient to build a separate road for every car. Furthermore, one would expect a road to be shared by many cars, which helps to explain why multithreading makes much more efficient use of computer resources. However, even though a given road is shared among many cars, it does not mean that two cars can occupy the same spot on that road at the same time—that is quite obviously an undesirable situation. So cars have to take turns and yield to one another to be able to share the same road, very much like threads have to share a CPU core. It may feel like the cars are using a given road in parallel, but strictly speaking they are actually doing it concurrently. Finally, there is no guarantee that the car that started its journey earlier will get to where it wants to go sooner or later than another car, considering unpredictable circumstances such as being stuck in traffic. This is similar to a concurrent thread that may have to wait for a CPU time slice, if the CPU time has to be shared with many other threads and tasks on the computer. An attempt to control the exact execution order, to ensure that a certain thread gets priority, can be compared to stopping all traffic to yield to an ambulance or a police car—while they get priority, everyone else is stopped, causing overall performance to degrade. It may be tolerable for extraordinary cases, but it would be a traffic disaster if the policy for using the road was to prioritize each and every car on the road. This means that it is best to embrace the stochastic nature of concurrent code execution and try not to control the exact execution order, or at least only do it in exceptional cases.

22.2 Runtime Organization for Thread Execution

Most JVM implementations run as a single process, but allow multiple threads to be created. Runtime organization for thread execution in the JVM is depicted in Figure 22.1. The JVM has designated memory areas, called *runtime data areas*, that are deployed for various purposes during program execution. Figure 22.1 shows data areas that are created specifically for each thread and are private to each thread. The figure also shows data areas that are shared by all threads, called *shared memory*.

Figure 22.1 *Runtime Data Areas*

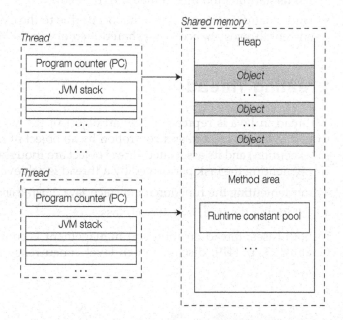

Each thread has the following data areas, which are private to the thread:

- *JVM stack*: A JVM stack (also known as *execution stack, call stack,* or *frame stack*) is created for each thread when the thread starts, and is used for bookkeeping method executions in the thread, as explained in §7.1, p. 365. This is also where all local variables for each active method invocation are stored. Note that each thread takes care of its own exception handling, and thus does not affect other threads.

- *Program counter* (PC): This register is created for each thread when the thread starts, and stores the address of the JVM instruction currently being executed.

The following data areas are shared by all threads:

- *Heap*: This shared memory space is where objects are created, stored, and garbage collected.

- *Method area*: This is created when the JVM starts. It stores the runtime constant pool, field and method information, static variables, and method bytecode for each of the classes and interfaces loaded by the JVM.

- *Runtime constant pool*: In addition to storing the constants defined in each class and interface, this also stores references to all methods and fields. The JVM uses the information in this pool to find the actual address of a method or a field in memory.

Threads make the runtime environment asynchronous, allowing different tasks to be performed concurrently. Using this powerful paradigm in Java centers on understanding the following aspects of multithreaded programming:

- Creating threads and providing the code that gets executed by a thread (p. 1370)

- Understanding the thread lifecycle (p. 1380)

- Understanding thread issues that occur due to the execution model where concurrent threads are accessing shared memory (p. 1408)

22.3 Creating Threads

A thread in Java is represented by an object of the java.lang.Thread class. Every thread in Java is created and controlled by an object of this class. Often the thread (of execution) and its associated Thread object are thought of as being synonymous. Implementing the task performed by a thread is achieved in one of two ways:

- Implementing the functional interface java.lang.Runnable

- Extending the java.lang.Thread class

In both cases, thread creation and management is controlled by the application. Chapter 23, p. 1419, discusses high-level concurrency features that abstract the drudgery of thread creation and management, facilitating the building of massively concurrent applications.

Implementing the Runnable Interface

The Runnable functional interface has the following specification, comprising a single abstract method declaration:

```
@FunctionalInterface
public interface Runnable {
  void run();
}
```

A thread, which is created based on an object that implements the Runnable interface, will execute the code defined in the public method run(). In other words, the code in the run() method defines an independent path of execution and thereby the entry and the exits for the thread. A thread ends when the run() method ends, either by normal completion or by throwing an uncaught exception. Note that the method run() does not return a value, does not take any parameters, and does not throw any checked exceptions.

The procedure for creating threads based on the Runnable interface is as follows:

1. Implement the Runnable interface, providing the run() method that will be executed by the thread. This can be done by providing a concrete or an anonymous class that implements the Runnable() interface. Since the interface is a functional interface, it can also be implemented by a lambda expression, typically for simple tasks.

2. An object of the Thread class is created by passing the Runnable implementation from step 1 as an argument in the Thread constructor call. The Thread object now has a Runnable object that implements the run() method.

3. The start() method is invoked on the Thread object created in step 2. The start() method returns immediately after a thread has been spawned. In other words, the call to the start() method is asynchronous.

When the thread, represented by the Thread object on which the start() method was invoked, gets to run, it executes the run() method of the Runnable object. This sequence of events is illustrated in Figure 22.2.

In the following code, the functional interface Runnable is implemented by a lambda expression that is passed to the Thread object. The code will create a thread and start the thread. When the thread gets to run, it will execute the print statement.

```
Thread thread = new Thread(
    () -> System.out.println("Harmonious threads create beautiful applications.")
);
thread.start();
```

Figure 22.2   *Spawning Threads Using a* Runnable *Object*

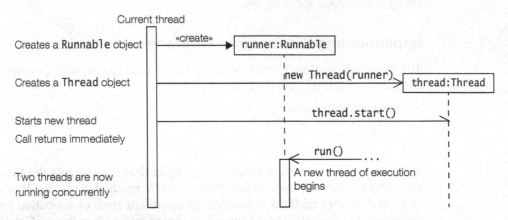

The following is a summary of selected constructors and methods from the
java.lang.Thread class:

Thread(Runnable threadTarget)
Thread(Runnable threadTarget, String threadName)

The argument threadTarget is the object whose run() method will be executed
when the thread is started. The argument threadName can be specified to give an
explicit name for the thread, rather than an automatically generated one.

void start()

Spawns a new thread—that is, the new thread will begin execution as a child
thread of the current thread. The spawning is done asynchronously as the call
to this method returns immediately. It throws an IllegalThreadStateException
if the thread is already started or it has already completed execution.

void run()

The Thread class implements the Runnable interface by providing an implementation of the run() method. This implementation in the Thread class does nothing and returns. Subclasses of the Thread class should override this method. If
the current thread is created using a separate Runnable object, the run() method
of this Runnable object is called.

static Thread currentThread()

Returns a reference to the Thread object of the currently executing thread.

final String getName()
final void setName(String name)

The first method returns the name of the thread. The second one sets the
thread's name to the specified argument.

```
final void setDaemon(boolean flag)
final boolean isDaemon()
```

The first method sets the status of the thread either as a daemon thread or as a normal thread (p. 1377), depending on whether the argument is true or false, respectively. The status should be set before the thread is started. The second method returns true if the thread is a daemon thread; otherwise, it returns false.

A slightly more elaborate example of creating a thread is presented in Example 22.1. The class Counter implements the Runnable interface. At (1), the class defines the run() method that constitutes the code to be executed in a thread. The while loop in the run() method executes as long as the current value is less than 5. In each iteration of the while loop, the old value and the new incremented value of the counter is printed, as shown at (3). Also, in each iteration, the thread will sleep for 500 milliseconds, as shown at (4). While it is sleeping, other threads may run (p. 1395).

The static method currentThread() in the Thread class can be used to obtain a reference to the Thread object associated with the current thread. We can call the getName() method on the current thread to obtain its name. An example of its usage, shown at (2), prints the name of the thread executing the run() method. Another example of its usage, shown at (5), prints the name of the thread executing the main() method.

The Client class in Example 22.1 uses the Counter class. It creates an object of the class Counter at (6). This Counter object is passed to two Thread objects at (7). The threads are started at (8). In other words, we have two threads that will increment the value in the same Counter object.

Both Thread A and Thread B are *child* threads of the *main* thread. They inherit the normal-thread status from the main thread (p. 1377). The output shows that the main thread finishes executing before the child threads. However, the program will continue running until the child threads have completed their execution of the run() method in the Counter object.

If a thread has been started or if it has completed, invoking the start() method again on the thread results in an IllegalThreadStateException, as shown at (9). Note that this does *not* terminate the thread that has already been started. If the thread has completed, a new thread must be created before the start() method can be called.

Since thread scheduling is not predictable (p. 1386) and Example 22.1 does not enforce any synchronization between the two threads in accessing the current value in the Counter object, the output shown may vary. The output from the two child threads is interspersed. The output also shows that the counter was incremented by 2 when Thread B executed for the first time! This is an example of *thread interference*. The challenge in multithreaded programming is to synchronize how shared data is accessed by the threads in the application.

Example 22.1   *Implementing the* Runnable *Interface*

```java
public class Counter implements Runnable {
  private int currentValue = 0;

  @Override
  public void run() {                            // (1) Thread entry point
    String threadName = Thread.currentThread().getName(); // (2)
    while (currentValue < 5) {
      System.out.printf("%s: old:%s new:%s%n",
                        threadName,              // (3) Print thread name,
                        this.currentValue,       //     old value,
                      ++this.currentValue);      //     new incremented value.
      try {
        Thread.sleep(500);                       // (4) Current thread sleeps.
      } catch (InterruptedException e) {
        System.out.println(threadName + " interrupted.");
      }
    }
    System.out.println("Exiting " + threadName);
  }
}
```

```java
public class Client {
  public static void main(String[] args) {
    String threadName = Thread.currentThread().getName();  // (5) main thread
    System.out.println("Method main() runs in thread " + threadName);

    // Create a Counter object:                            // (6)
    Counter counter = new Counter();

    // Create two threads with the same Counter:           // (7)
    Thread threadA = new Thread(counter, "Thread A");
    Thread threadB = new Thread(counter, "Thread B");

    // Start the two threads:                              // (8)
    System.out.println("Starting " + threadA.getName());
    threadA.start();
//  threadA.start();                                       // (9) IllegalThreadStateException
    System.out.println("Starting " + threadB.getName());
    threadB.start();

    System.out.println("Exiting Thread " + threadName);    // (10)
  }
}
```

Probable output from the program:

```
Method main() runs in thread main
Starting Thread A
Starting Thread B
Exiting Thread main
Thread B: old:0 new:2
Thread A: old:0 new:1
```

```
Thread B: old:2 new:3
Thread A: old:3 new:4
Thread B: old:4 new:5
Exiting Thread A
Exiting Thread B
```

Extending the Thread Class

A class can also extend the Thread class to create a thread. A typical procedure for doing this is as follows (see Figure 22.3):

1. A concrete or an anonymous class extending the Thread class overrides the run() method from the Thread class to define the code executed by the thread.

2. This subclass may call a Thread constructor explicitly in its constructors to initialize the thread, using the super() call.

3. The start() method inherited from the Thread class is invoked on an object of the class to make the thread eligible for running. This method should never be overridden.

Figure 22.3 *Spawning Threads—Extending the* Thread *Class*

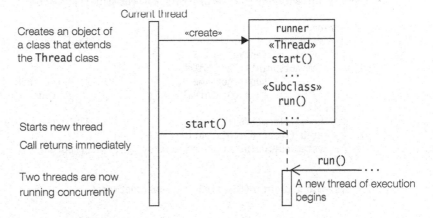

The simple example below shows an anonymous class that extends the Thread class and overrides the run() method from the Thread superclass. The code will create a thread and start the thread:

```
(new Thread() {
    @Override
    public void run() {
        System.out.println("Harmonious threads create beautiful applications.")
    }
}
).start();
```

In Example 22.2, the Counter class from Example 22.1 has been modified to illustrate creating a thread by extending the Thread class. The program output shows that the Client class creates two threads and exits, but the program continues running until the child threads have completed execution. The two child threads are independent, each having its own counter and executing its own run() method. Again note that the main thread finished execution before the child threads, but the JVM does not terminate before the child threads are done.

The Thread class implements the Runnable interface, which means that this approach is not much different from implementing the Runnable interface directly. The main difference is that the roles of the Runnable object and the Thread object are combined in a single object by extending the Thread class.

In the previous two examples, the code to create the Thread object, to set the thread name, and to call the start() method to initiate the thread execution is in the client code. In Example 22.2, however, setting the name and starting the thread can be placed in the constructor of the Counter subclass, as it inherits from the Thread class—an exercise the studious reader is encouraged to undertake.

Example 22.2 *Extending the* Thread *Class*

```java
public class Counter extends Thread {
  public int currentValue;
  public Counter() { this.currentValue = 0; }
  public int getValue() { return this.currentValue; }

  @Override
  public void run() {                            // (1) Override from superclass.
    while (this.currentValue < 5) {
      System.out.printf("%s: %s%n",
                    super.getName(),             // (2) Print thread name,
                    this.currentValue++);        //     current value, and increment.
      try {
        Thread.sleep(500);                       // (3) Current thread sleeps.
      } catch (InterruptedException e) {
        System.out.println(super.getName() + " interrupted.");
      }
    }
    System.out.println("Exiting " + super.getName());
  }
}
```

```java
public class Client {
  public static void main(String[] args) {
    String threadName = Thread.currentThread().getName();        // (4)
    System.out.println("Method main() runs in thread " + threadName);

    // Create two Counter objects that extend the Thread class:      (5)
    Counter counterA = new Counter();
    Counter counterB = new Counter();

    // Set the names for the two threads:                            (6)
    counterA.setName("Counter A");
    counterB.setName("Counter B");
```

```
    // Mark the threads as daemon threads:                            (7)
 // counterA.setDaemon(true);
 // counterB.setDaemon(true);

    // Start the two threads:                                        // (8)
    System.out.println("Starting " + counterA.getName());
    counterA.start();
    System.out.println("Starting " + counterB.getName());
    counterB.start();

    System.out.println("Exiting " + threadName);
  }
}
```

Probable output from the program:

```
Method main() runs in thread main
Starting Counter A
Counter A: 0
Starting Counter B
Exiting main
Counter B: 0
Counter A: 1
Counter B: 1
Counter B: 2
Counter A: 2
Counter A: 3
Counter B: 3
Counter A: 4
Counter B: 4
Exiting Counter B
Exiting Counter A
```

When creating threads, there are a few reasons why implementing the Runnable interface may be preferable to extending the Thread class:

- Extending the Thread class means that the subclass cannot extend any other class, whereas a class implementing the Runnable interface has this option.

- Extending the Thread class also means that the task of the thread—that is, executing the run() method—cannot be shared by several threads. This does not mean that the threads cannot access shared resources through their run() methods—which is typical in multithreaded applications.

- A class might only be interested in being runnable, and therefore, inheriting the full overhead of the Thread class would be excessive.

Types of Threads

The runtime environment distinguishes between *normal threads* (also called *user threads*) and *daemon threads*. As long as a normal thread is alive—meaning that it has not completed executing its task—the JVM does not terminate. A daemon thread is at the mercy of the runtime system: It is stopped if no more normal threads are running, thus terminating the program. Daemon threads exist only to serve normal threads. It is not a good strategy to run any clean-up code in daemon threads, which might not get executed if a daemon thread is stopped.

Uncommenting the statements at (7) in Example 22.2:

```
counterA.setDaemon(true);
counterB.setDaemon(true);
```

illustrates the daemon nature of threads. The program execution will now terminate after the main thread has completed, without waiting for the daemon Counter threads to finish normally:

```
Method main() runs in thread main
Starting Counter A
Starting Counter B
Counter A: 0
Counter B: 0
Exiting main
```

When a standalone application is run, a normal thread is automatically created to execute the main() method of the application. This thread is called the *main thread*. If no other normal threads are spawned, the program terminates when the main() method finishes executing. All other threads, called *child* threads, are spawned from the main thread, inheriting its normal-thread status. The main() method can then finish, but the program will keep running until all normal threads have completed. The status of a spawned thread can be set as either daemon or normal, but this must be done before the thread is *started*. Any attempt to change the status after the thread has been started throws an unchecked IllegalThreadState-Exception. A child thread inherits the thread status of its parent thread.

When a GUI application is started, a special thread is automatically created to monitor the user–GUI interaction. This normal thread keeps the program running, allowing interaction between the user and the GUI, even though the main thread might have completed after the main() method finished executing.

 ## Review Questions

22.1   What will be the result of attempting to compile and run the following program?

```
public class MyClass extends Thread {
  public MyClass(String s) { msg = s; }
  String msg;
  public void run() {
    System.out.println(msg);
  }

  public static void main(String[] args) {
    new MyClass("Hello");
    new MyClass("World");
  }
}
```

Select the one correct answer.

(a) The program will fail to compile.
(b) The program will compile without errors and will print Hello and World, in that order, every time it is run.
(c) The program will compile without errors, and will print a never-ending stream of Hello and World.
(d) The program will compile without errors, and will print Hello and World when run, but the order is unpredictable.
(e) The program will compile without errors, and will simply terminate without any output when run.

22.2 What will be the result of attempting to compile and run the following program?

```java
class R1 implements Runnable {
  public void run() {
    System.out.print(Thread.currentThread().getName());
  }
}
public class R2 implements Runnable {
  public void run() {
    new Thread(new R1(),"|R1a|").run();
    new Thread(new R1(),"|R1b|").start();
    System.out.print(Thread.currentThread().getName());
  }

  public static void main(String[] args) {
    new Thread(new R2(),"|R2|").start();
  }
}
```

Select the one correct answer.

(a) The program will fail to compile.
(b) The program will compile without errors, and will print |R1a| twice and |R2| once, in some order, every time it is run.
(c) The program will compile without errors, and will print |R1b| twice and |R2| once, in some order, every time it is run.
(d) The program will compile without errors, and will print |R1b| once and |R2| twice, in some order, every time it is run.
(e) The program will compile without errors, and will print |R1a| once, |R1b| once, and |R2| once, in some order, every time it is run.

22.3 What will be the result of attempting to compile and run the following program?

```java
public class Threader extends Thread {
  Threader(String name) {
    super(name);
  }
  public void run() throws IllegalThreadStateException {
    System.out.println(Thread.currentThread().getName());
    throw new IllegalThreadStateException();
  }
```

```
        public static void main(String[] args) {
            new Threader("|T1|").start();
        }
    }
```

Select the one correct answer.

(a) The program will fail to compile.

(b) The program will compile without errors, will print |T1|, and will terminate normally every time it is run.

(c) The program will compile without errors, will print|T1|, and will throw an unchecked IllegalThreadStateException every time it is run.

(d) None of the above

22.4 Thread Lifecycle

Before diving into the lifecycle of a thread, a few important thread-related concepts should be understood.

Objects, Monitors, and Locks

In Java, *each* object has a *monitor* associated with it—including arrays. A thread can *lock* and *unlock* a monitor, but only one thread at a time can *acquire* the lock on a monitor. The thread that acquires the lock is said to *own* the lock and has exclusive access to the object whose monitor was locked. Any other threads trying to acquire the lock are *blocked* and placed in the *entry set* of the monitor until the lock is *released*. At that time, if the entry set is not empty, a blocked thread is allowed to acquire the lock at the discretion of the JVM, based on the thread scheduling policy in effect. The locking mechanism thus implements *mutual exclusion* (also known as *mutex*).

It should be made clear that programs should not make any assumptions about the order in which threads are granted ownership of a lock while waiting in the entry set of the monitor providing the lock. Thread state transitions for lock acquisition are explained later (p. 1388).

The locking mechanism on a monitor is referred to by various names in the literature: *intrinsic lock, monitor lock, object-level lock, monitor*, or just *lock*. Conceptually, the lock is on the object, and therefore we will refer to this locking mechanism provided by a monitor associated with an object as the *object lock* or just *lock*, when it is clear which lock is being referred to.

Classes also have a *class lock* (a.k.a. *class-level lock*) that is analogous to the object lock. Such a lock is actually a lock on the java.lang.Class object that represents the class at runtime in the JVM. Given a class A, the reference A.class denotes this unique Class object. The class lock can be used in much the same way as an object lock to implement mutual exclusion.

The following static method of the Thread class can be used to determine whether the current thread holds a lock on a specific object:

```
static boolean holdsLock(Object obj)
```

Thread States

Understanding the lifecycle of a thread can be beneficial when programming with threads. Threads can exist in different states. Just because the start() method has been called on the thread, it does not mean that the thread has access to the CPU and can start executing straightaway. Several factors determine how it will proceed.

Figure 22.4 shows the states and the transitions in the lifecycle of a thread. The figure shows the main transitions that occur during the lifecycle of a thread—in particular, transitions pertaining to *blocked I/O* (p. 1405) and *thread interruption* (p. 1393) have been omitted.

The thread states are represented by enum constants and summarized in Table 22.1. The Thread class provides the getState() method to determine the state of the current thread. The method returns a constant of type Thread.State (i.e., the type State is a static inner enum type declared in the Thread class).

Figure 22.4 *Thread States*

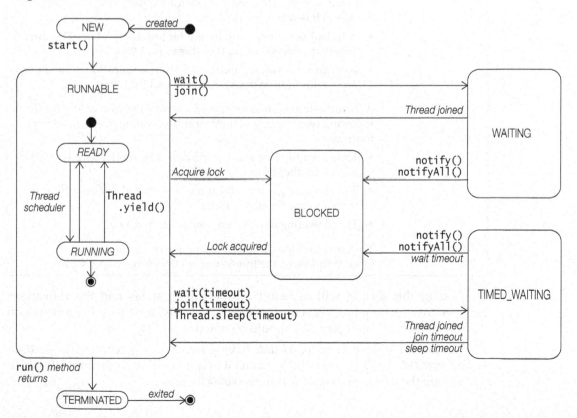

Table 22.1   *Thread States Defined by the* `Thread.State` *Enum Type*

Constant in the Thread.State enum type (see Figure 22.4)	Description of the state
NEW	A thread in this state has been created, but it has not yet started. A thread is started by calling its `start()` method (p. 1370).
RUNNABLE	The RUNNABLE states can be characterized by two *substates* which are not observable: • *READY substate*: A thread starts life in the *READY* substate (p. 1386), and also when it transitions from a *non-runnable state* to the RUN-NABLE state. • *RUNNING substate*: If a thread is in the *RUNNING* substate, it means that the thread is currently executing (p. 1386), and is deemed the *running thread*. From the *RUNNING* substate, a thread can transition either to the *READY* substate, to a non-runnable state, or to the TERMINATED state.
BLOCKED	A thread is blocked while waiting to acquire a lock (p. 1380, p. 1388). A thread is blocked while waiting for I/O (p. 1405).
WAITING	A thread is in this state indefinitely for the following reasons, until the action it is waiting for occurs: • A thread is waiting indefinitely for join completion: The thread awaits completion of another thread (p. 1402). • A thread is waiting indefinitely for notification: The thread awaits notification from another thread (p. 1396).
TIMED_WAITING	A thread is in this state for at least a *specified amount of time* for the following reasons, unless the action it is waiting for occurs before timeout: • Timed waiting for join completion: The thread awaits completion of another thread (p. 1402). • Timed waiting for notification: The thread awaits notification from another thread (p. 1396). • Timed waiting to wake up from sleep (p. 1395).
TERMINATED	The `run()` method completed execution or terminated. Once in this state, the thread can never run again (p. 1405).

The rest of this section will expound on the thread states and the transitions between them during the lifecycle of a thread. However, the following remarks on the thread lifecycle in Figure 22.4 should be noted.

• The RUNNABLE state is a *compound state* having two *non-observable substates*: *READY* and *RUNNING*. Being *non-observable* means it is not possible to distinguish which substate the thread is in once it is in the RUNNABLE state.

- The following states are characterized as *non-runnable* states: BLOCKED, WAITING, and TIMED_WAITING. A *running thread*—one in the *RUNNING* substate—can transit to one of the non-runnable states, depending on the circumstances. A thread remains in a non-runnable state until a specific transition occurs. A thread does not go directly to the *RUNNING* substate from a non-runnable state, but transits first to the *READY* substate.

Selected methods from the Thread class are presented below. Examples of their usage are presented in subsequent sections.

```
final boolean isAlive()
```

This method can be used to find out if a thread is alive or dead. A thread is *alive* if it has been started but not yet terminated—that is, it is not in the TERMINATED state.

```
Thread.State getState()
```

Returns the state of this thread (Table 22.1). It should be used for monitoring the state and not for synchronizing control.

```
final int getPriority()
final void setPriority(int newPriority)
```

The first method returns the priority of a thread (p. 1385). The second method changes its priority. The priority set will be the minimum of the specified newPriority and the maximum priority permitted for this thread. There is no guarantee that a thread with a higher priority will be chosen to run.

```
static void yield()
```

Causes the current thread to temporarily pause its execution and, thereby, allow other threads to execute. It is up to the JVM to decide if and when this transition will take place. The transition is from the *RUNNING* substate to the *READY* substate in the RUNNABLE state (Figure 22.4).

```
static void sleep(long millisec) throws InterruptedException
static void sleep(long millis, int nanos) throws InterruptedException
```

The current thread sleeps for at least the specified time before it becomes eligible for running again. The transition is from the *RUNNING* substate of the RUNNABLE state to the TIMED_WAITING state (Figure 22.4).

```
final void join() throws InterruptedException
final void join(long millisec) throws InterruptedException
```

A call to any of these two methods invoked on a thread will wait and not return until either the thread has completed or it is timed out after the specified time, respectively. In Figure 22.4, the transition is from the *RUNNING* substate of the RUNNABLE state to the WAITING state for the first method and to the TIMED_WAITING state for the second method.

```
static Map<Thread, StackTraceElement[]> getAllStackTraces()
```

Returns a map of stack traces for all alive threads. Keep in mind that each thread has its own JVM stack for method execution. The map can be used, for example, to extract a set of all alive threads.

Example 22.3 illustrates transitions between thread states. A thread at (1) sleeps a
little at (2) and then does some computation in a loop at (3), after which the thread
terminates. The main() method monitors the thread in a loop at (4), printing the
thread state returned by the getState() method. The output shows that the thread
starts off in the NEW state and goes through the RUNNABLE state when the run() method
starts to execute, and then transits to the TIMED_WAITING state to sleep. On waking
up, it computes the loop in the RUNNABLE state, and transits to the TERMINATED state
when the run() method completes execution.

Example 22.3 *Thread States*

```java
public class ThreadStates {

  private static Thread t1 = new Thread("T1") {      // (1)
    @Override public void run() {
      try {
        sleep(1);                                    // (2)
        for (int i = 10000; i > 0; i--) {;}          // (3)
      } catch (InterruptedException ie) {
        ie.printStackTrace();
      }
    }
  };

  public static void main(String[] args) {
    System.out.println(t1.getState());               // (4)
    t1.start();
    while (true) {                                    // (5)
      Thread.State state = t1.getState();
      System.out.println(state);
      if (state == Thread.State.TERMINATED) {
        break;
      }
    }
  }
}
```

Probable output from the program:

```
NEW
RUNNABLE
TIMED_WAITING
...
TIMED_WAITING
RUNNABLE
...
RUNNABLE
TERMINATED
```

Thread Priorities

Threads are assigned priorities that the thread scheduler *can* use to determine how the threads will be scheduled. The thread scheduler can use thread priorities to determine which thread gets to run. The thread scheduler favors giving CPU time to the thread with the highest priority in the *READY* substate. This is not necessarily the thread that has been in the *READY* substate the longest time. Heavy reliance on thread priorities for the behavior of a program can make the program unportable across platforms, as thread scheduling is host platform–dependent.

Selective priorities are defined by enum constants in the Thread class, shown in Table 22.2.

Table 22.2 *Selective Priorities Defined by the* Thread *Class*

Enum type java.lang.Thread	Value	Description
MIN_PRIORITY	0	Lowest priority
NORM_PRIORITY	5	Default priority
MAX_PRIORITY	10	Highest priority

A thread inherits the priority of its parent thread. The priority of a thread can be set using the setPriority() method and read using the getPriority() method, both of which are defined in the Thread class. The following code sets the priority of the thread myThread to the minimum of two values: maximum priority and current priority incremented to the next level. It also shows the default text representation of a thread, [*thread_name*, *priority*, *parent_thread_name*].

```
Thread myThread = new Thread(() ->
    System.out.println(Thread.currentThread() + ": Don't mess with my priority!")
);
System.out.println(myThread);
myThread.setPriority(Math.min(Thread.MAX_PRIORITY, myThread.getPriority() + 1));
myThread.start();
```

Output from the code:

```
Thread[Thread-0,5,main]
Thread[Thread-0,6,main]: Don't mess with my priority!
```

The setPriority() method is an *advisory* method, meaning that it provides a hint from the program to the JVM, which the JVM is in no way obliged to honor. A thread with higher priority is not guaranteed to complete its work faster than a thread with lower priority. The method can be used to fine-tune the *performance* of the program, but should not be relied upon for the *correctness* of the program.

Thread Scheduler

Schedulers in JVM implementations usually employ one of the following two strategies, which come into play in the RUNNABLE state:

- Preemptive scheduling

  If a thread with a higher priority than the current running thread moves to the *READY* substate, the current running thread can be *preempted* (moved from the *RUNNING* substate to the *READY* substate) to let the higher-priority thread execute.

- Time-sliced or round-robin scheduling

  A running thread is allowed to execute for a fixed length of time in the *RUNNING* substate, after which it moves to the *READY* substate to await its turn to run again.

It should be emphasized that thread schedulers are implementation- and platform-dependent; therefore, how threads will be scheduled is unpredictable, at least from platform to platform.

Starting a Thread

After a thread has been created, the thread is in the NEW state (Figure 22.5). Only after its start() method has been called, can the thread do useful work. This method is asynchronous—that is, it returns immediately. The newly created thread transits to the *READY* substate, waiting its turn to execute on the CPU at the discretion of the thread scheduler. The getState() method on this thread will return the value Thread.State.RUNNABLE. For a thread that is created but not started, the getState() method will return the value Thread.State.NEW. Details of creating and starting a thread were covered in an earlier section (p. 1370).

Figure 22.5 *Starting a Thread*

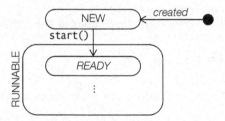

Running and Yielding

Once in the *READY* substate, the thread is eligible for running—that is, it waits for its turn to get CPU time. The thread scheduler decides which thread runs and for how long. Figure 22.6 illustrates the transitions between the *READY* and *RUNNING* substates. The thread transits from the *READY* substate to the *RUNNING* substate when it is its turn to run. The getState() method on this thread will return the value Thread.State.RUNNABLE.

A call to the static method yield(), defined in the Thread class, may cause the current thread in the *RUNNING* substate to transit to the *READY* substate. If this happens, the thread is then at the mercy of the thread scheduler as to when it will run again. It is possible that if there are no threads in the *READY* substate, this thread can continue executing. If there are other threads in the *READY* substate, their priorities can influence which thread gets to execute.

As with the setPriority() method, the yield() method is also an advisory method, and therefore comes with no guarantees that the JVM will honor the call. A call to the yield() method does *not* affect any locks that the thread might hold.

Figure 22.6 *Running and Yielding*

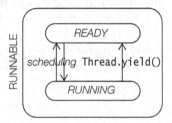

By calling the static method yield(), the running thread gives other threads in the *READY* substate a chance to run. A typical example where this can be useful is when a user has given some command to start a CPU-intensive computation, and has the option of cancelling it by clicking a CANCEL button. If the computation thread hogs the CPU and the user clicks the CANCEL button, chances are that it might take awhile before the thread monitoring the user input gets a chance to run and take appropriate action to stop the computation. A thread running such a computation should do the computation in increments, yielding between increments to allow other threads to run. This is illustrated by the following run() method:

```
public void run() {
  try {
    while (!done()) {
      doLittleBitMore();
      Thread.yield();                      // Current thread yields.
    }
  } catch (InterruptedException ie) { // Clean up if the thread is interrupted.
    doCleaningUp();
  }
}
```

Executing Synchronized Code

Threads share the same memory space—that is, they can share resources. However, there are critical situations where it is desirable that only one thread at a time has access to a shared resource. For example, crediting and debiting a shared bank account concurrently among several users without proper discipline will jeopardize the integrity of the account data. Java provides the concept of *synchronization* in order to control access to shared resources. It is one of the mechanisms that Java provides to write *thread-safe code* (§23.4, p. 1451).

The keyword synchronized and the intrinsic lock mechanism (p. 1380) form the basis for implementing synchronized execution of code. We refer to this as *intrinsic locking* (also referred to as *built-in synchronization*). There are two ways in which execution of code can be synchronized: by declaring synchronized *methods* or by using synchronized *statements*. The code that is synchronized to execute by one thread at a time is often referred to as a *critical section*.

Acquiring the Object Lock

In order to execute synchronized code, a thread must first acquire the lock of the relevant object, as illustrated in Figure 22.7. If this lock is not available, the thread transits from the *RUNNING* substate to the BLOCKED state. The thread is put in the *entry set* of the object. Threads in the BLOCKED state are grouped according to the object whose lock they are waiting for. The getState() method on a blocked thread in this state will return the value Thread.State.BLOCKED.

If there are several threads waiting for the same object lock, one is chosen at the discretion of the thread scheduler. It then transits to the *READY* substate where it takes its turn to run again.

Example 22.4 illustrates acquiring the lock in order to synchronize on a shared resource.

Figure 22.7 *Blocked for Lock Acquisition*

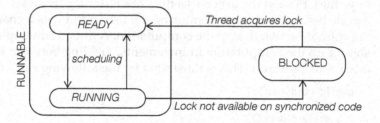

Synchronized Methods

If the methods of an object should only be executed by one thread at a time, then the declaration of all such methods should be specified with the keyword synchronized. A thread wishing to execute a synchronized method must first acquire the object lock before it can execute the method on the object. This is simply achieved by calling the method. If the lock is already held by another thread, the calling thread waits in the entry set of the object lock, as explained earlier. No particular action on the part of the program is necessary to acquire the lock. A thread releases the lock on method return, regardless of whether the synchronized method completed execution normally or threw an uncaught exception. In both cases, if there are any blocked threads in the entry set, one is chosen to acquire the lock. In case of an uncaught exception, the exception is propagated through the JVM stack of the thread that released the lock.

Synchronized methods are useful in situations where methods can manipulate the state of a shared object in ways that can corrupt the state if executed concurrently.

Example 22.4 is a reworking of the counter implementation from Example 22.1. The CounterX class defines the synchronized method increment() at (1a) that prints the old value and the new incremented value in the counter.

The main() method in the SynchronizedMethodDemo class creates a CounterX object at (2) and a Runnable at (3) that calls the increment() method five times on this CounterX object. Two threads are created and started at (4) and (5) that will each call the synchronized increment() method on the *same* CounterX object five times—in contrast to Example 22.1, where each thread had its own counter.

From the output shown in Example 22.4, we can see that the main thread exits right after creating and starting the threads. The output shows that the two threads run mutually exclusive of each other. Thread-0 increments the counter to 5 and Thread-1 increments it further to 10.

It is instructive to run Example 22.4 with (1a) commented out and (1b) uncommented. We see from the output that the execution of the threads is interleaved, and some results look dubious (Thread-1: old:0 new:2). Non-synchronized incrementing of the value in the counter between the two threads is a disaster waiting to happen. This is an example of what is called a *race condition* (also known as *thread interference*). It occurs when two or more threads simultaneously update a shared value and, due to the scheduling of the threads, can leave the value in an undefined or inconsistent state.

Running the program in Example 22.4 with the synchronized version of the increment() at (1a) avoids any race conditions. The lock is only released when the synchronized method exits, guaranteeing a mutually exclusive increment of the counter by each thread.

Example 22.4 *Mutual Exclusion*

```
class CounterX {
  private int counter = 0;

  public synchronized void increment() {                          // (1a)
//public void increment() {                                       // (1b)
    System.out.println(Thread.currentThread().getName()
                + ": old:" + counter + " new:" + ++counter);
  }
}
```

```
public class SynchronizedMethodDemo {
  public static void main(String[] args) {
    CounterX counter = new CounterX();                            // (2)
    Runnable r = () -> {                                          // (3)
      for (int i = 0; i < 5; i++) {
        counter.increment();
      }
```

```
        System.out.println("Exiting " + Thread.currentThread().getName());
      };
      new Thread(r).start();                                            // (4)
      new Thread(r).start();                                            // (5)
      System.out.println("Exiting thread " + Thread.currentThread().getName());
   }
}
```

Probable output from the program when run with (1a):

```
Exiting thread main
Thread-0: old:0 new:1
Thread-0: old:1 new:2
Thread-0: old:2 new:3
Thread-0: old:3 new:4
Thread-0: old:4 new:5
Exiting Thread-0
Thread-1: old:5 new:6
Thread-1: old:6 new:7
Thread-1: old:7 new:8
Thread-1: old:8 new:9
Thread-1: old:9 new:10
Exiting Thread-1
```

Probable output from the program when run with (1b):

```
Thread-1: old:0 new:2
Thread-1: old:2 new:3
Exiting thread main
Thread-0: old:0 new:1
Thread-1: old:3 new:4
Thread-0: old:4 new:5
Thread-0: old:6 new:7
Thread-1: old:5 new:6
Thread-1: old:8 new:9
Exiting Thread-1
Thread-0: old:7 new:8
Thread-0: old:9 new:10
Exiting Thread-0
```

Reentrant Synchronization

While a thread is inside a synchronized method of an object, all other threads that wish to execute this synchronized method or any other synchronized method of the object will have to wait in the entry set. This restriction does not apply to the thread that already has the lock and is executing a synchronized method of the object. Such a thread can invoke, directly or indirectly, other synchronized methods of the object without being blocked—that is, once a thread has a lock on an object, it can acquire the lock on the same object several times, called *reentrant synchronization*. The non-synchronized methods of the object can always be called at any time by any thread.

Examples of reentrant synchronization can be found in §23.4, p. 1460.

Synchronization on Class Lock

Static methods synchronize on the *class lock*. Acquiring and releasing a class lock by a thread in order to execute a static synchronized method is analogous to that of an object lock for a synchronized instance method. A thread acquires the class lock before it can proceed with the execution of any static synchronized method in the class, blocking other threads wishing to execute any static synchronized methods in the same class. The blocked threads wait in the entry set of the class lock. This does not apply to static, non-synchronized methods, which can be invoked by any thread. A thread acquiring the lock of a class to execute a static synchronized method has no effect on any thread acquiring the lock on any object of the class to execute a synchronized instance method. In other words, synchronization of static methods in a class is independent from the synchronization of instance methods on objects of the class.

A subclass decides whether the new definition of an inherited synchronized method will remain synchronized in the subclass.

Synchronized Statements

Whereas execution of synchronized methods of an object is synchronized on the lock of the object, the synchronized statement allows execution of arbitrary code to be synchronized on the lock of an *arbitrary object*. The general form of the synchronized statement (also called *synchronized block*) is as follows:

```
synchronized (object_reference_expression) { code_block }
```

The *object reference expression* must evaluate to a non-null reference value; otherwise, a NullPointerException is thrown. The *code block* is usually related to the object whose lock is acquired. This is analogous to a synchronized method, where the execution of the method is synchronized on the lock of the current object. The following code is equivalent to the synchronized increment() method in the CounterX class in Example 22.4:

```
public void increment() {
  synchronized(this) {                                    // Synchronized statement
    System.out.println(Thread.currentThread().getName()
        + ": current: " + counter + " new:" + ++counter);
  }
}
```

Once a thread has entered the code block after acquiring the lock on the specified object, no other thread will be able to execute the code block, or any other code requiring the same object lock, until the lock is released. This happens when the execution of the code block completes normally or an uncaught exception is thrown. In contrast to synchronized methods, this mechanism allows fine-grained synchronization of code on arbitrary objects.

The object reference expression in the synchronized statement is mandatory. A class can choose to synchronize the execution of a part of a method by using the this reference and putting the relevant code of the method in the synchronized statement.

The curly brackets of the block cannot be omitted, even if the code block has just one statement.

```
class SmartClient {
  BankAccount account;
  // ...
  public void updateTransaction() {
    synchronized (account) {        // (1) synchronized statement
      account.update();             // (2)
    }
  }
}
```

In the example above, the code at (2) in the synchronized statement at (1) is synchronized on the BankAccount object. If several threads were to concurrently execute the method updateTransaction() on an object of SmartClient, the statement at (2) would be executed by one thread at a time only after synchronizing on the BankAccount object associated with this particular instance of SmartClient.

Inner classes can access data in their enclosing context (§9.1, p. 491). An inner object might need to synchronize on its associated outer object in order to ensure integrity of data in the latter. This is illustrated in the following code where the synchronized statement at (5) uses the special form of the this reference to synchronize on the outer object associated with an object of the inner class. This setup ensures that a thread executing the method incr() in an inner object can only access the private double field count at (2) in the synchronized statement at (5) by first acquiring the lock on the associated outer object. If another thread has the lock of the associated outer object, the thread in the inner object has to wait for the lock to be released before it can proceed with the execution of the synchronized statement at (5). However, synchronizing on an inner object and on its associated outer object are independent of each other, unless enforced explicitly, as in the following code:

```
class Outer {                    // (1) Top-level Class
  private double count;          // (2)

  protected class Inner {        // (3) Non-static member Class
    public void incr() {         // (4)
      synchronized(Outer.this) { // (5) Synchronized statement on Outer object
        ++count;                 // (6)
      }
    }
  }
}
```

A synchronized statement can also be specified on a class lock:

```
synchronized (<class_name>.class) { <code_block> }
```

The statement synchronizes on the lock of the object denoted by the reference *class_name*.class. This object (of type Class) represents the class at runtime. A static synchronized method classAction() in class A is equivalent to the following declaration:

```
static void classAction() {
  synchronized (A.class) {          // Synchronized statement on class A
```

```
        // ...
    }
}
```

In summary, a thread can acquire a lock by carrying out the following actions:

- By executing a synchronized instance method of an object of a class.
- By executing a static synchronized method of a class (in which case, the object is the Class object representing the class in the JVM).
- By executing the body of a synchronized statement that synchronizes either on an object of a class, or on the Class object representing a class in the JVM.
- Intrinsic locking does not provide any guarantees as to which thread among the waiting threads will acquire the intrinsic lock.
- Intrinsic lock acquisition is rigid: Either the thread acquires the intrinsic lock immediately if it is available, or the thread has to wait its turn among the waiting threads. There is no other lock acquisition policy—for example, timed waiting.
- An intrinsic lock is acquired and released in the same synchronized code—for example, in a synchronized method. It cannot be acquired or released in separate methods.

Interrupt Handling

The purpose of interrupts is to allow threads to inform each other when the task they are running might need attention. For example, a thread might be hoarding crucial resources or might have become unresponsive. Whatever corrective action is required is then at the discretion of the thread that is interrupted. Simply catching and ignoring an InterruptedException is not recommended.

The following selected methods from the Thread class can be used for handling interrupts in threads.

void interrupt()

Interrupts the thread on which it is invoked.

If the thread is in a non-runnable state, either blocked or waiting, the *interrupt status* of the thread is *cleared* and the thread will receive an InterruptedException when it gets to run.

For a thread that is in the RUNNABLE state, the *interrupt status* of the thread will be *set*.

boolean isInterrupted()

Checks whether this thread has been interrupted. The *interrupt status* of the thread is *not* affected.

static boolean interrupted()

Checks whether the current thread has been interrupted. The *interrupt status* of the thread is cleared.

A thread can be interrupted by invoking the method interrupt(). A thread can also invoke this method on itself. How the interrupt manifests in the interrupted thread depends on the state the thread is in when the interrupt() method is invoked. Example 22.5 illustrates the two main scenarios that show how a thread can discover if it has been interrupted—and which a thread should be prepared to handle.

In Example 22.5, the main() method creates and starts a thread at (1) that executes the task defined at (3). The main thread uses an infinite loop at (2) in which it tries to send an interrupt to the worker thread by calling the interrupt() method. Sending an interrupt is dependent on the condition in the if statement being a random even number. If it cannot send an interrupt, the main thread sleeps for awhile before continuing to execute the infinite loop. The main thread exits the infinite loop (and terminates) when it has sent an interrupt to the worker thread.

The task executed by the worker thread is defined by the lambda expression at (3). The task executes an infinite while loop at (4) that illustrates how a thread can discover it has received an interrupt:

- An if statement at (5), which is used to determine if the thread has been interrupted. This corresponds to the first scenario in the output.

  If any interrupt is sent to the current thread by calling its interrupt() method while it is running, the interrupt status of the thread will be set. Calling the isInterrupted() method on the current thread in the if statement will then return true.

- A try-catch block at (6) in which the thread sleeps, and catches any Interrupted-Exception that is thrown in response to receiving an interrupt while it was asleep. This corresponds to the second scenario in the output.

  If the interrupt() method was called on the thread while it was sleeping, it will result in the interrupt status being cleared and an InterruptedException being thrown in the try block when the thread runs again. Appropriate action can be taken to mitigate the interrupt in the catch block at (7) in which this exception is caught.

- -

Example 22.5 *Interrupt Handling*

```java
public class InterruptHandling {
  public static void main(String[] args) throws InterruptedException {
    Thread worker = new Thread(task, "worker");              // (1)
    worker.start();
    while (true) {                                            // (2)
      if ((int)(Math.random()*100) % 2 == 0) {
        worker.interrupt();
        break;
      }
      Thread.sleep(2);
    }
  }
```

```java
    private static Runnable task = () -> {                        // (3)
      Thread ct = Thread.currentThread();
      String threadName = ct.getName();
      while (true) {                                              // (4)
        System.out.println(threadName + " performing task");

        if (ct.isInterrupted()) {                                // (5)
          System.out.println(threadName + ": interrupted flag is "
                              + ct.isInterrupted());
          System.out.println(threadName + " terminating");
          return;
        }

        try {                                                    // (6)
          Thread.sleep(2);
        } catch (InterruptedException e) {                       // (7)
          System.out.println(threadName + " caught " + e);
          System.out.println(threadName + ": interrupted flag is "
                              + ct.isInterrupted());
          System.out.println(threadName + " terminating");
          return;
        }
      }
    };
  }
```

Probable output from the program—first scenario:

```
worker performing task
worker: interrupted flag is true
worker terminating
```

Probable output from the program—second scenario:

```
worker performing task
worker performing task
worker caught java.lang.InterruptedException: sleep interrupted
worker: interrupted flag is false
worker terminating
```

Sleeping and Waking Up

Transitions by a thread that is sleeping and waking up are illustrated in Figure 22.8.

A call to the static method sleep() in the Thread class will cause the *currently running* thread to temporarily pause its execution and transit to the TIMED_WAITING state. The getState() method on this thread will return the value Thread.State.TIMED_WAITING.

The thread is *guaranteed* to sleep for *at least* the time specified in its argument, before transitioning to the *READY* substate where it takes its turn to run again. It might sleep a little longer than the specified time, but it will not sleep indefinitely.

Figure 22.8 *Sleeping and Waking Up*

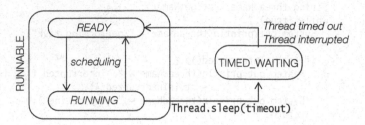

If a thread is interrupted while sleeping, it will throw a checked InterruptedException when it awakes and gets to execute. The idiom is to call the sleep() method in a try-catch block that handles the InterruptedException. The sleep() method does *not* release any locks that the thread might have.

There are two overloaded versions of the sleep() method in the Thread class, allowing time to be specified in milliseconds, and additionally in nanoseconds.

Usage of the sleep() method is illustrated in Examples 22.1, 22.2, and 22.4.

Thread Coordination

Before proceeding further with thread coordination using the wait() and notify()/ notifyAll() methods, it must be emphasized that these methods provide *low-level* thread coordination, which is error-prone and difficult to get right, and should be avoided in favor of the *high-level* concurrency support provided by the java.util.concurrent package (Chapter 23, p. 1419).

Waiting and notifying provide a means of coordination between threads that *synchronize on the same object*—also called *data access synchronization*. The threads execute wait() and notify() (or notifyAll()) methods *on the shared object* for this purpose. These final methods are defined in the Object class, and therefore are inherited by all objects. These methods can only be executed on an object whose lock the thread holds (i.e., in synchronized code); otherwise, the call will result in an IllegalMonitorStateException.

```
final void wait(long timeout) throws InterruptedException
final void wait(long timeout, int nanos) throws InterruptedException
final void wait() throws InterruptedException
```

A thread invokes the wait() method on the object whose lock it holds. The thread is added to the *wait set* of the current object.

```
final void notify()
final void notifyAll()
```

A thread invokes a notification method on the current object whose lock it holds to notify thread(s) that are in the wait set of the object.

Waiting

Coordination between threads is facilitated by waiting and notifying, as illustrated by Figures 22.9 and 22.10. A thread usually calls the wait() method on the object whose lock it holds because a condition for its continued execution was not met. The thread leaves the *RUNNING* substate and transits to the WAITING or TIMED_WAITING state, depending on whether a timeout was specified in the call. The thread releases ownership of the object lock.

Figure 22.9 *Timed Waiting and Notifying*

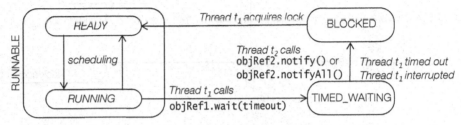

objRef1 and objRef2 are aliases

Transitioning to a waiting state and releasing the object lock are completed as one *atomic* (non-interruptible) operation. The releasing of the lock of the shared object by the thread allows other threads to run and execute synchronized code on the same object, after acquiring its lock.

Note that the waiting thread releases only the lock of the object on which the wait() method was invoked. It does not release any other object locks that it might hold, which will remain locked while the thread is waiting.

Each object has a *wait set* containing threads waiting for notification. Threads in a waiting state are grouped according to the object whose wait() method they invoked.

Figure 22.10 shows a thread t_1 that first acquires a lock on the shared object, and afterward invokes the wait() method on the shared object. This releases the object lock, the thread t_1 is added to the wait set of the object, and the thread waits to be notified in the WAITING state. While the thread t_1 is waiting, another thread t_2 can acquire the lock on the shared object for its own purpose.

Depending on whether a timeout was specified or not in the call to the wait() method, a call to the getState() method on thread t_1 while it is in a waiting state will return the value Thread.State.TIMED_WAITING or Thread.State.WAITING, respectively.

A thread in a waiting state can be awakened by the occurrence of any one of these events:

- Another thread invokes the notify() method on the object of the waiting thread, and the waiting thread is selected as the thread to be awakened.
- The waiting thread times out if it was a timed wait.
- Another thread interrupts the waiting thread.
- A spurious wakeup occurs.

Figure 22.10 *Thread Coordination*

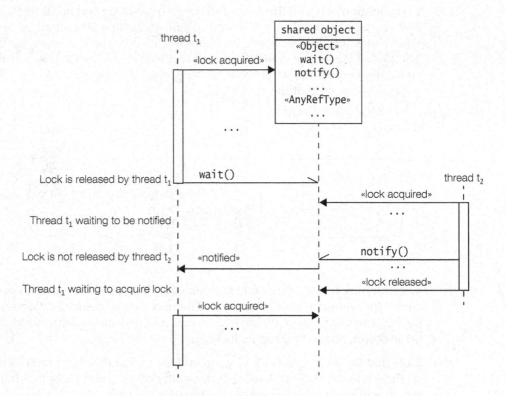

Notified

Invoking the `notify()` method on an object wakes up a single thread that is waiting for the lock of this object. The selection of a thread to awaken is dependent on the thread policies implemented by the JVM. On being *notified*, a waiting thread first transits to the BLOCKED state to acquire the lock on the object, and not directly to the *READY* substate of the RUNNABLE state. The thread is also removed from the wait set of the object. Note that the object lock is not released when the notifying thread invokes the `notify()` method. The notifying thread releases the lock at its own discretion, and the awakened thread will not be able to run until the notifying thread releases the object lock.

When the notified thread obtains the object lock, it is enabled for execution, waiting in the *READY* substate for its turn to execute again. Finally, when it does execute, the call to the `wait()` method returns and the thread can continue with its execution.

From Figure 22.10 we see that thread t_2 does not release the object lock when it invokes the `notify()` method. Thread t_1 is forced to wait in the BLOCKED state for lock acquisition. It is shown no privileges, and must compete with any other threads blocked for lock acquisition.

A call to the notify() method has no effect if there are no threads in the wait set of the object.

In contrast to the notify() method, the notifyAll() method wakes up *all* threads in the wait set of the shared object. They will all transit to the BLOCKED state, and contend for the object lock as explained earlier.

It should be stressed that a program should not make any assumptions about the order in which threads awaken in response to the notify() or notifyAll() method, or transit to the BLOCKED state for lock acquisition.

Timed-out

The wait() call can specify the time the thread should wait before being timed out, if it was not awakened by being notified or interrupted. The timed-out thread transits to the BLOCKED state and competes to acquire the lock as explained above. Note that the awakened thread has no way of knowing whether it was timed out or awakened by one of the notification methods.

If no timeout is specified in the call to the wait() method, the thread waits indefinitely in the WAITING state until it is notified, interrupted, or awakened spuriously.

Interrupted

This means that another thread invoked the interrupt() method on the waiting thread. The awakened thread is enabled as previously explained, but the return from the wait() call will result in an InterruptedException if and when the awakened thread finally gets a chance to run. The code invoking the wait() method must be prepared to handle this checked exception (p. 1393).

Spurious Wakeup

In very rare cases, a thread in a waiting state is awakened by what is called a *spurious wakeup*, which is not due to familiar events like being notified, timed out, or interrupted, but due to deep-level system signals warranting a wakeup call to the waiting threads. The condition on which the thread was waiting might not have been fulfilled when the thread wakes up from a spurious wakeup, and should therefore be rechecked when the thread gets to run. This is done by testing the condition in a loop that contains the wait() call, as the thread can go right back to waiting if the condition is not satisfied.

```
while (conditionNotSatisfied()) {
  ...
  wait();
  ...
}
// Proceed ...
```

Using Wait and Notify

The idiom is to call the wait() method in a try-catch block inside a loop, guarded by a condition that the thread expects to be set by notification.

In Example 22.6, the main() method of the class WaitNotifyScenario creates and starts four daemon threads that are manipulating the same MessageDisplay object. Two of them are continuously trying to set a message in the message display, while the other two are continuously trying to print whatever message is in the display.

Since the threads manipulate the same MessageDisplay object, and the setMessage() and displayMessage() methods in the class MessageDisplay are synchronized, it means that the threads synchronize on the same MessageDisplay object. In other words, the mutual exclusion of these operations is guaranteed on the same MessageDisplay object.

Example 22.6 *Waiting and Notifying*

```java
class MessageDisplay {
  private String message;

  public synchronized void displayMessage() {
    String threadName = Thread.currentThread().getName();
    while (this.message == null) {                          // No message?
      try {
        wait();                                             // (1)
      } catch (InterruptedException e) {
        e.printStackTrace();
      }
    }
    System.out.println(threadName + ": " + this.message);   // Display message.
    this.message = null;                                    // Remove message.
    notifyAll();                                            // (2)
  }

  public synchronized void setMessage(String message) {
    String threadName = Thread.currentThread().getName();
    while (this.message != null) {                          // Message present?
      try {
        wait();                                             // (3)
      } catch (InterruptedException e) {
        e.printStackTrace();
      }
    }
    this.message = message;                                 // Set new message.
    System.out.println(threadName + ": Message set is " + this.message);
    notifyAll();                                            // (4)
  }
}
```

```
public class WaitNotifyScenario {
    public static void main(String[] args) throws InterruptedException {
        MessageDisplay md = new MessageDisplay();
        Thread t1 = new Thread(() -> { while (true) md.setMessage("Hi!"); }, "t1");
        t1.setDaemon(true);
        t1.start();
        Thread t2 = new Thread(() -> { while (true) md.setMessage("Howdy!"); }, "t2");
        t2.setDaemon(true);
        t2.start();
        Thread t3 = new Thread(() -> { while (true) md.displayMessage(); }, "t3");
        t3.setDaemon(true);
        t3.start();
        Thread t4 = new Thread(() -> { while (true) md.displayMessage(); }, "t4");
        t4.setDaemon(true);
        t4.start();
        Thread.sleep(5);
        System.out.println("Exit from main.");
    }
}
```

Probable output from the program (*edited to fit on the page*):

```
t0: t1: Message set is Hi!
t3: Hi!
...
t2: Message set is Howdy!
t3: Howdy!
t1: Message set is Hi!
t3: Hi!
t2: Message set is Howdy!
t4: Howdy!
...
Exit from main.
t1: Message set is Hi!
t3: Hi!
t2: Message set is Howdy!
t4: Howdy!
t1: Message set is Hi!
```

Example 22.6 illustrates how threads waiting as a result of calling the wait() method on an object are notified by another thread calling the notifyAll() method on the same object, in order for a waiting thread to start running again.

One usage of the wait() call is shown in Example 22.6 at (1) in the synchronized displayMessage() method. When a thread executing this method on the Message-Display object finds that there is no message (this.message == null), it invokes the wait() method in order to wait for a thread to set a message.

Another use of the wait() call is shown at (3) in the synchronized setMessage() method. When a thread executing this method on the MessageDisplay object finds that there is already a message (this.message != null), it invokes the wait() method to wait for a thread to display and remove the message.

When a thread executing the synchronized method setMessage() on the Message-Display object successfully sets a message, it calls the notifyAll() method at (4). The wait set of the MessageDisplay object may contain any waiting threads that have earlier called the wait() method at either (1) or (3) on this MessageDisplay object. A single thread from the wait set is enabled for running. If this thread was executing a displayMessage() operation, it now has a chance of being successful because a message is available for display at the moment. If this thread was executing a setMessage() operation, it can try again to see if the previous message has been removed so that a new message can be set.

When a thread executing the synchronized method displayMessage() on the Message-Display object successfully prints and removes the message, it calls the notifyAll() method at (2). Again assuming that the wait set of the MessageDisplay object is not empty, one thread from the set is arbitrarily chosen and enabled. If the notified thread was executing a setMessage() operation, it now has a chance of succeeding because there is no message in the MessageDisplay object at the moment.

Note that the waiting condition at (1) for the displayMessage() operation is executed in a loop. A waiting thread that has been notified is not guaranteed to run right away. Before it gets to run, another thread may synchronize on the MessageDisplay object and remove the message. If the notified thread was waiting to display the message, it would now incorrectly try to display a nonexisting message because the condition was not tested after notification. The loop ensures that the condition is always tested after notification, sending the thread back to the waiting state if the condition is not met. To avert the analogous danger of setting a message if one already exits in the MessageDisplay object, the waiting condition at (3) for the setMessage() operation is also executed in a loop.

The output from Example 22.6 shows the behavior of the threads that set and print the message in the shared MessageDisplay object, respectively. The two operations of setting the message and displaying/removing the message are performed in lockstep.

The four threads created are daemon threads. They will be terminated if they have not completed when the main thread dies, thereby stopping the execution of the program.

Joining

A thread can invoke the overloaded method join() (from the Thread class) on another thread in order to wait for the other thread to complete its execution before continuing—that is, the first thread waits for the second thread to *join it after completion*.

A running thread t_1 invokes the method join() on a thread t_2. The join() call has no effect if thread t_2 has already completed. If thread t_2 is still alive, thread t_1 transits to one of the two waiting states. Depending on whether a timeout was specified or not in the call to the join() method, a call to the getState() method on thread t_1

while it is waiting for join completion will return the value Thread.State.TIMED-_WAITING or Thread.State.WAITING, respectively.

Thread t_1 waits in a waiting state until one of these events occurs (Figure 22.11):

- Thread t_2 completes.

  In this case, thread t_1 moves to the *READY* substate, and when it gets to run, it will continue normally after the call to the join() method.

- Thread t_1 is timed out.

  The time specified in the argument of the join() method call has elapsed without thread t_2 completing. In this case as well, thread t_1 transits from the TIMED_WAITING state to the *READY* substate. When it gets to run, it will continue normally after the call to the join() method.

  If the no-argument join() method was called, there is no timeout for thread t_1 in the WAITING state. It waits indefinitely in this state for one of the other events to occur.

- Thread t_1 is interrupted.

  Some thread interrupted thread t_1 while it was waiting for join completion. Thread t_1 transits to the *READY* substate, but when it gets to execute, it will now receive an InterruptedException.

Figure 22.11 *Timed Joining of Threads*

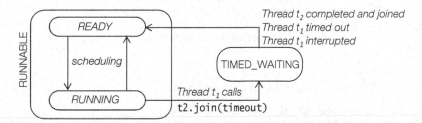

Example 22.7 illustrates joining of threads. The AnotherClient class below uses the Counter class, which extends the Thread class, from Example 22.2. It creates two threads that are enabled for execution. The main thread invokes the join() method on the Counter A thread. If the Counter A thread has not already completed, the main thread transits to the WAITING state, as no timeout is specified. When the Counter A thread completes, the main thread will be enabled for running. Once the main thread is running, it continues with execution after (5). A parent thread can call the isAlive() method to find out whether its child threads are alive, before terminating itself. The call to the isAlive() method on the Counter A thread at (6) correctly reports that the Counter A thread is not alive. A similar scenario transpires between the main thread and the Counter B thread. At most, the main thread passes through the WAITING state twice.

Example 22.7 *Joining of Threads*

```
class Counter extends Thread { /* See Example 22.2, p. 1376. */ }
```

```
public class AnotherClient {
  public static void main(String[] args) {

    // Create two Counter threads, set their names, and start them:    // (4)
    Counter counterA = new Counter();
    Counter counterB = new Counter();
    counterA.setName("counterA");
    counterB.setName("counterB");
    counterA.start();
    counterB.start();

    try {
      System.out.println("Wait for the child threads to finish.");
      counterA.join();                                                 // (5)
      if (!counterA.isAlive()) {                                       // (6)
        System.out.println("Counter A not alive.");
      }
      counterB.join();                                                 // (7)
      if (!counterB.isAlive()) {
        System.out.println("Counter B not alive.");
      }
    } catch (InterruptedException ie) {
      System.out.println("main thread interrupted.");
    }
    System.out.println("Exiting from main thread.");
  }
}
```

Probable output from the program:

```
Wait for the child threads to finish.
counterB: 0
counterA: 0
counterA: 1
counterB: 1
counterA: 2
counterB: 2
counterA: 3
counterB: 3
counterA: 4
counterB: 4
Exiting counterB
Exiting counterA
Counter A not alive.
Counter B not alive.
Exiting from main thread.
```

Blocking for I/O

A running thread, on executing a *blocking operation* requiring a resource (like a call to an I/O method), will transit to the BLOCKED state (Figure 22.12). The getState() method on this thread will return the value Thread.State.BLOCKED. When the thread can complete the blocking operation, it proceeds to the *READY* substate. An example is a thread reading from the standard input terminal, that blocks until input is provided:

```
int input = System.in.read();
```

Figure 22.12 *Blocked for I/O*

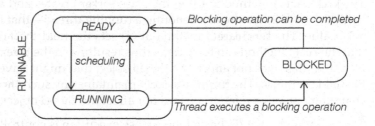

Thread Termination

A thread can transit to the TERMINATED state from the RUNNABLE state (Figure 22.13). The thread terminates when it finishes executing its run() method, either by returning normally or by throwing an exception. Once in this state, the thread cannot be resurrected. There is no way the thread can be enabled for running again, not even by calling the start() method again on the thread object. The getState() method on this thread will return the value Thread.State.TERMINATED.

Figure 22.13 *Thread Termination*

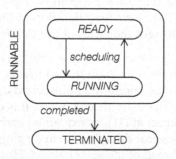

The *main thread* is special in that it is started and terminated when the main() method starts and stops execution, respectively.

It might be tempting to call the System.exit() method to terminate a thread, but this can be rather drastic. A call to this method terminates the *process* in which the JVM is running, and as a consequence, terminating all threads that might still be alive in the JVM.

Controlling a Thread

Example 22.8 illustrates a typical scenario where a thread can be controlled by one or more threads. Work is performed by a loop body, which the thread executes continuously. It should be possible for other threads to start and stop the *worker* thread. This functionality is implemented by the class Worker at (1), which has a private field theThread declared at (2) to keep track of the Thread object executing its run() method at (5).

The kickStart() method at (3) in the class Worker creates and starts a thread if the field theThread is not already denoting a running thread—that is, if the field has the null value. The terminate() method at (4) sets the field theThread to null to signal that the run() method can terminate, thus resulting in the thread being terminated. Note that this does not affect any Thread object that might have been referenced by the field theThread. The runtime system maintains any such Thread object; therefore, changing one of its references does not affect the Thread object.

The run() method at (5) has a loop whose execution is controlled by a special condition. The condition tests to see whether the Thread object referenced by the reference theThread and the Thread object currently running are one and the same. This is bound to be the case if the reference theThread has the same reference value that it was assigned when the thread was created and started in the kickStart() method. The condition will then be true, and the body of the loop will execute. However, if the value in the reference theThread has changed, the condition will be false. In that case, the loop will not execute, the run() method will complete, and the thread will terminate. This idiom is generally recommended to terminate a thread.

A client can control the thread implemented by the class Worker, using the kickStart() and the terminate() methods. The client is able to terminate the running thread at the start of the next iteration of the loop body by calling the terminate() method that changes the value of the theThread reference to null.

In Example 22.8, a Worker object is first created at (8) and a thread started on this Worker object at (9). The main thread invokes the sleep() method at (10) to temporarily cease its execution for 2 milliseconds, giving the thread of the Worker object a chance to run. The main thread, when it is executing again, terminates the thread of the Worker object at (11), as explained earlier. This simple scenario can be generalized where several threads, sharing a single Worker object, could be starting and stopping the thread of the Worker object. However, this generalization also requires that the field theThread is declared volatile in order to avoid memory consistency errors (p. 1414).

Example 22.8 *Thread Termination*

```
public class Worker implements Runnable {                    // (1)
  private Thread theThread;                                  // (2)

  public void kickStart() {                                  // (3)
    if (theThread == null) {
      theThread = new Thread(this);
      theThread.start();
    }
  }

  public void terminate() {                                  // (4)
    theThread = null;
  }

  @Override
  public void run() {                                        // (5)
    while (theThread == Thread.currentThread()) {            // (6)
      System.out.println("Going around in loops.");
    }
  }
}
```

```
public class Controller {
  public static void main(String[] args) {                   // (7)
    Worker worker = new Worker();                             // (8)
    System.out.println("Start the worker.");
    worker.kickStart();                                      // (9)
    try {
      Thread.sleep(2);                                       // (10)
    } catch(InterruptedException ie) {
      ie.printStackTrace();
    }
    System.out.println("Stop the worker.");
    worker.terminate();                                      // (11)
  }
}
```

Probable output from the program:

```
Start the worker.
Going around in loops.
Going around in loops.
...
Going around in loops.
Going around in loops.
Stop the worker.
Going around in loops.
```

Deprecated Thread Methods

There are a few operations defined by the Thread class that are not recommended for use and are now marked as @Deprecated. These include the following methods of the Thread class:

```
final void resume()
final void stop()
final void suspend()
```

Their initial design intention was to control the thread lifecycle. However, Java concurrency design has changed since these operations were introduced. The new concurrency API allows concurrent programming at a higher level than controlling the threads. The legacy approach to controlling threads was to force a thread to become suspended, to resume, or to stop. Deprecated concurrency methods are likely to result in memory corruption. The code in this chapter does not use any of the deprecated methods.

22.5 Thread Issues

In this section, we briefly outline some problems that occur often in multithreaded applications. Although some solutions are mentioned, there is no silver bullet that will solve all such problems. In the worst-case scenario, the application may need to be redesigned all over again.

Liveness and Fairness

Multithreaded applications strive for *liveness* and *fairness*.

The *fairness property* of a multithreaded application refers to threads in the application getting a fair chance to run—so that all threads in the application can make progress in their work, and no thread monopolizes the CPU at the expense of others.

The *liveness property* of a multithreaded application refers to the ability of the threads to execute in a *timely manner*—meaning performing as expected and making continuous progress in their work.

The rest of this section describes three liveness issues common in multithreaded applications: *deadlock*, *livelock*, and *starvation*.

Deadlock

A *deadlock* is a situation where threads are holding locks on objects that other threads need—a thread is waiting for an object lock that another thread holds, and this second thread is waiting for an object lock that the first thread holds. Since each thread is waiting for the other thread to release a lock, they both remain waiting forever in a waiting state and never make any progress. The threads are said to be *deadlocked*.

A deadlock is depicted in Figure 22.14. Thread t_1 has a lock on object o_1, but cannot acquire the lock on object o_2. Thread t_2 has a lock on object o_2, but cannot acquire the lock on object o_1. They can only proceed if one of them releases a lock the other one wants, which is never going to happen.

Figure 22.14 *Deadlock*

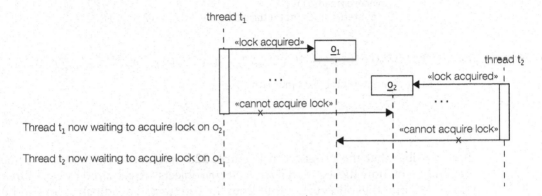

The situation in Figure 22.14 is implemented in Example 22.9. Thread t_1 at (3) tries to synchronize at (4) and (5), first on string o_1 at (1), then on string o_2 at (2), respectively. The thread t_2 at (6) does the opposite. It synchronizes at (7) and (8), first on string o_2 and then on string o_1, respectively. A deadlock can occur as explained previously, and the print statement at (11) will never be executed.

However, the potential of a deadlock in the situation in Example 22.9 is easy to fix. If the two threads acquire the locks on the objects in the same order, then mutual lock dependency is avoided and a deadlock can never occur. This means having the same locking order at (4) and (5) as at (7) and (8). In general, the cause of a deadlock is not always easy to discover, let alone easy to fix.

Example 22.9 *Deadlock*

```java
public class DeadLockDanger {
  public static void main(String[] args) {
    String o1 = "o1 " ;                                         // (1)
    String o2 = "o2 ";                                          // (2)

    Thread t1 = (new Thread("t1") {                             // (3)
      @Override
      public void run() {
        String threadName = Thread.currentThread().getName();
        while (true) {
          synchronized(o1) {                                    // (4)
            System.out.println(threadName + " acquired " + o1);
            synchronized(o2) {                                  // (5)
              System.out.println(threadName + ": " + o1 + o2);
    }}}}});
```

```
      Thread t2 = (new Thread("t2") {                                // (6)
        @Override
        public void run() {
          String threadName = Thread.currentThread().getName();
          while (true) {
            synchronized(o2) {                                       // (7)
              System.out.println(threadName + " acquired " + o2);
              synchronized(o1) {                                     // (8)
                System.out.println(threadName + ": " + o2 + o1);
        }}}}});

      t1.start();                                                    // (9)
      t2.start();                                                    // (10)
      System.out.println("Exiting main.");                           // (11)
    }
  }
```

It is possible that the program in Example 22.9 might run without a deadlock, depending on how the locks on the two String objects are acquired by each thread. However, after the following output from the program, a deadlock occurs and the program never terminates:

```
t1 acquired o1
t2 acquired o2
```

Livelock

Two threads may result in a livelock, if the response by a thread to another thread's action is always to undo or revert the consequences of the action. The threads are responding to each other, but are blocked in making any progress. The combined actions of the threads make it impossible for them to complete their tasks, making it impossible for the threads to terminate. This situation is different from a deadlock, where the threads are blocked, waiting for locked shared resources to become available.

An example of a livelock is when two guests (i.e., two threads) are trying to enter through a door, but there is only one door key and only one guest at a time can use it. Each guest is too polite, and insists on giving the key to the other if the other wants to enter. In other words, if one guest hands the key to the other, the other hands it right back. This situation will continue indefinitely, with neither guest thereby entering through the door. We have a livelock because of handing the key back and forth.

Example 22.10 provides another example of a livelock. Two threads are created at (11) and (12). In the first one, a customer makes a payment to a seller, and in the second one, the seller ships an item to the customer.

The Customer class at (1) has a flag (paymentMade) to mark that payment has been made. In the makePaymentTo() method, the customer continuously checks whether the seller has sent the shipment. If the seller has not, the customer waits before checking again. Once the seller has shipped the item, the customer marks at (4) that the payment has now been made.

On the other hand, the Seller class at (6) has a flag (itemShipped) to record that shipment has been sent. In the shipTo() method, the seller continuously checks whether the customer has paid. If the customer has not, the seller waits before checking again. Once the customer has paid, the seller marks at (5) that the shipment has been sent.

Output from running the program shows that the customer is waiting for shipment from the seller, and the seller is waiting for payment from the customer. Neither thread is able to make progress because the seller cannot send the shipment before the customer has paid, and the customer cannot pay before the shipment has been sent. Each is expecting a confirmation from the other, which never arrives. They need to renegotiate their contract, and one of them will have to trust the other.

Example 22.10 *Livelock*

```java
public class Customer {                                        // (1)
  private boolean paymentMade = false;                         // (2)

  public void makePaymentTo(Seller seller) {                   // (3)
    while (!seller.hasShipped()) {
      System.out.println("Customer: waiting for shipment from seller");
      try {
        Thread.sleep(1000);
      } catch (InterruptedException ex) {
        ex.printStackTrace();
      }
    }
    System.out.println("Customer: payment made");
    this.paymentMade = true;                                   // (4)
  }

  public boolean hasPaid() {
    return this.paymentMade;
  }
}
```

```java
public class Seller {                                          // (5)
  private boolean itemShipped = false;                         // (6)

  public void shipTo(Customer customer) {                      // (7)
    while (!customer.hasPaid()) {
      System.out.println("Seller: waiting for payment from customer");
      try {
        Thread.sleep(500);
      } catch (InterruptedException ex) {
        ex.printStackTrace();
      }
    }
```

```
      }
      System.out.println("Seller: item shipped");
      this.itemShipped = true;                                    // (8)
    }

    public boolean hasShipped() {
      return this.itemShipped;
    }
  }
```

```
  public class LivelockShipment {
    public static void main(String[] args) {
      Customer customer = new Customer();
      Seller seller = new Seller();

      new Thread(() -> customer.makePaymentTo(seller)).start();    // (9)
      new Thread(() -> seller.shipTo(customer)).start();           // (10)
    }
  }
```

Output from the program:

```
...
Seller: waiting for payment from customer
Customer: waiting for shipment from seller
Seller: waiting for payment from customer
Seller: waiting for payment from customer
Customer: waiting for shipment from seller
Seller: waiting for payment from customer
...
```

Starvation

A thread can *starve* because it is unsuccessfully waiting for its turn to be able to proceed with its execution. In addition to deadlock and livelock that result in starvation, some other situations where starvation can occur are the following:

- *Unfair priority scheduling*: Higher-priority threads monopolize the CPU, and low-priority threads starve in the READY substate.

- *Indefinite waiting for join to complete*: A thread that executed a no-timeout join() call can starve in the WAITING state if the thread it is waiting for never completes.

- *Indefinite waiting in the entry set of the object lock*: A thread can starve in the BLOCKED state if other threads get chosen before it to acquire the object lock to enter synchronized code.

- *Indefinite waiting in the wait set of an object*: A thread that executed a no-timeout wait() call can starve in the WAITING state if it never gets notified. It can also starve in this state if other threads get chosen on notification before it does, and it never gets to compete for object lock acquisition.

Example 22.11 provides another example of starvation. The Hole class at (1) provides the synchronized method dig() to dig a hole. The class Diggers creates a Hole object and starts five threads to dig this hole. The output shows that the thread that first acquires the lock to execute the synchronized dig() method in the Hole object monopolizes the CPU, and the other threads do not get a chance to run—they wait and starve.

The starvation scenario in Example 22.11 can be remedied by making a thread wait between digging—implemented by the try-catch block at (3) with the call to the *timed* wait() method. The call to the wait() method will result in the current thread transiting to the TIMED_WAITING state and releasing the lock on the Hole object, thus making it possible for other waiting threads to run. On the other hand, a call to the sleep() method does not release the lock and will still result in thread starvation.

- -

Example 22.11 *Starvation*

```
public class Hole {                                                 // (1)
  public synchronized void dig() {
    String threadName = Thread.currentThread().getName();
    while (true) {                                                  // (2)
      System.out.println(threadName + " digging the hole.");
//    try {                                                         // (3)
//      wait(1);
//    } catch (InterruptedException ex) {
//      ex.printStackTrace();
//    }
    }
  }
}
```

- -

```
public class Diggers {
  public static void main(String[] args) {
    Hole hole = new Hole();                                         // (4)
    for (int i = 0; i < 5; i++) {                                   // (5)
      new Thread(() -> hole.dig()).start();
    }
  }
}
```

Probable output from the program:

```
...
Thread-0 digging the hole.
Thread-0 digging the hole.
Thread-0 digging the hole.
Thread-0 digging the hole.
Thread-0 digging the hole.
Thread-0 digging the hole.
...
```

- -

Memory Consistency Errors

In a multithreaded application, there is a potential danger that changes made by one thread to shared data might not be *visible* to the other threads, resulting in inconsistent views of the shared data. When this happens, it is known as a *memory consistency error*.

Causes of memory consistency errors are too complex to go into here. The following simple example gives an idea of how they can manifest. Two threads have access to a shared counter.

```
int counter = 0;
```

```
// Thread A                                           // Thread B
...                                                   ...
counter = 1;                                          ...
System.out.println("Thread A:" + counter);            System.out.println("Thread B:" + counter);
...                                                   ...
```

Thread A set the counter value to 1 and prints it value. We can safely assume that the value printed would be 1—that is, the value in the counter set by the preceding assignment statement. However, if the print statement is executed by thread B, there is no guarantee that the change in the counter value in thread A will be visible to thread B—it might print 0 or 1—unless it can be established that a change of value in thread A occurred before being printed in thread B.

Happens-Before Relationship

The *happens-before relationship* helps to combat memory consistency errors. It is important in guaranteeing that *one action is ordered before another* in a multithreaded runtime environment. More importantly, the first action is *visible* to the second one, meaning that the *results* of the first action are evident to the second action. The relationship is *transitive*: If action A happens-before action B, and action B happens-before action C, then action A happens-before action C.

Little is guaranteed in a multithreaded environment, and therefore, the happens-before relationship is important in ascertaining certain properties about multithreaded applications. Here are some important rules pertaining to multithreaded applications in Java:

- *Object lock rule*: An unlock action on a monitor happens-before every subsequent lock action on that monitor.
- *Volatile field rule*: A write to a volatile field happens-before every subsequent read of that field (§23.4, p. 1453).
- *Thread start rule*: A call to the Thread.start() method on a thread happens-before any actions in the started thread.
- *Thread termination rule*: All actions in a thread happen-before any other thread can detect that the thread has terminated, either by successfully returning from

a `Thread.join()` method call or by a `Thread.isAlive()` method call returning `false` on that thread.

- *Thread interruption rule*: A thread calling the `Thread.interrupt()` method on another thread happens-before the interrupted thread detects the interrupt, either by having an `InterruptedException` thrown, or by invoking the `Thread.isInterrupted()` or the `Thread.interrupted()` method on itself.

 Review Questions

22.4 Which of the following statements are guaranteed to be true about the following program?

```java
public class ThreadedPrint {
  static Thread makeThread(String id, boolean daemon) {
    Thread t = new Thread(() -> System.out.println(id), id);
    t.setDaemon(daemon);
    t.start();
    return t;
  }

  public static void main(String[] args) {
    Thread a = makeThread("A", false);
    Thread b = makeThread("B", true);
    System.out.println("End");
  }
}
```

Select the two correct answers.

(a) The letter A is always printed.
(b) The letter B is always printed.
(c) The letter A is never printed after End.
(d) The letter B is never printed after End.
(e) The program might print B, End, and A, in that order.

22.5 Which of the following statements are true about the synchronized statement? Select the two correct answers.

(a) If the expression in a synchronized statement evaluates to `null`, a `NullPointerException` will be thrown.

(b) The lock is only released if the execution of the synchronized statement terminates normally.

(c) Several synchronized statements, synchronizing on the same object, can be executed concurrently.

(d) Synchronized statements cannot be nested.

(e) The block notation, {}, cannot be omitted even if there is only a single statement to execute in a synchronized statement.

22.6 Given the following program, which code modifications will result in *both* threads being able to participate in printing one smiley face (:-)) on a line continuously?

```
public class Smiley extends Thread {

    public void run() {                              // (1)
      while (true) {                                 // (2)
        try {                                        // (3)
          System.out.print(":");                     // (4)
          sleep(100);                                // (5)
          System.out.print("-");                     // (6)
          sleep(100);                                // (7)
          System.out.println(")");                   // (8)
          sleep(100);                                // (9)
        } catch (InterruptedException e) {
          e.printStackTrace();
        }
      }
    }

    public static void main(String[] args) {
      new Smiley().start();
      new Smiley().start();
    }
}
```

Select the two correct answers.

(a) Synchronize the run() method at (1) with the keyword synchronized.

(b) Synchronize the while loop at (2) with a synchronized(Smiley.class) statement.

(c) Synchronize the try-catch construct at (3) with a synchronized(Smiley.class) statement.

(d) Synchronize the statements from (4) to (9) with a synchronized(Smiley.class) statement.

(e) Synchronize each statement at (4), (6), and (8) individually with a synchronized (Smiley.class) statement.

22.7 Which of the following events will cause a thread to terminate?
Select the one correct answer.

(a) The method sleep() is called.

(b) The method wait() is called.

(c) Execution of the start() method ends.

(d) Execution of the run() method ends.

(e) Execution of the thread constructor ends.

22.8 Which of the following statements are true about the following code?

```
public class Joining {
  static Thread createThread(final int i, final Thread t1) {
    Thread t2 = new Thread() {
      public void run() {
        System.out.println(i+1);
```

```
                    try {
                      t1.join();
                    } catch (InterruptedException ie) {
                    }
                    System.out.println(i+2);
                  }
                };
                System.out.println(i+3);
                t2.start();
                System.out.println(i+4);
                return t2;
              }

              public static void main(String[] args) {
                createThread(10, createThread(20, Thread.currentThread()));
              }
            }
```

Select the two correct answers.

(a) The first number printed is 13.
(b) The number 14 is printed before the number 22.
(c) The number 24 is printed before the number 21.
(d) The last number printed is 12.
(e) The number 11 is printed before the number 23.

22.9 What can be guaranteed by calling the method yield()?
Select the one correct answer.

(a) All lower-priority threads will be granted CPU time.
(b) The current thread will sleep for some time while some other threads run.
(c) The current thread will not continue until other threads have terminated.
(d) The thread will wait until it is notified.
(e) None of the above

22.10 In which class or interface is the notify() method defined?
Select the one correct answer.
(a) Thread
(b) Object
(c) Appendable
(d) Runnable

22.11 What will be the result of invoking the wait() method on an object without ensuring that the current thread holds the lock on the object?
Select the one correct answer.

(a) The code will fail to compile.
(b) Nothing special will happen.
(c) An IllegalMonitorStateException will be thrown if the wait() method is called and the current thread does not hold the lock of the object.
(d) The thread will be blocked until it gains the lock of the object.

22.12   What will be the result of compiling and running the following program?

```java
public class Tank {
  private boolean isEmpty = true;

  public synchronized void emptying() {
    pause(true);
    isEmpty = !isEmpty;
    System.out.println("emptying");
    notify();
  }

  public synchronized void filling() {
    pause(false);
    isEmpty = !isEmpty;
    System.out.println("filling");
    notify();
  }

  private void pause(boolean flag) {
    while (flag ? isEmpty : !isEmpty) {
      try {
        wait();
      } catch (InterruptedException ie) {
        System.out.println(Thread.currentThread().getName() + " interrupted.");
      }
    }
  }

  public static void main(String[] args) {
    final Tank token = new Tank();
    new Thread(() -> {for(;;) token.emptying();}, "A").start();
    new Thread(() -> {for(;;) token.filling();}, "B").start();
  }
}
```

Select the one correct answer.

(a) The program will compile and continue running once started, but will not print anything.

(b) The program will compile and continue running once started, printing only the string "emptying".

(c) The program will compile and continue running once started, printing only the string "filling".

(d) The program will compile and continue running once started, always printing the string "filling" followed by the string "emptying".

(e) The program will compile and continue running once started, printing the strings "filling" and "emptying" in some order.

Concurrency: Part II 23

 Chapter Topics

- Understanding the inheritance hierarchy of the main interfaces of the Executor Framework: Executor, ExecutorService, and Scheduled-ExecutorService interfaces
- Using time units for time durations defined by the TimeUnit enum type
- Using a thread-local pseudorandom number generator defined by the ThreadLocalRandom class
- Creating executor services and scheduled executor services using methods of the Executors utility class
- Understanding the lifecycle of an executor service: RUNNING, SHUTDOWN, and TERMINATION states
- Controlling shutdown and termination of an executor service
- Defining tasks that do not return a result and those that do using the Runnable and the Callable<V> functional interfaces, respectively
- Submitting and invoking tasks using an executor service
- Handling task results using the Future<V> interface
- Scheduling tasks with a scheduled executor service
- Understanding task cancellation in an executor service
- Understanding the basics of solving divide-and-conquer problems using the Fork/Join Framework
- Understanding the implications of immutability
- Using the keyword volatile for visibility of shared fields to avoid memory contention errors
- Using atomic variables for mutually exclusive operations on shared single fields
- Using programmatic locking provided by reentrant locks and reentrant read-write locks to implement mutually exclusive operations on shared resources

- Using special-purpose synchronizers, such as the cyclic barrier and the count-down latch, to control thread execution behavior
- Using synchronized collections and maps for mutually exclusive operations on collections
- Using concurrent collections, concurrent maps, blocking queues, and copy-on-write collections for mutually exclusive operations on collections and maps

Java SE 17 Developer Exam Objectives	
[8.1] Create worker threads using Runnable and Callable, manage the thread lifecycle, including automations provided by different Executor services and concurrent API ○ *Creating worker threads with the* Callable *functional interface, and managing concurrency using executor services of the Concurrency API are covered in this chapter.* ○ *For the* Runnable *functional interface and the thread lifecycle, see* §22.3, p. 1371, *and* §22.4, p. 1380.	§23.2, p. 1423
[8.2] Develop thread-safe code, using different locking mechanisms and concurrent API	§23.4, p. 1451 *to* §23.7, p. 1482
[8.3] Process Java collections concurrently including the use of parallel streams ○ *Processing collections concurrently is covered in this chapter.* ○ *For parallel streams, see* §16.9, p. 1009.	§23.7, p. 1482
Java SE 11 Developer Exam Objectives	
[8.1] Create worker threads using Runnable and Callable, and manage concurrency using an ExecutorService and java.util.concurrent API ○ *Creating worker threads with the* Callable *functional interface, and managing concurrency using executor services of the Concurrency API are covered in this chapter.* ○ *For the* Runnable *functional interface, see* §22.3, p. 1371.	§23.2, p. 1423
[8.2] Develop thread-safe code, using different locking mechanisms and java.util.concurrent API	§23.4, p. 1451 *to* §23.7, p. 1482

Low-level support for creating, starting, and coordinating threads in multi-threaded applications is discussed in Chapter 22, p. 1365. This low-level approach to enforce correct execution order for concurrent threads inherently increases code complexity, potentially impacts performance, and is not always scalable. This chapter deals with high-level support for multithreaded programming that alleviates many of these problems in designing multithreaded applications. This support is primarily provided by the java.util.concurrent package and its subpackages: The Executor Framework, the Fork/Join Framework, locking mechanisms, lock-free algorithms, and concurrent collections.

23.1 Utility Classes TimeUnit and ThreadLocalRandom

This section can be skipped on the first reading, and can be read if and when the need arises while working through this chapter.

Before diving into high-level concurrency support provided by the java.util.concurrent package, we begin by providing an overview of two utility classes whose methods are used in many of the examples presented in this chapter.

The TimeUnit Enum Type

The enum type java.util.concurrent.TimeUnit represents *time units* at different levels of granularity, from nanoseconds to days, as shown in Table 23.1.

A TimeUnit can be used to indicate the time unit in which a numerical value should be interpreted as a time duration. Many time-based methods interpret their timing parameter according to the time unit specified by this enum type. In the code below, the numerical value 2 will be interpreted by the awaitTermination() method as two seconds.

```
boolean allTerminated = executor.awaitTermination(2, TimeUnit.SECONDS);
```

Note that a TimeUnit enum constant does not maintain any time information, like date or time of day.

Table 23.1   *Constants Defined by the* java.util.concurrent.TimeUnit *Enum Type*

Constants defined by java.util.concurrent. TimeUnit enum type	Description of the time unit
NANOSECONDS	Representing one-thousandth of a microsecond
MICROSECONDS	Representing one-thousandth of a millisecond
MILLISECONDS	Representing one-thousandth of a second
MINUTES	Representing 60 seconds
SECONDS	Representing 1 second

Table 23.1 *Constants Defined by the* `java.util.concurrent.TimeUnit` *Enum Type (Continued)*

Constants defined by java.util.concurrent. TimeUnit enum type	Description of the time unit
HOURS	Representing 60 minutes
DAYS	Representing 24 hours

The enum type `TimeUnit` also provides convenience methods that call the methods `Thread.sleep()`, `Thread.join()`, and `Object.wait()`, allowing the timeout for these methods to be specified in different time units. For example, the following method calls are equivalent:

```
TimeUnit.SECONDS.sleep(1);            // 1 second.
TimeUnit.MILLISECONDS.sleep(1000);    // 1000 milliseconds.
Thread.sleep(1000);                   // 1000 milliseconds.
```

Following convenience methods are defined in the `TimeUnit` enum type:

```
void sleep(long timeout)                          throws InterruptedException
void timedJoin(Thread thread, long timeout) throws InterruptedException
void timedWait(Object obj, long timeout)    throws InterruptedException
```

Call the `Thread.sleep(long millis)` method, the `Thread.join(long millis)` method, and the `Object.wait(long millis)` method, respectively, where the specified `timeout` is converted to milliseconds using this time unit.

The `ThreadLocalRandom` **Class**

Some examples in this chapter make use of a *pseudorandom generator*. The class `java.util.concurrent.ThreadLocalRandom` provides a pseudorandom generator that is confined to the current thread—that is, it is local to the thread. The `ThreadLocalRandom` class extends the `java.util.Random` class, and provides methods that return uniformly distributed numerical values. The `ThreadLocalRandom` class is particularly recommended for concurrent tasks, instead of using a shared object of the `Random` class, as it entails less overhead and resource contention.

The code below illustrates use of the class in a task that simulates a dice. The `current()` static method of the class returns the `ThreadLocalRandom` object associated with the current thread.

```
int diceValue = ThreadLocalRandom.current().nextInt(1, 7);   // [1, 6]
```

In addition, the `ThreadLocalRandom` class provides methods that return numerical streams whose elements are uniformly distributed pseudorandom numbers. The code below creates an `int` stream of 100 randomly generated `int` values which are in the interval [1, 6], and counts the number of times the dice value 6 occurs in the stream.

```
long count = ThreadLocalRandom.current()
                      .ints(100, 1, 7).filter(i -> i == 6).count();
```

Following selected methods are defined in the ThreadLocalRandom enum type:

```
static ThreadLocalRandom current()
```
Returns the ThreadLocalRandom object associated with the current thread.

```
int nextInt(int bound)
int nextInt(int origin, int bound)
```
The two methods return a pseudorandom, uniformly distributed int value between [0, bound) and [origin, bound), respectively, where [n, m) defines a half-open interval, where the end value is excluded.

The class ThreadLocalRandom also defines the analogous methods nextLong(), nextFloat(), and nextDouble() for the primitive types long, float, and double, respectively.

```
IntStream ints()
IntStream ints(long streamSize)
IntStream ints(int randomNumberOrigin, int randomNumberBound)
IntStream ints(long streamSize, int randomNumberOrigin,
               int randomNumberBound)
```
Each method returns a stream of pseudorandom int values.

The first method returns an unlimited number of pseudorandom int values in the stream, which can be any legal int value.

The second method returns streamSize pseudorandom int values in the stream, which can be any legal int value.

The third method returns unlimited pseudorandom int values in the stream, which are in the half-open interval [randomNumberOrigin, randomNumberBound).

The fourth method returns streamSize pseudorandom int values in the stream, which are in the half-open interval [randomNumberOrigin, randomNumberBound).

The class ThreadLocalRandom also defines the analogous methods longs() and doubles() for the primitive types long and double that return LongStream and DoubleStream, respectively.

23.2 The Executor Framework

Executors provide a high-level approach to launching tasks and managing threads. Tasks are executed asynchronously by threads in a multithreaded environment, where a *task* defines a unit of work—that is, a task is a set of instructions executed by a thread.

Internally, an executor maintains a *thread pool* that utilizes a number of reusable threads that are assigned tasks from a task queue, according to the execution policy of the executor. The threads maintained by a thread pool are also known as *worker threads*. A worker thread remains alive after executing a task, and can be assigned another task that is waiting to be executed.

Executors allow the *submission of tasks* for execution to be decoupled from the actual *execution of tasks*. The application defines and submits the tasks to the executor which manages their execution by assigning them to threads. The executor provides the necessary support for managing its lifecycle that comprises creating the executor, submitting tasks, managing the outcome of task execution, and shutting down the executor.

Figure 23.1 shows the interfaces in the java.util.concurrent package that define the characteristics of executors from basic to more advanced executors. The Executors utility class provides static methods that create various kinds of executors that not only implement the executor interfaces shown in Figure 23.1, but also implement various policies for task execution (Table 23.2, p. 1426).

Figure 23.1 *Executor Interfaces in the* java.util.concurrent *Package*

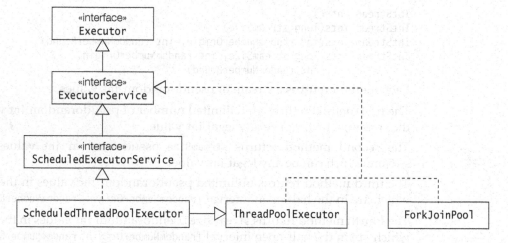

The Executor Interface

The java.util.concurrent.Executor interface defines a basic executor. This executor executes a Runnable task that is passed to its execute() method. Technically, the Executor interface is a functional interface as it has a single abstract method. However, it is not annotated as such in the Java SE Platform API documentation, as it is recommended to use the more versatile executors that extend the Executor interface (Figure 23.1).

The SimpleExecutor class below implements the Executor interface. Its execute() method shows two implementations, (1a) and (1b), for executing a Runnable task. Typically, an executor delegates the task to a new thread for asynchronous execution as shown at (1a). It can also be executed synchronously by calling the run() method on the task as shown at (1b).

```
class SimpleExecutor implements Executor {
  @Override
  public void execute(Runnable task) {
```

```
      new Thread(task).start();            // (1a) Asynchronous call
//    task.run();                          // (1b) Synchronous call. Not recommended.
  }
}
// Client code
SimpleExecutor executor = new SimpleExecutor();
Runnable task = () -> System.out.println("Executing task ...");
executor.execute(task);
```

The essence of the basic executor is to replace the following code for running a task in a thread:

```
new Thread(task).start();
```

with the following code using an executor, where the actual execution is managed by the executor, abstracting away the management of the underlying thread:

```
executor.execute(task);
```

Typically, the tasks are executed by a *thread pool* maintained by the executors provided by the Executors utility class.

The following method is defined in the Executor interface:

```
void execute(Runnable task)
```

Executes the given task at some time in the future. The task may execute in a new thread, in a worker thread, or in the calling thread, at the discretion of the Executor implementation. Note that this method does not return a value and it does not specify any throws clause with checked exceptions.

The Executors **Class**

The java.util.concurrent.Executors class provides factory and utility methods for the interfaces defined in the java.util.concurrent package. In particular, it provides factory methods that return versatile implementations of the ExecutorService (p. 1427) and the ScheduledExecutorService (p. 1440) interfaces shown in Figure 23.1. The executor services created by the methods of the Executors class are summarized in Table 23.2, showing the respective static methods, the task execution policy of the executor services they create, and examples where they are used. For many applications, these executor services will be adequate, and examples in this chapter make heavy use of them.

In addition, the java.util.concurrent.ThreadPoolExecutor class, shown in Figure 23.1, provides constructors to create even more versatile executors with various properties such as minimum and maximum pool size, keep-alive time for idle threads, a blocking queue for managing tasks, and a handler for tasks that cannot be executed.

Table 23.2   *Selected Executor Services Provided by the* Executors *Utility Class*

The static method that creates an executor that implements the ExecutorService interface (p. 1427), and the executor's task execution policy	Description of the ExecutorService implementation
Single Thread Executor newSingleThreadExecutor() *Task execution policy*: tasks executed sequentially by a single thread. *(Example 23.5, p. 1446)*	Provides a single worker thread to which tasks can be assigned. If this single thread terminates due to a failure, a new thread will take its place if needed. Tasks in the queue are guaranteed to execute sequentially. Logically it is an equivalent of a fixed thread pool of size 1, but it cannot be reconfigured to use additional threads.
Fixed Thread Pool newFixedThreadPool(int nThreads) *Task execution policy*: tasks executed concurrently by a fixed number of threads. *(Example 23.1, p. 1429)* *(Example 23.2, p. 1438)*	Provides a thread pool of fixed size. The number of threads actively processing tasks is, at the most, equal to the pool size. The number of tasks submitted can be greater than the pool size, but some tasks may have to wait in the queue for threads to become available within the pool. If a thread terminates due to a failure, a new thread will take its place if needed. Pool threads are reused as required to execute the submitted tasks. They remain blocked when not executing a task.
Work Stealing Pool newWorkStealingPool() newWorkStealingPool(int parallelism) *Task execution policy*: tasks executed concurrently while attempting to maintain its target parallelism level.	Provides a thread pool that tries to maintain its *target parallelism level*—that is, the maximum number of threads executing, or those available to execute tasks. The actual number of threads can vary dynamically. It makes no guarantees about the order in which the tasks will be executed. The first method uses the number of available processors as its target parallelism level.
Cached Thread Pool newCachedThreadPool() *Task execution policy*: tasks executed concurrently by a thread pool whose size can vary dynamically with the number of tasks remaining to execute.	Provides a thread pool whose size may vary dynamically. Submitted tasks reuse available threads in the pool. Additional threads are created as needed when no threads are available. Unused threads eventually time out and are removed from the cache, so a pool that remains idle for long enough will not consume any resources.

Table 23.2 *Selected Executor Services Provided by the* Executors *Utility Class (Continued)*

The static method that creates an executor that implements the ScheduledExecutorService interface (p. 1440), and the executor's task execution policy	Description of the ScheduledExecutorService implementation
Single Thread Scheduled Executor newSingleThreadScheduledExecutor() *Task execution policy*: tasks executed sequentially by a single thread according to the schedule policy specified for each task. *(Example 23.5, p. 1446)*	Provides a single worker thread that works very much like a combination of a scheduled thread pool of size 1 and a single thread executor. It can execute submitted tasks sequentially, using a single thread, but with a specified delay; or periodically, based on a schedule. The schedule is specified individually for each task when it is submitted to the executor.
Scheduled Thread Pool newScheduledThreadPool(int corePoolSize) *Task execution policy*: tasks executed concurrently by a fixed number of threads, according to the schedule policy specified for each task. *(Example 23.3, p. 1441)* *(Example 23.5, p. 1446)*	Provides a thread pool of a fixed size, that can execute submitted tasks with a specified delay or periodically, based on a schedule. The schedule is specified individually for each task when it is submitted to the executor.

The ExecutorService **Interface**

Table 23.2 lists the executor services provided by the factory methods of the Executors class. An *executor service* implements the ExecutorService interface that extends the Executor interface with methods that provide the following functionality:

- Flexibly submitting tasks to the executor service and handling the results returned (p. 1436)

  In addition to the execute() method, an executor service provides the overloaded methods submit(), invokeAll(), and invokeAny() for submitting tasks. The Future<V> interface provides methods to handle the execution status and the results returned by tasks (p. 1435). The Callable<V> functional interface can be used to implement tasks that return a value (p. 1434).

- Managing the *executor lifecycle*

  The ExecutorService interface provides methods to manage the lifecycle of an executor (Figure 23.2). Once an executor service is created, for example, by static methods of the Executors class, it is in the RUNNING state, ready to accept tasks for execution. As an executor service is a precious resource, it must be shut down by calling its shutdown() or shutdownNow() method. An executor service in the SHUTDOWN state does not accept new tasks, which are discarded. However, although the executor service might be shut down, some of its threads might still be executing tasks and other tasks might be waiting to be executed. Only when all tasks have completed does the executor service transition to the TERMINATED state. The methods isShutdown() and isTerminated() can be used to check if the executor service is in the SHUTDOWN or TERMINATED state, respectively. The method awaitTermination(), called on an executor service after it is shut down, can be used to wait for threads to complete their tasks. See Example 23.1, p. 1429.

Figure 23.2 *Executor Service Lifecycle*

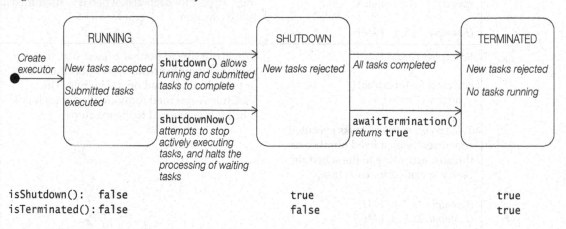

```
isShutdown():   false                           true                true
isTerminated(): false                           false               true
```

Following are selected methods of the ExecutorService interface for shutting down and terminating an executor service:

void shutdown()

Starts an orderly shutdown in which previously submitted tasks are executed, but new tasks are rejected. This method does *not* wait for already submitted tasks to complete execution. A shutdown request on an executor that is already shut down has no additional effect.

List<Runnable> shutdownNow()

Attempts to stop all actively executing tasks, and halts the processing of waiting tasks. It returns a list of the tasks that were awaiting execution.

This method does *not* wait for actively executing tasks to terminate.

This method at best attempts to stop processing of actively executing tasks—however, there are no guarantees. Typically, task cancellation will be triggered via Thread.interrupt(), so any task failing to respond to interrupts may never terminate (§22.4, p. 1393).

```
boolean isShutdown()
```

Returns true if this executor has been shut down—that is, a shutdown request has already been invoked on the executor.

```
boolean awaitTermination(long timeout, TimeUnit unit)
                    throws InterruptedException
```

Blocks until one of these events occurs first: All tasks have completed execution after a shutdown request, or the timeout occurs, or the current thread is interrupted. This method should be called after calling the shutdown() method.

```
boolean isTerminated()
```

Returns true if *all* tasks have completed following shutdown. It never returns true unless a shutdown request has already been invoked on the executor.

Using an Executor Service

The idiom for using an executor service is embodied in the following steps that are illustrated in Example 23.1:

- *Create the executor service.*
- *Submit tasks to the executor service.*
- *Shut down and terminate the executor service.*

Example 23.1 *Executor Lifecycle*

```java
package executors;
import java.util.concurrent.*;

public class ExecutorLifecycle {

  // Task: dice roll.
  private static final Runnable diceRoll = () -> {          // (1)
    int diceValue = ThreadLocalRandom.current().nextInt(1, 7);   // [1, 6]

    String threadName = Thread.currentThread().getName();
    System.out.println(threadName + " => dice value: " + diceValue);
    try {
      TimeUnit.MILLISECONDS.sleep(100);
    } catch (InterruptedException e) {
      System.out.println(threadName + ": " + e);
    }
  };

  public static void main(String[] args) {
    System.out.printf("%50s   %s%n", "isShutdown()", "isTerminated()");
    // Create the executor service:
    ExecutorService es = Executors.newFixedThreadPool(3);        // (2)
    try {                                                        // (3)
      checkStates(es, "Before execute() at (4): ");
```

```java
      // Submit tasks:
      es.execute(diceRoll);                                    // (4)
      es.execute(diceRoll);
      es.execute(diceRoll);
      checkStates(es, "After execute() at (4): ");
    } finally {                                                // (5)
      // Shut down the executor service:
      checkStates(es, "Before shutdown() at (6a): ");
      es.shutdown();                                           // (6a)
      checkStates(es, "After shutdown() at (6a): ");

//    checkStates(es, "Before shutdownNow() at (6b): ");
//    es.shutdownNow();                                        // (6b)
//    checkStates(es, "After shutdownNow() at (6b): ");
    }
    // Second phase of shutdown:
//  awaitAndShutdownNow(es, 2, TimeUnit.SECONDS);              // (7a)
//  awaitAndShutdownNow(es, 1, TimeUnit.MILLISECONDS);         // (7b)
  }

  private static void checkStates(ExecutorService es, String msg) {   // (8)
    System.out.printf("%-40s %-5s          %-5s%n",
        msg, es.isShutdown(), es.isTerminated());
  }

  private static void awaitAndShutdownNow(                     // (9)
      ExecutorService es, int timeout, TimeUnit timeunit) {
    try {
      // Timed wait for tasks to complete execution:
      if (!es.awaitTermination(timeout, timeunit)) {          // (10)
        // Attempt to cancel any uncompleted and waiting tasks:
        checkStates(es, "Before shutdownNow() at (11): " );
        es.shutdownNow();                                     // (11)
        checkStates(es, "After shutdownNow() at (11): " );
        // Timed wait for tasks to be cancelled:
        while (!es.awaitTermination(timeout, timeunit)) {     // (12)
          System.out.println("All tasks not yet completed at (12).");
        }
      }
      checkStates(es, "After awaitTermination() at (10): " );
    } catch (InterruptedException ie) {                       // (13)
      // Attempt to cancel any uncompleted and waiting tasks:
      es.shutdownNow();                                       // (14)
      // Reinstate the interrupt status.
      Thread.currentThread().interrupt();
      checkStates(es, "After interruption: ");
    }
  }
}
```

Probable output from the program when calling the shutdown() method at (6a):

	isShutdown()	isTerminated()
Before execute() at (4):	false	false
After execute() at (4):	false	false
Before shutdown() at (6a):	false	false

```
pool-1-thread-3 => dice value: 6
pool-1-thread-1 => dice value: 2
pool-1-thread-2 => dice value: 1
After shutdown() at (6a):                    true              false
```

Probable output from the program when calling the shutdownNow() method at (6b):

```
                                      isShutdown()    isTerminated()
Before execute() at (4):                  false            false
After execute() at (4):                   false            false
pool-1-thread-3 => dice value: 4
pool-1-thread-2 => dice value: 5
pool-1-thread-1 => dice value: 5
Before shutdownNow() at (6b):             false            false
After shutdownNow() at (6b):              true             false
pool-1-thread-3: java.lang.InterruptedException: sleep interrupted
pool-1-thread-1: java.lang.InterruptedException: sleep interrupted
pool-1-thread-2: java.lang.InterruptedException: sleep interrupted
```

Example 23.1 implements the necessary steps for using an executor service:

- *Create the executor service.*

  The utility class Executors provides methods for creating a wide range of executor services (Table 23.2). Appropriate executor service is created based on the desired task execution policy. In Example 23.1, a fixed thread pool with three worker threads is created at (2) to execute three tasks.

  ```
  ExecutorService es = Executors.newFixedThreadPool(3);
  ```

- *Submit tasks to the executor service.*

  The task submitted to the executor service is defined as Runnable at (1). It simulates a dice roll, and when executed, it prints the dice value. The executing thread then sleeps for 100 milliseconds to prolong the execution time for the task to illustrate executor shutdown and termination.

  The tasks are submitted to the executor service using the execute() method—other methods are explored later (p. 1436, p. 1440). Each call to the execute() method will result in a new task being submitted. The implementation of the Runnable diceRoll will be executed three times, each time as a separate task.

  ```
  es.execute(diceRoll);                                                  // (4)
  es.execute(diceRoll);
  es.execute(diceRoll);
  ```

- *Shut down and terminate the executor service.*

  When the executor service is no longer needed, it should be closed properly so that resources associated with the executor service can be reclaimed. As an executor service is not AutoCloseable, we cannot use the try-with-resources statement. The simplest shutdown procedure involves either calling the shutdown() or shutdownNow() method for this purpose. Calling either of these methods shuts down the executor service, after which any attempts to submit new tasks to the executor service will be rejected. However, the shutdown() method will allow actively executing tasks and any waiting tasks to complete, but the `shutdown-Now()` method will attempt to cancel actively executing tasks and halt the processing of any waiting tasks.

The shutdown procedure is typically performed in a `finally` block associated with a `try` block containing the code that uses the executor service. This setup ensures that the executor service will always be shut down no matter how the tasks execute.

The method `checkStates()` at (9) in Example 23.1 is used to determine whether the executor service has been shut down and/or terminated at various stages in the execution, as can be seen in the program output.

The code below from Example 23.1 sketches the steps involved in using an executor:

```
// Create the executor service:
ExecutorService es = Executors.newFixedThreadPool(3);
try {                                                   // (3)
  // Submit tasks:
  es.execute(diceRoll);                                 // (4)
  es.execute(diceRoll);
  es.execute(diceRoll);
} finally {                                             // (5)
  // Shut down the executor service:
  es.shutdown();                                        // (6a)

//es.shutdownNow();                                     // (6b)
}
```

Two scenarios are shown in the output from the program in Example 23.1, corresponding to using the `shutdown()` and the `shutdownNow()` methods at (6a) and (6b), respectively. These methods do *not* wait for previously submitted tasks to complete execution before returning. Note that the `isTerminated()` method returns `false` after shutdown as one or more threads might not have completed execution—in this particular case, most probably waiting for sleep to time out. It is also important to note that the JVM will not terminate until all active threads in the thread pool have completed execution—analogous to normal threads in an application.

In the output, we see that the default name of a worker thread is composed of a thread pool number and a thread number—for example, `pool-1-thread-3`.

The output from the program when calling the `shutdown()` method at (6a) shows that the executor service did shut down, but the executor service did *not* terminate as some tasks continued execution—the method `isTerminated()` returned `false` when called after return from the `shutdown()` method. However, any running or submitted tasks were allowed to complete execution before the JVM terminated—in this particular case, threads were allowed to sleep until timed out.

In contrast, calling the `shutdownNow()` method cancels any executing and pending tasks. The `shutdownNow()` method does not wait for pending tasks to terminate.

From the output, we can see that calling the isTerminated() method on the executor returns false, as the executor has not terminated because all pending tasks have not been cancelled yet. The output from the program shows that, when cancelled, all three threads were interrupted while asleep. The Interrupted-Exception being caught and handled when the threads woke up and continued execution resulted in the tasks completing execution and the JVM being able to terminate.

Controlling Shutdown and Termination of an Executor Service

The ExecutorService interface provides the awaitTermination() method, which in conjunction with the shutdown methods, allows more refined control over pending tasks at shutdown.

Further control in shutting down and terminating an executor service is implemented by the awaitAndShutdownNow() method defined at (9) in Example 23.1. This method utilizes both the awaitTermination() method and the shutdownNow() method of the executor service. The executor service to shut down and the timeout to wait for pending tasks to complete are passed as parameters to the awaitAndShutdown-Now() method.

The awaitAndShutdownNow() method first calls the awaitTermination() method at (10) that blocks until one of the following events occurs:

* The awaitTermination() method returns true, indicating that all tasks have completed, and thereby the executor service has been shut down and terminated.

* The awaitTermination() method returns false, indicating that there are still uncompleted tasks. The shutdownNow() method is called at (11) to cancel any uncompleted and waiting tasks. The awaitTermination() method is called again in a while loop at (12) to wait for any tasks still pending completion. This loop terminates when all tasks have completed; if the current thread is interrupted while awaiting task completion, the control goes to (13).

* The current thread is interrupted while waiting for the blocking call to the awaitTermination() method to return, in which case the InterruptedException thrown is caught by the catch block at (13). A further attempt is made in the catch block to cancel any pending tasks by calling the shutdownNow() method at (14).

The awaitAndShutdownNow() method at best makes an attempt at allowing pending tasks to complete after shutdown. It is called at (7a) and (7b) in Example 23.1 to illustrate shutting down an executor service and controlling any of its pending tasks. (For this discussion, (6b) is commented out in Example 23.1.)

The duration of the wait for pending tasks in the call to the awaitTermination() method impacts the fate of the pending tasks. The following call:

```
awaitAndShutdownNow(es, 2, TimeUnit.SECONDS);                          // (7a)
```

can result in the following output from the program, showing that two seconds of waiting was sufficient for all tasks to complete execution at (10), causing the executor service to terminate:

	isShutdown()	isTerminated()
Before execute() at (4):	false	false
After execute() at (4):	false	false
Before shutdown() at (6a):	false	false
pool-1-thread-2 => dice value: 4		
pool-1-thread-3 => dice value: 1		
pool-1-thread-1 => dice value: 2		
After shutdown() at (6a):	true	false
After awaitTermination() at (10):	true	true

However, the following call:

```
awaitAndShutdownNow(es, 1, TimeUnit.MILLISECONDS);                          // (7b)
```

can result in the following output from the program, showing that a one-millisecond wait was insufficient for all tasks to complete execution at (10), resulting in the shutdownNow() method at (11) being called. Any pending tasks are thus interrupted and the InterruptedException is handled by each task. The awaitTermination() method returns true when called in the while loop at (12), indicating that the interrupted tasks completed their execution:

	isShutdown()	isTerminated()
Before execute() at (4):	false	false
After execute() at (4):	false	false
Before shutdown() at (6a):	false	false
pool-1-thread-2 => dice value: 3		
pool-1-thread-1 => dice value: 1		
pool-1-thread-3 => dice value: 1		
After shutdown() at (6a):	true	false
Before shutdownNow() at (11):	true	false
After shutdownNow() at (11):	true	false
pool-1-thread-3: java.lang.InterruptedException: sleep interrupted		
pool-1-thread-2: java.lang.InterruptedException: sleep interrupted		
pool-1-thread-1: java.lang.InterruptedException: sleep interrupted		
After awaitTermination() at (10):	true	true

Defining Tasks That Return a Result

Implementations of the java.util.concurrent.Callable<V> functional interface represent tasks that are designed to be executed by threads—analogous to implementations of the java.lang.Runnable functional interface. Whereas we can create and start a thread by passing a Runnable to a constructor of the Thread class, this is not possible with a Callable<V> implementation, as Thread constructors do not accept a Callable<V> object. In order to execute an implementation of the Callable<V> functional interface as a task in a thread, we can use an executor service—a topic which we explore thoroughly later (p. 1436).

In contrast to the Runnable interface, the Callable<V> interface is generic. As opposed to the void run() method of the Runnable interface, the call() method of the Callable<V> interface returns a result from the task it represents and can throw checked exceptions. As it is a functional interface, the implementation of its sole method call() can be provided by a lambda expression.

An executor service provides bulk execution of tasks grouped in a collection using its methods invokeAny() and invokeAll() (p. 1439). Such bulk tasks can only be implemented as Callable<V> tasks, and not as Runnable tasks.

Typically, a Runnable is used for long-running tasks, such as a server, whereas a Callable<V> is a one-shot task that needs to compute and return a result.

The code at (1) implements a Callable<Integer> that simulates a dice using a Random object (§8.7, p. 482). The method call() is invoked directly on this implementation at (2) to roll the dice. Later we will see how we can obtain the value of a dice roll asynchronously in a thread using an executor service (p. 1438).

```
Random rng = new Random();
Callable<Integer> dice = () -> rng.nextInt(1,7);  // (1)
try {
  Integer diceValue = dice.call();       // (2)
  System.out.println(diceValue);         // Prints a value in the interval [1,6].
} catch (Exception ex) {
  ex.printStackTrace();
}
```

The following method is defined in the Callable<V> functional interface:

V call() throws Exception

Computes a result, or throws an exception if unable to do so.

Representing Task Results

A Future<V> object represents the result of a task that is asynchronously executed—that is, it represents the result of a task that is executed sometime in the future after its submission. For example, methods for submitting or scheduling tasks with an executor service return immediately. When a submitted task is executed sometime in the future, its result is returned in a Future<V> object that can be queried to obtain the result. A Future<V> object also provides methods to determine whether the task it represents completed normally or was cancelled (p. 1444).

The API of the Future<V> interface shown below provides references to examples that compute task results.

V get() throws InterruptedException, ExecutionException
V get(long timeout, TimeUnit unit)
        throws InterruptedException, ExecutionException, TimeoutException

The first method blocks if necessary for the computation to complete, and then retrieves the result contained in this Future<V> object. In other words, the method does not return unless the task completes execution.

The second method blocks if necessary at most for the duration of the specified timeout in order for the computation to complete, and then retrieves the result contained in this Future<V> object, if one is available.

Calling these methods on a computation that has been cancelled, throws a java.util.concurrent.CancellationException. See Example 23.5, p. 1446.

`boolean cancel(boolean mayInterruptIfRunning)`

Attempts to cancel the execution of the task this Future<V> object represents.

If this task is already completed or cancelled, or if could not be cancelled, the method has no effect. Otherwise, if this task has not started when the method is called, this task is never run.

If the task has already started, then the mayInterruptIfRunning parameter determines whether the thread executing this task is interrupted in an attempt to stop the task. If the mayInterruptIfRunning parameter is true, the thread executing the task is interrupted; otherwise, the task is allowed to complete.

This method returns false if the task could not be cancelled, typically because it has already completed; otherwise, it returns true. However, the return value from this method does not necessarily indicate whether the task is now cancelled. For that purpose, the isCancelled() method should be used. See Example 23.5, p. 1446.

`boolean isCancelled()`

Returns true if this task was *cancelled* before it completed normally. See Example 23.5, p. 1446.

`boolean isDone()`

Returns true if this task *completed*. Note that completion implies either normal termination, or an exception, or cancellation.

Submitting Tasks and Handling Task Results

Tasks executed by executor services are represented by implementations of either the Runnable or the Callable<V> functional interface. The following selected methods of the ExecutorService interface can be used for submitting tasks to an executor service:

```
Future<?> submit(Runnable task)
<V> Future<V> submit(Runnable task, V result)
<V> Future<V> submit(Callable<V> task)
```

All three methods submit a task for execution to the executor service. The first two methods submit a Runnable task, but the last one submits a value-returning Callable<V> task.

All three methods return a Future<V> object that represents the task. On *success-ful* execution of the task, the isDone() method of the Future<V> object will return true. The value returned in the Future<V> object can be obtained by calling the get() method on the Future<V> object. The Future object will contain the value null, or the specified result in the call, or the result of executing the value-returning Callable<V> task, respectively, for the three methods. See Example 23.2, p. 1438.

```
<V> List<Future<V>> invokeAll(Collection<? extends Callable<V>> tasks)
                            throws InterruptedException
<V> List<Future<V>> invokeAll(Collection<? extends Callable<V>> tasks,
                            long timeout, TimeUnit unit)
                            throws InterruptedException
```

Executes the given tasks and returns a list of Future<V> holding their status and results when *all* complete, or if the timeout expires first as in the second method. The isDone() method on each Future<V> object in the returned list of Future<V> instances will return true.

Upon return from the second method, any uncompleted tasks are cancelled through interruption. A *completed task* is one that has terminated either normally or by throwing an exception. The order of the Future<V> instances returned is the same as the Callable<V> tasks in the collection passed as a parameter to the methods. See Example 23.2, p. 1438.

```
<V> V invokeAny(Collection<? extends Callable<V>> tasks)
                throws InterruptedException, ExecutionException
<V> V invokeAny(Collection<? extends Callable<V>> tasks,
                long timeout, TimeUnit unit)
                throws InterruptedException, ExecutionException,
                TimeoutException
```

Executes the given tasks, returning the result of the first one that has *completed successfully without throwing an exception*, if any do succeed—or before the given timeout elapses in the case of the second method. Upon return, any uncompleted tasks are cancelled. See Example 23.2, p. 1438.

Submitting Tasks Individually

Example 23.2 illustrates submitting tasks *individually* and handling the task result. A Runnable task is defined at (1) that prints a dice value, and a Callable<Integer> task is defined at (2) that returns a dice value. We can of course call the run() and the call() methods to execute the Runnable printDiceValue and the Callable<Integer> diceRoll, respectively, but we would like to execute these tasks in a thread. For this purpose, a fixed thread pool is created at (3) in Example 23.2. Recall that this executor service reuses threads, and tasks may have to wait if all threads are occupied.

The overloaded submit() method of the ExecutorService interface can be used to submit tasks to the executor service. When a task submitted by these methods is executed asynchronously sometime in the future, the status or the result of executing the task is returned in a Future<V> object. The get() method of the Future<V>

interface can be used to extract the value contained in a Future<V> object. However, note that the get() method will block the current thread until the task has completed. A timed version of the get(timeout, timeunit) method can also be used if there is a risk of waiting indefinitely.

The Runnable printDiceValue is submitted to the executor service at (4). The get() method, called at (5) to extract the value in the Future<?> object, blocks for the task to complete, if necessary. Since a Runnable does not return a value, the get() method returns the literal value null to indicate successful completion of the task. In this particular case, the type of the object returned is Future<?>, which is parameterized with the ? wildcard to express that it contains an object of some unknown type.

The Callable<Integer> diceValue is submitted to the executor service at (6). The Integer result of executing this callable will be returned in a Future<Integer> object and can be extracted by calling the get() method on this object. The get() method blocks if the task has not completed execution.

- -

Example 23.2 *Submitting Tasks and Handling Task Results*

```java
package executors;
import java.util.List;
import java.util.concurrent.*;
import java.util.stream.Collectors;

public class TaskExecution {

  public static void main(String[] args) {
    // Runnable:
    Runnable printDiceValue = () ->                                    // (1)
      System.out.println("Execution of Runnable: "
                          + ThreadLocalRandom.current().nextInt(1,7));

    // Callable<V>:
    Callable<Integer> diceRoll =                                       // (2)
        () -> ThreadLocalRandom.current().nextInt(1,7);

    // Executor service:
    ExecutorService exs = Executors.newFixedThreadPool(3);            // (3)
    try {
      // Executing Runnable in a thread:
      Future<?> rfuture = exs.submit(printDiceValue);                  // (4)
      Object result = rfuture.get();                                   // (5)
      System.out.println("Result of Runnable: " + result);

      // Executing Callable<V> in a thread:
      Future<Integer> cfuture = exs.submit(diceRoll);                  // (6)
      Integer diceValue = cfuture.get();                              // (7)
      System.out.println("Result of Callable: " + diceValue);

      // Executing bulk tasks:
      List<Callable<Integer>> callables                               // (8)
          = List.of(diceRoll, diceRoll, diceRoll);
```

```
      List<Future<Integer>> allFutures = exs.invokeAll(callables);     // (9)
      List<Integer> resultList = allFutures.stream()                    // (10)
        .map(future -> {
          try {
            return future.get();
          } catch(InterruptedException | ExecutionException ie) {
            throw new IllegalStateException(ie);
          }
        })
        .toList();
      System.out.println("Result of invokeAll(): " + resultList);

      Integer anyResult = exs.invokeAny(callables);                    // (11)
      System.out.println("Result of invokeAny(): " + anyResult);
    } catch(InterruptedException | ExecutionException ie) {
      ie.printStackTrace();
    } finally {
      exs.shutdown();
    }
  }
}
```

Probable output from the program:

```
Execution of Runnable: 4
Result of Runnable: null
Result of Callable: 2
Result of invokeAll(): [1, 3, 6]
Result of invokeAny(): 3
```

Invoking Tasks Collectively

Example 23.2 also illustrates invoking tasks *collectively* and handling the task results. An executor service defines the blocking methods invokeAll() and invokeAny() that allow a collection of Callable<V> tasks to be executed—thus implementing *bulk task execution*.

A list of Callable<Integer> tasks is defined at (8) in Example 23.2, where each task is represented by the Callable<Integer> diceRoll defined at (2). The list represents tasks for rolling three dice. This list is executed by calling the invokeAll() method of the executor service at (9). In contrast to the submit() method, the invokeAll() method *blocks* until *all* tasks have completed, and their results are returned in a list of Future<Integer> objects. The order of the Future<Integer> objects in the result list corresponds to the order of the tasks in the task list. The resulting list of Future<Integer> objects is processed in a stream at (10) to extract the result (i.e., an Integer) from each Future<Integer> object using the get() method, and the results are collected in a list of Integer that represents the results of throwing three dice.

On the other hand, the list of Callable<Integer> tasks is executed at (11) using the invokeAny() blocking method, which returns the result of the *first* task that completes successfully without throwing an exception. On return, any tasks not completed are cancelled. Note that the invokeAny() method does *not* return the result in a Future<Integer> object.

Only Callable<V> tasks can be executed in bulk, as Runnable tasks cannot be passed as a parameter to the invoke methods.

The ScheduledExecutorService **Interface**

A ScheduledExecutorService is an ExecutorService that schedules tasks to be executed after a given delay or to be executed periodically. Table 23.2 shows scheduled executor services provided by the factory methods of the Executors class.

The methods of the ScheduledExecutorService interface that schedule tasks return an object that implements the ScheduledFuture<V> interface. This interface extends the Future<V> interface, and thus provides methods to retrieve task results, to check execution status, or to cancel task execution.

Scheduling One-Shot Tasks

The overloaded schedule() method of the ScheduledExecutorService interface allows either a Runnable or a Callable<V> task to be scheduled for execution *only once after a specified delay*—that is, the schedule() methods execute *scheduled one-shot tasks*. The overloaded schedule() method of the ScheduledExecutorService interface is the analog of the overloaded submit() method of the ExecutorService interface for executing Runnable and Callable<V> tasks. These methods do not block—that is, they do not wait for the task to complete execution.

The following methods are defined in the ScheduledExecutorService interface that extends the ExecutorService interface:

ScheduledFuture<?> schedule(Runnable task, long delay, TimeUnit unit)
Schedules a one-shot task that becomes enabled after the given delay. The method returns a ScheduledFuture<?> object representing pending completion of the task and whose get() method will return null upon completion.

<V> ScheduledFuture<V> schedule(Callable<V> callable, long delay,
                                         TimeUnit unit)
Schedules a value-returning one-shot task that becomes enabled after the given delay. The method returns a ScheduledFuture<V> object which can be used to extract the result computed by the scheduled task or to cancel the scheduled task.

Example 23.3 illustrates scheduling one-shot Runnable and Callable<V> tasks for execution using a scheduled executor service. The example uses a *scheduled* thread pool with two threads that is created at (1) by calling the newScheduledThreadPool() factory method of the Executors class.

The Runnable task defined at (2) is passed to the schedule() method of the scheduled executor service at (3) to be executed once after a delay of 500 milliseconds. The get()

method invoked on the resulting ScheduledFuture<?> object returns the value null, as expected, after execution of the Runnable task to indicate successful completion.

The Callable<String> task defined at (4) is passed to the schedule() method of the scheduled executor service at (5) to be executed once after a delay of one second. In this case, the get() method invoked on the resulting ScheduledFuture<String> object returns a String value after successful completion of the task.

Example 23.3 *Executing Scheduled One-Shot Tasks*

```java
package executors;
import java.util.concurrent.*;

public class ScheduledOneShotTasks {
  public static void main(String[] args) {
    ScheduledExecutorService ses = Executors.newScheduledThreadPool(2);  // (1)
    try {
      // Schedule a one-shot Runnable:
      Runnable runnableTask                                              // (2)
          = () -> System.out.println("I am a one-shot Runnable task.");
      ScheduledFuture<?> scheduledRunnableTaskFuture                     // (3)
          = ses.schedule(runnableTask, 500, TimeUnit.MILLISECONDS);
      System.out.println("Runnable result: " + scheduledRunnableTaskFuture.get());

      // Schedule a one-shot Callable<String>:
      Callable<String> callableTask
          = () -> "I am a one-shot Callable task.";                      // (4)
      ScheduledFuture<String> scheduledCallableTaskFuture
          = ses.schedule(callableTask, 1, TimeUnit.SECONDS);            // (5)
      System.out.println("Callable result: " + scheduledCallableTaskFuture.get());
    } catch (InterruptedException | ExecutionException exc) {
      exc.printStackTrace();
    } finally {
      ses.shutdown();
    }
  }
}
```

Probable output from the program:

```
I am a one-shot Runnable task.
Runnable result: null
Callable result: I am a one-shot Callable task.
```

Scheduling Periodic Tasks

The ScheduledExecutorService interface provides two methods that can be used to schedule a Runnable task that should be executed periodically either after a fixed delay or at a fixed rate, with the first task execution commencing after an initial delay—in other words, scheduling *periodic tasks* for execution. No analogous methods are provided by the ScheduledExecutorService interface for Callable<V> tasks.

```
ScheduledFuture<?> scheduleWithFixedDelay(Runnable task, long initialDelay,
                                          long delay, TimeUnit unit)
ScheduledFuture<?> scheduleAtFixedRate(Runnable task, long initialDelay,
                                       long period, TimeUnit unit)
```

The scheduleWithFixedDelay() method schedules a periodic task that becomes enabled first after the given initial delay, and subsequently with the given delay *between the termination of one execution and the commencement of the next.* This means that the time interval between the *start* of two consecutive task executions is the sum of the execution time of the first task execution and the specified delay between them.

The scheduleAtFixedRate() method schedules a task that becomes enabled periodically for execution, with the first task execution commencing after the initial delay. This means that the time *between the start of two consecutive task executions is equal to the* period. Note that a new task execution commences after each period, regardless of whether or not the previous task execution has finished.

For both methods, task executions continue indefinitely, unless one of the following events occurs: The task is cancelled via the returned future, or the executor shuts down, or an exception is thrown during task execution. The isDone() method on the returned future will then return true.

Example 23.4 illustrates scheduling Runnable tasks for repeated execution using a scheduled executor service. The Runnable task to be repeatedly executed is defined at (1). It prints information at the start and just before finishing its execution, which also includes the current time, by calling the auxiliary method printTimestamp() defined at (2). In between printing the information, the Runnable task sleeps for one second.

First scheduling a periodic task to be run with *a fixed delay* is illustrated in the main() method. An appropriate scheduled executor service is created at (3), namely, a scheduled thread pool of size 4. The method scheduleWithFixedDelay() is called at (4), passing the task, the initial delay of one second before commencement of the first task, and a fixed delay of three seconds between the end of one task execution and the start of the next one. The main thread sleeps for 15 seconds at (5) to allow the periodic task to be scheduled and executed. And finally the scheduled executor service is shut down at (6), which will allow the executing task to complete and the executor service to terminate. Without the shutdown, the periodic task would continue to be scheduled for execution. The output from the program shows that for the fixed delay, the delay between the finishing time of a task execution and the start time of the next one is approximately three seconds as it was specified—ignoring the nanoseconds in the current time.

Analogously, the scenario above is repeated for scheduling *a periodic task* to be executed at a fixed rate in the main() method. A new scheduled executor service is created at (7) for this purpose. This time the method scheduleAtFixedRate() is called at (8), passing the task, the initial delay of one second before commencement of the first task, and a fixed rate of three seconds between the *start* of each task execution.

The main thread sleeps for 10 seconds at (9) to allow the periodic task to be executed. The shutdown() method at (10) takes care of terminating the periodic task and the executor. The output from the program shows that for the fixed rate, the time between the start time of two consecutive task executions is approximately three seconds—again, ignoring the nanoseconds in the current time.

Example 23.4 *Executing Scheduled Periodic Tasks*

```java
package executors;
import java.time.LocalTime;
import java.time.format.DateTimeFormatter;
import java.util.concurrent.*;

public class ScheduledPeriodicTasks {

  private static Runnable task = () -> {                               // (1)
    printTimestamp(" Start:  I am on it!");
    try {
      TimeUnit.SECONDS.sleep(1);
    } catch (InterruptedException exc) {
      System.out.println(exc);
    }
    printTimestamp(" Finish: I am not on it!");
  };

  private static void printTimestamp(String msg) {                    // (2)
    String threadName = Thread.currentThread().getName();
    String ts = LocalTime.now().format(DateTimeFormatter.ofPattern("HH:mm:ss"));
    System.out.println(threadName + ": " + ts + msg);
  }

  public static void main(String[] args) {
    // Schedule a periodic task with fixed delay:
    ScheduledExecutorService ses1 = Executors.newScheduledThreadPool(4);  // (3)
    try {
      System.out.println("Fixed delay:");
      ses1.scheduleWithFixedDelay(task, 1, 3, TimeUnit.SECONDS);       // (4)
      TimeUnit.SECONDS.sleep(15);                                     // (5)
    } catch (InterruptedException e) {
      e.printStackTrace();
    } finally {
      ses1.shutdown();                                               // (6)
    }

    // Schedule a periodic task at fixed rate:
    ScheduledExecutorService ses2 = Executors.newScheduledThreadPool(4);  // (7)
    try {
      System.out.println("\nFixed rate:");
      ses2.scheduleAtFixedRate(task, 1, 3, TimeUnit.SECONDS);         // (8)
      TimeUnit.SECONDS.sleep(10);                                    // (9)
    } catch (InterruptedException e) {
      e.printStackTrace();
```

```
    } finally {
      ses2.shutdown();                                              // (10)
    }
  }
}
```

Probable output from the program:

```
Fixed delay:
pool-1-thread-1: 12:55:54 Start:  I am on it!
pool-1-thread-1: 12:55:55 Finish: I am not on it!
pool-1-thread-1: 12:55:58 Start:  I am on it!
pool-1-thread-1: 12:55:59 Finish: I am not on it!
pool-1-thread-2: 12:56:02 Start:  I am on it!
pool-1-thread-2: 12:56:03 Finish: I am not on it!
pool-1-thread-1: 12:56:06 Start:  I am on it!
pool-1-thread-1: 12:56:07 Finish: I am not on it!

Fixed rate:
pool-1-thread-2: 12:56:09 Start:  I am on it!
pool-1-thread-2: 12:56:10 Finish: I am not on it!
pool-1-thread-4: 12:56:12 Start:  I am on it!
pool-1-thread-4: 12:56:13 Finish: I am not on it!
pool-1-thread-4: 12:56:15 Start:  I am on it!
pool-1-thread-4: 12:56:16 Finish: I am not on it!
pool-1-thread-4: 12:56:18 Start:  I am on it!
pool-1-thread-4: 12:56:19 Finish: I am not on it!
```

Task Cancellation

Task cancellation is an important aspect of controlling task execution. Here we look at scenarios for cancelling tasks by invoking the cancel() method of the Future<V> object that represents the task after the task has been submitted to the executor. The effect of the cancel() method on the task depends on what stage the task is in when the cancel() method is called.

- *The task is in the queue, waiting to be assigned to a thread.*

  Calling the cancel() method on the Future<V> object that represents the task removes the task from the queue—thus cancelling the task.

- *The task is being executed by a thread.*

  Calling the cancel() method on the Future<V> object that represents the task sends an *interrupt signal* to the thread, the outcome of which depends on how the task handles the signal. In this section, we take a closer look at how cancellation can be organized programmatically when the thread that is executing a task is stopped by calling the cancel() method. See also the discussion on handling interrupt signals when a thread is interrupted by calling the Thread.interrupt() method (§22.4, p. 1393).

- *The task has completed execution.*

  Calling the cancel() method on the Future<V> object that represents the task has no effect on the task.

Example 23.5 illustrates task cancellation by calling the cancel() method on the Future<V> object that represents the task.

A computation-intensive task is defined by the bigFactorial() method at (1) to iteratively compute the factorial of a BigInteger. In each iteration of its for(;;) loop, the method checks at (2) whether the thread executing the method has been interrupted. If that is the case, it throws an InterruptedException. This terminates the for(;;) loop. The exception is caught and handled by the catch block at (3), causing the method to return normally. If there is no interrupt signal, the for(;;) loop continues the factorial computation. It is important that the task defines an appropriate action when the thread is interrupted.

The timedTaskCancellation() method at (4) illustrates using the timed get() method at (7) to wait for the task submitted at (6) to either finish execution and print the result at (8), or time out and throw a TimeoutException if the task did not complete execution. The output from the program shows that a TimeoutException was thrown. This exception is caught by the catch block at (9). The task is cancelled in the catch block by calling the cancel() method on the Future<BigInteger> object at (10). Since the cancel() method at (10) is called with the value true, the thread executing the task represented by the future is interrupted in an attempt to stop the task. The cancel() method returns true, indicating that the thread was interrupted. Whether the task is now cancelled is determined by the calling the isCancelled() method of the Future<BigInteger> object at (11) that returns the value true, verifying the cancellation. As only a single task is executed in the scenario above, we have used a single thread executor that is created at (5). The output from this scenario depends on the execution time to compute the factorial for the specified number at (6) and the duration of the timeout in the get() method at (7).

The scheduledTaskCancellation() method at (13) illustrates how to cancel a submitted task by scheduling a second task to do the cancellation, if necessary. As there are two tasks involved, a scheduled thread pool of size 2 is created at (14). The first task is submitted at (15) to compute the factorial of a big number. A second task is scheduled at (16) to call the cancel() method on the Future<BigInteger> object representing the first task, after a delay of 10 milliseconds. If the first task has completed before the cancel() method is called, it has no effect on the first task. However, if the first task has not completed execution before the second task executes, the cancel() method will send an interrupt signal to the thread of the first task in an attempt to stop it. The output from the program shows that the first task was interrupted by the scheduled task. The isCancelled() method called on the Future<BigInteger> object at (18) confirms that the task was indeed cancelled. The output in this case depends on the execution time to compute the factorial for the specified number at (15) and the delay specified in the schedule() method at (16), before the call to the cancel() method is executed.

In summary, task cancellation is dependent on exploiting the thread interrupt system and providing an appropriate action in the interrupted thread executing the task.

Example 23.5 *Task Cancellation*

```java
package executors;
import java.math.BigInteger;
import java.util.concurrent.*;

public class TaskCancellation {

  // Computation-intensive task:
  private static BigInteger bigFactorial(int number) {          // (1)
    String threadName = Thread.currentThread().getName();
    BigInteger factorial = BigInteger.ONE;
    try {
      for (int i = 2; i <= number; i++) {
        factorial = factorial.multiply(BigInteger.valueOf(i));
        if (Thread.interrupted()) {                             // (2)
          throw new InterruptedException();
        }
      }
      System.out.println(threadName + " completed.");
    } catch (InterruptedException e) {
      System.out.println(threadName + " interrupted.");         // (3)
    }
    return factorial;
  }

  private static void timedTaskCancellation() {                 // (4)
    System.out.println("Timed task cancellation:");
    int number = 100000;
    long timeout = 1;
    TimeUnit unit = TimeUnit.SECONDS;
    System.out.println("NUMBER: " + number + ", "
                       + "TIMEOUT: " + timeout + " " + unit);
    ExecutorService exs = Executors.newSingleThreadExecutor();  // (5)
    Future<BigInteger> future = null;
    try {
      future = exs.submit(() -> bigFactorial(number));          // (6)
      BigInteger result = future.get(timeout, unit);            // (7)
      System.out.println("Factorial: " + result);              // (8)
    } catch (TimeoutException e) {                              // (9)
      System.out.println(e);
      System.out.println("cancel(true):  " + future.cancel(true));    // (10)
      System.out.println("isCancelled(): " + future.isCancelled());   // (11)
    } catch (InterruptedException | ExecutionException e) {
      System.out.println(e);                                   // (12)
    } finally {
      exs.shutdown();
    }
  }

  private static void scheduledTaskCancellation() {             // (13)
    System.out.println("Scheduled task cancellation:");
    int number = 100000;
    long delay = 10;
```

```
    TimeUnit unit = TimeUnit.MILLISECONDS;
    System.out.println("NUMBER: " + number + ", DELAY: " + delay + " " + unit);
    ScheduledExecutorService ses = Executors.newScheduledThreadPool(2);    // (14)
    try {
      Future<BigInteger> future = ses.submit(() -> bigFactorial(number)); // (15)
      ses.schedule(() -> future.cancel(true), delay, unit);               // (16)
      TimeUnit.SECONDS.sleep(1);                                          // (17)
      System.out.println("isCancelled(): " + future.isCancelled());      // (18)
    } catch (InterruptedException e) {
      System.out.println(e);
    } finally {
      ses.shutdown();
    }
  }

  public static void main(String[] args) {
    timedTaskCancellation();
    System.out.println();
    scheduledTaskCancellation();
  }
}
```

Probable output from the program:

```
Timed task cancellation:
NUMBER: 100000, TIMEOUT: 1 SECONDS
java.util.concurrent.TimeoutException
pool-1-thread-1 interrupted.
cancel(true):  true
isCancelled(): true

Scheduled task cancellation:
NUMBER: 100000, DELAY: 10 MILLISECONDS
pool-2-thread-1 interrupted.
isCancelled(): true
```

23.3 The Fork/Join Framework

To harness the benefits of multicore architectures, the Fork/Join Framework in the java.util.concurrent package provides support for parallel programming that allows computations to run in parallel on multiple processors. In this section we provide an introduction to this framework which is also the basis of parallel streams (§16.9, p. 1009), but it is also worth exploring further in its own right.

The Fork/Join Framework is specially suited for problems that can be solved by the *divide-and-conquer* problem-solving paradigm. This technique is prominent in processing data in large arrays and collections—for example, in designing sorting and searching algorithms. The main step in a divide-and-conquer algorithm is to divide the task repeatedly into subtasks of the same type until the task size is smaller than a given threshold, such that a subtask can be solved directly. A simplified divide-and-conquer algorithm to solve a problem is presented below. When the task can be solved directly, this is called the *base case*. Otherwise, the algorithm proceeds with dividing the task into subtasks, solving each subtask recursively, and combining the results from each subtask, all the time the idea being that each subtask gets smaller and moves toward the base case. Solving a subtask recursively is referred to as *forking*, and combing the results of subtasks is referred to as *joining*, hence the name Fork/Join Framework.

```
if (taskSize < threshold)
    solve task directly                     // Base case
else {
    divide task into subtasks               // Divide
    solve each subtask recursively          // Conquer
    combine results from each subtask       // Combine
}
```

Each subtask is solved by invocation of the divide-and-conquer algorithm recursively. The subtasks are candidates for *parallel processing*. The Fork/Join Framework facilitates both the management of threads and the use of available processors for parallel processing of subtasks.

Abstract classes shown in Table 23.3 can be extended to define tasks. The abstract classes RecursiveAction and RecursiveTask<V> provide the abstract method compute() that defines the computation of the task. This method emulates the divide-and-conquer paradigm.

There are different ways to fork a subtask. One convenient way is to use the overloaded invokeAll() static method of the ForkJoinTask<V> class. This static method initiates the execution of the tasks and awaits their completion, returning any results, if necessary.

The overall execution of tasks is managed by the specialized executor service, ForkJoinPool, shown in Figure 23.1. It is used analogous to the executors encountered in the Executor Framework. The initial task can be submitted to the fork-join pool by calling the invoke() method that commences the performing of the task.

Table 23.3 *Task-Defining Classes*

Classes in the java.util.concurrent package to define tasks	Description
ForkJoinTask<V>	Abstract class that defines a task
RecursiveAction extends ForkJoinTask<Void>	Abstract class that should be extended to define a task that does not return a value
RecursiveTask<V> extends ForkJoinTask<V>	Abstract class that should be extended to define a task that returns a value

Example 23.6 illustrates using the Fork/Join Framework. It counts the number of values in an array of random integers that satisfy a given predicate—in this particular case, all numbers divisible by 7. The FilterTask class at (1) extends the RecursiveTask<Integer> abstract class to define a task for this purpose. It implements the compute() method at (2) that mimics the divide-and-conquer algorithm.

The array to filter for numbers divisible by 7 is successively divided into two equal subarrays given by the indices fromIndex, toIndex, and middle. If the size of a subarray is less than the threshold, the base case at (3) is executed. It constitutes iterating over the subarray to do the counting, and returning the result. Note that the base case does not entail further subdivision of the task.

If the size of the array is over the threshold, two new filter tasks are created at (4) with two equal subarrays from the current subarray. The two new filter tasks are forked at (5) by calling the invokeAll() static method. Recursion occurs when the two subtasks are executed and their compute() method is called. The result returned from each subtask can be obtained by calling the inherited join() method from the superclass ForkJoinTask. These results are combined at (6) to return the combined result of the current subarray.

The main() method of the ForkJoinDemo class shows the steps to set up the fork-join pool for execution. The initial task is created at (9). The fork-join pool is create at (10) and invoked on the task at (11) to initiate the computation. The invoke() method returns the combined result of all the subtasks that were created in executing the initial task.

The powerful paradigm of parallel streams is evident from the stream-based solution at (12) when compared with the solution using the Fork/Join Framework explicitly.

Example 23.6 *Filtering Values Using Fork/Join Framework*

```java
package forkjoin;

import java.util.Random;
import java.util.concurrent.*;
import java.util.function.IntPredicate;
import java.util.stream.IntStream;

class FilterTask extends RecursiveTask<Integer> {                    // (1)
    public static final int THRESHOLD = 10_000;
    private int[] values;
    private int fromIndex;
    private int toIndex;
    private IntPredicate predicate;

    public FilterTask(int[] values, int fromIndex, int toIndex,
                      IntPredicate predicate) {
        this.values = values;
        this.fromIndex = fromIndex;
        this.toIndex = toIndex;
```

```java
            this.predicate = predicate;
        }

        @Override
        protected Integer compute() {                                    // (2)
            if (toIndex - fromIndex < THRESHOLD) {
                // The base case:                                        (3)
                var count = 0;
                for (int i = fromIndex; i < toIndex; i++) {
                    if (predicate.test(values[i])) {
                        ++count;
                    }
                }
                return count;
            } else {
                // Create subtasks:                                      (4)
                var middel = fromIndex + (toIndex - fromIndex) / 2;
                var subtask1 = new FilterTask(values, fromIndex, middel, predicate);
                var subtask2 = new FilterTask(values, middel, toIndex, predicate);
                // Fork and execute the subtasks. Await completion.      (5)
                ForkJoinTask.invokeAll(subtask1, subtask2);
                // Combine the results returned by subtasks.             (6)
                return subtask1.join() + subtask2.join();
            }
        }
    }

    public class ForkJoinDemo {
        public static void main(String[] args) {
            // Set up the array with the random int values:             (7)
            final int SIZE = 1_000_000;
            int[] numbers = new Random().ints(SIZE).toArray();

            // Predicate to filter numbers divisible by 7:              (8)
            IntPredicate predicate = i -> i % 7 == 0;

            // Create the initial task.                                  (9)
            var filterTask = new FilterTask(numbers, 0, numbers.length, predicate);
            // Create fork-join pool to manage execution of the task.    (10)
            var pool = new ForkJoinPool();
            // Perform the task, await completion, and return the result: (11)
            var result = pool.invoke(filterTask);
            System.out.println("Fork/Join:      " + result);

            // Solution using parallel stream:                           (12)
            System.out.println("Parallel stream: " +
                            IntStream.range(0, numbers.length).parallel()
                                    .map(i -> numbers[i]).filter(predicate).count());
        }
    }
```

Probable output from the program:

```
    Fork/Join:      142733
    Parallel stream: 142733
```

23.4 Writing Thread-Safe Code

Thread-safety is a critical property of a concurrent application. Threads can generally execute their tasks concurrently without impending each other, unless they are sharing resources. Generally speaking, a shared resource can be any data that is visible to more than one thread. This could be an object or a primitive value, which multiple threads can access concurrently.

Each thread has its own execution stack that contains local variables of active methods during execution (§22.2, p. 1369). Any variable allocated on this stack is only visible to the thread that owns this stack, and is therefore automatically thread-safe. On the other hand, objects are placed in a heap which is shared by all threads. These objects are considered to be potentially visible to all threads. A thread can access any object in a heap if it has a reference to it. The challenge is to avoid thread interference (or race conditions) when concurrent threads are accessing a shared object.

As a running example, we will use different implementations of a counter to illustrate various approaches to achieving thread-safety. Example 23.7 shows the interface ICounter at (1) that is implemented by a counter. The interface defines the two methods increment() and getValue() to increment and read the value in a counter, respectively.

The class TestCounters at (3) tests various counter implementations from (5) to (10) in the main() method at (4) by calling the method runIncrementor() defined at (11). This method creates a Runnable incrementor at (12) that calls the increment() method of a counter a fixed number of times (NUM_OF_INCREMENTS). The incrementor is submitted a fixed number of times to an executor service in the try block at (13), corresponding to the size of the thread pool of the executor service (POOL_SIZE). All together, a counter is incremented 10,000 times (NUM_OF_INCREMENTS*POOL_SIZE).

The output shown in Example 23.7 is for the various counter implementations that will be discussed in this section. First up is an unsafe counter implementation at (2) which is not thread-safe, as we can see from the incorrect result in the output. The cause can be attributed to thread interference (§22.4, p. 1388) and memory consistency errors (§22.5, p. 1414) when accessing the shared counter field by the concurrent threads. We look at different solutions (in addition to the synchronized code) to implement mutually exclusive access of a shared object in a concurrent application.

Example 23.7 *Testing Counter Implementations*

```
package safe;
/** Interface that defines a basic counter. */
interface ICounter {                                              // (1)
  void increment();
  int getValue();
}
```

```
package safe;
public class UnsafeCounter implements ICounter {                       // (2)
  private int counter = 0;

  @Override public int getValue()   { return counter; }
  @Override public void increment() { ++counter; }
}
```

```
package safe;
import java.util.concurrent.*;
import java.util.stream.IntStream;

public class TestCounters {                                            // (3)
  private static final int NUM_OF_INCREMENTS = 1000;
  private static final int POOL_SIZE = 10;

  public static void main(String[] args) throws InterruptedException { // (4)

    UnsafeCounter usc = new UnsafeCounter();                           // (5)
    runIncrementor(usc);
    System.out.printf("Unsafe Counter: %24d%n", usc.getValue());

    VolatileCounter vc = new VolatileCounter();                        // (6)
    runIncrementor(vc);
    System.out.printf("Volatile Counter: %22d%n", vc.getValue());

    SynchronizedCounter sc = new SynchronizedCounter();                // (7)
    runIncrementor(sc);
    System.out.printf("Synchronized Counter: %18d%n", sc.getValue());

    AtomicCounter ac = new AtomicCounter();                            // (8)
    runIncrementor(ac);
    System.out.printf("Atomic Counter: %24d%n", ac.getValue());

    ReentrantLockCounter rlc = new ReentrantLockCounter();             // (9)
    runIncrementor(rlc);
    System.out.printf("Reentrant Lock Counter: %16d%n", rlc.getValue());

    ReentrantRWLockCounter rwlc = new ReentrantRWLockCounter();        // (10)
    runIncrementor(rwlc);
    System.out.printf("Reentrant Read-Write Lock Counter: %d%n", rwlc.getValue());
  }

  public static void runIncrementor(ICounter counter) {                // (11)
    // A Runnable incrementor to call the increment() method of the counter
    // a fixed number of times:
    Runnable incrementor = () -> {                                     // (12)
      IntStream.rangeClosed(1, NUM_OF_INCREMENTS).forEach(i->counter.increment());
    };

    // An executor service to manage a fixed number of incrementors:
    ExecutorService execService = Executors.newFixedThreadPool(POOL_SIZE);

    // Submit the incrementor to the executor service. Each thread executes
    // the same incrementor, and thereby increments the same counter.
```

```
        try {                                                          // (13)
          IntStream.range(0, POOL_SIZE).forEach(i -> execService.submit(incrementor));
        } finally {
          execService.shutdown();
        }
        // Wait for all tasks to complete.
        try {
          while (!execService.awaitTermination(1, TimeUnit.SECONDS));
        } catch (InterruptedException e) {
          execService.shutdownNow();
        }
      }
    }
```

Probable output from the program:

```
Unsafe Counter:                    8495
Volatile Counter:                  8765
Synchronized Counter:              10000
Atomic Counter:                    10000
Reentrant Lock Counter:            10000
Reentrant Read-Write Lock Counter: 10000
```

Immutability

We have seen how to implement thread-safe access to shared resources in synchronized code that uses intrinsic locks (§22.4, p. 1387). However, if the shared resource is an immutable object, thread-safety comes for free.

An object is *immutable* if its state cannot be changed once it has been constructed. Since its state can only be read, there can be no thread interference and the state is always consistent.

Examples of immutable classes in the Java SE Platform API and designing immutable classes are discussed in §6.7, p. 356.

Volatile Fields

To optimize the execution of compiled code, the compiler performs optimizations on the bytecode. Typical optimizations are instruction reordering, method call inlining, and loop optimizations. For multithreaded applications, thread-specific optimizations can also be performed. It is quite common for threads to create their own private cached copies of variables (called *thread-local* variables) for performance reasons. Values of thread-local variables are synchronized with the values of their master variables in main memory at various times—for example, when a thread enters or exits synchronized code. Declaring a field as volatile informs the compiler that the field will be modified by different threads, and all reads and writes to the field should be reflected in the master copy in main memory. Without the volatile modifier, there is no guarantee that the latest value in a shared field will be visible to the different threads. The *visibility* of a shared volatile field is guaranteed by the following rule:

- *Volatile Field Rule:* A write to a volatile field *happens-before* every subsequent read of that field (§22.5, p. 1414).

The rule implies that a read on a volatile field will always see the value from the latest write on the volatile field. Without the volatile modifier, the threads may see different values in the shared field. The class NonVolatileDemo in Example 23.8 illustrates the potential problem that can occur with visibility when different threads share data. The boolean field stopThread at (1) is used in the run() method at (3) of each child thread spawned in the loop at (2) to stop the thread when the field value becomes true. The main thread sets this value after sleeping for a little while. If the threads are using thread-local copies of the field stopThread, there is no guarantee when these threads will get to see the updated value, and therefore, might continue executing forever.

The class VolatileDemo in Example 23.8 declares the field stopThread at (6) to be volatile. This is a typical use of the volatile modifier: to flag a condition to different threads. When the value is updated in the main thread, the child threads will see the updated value on the next read of the field, and are guaranteed to terminate.

Example 23.8 *Visibility of Shared Data*

```
package safe;
/** Potential problem with visibility of shared data. */
public class NonVolatileDemo {

  private static boolean stopThread = false;                 // (1)

  public static void main(String[] args) throws InterruptedException {
    for (int i = 0; i < 2; i++) {                            // (2)
      new Thread(() -> {
        while (!stopThread) {                                // (3)
          System.out.println(Thread.currentThread().getName()
                        + ": Get me out of here!");
        }
      }, "T" + i).start();
    }
    Thread.sleep(1);                                         // (4)
    stopThread = true;                                       // (5)
  }
}
```

```
package safe;
/** Volatile field to guarantee visibility of shared data. */
public class VolatileDemo {

  private static volatile boolean stopThread = false;     // (6)
```

```
// The main() method remains the same as in the NonVolatileDemo class.

}
```

Probable output from each of the programs:

```
...
T0: Get me out of here!
T0: Get me out of here!
T0: Get me out of here!
T1: Get me out of here!
...
```

All *reads* and *writes* are *atomic actions* for all volatile fields, regardless of whether they are object references or are of primitive data types. An *atomic action* is guaranteed to be performed by a thread without any interleaving—that is, without any race conditions. Such an action either performs in its entirety or not at all—akin to a database transaction. Most program actions are not actually atomic; even something as simple as an arithmetic operator takes more than one CPU cycle, and therefore can be interrupted before the action completes.

Note that atomicity holds only for read and write operations, not for non-atomic operations like the increment operator (++), that are actually executed in several steps. For example, the expression ++i is equivalent to the following code:

```
int tmp = i;
tmp = tmp + 1;
i = tmp;
```

The expression ++i actually is being evaluated as a read of the value in i, and then a write to i after the value has been incremented by 1. If i was a shared volatile field, a different thread could read it between the atomic read and write operations, resulting in potential memory consistency errors, unless intermediate values in i did not matter. Computing the next value in i is dependent on the previous value in i. Declaring a variable with such data dependencies as volatile may not be adequate, as demonstrated by Example 23.9 that implements the counter as a volatile field. Not surprisingly, the output from the program shows an incorrect result of incrementing the counter due to memory consistency errors.

The volatile keyword is enough to combat memory consistency problems. That is, it solves the visibility problem (writing to main memory), but not interleaving of operations on a shared variable (i.e., thread interference/race conditions). Solving both problems requires mutual exclusion. We explore solutions for implementing mutual exclusion other than synchronized code later in this section: atomic variables for mutual exclusion on shared single variables (p. 1456) and programmatic locks for mutual exclusion on shared resources (p. 1460).

Example 23.9 *Volatile Counter*

```
package safe;
public class VolatileCounter implements ICounter {
  private volatile int counter = 0;

  @Override public int getValue()   { return counter; }
  @Override public void increment() { ++counter; }
}
```

Probable output from the program in Example 23.7, p. 1451:

```
Volatile Counter:                    87672
```

There is no need to use a volatile field unless it is shared between threads, or if only atomic reads and writes are necessary on a field. A field of primitive type long or double does not guarantee atomic reads and writes, unless it is declared volatile. Also, a final field cannot be declared volatile, as it is immutable.

It is worth noting the differences between the volatile and the synchronized keywords. The keyword volatile is only applicable to fields, whereas the keyword synchronized is only applicable to a statement block or method. A synchronized statement cannot synchronize on null, but a volatile field may be null.

Since there are no locks involved when accessing a volatile field, there is no blocking of threads either. Performance overhead is also lightweight, compared to synchronized code which is bound by the whole regime of thread management, although the keyword signals to the compiler *not* to undertake certain optimizations. And while the volatile keyword cannot replace synchronized code in all situations, it is more efficient in certain situations where the visibility and atomicity of a shared field are overriding factors.

Atomic Variables

Unless the action on a shared volatile variable is atomic, thread-safety cannot be guaranteed because of potential race conditions. Non-atomic actions (such as the use of the increment operator) by different threads can result in interleaving of constituent actions like read, update, and write.

Shared lock-free thread-safe variables are implemented by the classes in the java.util.concurrent.atomic package (Table 23.4). The classes provide methods that implement *atomic actions*. The classes and the variables that denote their instances are called *atomic classes* and *atomic variables*, respectively.

Atomic variables also behave as if they are volatile, so there is no need to declare them explicitly with the volatile keyword—that is, the atomic actions of the atomic classes guarantee visibility of an atomic variable to other threads.

The atomic classes thus implement *non-blocking lock-free synchronization* of atomic variables by a predefined set of atomic actions, ensuring visibility and avoiding race conditions.

Table 23.4   *Selected Atomic Classes*

Atomic classes in the java.util.concurrent.atomic package	Mutable value that may be updated atomically
AtomicBoolean	A boolean value
AtomicInteger implements Number	An int value
AtomicLong implements Number	A long value
AtomicReference<V>	An object reference

Example 23.11 illustrates a thread-safe counter implemented using the Atomic-Integer class. The counter field is declared at (1) as an AtomicInteger and initialized to 0. The getValue() and increment() methods at (2) and (3) delegate their operation to appropriate atomic methods of the AtomicInteger class. As the name implies, the get() method atomically returns the current value of the counter. The increment-AndGet() method atomically increments the counter and returns the new value (that is ignored in this example). The incrementAndGet() method entails more than one action, but none of them can be interrupted. The output shows that the counter was correctly incremented by the threads.

To understand how some of the atomic operations are implemented, we take a look at the while loop at (5), which implements the equivalent of the incrementAndGet() method at (4).

The strategy used in the while loop is known as *CAS: Compare and Set*, after the method called at (8). The compareAndSet() method will not set the counter to the new value unless the current value is equal to the expected value.

Assume that the current value in the counter is 100. Referring to the numbered lines in the code:

(6) The expected value is 100 (i.e., the current counter value).

(7) The new value is 101, after incrementing the expected value.

(8) The call to the compareAndSet() method in the conditional expression of the if statement returns true, since the current value (100) is equal to the expected value (100). The new value (101) is set in the counter—that is, it is correctly incremented by 1 from the previous value.

(9) The loop terminates.

Assume that by the time the current value is read again for comparison at (8) by the compareAndSet() method, it has been changed to 105 by another thread. This is possible by another thread in the time between the counter value is accessed at (6) by the get() method and then again at (8) by the compareAndSet() method—that is, there is a potential race condition.

(8) The call to the compareAndSet() method in the conditional expression of the if statement returns false, since the current value (105) is not equal to the expected value (100). The value in the counter is not changed as it could corrupt the state of the counter, and the loop continues until the counter value is correctly incremented by 1.

The while loop ensures that the value is always incremented by 1 from the previous value. Many of the methods in the atomic classes use a similar strategy to implement atomic operations.

It goes without saying that the AtomicInteger class should not be used as a replacement for the Integer class. We leave the inquisitive reader to explore the Atomic API further at leisure.

Example 23.10 *Atomic Counter*

```java
package safe;
import java.util.concurrent.atomic.AtomicInteger;

public class AtomicCounter implements ICounter {
  private AtomicInteger counter = new AtomicInteger(0);                    // (1)

  @Override
  public int getValue() {                                                 // (2)
    return counter.get();
  }

  @Override
  public void increment() {                                               // (3)
    counter.incrementAndGet();                                            // (4)
//  while (true) {                                                        // (5)
//    int expectedValue = counter.get();                                 // (6)
//    int newValue = expectedValue + 1;                                  // (7)
//    if (counter.compareAndSet(expectedValue, newValue)) {// (8) Compare and Set.
//      return;                                                          // (9)
//    }
//  }
  }
}
```

Output from the program in Example 23.7, p. 1451:

```
Atomic Counter:                10000
```

The AtomicInteger class provides the following constructors:

```
AtomicInteger()
AtomicInteger(int initialValue)
```

Create a new AtomicInteger with initial value 0 or with the given initial value, respectively.

Selected atomic methods from the `AtomicInteger` class are presented below.

```
int get()
```
Returns the current value.

```
void set(int newValue)
```
Sets the value to newValue.

```
int getAndSet(int newValue)
```
Atomically sets the value to newValue and returns the old value.

```
boolean compareAndSet(int expectedValue, int newValue)
```
Atomically sets the value to newValue if the current value == expectedValue, returning true if the operation was successful; otherwise, it returns false.

```
int addAndGet(int delta)
int getAndAdd(int delta)
```
Atomically adds the given value to the current value, returning the updated value or the previous value, respectively.

```
int decrementAndGet()
int getAndDecrement()
```
Atomically decrements the current value, returning the updated value or the previous value, respectively.

```
int incrementAndGet()
int getAndIncrement()
```
Atomically increments the current value, returning the updated value or the previous value, respectively.

```
int accumulateAndGet(int x, IntBinaryOperator accumulatorFunction)
int getAndAccumulate(int x, IntBinaryOperator accumulatorFunction)
```
Atomically updates the current value with the results of applying the given function to the current and given values, returning the updated value or the previous value, respectively.

```
int updateAndGet(IntUnaryOperator updateFunction)
int getAndUpdate(IntUnaryOperator updateFunction)
```
Atomically updates the current value with the results of applying the given function, returning the updated value or the previous value, respectively.

```
int    intValue()
double doubleValue()
float  floatValue()
long   longValue()
```
Returns the current value of this `AtomicInteger` as an int, double, float, and long after a widening primitive conversion, if necessary, respectively.

Intrinsic Locking Revisited

Intrinsic locking provides a blocking, lock-based, thread-safe solution for concurrent threads accessing mutable shared resources. The keyword synchronized is used to implement critical sections of code (synchronized methods/blocks) that rely on intrinsic locks to guarantee mutual exclusion to a single thread at a time (§22.4, p. 1387). Race conditions are thus avoided by mutual exclusion guaranteed by the critical section. The happens-before object lock rule (in this case for intrinsic locks) guarantees that any updates to the shared data done by one thread in a critical section will be visible to any other thread in another critical section guarded by the same intrinsic lock—thus eliminating memory consistency errors (§22.5, p. 1414).

Example 23.11 is an implementation of a thread-safe counter using synchronized methods for this particular case. Note that it is not necessary to declare the counter field as volatile, as both visibility and absence of race conditions are guaranteed by the synchronized code. The two operations on the counter are implemented as synchronized methods that are mutually exclusive, ensuring thread-safe use of the counter when accessed by different threads.

- -

Example 23.11 *Synchronized Counter*

```
package safe;
public class SynchronizedCounter implements ICounter  {
  private int counter = 0;

  @Override public synchronized int getValue() { return counter; }
  @Override public synchronized void increment() { counter++; }
}
```

Output from the program in Example 23.7, p. 1451:

```
Synchronized Counter:              10000
```

- -

Programmatic Locking

The Lock API in the java.util.concurrent.locks package provides flexible programmatic locking mechanisms that can be used to ensure thread-safety of shared mutable resources accessed by concurrent threads.

Intrinsic locking is based on the *acquire-release lock paradigm* to implement mutual exclusion. This paradigm is also the basis of locking mechanisms for mutual exclusion provided by the Lock API. This API also allows more control over *lock acquisition* (i.e., how the lock should be acquired) and *lock disciplines* (i.e., how to choose a thread among the waiting threads to acquire a released lock). Programmatic locking is thus more flexible, and can prevent threads from potential resource starvation (§22.5, p. 1412).

Selected interfaces and classes from the Lock API are shown in Figure 23.3. The main interfaces are Lock and ReadWriteLock that are implemented by the ReentrantLock and the `ReentrantReadWriteLock` classes, respectively. The `ReentrantReadWriteLock` class defines two nested classes, `ReadLock` and `WriteLock`, that implement the `Lock` interface. We explore the Lock API in the next section.

Figure 23.3   *Selected Interfaces and Classes in the Lock API*

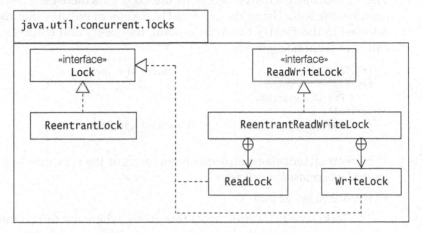

Reentrant Lock

The `ReentrantLock` class implements the `Lock` interface. Instances of the `Reentrant-Lock` class are basically analogous to intrinsic locks. A thread needs to *lock* a `ReentrantLock` instance in order to gain exclusive access to a critical section guarded by the `ReentrantLock` instance. Afterward, the `ReentrantLock` instance must be *unlocked* so that other threads can try to gain access to the critical region.

The `ReentrantLock` class provides two constructors to create locks, with or without a *fairness policy*, as shown below at (1) and (2), respectively. The fairness policy is specified by the value true in the constructor. In this case, the *acquisition order* is that the longest-waiting thread for the lock is chosen to acquire the released lock. Otherwise, no guarantees are given as to how a thread will be chosen from the threads waiting to acquire the lock.

```
Lock frl = new ReentrantLock(true);  // (1) Fair reentrant lock
Lock rl = new ReentrantLock();       // (2) Reentrant lock with no fairness policy
```

`ReentrantLock()`

Creates an instance of `ReentrantLock`. This `ReentrantLock` instance does *not* use a fairness policy, and it is equivalent to `ReentrantLock(false)`.

`ReentrantLock(boolean fair)`

Creates an instance of `ReentrantLock` with the given fairness policy. The fair ordering policy is implied by the value true, allowing the longest-waiting thread to acquire the lock when it is released.

The basic idiom to use a reentrant lock for mutual exclusion is shown below. A thread first *locks* the ReentrantLock instance at (1) by calling the lock() method—we say that the thread *acquires* the lock. At (2), the thread *unlocks* the ReentrantLock instance by calling the unlock() method—we say that the thread *releases* the lock. The thread has exclusive access to the code executed between (1) and (2) if it acquires the lock. Using the try-finally statement ensures that the lock is always released in the finally block. In general, the lock() and unlock() methods can be called in separate methods.

```
frl.lock();                    // (1) Acquire the lock.
try {
// Exclusive access...
} finally {
  frl.unlock();                // (2) Release the lock.
}
```

The ReentrantLock class implements methods of the Lock interface that define different *lock acquisition policies*.

- *Unconditional locking*

  The lock() method implements this policy, where the thread must unconditionally wait to acquire the lock if it is not available immediately.

  ```
  frl.lock();                                          // Unconditional locking.
  try { /* Lock acquired. Can access the resource. */ }
  finally { frl.unlock(); }
  ```

- *Polled locking*

  The tryLock() method implements this policy, where the call will return immediately with the value false if the lock is not available. The value true is returned if the lock is acquired.

  ```
  if (frl.tryLock()) {                                 // Polled locking.
    try { /* Lock acquired. Can access the resource. */ }
    finally { frl.unlock(); }
  } else { /* Lock was not acquired. */ }
  ```

- *Timed locking*

  The tryLock(timeout, timeunit) method will also return false if the thread is not able to acquire the lock in the specified time. If the thread is interrupted while waiting for the lock, it will throw an InterruptedException.

  ```
  try {
    if (frl.tryLock(100, TimeUnit.MILLISECONDS)) {     // Timed locking.
      try { /* Lock acquired. Can access the resource. */ }
      finally { frl.unlock(); }
    } else { /* Lock was not acquired. */ }
  } catch (InterruptedException iex) { iex.printStackTrace(); }
  ```

- *Interruptible locking*

  The lockInterruptibly() method throws an InterruptedException if the thread is interrupted while acquiring the lock or while waiting for the lock.

```
try {
  frl.lockInterruptibly();                            // Interruptible locking.
  try { /* Lock acquired. Can access the resource. */ }
  finally { frl.unlock(); }
} catch (InterruptedException iex) { iex.printStackTrace(); }
```

More details are provided below about the lock acquisition policy implemented by the methods mentioned above. These methods are defined by the Lock interface and implemented by the ReentrantLock class.

void lock()

If the lock is not held by another thread, the *lock hold count* is set to 1 and the method returns immediately.

If the current thread already holds the lock, the lock hold count is incremented by 1 and the method returns immediately.

If the lock is held by another thread, the thread waits until the lock is acquired, at which point the lock hold count is set to 1.

void unlock()

If the current thread is the holder of this lock, the lock hold count is decremented. If the lock hold count now has the value 0, the lock is released.

If the current thread is not the holder of this lock, then an IllegalMonitorState-Exception is thrown.

Note that a lock action on a lock must be matched by an unlock action.

The thread must make sure that an acquired lock is released after use, typically in the finally block of a try-finally statement.

boolean tryLock()

If the lock is not held by another thread, the *lock hold count* is set to 1 and the method returns true. This method does not honor fairness—it does not care if there are any threads already waiting for this lock.

If the current thread already holds the lock, the lock hold count is incremented by 1 and the method returns true.

If the lock is held by another thread, the method returns immediately with the value false.

boolean tryLock(long time, TimeUnit unit) throws InterruptedException

Acquires the lock if it is free within the given waiting time and the current thread has not been interrupted. In this case, the lock hold count is set to 1 and the value true is returned. The method respects the fair ordering policy if one has been specified for this lock.

If the current thread already holds the lock, the lock hold count is incremented by 1 and the method returns true.

If the current thread is interrupted while waiting to acquire the lock, an InterruptedException is thrown.

If timed out, the method returns the value false.

```
void lockInterruptibly() throws InterruptedException
```

If the lock is not held by another thread and the current thread is not interrupted, the *lock hold count* is set to 1 and the method returns immediately.

If the current thread already holds the lock, the lock hold count is incremented by 1 and the method returns immediately.

If the lock is held by another thread, the current thread waits for the lock. If the lock is acquired by the current thread while waiting, the lock hold count is set to 1.

If the current thread is interrupted while waiting to acquire the lock, an `InterruptedException` is thrown.

The following selected methods for querying a lock are only defined by the `ReentrantLock` class:

```
boolean isFair()
```
Returns `true` if this lock has the fairness policy set to `true`.

```
boolean isLocked()
```
If the lock is held by any thread, this method returns `true`; otherwise, it returns `false`.

```
int getQueueLength()
```
Returns an estimate of the number of threads waiting to acquire this lock.

```
boolean hasQueuedThreads()
```
Returns `true` if any threads are waiting to acquire this lock; otherwise, it returns `false`.

```
boolean hasQueuedThread(Thread thread)
```
Returns `true` if the given thread is waiting to acquire this lock; otherwise, it returns `false`.

Example 23.12 illustrates using a reentrant lock to implement a thread-safe counter. The class `ReentrantLockCounter` at (1) implements the `ICounter` interface (Example 23.7). It defines a counter whose value can be read by the method `getValue()` at (1), and incremented by the method `increment()` at (5). The class instantiates a `ReentrantLock` instance at (2) that is used in the two methods to implement exclusive access to the counter field.

The `getValue()` method at (4) acquires the `rl` lock, reads and stores the current counter value locally, unlocks the `rl` lock, and returns the locally stored counter value. The `increment()` method at (5) acquires the `rl` lock, increments the counter, calls the `getValue()` method (ignoring the returned value), and releases the `rl` lock. The setup with the locks ensures that any read or write operation will have exclusive access to the counter field. When testing the `ReentrantLockCounter` class with Example 23.7, p. 1451, the output shows that the counter was incremented correctly by the threads.

Note that the expression of a return statement in a try block is evaluated first and its value stored locally, before the finally block is executed. The stored result is returned after the completion of the finally block.

Intrinsic locks are *reentrant*: A thread that has acquired an intrinsic lock can acquire the same intrinsic lock again immediately (§22.4, p. 1390). This is also true of the locks implemented by the ReentrantLock class. In other words, explicit locks implemented by the ReentrantLock class are reentrant, as their name implies. The following code relies on the lock being reentrant:

```
frl.lock();
frl.lock();
// Access the resource. Lock hold count is 2.
frl.unlock();
frl.unlock();
```

Example 23.12 also illustrates the reentrant nature of explicit locks. The increment() method of the ReentrantLockCounter class calls the method getValue(). The current thread already holds the rl lock when the getValue() method is called. The get-Value() method also calls the lock() method on the rl lock. If rl was not reentrant, the current thread would not be able to proceed in the getValue() method and would starve waiting for the lock to become available, as it already has been acquired by the current thread. The reentrant nature of the rl lock allows the current thread to reacquire the lock and execute the getValue() method.

Example 23.12 *Reentrant Lock Counter*

```
package safe;
import java.util.concurrent.locks.*;

public class ReentrantLockCounter implements ICounter {          // (1)

  private Lock rl = new ReentrantLock();                         // (2)
  private int counter = 0;                                       // (3)

  @Override
  public int getValue() {                                        // (4)
    rl.lock();
    try {
      return counter;
    } finally { rl.unlock(); }
  }

  @Override
  public void increment() {                                      // (5)
    rl.lock();
    try {
      counter++;                                                 // (6)
      getValue();                                                // (7)
    } finally { rl.unlock(); }
  }
}
```

Output from the program in Example 23.7, p. 1451:

```
Reentrant Lock Counter:              10000
```

Reentrant Read-Write Lock

The explicit lock implemented by the ReentrantLock class is *mutually exclusive*—that is, only one thread at a time can obtain the lock and thereby access the shared data. There are cases where shared data is read more often than it is modified—that is, there are more *readers* (or *reader threads*) than *writers* (or *writer threads*) accessing the shared data. Taking into consideration such behavior to improve the level of concurrency would be a challenge using a mutually exclusive lock, as the lock acquisition is exclusive, irrespective of whether it is a read or a write operation.

The ReadWriteLock interface provides a more flexible and sophisticated locking mechanism than a mutually exclusive lock for accessing shared data. Figure 23.3 shows that the ReentrantReadWriteLock class implements the ReadWriteLock interface. It implements a *read-write lock* that actually maintains *a pair of associated locks*, one for read operations and one for write operations. The *read lock* is an instance of the ReadLock inner class and the *write lock* is an instance of the WriteLock inner class, both of which implement the Lock interface. The ReadWriteLock interface defines the methods to obtain the read and the write lock of a read-write lock.

The following methods are defined in the ReadWriteLock interface:

```
Lock readLock()
Lock writeLock()
```

These methods are implemented by inner classes in the ReentrantReadWriteLock class:

```
ReentrantReadWriteLock.ReadLock readLock()
ReentrantReadWriteLock.WriteLock writeLock()
```

Return the lock used for reading and for writing, respectively. The inner classes ReadLock and WriteLock implement the Lock interface.

The ReentrantReadWriteLock class provides the following constructors to create read-write locks with or without a fairness policy:

```
ReentrantReadWriteLock()
```

Creates an instance of ReentrantLock with non-fair ordering policy—imposing no ordering for lock access. A non-fair lock may be acquired by a thread at the expense of other waiting reader and writer threads.

```
ReentrantReadWriteLock(boolean fair)
```

Creates an instance of ReentrantLock with the given fairness policy. The value true indicates to use a fair ordering policy.

The basic idea behind a read-write lock is that a thread can use its read and write locks to perform thread-safe read and write operations on shared data, respectively. A thread is bound by the following lock acquisition rules for the read lock and the write lock of a read-write lock:

- *The read lock*: Only if no thread holds *the write lock* can a thread acquire the read lock. This means that the read lock can be shared by several reader threads—that is, a group of reader threads can access the shared data concurrently, as long as the write lock is not held by any thread.

- *The write lock*: Only if no thread holds *the write lock or the read lock* can a thread acquire the write lock. The write lock is thus mutually exclusive for writer threads—only one writer thread at a time can access the shared data.

Since the inner classes ReadLock and WriteLock implement the Lock interface, the lock acquisition policies of the Lock interface discussed earlier (p. 1462) are applicable to the read lock and the write lock, bearing in mind the specialized lock acquisition rules mentioned above for the read-write lock:

- *Unconditional locking* using the blocking lock() method
- *Polled locking* using the non-blocking tryLock() method
- *Timed locking* using the tryLock(timeout, timeunit) method
- *Interruptible locking* using the lockInterruptibly() method

As with any implementation of the Lock interface, the read lock and the write lock of a read-write lock must be released when done:

- *Released* using the unlock() method

- -

Example 23.13 *Reentrant Read-Write Lock Counter*

```java
package safe;
import java.util.OptionalInt;
import java.util.concurrent.locks.*;

public class ReentrantRWLockCounter implements ICounter {

  private ReadWriteLock rwl = new ReentrantReadWriteLock();        // (1)
  private Lock readLock = rwl.readLock();                          // (2)
  private Lock writeLock = rwl.writeLock();                        // (3)
  private int counter = 0;

  @Override
  public int getValue() {                                         // (4)
    readLock.lock();
    try {
//      System.out.println(Thread.currentThread().getName() + ": " + counter);
      return counter;
    } finally { readLock.unlock(); }
  }
```

```
    @Override
    public void increment() {                                 // (5)
      writeLock.lock();
      try {
        counter++;
      } finally { writeLock.unlock(); }
    }

    public int incrementAndGet() {                            // (6)
      writeLock.lock();                  // Acquire write lock.
      try {
        return ++counter;                                     // (7)
//      ++counter;                       // Increment.         // (8)
//      return getValue();               // Get the new value. // (9)
      } finally { writeLock.unlock(); } // Release write lock.
    }

    public int getAndIncrement() {                            // (10)
      writeLock.lock();                  // Acquire write lock.
      try {
        return counter++;                // Get and increment. // (11)
      } finally { writeLock.unlock(); } // Release write lock.
    }

    public boolean incrIfPossible() {                         // (12)
      if (writeLock.tryLock()) {         // Attempts to acquire the write lock.
        try {                            // Write lock acquired.
          counter++;
          return true;
        } finally { writeLock.unlock(); } // Write lock released.
      } else {                           // Write lock not acquired.
        return false;
      }
    }

    public OptionalInt getIfPossible() {                      // (13)
      if (readLock.tryLock()) {          // Attempts to acquire the read lock.
        try { return OptionalInt.of(counter); }
        finally { readLock.unlock(); }   // Read lock released.
      } else {                           // Read lock not acquired.
        return OptionalInt.empty();
      }
    }
  }
```

Output from the program in Example 23.7, p. 1451:

```
Reentrant Read-Write Lock Counter: 10000
```

- -

In Example 23.13, the class ReentrantRWLockCounter implements a thread-safe counter using a ReentrantReadWriteLock. It is a reworking of the counter in Example 23.12 that uses a ReentrantLock. In Example 23.13, the write lock allows mutually exclusive access to write operations and the read lock is shared concurrently by read operations. The numbered comments below correspond to the numbered code lines in Example 23.13.

(1)–(3) A non-fair `ReentrantReadWriteLock` is created, and its read and write locks obtained.

(4) The read lock acquired by a thread in the `getValue()` method ensures that the counter can be read safely, as no other thread can hold the write lock to modify the counter. This approach allows concurrent read operations and prevents concurrent write operations on the mutable counter, making it thread-safe. The read lock is guaranteed to be released in the `finally` block of the `try-finally` statement.

(5) The `increment()` method uses the write lock to provide exclusive access to increment the counter.

(6) The `incrementAndGet()` method shows that it is safe to increment *and* read the counter when the thread holds the write lock, as no other thread can access the counter. The `return` statement at (7) is equivalent to the statements at (8) and (9). The call to the `getValue()` method at (9) acquires the read lock to read the counter value, while the current write thread is still holding the write lock. This illustrates the reentrant nature of the read-write lock, which allows a thread holding the write lock to acquire the read lock.

(10) The `getAndIncrement()` method shows that it is safe to read *and* increment the counter when the thread holds the write lock, as no other thread can access the counter.

(12) The `incrIfPossible()` method illustrates polling for the write lock. It uses the non-blocking `tryLock()` method in an attempt to acquire the write lock. If successful, it increments the counter, releases the write lock, and returns `true`. Otherwise, it returns `false`.

(13) The `getIfPossible()` method illustrates polling for the read lock. It uses the non-blocking `tryLock()` method in an attempt to acquire the read lock. If successful, it releases the read lock, and returns an `OptionalInt` with the value of the counter. Otherwise, it returns an empty `OptionalInt`, since the read lock could not be acquired.

Note that the methods in Example 23.13 implement *atomic actions*. When testing the `ReentrantRWLockCounter` class with Example 23.7, p. 1451, the output shows that the counter was incremented correctly by the threads.

The `ReentrantReadWriteLock` class also provides miscellaneous methods that can be used to query a read-write lock:

```
boolean isFair()
```
Determines whether this lock has its fairness policy set to `true`.

```
int getReadHoldCount()
int getWriteHoldCount()
```
Queries the number of reentrant read holds and reentrant write holds on this lock by the current thread, respectively.

```
boolean isWriteLockedByCurrentThread()
```
If the write lock is held by the current thread, returns true; otherwise, it returns ·false.

The fairness policy comes into play when the currently held lock is released and there are threads waiting for a lock. For a read-write lock, there may be both writer threads and reader threads waiting to acquire a lock. The following aspects of a read-write lock's fairness policy should be noted:

- In order to assign the read lock, the fairness policy basically chooses between *one longest-waiting writer thread* among any waiting writer threads to assign the write lock and *the longest-waiting group of reader threads* among any waiting reader threads. Whichever of these has waited the longest is chosen.

- A thread can only acquire a fair read lock if both the write lock is free and there are no waiting writer threads. The thread will only acquire the read lock after the oldest currently waiting writer thread has acquired and released the write lock.

- A thread can only acquire a fair write lock if both the read lock and write lock are free; otherwise, it will block.

Analogous to the tryLock() methods of the ReentrantLock class, the tryLock() methods of the inner classes ReadLock and WriteLock do not honor the fairness policy, acquiring the lock immediately if available, regardless of any waiting threads.

Analogous to the reentrant nature of a ReentrantLock, the read-write lock allows both reader and writer threads to reacquire its read lock or write lock. Note that a thread that holds the write lock can acquire the read lock, but not vice versa. A reader thread that tries to acquire the write lock will block and never succeed.

Although a ReentrantReadWriteLock allows a greater level of concurrency to access shared data than a ReentrantLock, many factors can influence the performance of a read-write lock. Profiling is recommended to gauge the impact of such factors as its premises of more frequent reads than writes, duration of read and write operations, and number of cores available to leverage parallel execution. However, other thread-safe solutions provided by the Concurrency API for accessing shared data should also be considered.

23.5 Special-Purpose Synchronizers

The java.util.concurrent package provides classes that implement useful special-purpose synchronization idioms that impose specific behavior on how threads can collectively make progress through some algorithm. We consider two such classes in this section: CyclicBarrier and CountDownLatch.

Cyclic Barrier

The java.util.concurrent.CyclicBarrier class implements a *barrier* upon which a set of threads have to synchronize before they are all allowed to proceed. The threads may need to wait for one another until all threads reach the barrier. When this happens the barrier will *trip*, allowing them to continue. The barrier is *cyclic*, as the same barrier can be reused after the waiting threads have been released.

The following constructors of the CyclicBarrier class can be used to create a barrier.

```
CyclicBarrier(int parties)
CyclicBarrier(int parties, Runnable barrierAction)
```

Both methods create a barrier that will trip when the specified number of parties (i.e., threads) are waiting for it—that is, when these invoke the await() method on it.

The barrier created by the second method will execute the given *barrier action* when the barrier is tripped. This action is performed by the *last* thread arriving at the barrier.

The declaration at (1) below creates a barrier that will trip when three threads synchronize on it. The declaration at (2) creates a barrier that will trip when five threads are waiting for it. In addition, a *barrier action* is defined that will be performed when the barrier is tripped. Typically, a barrier action can be used for consolidating any results computed by the threads thus far.

```
CyclicBarrier barrier1 = new CyclicBarrier(3);                          // (1)
CyclicBarrier barrier2 = new CyclicBarrier(5, () ->
        System.out.println("All results accumulated."));               // (2)
```

A cyclic barrier is *shared* by the threads wishing to synchronize on it. When a thread wants to wait at the barrier, it calls the await() method on the barrier. This defines a *barrier point*. The call blocks at the barrier point until the number of threads required to trip the barrier is reached—that is, the remaining threads also invoke the await() method. Otherwise, the barrier will not trip as long as the number of waiting threads is less than the number required by the barrier.

```
// Thread t1 waits on barrier1 at this barrier point.
barrier1.await();              // Can continue when the barrier is tripped.
...

// Thread t2 waits on barrier1 at this barrier point.
barrier1.await();              // Can continue when the barrier is tripped.
...

// Thread t3 waits on barrier1 at this barrier point.
barrier1.await();              // Can continue when the barrier is tripped.
...
```

The barrier barrier1 is tripped when any three threads invoke the await() method on this barrier—for example, threads t1, t2, and t3, as shown above. When tripped, the waiting threads can proceed, and the cyclic barrier resets itself and can be tripped again.

The CyclicBarrier class also defines methods to query and reset a barrier.

```
int await() throws InterruptedException, BrokenBarrierException
int await(long timeout, TimeUnit unit) throws InterruptedException,
                                               BrokenBarrierException,
                                               TimeoutException
```

Both methods wait until all parties have invoked the await() method on this barrier, or until the specified waiting time elapses, as in the second method.

These methods return the *arrival index* of the current thread, index N-1 for the first thread to arrive and 0 for the last thread to arrive, where N is the number of parties required to trip this barrier.

An InterruptedException is thrown if the current thread was interrupted while waiting.

A BrokenBarrierException is thrown if another thread was interrupted or timed out while the current thread was waiting, or the barrier was reset, or the barrier was broken when the await() method was called, or any barrier action failed due to an exception.

A TimeoutException is thrown if any specified timeout elapses. The barrier is then broken.

```
int getParties()
```

Returns the number of parties required to trip this barrier.

```
boolean isBroken()
```

Queries whether this barrier is in a *broken state*. A barrier can break due to an interruption, a timeout, the last reset, or a failed barrier action due to an exception. It returns true if any of the parties broke the barrier; otherwise, it returns false.

```
void reset()
```

Resets the barrier to its initial state—that is, the wait count of the barrier is set to 0. Any parties currently waiting at this barrier will return with a Broken-BarrierException.

Example 23.14 illustrates using a single cyclic barrier that is shared by three threads. The barrier is declared at (2), requiring three parties and having the barrier action at (1) being performed when the barrier is tripped. The task declared at (3) calls the await() method on the barrier when it wants to synchronize on the barrier. Note the checked exceptions that can be thrown by the await() method. The threads are created and started at (4).

The output from Example 23.14 shows that each thread waited at the barrier point and announced it was released after the barrier tripped. The barrier action is performed by thread T2 that was the last one to arrive at the barrier point.

Example 23.14 *Cyclic Barrier*

```java
package synchronizers;
import java.util.concurrent.BrokenBarrierException;
import java.util.concurrent.CyclicBarrier;

public class CyclicBarrierDemo {
  public static final int PARTIES = 3;

  public static void main(String args[]) {
    Runnable barrierAction =  () ->                                        // (1)
        System.out.println("Barrier action by "
                        + Thread.currentThread().getName()
                        + ": All tasks are released.");

    CyclicBarrier barrier = new CyclicBarrier(PARTIES, barrierAction);     // (2)

    Runnable task = () -> {                                                // (3)
      String threadName = Thread.currentThread().getName();
      try {
        System.out.println(threadName + " is now waiting");
        barrier.await();                                   // Barrier point.
        System.out.println(threadName + " is now released");
      } catch (BrokenBarrierException | InterruptedException e) {
        e.printStackTrace();
      }
    };

    for (int i = 0; i < PARTIES; i++) {                                    // (4)
      new Thread(task, "T" + (i+1)).start();
    }
  }
}
```

Probable output from the program:

```
T1 is now waiting
T3 is now waiting
T2 is now waiting
Barrier action by T2: All tasks are released.
T2 is now released
T1 is now released
T3 is now released
```

Threads can of course share more than one barrier, having a different number of parties and different barrier actions.

Once a barrier is tripped, its thread wait count is reset to zero, and the barrier can be used again to implement a barrier point by calling the await() method.

If more threads than the required number invoke the await() method, then the required number of threads will cause the barrier to trip. This will allow the required number to continue and will reset the wait count, and the extra threads will have to wait for the barrier to trip again.

The cyclic barrier implements the *all-or-none model*. Either all waiting threads successfully continue execution past the await() method, or none do. If one thread waiting at a barrier point leaves prematurely—which could be due to an interruption, timeout, or failure—then all other waiting threads also leave abnormally via the checked java.util.concurrent.BrokenBarrierException. In this case, the barrier is said to be *broken*. The method isBroken() can be used to determine whether this is the case. A broken barrier can be reset and reused.

Count-Down Latch

The java.util.concurrent.CountDownLatch class implements a *count-down latch* that allows one or more threads to wait until the latch goes up, and then the waiting threads are allowed to proceed. The latch goes up depending on one or more other threads performing a specific number of countdown operations.

The CountDownLatch class provides the following constructor to create a count-down latch.

CountDownLatch(int count)

Creates a CountDownLatch initialized with the given count. The count specifies the number of times the countDown() method must be invoked to raise the latch to allow threads waiting on the await() method to pass through.

A count-down latch is created with an initial count. One or more threads can call the await() method of the latch to wait until the count reaches zero. The count is decremented by calls to the countDown() method of the latch by one or more other threads. Note that it is the number of calls to the countDown() method that raises the latch, independent of the number of threads involved. The countDown() method is used in tandem with the await() method to operate the latch. The latch can only go up once, and therefore cannot be reused.

void await() throws InterruptedException
boolean await(long timeout, TimeUnit unit) throws InterruptedException

Both methods cause the current thread to wait until one of the following events occurs: The latch count reaches 0, the thread is interrupted, or if any specified waiting time has elapsed.

In the first method, it is possible that the current thread may wait forever, if the count never reaches 0.

The second method returns true if the count reached 0 and false if the waiting time elapsed before the count reached 0.

void countDown()

Decrements the current count of the latch if it is greater than 0, releasing all waiting threads if the new count reaches 0. Nothing happens if the current count is already 0.

Given that the latch below is shared by threads t1, t2, and t3:

```
CountDownLatch latch = new CountDownLatch(3);     // (1) Latch count is 3.
```

Threads t1 and t2 call the await() method and wait at (2) and (3), respectively, for the latch to be raised:

```
// Thread t1:
latch.await();              // (2) Waiting for latch to be raised.
...

// Thread t2:
latch.await();              // (3) Waiting for latch to be raised.
...
```

Thread t3 calls the countDown() method on the latch, decrementing the count each time. Note that the thread calling the countDown() method does *not* wait for the count to reach 0. The count reaches 0 when the call at (4) is executed, upon which the latch is raised, and waiting threads t1 and t2 can continue execution past the await() method call.

```
// Thread t3:
latch.countDown();
...
latch.countDown(),
...
latch.countDown();          // (4) Count reaches 0. Latch released at (2) and (3).
...
```

Example 23.15 illustrates a typical scenario where an administrator thread (in this case, the main thread) submits tasks (defined by the Task class at (7)) to individual threads and uses two count-down latches to start and wait for the tasks to finish.

The two latches, startLine and finishLine, are declared at (1) and (2), respectively. The startLine latch is an *on/off latch* with a count of 1. All submitted tasks invoke the await() method at (9) to wait until the startLine latch is raised by the main thread by invoking the countDown() method at (5) to decrement the count to 0.

The finishLine latch is a latch with a count of N. It is the converse of the startLine latch. All submitted tasks count down the finishLine latch by invoking the count-Down() method at (10) and continue execution. The main method invokes the await() on the finishLine latch and waits until the latch is raised by all submitted tasks, decrementing the count to 0.

Example 23.15 *Count-Down Latch*

```
package synchronizers;
import static java.lang.System.out;
import java.util.concurrent.*;

public class CountDownLatchTest {
  public static final int N = 3;

  public static void main(String[] args) throws InterruptedException {
    CountDownLatch startLine = new CountDownLatch(1);          // (1)
```

```
        CountDownLatch finishLine = new CountDownLatch(N);          // (2)

        ExecutorService es = Executors.newFixedThreadPool(N);       // (3)
        String threadName = Thread.currentThread().getName();
        try {
          for (int i = 0; i < N; ++i) {    // (4) Submit tasks.
            es.submit(new Task(startLine, finishLine));
          }
          out.println(threadName + ": Let all tasks proceed.");
          startLine.countDown();           // (5) Count down to let all tasks proceed.
          finishLine.await();              // (6) Wait for all tasks to finish.
          out.println(threadName + ": All tasks done.");
        } finally {
          es.shutdown();
        }
      }
    }

    class Task implements Runnable {                                // (7)
      private final CountDownLatch startLine;
      private final CountDownLatch finishLine;

      public Task(CountDownLatch start, CountDownLatch finish) {
        this.startLine = start;
        this.finishLine = finish;
      }

      @Override
      public void run() {                                           // (8)
        String threadName = Thread.currentThread().getName();
        try {
          out.println(threadName + ": Waiting to proceed.");
          startLine.await();                    // (9) Wait to proceed.
          out.println(threadName + ": Running ... ");
          finishLine.countDown();               // (10) Count down the latch & continue.
          out.println(threadName + ": Latch count decremented.");
        } catch (InterruptedException ex) {
          ex.printStackTrace();
        }
      }
    }
```

Probable output from the program:

```
    main: Let all tasks proceed.
    pool-1-thread-3: Waiting to proceed.
    pool-1-thread-2: Waiting to proceed.
    pool-1-thread-1: Waiting to proceed.
    pool-1-thread-1: Running ...
    pool-1-thread-2: Running ...
    pool-1-thread-2: Latch count decremented.
    pool-1-thread-3: Running ...
    pool-1-thread-1: Latch count decremented.
    pool-1-thread-3: Latch count decremented.
    main: All tasks done.
```

23.6 Synchronized Collections and Maps

The primary goal of the Collections Framework is to provide support for efficient computation on collections that can be used in single-threaded applications. In the rest of this chapter we explore the support provided by the Collections Framework and the Concurrency Framework to create thread-safe collections that can be used in multithreaded applications. We start with *synchronized collections* provided by the java.util package, and explore *concurrent collections* found in the java.util.concurrent package in the next section (p. 1482).

By a *thread-safe collection* we mean a collection whose elements can be processed by concurrent threads without ever being in an inconsistent state.

Unmodifiable collections cannot be changed structurally (add and remove operations are prohibited) and their elements cannot be replaced (throw an Unsupported-OperationException), making the unmodifiable collection immutable (§12.2, p. 649). This guarantees that an unmodifiable collection is thread-safe, and multiple reader threads can safely access the elements concurrently as long as it is done via the unmodifiable collection.

```
// Thread-safe unmodifiable list:
List<String> list = List.of("Tom", "Dick", "Harriet");
list.add("Harry");                          // UnsupportedOperationException
list.set(0, "Tommy");                       // UnsupportedOperationException
list.remove("Dick");                        // UnsupportedOperationException
System.out.println(list.get(0));            // "Tom"
```

Unmodifiable views of collections are backed by an underlying collection, where changes in the underlying collection are reflected in the view (§15.11, p. 856). Such a view also cannot be modified, and only query methods are passed to the underlying collection. The view can be considered effectively immutable, and thus thread-safe, if the backing collection is effectively immutable, or if the only reference to the backing collection is through the unmodifiable view. An example of such an unmodifiable view is given below:

```
// Effectively immutable list view:
List<Integer> list = new ArrayList<>();
list.add(2021); list.add(2022);
List<Integer> immutablelist = Collections.unmodifiableList(list);
immutablelist.add(2023);                    // UnsupportedOperationException
immutablelist.set(0, 2023);                 // UnsupportedOperationException
immutablelist.remove(2021);                 // UnsupportedOperationException
System.out.println(immutablelist.get(0));   // 2021
```

It is worth keeping in mind that a thread-safe collection does not imply that its elements are thread-safe. It might be necessary to employ an appropriate synchronization mechanism on the elements in order to modify them in a thread-safe way.

The java.util.Collections class provides methods to create *synchronized collections* that are thread-safe. Actually, these collections are *synchronized views of collections* as they are backed by an *underlying collection*. The methods provided accept a collection and return a view of this collection in which the getter and setter methods use synchronized blocks to delegate operations to the underlying collection—that is, the methods provide a synchronized wrapper around the underlying collection. A single intrinsic lock on the synchronized collection implements mutual exclusion of operations, but this can potentially become a point of contention among threads. Synchronized collections also incur the performance penalty associated with intrinsic locking. Other thread-safe solutions explored in this chapter should be considered before settling on using a synchronized view to make a collection thread-safe.

```
static <E> Collection<E>   synchronizedCollection(Collection<E> c)
static <E> List<E>         synchronizedList(List<E> list)
static <E> Set<E>          synchronizedSet(Set<E> set)
static <E> SortedSet<E>    synchronizedSortedSet(SortedSet<E> set)
static <E> NavigableSet<E> synchronizedNavigableSet(NavigableSet<E> set)
```

Return a synchronized (thread-safe) *view* collection that has the same type as the specified backing collection. It is imperative that any access to the backing collection is accomplished through the returned collection (or its views) to guarantee serial access.

Analogous to an unmodifiable view collection (§15.11, p. 856), the synchronized collection returned by the synchronizedCollection() method does not delegate the equals() and the hashCode() methods to the backing collection. Instead, the returned collection uses the corresponding methods inherited from the Object class. This is to safeguard the contract of these methods when the backing collection is a set or a list. However, the synchronized collections returned by the other methods above do not exhibit this behavior.

```
static <K,V> Map<K,V>       synchronizedMap(Map<K,V> map)
static <K,V> SortedMap<K,V> synchronizedSortedMap(SortedMap<K,V> map)
static <K,V> NavigableMap<K,V>
                            synchronizedNavigableMap(NavigableMap<K,V> map)
```

Return a synchronized (thread-safe) *view* map that has the same type as the backing map that is specified. It is imperative that any access to the backing map is accomplished through the synchronized map (e.g., its key, entry, or values views) to guarantee thread-safe serial access.

We use the synchronized list as an example in this section. For using the other synchronized collections and maps, familiarity with their unsafe counterparts will go a long way. For the most part, the synchronized collections provide mutually exclusive operations corresponding to the operations on their unsafe counterparts.

Serial Access

In order to guarantee thread-safety, *all* access to elements of the underlying collection should be through the synchronized collection. Although getter and setter methods are synchronized in a synchronized collection, this is *not* the case for methods that implement *serial access* (e.g., iteration using an iterator or a stream).

As multiple methods can be called for an operation on a synchronized collection when using the iterator, we need to ensure that these are executed as a single mutually exclusive operation. Iteration thus requires a coarse-grained manual synchronization on the synchronized collection for deterministic results. A more general case of coarse-grained synchronization is discussed in the next subsection (p. 1480).

Example 23.16 illustrates the idiom used for serial access over a synchronized collection. A synchronized list is created at (1) and populated. A Runnable is implemented at (2) to remove a certain year from the synchronized list.

Serial access over the synchronized list is attempted using an explicit iterator. However, serial access operations are all done in a synchronized block requiring the intrinsic lock on the synchronized list, as at (3). Obtaining the iterator is also done in the synchronized block. All modifications must be made through the iterator. Iterator methods are used to process the synchronized list, including removing elements. Keep in mind that next() and remove() methods of the iterator work in lockstep. The current element from each iteration can be processed safely. This idiom also applies when using a for(:) loop for serial access, as this loop internally is translated to an iterator.

The program in Example 23.16 is run with three threads that execute the Runnable eliminator. With manual synchronization on the synchronized list at (3), the threads execute as expected. One of the threads removed the year 2021 from the list and thus modified the list. As there was only one occurrence of the year 2021, the other two threads did not modify the list. With no manual synchronization on the synchronized list, the results are unpredictable. Most likely one or more exceptions will be thrown.

Regardless of manually synchronizing on the synchronized collection, as in Example 23.16, any modification made directly on the *underlying* collection during serial access will result in the runtime java.util.ConcurrentModificationException.

Example 23.16 *Serial Access in Synchronized Views of Collections*

```java
package synced;
import java.util.*;
import java.util.stream.IntStream;

public class SerialAccessThreads  {

  public static void main(String[] args) throws InterruptedException {
    List<Integer> years = Collections.synchronizedList(new ArrayList<>()); // (1)
    years.add(2024); years.add(2023); years.add(2021); years.add(2022);

    Runnable eliminator = () -> {                                          // (2)
      boolean found = false;
      synchronized(years) {                                               // (3)
        Iterator<Integer> iteratorA = years.iterator();                   // (4)
        while (iteratorA.hasNext()) {
          if (iteratorA.next().equals(2021)) {                            // (5)
```

```
            iteratorA.remove();                                   // (6)
            found = true;
          }
        }
      }                                                            // (7)
      System.out.println("List modified: " + found);
    };
    IntStream.rangeClosed(1, 3).forEach(i -> new Thread(eliminator).start());
  }
}
```

Probable output from the program with manual synchronization for serial access:

```
List modified: false
List modified: true
List modified: false
```

Probable output from the program without manual synchronization for serial access (comment out lines at (2) and (7)) (*output edited to fit on the page*):

```
Exception in thread "Thread-1"
Exception in thread "Thread-2"
Exception in thread "Thread-0" java.lang.NullPointerException:
    Cannot invoke "java.lang.Integer.equals(Object)" because the return value of
    "java.util.Iterator.next()" is null
    ...
```

Compound Mutually Exclusive Operations

A compound operation that requires multiple operations on a synchronized collection is not guaranteed to be thread-safe just because the individual operations are mutually exclusive. Concurrent threads executing such a compound operation can interleave the individual operations, as in the case of a compound arithmetic operator. Example 23.17 illustrates implementing a compound mutually exclusive operation on a synchronized list using coarse-grained synchronization.

The class DoubleAct has a synchronized list (names) declared at (1), and provides two methods add() and removeFirst() at (2) and (3) to maintain this list.

The Client class uses the DoubleAct class. An instance of the DoubleAct class is populated at (10) in the main() method. A Runnable (remover) is implemented by the lambda expression at (11). It calls the removeFirst() method at (12) and prints the retrieved name. Three threads are created at (13) that execute the Runnable remover, calling the removeFirst() method on the shared DoubleAct instance. Since there are only two elements in the list, two of the threads should print one name each, and one of them should return null.

The method removeFirst() at (3) uses two mutually exclusive methods of the synchronized list. The intent is to return the element at index 0 if the list is not empty; otherwise, the value null. The method size() returns the current size of the synchronized list, and the method remove() deletes the element at index 0. The calls to these methods can be interleaved by concurrent threads executing the removeFirst()

method between the time the list size is determined and the first element is removed, unless appropriate steps are taken.

```
// Thread t1                                    // Thread t2
...                                            ...

if (name.size() > 0) // true                   ...

...                                            if (name.size() > 0) // true

return remove(0);     // Size 0                ...

...                                            return remove(0);     // Exception!
```

The recommended solution is to use a synchronized block on the synchronized list, as shown at (4), to guarantee that the method removeFirst() has exclusive access to the synchronized list, until the individual exclusive operations have completed. Example 23.17 shows output for both scenarios that we have sketched above. Note that the reentrant nature of the intrinsic lock on the synchronized list allows nested locking on the list for the individual exclusive operations.

Example 23.17 *Compound Mutually Exclusive Operation*

```
package synced;
import java.util.*;

public class DoubleAct {
  // Synchronized list:                                                  (1)
  private List<String> names = Collections.synchronizedList(new ArrayList<>());

  public void add(String name) { names.add(name); }                // (2)

  public String removeFirst() {                                    // (3)
    synchronized(names) {                                          // (4)
      if (names.size() > 0) {                                      // (5)
        try { Thread.sleep(1); }                                   // (6)
        catch(InterruptedException e) { e.printStackTrace(); }
        return names.remove(0);                                    // (7)
      } else { return null; }                                      // (8)
    }                                                              // (9)
  }
}
```

```
package synced;
import java.util.stream.IntStream;

public class Client {                                              // (9)
  public static void main(String[] args) {
    DoubleAct da = new DoubleAct();
    da.add("Laurel"); da.add("Hardy");                            // (10)
    Runnable remover = () -> {                                     // (11)
      String name = da.removeFirst();                             // (12)
      System.out.println(name);
    };
```

```
    IntStream.rangeClosed(1, 3).forEach(i -> new Thread(remover).start());// (13)
  }
}
```

Probable output from the program:

```
Laurel
Hardy
null
```

Probable output from the program when (4) and (9) are commented out (*output edited to fit on the page*):

```
Laurel
Hardy
Exception in thread "Thread-1" java.lang.IndexOutOfBoundsException:
    Index 0 out of bounds for length 0
    at ...
    at synced.DoubleAction.removeFirst(DoubleAction.java:15)
    at ...
```

23.7 Concurrent Collections and Maps

Most of the collections in the java.util package are not thread-safe—executing concurrent operations on them is courting disaster. Exceptions to this are the legacy Vector and Hashtable classes, but these use a single lock, allowing only one thread at a time to execute an operation on the collection while other threads are blocked. The *synchronized collections* created by methods in the java.util.Collections class are not much better, as they are just thread-safe wrappers around a backing collection, again providing only mutually exclusive operations on the backing collection. However, the *concurrent collections* provided by the java.util.concurrent package use special-purpose locking mechanisms to enable multiple threads to operate concurrently, without explicit locking on the collection and with minimal contention. The concurrent collections offer greater flexibility and higher scalability compared to the collections in the java.util package, when concurrent access is crucial for multiple threads sharing objects stored in a collection.

We assume familiarity with the Collections Framework, especially the core interfaces in the java.util package (Chapter 15, p. 781), as these are implemented by the concurrent collections to provide thread-safety and atomicity of operations defined by these interfaces:

Collection	(§15.3, p. 863)		Queue	(§15.6, p. 877)
List	(§15.3, p. 863)		Deque	(§15.7, p. 884)
Set	(§15.4, p. 867)		Map	(§15.8, p. 894)
NavigableSet	(§15.5, p. 874)		NavigableMap	(§15.10, p. 909)

It is also important to note that concurrent collections avoid memory consistency errors by defining a happens-before relationship that essentially states that an action by a thread to place an object into a concurrent collection happens-before a subsequent action to access or remove that object from the collection by another thread.

The concurrent collections and maps in the java.util.concurrent package can be categorized as follows:

- *Concurrent collections (p. 1485)*
- *Concurrent maps (p. 1490)*
- *Blocking queues (p. 1495)*
- *Copy-on-write collections (p. 1501)*

The following aspects about collections and maps should be noted, as they can be crucial in selecting an appropriate collection for maintaining the elements:

- *Non-blocking or blocking*

  Operations on a *non-blocking collection* do not use any locking mechanism (are *lock-free*) to access elements of the collection, allowing multiple threads to execute concurrently, in contrast to a *blocking collection* in which operations can block to acquire a lock before they can proceed, because only one thread at a time is allowed.

  Collections with Concurrent as a prefix to their name are all non-blocking—for example, a ConcurrentHashMap. All queues implementing the BlockingQueue<E> interface, not surprisingly, are blocking collections. The names of many queues reveal their blocking nature—for example, a LinkedBlockingQueue.

- *Unbounded and bounded*

  A *bounded collection* has a *fixed capacity* that defines the maximum number of elements allowed in the collection and is usually specified when the collection is created. When the collection is full, some operations, such as adding an element, will block until there is space in the collection. *Unbounded collections* are not bounded by any capacity restriction. *Optionally bounded collections* can be instantiated to behave either as bounded or as unbounded.

  An ArrayBlockingQueue is a bounded queue, whereas a ConcurrentLinkedQueue is unbounded, but a LinkedBlockingDeque can be optionally bounded.

- *The* null *value*

  Some collections allow the null value, and others do not. All concurrent collections, blocking queues, and concurrent maps do *not* allow the null value as elements, whereas the copy-on-write collections do.

- *Duplicate elements*

  All collections that embody the concept of a set do not allow duplicates—for example, a CopyOnWriteArraySet. All maps (e.g., a ConcurrentHashMap) do not allow duplicate keys which would violate the concept of hashing values. However, all queues allow duplicates—for example, a LinkedBlockingDeque.

- *Ordering*

  Elements in some concurrent sets and maps do not have any ordering—for example, a CopyOnWriteArraySet or a ConcurrentHashMap.

  Some sets and maps keep their elements and entries in *sort order*, according to either their natural ordering or a total ordering defined by a comparator on the elements or the keys, respectively. Examples of concurrent sorted collections are a ConcurrentSkipListSet and a ConcurrentSkipListMap.

  Insertion ordering is the order in which the elements are inserted into the collection—as used by a CopyOnWriteArrayList for its elements.

  FIFO (*First-In-First-Out*) order is maintained by some thread-safe queues, such as a LinkedBlockingQueue and a ConcurrentLinkedQueue. Other queues have a more specialized ordering, like a DelayQueue.

  Not surprisingly, some thread-safe deques exhibit both FIFO and LIFO (*Last-In-First-Out*) order for their elements depending on how the deque is used—for example, a LinkedBlockingDeque.

- *Iterator behavior during serial access*

  Serial access is implemented differently for different categories of concurrent collections. It is important to understand the behavior of the iterator provided by these collections. An iterator has to address situations where modifications are made to the collection, outside the control of the iterator, that might render the state of the collection inconsistent—for example, removing or inserting elements during iteration. Iterators can be classified according to the response they provide in this situation, which is referred to as *concurrent modification*:

  - *Weakly consistent iterator*

    Most of the concurrent collections, and especially queues, provide an iterator that is *weakly consistent* during serial access. Such an iterator is created on a clone of the collection, and will always traverse elements that existed at the time the iterator was constructed only once. It *may not* reflect all subsequent modifications made to the collection after the iterator is constructed. It will also not throw a ConcurrentModificationException, and can execute concurrently with other operations on the collection. Weakly consistent iterators also provide guarantees against repeated elements occurring, and guard against a variety of errors and from infinite loops occurring during traversal.

    Weakly consistent iterators are also informally referred to as *fail-safe* iterators.

  - *Snapshot-style iterator*

    A CopyOnWriteArrayList, which is based on a thread-safe version of an ArrayList, uses *snapshot-style iterators* for serial access. The name of the iterator reflects that it iterates over a snapshot of the underlying array taken at the time the iterator is created. Concurrent multiple *read* operations on this array snapshot are thread-safe as this snapshot of the array cannot be changed, but any *write* operation is done on a *new copy* of the array. An iterator is always created on the most current modified array. A snapshot iterator does *not* reflect any changes made in the copy of the array—in contrast to a weakly consistent iterator that may reflect such changes.

- *Fail-fast iterator*

  At the start of each iteration, a fail-fast iterator detects whether the collection has been modified. If that is the case, it throws a ConcurrentModification-Exception. In other words, it fails as soon as possible at the next iteration. It is perfectly safe during iteration to use the Iterator.remove() method to delete the current element, but not with the Collection.remove() method.

Thread-unsafe collections from the java.util package exhibit this behavior, as do the PriorityBlockingQueue and DelayDeque classes in the java.util.concurrent package.

Concurrent Collections

Concurrent sets, queues, and deques are implemented by the classes Concurrent-SkipListSet, ConcurrentLinkedQueue, and ConcurrentLinkedDeque, respectively. These thread-safe classes implement the corresponding NavigableSet, Queue, and Deque interfaces in the java.util package, as shown in Figure 23.4 and summarized in Table 23.5. Their characteristics are summarized in Table 23.6. These concurrent collections are *unbounded* and *non-blocking*. They do not allow null values and have a weakly consistent iterator. As they are unbounded, their insert operation will always succeed. Also worth noting is that their *bulk operations* (addAll(), removeIf(), forEach()) are not guaranteed to perform atomically.

Figure 23.4 *Concurrent Collections in the* java.util.concurrent *Package*

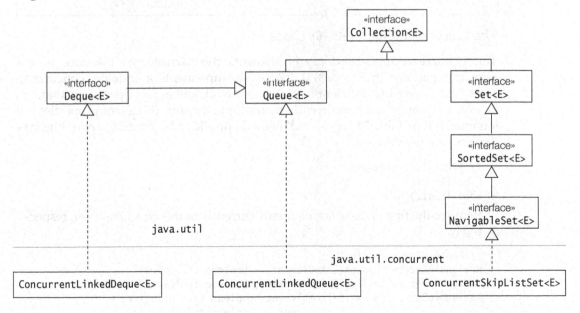

Table 23.5 *Concurrent Collections in the* `java.util.concurrent` *Package*

Concurrent collections	Description
`ConcurrentSkipListSet<E>` implements `NavigableSet<E>`	An unbounded, non-blocking, concurrent `NavigableSet` implementation that internally uses a `ConcurrentSkipListMap`. Elements are sorted according to the natural ordering or by a comparator that is provided in the constructor.
`ConcurrentLinkedQueue<E>` implements `Queue<E>`	An unbounded, non-blocking, concurrent queue based on linked nodes.
`ConcurrentLinkedDeque<E>` implements `Deque<E>`	An unbounded, non-blocking, concurrent deque based on linked nodes.

Table 23.6 *Characteristics of Concurrent Collections*

Concurrent collections	null value	Duplicates	Ordering	Kind of iterator
`ConcurrentSkipListSet<E>` implements `NavigableSet<E>`	No	No	Sort order	Weakly consistent
`ConcurrentLinkedQueue<E>` implements `Queue<E>`	No	Yes	FIFO order	Weakly consistent
`ConcurrentLinkedDeque<E>` implements `Deque<E>`	No	Yes	LIFO/ FIFO order	Weakly consistent

The `ConcurrentSkipListSet<E>` Class

The `ConcurrentSkipListSet` class implements the `NavigableSet` interface in the java.util package (§15.5, p. 811). The class implements a scalable, concurrent, sorted set. It provides efficient insertion, removal, and access operations that can be executed safely and concurrently by multiple threads. Its salient properties are summarized in Table 23.6. Selected methods provided by the `ConcurrentSkipList-Set` class are listed below.

```
// First-last elements
E pollFirst()
E pollLast()
```

Remove the first and the last elements currently in this concurrent set, respectively.

```
// Range-view operations
NavigableSet<E> headSet(E toElement,   boolean inclusive)
NavigableSet<E> tailSet(E fromElement, boolean inclusive)
NavigableSet<E> subSet(E fromElement, boolean fromInclusive,
                       E toElement,   boolean toInclusive)
```

Return different views of the underlying concurrent set, depending on the bound elements.

```
// Closest-matches
E ceiling(E e)
E floor(E e)
E higher(E e)
E lower(E e)
```

Determine closest-match elements according to various criteria.

```
// Reverse order
Iterator<E> descendingIterator()
NavigableSet<E> descendingSet()
```

The first method returns a reverse-order iterator for this concurrent set. The second method returns a reverse-order view of the elements in the set.

The ConcurrentLinkedQueue<E> *Class*

The ConcurrentLinkedQueue class implements the Queue interface, as shown in Figure 23.6. No new methods are defined, and existing methods of the Queue interface (§15.6, p. 814) are implemented as shown in Table 23.7. Note that since it is an unbounded queue, the insert operations will always succeed.

Table 23.7   *Selected Methods in the* ConcurrentLinkedQueue *Class*

Operation	Throws exception	Returns special value
Insert at the tail	add(e) *will never throw* IllegalArgumentException	offer(e) *will never return* false
Remove from the head	remove() *can throw* NoSuchElementException	poll() *returns* null *if empty*
Examine element at the head	element() *can throw* NoSuchElementException	peek() *returns* null *if empty*

The ConcurrentLinkedDeque<E> *Class*

The ConcurrentLinkedDeque class implements the Deque interface, as shown in Figure 23.6. No new methods are defined, and existing methods of the Deque interface (§15.7, p. 821) are implemented as shown in Table 23.8. Note that since it is an unbounded deque, the insert operations will always succeed. Methods inherited from the Queue interface are marked with an asterisk (*) in Table 23.8.

Table 23.8   *Selected Methods in the* ConcurrentLinkedDeque *Class*

Insert at the head	Insert at the tail	Runtime behavior on failure
offerFirst(e)	offerLast(e), offer(e)*	*Never returns* false
addFirst(e)	addLast(e), add(e)*	*Never throws* IllegalStateException

Table 23.8   *Selected Methods in the* ConcurrentLinkedDeque *Class (Continued)*

Remove from the head	Remove from the tail	Runtime behavior on failure
pollFirst(), poll()*	pollLast()	*Returns* null *if empty*
removeFirst(), remove()*	removeLast()	*Throws* NoSuchElementException
Examine at the head	**Examine at the tail**	**Runtime behavior on failure**
peekFirst(), peek()*	peekLast()	*Returns* null *if empty*
getFirst(), element()*	getLast()	*Throws* NoSuchElementException

Example 23.18 illustrates the iterator of a ConcurrentSkipListSet (declared at (1)) that is weakly consistent during traversal. The idea is to have two tasks operating on the concurrent sorted set: one repeatedly creating an iterator to traverse the elements of the collection and summing them (2), and another continuously removing elements from the set (5).

The utility class ConcUtil declares the auxiliary method snooze() that is used to put a thread to sleep. If interrupted, the exception is caught and the interrupt reinstated so that the caller of the snooze() method can take the appropriate action. This method is also used in other examples in this section.

The Runnable sumValues at (2) repeatedly creates an iterator at (3) to sum the values in the set at the time the iterator is created, and prints the result. It snoozes a little after each traversal of the set. The thread determines at (4) whether it has been interrupted. If interrupted, the infinite loop terminates, thereby terminating the thread.

The Runnable removeValues at (5) polls the set and prints the value, snoozing after each polling operation. It also detects whether it has been interrupted, terminating the infinite loop at (6) if that is the case.

The main() method instantiates and initializes a ConcurrentSkipListSet at (7) with random numbers between 0 and 1000. The two tasks are submitted to a service executor at (8). The main thread snoozes a little to allow the tasks to run. The call to the shutdownNow() method at (10) leads to any thread running to be interrupted, and the threads taking appropriate action to terminate their execution as described above.

The output from the program shows that only elements that are in the ConcurrentSkipListSet instance at the time the iterator is created contribute to the sum, and the sum drops correctly as elements are removed.

Example 23.18 *Concurrent Collections*

```
package concurrent;
import java.util.concurrent.TimeUnit;
```

```java
public class ConcUtil {
  public static void snooze(int timeout, TimeUnit unit) {
    String threadName = Thread.currentThread().getName();
    try {
      unit.sleep(timeout);
    } catch (InterruptedException ex) {
      System.out.println(threadName + ": " + ex);
      Thread.currentThread().interrupt();          // Reinstate interrupt status.
    }
  }
}
```

```java
package concurrent;
import java.util.*;
import java.util.concurrent.*;

public class ConcurrentSkipListSetDemo {

  private static ConcurrentSkipListSet<Integer> set;                    // (1)

  private static Runnable sumValues = () -> {                           // (2)
    String threadName = Thread.currentThread().getName();
    while (true) {
      int sum = 0;
      for (Integer v : set) {                                          // (3)
        sum += v;
      }
      System.out.printf(threadName + ": sum%9d%n", sum);
      ConcUtil.snooze(2, TimeUnit.SECONDS);
      if (Thread.interrupted()) break;                                 // (4)
    }
  };

  private static Runnable removeValues = () -> {                        // (5)
    String threadName = Thread.currentThread().getName();
    while (true) {
      Integer value = set.pollFirst();
      if (value == null) continue;
      System.out.printf(threadName + ": removed%5d%n", value);
      ConcUtil.snooze(2, TimeUnit.SECONDS);
      if (Thread.interrupted()) break;                                 // (6)
    }
  };

  public static void main(String[] args) {
    // Create and populate the set:                                      (7)
    set = new ConcurrentSkipListSet<>();
    new Random().ints(10, 0, 1000).forEach(val -> set.add(val));
    System.out.println(set);

    // Create an executor service to execute two tasks:                  (8)
    ExecutorService exs = Executors.newFixedThreadPool(2);
    try {
      exs.submit(sumValues);
      exs.submit(removeValues);
```

```
            ConcUtil.snooze(5, TimeUnit.SECONDS);                        // (9)
        } finally {
            System.out.println("Shutting down now.");
            exs.shutdownNow();                                           // (10)
        }
    }
}
```

Probable output from the program:

```
[20, 100, 236, 263, 299, 359, 548, 552, 591, 686]
pool-1-thread-1: sum      3654
pool-1-thread-2: removed   20
pool-1-thread-1: sum      3634
pool-1-thread-2: removed  100
pool-1-thread-1: sum      3534
pool-1-thread-2: removed  236
Shutting down now.
pool-1-thread-1: java.lang.InterruptedException: sleep interrupted
pool-1-thread-2: java.lang.InterruptedException: sleep interrupted
```

Concurrent Maps

Figure 23.5 shows the inheritance hierarchy of concurrent maps in the java.util
.concurrent package. Note the interfaces ConcurrentMap<K,V> and ConcurrentNavigable-
Map<K,V> that extend the thread-unsafe map interfaces in the java.util package.
Their implementations, ConcurrentHashMap<K,V> and ConcurrentSkipListMap<K,V>,

Figure 23.5 *Concurrent Maps in the* java.util.concurrent *Package*

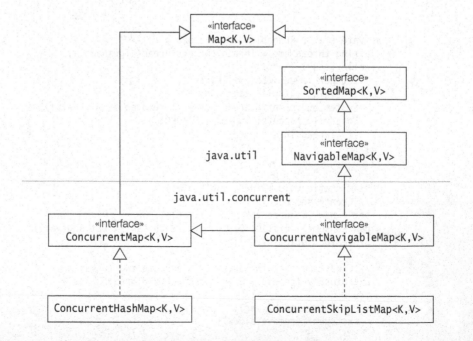

provide efficient unsorted and sorted concurrent maps, respectively. The concrete map implementations are summarized in Table 23.9, together with their characteristics in Table 23.10.

Table 23.9　*Concurrent Maps in the* `java.util.concurrent` *Package*

Concurrent maps	Description
interface ConcurrentMap<K,V> extends Map<K,V>	A Map providing thread-safety and atomicity guarantees
ConcurrentHashMap<K,V> implements ConcurrentMap<K,V>	A hash table implementation supporting full concurrency of retrievals and high expected concurrency for updates
interface ConcurrentNavigableMap<K,V> extends ConcurrentMap<K,V>, NavigableMap<K,V>	A ConcurrentMap supporting NavigableMap operations, and recursively so for its navigable sub-maps
ConcurrentSkipListMap<K,V> implements ConcurrentNavigableMap<K,V>	A scalable concurrent ConcurrentNavigableMap implementation that is highly efficient for traversal

Table 23.10　*Characteristics of Concurrent Maps*

Concurrent maps	null value	Dupli-cates	Ordering	Kind of iterator
ConcurrentHashMap<K,V> implements ConcurrentMap<K,V>	Not allowed as key or values	Unique keys	No order	Weakly consistent
ConcurrentSkipListMap<K,V> implements ConcurrentNavigableMap<K,V>	Not allowed as key or values	Unique keys	Key sort order	Weakly consistent

The ConcurrentMap<K,V> *Interface*

In order to maintain the guarantees of thread-safety and atomicity of operations, the ConcurrentMap<K,V> overrides the methods shown below from the Map<K,V> interface, and stipulates that concurrent implementations will honor these guarantees—as exemplified by the ConcurrentHashMap<K,V> class, affording efficient concurrent insertion and lookup. Details on these overridden methods can be found in the Map<K,V> interface (§15.8, p. 831).

The implementation of the ConcurrentHashMap<K,V> class conceptually divides the map into *segments* (also called *sub-maps*) that can be independently locked by a thread, thus allowing several threads to perform operations on the map concurrently.

```
interface ConcurrentMap<K,V> extends Map<K, V>  // §15.8, p. 831.

default V compute(K key,
                  BiFunction<? super K,? super V,? extends V> remapFunction)
default V computeIfAbsent(K key,
                         Function<? super K,? extends V> mappingFunction)
default V computeIfPresent(K key,
                  BiFunction<? super K,? super V,? extends V> remapFunction)

default void forEach(BiConsumer<? super K,? super V> action)

default V getOrDefault(Object key, V defaultValue)

default V merge(K key, V value,
                BiFunction<? super V,? super V,? extends V> remapFunction)

V putIfAbsent(K key, V value)
boolean remove(Object key, Object value)

V        replace(K key, V value)
boolean replace(K key, V oldValue, V newValue)
default void replaceAll(BiFunction<? super K,? super V,? extends V> func)
```

The ConcurrentNavigableMap<K,V> *Interface*

A concurrent, sorted map is defined by the ConcurrentNavigableMap<K,V> interface that extends both the ConcurrentMap<K,V> and the NavigableMap<K,V> interfaces. It overrides the methods shown below from its superinterfaces. Details on these overridden methods can be found in the ConcurrentMap<K,V> interface (p. 1491) and in the NavigableMap<K,V> interface (§15.10, p. 845).

The ConcurrentSkipListMap<K,V> class is an efficient implementation of the Concurrent-NavigableMap<K,V> class. This implementation is based on a concurrent variant of a *skip list* that is organized as a hierarchy of linked lists with subsequences of elements that are sorted, allowing efficient traversal, but at the extra cost of insertions in the skip list.

```
interface ConcurrentNavigableMap<K,V> extends ConcurrentMap<K,V>,
                                               NavigableMap<K,V>
NavigableSet<K> descendingKeySet()
ConcurrentNavigableMap<K,V> descendingMap()
```

Return a reverse-order NavigableSet view of the keys or a reverse-order ConcurrentNavigableMap of the entries contained in this map, respectively.

```
ConcurrentNavigableMap<K,V> headMap(K toKey)
ConcurrentNavigableMap<K,V> headMap(K toKey, boolean inclusive)
```

Return a view of the portion of this map whose keys are strictly less than toKey or are less than or equal to toKey, if inclusive is true is specified.

```
NavigableSet<K> keySet()
NavigableSet<K> navigableKeySet()
```

Return a NavigableSet view of the keys contained in this map. These methods are equivalent.

```
ConcurrentNavigableMap<K,V> subMap(K fromKey, K toKey)
ConcurrentNavigableMap<K,V> subMap(K fromKey, boolean fromInclusive,
                                    K toKey, boolean toInclusive)
```

Return a view of the portion of this map whose keys range from fromKey, inclusive, to toKey, exclusive, or from fromKey to toKey, where inclusion of the interval keys is explicitly specified.

```
ConcurrentNavigableMap<K,V> tailMap(K fromKey)
ConcurrentNavigableMap<K,V> tailMap(K fromKey, boolean inclusive)
```

Return a view of the portion of this map whose keys are greater than or equal to fromKey, or are greater than or equal to fromKey, if inclusive is true is specified.

Example 23.19 illustrates using the ConcurrentHashMap<K,V> class. A frequency map is created for rolling a dice at (3) and (4). A reader, declared as diceResultsReader at (1), repeatedly creates a new key set of the map and prints its contents. A remover, declared as diceResultRemover at (2), continuously removes the entry for a random dice result from the map. Both the reader and the remover take a snooze after printing the contents and removing an entry, respectively. All threads terminate on being interrupted, as the shutdownNow() method will initiate cancellation of all tasks at (6).

One reader and two removers are submitted to the service executor at (5). The output shows that the map contents reflect correctly that entries are removed and printed concurrently.

. . . .

Example 23.19 *Using a Concurrent Map*

```java
package concurrent;
import java.util.*;
import java.util.concurrent.*;
import java.util.function.Function;
import java.util.stream.Collectors;

public class ConcurrentHashMapDemo {

  private static ConcurrentHashMap<Integer, Long> map;
  public static final int NUM_OF_THROWS = 1000;

  private static Runnable diceResultsReader = () -> {                      // (1)
    String threadName = Thread.currentThread().getName();
    while (true) {
      ConcurrentHashMap.KeySetView<Integer, Long> keySetView = map.keySet();
      String output = "";
      for (Integer key : keySetView) {
        Long value = map.get(key);
        output += " " + "<" + key + "," + value + ">";
      }
      System.out.println(threadName + ": {" + output + " }");
      ConcUtil.snooze(1000, TimeUnit.MILLISECONDS);
      if (Thread.interrupted()) break;
    }
  };
```

```java
private static Runnable diceResultRemover = () -> {          // (2)
  String threadName = Thread.currentThread().getName();
  while (true) {
    ConcUtil.snooze(500, TimeUnit.MILLISECONDS);
    if (Thread.interrupted()) break;
    Integer key = ThreadLocalRandom.current().nextInt(1, 7);  // [1, 6]
    Long value = map.remove(key);
    if (value == null) continue;
    String removedEntry = threadName + ": removed "
                        + "<" + key + "," + value + ">";
    System.out.println(removedEntry);
  }
};

public static void main(String[] args) throws InterruptedException {
  map = new ConcurrentHashMap<>(6);                          // (3)
  new Random().ints(NUM_OF_THROWS, 1, 7)                     // (4)
              .boxed()
              .parallel()
              .collect(Collectors.groupingByConcurrent(
                Function.identity(),
                () -> map,
                Collectors.counting()));

  ExecutorService exs = Executors.newFixedThreadPool(3);
  try {
    exs.submit(diceResultsReader);                           // (5)
    exs.submit(diceResultRemover);
    exs.submit(diceResultRemover);
    ConcUtil.snooze(5, TimeUnit.SECONDS);
  } finally {
    exs.shutdownNow();                                       // (6)
  }
}
}
```

Probable output from the program:

```
pool-1-thread-1: { <1,160> <2,159> <3,170> <4,178> <5,158> <6,175> }
pool-1-thread-2: removed <1,160>
pool-1-thread-3: removed <6,175>
pool-1-thread-2: removed <5,158>
pool-1-thread-1: { <2,159> <3,170> <4,178> }
pool-1-thread-2: removed <4,178>
pool-1-thread-1: { <2,159> <3,170> }
pool-1-thread-1: { <2,159> <3,170> }
pool-1-thread-2: removed <2,159>
pool-1-thread-1: { <3,170> }
pool-1-thread-2: removed <3,170>
pool-1-thread-1: java.lang.InterruptedException: sleep interrupted
pool-1-thread-2: java.lang.InterruptedException: sleep interrupted
pool-1-thread-3: java.lang.InterruptedException: sleep interrupted
```

Blocking Queues

Queues (and deques) are the indisputable choice when choosing a collection to manage shared data in producer-consumer problems. The interfaces for thread-unsafe queues (Queue, Deque) in the java.util package have been enhanced in the java.util.concurrent package to provide a wide variety of blocking queues that are thread-safe (Figure 23.6). These thread-safe queues are *blocking* because a thread *blocks* when trying to add an element and the queue is full, or when trying to remove an element and the queue is empty.

Figure 23.6 *Blocking Queues in the* java.util.concurrent *Package*

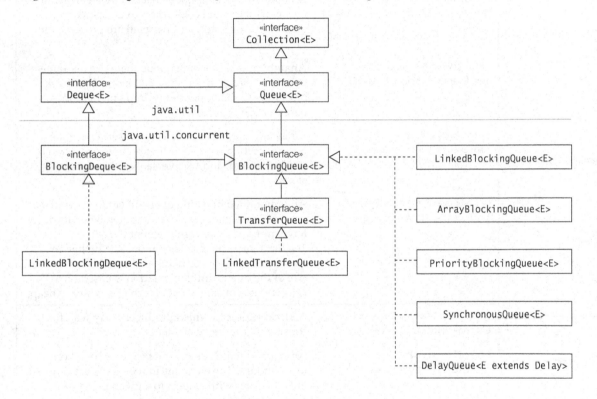

A summary of interfaces and classes that implement blocking queues and deques provided by the java.util.concurrent package is given in Table 23.11. Salient characteristics of these queues and deques are summarized in Table 23.12. None of the queues or deques allow a null value for an element, but they do allow duplicates. Being queues, FIFO ordering is the norm and a majority of them are weakly consistent when it comes to serial access.

Table 23.11   *Blocking Queues in the* `java.util.concurrent` *Package*

Blocking queues	Description
interface BlockingQueue<E> extends Queue<E> (Table 23.13)	A `Queue` that additionally supports operations that wait for the queue to become non-empty when retrieving an element, and wait for space to become available in the queue when storing an element.
LinkedBlockingQueue<E> implements BlockingQueue<E>	An optionally bounded blocking queue based on linked nodes.
ArrayBlockingQueue<E> implements BlockingQueue<E>	A bounded blocking queue backed by an array. A fairness policy can be specified so that threads blocked for insertion and removal are processed in FIFO order.
PriorityBlockingQueue<E> implements BlockingQueue<E>	An unbounded blocking queue that uses the same ordering rules as class `PriorityQueue` and supplies blocking retrieval operations. Implementation is based on a binary heap.
SynchronousQueue<E> implements BlockingQueue<E>	A blocking queue in which each insert operation must wait for a corresponding remove operation by another thread, and vice versa. No elements are stored.
DelayQueue<E extends Delayed> implements BlockingQueue<E>	An unbounded blocking queue of `Delayed` elements, in which an element can only be taken when its delay has expired. Elements implement the `java.util.concurrent.Delay` interface. Whether an element is available or not, it still counts toward the size of the queue. Implementation is based on a `PriorityQueue` instance that in turn uses a binary heap.
interface TransferQueue<E> extends BlockingQueue<E>	A `BlockingQueue` in which producers may wait for consumers to receive elements.
LinkedTransferQueue<E> implements TranferQueue<E>	An unbounded blocking `TransferQueue` based on linked nodes. The elements in the queue are ordered in FIFO order with respect to a given producer waiting for consumers.
interface BlockingDeque<E> extends BlockingQueue<E>, Deque<E> (Table 23.14)	A `Deque` that additionally supports blocking operations that wait for the deque to become non-empty when retrieving an element, and wait for space to become available in the deque when storing an element.
LinkedBlockingDeque<E> implements BlockingDeque<E>	An optionally bounded blocking deque based on doubly linked nodes.

Table 23.12 *Characteristics of Blocking Queues*

Blocking queues	null value	Duplicates	Ordering	Kind of iterator
LinkedBlockingQueue<E> implements BlockingQueue<E>	No	Allowed	FIFO order	Weakly consistent
ArrayBlockingQueue<E> implements BlockingQueue<E>	No	Allowed	FIFO order	Weakly consistent
PriorityBlockingQueue<E> implements BlockingQueue<E>	No	Allowed	Natural ordering	Fail-fast
SynchronousQueue<E> implements BlockingQueue<E>	No	Not applicable	Not applicable	Not applicable
DelayQueue<E extends Delayed> implements BlockingQueue<E>	No	Allowed	Longest-delayed order	Fail-fast
LinkedTransferQueue<E> implements TranferQueue<E>	No	Allowed	FIFO order	Weakly consistent
LinkedBlockingDeque<E> implements BlockingDeque<E>	No	Allowed	FIFO/LIFO order	Weakly consistent

The BlockingQueue<E> *Interface*

The java.util.concurrent.BlockingQueue interface extends the java.util.Queue interface, as shown in Figure 23.6. Compared to the operations shown for the Queue interface in Table 23.7, the BlockingQueue interface provides new insert and remove operations that can block or can time out—shown in the two rightmost columns in Table 23.13. Classes that implement the BlockingQueue interface are shown in Table 23.11, where general-purpose queues are listed at the top, down to more specialized thread-safe queues. The LinkedBlockingQueue class represents the all-round queue of choice in most cases.

Table 23.13 *Selected Methods in the BlockingQueue Interface*

Operation	Throws exception	Returns special value	Blocks	Times out
Insert at the tail	add(e) *can throw* IllegalArgument-Exception	offer(e) *returns* true *or* false	put(e) *blocks if no space*	offer(e, time, unit) *waits if necessary for specified time if no space*

Table 23.13   *Selected Methods in the* `BlockingQueue` *Interface (Continued)*

Operation	Throws exception	Returns special value	Blocks	Times out
Remove from the head	`remove()` *can throw* `NoSuchElement-Exception`	`poll()` *returns head element or* `null`	`take()` *blocks if empty*	`poll(time, unit)` *waits if necessary for specified time for head element, and returns* `null` *if no element becomes available*
Examine element at the head	`element()` *can throw* `NoSuchElement-Exception`	`peek()` *returns head element or* `null`	*Not applicable*	*Not applicable*

The `TransferQueue<E>` Interface

The `TransferQueue` interface extends the `BlockingQueue` interface to provide queues where producers wait for consumers to receive elements (Figure 23.6). The interface defines additional methods to utilize this property.

```
void transfer(E e)
boolean tryTransfer(E e)
boolean tryTransfer(E e, long timeout, TimeUnit unit)
```

The first method transfers the element to a consumer, waiting if necessary to do so.

The second method transfers the element to a waiting consumer immediately, if possible. It returns `true` if the element was transferred; otherwise, it returns `false`.

The third method transfers the element to a consumer if it is possible to do so before the timeout elapses. It returns `true` if successful, and `false` if the specified waiting time elapses before completion, in which case the element is not left enqueued.

```
boolean hasWaitingConsumer()
int getWaitingConsumerCount()
```

The first method returns `true` if there is at least one consumer waiting to receive an element via `BlockingQueue.take()` or a timed poll.

The second method returns an estimate of the number of consumers waiting to receive elements via `BlockingQueue.take()` or a timed poll.

The `BlockingDeque<E>` Interface

The `java.util.concurrent.BlockingDeque` interface extends both the `java.util.Deque` interface and the `BlockingQueue` interface, as shown in Figure 23.6. Compared to the operations shown for the `ConcurrentLinkedDeque` interface in Table 23.8, the `Blocking-Deque` interface provides new insert and remove operations, both at the head and tail of a deque, that can block or can time out—shown in the light-gray rows in Table 23.14. Methods inherited from the BlockingQueue interface are marked with an asterisk (*) in Table 23.14. The LinkedBlockingDeque class that implements the BlockingDeque interface is shown in Table 23.11. This class represents an all-round implementation of a blocking deque.

Table 23.14 *Selected Methods in the* BlockingDeque *Interface*

Insert at the head	Insert at the tail	Runtime behavior on failure
offerFirst(e)	offerLast(e), offer(e)*	*Returns* false *if full*
addFirst(e)	addLast(e), add(e)*	*Throws* IllegalStateException
putFirst(e)	putLast(e), put(e)*	*Blocks if full*
offerFirst(e, time, unit)	offerLast(e,time,unit), offer(e, time, unit)*	*Times out*
Remove from the head	**Remove from the tail**	**Runtime behavior on failure**
pollFirst(), poll()*	pollLast()	*Returns* null *if empty*
removeFirst(), remove()*	removeLast()	*Throws* NoSuchElementException
takeFirst(), take()*	takeLast()	*Blocks if empty*
pollFirst(time, unit), poll(time, unit)*	pollLast(time, unit)	*Times out*
Examine at the head	**Examine at the tail**	**Runtime behavior on failure**
peekFirst(), peek()*	peekLast()	*Returns* null *if empty*
getFirst(), element()*	getLast()	*Throws* NoSuchElementException

Example 23.20 demonstrates using the LinkedBlockingQueue class that implements the BlockingQueue interface. A producer is defined at (2) that puts a fixed number of random values (between 0 and 100) in the blocking queue. Note that the put() call at (3) can block. The thread sleeps for a little while after each put() operation. When done, it puts a *poison value* (which is not a legal value) in the queue at (4), that is interpreted as no more values are in the queue.

A consumer is defined at (5) that continuously takes a value from the blocking queue at (7) and prints it. It sleeps for a little while after each take() operation that can block. Before taking a value, it checks at (6) to see if the value at the head of the queue is the poison value. If so, the infinite loop is terminated, and thereby the consumer as well.

The LinkedBlockingQueue class is instantiated at (8). Note that the blocking queue is bounded, but the number of values to put in the queue is greater than its capacity—which can result in the put() operation to block if the queue is full. A service executor is created at (9). One producer and two consumers are submitted to the service executor at (10). The call to the shutdown() method at (11) allows threads to complete execution.

The output from the program shows that the producer puts the values in the blocking queue and the two consumers take the values and process them.

Example 23.20 *Linked Blocking Queue*

```java
package concurrent;
import java.util.concurrent.*;

public class LinkedBlockingQueueDemo {

  public static final int UPPER_BOUND = 3;
  public static final int NUM_OF_VALUES = 5;
  public static final int STOP_VALUE = -1;

  private static BlockingQueue<Integer> queue;                        // (1)

  private static Runnable producer = () -> {                          // (2)
    String threadName = Thread.currentThread().getName();
    ThreadLocalRandom tlrng = ThreadLocalRandom.current();
    try {
      for (int i = 0; i < NUM_OF_VALUES; i++) {
        Integer value = tlrng.nextInt(100);
        queue.put(value);                                             // (3)
        System.out.println(threadName + ": put " + value);
        Thread.sleep(tlrng.nextInt(200));
      }
      queue.put(STOP_VALUE);                                          // (4)
      System.out.println(threadName + ": done.");
    } catch (InterruptedException ie) {
      ie.printStackTrace();
    }
  };

  private static Runnable consumer = () -> {                          // (5)
    String threadName = Thread.currentThread().getName();
    ThreadLocalRandom tlrng = ThreadLocalRandom.current();
    while (true) {
      try {
        Integer head = queue.peek();                                 // (6)
        if (head != null && head.equals(STOP_VALUE)) {
            System.out.println(threadName + ": done.");
            break;
        }
        Integer value = queue.take();                                // (7)
        System.out.println(threadName + ": processing " + value);
        Thread.sleep(tlrng.nextInt(1000));
      } catch (InterruptedException ie) {
        ie.printStackTrace();
      }
    }
  };
```

```
        public static void main(String[] args) {
            queue = new LinkedBlockingQueue<>(UPPER_BOUND);          // (8)
            ExecutorService exs = Executors.newFixedThreadPool(3);   // (9)
            try {
                exs.submit(producer);                                // (10)
                exs.submit(consumer);
                exs.submit(consumer);
            } finally {
                exs.shutdown();                                      // (11)
            }
        }
    }
```

Probable output from the program:

```
pool-1-thread-1: put 43
pool-1-thread-2: processing 43
pool-1-thread-1: put 84
pool-1-thread-3: processing 84
pool-1-thread-1: put 60
pool-1-thread-3: processing 60
pool-1-thread-1: put 55
pool-1-thread-1: put 17
pool-1-thread-3: processing 55
pool-1-thread-1: done.
pool-1-thread-3: processing 17
pool-1-thread-2: done.
pool-1-thread-3: done.
```

Copy-on-Write Collections

The copy-on-write collections comprise special-purpose concurrent lists and sets that are recommended when read operations vastly outnumber mutative operations on the collection. The classes CopyOnWriteArrayList and CopyOnWriteArraySet implement the List and the Set interfaces in the java.util package (Figure 23.7). A summary of the copy-on-write classes in the java.util.concurrent package is given in Table 23.15. Salient characteristics of these collections are summarized in Table 23.16.

Figure 23.7   *Copy-on-Write Collections in the* java.util.concurrent *Package*

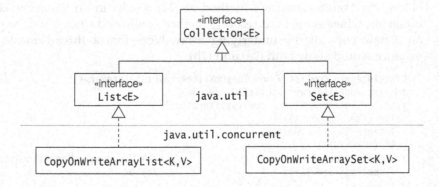

Table 23.15 *Copy-on-Write Collections in the* `java.util.concurrent` *Package*

Copy-on-write collections	Description
`CopyOnWriteArrayList<E>` `implements List<E>`	A thread-safe variant of `ArrayList` in which all mutative operations (add, set, etc.) are implemented by making a fresh copy of the underlying array.
`CopyOnWriteArraySet<E>` `implements Set<E>`	A Set that uses an internal `CopyOnWriteArrayList` for all of its operations.

Table 23.16 *Characteristics of Copy-on-Write Collections*

Copy-on-write collections	null value	Duplicates	Ordering	Kind of iterator
`CopyOnWriteArrayList<E>` `implements List<E>`	Yes	Yes	Insertion order	Snapshot-style
`CopyOnWriteArraySet<E>` `implements Set<E>`	Yes	No	No order	Snapshot-style

The `CopyOnWriteArrayList<E>` *Class*

The `CopyOnWriteArrayList` class implements the `java.util.List` interface (§15.3, p. 801), providing a thread-safe list that is recommended for a vast number of concurrent read and traversal operations. It uses an underlying array to implement its operations. By default, such a list is immutable, guaranteeing thread-safety of concurrent operations. Any mutative operation (add, set, remove, etc.) is done on a new *copy* of its entire underlying array which then supersedes the previous version for subsequent operations. For efficiency reasons, the list size should be kept small and modifications should be minimized, as they are expensive, incurring the copying cost of its underlying array and extra space.

Traversal via snapshot-style iterators is efficient and thread safe—there is no need for any external synchronization, since it relies on the immutable state of the underlying array at the time the iterator is constructed (Example 23.21). Note that immutability of the list during traversal rules out the `remove()` operation of the iterator, as this can invalidate its snapshot traversal guarantee if allowed. In the code below, the `Iterator.remove()` method at (2a) results in an `UnsupportedOperation-Exception`, whereas the `List.remove()` method is allowed since it will be performed on a new copy of the underlying array. Note that a thread-unsafe `ArrayList` instance would allow both (2a) and (2b).

```
List<Integer> cowlist = new CopyOnWriteArrayList<Integer>();          // (1a)
cowlist.addAll(Arrays.asList(10, 20, 30));
Iterator<Integer> iter = cowlist.iterator();
while (iter.hasNext()) {
  Integer i = iter.next();
  if (i == 20) {
// iter.remove();                          // (2a) UnsupportedOperationException
    cowlist.remove(i);                     // (2b) OK
```

```
      continue;
    }
    System.out.print(i + " ");              // With (2b): 10 30
  }
```

In addition to the methods of the List interface, the following useful methods are also defined by the CopyOnWriteArrayList class:

boolean addIfAbsent(E e)

Appends the element, if not present.

int addAllAbsent(Collection<? extends E> c)

Appends to the end of this list all of the elements in the specified collection that are not already contained in this list.

The CopyOnWriteArraySet<E> *Class*

The CopyOnWriteArraySet class implements the java.util.Set interface (§15.4, p. 804). It does not implement any additional methods. Internally it uses a CopyOnWriteArrayList, and therefore shares the same basic properties with the list, except that, being a set, it does not allow duplicates and its elements have no ordering.

Example 23.21 illustrates the snapshot-style iterator of a CopyOnWriteArrayList. Such a list is created at (1) and populated with three values. A task to traverse the list and print its elements is defined by the Runnable iter at (2). Two threads are created at different times to execute this task at (4) and (6), respectively. The main thread modifies the list by adding a new value and removing a value after the start of the first thread. The output shows that the result from the first thread is not affected by the modifications done by the main thread, as its iterator only traverses those elements that were in the list when the iterator was created. The result from the second thread shows the state of the list when it was created—that is, after the list was modified by the main thread.

Example 23.21 *Copy-on-Write Array List*

```
package concurrent;
import java.util.*;
import java.util.concurrent.*;

public class CopyOnWriteArrayListDemo {

  public static void main(String[] args) {
    List<Integer> cowlist = new CopyOnWriteArrayList<Integer>();      // (1)
    cowlist.addAll(Arrays.asList(1, 2, 3));

    Runnable iter = () -> {                                           // (2)
      String threadName = Thread.currentThread().getName();
      for (Integer i : cowlist) {
        System.out.println(threadName + ": " + i);
        ConcUtil.snooze(1, TimeUnit.SECONDS);
      }
    };
```

```
        // First iterator:
        new Thread(iter, "Iterator A").start();                        // (4)

        // Snooze, add, and remove in main thread.                     // (5)
        ConcUtil.snooze(1, TimeUnit.SECONDS);
        Integer newValue = 4;
        cowlist.add(newValue);
        System.out.println("New value added: " + newValue);
        Integer first = cowlist.remove(0);
        System.out.println("Value removed:   " + first);

        // Second iterator:
        new Thread(iter, "Iterator B").start();                        // (6)
    }
}
```

Probable output from the program:

```
Iterator A: 1
New value added: 4
Iterator A: 2
Value removed: 1
Iterator B: 2
Iterator A: 3
Iterator B: 3
Iterator B: 4
```

 Review Questions

23.1 Which of the following statements is true?
Select the one correct answer.

(a) A single thread executor service cannot be used to schedule tasks.
(b) A fixed thread pool is configured with a given level of parallelism.
(c) A scheduled executor service allows a task to be run with a specified delay.
(d) A cached thread pool implements a work-stealing mechanism.

23.2 Which of the following statements is true?
Select the one correct answer.

(a) The executor service's shutdown() method cancels all tasks that are still running.
(b) The executor service's shutdown() method disables new tasks from being submitted.
(c) The executor service's awaitTermination() method cannot be interrupted.
(d) The executor service's shutdownNow() method awaits termination of tasks that are still running.

23.3 Which of the following statements is true about the `ReentrantReadWriteLock` class?
Select the one correct answer.

(a) Its read lock prevents concurrent read operations from reading inconsistent data.
(b) Its write lock prevents concurrent read operations from reading inconsistent data.
(c) Its write lock acquisition cannot be interrupted.
(d) Its read lock acquisition cannot be interrupted.

23.4 Given the following code:

```
var values = List.of("1", "2", "3", "4", "5", "6", "7", "8");
var list1 = new CopyOnWriteArrayList<Integer>();
for (String value: values) {
    new Thread(() -> {
        list1.add(Integer.valueOf(value));
    }).start();
}
System.out.println(list1);

var list2 = values.parallelStream().map(v->Integer.valueOf(v))
                                .toList();
System.out.println(list2);

var list3 = new ArrayList<Integer>();
values.parallelStream().map(v->Integer.valueOf(v)).forEach(v->list3.add(v));
System.out.println(list3);
```

Which lists will always print the same values as in the initial list?
Select the one correct answer.

(a) list1
(b) list2
(c) list3
(d) list1 and list2
(e) list2 and list3
(f) list1 and list3
(g) All of the lists
(h) None of the lists

23.5 Which of the following statements is true?
Select the one correct answer.

(a) Synchronized collections provide a synchronized `iterator()` method.
(b) Copy-on-write collections provide a synchronized `iterator()` method.
(c) Immutable collections provide a synchronized `iterator()` method.
(d) Synchronized collections require the programmer to implement a synchronized `iterator()` method.
(e) Copy-on-write collections require the programmer to implement a synchronized `iterator()` method.
(f) Immutable collections require the programmer to implement a synchronized
`iterator()` method.

23.6   Which of the following statements is true about atomic variables?
Select the one correct answer.

(a) Atomic variables represent the smallest indivisible unit of data.
(b) Atomic variables ensure memory consistency using synchronized operations.
(c) Atomic variables provide methods that can throw an `InterruptedException`.
(d) Atomic variables do not utilize an intrinsic locking mechanism.

23.7   Given the following code:

```java
import java.util.*;
import java.util.concurrent.*;
import java.util.concurrent.atomic.*;
public class RQ7 {
  public static void main(String[] args) {
    AtomicLong aValue = new AtomicLong(0);
    Callable<Number> c = () -> {
      AtomicLong value = aValue;
        return value.incrementAndGet();
      };

    Collection<Callable<Number>> cc = List.of(c, c, c);
    ExecutorService es = Executors.newFixedThreadPool(2);
    List<Future<Number>> futures = null;
    try {
      futures = es.invokeAll(cc);
    } catch (InterruptedException e) {
      e.printStackTrace();
    }
    es.shutdown();

    futures.stream().mapToLong(v-> {
    try {
      return v.get().longValue();
    }catch(Exception e) {
      return -1;
    }}).forEach(v->System.out.print(v));
    System.out.print(aValue);
  }
}
```

Which of the following output can be produced by this program?
Select the two correct answers.

(a) 1233
(b) 2133
(c) 1122
(d) 2122
(e) 2123

23.8   Given the following code:

```java
import java.util.concurrent.locks.*;
public class RQ8 {
  public static void main(String[] args) {
```

```
            ReentrantReadWriteLock rwl = new ReentrantReadWriteLock();
            Lock rl = rwl.readLock();
            Lock wl = rwl.writeLock();
            try {
              rl.lock();
              System.out.println("Read lock acquired");
              if (wl.tryLock()) {
                System.out.println("Write lock acquired");
              }
            } catch(Exception e) {
              System.out.println("Lock acquisition failed");
            } finally {
              rl.unlock();
              if (rwl.isWriteLocked()) {
                wl.unlock();
                System.out.println("Write lock released");
              }
            }
            System.out.println("The end");
          }
        }
```

What is the result?
Select the one correct answer.

(a) Read lock acquired
     The end

(b) Read lock acquired
     Write lock acquired
     Write lock released
     The end

(c) Read lock acquired
     Lock acquisition failed
     The end

(d) Lock acquisition failed
     The end

(e) Lock acquisition failed
     Write lock released
     The end

23.9   Given the following code:

```
        public class RQ9 {
          private static volatile int counter = 10;
          public static void main(String[] args) {
            Runnable r = () -> counter--;
            while (counter > 0) {
              new Thread(r).start();
              System.out.print(counter);
            }
          }
        }
```

What is the result?

Select the one correct answer.

(a) Either 9876543210 or 876543210-1 or 987654321
(b) Either 9876543210 or 10987654321 or 987654321
(c) 9876543210
(d) The result is unpredictable.

23.10 Given the following code:

```java
import java.util.concurrent.*;
public class RQ10 {
  public static void main(String[] args) {
    try {
      ExecutorService es = Executors.newFixedThreadPool(2);
      Future<?> f1 = es.submit(() -> "acme");
      Future<?> f2 = es.submit(() -> {}); // (1)
      es.shutdown();                       // (2)
      Object o1 = f1.get();
      Object o2 = f2.get();                // (3)
      System.out.println(o1 + " " + o2);  // (4)
    } catch (InterruptedException | ExecutionException e) {
      e.printStackTrace();
    }
  }
}
```

What is the result?
Select the one correct answer.

(a) An exception is thrown at (1).
(b) An exception is thrown at (2).
(c) An exception is thrown at (3).
(d) An exception is thrown at (4).
(e) acme null
(f) acme

23.11 Given the following code:

```java
import java.util.*;
import java.util.concurrent.*;
import java.util.stream.*;

public class RQ11 {
  public static void main(String[] args) {
    Map<Integer, String> map =
        new ConcurrentHashMap<>(Map.of(1,"a",2,"b",3,"c",4,"d",5,"e"));
    List<Future<String>> results = new CopyOnWriteArrayList<>();

    ExecutorService es = Executors.newFixedThreadPool(3);
    for (int i = 1; i <= map.size(); i++) {
      final int key = i;
      Future<String> f = es.submit(() -> map.get(key).toUpperCase());
      if (i % 2 != 0) {
        f.cancel(true);
      }
```

```
        results.add(f);
    }
    es.shutdown();
    String result = (results.stream().allMatch(r -> r.isDone()))
        ? results.stream().filter(r -> !r.isCancelled()).map(r -> {
            try {
                return r.get();
            } catch (InterruptedException | ExecutionException e) {
                return "X";
            }
        }).collect(Collectors.joining())
        : "Z";
    System.out.println(result);
    }
}
```

Which of the following statements are true about the result of this program? Select the two correct answers.

(a) The program terminates with an exception.
(b) The program only prints the letters B or D.
(c) The program never prints the letters B or D.
(d) The program only prints the letters A, C, or E.
(e) The program never prints the letters A, C, or E.
(f) The program may print the letters A, B, C, D, or E.
(g) The program may print the letter X.
(h) The program may print the letter Z.

Database Connectivity 24

 Chapter Topics

- Understanding the basics of relational databases: relational tables and SQL
- Understanding the role of the JDBC driver, and establishing a database connection using such a driver
- Understanding the handling of JDBC resources, and closing them in a responsible way
- Writing code to create and execute SQL statements: basic statement, prepared statement, and callable statement in the JDBC API
- Writing code to process query results, including customizing the result set returned by a query
- Discovering database capabilities and reading result set metadata
- Writing code to implement transaction control

Java SE 17 Developer Exam Objectives	
[11.1] Implement localization using locales, resource bundles, parse and format messages, dates, times, and numbers including currency and percentage values	§24.1, p. 1512, to §24.8, p. 1545.
Java SE 11 Developer Exam Objectives	
[11.1] Connect to and perform database SQL operations, process query results using JDBC API	§24.1, p. 1512, to §24.8, p. 1545.

Database is a general term that describes organized data storage, controlled by a *Database Management System* (DBMS). There are many different such systems from different providers and vendors, both commercial and open source.

The responsibilities of a DBMS typically include tasks such as secure and control data access, keep data safe and consistent, and query the data. Databases can be classified by the way in which they store information, such as hierarchical, network, object, and relational, each with their own advantages and disadvantages. Many modern DBMS present a mix of different database features and capabilities.

This chapter discusses how to develop Java applications that use a relational database, which is one of the most commonly used database models. The Java Database Connectivity (JDBC) specification allows development of Java applications that can leverage a relational database independent of a specific DBMS.

The coverage of JDBC in this chapter is in no way exhaustive. The topics covered provide the basic essentials to write Java applications that use the JDBC API to interact with a relational database in an independent way. Prior knowledge of databases is advantageous, but not essential, as the basics are covered in this chapter. However, to be proficient, the large body of literature and software in this area should be consulted.

24.1 Introduction to Relational Databases

Relational databases are based on the *relational model* that provides a standardized way to represent and query data. The data is stored in *tables* and queried using a *query language*.

Relational Tables

Relational databases store information in *tables*. Each table is designed to represent a business entity that applications need to store information about. Each table is composed of *columns* (a.k.a. *attributes*). Each column represents specific information that describes a specific characteristic of a business entity that the table represents.

Each column has a *name* and describes information of a specific *type*, such as fixed- or variable-length character data (type CHAR or VARCHAR), numeric values (type NUMBER or INTEGER), date and time values (type DATE or TIMESTAMP), and many other types. Different database providers may support different data types.

Each table may be defined with a number of *constraints* that enforce business rules associated with this entity. For example, constraints may be used to enforce uniqueness of column values (PRIMARY KEY), or that these values must always be present (NOT NULL), or that they are restricted to a specific list or range of values. Different database providers may support different constraint types.

Actual business data is stored in tables as *rows* (a.k.a. *tuples*). Each row is composed of values that follow the exact structure of columns defined by a given table.

As an example, a music catalogue application needs to store information about music compositions in a database. Let us assume that each composition has the following attributes:

- An International Standard Recording Code (*ISRC*), which uniquely identifies a composition
- A title
- A duration

Thus to store this information in a relational database would require a compositions table with isrc, title, and duration columns. Assume that all of these are mandatory pieces of information for every composition object, and that isrc and title are both of type VARCHAR, and duration is of type INT. The definition of the compositions table is shown in Table 24.1.

Table 24.1 *Definition of the* compositions *Table*

Column name	Column type	Column constraints
isrc	VARCHAR(12)	PRIMARY KEY
title	VARCHAR(40)	NOT NULL
duration	INT	NOT NULL

Note that column types often specify specific length or precision characteristics—for example, VARCHAR(12) in Table 24.1. Also, a PRIMARY KEY constraint is usually implicitly mandatory NOT NULL (does not allow null values). In Table 24.1, the isrc column name uniquely identifies a composition, hence its constraint is PRIMARY KEY and implicitly NOT NULL. The other two column names title and duration are mandatory for each composition, hence their constraint is also NOT NULL.

Table 24.2 shows example data (four rows) stored in the compositions table, which satisfies the *table definition* given in Table 24.1. Each row in Table 24.2 represents a unique music composition.

A table definition can be loosely compared to a class that describes a number of attributes, and a row can be compared to an object (instance) of that specific class. A spreadsheet is another example of organizing data in rows and columns.

Table 24.2 *Data in the* compositions *Table*

isrc	title	duration
ushm91736697	Vacation	231
ushm91736698	Rage	308
ushm91736699	Why Don't	178
ushm91736700	Something Happened	147

Basic SQL Statements

Structured Query Language (SQL) is used to perform relational database operations. Despite the existence of an ANSI (American National Standards Institute) SQL standard, different database providers may provide SQL implementations that are not exactly the same and may contain nuanced differences and proprietary additions.

SQL statements can be logically grouped into a number of languages, in which they are identified by SQL keywords:

- *Data Manipulation Language* (*DML*) comprises the SELECT, INSERT, UPDATE, and DELETE statements, used to query, create, modify, and remove table rows. Sometimes the SELECT statement is described to be in its own *Data Query Language* (*DQL*) group.

- *Data Definition Language* (*DDL*) comprises the CREATE, ALTER, and DROP statements, whose purpose is to create, modify, and remove tables. We will refer to the CREATE, ALTER, and DROP statements as *DDL operations*.

- *Transaction Control Language* (*TCL*) comprises the COMMIT and ROLLBACK statements, whose purpose is to save or undo pending changes, respectively.

Often the INSERT, SELECT, UPDATE, and DELETE statements (in that order) are referred to as *CRUD operations*, denoting the *Create, Read/Retrieve, Update*, and *Delete* operations implied by the acronym, respectively. Note the name mismatch of the CRUD operations and the SQL statements is implied. In particular, the set of CRUD operations does *not* include the CREATE statement in SQL that creates relational tables.

The rest of this subsection presents basic syntax patterns and examples of creating relational tables and the CRUD operations in SQL. Note that the semicolon (;) is a *statement terminator* in SQL.

The CREATE *Statement*

The CREATE statement can be used to create a new table in the database:

```
CREATE TABLE table_name (column_definitions);
```

where *table_name* is the name of the table to be created, and *column_definitions* is a comma-delimited list that describes each column in this table:

```
column_name column_type constraints, ...
```

The following statement creates an empty compositions table:

```
CREATE TABLE compositions (isrc VARCHAR(12) PRIMARY KEY,
                           title VARCHAR(40) NOT NULL, duration INT NOT NULL);
```

The CREATE statement above will create an empty relational table whose columns will correspond to the table shown in Table 24.2.

The INSERT Statement

The INSERT statement can be used to insert a new row into a table:

```
INSERT INTO table_name VALUES (actual_values);
```

where *actual_values* in the VALUES clause is a comma-delimited list that provides values for the columns of the table specified by *table_name*.

The following statement inserts a new row into the compositions table:

```
INSERT INTO compositions VALUES ('ushm91736697', 'Vacation', 231);
```

The number of rows in the compositions table increases by 1. By default, the values specified are interpreted in the same order as the columns are defined in the table. Note that string literals in SQL are enclosed in single quotes (').

The SELECT Statement

The SELECT statement can be used to query or read rows from the database:

```
SELECT column_list FROM table_name WHERE row_filter;
```

The *column_list* is a comma-delimited list of column names, whose values are selected from the table specified with *table_name* in the FROM clause. The '*' symbol can be used as *column_list* to specify that all columns should be included in the returned result. A list of conditions is specified by *row_filter* in the WHERE clause to determine which specific rows should be selected. Such conditions may be constructed using a variety of operators to compare column values, such as = (*equals*), > (*greater than*), < (*less than*), LIKE (which can use "%" wildcards), and many others. Conditions in *row_filter* can be combined using AND and OR operators.

```
column_name = some_value AND column_name LIKE some_value
```

The following statement selects values of isrc and title for all rows in the compositions table whose duration is greater than 200 and whose title starts with 'V':

```
SELECT isrc, title FROM compositions WHERE duration > 200 AND title LIKE 'V%';
```

Applied to Table 24.2, the above query will return the values of isrc and title in the first row, which is the only row that meets the *row_filter* criteria—that is, (ushm91736697, Vacation).

The WHERE clause is optional. In that case, the values of *column_list* in the entire table are returned.

```
SELECT * FROM compositions;
```

The above SELECT statement will return all the rows in the specified table.

The UPDATE Statement

The UPDATE statement can be used to update specific rows in a table. In other words, this statement modifies zero or more rows in the table:

```
UPDATE table_name SET column_name_value_pairs WHERE row_filter;
```

where *column_name_value_pairs* in the SET clause is a comma-delimited list of pairs of column names and values:

```
column_name = column_value, ...
```

and *row_filter* in the WHERE clause specifies a list of conditions to indicate which specific rows should be updated.

All rows that meet the *row_filter* criteria in *table_name* will have their columns specified in the *column_name_value_pairs* set to the corresponding values in *column_name_value_pairs*.

The following statement updates a duration value for an existing row in the compositions table:

```
UPDATE compositions SET duration = 240 WHERE isrc LIKE '%91736697'
                                             OR duration > 231;
```

The above UPDATE statement will update the first row (isrc '91736697') in Table 24.2 by setting the duration to 240.

The WHERE clause is optional. When omitted, all rows will have their columns specified in the *column_name_value_pairs* set to the corresponding values in *column_name_value_pairs*.

```
UPDATE compositions SET duration = 250;
```

The above UPDATE statement will update the duration column for all rows to 250 in Table 24.2.

The DELETE *Statement*

The DELETE statement can be used to delete specific rows in a table that meet the criteria in the WHERE clause. This statement deletes zero or more rows from the specified table:

```
DELETE FROM table_name WHERE row_filter;
```

where *row_filter* in the WHERE clause is the criteria for which rows should be deleted from *table_name* in the FROM clause.

The following statement deletes a row from the compositions table:

```
DELETE FROM compositions WHERE isrc = 'ushm91736697';
```

The row with isrc having the value 'ushm91736697' in the compositions table will be deleted from Table 24.2.

The WHERE clause is optional. Care must be taken, as omitting it will delete all rows from the table.

```
DELETE FROM compositions;
```

There are many other statements available in SQL described by the ANSI SQL standard and additional statements which may be implemented by database providers.

This book does not have a goal of covering SQL in detail, but provides a brief introduction to ensure a minimum level of understanding of how relational databases operate and thereby an understanding of how Java programs interact with relational databases.

Java certification focuses on Java, not on SQL. However, it is essential to learn database concepts and understand SQL if one wants to work with relational databases.

24.2 Introduction to JDBC

The *Java Database Connectivity* (JDBC) protocol provides database interaction capabilities for Java programs. The JDBC specification is not database provider specific, allowing Java programs to interact with any database.

The *JDBC API* is defined in the java.sql package. It comprises a number of interfaces that Java programs use to represent database connections, SQL statements, query results, and much more.

The JDBC API is implemented by a number of database-specific *JDBC drivers*. The job of a JDBC driver is to provide database-specific, native protocol implementation of the JDBC API. For example, Oracle, MySQL, DerbyDB, and others provide JDBC drivers that all implement the same JDBC API, but in a different database-specific manner.

A Java application can dynamically load the JDBC driver as required and connect to different databases, provided that the JDBC driver is present in the class path or module path of the application.

Figure 24.1 illustrates the layered approach to database connectivity. Java developers write code that utilizes JDBC interfaces defined by the java.sql package. These interfaces are implemented by different JDBC drivers. Java developers should only write code that utilizes JDBC API interfaces and not use JDBC drivers directly, so that software portability is not compromised. This allows Java applications to maintain database-provider neutrality, and potentially switch JDBC drivers and database providers without modifying application code. This approach is designed to decouple the application code from specific database providers, potentially

Figure 24.1 *Layered Database Connectivity*

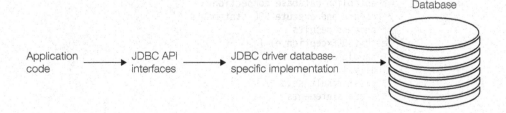

allowing the application to switch between different databases and even use different databases at the same time.

In order to connect to a database, the Java application has to perform the following tasks:

1. Ensure that the relevant JDBC driver is available in the class path or module path of the application.

2. Load the JDBC driver to memory.

3. Establish the database connection.

Once a database connection is established, a typical interaction scenario with the database proceeds as follows:

1. *Create* SQL statements.

2. *Execute* SQL statements.

3. *Process* query results.

4. *Close* the JDBC resources.

Closing JDBC Resources

It is important to ensure that all JDBC resources are properly closed once they are no longer needed.

All JDBC API methods can throw a java.sql.SQLException. A SQLException is a checked exception, which in addition to the usual Java error message, also wraps up database error information such as the SQL state and an error code.

The skeletal code below will always catch the SQLException and handle it:

```
try {
/* execute JDBC operations */
} catch (SQLException e) {
  String state = e.getSQLState();
  int code = e.getErrorCode();
}
```

The logic of the JDBC application can be generalized with the following skeletal code:

```
try {
  /* establish database connection   */
  /* create and execute SQL statements */
  /* process results                 */
} catch (SQLException e) {
  /* handle any errors */
} finally {
  /* close result sets */
  /* close statements  */
```

```
    /* close connection  */
}
```

It is important to remember that the closing order of these objects is significant: First close any result set objects, then close statements, and then close connections. No Java exceptions are actually produced if you try to close in a different order. However, this would prevent resources from being promptly released and thus can result in memory leaks.

JDBC interfaces that represent connection, statement, and result set objects all implement the AutoCloseable interface. Therefore, they can be used in the try-with-resources construct, in which case they are automatically closed in the implicit finally block inserted by the compiler, as shown below.

```
try (/* establish database connection     */
    /* create and execute SQL statements */)
{
  /* process results */
} catch (SQLException e) {
  /* handle any exceptions */
} /* implicit finally block closes resources*/
```

24.3 Establishing a Database Connection

Interaction between the application and the database is in the context of a *connection*. Database connections are represented by the java.sql.Connection interface. JDBC drivers provide database-specific implementations of this interface.

The class java.sql.DriverManager provides the overloaded factory method get-Connection() that initializes and returns a database Connection object.

```
static Connection getConnection(String jdbcURL)
static Connection getConnection(String jdbcURL, String username,
                                String password)
static Connection getConnection(String jdbcURL, Properties info)
```

All versions of the getConnection() method require a JDBC URL and all throw a SQLException. Additional information may be required to establish a database connection, such as username and password, or other means of authentication such as digital signatures that can be set using the Properties object (§18.2, p. 1100). Note also that the Connection object returned is AutoCloseable, and therefore it is best handled in a try-with-resources construct to ensure that the connection is closed when done.

JDBC URL

The general syntax of the *JDBC URL* is as follows:

```
protocol:provider:driver_type:database_specific_connection_details
```

The *protocol* is always specified as "jdbc". Other details may vary depending on the database provider. For example, to connect to the Apache Derby database you need to specify the *provider* as "derby", followed by the description of where this database is located, which would include *host*, *port*, and *database name* information.

```
jdbc:derby:localhost:1521:musicDB
```

The example below shows a more sophisticated JDBC driver that may provide different connectivity mechanisms, each identified by an appropriate *subprotocol*. In this case, the JDBC URL example shows how one can specify an Oracle database connection using the most frequently used *thin* protocol implementation that provides enhanced security features.

```
jdbc:oracle:thin:@localhost:1521:musicDB
```

Not all JDBC drivers provide alternative connectivity methods. In the Oracle JDBC driver case, alternative connectivity mechanisms, such as *thin*, *OCI*, or *kprb*, can be used. This could be the case with many other providers of JDBC drivers. In the case of a Derby database, it can be accessed as a separate process or be embedded inside a Java program, which would make the JDBC URL look different. It is best to refer to JDBC driver-specific documentation to identify available choices and the rationale behind selecting one or the other connectivity mechanism.

Getting a Database Connection

To create a connection to a Derby database, the following code can be emulated:

```
String jdbcURL  = "jdbc:derby:localhost:1521:musicDB";
String username = "joe";
String password = "welcome1";
try (Connection connection = DriverManager.getConnection(jdbcURL,
                                            username, password)) {

  /* use the connection. */
} catch (SQLException e) {
  e.printStackTrace();
}
```

A portion of the URL that indicates a driver instructs the DriverManager to load the appropriate driver implementation to memory. This of course would fail if this JDBC driver is not found in the class path or module path.

Connecting to the musicDB *Database*

We will use the musicDB database which consists of the compositions table shown in Table 24.2. Instructions for downloading the files for the musicDB database and the Derby JAR files can be found on this book's website. The structure of the working directory is assumed to be the following:

```
Working directory
│
├── db-derby-10.15.2.0-lib/   <== Directory with the Apache Derby distribution
│   │
│   └── lib/                   <== Directory with the Derby JAR files
│
├── musicDB/                   <== Directory with the musicDB database files
│
├── dbDemo/                    <== Package with examples used in this chapter
│   │
│   ├── JDBCConnection.java
│   │
... ...
```

Example 24.1 shows how to obtain a connection to the musicDB database. Note that in the JDBC URL, the relative path of the musicDB directory in the working directory is musicDB. The class path must also be set to access the Derby JAR files. In the code below, the implicit finally clause of the try-with-resources statement guarantees to close the connection when done.

Example 24.1 *Connecting to the* musicDB *Database*

```java
package dbDemo;
import java.sql.Connection;
import java.sql.DriverManager;
import java.sql.SQLException;

public class JDBCConnection {
  public static void main(String[] args) {
    final String jdbcURL = "jdbc:derby:musicDB";
    try (Connection connection = DriverManager.getConnection(jdbcURL)) {
      /* use the connection. */
      System.out.println(connection);
    } catch (SQLException e) {
      e.printStackTrace();
    }
  }
}
```

Probable output from the program:

```
org.apache.derby.impl.jdbc.EmbedConnection@1201454821 (XID = 1301),
(SESSIONID = 1), (DATABASE = musicDB), (DRDAID = null)
```

Legacy JDBC Driver Management

Prior to JDBC version 4.0, drivers had to be loaded into memory explicitly, before using them to establish database connections. There are several ways in which this could be achieved:

- Instantiate and register the database-specific JDBC driver class using the `java.sql.DriverManager.registerDriver()` method:

```
DriverManager.registerDriver(new oracle.jdbc.driver.OracleDriver());
```

- Load a database-specific JDBC driver class using the `java.lang.Class.forName()` method:

```
try {
  Class.forName("oracle.jdbc.driver.OracleDriver");
} catch (ClassNotfoundException c) { }
```

- Load a database-specific JDBC driver class using the command-line `-D` option:

```
java –Djdbc.drivers=oracle.jdbc.driver.OracleDriver ...
```

From JDBC 4.0 onward, JDBC drivers are automatically loaded, and no explicit driver loading or registration is required. However, old-style code would still function for backward compatibility reasons.

24.4 Creating and Executing SQL Statements

The JDBC API defines three interfaces that represent SQL *statements*:

- `java.sql.Statement` represents a basic statement (p. 1523). This type of statement can be used to execute any SQL operation, such as CRUD or DDL operations. However, it is associated with performance and security issues. Thus it is not generally recommended, except for very simple operations that do not require dynamic parameterization and that are not reused within a program.
- `java.sql.PreparedStatement` is a subinterface of the `Statement` interface, that represents a statement capable of *substitutional parameterization* (p. 1526). This type of statement has the same capabilities as a basic statement, but is considered to be better from both performance and security perspectives, and thus is a recommended choice for representing SQL operations in general.
- `java.sql.CallableStatement` is a subinterface of the `PreparedStatement` interface, that represents a statement that invokes a *stored procedure* or *function* (p. 1530) and is also capable of *substitutional parameterization*.

The result of executing a `SELECT` statement is a table of rows represented by the following interface:

- `java.sql.ResultSet` that represents a table whose contents can be read and processed

All statements are created using a previously initialized JDBC connection object. A statement is created using one of the methods of the `Connection` interface shown below. Depending on the method, a specific statement is returned. Note that the statement object returned is AutoCloseable, and should be used in a try-with-resources statement to ensure proper closing of recourses such objects represent.

The following methods are defined in the Connection interface:

```
Statement          createStatement()
PreparedStatement prepareStatement(String sql)
CallableStatement prepareCall(String sql)
```

For overloaded versions of these methods in the Connection interface that can be used to customize the result set, see p. 1541.

Basic Statement

We first look at how to create and execute a basic statement. A Statement object should first be obtained from the Connection object. Note the declarations in the header of the try-with-resources statement that obtain a Connection object and create a Statement object, respectively. The try-with-resources statement will ensure that these resources are closed in the right order—that is, the reverse of their declarations.

```
try (Connection connection = DriverManager.getConnection(jdbcURL);
    Statement statement
        = connection.createStatement()) { // Obtain a Statement object.
  /* execute a query */
} catch (SQLException e) {
  e.printStackTrace();
}
```

Once a statement has been obtained, the following methods of the Statement interface can be used to execute and process a SQL query.

boolean execute(String sql)

The execute() method can be called to execute any operation, returning a boolean value which is true for the SELECT statement, false otherwise.

ResultSet executeQuery(String sql)

The executeQuery() method can only be called to execute SELECT statements, returning a ResultSet that is the result of executing the query. A ResultSet is also AutoCloseable and must be closed when done. Passing a non-SELECT operation will throw a SQLException.

int executeUpdate(String sql)

The executeUpdate() method can be called to execute any operations, except SELECT operations, returning an int value indicating the number of rows affected by the non-SELECT operation. Passing a SELECT operation will throw a SQLException.

ResultSet getResultSet()

Returns the ResultSet that was the result of executing a SELECT query using the current statement.

int getUpdateCount()

Returns the number of rows that were affected by the execution of a non-SELECT query using the current statement.

An appropriate execute method can be called depending on the type of SQL statement and on passing the SQL operation as a String parameter. The code below executes a SELECT query by calling the execute() method of the Statement interface, as shown at (1). This method returns a boolean value. The output from the code at (2) indicates that a SELECT query was processed.

```
final String jdbcURL = "jdbc:derby:musicDB";
try (Connection connection = DriverManager.getConnection(jdbcURL);
    Statement statement
        = connection.createStatement()) {       // Obtain a Statement object.
    String sql = "select * from compositions";   // SELECT query: select all rows.
    boolean isSelectStmt = statement.execute(sql);        // (1) Execute the query
    System.out.println("SELECT statement? " + isSelectStmt);// (2) SELECT statement?
                                                  //        true
} catch (SQLException e) {
    e.printStackTrace();
}
```

When calling the execute() method with a SQL statement as a String parameter, it might not be possible to know a priori what type of SQL statement will be executed. However, this method would return true if the statement happens to be a SELECT query; otherwise, it returns false. As shown in the code below, which analyzes the resulting value in an if statement, a ResultSet object can be retrieved or the number of rows affected by the statement, depending on the result.

```
boolean isSelectStmt = statement.execute(sql);
if (isSelectStmt) {
  try (ResultSet resultSet
          = statement.getResultSet()) { // SELECT statement: retrieve ResultSet.
    System.out.println("SELECT statement: processing ResultSet");
  }
} else {                                           // Update statement:
  int rowCount = statement.getUpdateCount();       // Retrieve the number of
                                                   // rows affected.
  System.out.println("Update statement: Rows affected " + rowCount);
}
```

The method executeQuery() is used exclusively to execute a SELECT query. This method returns a ResultSet object that represents the rows retrieved as a result of executing the query. As a ResultSet is AutoCloseable, the method is called in a nested try-with-resources statement at (1) to ensure closure of the ResultSet.

```
try (Connection connection = DriverManager.getConnection(jdbcURL);
    Statement statement
        = connection.createStatement()) {         // Obtain a Statement object.
    String sql = "select * from compositions";    // SQL query: select all rows.
```

```
    try (ResultSet resultSet
            = statement.executeQuery(sql)) {    // (1) Nested try-with-resources
      System.out.println("Processing ResultSet");
    }
  } catch (SQLException e) {
    e.printStackTrace();
  }
```

The method executeUpdate() can be used to execute any SQL statement except a SELECT statement. An int value indicating the number of rows affected by the statement is returned as a result. The code below doubles the duration of each composition in the compositions table.

```
  try (Connection connection = DriverManager.getConnection(jdbcURL);    // (1)
       Statement statement = connection.createStatement()) {            // (2)
    String sql = "update compositions set duration = duration * 2";     // (3)
    int count = statement.executeUpdate(sql);                           // (4)
    System.out.println("Rows modified: " + count);
  } catch (SQLException e) {
    e.printStackTrace();
  }
```

The code above illustrates the procedure to use a basic statement. The numbered comments below correspond to the numbered lines in the code:

(1) Create a Connection with the DriverManager.getConnection() method.

(2) Obtain a Statement from the connection by calling its createStatement() method.

(3) Formulate a SQL operation.

(4) Call the appropriate execute method of the statement, passing the SQL operation as the String parameter.

SQL Injection

Passing the SQL operation as a string in the execute method presents the risk of a *SQL injection*, as malicious SQL code can be injected into the query string. Assume that there is a basic statement that queries a table, where the query is dependent on a value:

```
  ResultSet resultSet = statement.executeQuery(
      "select * from compositions where title like '" + value + "'");
```

A user may try to exploit this code by submitting a malicious value, such as the following:

```
  String value = "SomeValue'; drop table compositions;";
```

The above query would be equivalent to the following statement, where the SELECT operation would be executed, followed by dropping the compositions table:

```
  ResultSet resultSet2 = statement.executeQuery(
      "select * from compositions where title like '" +
      "SomeValue'; drop table compositions;");
```

To address this issue, one can use either a PreparedStatement object or the Statement .enquoteLiteral() method to sanitize the parameter value.

Prepared Statement

In contrast to the Statement object, which defines the SQL operation as a String
parameter to the execute method, a PreparedStatement defines a SQL operation
immediately at the point when the prepared statement is created with the prepare-
Statement() method. In other words, the SQL operation string is passed as an argument in the prepareStatement() method call, as shown at (1). The prepared statement
executes the precompiled SQL operation at (2) by calling the execute() method.

```
String sql = "select * from compositions where duration > 200"; // SQL operation
try (Connection connection
        = DriverManager.getConnection(jdbcURL);                    // Get connection
    PreparedStatement pStatement
        = connection.prepareStatement(sql)) {                    // (1) Prepare statement
  boolean result = pStatement.execute();                         // (2) Execute
  System.out.println(result);
} catch (SQLException e) {
  e.printStackTrace();
}
```

Substitutional Parameterization

Consider the following code:

```
String sql = "select * from compositions where duration > ?"; // (1) SQL operation
                                                              // with 1 marker parameter.
PreparedStatement pStatement
  = connection.prepareStatement(sql);                        // (2) A prepared statement
```

The SQL operation at (1) now contains a *marker parameter* (also known as *bind
parameter* or *bind variable*). Prepared statements use *positional notation* where each
question mark (?) indicates the position of a marker parameter starting with 1 from
left to right. This could be any SQL operation, such as an INSERT, UPDATE, or DELETE
statement with appropriate marker parameters. The SQL operation with marker
parameters is passed as an argument to the prepareStatement() method to precom-
pile this SQL operation into a prepared statement, as shown at (2).

However, before a prepared statement can be executed, all its parameters must be
set—that is, all marker parameters must be substituted with a value. One can use
the set methods of the PreparedStatement interface that are provided for all standard
JDBC types to set the value of a marker parameter (see below).

```
pStatement.setInt(1,200);          // Sets the value of the marker parameter
                                   // at position 1 to 200.
```

Alternatively, the method setObject() can be used to supply a value and explicitly
indicate the desired SQL type:

```
pStatement.setObject(1, 200, Types.INTEGER);
```

There is no requirement that parameters should be set in any specific order, as long
as all parameters are set before executing the statement. Note that the position
counter in JDBC is not 0-based as in the rest of the Java language, but starts at 1,

which is typical in the database world. The driver converts the value of the Java data type in the method call to the corresponding value of the SQL data type. All parameter-setting methods throw a SQLException if the parameter index does not correspond to a marker parameter, or if it is called on a prepared statement that is already closed.

The PreparedStatement interface is a subinterface of the Statement interface. Once a prepared statement has been obtained with its precompiled SQL operation and values for its marker parameters have been supplied, the execute methods of the PreparedStatement interface can be used to execute the SQL operation. These execute methods are analogous to the corresponding methods in the Statement interface. Note that since the SQL operation to execute is already precompiled with the prepared statement, the execute methods of the PreparedStatement interface do not take any parameter. Specifying an argument will throw a SQLException, as will any marker parameter that is not substituted with a value.

```
boolean execute()
ResultSet executeQuery()
int executeUpdate()
```

The PreparedStatement interface provides the following set methods for setting the values of marker parameters:

```
void setString(int index, String value)
```
Sets a String value for the parameter designated by the index.

```
void setBoolean(int index, boolean value)
```
Sets a boolean value for the parameter designated by the index.

```
void setInt(int index, int value)
```
Sets an int value for the parameter designated by the index.

```
void setLong(int index, long value)
```
Sets a long value for the parameter designated by the index.

```
void setDouble(int index, double value)
```
Sets a double value for the parameter designated by the index.

```
void setBigDecimal(int index, BigDecimal value)
```
Sets a BigDecimal value for the parameter designated by the index.

```
void setDate(int index, Date value)
```
Sets a Date value for the parameter designated by the index.

```
void setObject(int index, Object value, int sqlType)
```
Sets any Object value for the parameter designated by the index, and the required SQL type which is a named constant in the java.sql.Types class—for example, Types.INTEGER, Types.DATE, or Types.VARCHAR.

Example 24.2 *Executing a Prepared Statement*

```
package dbDemo;
import java.sql.*;

public class XQTPreparedStatement {
  public static void main(String[] args) {
    final String jdbcURL = "jdbc:derby:musicDB";
    String sql = "select * from compositions where duration > ?";     // (1)
    try (Connection connection = DriverManager.getConnection(jdbcURL);    // (2)
        PreparedStatement pStatement = connection.prepareStatement(sql);) { // (3)
      pStatement.setInt(1, 200);                                        // (4)
      boolean result = pStatement.execute();                           // (5)
      System.out.println(result);
    } catch (SQLException e) {
      e.printStackTrace();
    }
  }
}
```

Probable output:

```
true
```

The procedure to use a prepared statement is illustrated by Example 24.2. The numbered comments below correspond to the numbered lines of code in the example.

(1) Formulate a SQL operation with marker parameters.

(2) Create a `Connection` with the `DriverManager.getConnection()` method.

(3) Create a `PreparedStatement` from the connection by calling its `prepareStatement()` method and passing the SQL operation as a parameter.

(4) Set the values of all marker parameters.

(5) Call the appropriate execute method of the prepared statement.

Note that a prepared statement can be reused by substituting different values for its marker parameters. In the try-with-resources statement in Example 24.2, we can include the following code to change the condition in the WHERE clause at (1) by substituting another value for the marker parameter before executing the prepared statement:

```
pStatement.setInt(1, 100);
result = pStatement.execute();
```

Substitutional parameterization allows SQL operations to be precompiled and reused, leading to more efficient execution. Supplying values using marker parameters is more flexible, faster, and safer than using a basic statement because the prepared statement is precompiled and marker parameters are not prone to SQL injection.

Example 24.3 illustrates prepared statements to execute INSERT, UPDATE, and DELETE statements with marker parameters that are defined first. A database connection and three prepared statements are created in the header of the try-with-resources statement, respectively. The marker parameters are set in each prepared statement, before the statement is executed using the executeUpdate() method of the Prepared-Statement interface. The program prints three integers that indicate the number of rows affected by each SQL operation, which of course is dependent on the data in the compositions table.

Example 24.3   *Prepared Statement to Execute* INSERT, UPDATE, *and* DELETE

```java
package dbDemo;
import java.sql.DriverManager;
import java.sql.SQLException;

public class PreparedStatementExecuteUpdate {
  public static void main(String[] args) {

    final String insSql = "insert into compositions VALUES(?, ?, ?)";
    final String updSql = "update compositions set title = ? where title = ?";
    final String delSql = "delete from compositions where duration = ?";

    final String jdbcURL = "jdbc:derby:musicDB";
    try (var connection = DriverManager.getConnection(jdbcURL);
        var pStatement1 = connection.prepareStatement(insSql);
        var pStatement2 = connection.prepareStatement(updSql);
        var pStatement3 = connection.prepareStatement(delSql)) {

      pStatement1.setInt(3, 150);
      pStatement1.setString(2, "Java Jazz");
      pStatement1.setString(1, "ushm91736991");
      int result1 = pStatement1.executeUpdate();
      System.out.println(result1);

      pStatement2.setString(1, "Java Jive");
      pStatement2.setString(2, "Java Jazz");
      int result2 = pStatement2.executeUpdate();
      System.out.println(result2);

      pStatement3.setInt(1, 200);
      int result3 = pStatement3.executeUpdate();
      System.out.println(result3);
    } catch (SQLException e) {
      e.printStackTrace();
    }
  }
}
```

Probable output:

```
1
1
0
```

Callable Statement

The Callable interface is a subinterface of the PreparedStatement interface. Callable statements are very similar to prepared statements because both use marker parameters. The main difference is that callable statements are used to invoke *named stored procedures and stored functions that reside on the database side*. The difference between a function and a procedure is that a function is intended to return a value. Both are precompiled code on the database side and can be invoked via a callable statement on the application side.

Syntax of Calling Stored Procedures and Functions

The syntax for calling stored procedures and functions is shown below at (1) and (2), respectively. The parameter list of a stored procedure or function can have any number of marker parameters, but the value returned by a function call is assigned to the first marker on the left-hand side of the = sign.

```
String procedureCall
    = "{ call some_procedure(?,?) }";            // (1) Call a stored procedure.
String functionCall = "? = { call some_function(?) }"; // (2) Call a function.
CallableStatement cStatement1 = connection.prepareCall(procedureCall); // (3)
CallableStatement cStatement2 = connection.prepareCall(functionCall);  // (4)
```

Callable statements are prepared analogous to prepared statements by calling the prepareCall() factory method of the Connection interface, as shown at (3) and (4). The marker parameters in the call must be set up in accordance with the parameters of the stored procedure or function before executing the callable statement.

Three kinds of marker parameters can be specified in a call to a stored procedure or function on the database side: IN, OUT, and INOUT parameters.

IN Parameters

These parameters pass values to the stored procedure or function. These are marker parameters whose values are initialized with the inherited set*XXX*() methods from the superinterface PreparedStatement. The IN parameters for callable statements are handled exactly as those for prepared statements—a prepared statement has only IN parameters. The parameter index starts at 1. It goes without saying that IN parameters must be initialized before the callable statement is executed.

```
cStatement1.setString(1, "Hi");              // Set value of IN parameter
                                             // at marker 1
cStatement2.setObject(2, 42, Types.INTEGER); // Set value of IN parameter
                                             // at marker 2
```

OUT Parameters

These parameters are marker parameters that hold values returned by a stored procedure or a function. Before executing callable statements with OUT parameters, the registerOutputParameter() method of the callable statement should be used to specify the expected types of the values returned in the OUT parameters.

```
cStatement1.registerOutParameter(2, Types.VARCHAR); // Register SQL VARCHAR as
                                                    // type for the
                                                    // 2nd marker parameter.
cStatement2.registerOutParameter(1, Types.INTEGER); // Register SQL INTEGER as
                                                    // type for the
                                                    // 1st marker parameter.
```

> **void registerOutParameter(int parameterIndex, int sqlType)**
>
> Registers the type of the OUT parameter at the marker parameter index to be of the specified JDBC type. The JDBC type is a constant specified by java.sql.Types—for example, Types.INTEGER and Types.VARCHAR.

Note there can be several OUT parameters, and the *first* marker parameter of a stored function call must also register the expected type of its return value.

The Callable interface inherits the execute methods of the PreparedStatement interface. The code below executes callable statements.

```
boolean result1 = cStatement1.execute();
boolean result2 = cStatement2.execute();
```

After execution, the get*XXX*() methods of the CallableStatement interface can be used to retrieve OUT parameter values of relevant types, based on the parameter index.

```
String result1 = cStatement1.getString(2);     // Retrieve value of OUT parameter
                                               // at marker 2.
```

The generic method getObject() can also be used to retrieve OUT parameter values, specifying both an index and the expected Java type of the value (see below).

```
String result2 = cStatement2.getObject(1, Integer.class);// Retrieve value of OUT
                                                        // parameter at marker 1.
```

Following are selected get methods in the CallableStatement interface to retrieve values of OUT parameters:

> **String getString(int paramIndex)**
>
> Retrieves the value of the designated marker parameter as a String.

> **int getBoolean(int paramIndex)**
>
> Retrieves the value of the designated marker parameter as a boolean.

> **int getInt(int paramIndex)**
>
> Retrieves the value of the designated marker parameter as an int.

> **double getLong(int paramIndex)**
>
> Retrieves the value of the designated marker parameter as a long.

> **double getDouble(int paramIndex)**
>
> Retrieves the value of the designated marker parameter as a double.

> **BigDecimal getBigDecimal(int paramIndex)**
>
> Retrieves the value of the designated marker parameter as a BigDecimal.

```
Date getDate(int paramIndex)
```
Retrieves the value of the designated marker parameter as a Date.

```
<T> T getObject(int paramIndex, Class<T> type)
```
Retrieves the value of the designated marker parameter as an object of the indicated Java type.

INOUT Parameters

An INOUT parameter acts as both an IN parameter to pass a value to the stored procedure or function and an OUT parameter to return a value from the stored procedure or function. Before the execution of the callable statement, its value can be initialized with a set*XXX*() method as for an IN parameter and can register the JDBC type of the return value by calling the registerOutputParameter() method as for an OUT parameter. The returned values can be retrieved using the appropriate get*XXX*() method as we have seen for OUT parameters.

Example 24.4 illustrates the basics of calling stored procedures and functions. The nitty-gritty of creating and deploying stored methods and procedures is database specific, and beyond the scope of this book.

Example 24.4 *Stored Procedures and Functions*

```java
public void storedProcedureCall(Connection connection) {
  final String callProc
    = "{call longCompositionsProc(?, ?)}";             // (1) 1: IN 2:OUT
  try (CallableStatement cStmt = connection.prepareCall(callProc)) { // (2)
    int duration = 100;                                              // (3)
    cStmt.setInt(1, duration);                                       // (4)
    cStmt.registerOutParameter(2, Types.INTEGER);                    // (5)
    cStmt.execute();                                                 // (6)
    int returnedValue = cStmt.getInt(2);                             // (7)
    System.out.println("Compositions with duration greater than "
      + duration + ": " + returnedValue);
  } catch (SQLException e) {
    e.printStackTrace();
  }
}

public void storedFunctionCall(Connection connection) {
  final String callFunc
    = "? = {call longCompositionsFunc(?)}";            // (8) 1:OUT 2:IN
  try (CallableStatement cStmt = connection.prepareCall(callFunc)) {
    cStmt.registerOutParameter(1, Types.INTEGER);                    // (9)
    int duration = 100;
    cStmt.setInt(2, duration);                                       // (10)
    cStmt.execute();
    int returnedValue = cStmt.getInt(1);                             // (11)
    System.out.println("Compositions with duration greater than "
      + duration + ": " + returnedValue);
  } catch (SQLException e) {
```

```
            e.printStackTrace();
        }
    }
```

The two methods storedProcedureCall() and storedFunctionCall(), in Example 24.4, call a stored procedure and a stored function, respectively. Both the stored procedure named longCompositionsProc and the stored function named longCompositions-Func compute the number of rows in the compositions table whose duration is greater than the duration specified in the call. We assume that the stored procedure and function are implemented and deployed on the database side. The result returned will depend on the state of the compositions table. The numbered comments below correspond to the numbered lines in Example 24.4.

(1) The stored procedure longCompositionsProc has one IN and one OUT parameter designated by the marker positions 1 and 2, respectively.

(2) The prepareCall() method prepares a callable statement for the stored procedure call.

(3) The variable duration is declared and initialized with the value 100.

(4) The IN parameter at marker 1 is initialized with the value of the variable duration (100). We are interested in finding the number of rows with duration greater than 100.

(5) The OUT parameter at marker 2 is registered to return a value of JDBC type INTEGER which will be retrieved as a value of Java type int.

(6) The execute() method executes the stored procedure call in the callable statement.

(7) After execution, the int value returned in the OUT parameter at marker 2 can be retrieved. Of course, this value depends on the state of the database.

(8) The stored function longCompositionsCall has one IN and one OUT parameter designated by the marker positions 2 and 1, respectively.

(9) Note that the OUT parameter at marker 1 is reserved for the return value from the stored function call, but its JDBC type must be registered, in this case JDBC type INTEGER.

(10) The IN parameter at marker 2 is initialized with the value 100 as the lower limit for duration.

(11) After execution, the returned value at marker 1 can be retrieved.

24.5 Processing Query Results

A *result set* represents a table of rows that is the result of executing a database query. By default, it is not updatable—that is, it cannot be modified. SELECT queries can be executed by the different types of statements that we have encountered so far to create result sets (p. 1522). It is quite obvious that basic and prepared statements can produce such results, but it is also possible to get a result set as an output value from a stored procedure or function.

The first thing to note is that a ResultSet object is AutoCloseable. Of course, it will be automatically closed and its resources released if handled in a try-with-resources statement. However, it can be prudent to call its close() method to release its resources immediately after use rather than wait for it to happen automatically. This might improve overall performance and facilitate scalability of the application.

Traversing the Result Set

Associated with a result set is a *cursor* that indicates the current row in the table of rows associated with the result set. This cursor should not be confused with a *database cursor* which represents a ResultSet object itself in database terminology. Initially the cursor is positioned just before the first row. A result set can be traversed by moving the cursor forward by one row by calling the next() method of the ResultSet interface.

- If the next() method returns true, the cursor has been moved forward and the row it points to is now the current row whose column values can be read from the result set using the get methods of the ResultSet interface (p. 1537).
- If the next() method returns false, the cursor now points past the last row and there are no more rows to traverse in the result set.

A result set can only be traversed once from the first row to the last row. The next() method can be used as the condition of a while loop to process all rows in the result set.

```
while (resultSet.next()) {
  /* Process current row. */
}
```

An if statement can be used to determine whether the result set is empty or not. For example, a SELECT statement parameterized with a primary key value would expect to return a single row. However, it is also possible that no rows are returned if the marker parameter specifies a nonexistent key value. In any case, the next() method should be invoked to check if there are any rows in the result set.

```
if (resultSet.next()) {
  /* Result set not empty. */
}
```

Result Set Navigation Methods

The following methods of the ResultSet interface can be used to navigate a result set. By default, the cursor can only be moved in the forward direction by calling the next() method. The other navigation methods (previous(), next(), first(), last(), absolute(), and relative(int row)) can only be used if scrolling is first enabled by setting the appropriate ResultSet type (Table 24.3, p. 1539).

```
boolean next()
```

Returns true if it is possible to move the cursor forward by one row from its current position; otherwise, it returns false. The return value false implies that either the cursor is after the last row or the result set is empty. Calling the next() method after it returns false will throw a SQLException.

```
boolean previous()
```

Returns true if it is possible to move the cursor to the previous row from its current position; otherwise, it returns false. The return value false implies that either the cursor is before the first row or the result set is empty. In both case, the cursor does not point to a valid row—in which case, calling a method on the ResultSet that requires a valid row will throw a SQLException.

```
boolean first()
```

Returns true if it is possible to move the cursor to the first row; otherwise, it returns false. The return value false implies that the result set is empty.

```
boolean last()
```

Returns true if it is possible to move the cursor to the last row; otherwise, it returns false. The return value false implies that the result set is empty.

```
boolean absolute(int rowNumber)
```

If the specified row number is positive, the cursor is moved to the absolute row number with respect to the beginning of the result set. Calling absolute(1) is the same as calling first().

If the given row number is negative, the cursor is moved to the absolute row number with respect to the end of the result set. Calling absolute(-1) is the same as calling last().

If the row number is zero, the cursor is moved to before the first row.

An attempt to position the cursor beyond the first or the last row in the result set leaves the cursor before the first row or after the last row, respectively.

```
boolean relative(int rows)
```

A positive/negative value in rows moves the cursor that many rows forward/ backward from the current position, respectively. Attempting to move beyond the first or the last row in the result set will set the cursor before the first row or after the last row, respectively.

Calling the method relative(1) is the same as calling the method next().

Calling the method relative(-1) is the same as calling the method previous().

Calling relative(0) is valid, but does not change the cursor position.

Optimizing the Fetch Size

To optimize the processing of rows in the result set that resulted from executing a query, only a certain number of these rows are fetched at a time from the database when they are needed by the result set. The default number to fetch, called the default *fetch size*, is set by the Statement object that created the result set.

The fetch size achieves a balance between the time it takes to fetch a row (depending on the row size), the total number of rows, and the number of round trips necessary between the database and the application to fetch all the rows.

However, we can improve the performance of processing the result set by providing a hint about the fetch size in the setFetchSize() method. Setting the fetch size only provides the JDBC driver with a hint as to the number of rows that should be fetched at a time from the database when more rows are needed by the result set. Setting the fetch size value to 0 is ignored by the JDBC driver, and it will then decide what fetch size to use. The fetch size can be set at the level of the Statement or the ResultSet.

```
PreparedStatement statement
    = connection.prepareStatement("select * from compositions");
statement.setFetchSize(20);              // Rows would be downloaded 20 at a time.
ResultSet resultSet = statement.executeQuery();
while (resultSet.next()){
  /* Rows are processed one at a time regardless of the fetch size */
  if (/* some condition */) {
    resultSet.setFetchSize(10);          // Rows would be downloaded 10 at a time.
  }
}
```

Calling the next() method will still only move the cursor to the next row, if there are still rows in the result set to traverse, regardless of the actual fetch size that is set. In other words, the program logic does not change in any way regardless of the fetch size optimization.

Extracting Column Values from the Current Row

The column values of the current row indicated by the cursor can be extracted using the get methods provided by the result set (see below).

```
String strValue1 = resultSet.getString(1);               // Using column index.
String strValue2 = resultSet.getString("column_name");   // Using column name.
```

We can also use the getObject() generic method, specifying either the column index or the column name together with the corresponding SQL type.

```
String strValue3 = resultSet.getObject(1, String.class);
String strValue4 = resultSet.getObject("column_name", String.class);
```

If the result set is not processed in a try-with-resources statement, consider closing the result set explicitly as soon as possible, after it has been processed.

```
resultSet.close();
```

Result Set Methods to Extract Column Values of the Current Row

The following get methods of the ResultSet interface can be used to extract the column values of the current row indicated by the cursor in the result set. The column index or the column label can be passed as a parameter to designate the appropriate column in the table. The CallableStatement interface provides analogous get*XXX*() methods to retrieve values of OUT parameters (p. 1530).

Selected get methods from the ResultSet interface to extract column values of the current row are shown below:

```
String getString(int columnIndex)
String getString(String columnLabel)
```
Retrieve the value of the column as a String.

```
int getBoolean(int columnIndex)
int getBoolean(String columnLabel)
```
Retrieve the value of the column as a boolean.

```
int getInt(int columnIndex)
int getInt(String columnLabel)
```
Retrieve the value of the column as an int.

```
double getLong(int columnIndex)
double getLong(String columnLabel)
```
Retrieve the value of the column as a long.

```
double getDouble(int columnIndex)
double getDouble(String columnLabel)
```
Retrieve the value of the column as a double.

```
BigDecimal getBigDecimal(int columnIndex)
BigDecimal getBigDecimal(String columnLabel)
```
Retrieve the value of the column as a BigDecimal.

```
Date getDate(int columnIndex)
Date getDate(int columnLabel)
```
Retrieve the value of the column as a Date.

```
<T> T getObject(int columnIndex, Class<T> type)
<T> T getObject(int columnLabel, Class<T> type)
```
Retrieve the value of the column as an object of the indicated Java type.

- -

Example 24.5 *Processing a* ResultSet

```
package dbDemo;
import java.sql.DriverManager;
import java.sql.SQLException;
import java.time.Duration;

import static java.lang.System.out;
```

```
public class ResultSetProcessing {
  public static void main(String[] args) {
    final String jdbcURL = "jdbc:derby:musicDB";
    final String sql = "select * from compositions where duration > ?";   // (1)
    try (var connection = DriverManager.getConnection(jdbcURL);            // (2)
         var pStatement = connection.prepareStatement(sql);) {            // (3)
      pStatement.setInt(1, 0);                                            // (4)
      var resultSet = pStatement.executeQuery();
      try (resultSet) {                                                   // (5)
        while (resultSet.next()) {                                        // (6)
          String isrc = resultSet.getString(1);                          // (7)
          String title = resultSet.getObject(2, String.class);           // (8)
          int duration = resultSet.getInt("duration");                   // (9)
          out.println("[" + isrc + ", " + title + ", " + duration + "]"); // (10)
        }
      } // Closes the result set.
    } catch (SQLException e) {                                            // (11)
      e.printStackTrace();
    } // Closes the prepared statement and the connection.
  }
}
```

Probable output from the program:

```
[ushm91736697, Vacation, 231]
[ushm91736698, Rage, 308]
[ushm91736699, Why Don't, 178]
```

Example 24.5 illustrates the main steps in the interaction between a Java application and a relational database. The example uses the musicDB database that has been used so far to illustrate salient features of programming this interaction. The numbered comments below correspond to the numbered code lines in Example 24.5.

(1) Define the SELECT statement to execute, having one marker parameter for the second operand of the boolean expression.

(2) Use the try-with-resources statement to declare the resources and to close the connection and the prepared statement afterward. Obtain the connection to the database.

(3) Create the prepared statement in the header of the try-with-resources statement.

(4) Substitute the marker parameter with a value in the SELECT statement at (1).

(5) Use the nested try-with-resources statement to close the result set after processing it. The prepared statement is executed in the header of the try-with-resources statement, returning a result set. Any exception thrown will be propagated to the catch clause at (11) of the outer try-with-resources statement.

(6) The while loop processes the rows in the result set.

(7) Extract the column values of the current row denoted by the result set cursor by calling the appropriate get methods of the result set. Extract a string (isrc) from column 1 using the getString() method.

(8) Extract a string (title) from column 2 using the getObject() method.

(9) Extract an int value (duration) by column name using the getInt() method.

(10) Print the column values of the current row.

(11) Use the catch clause of the outer try-with-resources statement to catch any SQLException.

24.6 Customizing Result Sets

It is possible to customize certain features of the result set. Such features may not necessarily be available across all databases and in some cases may result in performance degradation. In this section we discuss possible customizations and what can be achieved by them.

The following features of the result set can be customized:

- *Result set type*: This feature allows customization of the *navigational direction* of the result set traversal and the *sensitivity* of the result set to reflect changes made in the underlying data while it remains open.

- *Result set concurrency*: This feature allows customization of the *updatability* of the result set—that is, whether the ResultSet object can be updated using the ResultSet interface.

- *Result set holdability*: This feature allows customization of whether the result set is retained or closed when the current transaction is committed.

Valid values for these features are defined by static constants in the ResultSet interface, shown in Table 24.3.

Table 24.3 *Selected Constants Defined in the* ResultSet *Interface*

Result set type constants	Description
TYPE_FORWARD_ONLY	The type for a ResultSet object whose cursor may only move *forward*. This is the default ResultSet type.
TYPE_SCROLL_INSENSITIVE	The type for a ResultSet object that is *scrollable* (i.e., the cursor can move forward and backward), but generally *not sensitive* to changes made to the underlying data while the ResultSet is open.
TYPE_SCROLL_SENSITIVE	The type for a ResultSet object that is *scrollable* and generally *sensitive* to changes made to the underlying data while the ResultSet is open.

Table 24.3   *Selected Constants Defined in the* ResultSet *Interface (Continued)*

Result set concurrency constants	Description
CONCUR_READ_ONLY	The concurrency for a ResultSet object that may *not* be updated—that is, it is read-only. In other words, *updatability* of the ResultSet object is not allowed. This is the default ResultSet concurrency.
CONCUR_UPDATABLE	The concurrency for a ResultSet object that may be updated. That is, *updatability* of the ResultSet is allowed.
Result set holdability constants	**Description**
CLOSE_CURSORS_AT_COMMIT	Open ResultSet objects with this *holdability* will be *closed* when the current transaction is committed. Such a ResultSet is said *not to be holdable*.
HOLD_CURSORS_OVER_COMMIT	Open ResultSet objects with this *holdability* will remain *open* when the current transaction is committed. Such a ResultSet said to be *holdable*.

Result Set Type

The *result set type* refers to the direction of navigation in the result set and whether changes in the underlying data get reflected in an open result set.

By default, the result set type is set to ResultSet.TYPE_FORWARD_ONLY, which makes the cursor move in the forward direction only, from before the first row and successively to after the last row. This essentially means that the traversal of the rows in the result set is only possible with the next() method. This option is considered to be a safe default choice for all result sets because forward-only progression through rows does *not* require the Java application to download the whole *database cursor* (i.e., all rows that comprise the result of the query on the database). It also allows the fetch size to be customized to achieve better performance, especially in a situation where the query might result in a large number of rows.

With the option ResultSet.TYPE_FORWARD_ONLY, the result set may reflect changes in the underlying database that occur while the result set is being processed. Not all databases are capable of reflecting changes.

Two other options (ResultSet.TYPE_SCROLL_INSENSITIVE, ResultSet.TYPE_SCROLL_SENSITIVE) are also available for the result set type, both of which enable scrolling—that is, the arbitrary navigation direction in the result set using the previous(), next(), first(), last(), absolute(), and relative() methods (p. 1534). The cursor can move both forward and backward relative to the current position, or to an absolute position. In order to jump to a particular row in the result set, the entire result set may need to be downloaded first from the database, which can result in performance degradation when dealing with very large result sets returned by the query.

The options ResultSet.TYPE_SCROLL_INSENSITIVE and ResultSet.TYPE_SCROLL_SENSITIVE make the result set *insensitive* and *sensitive*, respectively, to changes made in the underlying data source while the result set is open.

The DatabaseMetaData.supportsResultSetType() method can be called to determine whether a particular result set type is actually supported by the database (p. 1543).

Result Set Concurrency

The *result set concurrency* feature enables or disables whether the result set can be updated or not—that is, it indicates the *concurrency mode* of the result set. By default, the result set concurrency is set to ResultSet.CONCUR_READ_ONLY, which means the result set cannot be updated. Alternatively, updatability can be enabled by setting the result set concurrency to be ResultSet.CONCUR_UPDATABLE. This allows the result set to be modified.

The DatabaseMetaData.supportsResultSetConcurrency() method can be called to identify valid combinations of result set type and result set concurrency supported by the current JDBC driver (p. 1543).

Result Set Holdability

The *result set holdability* refers to whether the result set may remain open or be closed when the current transaction is committed (p. 1545). The default value for the result set holdability is actually database dependent. One option is Result-Set.HOLD_CURSORS_OVER_COMMIT, which allows the result sets (cursors) to remain open when the transaction is committed.

Alternatively, holdability can be set to ResultSet.CLOSE_CURSORS_AT_COMMIT, which indicates that ResultSet objects (cursors) should be closed upon commit. Closing cursors can result in better performance for some applications.

The DatabaseMetaData.supportsResultSetHoldability() method can be called to identify the holdability supported by the current JDBC driver (p. 1543).

Please note that not all databases and JDBC drivers support these customizations. Such customizations can be specified when the statement object is created by calling the relevant factory method of the Connection interface. Analogous methods with the same result set customizations are also available for a Statement and a Callable.

The following overloaded method is defined in the Connection interface:

```
PreparedStatement prepareStatement(String sql,
                    int resultSetType, int resultSetConcurrency,
                    int resultSetHoldability)
```

Example 24.6 illustrates using different `ResultSet` options. Note that in this example, the call to the `updateRow()` method will result in the column value of the underlying row in the database to be updated with the column value of the current row in the result set which was just updated. In other words, the `updateRow()` method commits the changes to the database and thereby the result set is also closed as we have specified `ResultSet.CLOSE_CURSORS_AT_COMMIT`. However, if the automatic commit is disabled, as shown at (1), the changes in the database due to the `updateRow()` method will not be committed and the result set will not be closed until an explicit call to the `commit()` method is executed, as shown at (2) (p. 1545).

Example 24.6   *Using* `ResultSet` *Options*

```java
package dbDemo;
import java.sql.DriverManager;

import java.sql.ResultSet;
import java.sql.SQLException;
public class ResultSetCustomization {
  public static void main(String[] args) {
    final String jdbcURL = "jdbc:derby:musicDB";
    try (var connection = DriverManager.getConnection(jdbcURL);
        var statement = connection.prepareStatement(
            "select duration from compositions where title = ?",
            ResultSet.TYPE_FORWARD_ONLY,          // Forward direction. May reflect
                                                  // database changes.
            ResultSet.CONCUR_UPDATABLE,           // Result set is updatable.
            ResultSet.CLOSE_CURSORS_AT_COMMIT     // Result set is closed on commit.
        )) {
      connection.setAutoCommit(false);           // (1) Disables automatic commit.
      statement.setString(1,"Vacation");
      try (ResultSet resultSet = statement.executeQuery();) {
        if (resultSet.next()) {                   // Moves forward one row.
          resultSet.updateInt("duration", 147);   // Updates the current row
                                                  // in the result set.
          resultSet.updateRow();                  // Updates the underlying
                                                  // database.

          System.out.println("Updated");
        }
        connection.commit();                      // (2) Also closes the result set.
      }
    } catch (SQLException e) {
      e.printStackTrace();
    }
  }
}
```

Possible program output:

```
Updated
```

24.7 Discovering Database and `ResultSet` Metadata

The JDBC API allows Java programs to interact with many different types of databases. Obviously, different database providers have different capabilities and default behaviors, and may or may not support certain SQL features. It is possible to obtain such information using the `java.sql.DatabaseMetaData` object. This object is obtained from the JDBC `Connection` and can be used to investigate various capabilities and many other properties, such as support for type, concurrency, and holdability of a result set.

Following selected methods from the `DatabaseMetaData` API can be used to examine the capabilities of a database:

`String getDatabaseProductName()`
Retrieves the name of this database product.

`String getDatabaseProductVersion()`
Retrieves the version number of this database product.

`String getSQLKeywords()`
Retrieves a comma-separated list of all SQL keywords supported by this database.

`boolean supportsResultSetType(int resultSettype)`
Retrieves whether this database supports the given result set type.

`boolean supportsResultSetHoldability(int holdability)`
Retrieves whether this database supports the given result set holdability.

`boolean supportsResultSetConcurrency(int resultSettype, int concurrency)`
Retrieves whether this database supports the given combination result set type/concurrency type.

In addition to the database metadata, a `ResultSetMetaData` object can be used to discover information about the structure of a given result set.

Following selected methods from the `ResultSetMetaData` API can be used to examine the structure of the result set:

`int getColumnCount()`
Returns the number of columns in this result set.

`String getColumnName(int column)`
Returns the name of the designated columns in this result set.

`int getColumnType(int column)`
Returns the type of the designated columns in this result set. The `int` value returned corresponds to the SQL type designated by constants in `java.sql.Types`. The values 12 and 4 represent the SQL types `VARCHAR` and `INTEGER`, respectively.

Example 24.7 prints various metadata about the database and the result set.

Example 24.7   *Discovering Metadata for the Database and* ResultSet

```java
package dbDemo;
import java.sql.DatabaseMetaData;
import java.sql.DriverManager;
import java.sql.ResultSet;
import java.sql.ResultSetMetaData;
import java.sql.SQLException;

public class DBMetadata {
  public static void main(String[] args) {
    final String jdbcURL = "jdbc:derby:musicDB";
    try (var connection = DriverManager.getConnection(jdbcURL)) {

      // Print various information about the database:
      DatabaseMetaData dbMetaData
          = connection.getMetaData();                      // Obtain DatabaseMetaData.
      String dbName              = dbMetaData.getDatabaseProductName();
      String dbVersion           = dbMetaData.getDatabaseProductVersion();
      String sqlKeywords         = dbMetaData.getSQLKeywords();
      boolean forwardOnly = dbMetaData.supportsResultSetType(
        ResultSet.TYPE_FORWARD_ONLY);
      boolean cursorOpen  = dbMetaData.supportsResultSetHoldability(
        ResultSet.HOLD_CURSORS_OVER_COMMIT);
      boolean forwardUpdate = dbMetaData.supportsResultSetConcurrency(
        ResultSet.TYPE_FORWARD_ONLY,
        ResultSet.CONCUR_UPDATABLE);

      System.out.println("Various info about the database:");
      System.out.println("Database name: " + dbName);
      System.out.println("Version: " + dbVersion);
      System.out.println("SQL keywords: " + sqlKeywords);
      System.out.println("TYPE_FORWARD_ONLY: " + forwardOnly);
      System.out.println("HOLD_CURSORS_OVER_COMMIT: " + cursorOpen);
      System.out.println("TYPE_FORWARD_ONLY/CONCUR_UPDATABLE: "
          + forwardUpdate);

      // Create a ResultSet and print its structure:
      String sql = "select * from compositions where duration > ?";
      try (var pStatement = connection.prepareStatement(sql);) {
        pStatement.setInt(1, 100);
        var resultSet = pStatement.executeQuery();
        try (resultSet){
          System.out.println("Structure of ResultSet:");
          ResultSetMetaData rsMetaData
              = resultSet.getMetaData();                   // Obtain ResultSetMetadata.
          int columnCount = rsMetaData.getColumnCount();
          System.out.println("Number of columns:" + columnCount);
          for (int i = 1; i <= columnCount; i++){
            String name = rsMetaData.getColumnName(i);
            int type = rsMetaData.getColumnType(i);   // Value of Types constant.
            System.out.println(name + ": " + type);
          }
        }
      }
```

```
        } catch (SQLException e) {
          e.printStackTrace();
        }
      }
    }
```

Probable output from the program:

```
Various info about the database:
Database name: Apache Derby
Version: 10.15.2.0 - (1873585)
SQL keywords: ALIAS,BIGINT,BOOLEAN,CALL,CLASS,COPY,DB2J_DEBUG,EXECUTE,… (EDITED)
TYPE_FORWARD_ONLY: true
HOLD_CURSORS_OVER_COMMIT: true
TYPE_FORWARD_ONLY/CONCUR_UPDATABLE: true
Structure of ResultSet:
Number of columns:3
ISRC: 12
TITLE: 12
DURATION: 4
```

24.8　Implementing Transaction Control

The JDBC protocol allows the application to control *database transactions*. A *transaction* is a set of statements that is executed as a logical unit. Either all changes due to the execution of statements in the transaction are committed to the database, or none of the changes made in the transaction are committed. A *commit* results in the changes made in the transaction being made permanent in the database. A commit thereby ends a transaction. A *rollback* results in undoing all changes made in the transaction—that is, restoring the database state to what it was before the transaction commenced. A *savepoint* defines a logical rollback point *within* a transaction. A *rollback* can be used to undo all changes made since a savepoint was set up in the transaction—that is, restoring the database state to what it was before the savepoint was set up.

By default, JDBC connections are in *auto-commit mode*, which means that commit occurs automatically when the statement processing completes successfully. To change this behavior, the following method call can be used:

```
connection.setAutoCommit(false);
```

Once auto-commit is turned off, transactions can be controlled using the rollback() and commit() methods of the Connection interface. Each transaction can include any number of insert, update, and delete actions and must end in either a commit that would make all pending transaction changes permanent, or a rollback if the pending transaction changes should be discarded. Some databases also support savepoints, which provides an ability to partially roll back a transaction, discarding only those pending changes that occurred in the transaction after the savepoint was set up. Whether a given database supports savepoints can be determined by calling the DatabaseMetaData.supportsSavepoints() method. It is important to remember that normal closing of a connection implicitly causes the transaction to commit. However, the transaction will be rolled back if the program terminates with an uncaught exception.

If an exception is intercepted, the Java runtime considers this exception to be successfully handled and therefore resumes normal execution after the catch block. It is worth reciting the mantra that the JDBC interfaces, including the Connection interface, implement AutoCloseable, which means that all statements and connections are closed implicitly following the execution of the try-with-resources statement. This implies that if the transaction was not explicitly rolled back inside the exception handler, then by default, the transaction will be committed.

Following selected methods of the java.sql.Connection interface can be used to control transactions:

```
void setAutoCommit(boolean autoCommit)
```

Enables or disables *auto-commit mode* of this connection. The value true enables auto-commit mode and false disables it.

```
Savepoint setSavepoint()
Savepoint setSavepoint(String name)
```

Create an unnamed or a named savepoint in the current transaction and returns the new Savepoint object that represents it, respectively.

```
void rollback()
void rollback(Savepoint savepoint)
```

Undo all changes made in the current transaction or all changes made since the named savepoint was set up in the current transaction, respectively.

```
void commit()
```

Makes all changes made since the previous commit/rollback permanent.

Example 24.8 *Controlling Transactions*

```java
package dbDemo;
import java.sql.DriverManager;
import java.sql.SQLException;
import java.sql.Savepoint;

public class Transactions {
  public static void main(String[] args) {
    final String jdbcURL = "jdbc:derby:musicDB";
    try (var connection = DriverManager.getConnection(jdbcURL)) {

      // SQL statements:
      final String insSql = "insert into compositions VALUES(?, ?, ?)";
      final String updSql = "update compositions set title = ? where title = ?";
      final String delSql = "delete from compositions where duration = ?";
```

```
                    // Create statements:
                    try (var insStatement = connection.prepareStatement(insSql);
                         var updStatement = connection.prepareStatement(updSql);
                         var delStatement = connection.prepareStatement(delSql);) {

                      connection.setAutoCommit(false);         // (1) Auto-commit disabled.
                      insStatement.setInt(3, 150);             // (2) Insert a new row.
                      insStatement.setString(2, "Java Jazz");
                      insStatement.setString(1, "ushm91736991");
                      int insResult = insStatement.executeUpdate();
                      System.out.println("INSERT: " + insResult);

                      updStatement.setString(1, "Java Jive");  // (3) Update an existing row.
                      updStatement.setString(2, "Rage");
                      int updResult = updStatement.executeUpdate();
                      System.out.println("UPDATE: " + updResult);

                      Savepoint savePoint = connection.setSavepoint(); // (4) Set a savepoint.
                      delStatement.setInt(1, 178);             // (5) Delete a row.
                      int delResult = delStatement.executeUpdate();
                      System.out.println("DELETE: " + delResult);

                      connection.rollback(savePoint);   // (6) Roll back to safepoint.
                      connection.commit();              // (7) Commits only (2) and (3).
                    } catch (SQLException e) {
                      connection.rollback();            // (8) Roll back any changes.
                    }
                  } catch (SQLException e) {
                    e.printStackTrace();
                  }
                }
              }
```

Output from the program:

```
INSERT: 1
UPDATE: 1
DELETE: 1
```

Example 24.8 illustrates how transactions can be controlled with commit and roll-back operations. The numbered comments below correspond to the numbered code lines in Example 24.8.

The following rows are in the compositions table at the start.

```
[ushm91736697, Vacation, 231]
[ushm91736698, Rage, 308]
[ushm91736699, Why Don't, 178]
```

(1) Auto-commit is disabled. A new transaction starts.

(2) A new row is inserted:

```
[ushm91736991, Java Jazz, 150}
```

(3) The title "Rage" of an existing row:

```
[ushm91736698, Rage, 308]
```

is updated to "Java Jive":

```
[ushm91736698, Java Jive, 308]
```

(4) A savepoint is set.

(5) The row with the duration 178 is deleted:

```
[ushm91736699, Why Don't, 178]
```

(6) A rollback is performed, rolling back the deletion of the row at (5) that was performed since the last savepoint was set up at (4).

(7) A commit is performed, committing the insertion at (2) and the update at (3), leaving the database in the following state and ending the transaction that started at (1):

```
[ushm91736697, Vacation, 231]
[ushm91736698, Java Jive, 308]
[ushm91736699, Why Don't, 178]
[ushm91736991, Java Jazz, 150]
```

(8) In case a SQLException is thrown in the inner try-with-resources statement, all changes are rolled back.

 Review Questions

24.1 Which of the following statements is true about the JDBC ResultSet?
Select the one correct answer.

(a) The method next() throws an exception when no rows were returned by the query.

(b) The method next() throws an exception when it is invoked more times than the number of rows in the result set.

(c) The method absolute(1) navigates to the first row of the result set, if there are rows in the result set.

(d) The method absolute(0) navigates to the first row of the result set, if there are rows in the result set.

24.2 What is the correct order in which the following JDBC resources are closed?
Select the one correct answer.

(a) Connection, Statement, ResultSet

(b) Statement, ResultSet, Connection

(c) ResultSet, Statement, Connection

(d) Closure order is irrelevant.

(e) Closure order is irrelevant when auto-commit mode is enabled.

24.3 Assume that a database has the following questions table with the specified columns and rows of data:

id	question	answer
(INTEGER, PRIMARY KEY)	(VARCHAR, NOT NULL)	(VARCHAR)
101	What was Deep Thought's answer?	42
103	Where is Wally?	
102	Is Waldo older than Wally?	He is younger.
106	Which one is Wally?	He is the one in a bobble hat.
107	Where am I?	Right here.

What will be the result of executing the following code (assuming that jdbcUrl, username, and password are correctly initialized)?

```
String findAnswers = "select * from questions where question like ?";
try (Connection c = DriverManager.getConnection(jdbcUrl, username, password);
    PreparedStatement ps = c.prepareStatement(findAnswers)) {
  ps.setString(1, "Where%");
  try (ResultSet rs = ps.executeQuery()) {
    while (rs.next()) {
      String question = rs.getObject(2, String.class);   // (1)
      String answer = rs.getObject(3, String.class);      // (2)
      answer = (answer == null) ? "No answer." : answer;  // (3)
      System.out.println(question + " - " + answer);
    }
  }
} catch (SQLException e) { e.printStackTrace(); }
```

Select the one correct answer.

(a) The program will print one line.
(b) The program will print two lines.
(c) The program will throw an exception at (1).
(d) The program will throw an exception at (2).
(e) The program will throw an exception at (3).

24.4 Assume that a database has the following questions table with the specified columns and rows of data:

id	question	answer
(INTEGER, PRIMARY KEY)	(VARCHAR, NOT NULL)	(VARCHAR)
101	What was Deep Thought's answer?	42
102	Where is Wally?	

What will be the result of executing the following code (assuming that `jdbcUrl`, username, and password are correctly initialized)?

```
String findQuestion = "select * from questions where id = ?";
int id = 103;
try (Connection c = DriverManager.getConnection(jdbcUrl, username, password);
     PreparedStatement ps = c.prepareStatement(findQuestion)) {
  ps.setInt(1, id);                                     // (1)
  try (ResultSet rs = ps.executeQuery()) {
    if (rs.next()) {                                    // (2)
      String question = rs.getObject(2, String.class);
      System.out.println(question);
    }
  }
} catch (SQLException e) { e.printStackTrace(); }
```

Select the one correct answer.

(a) The program will print one line.
(b) The program will print nothing.
(c) The program will throw an exception at (1).
(d) The program will throw an exception at (2).

24.5 Assume that a database has the following questions table with the specified columns and rows of data:

id	question	answer
(INTEGER, PRIMARY KEY)	(VARCHAR, NOT NULL)	(VARCHAR)
101	What was Deep Thought's answer?	42
102	Where is Wally?	

Which of the following statements is true about executing the following code (assuming that `jdbcUrl`, username, and password are correctly initialized)?

```
String findQuestion = "select question from questions where id = ?";
String provideAnswer = "update questions set answer = ? where id = ?";
int id = 102;
try (Connection c = DriverManager.getConnection(jdbcUrl, username, password);
     PreparedStatement ps1 = c.prepareStatement(findQuestion);
     PreparedStatement ps2 = c.prepareStatement(provideAnswer)) {
  c.setAutoCommit(false);
  ps2.setString(1, "Look and you will find!");
  ps2.setInt(2, id);
  ps2.executeUpdate();
  ps1.setInt(2, id);
  try (ResultSet rs = ps1.executeQuery()) {
    while (rs.next()) {
      String question = rs.getString(1);
      String answer = rs.getString(2);
      System.out.println(question + " - " + answer);
    }
  }
}
```

```
        c.commit();
    } catch (SQLException e) {
        e.printStackTrace();
    }
```

Select the one correct answer.

(a) The program updates one row, executes the query, and commits the transaction.

(b) The program updates one row, throws a SQLException, and commits the transaction.

(c) The program updates one row, throws a SQLException, and rolls back the transaction.

(d) The program throws a SQLException, executes the query, and commits the transaction.

(e) The program throws a SQLException, executes the query, and rolls back the transaction.

24.6 Which of the following statements is true about the following code (assuming that jdbcUrl, username, password, and sqlQuery are correctly initialized)?

```
try (Connection connection
        = DriverManager.getConnection(jdbcUrl, username, password);
    Statement statement = connection.createStatement();
    ResultSet resultSet = statement.executeQuery(sqlQuery)) {
  while (resultSet.next()) {
    /* Do nothing. */
  }
} catch (SQLException e) {
    e.printStackTrace();
}
```

Select the one correct answer.

(a) The program will attempt to close the connection, statement, and result set objects, in that exact order.

(b) The program will attempt to close the result set, statement, and connection objects, in that exact order.

(c) The program will attempt to close the statement, result set, and connection objects, in that exact order.

(d) The program will attempt to close the statement, connection, and result set objects, in that exact order.

(e) The program will attempt to close the connection, statement, and result set objects, in an undetermined order.

24.7 Which of the following statements is true?
Select the one correct answer.

(a) The method executeQuery() of the PreparedStatement interface accepts marker parameter values.

(b) Each PreparedStatement object represents a single SQL statement.

(c) Each PreparedStatement object represents one or more SQL statements.

(d) Setting new values for marker parameters in a PreparedStatement object will produce a new SQL statement.

24.8   Given the following code:

```
String findQuestion
    = "select question, answer from questions where answer is null";
String jdbcUrl = "jdbc:thin:oracle:@localhost:1521:qa";
String username = "joe";
String password = "welcome1";
try (Connection c = DriverManager.getConnection(jdbcUrl, username, password);
        PreparedStatement ps = c.prepareStatement(findQuestion,
            ResultSet.TYPE_FORWARD_ONLY,
            ResultSet.CONCUR_UPDATABLE,
            ResultSet.CLOSE_CURSORS_AT_COMMIT)) {
    c.setAutoCommit(false);
    try (ResultSet rs = ps.executeQuery()) {
      while (rs.next()) {
        rs.updateString("answer", "no answer");
        rs.updateRow();
      }
    }
    c.commit();
} catch (SQLException e) {
    e.printStackTrace();
}
```

Which of the following statements are true about this code (assuming the database supports all designated ResultSet features)?
Select the two correct answers.

(a) It selects all rows from the questions table that have no value set for the answer column.

(b) It updates all rows in the questions table that have no value set for the answer column.

(c) It sets the "no answer" value for the answer column in all rows in the questions table.

(d) It will roll back changes if an exception is thrown inside the while loop.

24.9   Given the following code:

```
String jdbcUrl = "jdbc:thin:oracle:@localhost:1521:qa";
String username = "joe";
String password = "welcome1";
try (Connection c = DriverManager.getConnection(jdbcUrl, username, password);
        var ps = c.prepareStatement(
                    "update questions set answer = ? where question = ?")) {
    ps.setString(2, "What?");                      // (1)
    try (ResultSet rs = ps.executeQuery()) {  // (2)
      while (rs.next()) {                           // (3)
        rs.setString(1, "42");                      // (4)
      }
    }
} catch (SQLException e) {
    e.printStackTrace();
}
```

Which of the following statements is true about this program?
Select the one correct answer.

(a) It updates rows in the questions table, setting the answer column value to "42".
(b) It throws an exception at (1).
(c) It throws an exception at (2).
(d) It throws an exception at (3).
(e) It throws an exception at (4).

24.10 Given the following code:

```
String jdbcUrl = "jdbc:thin:oracle:@localhost:1521:qa";
String username = "joe";
String password = "welcome1";
try (Connection c = DriverManager.getConnection(jdbcUrl, username, password);
    PreparedStatement ps = c.prepareStatement(
        "update questions set answer = ? where question = ?")) {
    ps.setString(2,"What?");          // (1)
    ps.setString(1,"42");             // (2)
    ps.execute();                     // (3)
} catch (SQLException e) {
    e.printStackTrace();
}
```

Which of the following statements is true about this program?
Select the one correct answer.

(a) It updates rows in the questions table, setting the answer column value to "42".
(b) It throws an exception at (1).
(c) It throws an exception at (2).
(d) It throws an exception at (3).

24.11 Which of the following statements are true?
Select the three correct answers.

(a) A given PreparedStatement can only be executed once.
(b) A given PreparedStatement can be executed multiple times.
(c) A given PreparedStatement can be executed using both execute() and execute-Query() methods.
(d) A given PreparedStatement can be executed using both execute() and execute-Update() methods.
(e) A given PreparedStatement can be executed using both executeUpdate() and executeQuery() methods.

24.12 Which of the following statements is true?
Select the one correct answer.

(a) All databases support forward-only type of result sets.
(b) Forward-only result sets automatically reflect database changes in an open result set.
(c) By default, result set objects are scroll sensitive.
(d) Result sets are always closed at commit.

24.13   Which of the following statements is true about `ResultSet` methods?
Select the one correct answer.

(a) Calling the method `relative(1)` is equivalent to calling the method `next()`.

(b) Calling the method `relative(1)` is equivalent to calling the method `absolute(0)`.

(c) Calling the method `relative(0)` is equivalent to calling the method `previous()`.

(d) Calling the method `relative(-1)` is equivalent to calling the method `absolute(-1)`.

Annotations 25

 Chapter Topics

- Understanding the role of annotations to specify metadata in the source code

- Declaring annotation types: marker annotation type, single-element annotation type, and multi-element annotation type

- Understanding the implications of declaring a value() element and default values in annotation types

- Applying annotations as instantiations of annotation type declarations with notations for normal, marker, and single-element annotations

- Understanding how the value() element and default values in an annotation type declaration influence its application in the source code

- Applying predefined meta-annotations in annotation type declarations to specify the retention (@Retention), the target (@Target), the inheritance (@Inherited), the documentation (@Documented), and the repeatability (@Repeatable) of an annotation type declaration

- Writing code to demonstrate use of standard predefined annotations to validate overriding (@Override) and functional interfaces (@FunctionalInterface), annotate deprecated code (@Deprecated), and suppress warnings (@SuppressWarnings, @SafeVarargs)

- Writing code to use the Reflection API to process annotations in a program at runtime

Java SE 17 Developer Supplementary Topic	
[12.2] Use Annotations such as Override, FunctionalInterface, Deprecated, SuppressWarnings, and SafeVarargs. ○ Note that this is a supplementary objective in the description of the Java SE 17 Developer exam.	§25.5, p. 1577

Java SE 11 Developer Exam Objectives	
[13.1] Create, apply, and process annotations	§25.1, p. 1557 to §25.6, p. 1587

Annotations allow information in the form of metadata to be added to the source code. Annotations provide information about the program, but are not considered to be a part of the program. Syntactically, annotations are a special kind of interfaces that are attached to various program elements in the source code, such as classes, variables, and methods. Tools can then process these annotations at the source level or process the class files into which they are compiled. Without such processing, the annotations do not actually do anything. The benefit of using annotations is only realized when appropriate tools are used to process them and analyze the metadata they represent. There are some existing annotations that are processed by the Java compiler, and even more annotation support is provided by various frameworks like Java EE/Jakarta and the Spring Framework.

It is important to note that annotations are optional and do not change the logic of the program. Augmenting the source code with annotations does not change the bytecode generated for the program. Thus the presence of annotations has no effect on the execution of the program by the JVM, only that they may be present in the class file.

This chapter covers declaring annotation types and applying annotations and utilizing the predefined annotations provided by the Java SE platform. It also provides a taste of processing annotations using the Reflection API.

25.1 Basics of Annotations

Support for annotations is provided by the Annotation API, which is located in the `java.lang.annotation` package. The contents of this package are used to declare annotation types—as we shall see in this chapter.

As subpackages are not automatically imported, the types in the subpackage `java.lang.annotation` of the `java.lang` package must be explicitly imported in order to access them by their simple names—for example, by including a type-import-on-demand statement:

```
import java.lang.annotation.*;
```

Annotations are types that are a special kind of interfaces, analogous to enum types that are a special kind of class. An annotation must be declared before it can be used: An *annotation type declaration* must be defined, and when *applied* to a program element, an *annotation* designates a specific invocation of an annotation type. The `java.lang.annotation.Annotation` interface is a common interface implicitly extend by all annotation types, analogous to all classes implicitly extending the `Object` class. However, an annotation type declaration cannot explicitly extend the `Annotation` interface. Typically, an annotation type is declared as a top-level type, but can be nested like static member types. An annotation type declaration is compiled as any other Java type declaration, resulting in a class file containing its bytecode.

```
// Annotation type declaration with the name Tag.
@interface Tag {}                    // Declaration always specified with
                                     // at-sign (@) preceding the keyword interface.
```

```
// Applying annotation @Tag which denotes the annotation type declaration Tag.
@Tag class Gizmo {                   // Always applied with at-sign (@) preceding
                                     // the annotation type name.
  @Tag void start() {}               // Another invocation of the annotation type Tag.
}
```

The code above shows the minimalistic declaration of an annotation type named
Tag and its application to a class named Gizmo. What is important to note is that an
annotation type declaration is specified with the at-sign (@) preceding the keyword
interface, and when applied to a program element, the at-sign (@) precedes the
annotation type name, and each application of the annotation to any program element denotes a different invocation of the annotation type. The rest of this chapter
will elaborate on defining annotation type declarations and applying annotations
to various program elements in the source code. The last section provides an introduction to *annotation processing*.

25.2 Declaring Annotation Types

An *annotation type declaration* specifies a new *annotation type*, and has a lot in common with an interface type. General syntax of an annotation type declaration is
shown below.

```
meta-annotations access_modifier @interface annotation_name // Annot type header
{ // Annotation type body with zero or more member declarations:

  annotation_type_element_declarations

  constant_variable_declarations

  enum_declarations
  class_declarations
  interface_declarations
}
```

We will use the annotation type declaration TaskInfo below to explain the syntax of
an annotation type declaration. The TaskInfo annotation type allows meta-infor-
mation to be specified about tasks on program elements: a description of the task,
people the task is assigned to, and the priority given to the task. The TaskInfo annotation type is meant to illustrate declaring annotation types, and is in no way
meant to replace task management tools.

```
import java.lang.annotation.Target;                      // (1)
import java.lang.annotation.ElementType;                 // (2)
import java.lang.annotation.Retention;                   // (3)
import java.lang.annotation.RetentionPolicy;             // (4)

@Target({ElementType.TYPE, ElementType.METHOD})          // (5) Meta-annotation
@Retention(RetentionPolicy.RUNTIME)                      // (6) Meta-annotation
```

```
public @interface TaskInfo {                        // (7)
    String taskDesc();                              // (8) Annotation type element
    String[] assignedTo();                          // (9) Annotation type element
    TaskPriority priority() default TaskPriority.NORMAL; // (10) Annot type element

    public enum TaskPriority { LOW, NORMAL, HIGH };    // (11) Nested enum type

    public static final String LOG_FILE = "./logs/Tasks.log"; // (12) const decl.
}
```

The *meta-annotations* specified in the annotation type header are annotations that are applied to the annotation type declaration to specify certain aspects of the declaration—that is, they allow metadata to be associated with the annotation type declaration (p. 1567). In the code above, these meta-annotations are defined by classes in the java.lang.annotation package, which are imported at (1) and (3), together with auxiliary enum types at (2) and (4). The meta-annotation @Target at (5) specifies which program elements the annotation type can be applied to. The targets specified for the TaskInfo annotation type are any type declaration (ElementType.TYPE) and methods (ElementType.METHOD). The @Retention meta-annotation specifies the retention policy: whether invocations of the annotation should be retained with the program element in the source file or in the class file, or made available at runtime. Applications of the TaskInfo annotation type on program elements will be available at runtime (RetentionPolicy.RUNTIME).

The *access modifier* that can be specified in the annotation type header is public, or there is no access modifier to indicate package accessibility—the same as with a normal interface. The TaskInfo annotation type is declared public.

Like any normal interface, an annotation type declaration is implicitly abstract, but seldom explicitly specified as such. Note also that an annotation type declaration cannot be generic and the extends clause is not permitted—in contrast to a normal interface.

The *simple name* of an annotation type shares the same namespace as simple names of normal classes and interfaces in a package—that is, a simple name of an annotation type should not conflict with any type declaration having the same simple name in the package.

The *annotation type body* can contain zero or more *member declarations*. These member declarations are analogous to the member declarations in a normal interface when it comes to constant variable declarations (which are implicitly public, static, and final) and nested type member declarations—but default, static, and private methods are not permitted. For example, the TaskInfo type annotation declaration declares a nested enum type named TaskPriority at (11) and a constant variable named LOG_FILE at (12).

In the rest of this section, we take a closer look at declaration of annotation type elements in the body of an annotation type, declared at (8), (9), and (10), as values provided for these annotation type elements when an annotation is applied to a program element determine the metadata that is associated with the program element.

Declaring Annotation Type Elements

The body of an *annotation type declaration* may contain declarations of *annotation type elements*. The syntax of an annotation type element declaration is shown below.

```
element_modifiers element_type method_name() default constant_expression;
```

A partial declaration of the TaskInfo annotation type is repeated below, showing the declaration of the three annotation type elements at (8), (9), and (10).

```
// ...
public @interface TaskInfo {                  // (7)
  String taskDesc();                          // (8) Required annotation element
  String[] assignedTo();                      // (9) Required annotation element
  TaskPriority priority() default TaskPriority.NORMAL;  // (10) Optional
                                              //          annotation element
  // ...
}
```

Each annotation type element specifies a *method declaration*, resembling the abstract method declaration in a normal interface. Each annotation type element is usually referred to as an *element* of the annotation type. The elements declared in an annotation type declaration constitute the *attributes* of the annotation type.

The *method declaration* in an element has a *return type* and a *method name*, and is *always* specified with an *empty formal parameter list*, as exemplified by the method declarations in the elements at (8), (9), and (10) in the TaskInfo annotation type declaration. Note that no formal parameters, type parameters, or a throws clause can be specified for a method declaration in an element. The name and the return type of the method declared in an element are referred to as *the name and the type of the element*, respectively. Only specific types can be declared as the type of an element (p. 1561).

Annotation types are characterized by the number of elements declared in their declaration.

- A *marker annotation type* is an annotation type with no elements, analogous to a marker interface. A marker annotation is typically used to indicate a specific purpose that does not require any elements. Earlier in this chapter we have seen the annotation type Tag, which is a marker annotation type. The notation for applying such an annotation type to program elements is straightforward: an at-sign (@) preceding the annotation name (p. 1565)—for example, @Tag. Ample examples of marker annotation types can be found throughout this chapter.

  ```
  @interface Tag {}                 // No element type declarations.
  ```

- A *single-element annotation type*, as the name suggests, is an annotation type with a single element. By convention, the method of a single-element annotation type is declared as value(). Various shorthand notations are offered when applying such annotation types to program elements (p. 1565).

```
@interface SecurityLevel {          // Single-element type declaration
  int value();
}
```

- *A multi-element annotation type*, as the name suggests, is an annotation type with more than one element. The TaskInfo annotation type is a multi-element annotation type, as it declares three elements. At the most, one method of an element in a multi-element annotation type can be declared as value(). Under certain conditions, a shorthand notation can be used when applying an annotation type declaration that has a value() element (p. 1563).

Element Modifiers for Annotation Type Elements

The modifiers allowed for an annotation type element are analogous to the modifiers that can be specified for an abstract method declaration in a normal interface. The only *access modifier* that can be specified for an annotation type element is public; otherwise, the accessibility is implicitly public. The modifier abstract is also implied, and typically not specified in the annotation type element declaration. The elements of the TaskInfo annotation type are implicitly public and abstract.

Element Type of Annotation Type Elements

The *element type* of an annotation type element can be any one of the following:

- A primitive type
- A String
- The class Class
- An enum type
- An annotation type
- A one-dimensional array whose element type is one of the above types

The code below illustrates declaring the element type of an annotation type element. An example of each type that is allowed as the return type of an annotation type element is shown, together with the specification of a default value for each annotation type element.

```
public @interface MultiElementAnnotationType {

  public enum Priority { LOW, NORMAL, HIGH };

  public int certificationLevel()    default 1;                      // int
  String date()                      default "2021-01-11";          // String
  Class<? extends PrettyPrinter> pp()
                          default AdvancedPrettyPrinter.class;       // type Class
  Priority priorityLevel()           default Priority.NORMAL;       // enum Priority
  Tag annotate()                     default @Tag;                   // Annotation type
  int[] value()                      default {10, 20, 30};          // Array, int[]
}
```

```
// Auxiliary classes:
class PrettyPrinter {}
class AdvancedPrettyPrinter extends PrettyPrinter {}
```

The declaration of the `ProblematicAnnotationType` annotation type below shows examples of illegal declarations of annotation type elements.

```
@interface ProblematicAnnotationType {
    StringBuilder message();             // Illegal return type.
    int[][] voting();                    // Only one-dimensional array allowed.
    String value;                        // Missing parentheses.
    private Thread.State state();         // Only public can be specified.
}
```

The code below shows an annotation which is used as an element type within another annotation. This relationship between annotations is sometimes described as a *contained annotation type* (1) and a *containing annotation type* (2). This relationship is further explored when we discuss repeatable annotations (p. 1575).

```
public @interface MusicMeta {           // (1) Contained annotation type
    String value();
}

public @interface ArtistMeta {          // (2) Containing annotation type
    MusicMeta value();                   // Annotation type from (1).
}
```

Defaults for Annotation Type Elements

An annotation type element declaration can declare a *default value* for an element using the optional `default` clause in the annotation type element declaration, as shown in the declaration of the `MultiElementAnnotationType` earlier. The default value is specified in the default clause as a *constant expression*—that is, the operands of the expression are all constants so that the compiler is able to determine its value at compile time. The constant expression must not be `null`. The declaration of the `Refactor` annotation type below shows examples of illegal default values.

```
@interface Refactor {
    int id()          default (int) (Math.random() * 10);// Not a const expression.
    String value()    default null;                      // Cannot be null.
    String deadline() default new String("2021-01-11");  // Not a const expression.
    String[] team()   default new String[] {"VJ", "PT"}; // Not a const expression.
}
```

An element that specifies a default value is called an *optional annotation element*. An element that does *not* specify a default clause is called a *required annotation element*. As we shall see when an annotation is applied to a program element, specifying a value for an optional annotation element can be omitted, in which case the default value in the declaration of the annotation type element is used. For a required annotation element, a value for the element *must* be specified when the annotation is applied to a program element. We see that the declaration of the `TaskInfo` annotation type below has two required annotation elements, at (8) and at (9), and one optional annotation element at (10).

```
    // ...
    public @interface TaskInfo {                    // (7)
      String taskDesc();                            // (8) Required annotation element
      String[] assignedTo();                        // (9) Required annotation element
      TaskPriority priority() default TaskPriority.NORMAL; // (10) Optional
                                                    //     annotation element
    // ...
    }
```

25.3 Applying Annotations

Once an annotation type has been compiled, it can be applied to program elements. An annotation is an application of an annotation type to a program element, and we refer to the annotation as being of that type. Which program elements an annotation can be applied to is typically determined by the meta-annotation @Target specified in the declaration of the annotation type (p. 1569). Each annotation refers to a specific invocation of an annotation type. An annotation is always specified with the at-sign (@) preceding the name of the annotation type, and usually provides values for the elements of the annotation type.

Multiple annotations of different types can be applied to a program element. Repeatable annotations are covered later (p. 1575).

Annotations can be characterized according to the *notation* that can be used when applied to a program element. We distinguish between three kinds of annotations:

- *Normal annotations*
- *Marker annotations*
- *Single-element annotations*

The last two annotations are special cases of normal annotations. Choosing which annotation to use depends on knowing what annotation type elements are declared in an annotation type declaration. The different kinds of annotations are discussed in this section.

Applying Normal Annotations

When a *normal annotation* is applied to a program element, in addition to the name of the annotation type being preceded by the at-sign (@), it can optionally specify a comma-separated list of element-value pairs enclosed in parentheses, (). Each pair has the syntax *element = value*. For each pair, the *element* and the *value* must be compatible with the method name and the return type of a method specified in an annotation type element.

The normal annotation for the annotation type TaskInfo (p. 1558) is applied to a class below, where each element-value pair associates a value with an element of the annotation type TaskInfo.

```
@TaskInfo(                                                      // Normal annotation
    taskDesc = "Class for monitoring nuclear reactor activity",      // Required
    assignedTo = {"Tom", "Dick", "Harriet"},                         // Required
    priority = TaskInfo.TaskPriority.HIGH                            // Optional
    )
class NuclearPlant {}
```

A normal annotation must contain element-value pairs for all required annotation elements in the annotation type—that is, for elements that do not specify a default value. Specifying the element-value pairs for optional annotation elements is obviously optional.

The order of the element-value pairs is irrelevant, but usually they are specified in the same order that the elements have in the annotation type declaration. Note also that a null value in an element-value pair will result in a compile-time error.

In the normal annotation below, the optional annotation element priority in the annotation type TaskInfo is omitted.

```
@TaskInfo(                                                              // Normal
annotation
    taskDesc = "Class for monitoring nuclear reactor activity",      // Required
    assignedTo = {"Tom", "Dick", "Harriet"}                          // Required
    )
class NuclearPlant {}
```

The above normal annotation is then equivalent to the normal annotation below, where the default value TaskInfo.TaskPriority.NORMAL of the optional annotation element priority is implied.

```
@TaskInfo(                                                              // Normal
annotation
    taskDesc = "Class for monitoring nuclear reactor activity",      // Required
    assignedTo = {"Tom", "Dick", "Harriet"},                         // Required
    priority = TaskInfo.TaskPriority.NORMAL                          // Implied
    )
class NuclearPlant {}
```

An *array element initializer*, $\{v_1, \ldots, v_n\}$, can be used to specify the values of array elements for annotation elements whose type is an array type. The curly brackets can be omitted when specifying the value for a *single-element array-valued element-value pair*—that is, where the type of the annotation type element is an array type, but only a single array element is specified in the annotation.

```
@TaskInfo(
    priority = TaskInfo.TaskPriority.LOW,
    taskDesc = "Start nuclear reactor",
    assignedTo = "Harriet"                     // Single-element array-valued element
    )
class NuclearPlant {}
```

Applying Marker Annotations

A *marker annotation* is a shorthand notation typically for use with marker annotation types, which have no elements in their type declaration.

```
// Marker annotation type
@interface Tag {}                              // No element type declarations
```

The marker annotation of annotation type Tag is applied to a class as shown below, with just the name of the annotation type preceded by the at-sign (@)—that is, the parentheses are omitted.

```
@Tag class Gizmo {}                            // Marker annotation
```

The normal annotation of annotation type Tag is applied to a class, where the empty list of element-value pairs is explicitly specified:

```
@Tag() class Gizmo {}                          // Normal annotation
```

A marker annotation can also be used if all elements are optional annotation elements in the annotation type declaration—that is, they specify default values.

```
// Annotation type declaration where all elements have default values.
@interface Option {
  Color color()  default Color.WHITE;  // Optional annotation element
  Size size()    default Size.M;       // Optional annotation element
  enum Color {RED, WHITE, BLUE}
  enum Size  {S, M, L, XL}
}
```

A marker annotation of annotation type Option is applied to the class below:

```
@Option                                        // Marker annotation
class Item {}
```

The above marker annotation is equivalent to the following normal annotation:

```
@Option(color = Option.Color.WHITE, size = Option.Size.M)  // Normal annotation
class Item {}
```

Applying Single-Element Annotations

A *single-element annotation* is a shorthand notation typically for use with single-element annotation types, whose only annotation type element is declared as a value() element. Single-element annotation will not work if the element in the single-element annotation type is not declared as a value() element. However, there is no requirement that the single element should be either required or optional. Note that there is no restriction on declaring a value() element for any annotation type, but that alone does not guarantee that single-element annotation can be used.

```
// Single-element annotation type
@interface Author {
  String value();                              // Single annotation type element
}
```

A single-element annotation of annotation type Author is applied to the class below, where only the value of the single value() element is specified:

```
@Author("Tom")                              // Single-element annotation
class Connection {}
```

The above single-element annotation is equivalent to the following normal annotation:

```
@Author(value = "Tom")                      // Normal annotation
class Connection {}
```

Single-element annotation can also be used if one element is declared as a value() element and *all other elements are optional annotation elements* in the annotation type declaration—that is, they specify default values.

```
//Annotation type declaration with a value() element and other elements with
default values.
@interface ExtraOption {
  int value();                          // Required annotation element
  Color color()  default Color.WHITE;   // Optional annotation element
  Size size()    default Size.M;        // Optional annotation element
  enum Color {RED, WHITE, BLUE}
  enum Size  {S, M, L, XL}
}
```

A single-element annotation of annotation type ExtraOption is applied to the class below:

```
@ExtraOption(10)                            // Single-element annotation
class ItemV2 {}
```

The above single-element annotation is equivalent to the following normal annotation:

```
@ExtraOption(value=10, color=ExtraOption.Color.WHITE,    // Normal annotation
            size=ExtraOption.Size.M)
class ItemV3 {}
```

Following is an example of using *array-valued single-element annotation*—that is, where the element type of the single annotation type element is an array type:

```
// Array-valued single-element annotation type declaration:
@interface Problems {
  String[] value();                          // Array-type value() element
}

@Problems({"Code smell", "Exception not caught"})  // Array-valued single-element
class ItemV4 {}                                    // annotation

@Problems(value = {"Code smell", "Exception not caught"})  // Normal annotation
class ItemV5 {}
```

Using a *single-element array-valued single-element annotation*—that is, where the element type of the single value() element is an array type, but only a single array element is specified in the annotation—is shown below.

```
@Problems("Code smell")   // Single-element array-valued single-element annotation
class ItemV6 {}

@Problems({"Code smell"}) // Single-element array-valued single-element annotation
class ItemV7 {}

@Problems(value = "Code smell")     // Normal annotation
class ItemV8 {}

@Problems(value = {"Code smell"})    // Normal annotation
class ItemV9 {}
```

25.4 Meta-Annotations

Meta-annotations are annotations that can be applied on an annotation type declaration to specify various aspects of the annotation when this annotation type is
applied in the source code. We discuss the purpose and usage of predefined meta-
annotations when declaring an annotation type, as they have implications on how
the annotation will be handled when applied in the source code.

@Retention: Specifies how this annotation is retained when applied, whether in the
source file, in the class file, or at runtime.

@Target: Specifies to which contexts in the source code this annotation can be
applied.

@Inherited: Indicates that all subclasses of a superclass that this annotation is
applied to will inherit this annotation.

@Repeatable: Indicates that this annotation can be used multiple times in the same
context.

@Documented: Indicates that this annotation should be included in the documentation generated by a tool like javadoc.

The @Retention **Meta-Annotation**

In the declaration of an annotation type, it is possible to specify how long the annotation will be retained, meaning whether it should be in the source file, in the class
file, or available at runtime.

In fact, each annotation is associated with one of three retention policies, controlled
by the meta-annotation type java.lang.annotation.Retention and the *retention policy
constants* defined by the enum type java.lang.annotation.RetentionPolicy shown in
Table 25.1 in increasing order of retention.

The meta-annotation type Retention is a *single-element meta-annotation type* that
specifies a value() element of enum type RetentionPolicy. Defining value() elements is covered elsewhere in this chapter (p. 1560).

```
import java.lang.annotation.Retention;
import java.lang.annotation.RetentionPolicy;
@Retention(value = RetentionPolicy.RUNTIME)   // Retention: In source code,
                                              // in class file, at runtime.
public @interface MusicMeta {}
```

The annotation type MusicMeta above needs to be retained at runtime so that it is possible to extract any information that is specified by this annotation. The Retention-Policy.RUNTIME enum constant provides the longest retention. If used in the source code, the @MusicMeta annotation will be recorded in the class file, and when loaded at runtime, it will be available through reflection. However, no provision has been made as yet in the MusicMeta annotation type declaration to provide any information. It is added to the annotation type declaration by specifying annotation type elements (p. 1560).

```
import java.lang.annotation.Retention;
import java.lang.annotation.RetentionPolicy;
@Retention(value = RetentionPolicy.SOURCE) // Retention: Only in the source code.
public @interface Override {}
```

The code above shows the declaration of the Override annotation type. This built-in annotation type when applied in the source code can be used by the compiler (p. 1578). Its declaration specifies the RetentionPolicy.SOURCE, meaning that the annotation will only be retained in the source code. In other words, it will not be recorded in the class file or be available at runtime.

The annotation type declarations shown above do not contain any annotation type elements. They are *marker annotation types*. The purpose of a marker annotation type is to indicate the presence of a feature, rather than convey any specific information. As the MusicMeta annotation type declaration stands, it is possible to discover at runtime that this annotation is used on a particular program element and take the appropriate action, whatever that might be. Use of the @Override marker annotation in the source code alerts the compiler to check that the criteria for overriding is satisfied by the method on which this annotation is applied, but the annotation is not recorded in the class file.

Table 25.1 *Retention Policy Values for the* @Retention *Meta-Annotation*

Constants defined by the RetentionPolicy enum type	Description
SOURCE	This retention policy implies that the annotation is only retained in the source code and is discarded by the compiler—that is, it is not recorded in the class file. The purpose of this annotation is to provide information for the compiler—for example, to validate source code, detect design errors, and suppress compiler warnings.

Table 25.1 *Retention Policy Values for the* @Retention *Meta-Annotation (Continued)*

Constants defined by the RetentionPolicy enum type	Description
CLASS	This retention policy implies that the annotation is recorded in the class file and thus retained by the compiler, but it is not intended to be used at runtime. That it, it need not be loaded by the JVM at runtime. The purpose of this annotation is to provide information for compile-time and deployment-time processing. It can be used by tools that process information to generate additional code—for example, deployment descriptors such as XML files used by Java EE/Jakarta. RetentionPolicy.CLASS is the default retention policy if no retention policy is specified on the annotation type declaration.
RUNTIME	This retention policy results in the annotation being recorded in the class file by the compiler. It is retained by the JVM and can be read at runtime via reflection.

The @Target **Meta-Annotation**

An annotation type declaration can specify the contexts in which the annotation is applicable. This is controlled by the meta-annotation type java.lang.annotation.Target and the *element type constants* defined by the enum type java.lang.annotation.Element-Type, shown in Table 25.2. The meta-annotation type Target is an *array-valued single-element meta-annotation type*—that is, it has a single value() element of type ElementType[] to specify contexts in which the annotation is applicable, meaning multiple ElementType values can be specified to indicate multiple contexts.

Table 25.2 *The* ElementType *Values for the* @Target *Meta-Annotation*

	Constants defined by the ElementType enum	Description
1.	ANNOTATION_TYPE	The annotation can be applied to annotation type declarations. @Tag @interface Status {}
2.	CONSTRUCTOR	The annotation can be applied to constructor declarations. @Tag public Item() {}
3.	FIELD	The annotation can be applied to field declarations, such as instance and static variables, or enum constants. @Tag public static final int YEAR = 2021; enum Size { @Tag S, @Tag M, @Tag L, @Tag XL }

Table 25.2   *The* ElementType *Values for the* @Target *Meta-Annotation (Continued)*

Constants defined by the ElementType enum	Description

4. LOCAL_VARIABLE	The annotation can be applied to local variable declarations, including loop variables of for statements and resource variables of try-with-resources statements.
	`@Tag String localBarber = "Director's Cut";`
	`for (@Tag int i : intArray) {}`
	`try (@Tag var resource = new CloseableResource()) {}`

5. METHOD	The annotation can be applied to method declarations (including elements of annotation types).
	`@Tag boolean passed() { return true; }`
	`@Tag String[] value();`

6. MODULE	The annotation can be applied to a module declaration in a module-info.java source file. `@Tag module com.passion {}`
7. PACKAGE	The annotation can be applied to a package declaration in a source file. Best practice is to specify package-related annotations in a file named package-info.java. `@Tag package com.passion.logic;`

8. PARAMETER	The annotation can be applied to formal and exception parameter declarations in constructors, methods, lambda expressions, and catch blocks.
	`double circleArea(@Tag double r) { return Math.PI*r*r; }`
	`Predicate<String> p = (@Tag var str) -> str.length() < 10;`
	`try {} catch (@Tag Exception ex) {}`

9. TYPE	The annotation can be applied to type declarations: class, interface (including annotation type), and enum declarations.
	`@Tag class Gizmo {}`
	`@Tag interface Reparable {}`
	`@Tag enum Direction {LEFT, RIGHT}`
	`@Tag @interface Validate {}`

10. TYPE_PARAMETER	The annotation can be applied to type parameter declarations of generic classes, interfaces, methods, and constructors.
	`class Box<@Tag E> {}`
	`interface Eatable<@Tag E> {}`
	`<@Tag E extends Comparable<E>> void comparison(E e) {}`
	`<@Tag E> Item(E e) {}`

Table 25.2 *The* `ElementType` *Values for the* `@Target` *Meta-Annotation (Continued)*

Constants defined by the ElementType enum		Description

11.	TYPE_USE	The annotation can be applied in any type context in declarations and expressions where a type can be used.
		`class X extends @Tag Y implements @Tag IZ {}`
		`java.lang. @Tag String strOp() { return "ok"; }`
		`@Tag int compute() { return (@Tag int) 3.14; }`
		`java.lang. @Tag Integer iRef1 = 100;`
		`@Tag Integer iRef2 = 100;`
		`void passItOn() throws @Tag Exception {}`
		`@Tag int[] array1;        // Annotates primitive type int`
		`int @Tag [] array2;       // Annotates array type int[]`
		`int @Tag [][] array3;     // Annotates array type int[][]`

The target values of the `ElementType` constants in Table 25.2 are categorized by the two contexts where annotations can be applied: *declaration context* and *type context*.

The target values of the `ElementType` constants from 1 to 10 in Table 25.2 indicate *declaration contexts*—that is, a context where a program element is declared. Annotations with these target values are called *declaration annotations*. For example, an annotation type declaration with the target value `ElementType.CONSTRUCTOR` is only applicable to a constructor declaration.

```
@Target(ElementType.CONSTRUCTOR)
@interface Tag {}
------------------------------------
class Item {
  @Tag public Item() {}      // Declaration context. Annotates constructor Item.
}
```

However, an annotation type declaration with the target value `ElementType.PARAMETER` is applicable to a parameter declaration in contexts where such parameter declarations are permitted. Note that several target values can be specified in the `@Target` meta-annotation.

```
@Target({ElementType.CONSTRUCTOR, ElementType.PARAMETER})
@interface Tag {}
-----------------------------------
double circleArea(@Tag double r) { // Declaration context. Annotates parameter r.
  return 5.0;
}
```

Note also that the context of the target value `ElementType.ANNOTATION_TYPE` and the context of the target value `ElementType.TYPE` are overlapping, as the latter not only includes annotation type declarations, but also other reference type declarations (class, interface, and enum).

The target value ElementType.TYPE_USE indicates *type contexts*—that is, where a type is used in a declaration or an expression. Annotations with this target value are called *type annotations*.

```
@Target(ElementType.TYPE_USE)
@interface Tag {}
---------------------------------
java.lang. @Tag Integer iRef1 = 100;        // (1) Type context. Annotates Integer.
@Tag Integer iRef2 = 100;                   // (2) Type context. Annotates Integer.
@Tag java.lang.Integer iRef3 = 100;         // (3) Declaration context.
                                            //     Compile-time error!
@Tag int compute() { return (@Tag int) 3.14; }// (4) Type context is int type.
@Tag void compute(int i) {}                 // (5) No return type specified.
                                            //       Compile-time error!
```

In both (1) and (2) above, @Tag is a type annotation on the type Integer, as this type is used in the declaration of the variables. The code at (3) does not compile, as the type annotation @Tag is used in a declaration context. Note how the position of the annotation changes the context of the annotation at (1) and (3). At (4), the type annotation @Tag is on the return type int of the non-void method. As the method at (4) is a void method, there is no return type that is applicable for the type annotation @Tag, so the compiler flags an error.

Consider the following annotation type with the target value ElementType.FIELD:

```
@Target(ElementType.FIELD)
@interface Tag {}
---------------------------------
java.lang. @Tag Integer iRef1 = 100; // (1a) Type context. Compile-time error!
@Tag Integer iRef2 = 100;            // (2a) Declaration context. Annotates iRef2.
@Tag java.lang.Integer iRef3 = 100;  // (3a) Declaration context. Annotates iRef3.
```

At both (2a) and (3a), the annotation @Tag is a declaration annotation on the field, as these are field declarations. The code at (1a) does not compile, as the declaration annotation @Tag is used in a type context.

An annotation can be both a declaration and a type annotation, as illustrated by the code below.

```
@Target({ElementType.TYPE_USE, ElementType.FIELD})
@interface Tag {}
---------------------------------
java.lang. @Tag Integer iRef1 = 100; // (1b) Type context. Annotates Integer.
@Tag Integer iRef2 = 100;            // (2b) Declaration and type context.
@Tag java.lang.Integer iRef3 = 100;  // (3b) Declaration context. Annotates iRef3.
```

An ElementType value can only occur once in the value() element of the meta-annotation @Target. The following specification of the value() element of the meta-annotation @Target will not compile.

```
@Target(value = {ElementType.METHOD, ElementType.FIELD,
                 ElementType.METHOD})        // Compile-time error!
@interface Tag {}
```

By default (when the @Target meta-annotation is not present on the annotation type declaration), the annotation can be applied in any declaration context *except type parameter declarations*. In addition, the annotation is *not permitted in any type contexts*.

```
@interface Tag {}                    // No target specified.
-----------------------------------------------------------------
@Tag class Box<@Tag E> {             // Class declaration: OK.
                                     // Type parameter: Compile-time error!
  <@Tag T> void doIt(T t) {}         // Type parameter: Compile-time error!
  void doTask() throws @Tag Exception {}    // Type context: Compile-time error!
  int iTod(double d) { return (@Tag int) d; }// Type context: Compile-time error!
  @Tag boolean flag;                         // Field declaration. OK.
}
```

An empty @Target(value = {}) annotation is allowed, shown at (1) below, but it does not allow the annotation to be directly applied to any program element, as shown at (3) below. However, this annotation can still be used as the type of an element in other annotation type declarations, as shown at (2), which can be applied normally, as shown at (4).

```
@Target({})                          // (1) Empty target.
@interface Exclusive {}

@interface ExtraExclusive {
  Exclusive value() default @Exclusive;    // (2) Annotation as element type.
}
-----------------------------------------------------------------
@Exclusive class Titanium {}         // (3) Compile-time error!
@ExtraExclusive class Krypton {}     // (4) OK.
```

The annotation type declaration below shows that the MusicMeta type annotation is applicable to any type (class, interface, and enum), method, or field.

```
import java.lang.annotation.Retention;
import java.lang.annotation.RetentionPolicy;
import java.lang.annotation.Target;
import java.lang.annotation.ElementType;

@Retention(RetentionPolicy.RUNTIME)
@Target(value = {ElementType.TYPE, ElementType.METHOD, ElementType.FIELD})
public @interface MusicMeta {}
```

The @MusicMeta annotation is applied below on a class at (1), on a field at (2), and on a method at (3), as permitted by the annotation type declaration shown above. Not surprisingly, applying it on a local variable at (4) results in a compile-time error.

```
@MusicMeta public class Composition {       // (1) On class
  @MusicMeta private String description;    // (2) On field
  @MusicMeta public void play() {           // (3) On method
//  @MusicMeta int volume;                  // (4) Compile-time error!
  }
}
```

The @Inherited **Meta-Annotation**

By default, an annotation applied on a class is not inherited by its subclasses. However, this can be changed by applying the meta-annotation @Inherited on the declaration of the annotation type. Such an annotation will automatically be inherited by subclasses when this annotation is present in their superclass. It has no effect if the annotation is applied to program elements other than classes. Note also that a class cannot inherit annotations from interfaces it implements, nor can a subinterface inherit annotations from superinterfaces it extends, regardless of the fact that these annotations are marked with the meta-annotation @Inherited.

The meta-annotation @Inherited is of type java.lang.annotation.Inherited, which is a *marker meta-annotation type.*

```
import java.lang.annotation.Inherited;
import java.lang.annotation.Retention;
import java.lang.annotation.RetentionPolicy;

@Retention(RetentionPolicy.RUNTIME)
@Inherited
public @interface Playable {}
```

```
@MusicMeta
@Playable
public class Composition {}
```

```
public class Song extends Composition {}
```

In the code above, the annotations @MusicMeta and @Playable are applied to the class Composition, but only the annotation @Playable is inherited by the subclass Song because only the @Playable annotation is applied to the meta-annotation @Inherited in its type declaration. This means that the Composition class has two annotations, but the subclass Song has only one, namely the inherited annotation @Playable.

The @Documented **Meta-Annotation**

By default, annotations are not processed by the javadoc tool when generating API documentation from the source code, unless the declaration of the annotation type is marked with the meta-annotation @Documented. This meta-annotation is of type java.lang.annotation.Documented which is a *marker meta-annotation type.*

```
import java.lang.annotation.*;
@Retention(RetentionPolicy.RUNTIME)
@Target(ElementType.TYPE)
@Documented                              // (1)
public @interface Pending {}
```

```
import java.lang.annotation.*;
@Retention(RetentionPolicy.RUNTIME)
@Target(ElementType.TYPE)
public @interface Verified {}            // (2)
```

```
@Documented
@Verified
public class Gizmo {}                           // (3)
```

In the code above, the declaration of the annotation type `Pending` is marked with the meta-annotation `Documented` at (1), but this is not the case for the declaration of the annotation type `Verified` at (2). Both annotations are applied to the class `Gizmo` at (3). As a result, the generated Javadoc documentation for the class `Gizmo` will only show the presence of the `@Pending` annotation, but not the `@Verified` annotation. Thus the `@Documented` annotation gives annotation developers full control over the process of including annotations in the generated API documentation.

For another example of using the meta-annotation `@Documented`, see the discussion about the `@Deprecated` annotation (Example 25.1, p. 1580).

The `@Repeatable` Meta-Annotation

There are situations where we would like to apply the same annotation multiple times on the same program element. This makes more sense if the annotation is not a marker annotation and we want to apply the annotation with different values.

The declaration of the `Choice` annotation type below declares two annotation type elements that specify the color and the size.

```
import java.lang.annotation.*;
enum Size {S, M, L, XL}
@Retention(RetentionPolicy.RUNTIME)
@interface Choice {
  String color();
  Size size() default Size.L;
}
```

We wish to apply the `@Choice` annotation multiple times to the class `Item` to indicate different combinations of color and size. However, the code below will not compile.

```
@Choice(color="Green", size=Size.S)             // Compile-time error!
@Choice(color="Yellow", size=Size.XL)           // Compile-time error!
@Choice(color="Red", size=Size.M)               // Compile-time error!
@Choice(color="White")                          // Compile-time error!
class Item {}
```

The compiler complains that the `@Choice` annotation is not *repeatable*. The declaration of the *Choice* annotation type must be declared with the meta-annotation `@Repeatable`, which is a *single-element meta-annotation* having the following declaration:

```
@Documented
@Retention(RUNTIME)
@Target(ANNOTATION_TYPE)
public @interface Repeatable {
  Class<? extends Annotation> value();  // Indicates the containing annot type
}
```

In order to apply the @Repeatable meta-annotation on an annotation type, the value of the *containing annotation type* must be supplied—that is, the Class object representing the containing annotation type in its single-element type declaration must be specified. Keep in mind that all annotation types implement the Annotation interface.

We can augment the declaration of the Choice annotation with the meta-annotation @Repeatable that specifies the containing annotation type Choices (which has not been declared as yet).

```
import java.lang.annotation.*;
enum Size {S, M, L, XL}
@Retention(RetentionPolicy.RUNTIME)
@Repeatable(Choices.class)       // @Repeatable specifies the container
                                 // annotation type Choices.
@interface Choice {
  String color();
  Size size() default Size.L;
}
```

The *containing annotation type* (Choices) of a *repeatable annotation type* (Choice) must declare a value() method whose return type is *an array of the repeatable annotation type* (Choice[]).

```
@Retention(RetentionPolicy.RUNTIME)
@interface Choices {
  Choice[] value();              // Return value is an array of Choice.
}
```

The upshot of the setup described above is that the multiple applications of a *repeatable annotation* (@Choice) will be stored in the *array of the repeatable annotation type* (Choice[]) declared in the *containing annotation type* (@Choices).

The multiple applications of the @Choice annotation on the class Item above will now compile. We can call the method AnnotationPrinter.printAllAnnotations() in Example 25.5, p. 1592, with the Class<Item> object Item.class to print the annotations on the class Item. (*Output shown below has been edited to fit on the page.*)

```
Annotations for 'class Item':
  @Choices(value={@Choice(size=S, color="Green"),
              @Choice(size=XL, color="Yellow"),
              @Choice(size=M, color="Red"),
              @Choice(size=L, color="White")})
  ...
```

A *Containing Annotation Type* (CAT) for a *Repeatable Annotation Type* (RAT) must satisfy the following conditions:

- *RAT* must specify *CAT*.class as the value of the single element of its meta-annotation @Repeatable.
- *CAT* must declare a value() annotation type element whose type is *RAT*[].
- Any additional annotation type elements declared in *CAT* must have a default value.

```
@Retention(RetentionPolicy.RUNTIME)
@interface Choices {
  Choice[] value();                    // Return value is an array of Choice.
  double minPrice() default 1.00;      // Must specify a default value.
}
```

- The retention policy for *CAT* is at least as long as the retention policy for *RAT*. For example, if *RAT* has retention policy RUNTIME, the retention policy for *CAT* cannot be CLASS or SOURCE. However, if *RAT* has retention policy CLASS, the retention policy for *CAT* can be CLASS or RUNTIME.

- *RAT* is applicable to at least the same kind of program elements as *CAT*—that is, the list of targets to which *RAT* can be applied cannot be shorter than the list of targets to which *CAT* can be applied. For example, if *CAT* is applicable to the targets METHOD and FIELD, then *RAT* must be applicable to at least these targets.

- If *RAT* has the meta-annotation @Documented, then so must *CAT*.

- If *RAT* has the meta-annotation @Inherited, then so must *CAT*.

In addition, it is a compile-time error if the meta-annotation @Repeatable in the repeatable annotation type does not specify a containing annotation type for the repeatable annotation type.

```
@Repeatable(Choices.class)            // Compile-time error since invalid return type
                                       // at (1).
@interface Choice {
  String color();
  Size size() default Size.L;
}

@Retention(RetentionPolicy.RUNTIME)
@interface Choices {
  String[] value();                    // (1) Invalid return type.
}
```

25.5 Selected Standard Annotations

The Java SE Platform API provides several predefined annotation types in the java.lang package that can readily be used in the source code. Selected predefined annotations are discussed in this section, but they should already be familiar as they have been previously used in this book. The reader is encouraged to consult the Java SE Platform API documentation for further details.

It is important to note that the standard annotations presented here are all optional, but programmers are encouraged to use them as they improve the quality of the code. If used, the compiler can aid in verifying certain aspects of the code at compile time.

The @Override **Annotation**

The marker annotation @Override can be used to indicate that *the annotated method in a subtype must override an inherited method from a supertype*. If that is not the case, the compiler issues an error.

```
public class A {
  public void doThings() {}
}
public class B extends A {
  @Override
  public void dothings() {}              // Wrong method name.
}
```

Without the @Override annotation, the class B above will compile successfully even though the method dothings() does not really override the method doThings() in the superclass A. With the @Override annotation, the compiler will flag an error that the method does not fulfill the criteria for overriding methods—in this case, the method names do not match.

Basically, the @Override annotation when applied to a method helps to catch any errors in an attempt to override some method in its supertype at compile time, ensuring that the overriding method satisfies the criteria for method overriding (§5.1, p. 196).

A common mistake is to inadvertently overload a method from the supertype when the intention is to override it. A classic example is the equals() method from the Object class that has the header:

```
public boolean equals(Object obj)
```

Instead, the method declaration at (1) is declared in the Gizmo class below, leading to subtle bugs in the code:

```
class Gizmo {
  public boolean equals(Gizmo obj) { // (1) Overloaded, as parameter doesn't match.
    // ...
  }
}
```

Best practices advocate that the @Override annotation is always used when overriding a method.

The API of the Override annotation type from the java.lang package is shown below:

```
@Target(ElementType=METHOD)
@Retention(RetentionPolicy=SOURCE)
public @interface Override
```

Note that the Override annotation type can only be applied to a method. Its retention policy is SOURCE, meaning it is discarded by the compiler once the code is validated—in other words, it is not recorded in the class file and therefore not available at runtime.

The @FunctionalInterface **Annotation**

The marker annotation @FunctionalInterface is designed to ensure that a given interface is indeed functional—that is, it contains exactly one abstract method that is either specified or inherited by the interface; otherwise, it will report an *error*.

```
@FunctionalInterface
public interface FIX {        // Compiles without errors.One abstract method.
  void doThings();
}

@FunctionalInterface
public interface FIXIt extends FIX {  // Compiles without errors. Abstract method
}                                     // inherited.

@FunctionalInterface
public interface FIY {        // Compile-time error! More than one abstract method.
  void doThings();
  void doOtherThings();
}

@FunctionalInterface
public interface FIZ {        // Compile-time error! No abstract method.
}
```

Without the @FunctionalInterface annotation, the interfaces above will compile successfully as they are all valid interface declarations. However, the presence of the @FunctionalInterface annotation will ensure that the interface has exactly one abstract method. For more details on declaring functional interfaces, see §13.1, p. 675.

It is not mandatory that all interfaces that have exactly one abstract method should be marked with the @FunctionalInterface annotation. For example, the Comparable<E> interface qualifies as a functional interface but is not marked with the @Functional-Interface annotation in the java.lang package API. Typically, only those interfaces whose implementation is provided by lambda expressions or method references are marked with this annotation. However, whether marked with this annotation or not, the compiler will treat interfaces with exactly one abstract method as functional interfaces.

The API of the FunctionalInterface annotation type from the java.lang package is shown below:

```
@Documented
@Retention(RUNTIME)
@Target(TYPE)
public @interface FunctionalInterface
```

Note that the annotation @FunctionalInterface can only be applied to a target that is a type declaration (ElementType.TYPE)—in particular, *only to an interface declaration*; otherwise, the compiler will flag an error. Its retention policy is RUNTIME, and therefore it is recorded in the class file and available at runtime. The javadoc tool will include the annotation in the documentation it generates, as the annotation has the meta-annotation @Documented.

The @Deprecated **Annotation**

The annotation @Deprecated is designed to discourage the use of certain declarations that were previously allowed. The deprecated code can be declarations of methods, constructors, fields, local variables, packages, modules, parameters, classes, interfaces, and enums, to which this annotation is applied.

It is typically used to indicate that certain code is considered legacy and should no longer be used for various reasons: API design changes, deficiencies in legacy implementations, availability of a better alternative approach that could be more stable, have better performance, and be less likely to cause errors or unwanted side effects. The purpose of the @Deprecated annotation is to caution developers that certain code is obsolete and is considered to be removed from future versions. However, the annotation does not prevent such obsolete code from being used in a program. Instead, the compiler can produce a deprecation warning when compiling code that utilizes declarations that have been marked as deprecated.

Although strictly not required, developers are strongly advised to document the reason for deprecating a program element using the Javadoc annotation @deprecated in a Javadoc comment. Usually such documentation should describe a reason why certain code has been deprecated and suggest an alternative replacement API, as well as point out any differences in the way this suggested API works or is supposed to be used.

There are two annotation type elements defined by the Deprecated annotation type:

```
String  since()      default "";
boolean forRemoval() default false;
```

The value of the since() element in the Deprecated annotation type is used to indicate the Java version when deprecation first occurred. The boolean value of the forRemoval() element, when set to true, indicates the intention to remove the code marked with this annotation in future versions—called *terminally deprecated*. If the value is false, the intent is to discourage the use of the deprecated program element, but it does not indicate an imminent intent to remove it—called *ordinarily deprecated*. As both annotation type elements are defined with default values, they can be omitted in the annotation, but it is strongly advised to provide this information for deprecated code.

Some IDEs show the name of the deprecated program element by a strikethrough, as shown in Example 25.1. The compiler can provide more details of deprecated code usage if the -deprecation or -Xlint:deprecation option is used to compile the code, as seen from the compiler output in Example 25.1. The warnings relate to the usage of the deprecated method initAuthentication() and the deprecated static field SIGN_IN_ATTEMPTS, respectively.

Example 25.1 *Using the* @Deprecated *Annotation*

```
class LoginHandler {
  /**
   * The field SIGN_IN_ATTEMPTS has now been deprecated,
```

```
     * and replaced by more appropriate name.
     * @deprecated Use ACCOUNT_LOCKOUT_THRESHOLD instead.
     */
    @Deprecated(since = "10", forRemoval = false)        // Ordinarily deprecated
    public static final int SIGN_IN_ATTEMPTS = 4;        // static field.
    public static final int ACCOUNT_LOCKOUT_THRESHOLD = 4;

    /**
     * The following method has now been deprecated.
     * @deprecated Use initTwoFactorAuthentication() instead
     */
    @Deprecated(since = "10", forRemoval = true)         // Terminally deprecated
    public void initAuthentication() { /* ...*/ }         // instance method.

    public void initTwoFactorAuthentication() { /* ... */ }
}

public class UserLogin {
    public static void main(String[] args) {
        LoginHandler lh = new LoginHandler();
        lh.initAuthentication();                          // Removal warning
        System.out.println(LoginHandler.SIGN_IN_ATTEMPTS); // Deprecation warning
    }
}
```

Compiling the program:
```
>javac -deprecation UserLogin.java
UserLogin.java:24: warning: [removal] initAuthentication() in LoginHandler has
been deprecated and marked for removal
        lh.initAuthentication();                          // Removal warning
           ^
UserLogin.java:25: warning: [deprecation] SIGN_IN_ATTEMPTS in LoginHandler has
been deprecated
        System.out.println(LoginHandler.SIGN_IN_ATTEMPTS); // Deprecation warning
                                        ^
2 warnings
```

The following example of a deprecated method can be found in the Object class
API:

```
@Deprecated(since="9")
protected void finalize() throws Throwable
```

The example above shows that the use of the finalize() method is discouraged
and appropriate documentation provides reasons for it, as well as suggests alternative approaches to implementing its functionality. Starting from Java 9, the compiler produces *a deprecation warning* when compiling classes that invoke or
override this method.

Other examples to note are the constructors of the wrapper classes which are now
deprecated (§8.3, p. 429).

The API of the Deprecated annotation type from the java.lang package is shown below:

```
@Documented
@Retention(RUNTIME)
@Target({CONSTRUCTOR,FIELD,LOCAL_VARIABLE,METHOD,PACKAGE,MODULE,PARAMETER,TYPE})
public @interface Deprecated
```

The primary use of the @Deprecated annotation is to mark code that is deprecated so that its use is discouraged. Its retention policy is RUNTIME so that it is retained by the compiler, making it possible to dynamically discover whether some code is deprecated through the use of the Reflection API. The contexts in which it can be used are practically all declarations.

As the declaration of the Deprecated annotation type specifies the meta-annotation @Documented, its use will also be documented by the javadoc tool as mentioned earlier. It is recommended to use this annotation in conjunction with the Javadoc annotation @deprecated in a Javadoc comment. A screenshot showing partial documentation generated for the deprecated method initAuthentication() of the Login-Handler class is shown in Figure 25.1.

Figure 25.1   *API Documentation of a Deprecated Method*

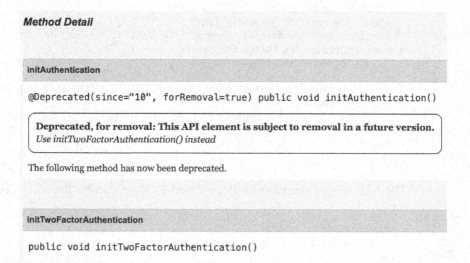

The @SuppressWarnings **Annotation**

The annotation @SuppressWarnings can be used to suppress different kinds of warnings from the compiler in code that would otherwise result in these warnings being issued (§11.13, p. 623).

The SuppressWarnings annotation type is an *array-valued single-element annotation type*—that is, it defines a value() element of type String[]. It is used to indicate which kinds of warnings should be suppressed. Typical kinds of warnings that can be specified for the value array are "unchecked" and "deprecation". *Unchecked warnings* caution about mixing legacy and generic code that might result in heap pollution (§11.13, p. 630). *Deprecation warnings* result from usage of deprecated code (p. 1580). Different Java compilers may provide different kinds of warnings that can be suppressed.

The @SuppressWarnings annotation can be applied at different nested levels of a program construct—for example, when it is applied to a class, it will suppress warnings of a specific kind for the entire class. It is advisable to apply the @SuppressWarnings annotation at the deepest nested level possible, such as a specific method, or a variable that may be the cause of the compiler warnings that a programmer wishes to suppress. Specifying the same kind of warning multiple times is permissible, but only the first occurrence of the name is applied and any other occurrences of this name are ignored.

In the code below, suppressing unchecked warnings in the method is redundant, as that is already the case since its class also suppresses unchecked warnings. However, deprecation warnings are only suppressed for the annotated method in the example below. Note also that the compiler will only suppress unchecked warnings relating to the declaration of the method, but it will *not* suppress any unchecked warnings at the call sites for this method, in contrast to the @SafeVarargs annotation (p. 1585).

```java
@SuppressWarnings("unchecked")
public class PhoneCenter {

  @SuppressWarnings({"unchecked", "deprecation"})
  public void callLandline() {}

}
```

Example 25.2 illustrates suppressing warnings with the @SuppressWarnings annotation. The intention is to suppress both unchecked and deprecation warnings. To show the potential problems in the code, it is first complied without the @SuppressWarnings annotation using appropriate compiler options. The compiler output shows two unchecked warnings and two deprecation warnings in the undisciplinedMethod() and the overridden finalize() method, respectively. With these issues in the code, it is hardly recommended to suppress the warnings using the @SuppressWarnings annotation; doing so will suppress them, but it will not solve the potential problems in the code.

- -

Example 25.2 *Using the @SuppressWarnings Annotation*

```java
import java.util.ArrayList;
import java.util.List;

@SuppressWarnings(value={"unchecked", "deprecation"})  // (1)
public class ATSuppressWarnings {
  /** Mixing legacy code and generic code. */
```

```
    public void undisciplinedMethod() {
      List wordList1 = new ArrayList<String>();   // Assigning parameterized type
                                                  // to raw type.
      List<String> wordList2 = wordList1;         // (2) Unchecked conversion
      wordList1.add("911");                       // (3) Unchecked call
      wordList2.add("119");                       // OK
    }

    /** Overriding and using a deprecated method. */
    @Override
    public void finalize() throws Throwable { // (4) Overriding a deprecated method.
      super.finalize();                       // (5) Usage of deprecated method.
    }
}
```

Compiling without the @SuppressWarnings annotation at (1) is shown below:

```
>javac -Xlint:unchecked -deprecation ATSuppressWarnings.java
ATSuppressWarnings.java:9: warning: [unchecked] unchecked conversion
      List<String> wordList2 = wordList1;         // (2) Unchecked conversion
                               ^
  required: List<String>
  found:    List
ATSuppressWarnings.java:10: warning: [unchecked] unchecked call to add(E) as a
member of the raw type List
      wordList1.add("911");                       // (3) Unchecked call
                ^
  where E is a type-variable:
    E extends Object declared in interface List
ATSuppressWarnings.java:16: warning: [deprecation] finalize() in Object has been
deprecated
    public void finalize() throws Throwable { // (4) Overriding a deprecated method.
                ^
ATSuppressWarnings.java:17: warning: [deprecation] finalize() in Object has been
deprecated
      super.finalize();                       // (5) Usage of deprecated method.
            ^
4 warnings
```

Suppressing warnings is generally considered to be potentially dangerous, as this might hide potential problems within the code. For example, suppressing deprecation warnings may result in a programmer not noticing that deprecated code is in use and may lead to the program not compiling in future versions of Java because the deprecated code has been removed. Regardless, the @SuppressWarnings annotation should not be used unless it has been manually verified that it is safe to do so. Any warnings not suppressed must always be looked into.

The API of the SuppressWarnings annotation type from the java.lang package is shown below:

```
@Target({TYPE,FIELD,METHOD,PARAMETER,CONSTRUCTOR,LOCAL_VARIABLE,MODULE})
@Retention(SOURCE)
public @interface SuppressWarnings
```

The annotation is primarily used for suppressing various warnings that the compiler would otherwise issue. Note that the annotation @SuppressWarnings can be applied to declarations of class, interface, enum type, fields, methods, parameters, constructors, local variables, and modules. Its retention policy is SOURCE and thus it is discarded by the compiler once the code is validated—in other words, it is not recorded in the class file and therefore not available at runtime.

The @SafeVarargs **Annotation**

The marker annotation @SafeVarargs is used to instruct the compiler to suppress unchecked warnings that would otherwise be issued if the declaration or the invocation of a variable arity method or constructor has a variable arity parameter of a non-reifiable element type, as this can lead to heap pollution (§11.13, p. 630).

It is entirely the responsibility of the programmer to ensure that the variable arity method or constructor is well formed to prevent *heap pollution* before using the @SafeVarargs annotation to suppress the warnings. Note that the @SafeVarargs annotation suppresses any unchecked warnings both for the declaration and all call sites of the variable arity method or constructor.

In order to prevent heap pollution occurring in a subclass, a variable arity method cannot be overridden. The compiler will only allow this annotation on a method that is either static, private, or final. Constructors are not a problem in this regard as they cannot be overridden.

Example 25.3 below illustrates using the @SafeVarargs annotation. It is compiled with and without the @SafeVarargs annotation at (1). The output without the @Safe-Varargs annotation shows that two warnings are generated: the first one where the method printList() is declared at (2) and the second one at the call site for this method at (3). Since the variable arity method printList() is well formed, there is no risk in using the annotation.

Example 25.3 *Using the @SafeVarargs Annotation*

```java
import java.util.ArrayList;
import java.util.List;
public class SafeVarargsTest{
  @SafeVarargs                                           // (1)
  private static void printList(List<String>... toys) { // (2) List<String>[]
    for (List<String> toy : toys) {
      System.out.println(toy);
    }
  }

  public static void main(String[] args) {
    List<String> tList = new ArrayList<String>();
    tList.add("vaporizer"); tList.add("slime gun");
    printList(tList);                                    // (3) new List<String>[]
  }
}
```

Without @SafeVarargs at (1):

```
>javac SafeVarargsTest.java
Note: SafeVarargsTest.java uses unchecked or unsafe operations.
Note: Recompile with -Xlint:unchecked for details.

>javac -Xlint:unchecked SafeVarargsTest.java
SafeVarargsTest.java:5: warning: [unchecked] Possible heap pollution from parame-
terized vararg type List<String>
  private static void printList(List<String>... toys) { // (2) List<String>[]
                                             ^
SafeVarargsTest.java:14: warning: [unchecked] unchecked generic array creation for
varargs parameter of type List<String>[]
    printList(tList);                                       // (3) new List<String>[]
            ^
2 warnings
```

With @SafeVarargs:

```
>javac SafeVarargsTest.java
>java SafeVarargsTest
[vaporizer, slime gun]
```

The API of the SafeVarargs annotation type from the java.lang package is shown below:

```
@Documented
@Retention(RUNTIME)
@Target({CONSTRUCTOR,METHOD})
public @interface SafeVarargs
```

The primary use of the @SafeVarargs marker annotation is to suppress unchecked warnings alerting to potential heap pollution that can result from a variable arity parameter of a non-reifiable element type in a variable arity method or constructor.

The @SafeVarargs marker annotation has the RUNTIME retention policy and is thus not discarded by the compiler, making it possible to dynamically discover it through the use of the Reflection API. It can be used to annotate the declaration of a constructor or a method—the compiler ensures that the method is either static, private, or final. Its use will also be documented by the javadoc tool.

Table 25.3 provides a summary of selected standard annotations.

Table 25.3 *Summary of Selected Standard Annotations*

Standard annotation	Kind of annotation	Retention policy	Element type values of target	Compiler action
@Override	*Marker annotation*	SOURCE	METHOD (*which must be an instance or abstract method*)	Error when criteria for overriding are not satisfied

Table 25.3   *Summary of Selected Standard Annotations (Continued)*

Standard annotation	Kind of annotation	Retention policy	Element type values of target	Compiler action
@FunctionalInterface	*Marker annotation*	RUNTIME	TYPE (*which must be an interface*)	Error when the interface does not have exactly one abstract method
@Deprecated	*Two elements:* String since() default ""; boolean forRemoval() default false;	RUNTIME	CONSTRUCTOR, FIELD, LOCAL_VARIABLE, METHOD, PACKAGE, MODULE, PARAMETER, TYPE	Warnings when deprecated code is used or overridden in non-deprecated code
@SuppressWarnings	*Single-element annotation:* String[] value();	SOURCE	CONSTRUCTOR, FIELD, LOCAL_VARIABLE, METHOD, MODULE, PARAMETER, TYPE	Warnings are suppressed
@SafeVarargs	*Marker annotation*	RUNTIME	CONSTRUCTOR, METHOD (*which must be* static, private, *or* final)	Error when no varargs parameter is specified or when applied to a method that is not either static, private, or final; otherwise warnings are suppressed

Other Annotations

Many other annotations used in various contexts are defined in the language. Additional annotations may be provided with various extended APIs that are not part of the core Java language, but nevertheless are often used in practical programming, especially in server-side Java applications deployed in the Java Enterprise Edition or Micro Profile environments. Examples include the Java Persistence (JPA), Container Dependency Injection (CDI), and Bean Validation APIs. These APIs go beyond the Java SE Edition and are therefore not on the Java SE certification exam. However, they are essential for developing real-world Java applications.

25.6 Processing Annotations

It is possible to discover annotations on program elements at runtime using the Reflection API found in the java.lang.reflect package. As this topic is beyond the scope of this book, we provide a brief introduction to the Reflection API—in particular, how to discover annotations on a class and its members.

Figure 25.2 shows a few selected classes and interfaces from the Reflection API. At runtime, an instance of the class Class<T> represents the type T in a Java program. Classes, interfaces, enums, annotations, and primitive types are all represented by Class objects at runtime. For example, the class NuclearPlant is represented by a Class object which can be referenced by NuclearPlant.class and whose type is Class<NuclearPlant> at compile time to ensure type-safety before type erasure removes the type parameter.

Figure 25.2   *Selected Types from the Reflection API*

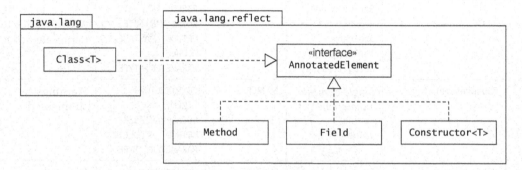

A Class<T> object representing a class can be queried for members that are declared in the class:

```
Constructor<?>[] cons = classobj.getDeclaredConstructors();
Method[] methods      = classobj.getDeclaredMethods();
Field[] fields        = classobj.getDeclaredFields();
```

The classes Class<T>, Method, Field, and Constructor<T> implement the java.lang.reflect.AnnotatedElement interface, as shown in Figure 25.2. The method getDeclaredAnnotations() of the AnnotatedElement interface can be used to obtain the annotations applied to an annotated element. All annotation types implicitly implement the java.lang.annotation.Annotation interface. The method getDeclared-Annotations() of the Annotation interface returns an array of Annotation containing the annotations applied to an annotated element. Using this method, we can obtain the annotations on a class or any member declared in the class.

```
Annotation[] annotations = annotatedElement.getDeclaredAnnotations();
```

If we are interested in a particular annotation on an annotated element, we can use the getDeclaredAnnotationsByType() method of the AnnotatedElement interface. The code below returns all @TaskInfo annotations applied on the NuclearPlant class. Since the @TaskInfo annotation is not repeatable, the array returned will have at most one TaskInfo object, which can be queried by calling the methods declared in the TaskInfo type declaration.

```
TaskInfo[] tias = NuclearPlant.class.getDeclaredAnnotationsByType(TaskInfo.class);
```

Of course, in order for an annotation to be discoverable at runtime, its retention policy must be RUNTIME.

In Example 25.4, the class `NuclearPlant` and its members are marked with annotations which have previously been declared in this chapter: `@Pending` and `@TaskInfo`. In addition, the standard annotations `@Deprecated` and `@Override` are also applied to some methods.

Example 25.4 *Processing Annotations*

```java
@Pending
@TaskInfo(
    priority   = TaskInfo.TaskPriority.HIGH,
    taskDesc   = "Class for running a nuclear reactor.",
    assignedTo = {"Tom", "Dick", "Harriet"}
    )
public class NuclearPlant {

  @Pending
  public NuclearPlant() {}

  @Deprecated(forRemoval = true, since = "8")
  public boolean outOfProduction;

  @Deprecated(since = "10")
  public void notInUse() {}

  @Pending
  @TaskInfo(
    taskDesc   = "Procedure for nuclear reactor shutdown",
    assignedTo = {"Tom", "Harriet"}
    )
  public void shutDownNuclearReactor() {}

  @TaskInfo(
    priority   = TaskInfo.TaskPriority.LOW,
    taskDesc   = "Exchange nuclear rods",
    assignedTo = {"Tom", "Dick"}
    )
  public void changeNuclearRods() {}

  @TaskInfo(
    priority   = TaskInfo.TaskPriority.LOW,
    taskDesc   = "Adjust nuclear fuel",
    assignedTo = {"Harriet"}
    )
  public void adjustNuclearFuel() {}

  @TaskInfo(
    taskDesc   = "Start nuclear reactor",
    assignedTo = "Dick"
    )
  public void startNuclearReactor() {}

  @Pending
  @Override
  public String toString() {
```

```
        return "TBD";
    }
}
```

. . . .

```
import static java.lang.System.out;

import java.lang.reflect.AnnotatedElement;
import java.util.Arrays;
import java.util.stream.Stream;

public class TaskInfoAnnotationProcessor {

  public static void printTaskInfoAnnotation(AnnotatedElement... elements) {// (1)
    Stream.of(elements)                                                    // (2)
      .filter(ae -> ae.isAnnotationPresent(TaskInfo.class))                // (3)
      .peek(ae -> out.printf("%s annotation for '%s':%n",                  // (4)
          TaskInfo.class.getName(), ae))
      .flatMap(ae -> Stream.of(
                      ae.getDeclaredAnnotationsByType(TaskInfo.class)))    // (5)
      .forEach(a -> {                                                      // (6)
        out.printf("  Task description: %s%n", a.taskDesc());
        out.printf("  Priority: %s%n", a.priority());
        out.printf("  Assigned to: %s%n", Arrays.toString(a.assignedTo()));
      });
  }

  public static void main(String[] args) {
    Class<?> classobj = NuclearPlant.class;                               // (7)
    printTaskInfoAnnotation(classobj);                                    // (8)
    printTaskInfoAnnotation(classobj.getDeclaredMethods());              // (9)
  }
}
```

Output from the program:

```
TaskInfo annotation for 'class NuclearPlant':
  Task description: Class for running a nuclear reactor.
  Priority: HIGH
  Assigned to: [Tom, Dick, Harriet]
TaskInfo annotation for 'public void NuclearPlant.shutDownNuclearReactor()':
  Task description: Procedure for nuclear reactor shutdown
  Priority: NORMAL
  Assigned to: [Tom, Harriet]
TaskInfo annotation for 'public void NuclearPlant.changeNuclearRods()':
  Task description: Exchange nuclear rods
  Priority: LOW
  Assigned to: [Tom, Dick]
TaskInfo annotation for 'public void NuclearPlant.adjustNuclearFuel()':
  Task description: Adjust nuclear fuel
  Priority: LOW
  Assigned to: [Harriet]
TaskInfo annotation for 'public void NuclearPlant.startNuclearReactor()':
  Task description: Start nuclear reactor
  Priority: NORMAL
  Assigned to: [Dick]
```

. . . .

In Example 25.4, the method `printTaskInfoAnnotation()` at (1) in the `TaskInfo-AnnotationProcessor` class can be used to specifically discover `TaskInfo` annotations on program elements. Its parameter is an array of `AnnotatedElement`—that is, it contains program elements that are presumably marked with annotations. A stream of `AnnotatedElement` to process each annotated element is created at (2) from the array of `AnnotatedElement` that is passed as an argument to the method. This stream is filtered at (3) to discard any annotated element that is not marked with the `TaskInfo` annotation. A header is printed at (4) to indicate which annotated element is being processed for `TaskInfo` annotation. At (5) the method `getDeclaredAnnotationsByType()` returns an array of `TaskInfo`, containing any `TaskInfo` annotations applied to the current annotated element. This array of `TaskInfo` is flattened to create a stream of `TaskInfo` annotations. The element values of a `TaskInfo` annotation are extracted at (6) by calling the methods specified in the annotation type elements declared in the `TaskInfo` annotation type.

The method `printTaskInfoAnnotation()` is called at (8) and (9) to process `TaskInfo` annotations for the class `NuclearPlant` and its methods, respectively. The program output shows the result of running this annotation processor on the `NuclearPlant` class.

In Example 25.5, the class `AnnotationPrinter` implements a more general annotation processor that prints all annotations applied on a class and its members. The numbers below refer to the numbered lines in the code in Example 25.5.

(1) The `printAllAnnotations()` method is passed the `Class` object of the class whose annotations should be printed.

(2) through (5): The method `printAnnotatedElements()` is successively called to print any annotations on the class, its constructors, its methods, and its fields.

(6) The method `printAnnotatedElements()` accepts elements that implement the `AnnotatedElement` interface. Recall that this is the case for the `Class<T>`, `Constructor<T>`, `Method`, and `Field` classes (Figure 25.2).

(7) A stream of `AnnotatedElement` is created.

(8) The name of the `AnnotatedElement` is printed.

(9) The method `getDeclaredAnnotations()` returns an array with the annotations applied to an `AnnotatedElement`, which is flattened into a stream of `Annotation`.

(10) The text representation of an `Annotation` is printed.

The program output shows the results of running the annotation processor on the `NuclearPlant` class. It is worth running this annotation processor on classes that we have seen in this chapter, keeping in mind that any annotation applied in the code must have `RetentionPolicy.RUNTIME` in order for it to be processed at runtime. For instance, the `@Override` annotation on the `toString()` method of the `NuclearPlant` class is not in the program output, as it has `RetentionPolicy.SOURCE`.

Example 25.5 *Annotation Processor*

```
import java.lang.annotation.Annotation;
import java.lang.reflect.AnnotatedElement;
import java.util.stream.Stream;

public class AnnotationPrinter {

  public static void printAllAnnotations(Class<?> classobj) {          // (1)
    printAnnotatedElements(classobj);                                  // (2)
    printAnnotatedElements(classobj.getDeclaredConstructors());        // (3)
    printAnnotatedElements(classobj.getDeclaredMethods());             // (4)
    printAnnotatedElements(classobj.getDeclaredFields());              // (5)
  }

  public static void printAnnotatedElements(AnnotatedElement... elements) {// (6)
    Stream.of(elements)                                                // (7)
      .peek(ae -> System.out.printf("Annotations for \'%s\':%n", ae))  // (8)
      .flatMap(ae -> Stream.of(ae.getDeclaredAnnotations()))           // (9)
      .forEach(a -> System.out.println("  " + a));                     // (10)
  }
}
```

```
public class AnnotationClient {
  public static void main(String[] args) {
    AnnotationPrinter.printAllAnnotations(NuclearPlant.class);
  }
}
```

Output from the program (*edited to fit on the page*):

```
Annotations for 'class NuclearPlant':
  @Pending()
  @TaskInfo(priority=HIGH, taskDesc="Class for running a nuclear reactor.",
            assignedTo={"Tom", "Dick", "Harriet"})
Annotations for 'public NuclearPlant()':
  @Pending()
Annotations for 'public void NuclearPlant.shutDownNuclearReactor()':
  @Pending()
  @TaskInfo(priority=NORMAL, taskDesc="Procedure for nuclear reactor shutdown",
            assignedTo={"Tom", "Harriet"})
Annotations for 'public void NuclearPlant.notInUse()':
  @java.lang.Deprecated(forRemoval=false, since="10")
Annotations for 'public void NuclearPlant.changeNuclearRods()':
  @TaskInfo(priority=LOW, taskDesc="Exchange nuclear rods",
            assignedTo={"Tom", "Dick"})
Annotations for 'public void NuclearPlant.adjustNuclearFuel()':
  @TaskInfo(priority=LOW, taskDesc="Adjust nuclear fuel", assignedTo={"Harriet"})
Annotations for 'public void NuclearPlant.startNuclearReactor()':
  @TaskInfo(priority=NORMAL, taskDesc="Start nuclear reactor",
            assignedTo={"Dick"})
Annotations for 'public java.lang.String NuclearPlant.toString()':
  @Pending()
Annotations for 'public boolean NuclearPlant.outOfProduction':
  @java.lang.Deprecated(forRemoval=true, since="8")
```

Review Questions

25.1 Which of the following statements are true about annotations?
Select the two correct answers.

(a) Annotations are compiled as classes.
(b) Annotations are used to provide metadata for Java program elements.
(c) An annotation cannot be applied to other annotations.
(d) An annotation cannot be an element type in another annotation.

25.2 Which of the following statements is true about the value of `ElementType` that can be specified for the meta-annotation `@Target` in an annotation type declaration—that is, the target of an annotation type?
Select the one correct answer.

(a) `ElementType.TYPE` means the annotation type cannot be applied to annotations.
(b) `ElementType.TYPE_PARAMETER` means the annotation type cannot be applied to generic types.
(c) `ElementType.FIELD` means the annotation type can be applied to constants.
(d) `ElementType.METHOD` means the annotation type can be applied to constructors.

25.3 Given the following code:

```
@Test3Annotation          // (1)
public class Test3 { }
```

Which of the following annotation types are compatible with the annotation applied at (1)?
Select the two correct answers.

(a) `public @interface Test3Annotation { }`

(b)
```
import static java.lang.annotation.ElementType.*;
import java.lang.annotation.*;
@Target(PACKAGE)
public @interface Test3Annotation { }
```

(c)
```
import static java.lang.annotation.ElementType.*;
import java.lang.annotation.*;
@Target({FIELD,TYPE})
public @interface Test3Annotation { }
```

(d)
```
import static java.lang.annotation.ElementType.*;
import java.lang.annotation.*;
@Target({PACKAGE,TYPE_USE})
public @interface Test3Annotation { }
```

(e) None of the above

25.4 Given the following code:

```
@interface Test4Annotation {
  int[] value() default {1,2,3};
}
```

and

```
// (1) INSERT ANNOTATION HERE
public class Test4 { }
```

Which of the following are incorrect ways to apply @Test4Annotation at (1)?
Select the two correct answers.

(a) `@Test4Annotation(value=7)`

(b) `@Test4Annotation(value=7,8,9)`

(c) `@Test4Annotation({7,8,9})`

(d) `@Test4Annotation`

(e) `@Test4Annotation()`

(f) `@Test4Annotation(8)`

(g) `@Test4Annotation(8,9)`

25.5   Given the following code:

```
@Test5Annotation
public class Test5<@Test5Annotation(value="a") T> {
  @Test5Annotation({"a","b"})
  private T var;
  public Test5(T var) {
    this.var = var;
  }
}
```

Which of the following annotation types is compatible with the annotation
@Test5Annotation?
Select the one correct answer.

(a) ```
import static java.lang.annotation.ElementType.*;
import java.lang.annotation.Target;
@Target({CONSTRUCTOR, FIELD, TYPE})
@interface Test5Annotation {
  String[] value() default {"x"};
}
```

(b) ```
import static java.lang.annotation.ElementType.*;
import java.lang.annotation.Target;
@Target({METHOD, FIELD, TYPE_PARAMETER, TYPE})
@interface Test5Annotation {
  String[] value() default "x";
}
```

(c) ```
import static java.lang.annotation.ElementType.*;
import java.lang.annotation.Target;
@Target({CONSTRUCTOR, FIELD, TYPE_PARAMETER, TYPE})
@interface Test5Annotation {
  String[] values() default {"x"};
}
```

(d) ```
import static java.lang.annotation.ElementType.*;
import java.lang.annotation.Target;
```

```
@Target({METHOD, FIELD, TYPE_PARAMETER})
@interface Test5Annotation {
  String[] values() default "x";
}
```

25.6 Which of the following statements is true about annotations being reflected in the class documentation generated by the javadoc tool?
Select the one correct answer.

(a) Annotations applied at the class level are reflected in the class documentation.

(b) Annotations applied at the method level are reflected in the class documentation.

(c) Annotations applied to public methods are reflected in the class documentation.

(d) Annotations are not reflected in the class documentation by default.

25.7 Which of the following annotation types are correctly declared?
Select the two correct answers.

(a)
```
public @interface Location {
    String value() default null;
    int[] coordinates default 1;
}
```

(b)
```
public @interface Location {
    String value() default "London";
    int[] coordinates() default 1;
}
```

(c)
```
public @interface Location {
    String value();
    int[] coordinates default {1,1};
}
```

(d)
```
public @interface Location {
    String value() default null;
    int[] coordinates default 1;
}
```

(e)
```
public @interface Location {
    String value();
    int[] coordinates() default {1,1};
}
```

25.8 Given the following code:

```
import static java.lang.annotation.ElementType.*;
import java.lang.annotation.Target;
@Target({FIELD, CONSTRUCTOR, TYPE})
public @interface Descriptor {
  String value();
  String[] details() default "";
}
```

Which of the following applications of this annotation type are valid?
Select the three correct answers.

(a) ```
    @Descriptor("Music to play")
    public interface Playable { }
    ```

(b) ```
    public enum Style {
        @Descriptor(value="Rock music", details={"listen"})
        ROCK,
        @Descriptor(value="POP music", details="dance")
        POP,
        @Descriptor(value="Jazz music", details={"listen", "dance"})
        JAZZ,
        @Descriptor("Classic music")
        CLASSIC;
    }
    ```

(c) ```
    public class Music {
        @Descriptor(value="Music to play")
        Music m = new Music();
    }
    ```

(d) ```
    @Descriptor("Music to play",details={"listen","dance"})
    public class Music {
        Music m = new Music();
    }
    ```

(e) ```
    public class Player {
        @Descriptor("Music to play")
        public static void main(String[] args) {
            Music m = new Music();
        }
    }
    ```

(f) ```
    public class Player {
        public static void main(String[] args) {
            @Descriptor(value="Music to play",details={"listen","dance"})
            new Music();
        }
    }
    ```

25.9 Given the following code:

```
import java.lang.annotation.*;
@Repeatable(Container.class)
public @interface Containee { int value(); }
```

and

```
public @interface Container {
    // (1) INSERT CODE HERE
}
```

Which of the following code fragments inserted at (1) will allow the annotation
types to compile?

Select the one correct answer.

(a) ```
String name();
Containee[] value();
```

(b)  ```
String name() default "x";
Containee[] value();
```

(c) ```
String name() default "x";
Containee[] values();
```

(d)  ```
String name() default "x";
Containee value() default @Containee;
```

(e) ```
String name() default "x";
Containee[] values() default {@Containee(1), @Containee(2)};
```

(f)  ```
String name();
Containee[] values() default {@Containee(1), @Containee(2)};
```

25.10   Given the following code:

```
@Folder("/data")
@Folder(value="/tmp", temp=true)
public class Storage { }
```

Which of the following declarations of the Folder and Folders annotation types is valid?

Select the one correct answer.

(a) ```
import java.lang.annotation.Repeatable;
@Repeatable(Folders.class)
public @interface Folder {
  String value();
  boolean temp() default false;
}
```

and

```
public @interface Folders {
  Folder[] paths();
}
```

(b) ```
import java.lang.annotation.Repeatable;
@Repeatable(Folders.class)
public @interface Folder {
  String value();
  boolean temp();
}
```

and

```
public @interface Folders {
  Folder[] value();
}
```

(c) ```
import java.lang.annotation.Repeatable;
@Repeatable(Folders.class)
public @interface Folder {
```
```

```
    String value();
    boolean temp() default false;
}
```

and

```
public @interface Folders {
    Folder[] value();
}
```

(d)
```
import java.lang.annotation.Repeatable;
@Repeatable(Folders.class)
public @interface Folder {
    String path();
    boolean temp() default true;
}
```

and

```
public @interface Folders {
    Folder[] value();
}
```

Secure Coding **26**

 Chapter Topics

- An overview of application security
- Identifying security threat categories
- Understanding denial-of-service (DoS) attacks and their mitigation
- Recognizing sensitive information leakages, and applying value obfuscation and data encryption
- Understanding code injection and the importance of input validation
- Understanding code corruption and its mitigation through practices of encapsulation, data integrity, robustness, judicious extensibility, and immutability
- Understanding the basics of Java security policies and how to execute privileged code
- Presenting additional security guidelines on accessing the file system, utilizing deserialization properly, and the importance of good class design practices

Java SE 11 Developer Exam Objectives	
[10.1] Develop code that mitigates security threats such as denial of service, code injection, input validation and ensure data integrity	§26.1, p. 1600 §26.2, p. 1602
[10.2] Secure resource access including filesystems, manage policies and execute privileged code	§26.3, p. 1608 §26.4, p. 1610

The topic of secure coding is marginal compared to the core topics of the Java SE 11 Developer exam. No attempt is made here to cover this important topic comprehensively in a single chapter. Selected topics in secure coding are covered to the extent of their relevance for Java SE 11 certification. We encourage the reader to consult literature on *software security* that encompasses essential security topics in developing secure and reliable systems, not just secure coding.

26.1 Application Security Overview

This chapter is quite different from other chapters in this book because of the nature of the topic that is covered here. So far this book has covered Java language constructs and APIs that programmers use to implement the business logic of the application. Application designers and architects describe business logic requirements as *functional requirements* (FRs). Such requirements must be implemented to satisfy the business reasons for this application and implement its functionality—in other words, they answer the question of *what* this application should do. However, there is more to application design than that. There is another set of requirements that application designers and architects should consider, known as *non-functional requirements* (NFRs). These include things that are not directly related to the question of *what* the application is supposed to do, but rather characterize *how* it is supposed to work—for example, application performance, scalability, user interface ergonomics, maintainability, and security.

Securing and protecting applications is an important NFR and is usually treated as a separate set of concerns in the overall development cycle. NFR-related design decisions are a complex set of considerations that have to be resolved by a fairly large group of participants, including system and application architects, application designers, and even business stakeholders, not just programmers. Programmers usually are responsible for implementing design and architecture decisions that are made for them. However, it is still quite beneficial for a programmer to be able to understand and appreciate the logic behind the NFRs. Therefore, a reasonable level of understanding of the security principles of application design is advised for any practical programmer. Such an appreciation may help programmers reduce cases when code they have written has to be adjusted or reengineered to satisfy NFRs, including security design decisions.

It is important to understand that security enforcement always comes at a price. This could be a direct financial cost of actually investing in designing, coding, and maintaining a secure environment, but also other overheads, such as decreased performance or decreased throughput of the application that could be caused by data encryption and decryption, or verification and validation of values, and so on.

Improving application security can have implications on its usability—for example, making it less convenient for users to access the application or use some of its functionality because security measures may require users to overcome extra hurdles, such as using two-factor authentication or connecting using virtual private network (VPN). Therefore, a cost-benefit analysis should always be performed as part of the application security design process.

The question that needs to be addressed is this: Is extra protection worth the increase in the up-front development investment, potential user inconvenience, increased maintenance costs, and possible adverse impact on performance and scalability? This is not an easy question to answer because it may involve considerations that go far beyond software design concerns. For example, data leaks caused by security breaches can carry financial and reputation risks for a company, or can even put the company in breach of regulatory requirements and thus have legal implications. Overall security design is often a compromise that is a reflection of a precarious and delicate balance between improved protection and the overhead that it entails.

Lastly, it should be noted that the overall security of the application can only be as good as its weakest link. There is no point in overinvesting in addressing a specific security concern if other related areas are not secured at a comparable level. Potential attackers will always look for the weakest link in the overall security model of the application. Don't forget that it is not just software, but also humans that could be the weak link in security. For example, people who are not careful about keeping their password secret could pose a significant security risk depending on their role in the organization, or what information they can access.

Many of these considerations go far beyond the scope of this book because they are considered to be a responsibility of designers and architects rather than programmers. Therefore, this chapter takes a much narrower approach and only discusses issues that have a direct impact on programmers' activities related to security implementation within an application.

It is also worth mentioning that many security concerns raised in this chapter are applicable to much more complex Java applications hosted in the Java Enterprise Edition (EE)/Jakarta and MicroProfile server environments. Thus many implementation details would fall outside the Java SE scope. However, a Java programmer should still have some degree of awareness of these issues and at least the basics techniques for how to remedy them because Java classes are portable between runtime environments, and thus some of the code written in the context of the Java SE application may eventually end up being used in the Java server environment. This chapter also avoids going into detail about environment management tasks, such as creating and maintaining SSL keys and managing keystore files, and instead keeps the reader focused on programmer-specific tasks related to security implementation. These extra topics may be of interest to developers who not only write code, but also are responsible for maintaining environments were the code will be executed. However, these topics are beyond the scope of Java SE certification.

26.2 Security Threat Categories

Security threats can be grouped into categories based on the nature of the threat and its impact on a system. Each category has its own characteristics that programmers need to be aware of, in order to address these security threats throughout the software lifecycle.

Denial-of-Service (DoS) Attacks

Denial-of-Service (DoS) attacks are a group of threats that are related to the way in which an application manages its resources—specifically, various attempts to exploit the lack of checks and restrictions around resource utilization. For example, a resource could be an open port, or a file, or memory allocation—in other words, something that an application needs for its operational requirements. The idea behind the DoS attack is to make requests to the application for its resources so that their availability for legitimate use is blocked. In DoS attack scenarios, the attacker is trying to exploit the lack of controls and restrictions that an application applies when it is allocating or accessing its resources.

The following scenarios are examples of DoS attacks:

- An attacker providing a very large file or document containing recursive references, causing the application to waste resources trying to parse such a document. This could cause the program to run out of memory, go into an infinite loop trying to handle the recursive execution, or simply slow down as it attempts to read a large document. In any case, this would impede this application's ability to process legitimate data from other sources.

- An attacker opening a connection to a port through which the application performs network interactions. Once this connection is established, the attacker can start sending or receiving information in the slowest possible manner, causing the application to block for read or write operations to complete. The attacker can also spawn a large number of such connections, with the eventual goal of causing this application to run out of its capacity to handle simultaneous connections and denying service from legitimate users.

Countermeasures that can remedy DoS attacks include the following:

- Checking file sizes before starting parsing
- Detecting recursive references and stopping data processing if such recursions occur
- Discarding suspicious documents
- Detecting how many connections a given client has opened concurrently
- Detecting and terminating excessively slow uploads and downloads
- Dropping suspicious connections
- Limiting access to program logic to only authenticated and authorized code

Sometimes it might be the case that a legitimate user struggles with a network connection due to poor network quality. This means that slow connections must still be handled by the program. Consider using asynchronous I/O capabilities to handle these types of slow connections. Asynchronous I/O is supported in Java Enterprise Edition (EE)/Jakarta and MicroProfile servers.

Sensitive Information Leakage

Sensitive information leakage is a group of threats that are related to the way in which an application maintains and transmits its data. This could be internal information storage as well as data exchanges and transmission of values across the network. Reasons behind this type of security vulnerability typically are the lack of value obfuscation, encryption, and information reduction.

For example, the application may have to handle sensitive values, such as personal information or financial details. Such values should be stored in a secure manner, and should not be transmitted through the network in clear text, or maybe not transmitted at all. Objects containing sensitive information should be expunged from memory as soon as possible. Sensitive information should not be written into logs, which includes omitting such information from exception logging. And of course, it is not recommended to serialize sensitive data. Consider performing selective serialization (§20.5, p. 1261), marking such variables as transient, or obfuscating values before serializing.

Nevertheless, sometimes programs do need to write sensitive data, or transmit it through the network. If that is the case, there are several techniques that should be considered to secure such data.

Value Obfuscation

Value obfuscation is a process of scrambling data, producing a digest value that can be used in place of the original data. The purpose of the digest is to act as a value substitution which is not supposed to be unscrambled.

```java
try {
  String creditCard = "12345678890";
  MessageDigest md = MessageDigest.getInstance("SHA-256");   // (1)
  byte[] digest = md.digest(creditCard.getBytes());          // (2)
  String hash = (new BigInteger(1, digest)).toString(16);    // (3)
} catch (NoSuchAlgorithmException e) {
  e.printStackTrace();
}
```

This example assumes that a credit card number needs to be obfuscated. The numbered comments below correspond to the numbered lines in the code:

(1) A `java.security.MessageDigest` object is created using the *SHA-256 digest algorithm*. The SHA algorithm is designed to take a variable-length input and produce a fixed-length digest result. In the case of the SHA-256 algorithm, the number 256 refers to the length of the result in bytes.

(2) A digest value in the form of a byte array is obtained from the original value.

(3) The digest value is represented as a string of fixed length.

Now this digest can be used in place of the original credit card number. It can be stored, or transmitted in the network.

Data Encryption

Another approach is to secure data using encryption. In order to perform encryption and decryption of information, a cipher algorithm and a key have to be selected. This key is then used to perform actual encryption and decryption actions, utilizing an appropriate cipher algorithm. The exact list of supported digest and encryption algorithms varies among different versions and implementations of Java, so developers should consult release-specific Java documentation for a full list of supported algorithms.

```java
try {
  String creditCard = "12345678890";
  SecretKey key = KeyGenerator.getInstance("AES").generateKey(); // (1)
  Cipher cipher = Cipher.getInstance("AES/GCM/NoPadding");       // (2)
  cipher.init(Cipher.ENCRYPT_MODE, key);                         // (3)
  byte[] encryptedValue = cipher.doFinal(creditCard.getBytes()); // (4)
  GCMParameterSpec ps = cipher.getParameters()
                              .getParameterSpec(GCMParameterSpec.class);
  cipher.init(Cipher.DECRYPT_MODE, key, ps);                     // (5)
  byte[] decryptedValue = cipher.doFinal(encryptedValue);        // (6)
} catch (GeneralSecurityException e) {
  e.printStackTrace();
}
```

The numbered comments below correspond to the numbered lines in the code:

(1) The key in this example is generated on the fly using the AES algorithm. However, often keys are created in advance and stored in secure SSL wallet files that implement password-protected key storage.

(2) A new javax.crypto.Cipher object is created that is associated with a cipher algorithm.

(3) A cipher is now associated with a key and initialized to be used for encryption.

(4) A value is encrypted using the previously initialized cypher. There are several methods provided by the Cipher class that can perform the encryption or decryption, such as update() and doFinal(). In simple cases, a single doFinal() method call can be used to perform encryption or decryption actions. In more complex scenarios, such as the need to handle large messages, multiple-part encryption or decryption mechanics can be used with intermediate actions performed by the update() method, before the invocation of the doFinal() method.

(5) Next, a cipher parameter specification object is acquired, which is used to set up the cipher for the decryption mode. Notice that the same key that was used for encrypting the values is now used to decrypt them.

(6) Finally, the cipher is used to decrypt the values.

Notice that the cipher encrypts and decrypts values as byte arrays, so any other type values should first be converted into a byte array before encryption can happen. After decryption completes, the byte array containing the decrypted value can be converted to the required type.

Finally, when exchanging information among different systems, consider only transmitting the minimal amount of data outside an application, if possible.

Code Injection and Input Validation

Code injection is a group of threats that are related to malicious code being injected into the application, instead of legitimate values that the application is supposed to be processing. Code injection is often related to interpreted programming languages, and situations when dynamically supplied code can be executed by the application. Usually, neither of these cases is applicable to a Java application because Java code is fully verified and compiled before execution. However, Java programs can pass executable code disguised as legitimate values that are the source of the code injection. Once again, there is a possibility that malicious executable code can be supplied instead of a regular data value that the application is supposed to handle, causing the application behavior to change when the malicious value is interpreted. Consider validating input values by checking value patterns to ensure that data appears legitimate. Also, consider sanitizing input values by modifying values in a way that prevents their interpretation as executable code.

SQL Injection

Consider the code below, which can be exploited for SQL injection (§24.4, p. 1525). It uses a basic JDBC Statement object at (1) to execute a query, but performs a simple concatenation to create the query string passed to the method.

```
final String jdbcURL = "jdbc:derby:musicDB";
try (Connection connection = DriverManager.getConnection(jdbcURL);
     Statement s = connection.createStatement()) {
  String value = "whatever";
  ResultSet rs = s.executeQuery("select * from songs where name like '"
                          + value + "'");                    // (1)
} catch (SQLException e) {
  e.printStackTrace();
}
```

The expectation is that this code snippet performs a query. However, this code can be exploited if the user submits a SQL statement as a parameter value, such as "Beatles'; drop table songs;". To avoid this problem, consider using a Prepared-Statement object (§24.4, p. 1526), which does not concatenate parameters, or using an enquoteLiteral(value) method provided by the Statement object to sanitize the parameter value.

Code Corruption

Code corruption is a group of threats that are related to the way in which Java code can be exploited by application developers. There is a possibility that the application logic can be broken because of a lack of encapsulation, or immutability, or loss of semantic cohesion when extending classes. Arguably, these types of issues could be considered general programming malpractice problems rather than security threats per se.

Encapsulation

A field that is declared as public allows developers to write code that reads and writes its value directly, which may result in data corruption and loss of integrity, even though relevant safe operations could be provided by the application. The issue is that a developer is not forced to invoke such operations if direct access to data is allowed due to lack of encapsulation.

```
public class SyncCounter {
  public int value;                                           // (1)
  public synchronized void increment()  { value++; }
  public synchronized int  getValue()   { return value; }
}
```

In the preceding code, the variable value at (1) should be private; otherwise, no enforcement of memory integrity would be possible. This principle is applicable to any operation—not just those that enforce synchronization (§22.4, p. 1387), but also those that validate values, or transform values, or perform any additional actions besides just setting or getting values.

Data Integrity

Restricting access to data via methods provides additional opportunities to improve overall program integrity. Operations can be used to validate values, and guard against erroneous values, such as number overflow (§2.8, p. 59). Consider using methods that guard against such overflows. It may be better for a program to throw an ArithmeticException, rather than silently overflow a numeric value.

```
int x = Integer.MAX_VALUE;
int y = x + 1;                          // (1)
int z = Math.addExact(x, 1);           // (2)
```

This example attempts to add 1 to the maximum int value. The code at (1) causes a value to overflow and wrap around (§2.8, p. 59), and the code at (2) throws an ArithmeticException when overflow occurs.

Similarly, a floating-point operation may result in positive or negative infinity, or result in *Not-a-number* (NaN) when attempting floating-point division by zero. Developers are advised to guard against such erroneous cases using simple boolean verification of operation results.

```
boolean veryLargeNum = Double.isInfinite(1/Double.MIN_VALUE); // (1)
boolean nan = Double.isNaN(0.1/0);                            // (2)
```

The code at (1) checks if the operation result is an infinitely large number, and the code at (2) checks if the operation result is NaN.

Robustness

Finally, it is worth considering guarding against references with a `null` value using an `Optional` object (§16.6, p. 940).

```
Optional<String> o = computeOptionalResult(); // (1)
String s = null;
if (o.isPresent()) {                          // (2)
  s = o.get();
}
s = o.orElse("Default");                      // (3)
s = o.orElseThrow();                          // (4)
```

The method at (1) returns an `Optional` object that can encapsulates an actual value. The caller is forced to check what value is in the `Optional` object and take appropriate action. Here are some example of such actions:

- Check whether the value is present before attempting to retrieve it from the `Optional` object.
- Substitute a default value if a value is not present in the `Optional` object.
- Throw a `NoSuchElementException` if the value is not present in the `Optional` object.

The common requirement for all of these cases to work is proper encapsulation to ensure that relevant validations and value corrections are actually applied by appropriate methods.

Extensibility

An example of a loss of semantic cohesion when extending classes is when a developer extends a class and overrides a method in such a way that the overriding method breaks semantic assumptions imposed by the supertype method (§5.1, p. 196). This may lead to erroneous interpretation of the behavior when using polymorphism. Other developers may expect the invoked method to adhere to certain semantics, but instead the invoked method would exhibit unexpected and possibly erroneous behavior.

Immutability

In order to avoid code corruption issues, consider using immutable design, declaring all variables that do not change value as `final` (§5.5, p. 225), as well as declaring classes and methods as `final` to prevent them from being overridden in all cases where extensibility is not required, or if certain method semantics are critical for application functionality.

```
public class Authenticator {
  public boolean authenticate() {           // (1)
    /* Perform authentication logic. */
  }
}
```

The method or even the entire class above could be made final to ensure that no other class can extend this class or override its methods. This would prevent overriding method implementations that can disable or compromise the actual authentication process. This principle is also applicable in many other cases, such as operations that validate values, ensure memory integrity, and so on.

26.3 Java Security Policies

Security policies are designed to impose restrictions on code execution and on access to resources. Security configuration settings are recorded in the properties file ${java.home}/conf/security/java.policy, where the environment variable java.home is the root directory of a Java runtime image, or a directory where the JDK is installed on a given machine. This configuration file contains properties defined as name-value pairs that describe general security settings, references to certificate keystore files, and references to other security policy files that can be found in other locations.

Here is an example of a configuration in the java.security properties file to reference policy files:

```
policy.url.1=file:${java.home}/conf/security/java.policy
policy.url.2=file:/anypath/java.policy
```

These Java security policy descriptors configure security restrictions and permissions. These restrictions and permissions define access to resources and permissions to execute code for a specific codebase. The term *codebase* describes a location where Java code is placed, such as a directory or a URL, but more typically JAR archives. Each security policy is defined as a *grant* that is associated with a specific digital signature and allows the origin of the code to be authenticated.

Here is an example of a java.policy file structure:

```
keystore "xyz.keystore";
grant codeBase "file:/application.jar" signedBy "abc" {
  permission java.net.SocketPermission "localhost:8080", "listen";
  permission java.io.FilePermission "/FileSystemPath", "read, write";
};
```

The example above defines a keystore description and specifies a number of permissions. The keystore file is a secure store that contains keys and certificates. It is used to look up the public keys and associate digital signatures with a given codebase. Keystores are created and maintained using a keytool utility.

A grant is configured for a specific codebase given by the location of a JAR file containing classes to which this grant should be applied. In other words, classes within this archive will be allowed to perform restricted actions described within this grant. To make sure this is a genuine JAR file, it can be signed using a signedBy property that references a relevant digital signature alias from the keystore.

In the grant specification, this policy descriptor defines a number of permissions. One permission allows classes contained within the codebase to listen on a certain address given by the host and the specified port. Another permission allows read and write access to a specific file system path. The exact nature of the permissions depends on the permission type, such as a socket or file permission used in this example. Custom permissions can also be created by extending the java.security .BasicPermission class.

Once security policies are defined, they can be verified.

```java
SocketPermission socketPermission
        = new SocketPermission("localhost:8080", "listen");     // (1)
FilePermission filePermission
        = new FilePermission("/FileSystemPath", "read, write"); // (2)
try {
    AccessController.checkPermission(socketPermission);          // (3)
    AccessController.checkPermission(filePermission);            // (4)
    // (5) ...
} catch(AccessControlException e) {
    // (6) ...
}
```

The numbered comments below correspond to the numbered lines in the code:

(1)–(2) A number of permission objects can be initialized to match permissions configured through the security policy descriptor.

(3)–(4) The AccessController class is used to validate whether such permissions were indeed granted to the given class. This is determined based on the class location within a codebase referenced by the relevant grant. The method checkPermission() throws an AccessControlException if corresponding permission was not granted.

(5) Once permissions are verified, the program can proceed to perform restricted actions.

(6) Handle exceptions that are thrown when requested access does not match permissions configured by the policies.

Executing Privileged Code

There are cases when it is not known which specific permissions must be verified—for example, when the program logic is supplied before the actual permission configuration has been created, or when such a configuration is expected to change in the future. In these cases, the program can use the Access-Controller.doPrivileged() method to execute the computation with privileges enabled. This method accepts an object that implements the PrivilegedAction or the PrivilegedExceptionAction interface, depending on whether this computation can potentially throw a checked exception.

```java
String content = AccessController.doPrivileged(
    new PrivilegedAction<String>() {
        @Override
```

```
      public String run() {                                    // (1)
        String result = null;
        try {
          result = Files.readString(Path.of("/FileSystemPath")); // (2)
        } catch (IOException ex) {
          // ...                                                  (3)
        }
        return result;
      }
    });
```

The numbered comments below correspond to the numbered lines in the code:

(1) The implementation of the `PrivilegedAction` interface must override the `run()` method.

(2) The implementation of the `run()` method contains logic that has access to restricted resources.

(3) Any checked exceptions thrown must be handled within the `run()` method. If checked exceptions are to propagate outside of the `run()` method, then the `PrivilegedExceptionAction` interface should be implemented instead.

The method `doPrivileged()` is overloaded and can accept additional parameters, including specific permissions that must be satisfied for the privileged action to succeed.

26.4 Additional Security Guidelines

Attention is drawn to some selected security guidelines in this section.

Accessing the File System

When accessing the file system or performing I/O operations, consider the following recommendations:

• Remove redundant elements from the path and convert it to a canonical form using the methods `normalize()` and `toRealPath()` to guard against directory traversal attacks, such as attempts to guess the directory structure by using relative paths (§21.3, p. 1297).

• Verify the file sizes and lengths of I/O streams before attempting to process information.

• Monitor I/O operations to detect excessive use of resources and terminate operations that process excessive amounts of data.

• Release resources as soon as possible, and terminate and time out long operations.

Deserialization

Be mindful of deserialization (§20.5, p. 1261), as it can create objects that are beyond the control of the application and that can bypass normal constructor invocations. Essentially, the deserialization process circumvents normal secure object creation, and thus must be considered a potential risk factor, especially if a serialized object arrived from an untrusted source. Thus it is a good idea to validate such objects as soon as they are created.

Class Design

Another important set of guidelines is related to class design.

- Always strive to enforce tight encapsulation using the most restrictive access permissions possible, also known as *principle of least privilege* (PoLP). Consider utilizing the Java Platform Module System for further reinforcement of encapsulation (§19.3, p. 1173), including restrictions imposed on the use of reflection (§19.8, p. 1191).

- Make objects immutable (§6.7, p. 356). Don't forget that even though a variable referencing an object can be marked as final, it does not mean that the object itself is immutable. It may be a good idea to create cloned object replicas of otherwise mutable objects to avoid unsafe memory mutable operations.

- When extending classes and overriding methods, carefully consider the semantics of the superclass methods to override. Also, remember that any modification made to a superclass, such as changing method implementation or introducing additional methods, may have a cascading effect on all its subclasses in the inheritance hierarchy (§5.1, p. 191).

- Always mark non-private classes and methods as final if they are not intended to be extended or overridden (§5.5, p. 225).

- Use factory methods to validate values before invoking a constructor to actually create an object.

- Avoid invoking overridden methods from constructors (§10.9, p. 555).

- Declare constructors as private if the class should not be instantiated.

Finally, consider never disabling bytecode verification with command-line options such as -Xverify:none or –noverify that protect bytecode against tampering and dangerous behavior.

 Review Questions

26.1   Which of the following can prevent DoS attacks?
Select the one correct answer.

(a) Obfuscating sensitive data
(b) Sanitizing input values

    (c) Terminating recursive data references

    (d) Encapsulating code

26.2 An input parameter containing executable code is an example of which of the following?
Select the one correct answer.

    (a) Lack of encapsulation

    (b) Mutable code

    (c) Code corruption

    (d) Code injection

26.3 Given the following code:

```java
public class RQ3 {
    public static void main(String[] args) {
        int z = Math.addExact(Integer.MAX_VALUE, 1);
        System.out.println(z);
    }
}
```

What is the result?
Select the one correct answer.

    (a) 2147483647

    (b) -2147483648

    (c) 2147483648

    (d) An `ArithmeticException`

26.4 Which of the following describes the meaning of the number 256 in the name of the SHA-256 algorithm?
Select the one correct answer.

    (a) A length of a public key used for encryption

    (b) A length of a private key used for encryption

    (c) A length of the resulting hash value

    (d) A length of the input value

26.5 What is the purpose of Java security policies?
Select the one correct answer.

    (a) To set restrictions on code execution and on access to resources

    (b) To set POSIX permissions for file system resources

    (c) To restrict access to data via security methods

    (d) To prevent code injections

26.6 Which of the following statements is true about privileged code execution?
Select the one correct answer.

    (a) The method `PrivilegedAction.run()` is expected to throw a checked exception if security constraints are violated.

(b) The method `AccessController.doPrivileged()` can handle checked exceptions thrown by the `PrivilegedAction.run()` method.

(c) Checked exceptions must be handled within the `PrivilegedAction.run()` method.

(d) Checked exceptions thrown by the `PrivilegedAction.run()` method can be propagated out of the `AccessController.doPrivileged()` method.

Taking the Java SE 17 and Java SE 11 Developer Exams

●●

Please note that all information presented in this appendix is valid as of November 2022. It is imperative that readers regularly visit the websites mentioned in this appendix, as Oracle is known to change practical information regarding the exam and the exam objectives intermittently.

The primary focus of this book is the *Java SE 17 Developer Exam* (*1Z0-829*) and the *Java SE 11 Developer Exam* (*1Z0-819*). Pertinent information about these two exams can be found here:

```
https://education.oracle.com/java-se-17-developer/pexam_1Z0-829

https://education.oracle.com/java-se-11-developer/pexam_1Z0-819
```

For authoritative information about the certification paths for Java SE, consult the following web page:

```
https://education.oracle.com/oracle-certification-path/product_267
```

Appendix B, p. 1623, and Appendix C, p. 1629, contain specific information about the objectives for the *Java SE 17 Developer* exam and the *Java SE 11 Developer* exam, respectively.

A.1 Preparing for the Exam

The goal of the exams is to test practical knowledge and usage of the Java programming language and specific APIs. The exams require a thorough understanding of both the syntax and the semantics of the language, including the use of its core APIs. The exams cover a wide variety of topics, as defined in the exam objectives (Appendix B, Appendix C). Central to the exams are language constructs, usage of the core API, and specific topics, with heavy emphasis on interpreting code scenarios.

The need for real-world experience prior to taking the exam cannot be stressed enough. It requires very thorough preparation to pass the exam without having some actual Java programming experience. This book is intended to be used as a study guide: to encourage readers to try out what they have learned every step of the way, and to test their newly acquired knowledge using the review questions provided in every chapter.

Experimenting with the examples in this book will give the reader a much better chance of passing the exam. Numbered examples in the book are complete Java programs, the source code for which is available on the companion book website. Whether one uses the tools in the JDK or an IDE (integrated development environment), it is the hands-on programming that is important. That said, tools in the JDK are preferred as preparation for the exam, as there is less reliance on programming support provided by an IDE.

When the reader feels ready, they should test their skills on the mock exam for Java SE 17 provided in Appendix E. This will give the reader an indication of how well they are prepared for the exam, and which topics need further study. The structure of the book should make it easy for the reader to focus on single topics, if necessary.

The exam is considered to be difficult, and it requires a fair amount of studying on the part of the candidate. Even seasoned Java programmers should invest some time in preparing for the exam. Simply having real-world experience is not enough to pass the exam.

It is highly recommended that exam candidates devise a study plan, incorporating the activities we mentioned previously. Disruptions in the study plan should be avoided, as this can result in revising the material already covered when you pick up the thread. The exam should be scheduled immediately after the study period, when the momentum from the preparation is at its maximum.

We also highly recommend joining an online Java certification community, such as Code Ranch (www.coderanch.com), which has dedicated active forums for the different Java certifications. All things Java are discussed in a friendly manner around the bonfire at this ranch, where greenhorns are especially welcomed. The forum for Java Programmer Certification can be found here:

```
https://coderanch.com/f/24/java-programmer-OCPJP
```

The following website provides more practice tests for OCP Java SE Developer certification at a nominal price:

```
https://enthuware.com/java-certification-mock-exams/oracle-certified-profes-
sional/ocp-java-17-exam-1z0-829
```

For answers to technical questions on Java, consult the following website:

```
https://stackoverflow.com
```

A.2 Registering for the Online Proctored Exam

The best way to find all pertinent up-to-date information for taking an exam is to visit the exam website, which provides all the relevant links on buying an exam, registering for the exam, and scheduling the exam.

A *certified Oracle account* is required to log on to the *Oracle CertView* certification portal, where pertinent information about the exam can be found. These steps can be accomplished at:

```
https://certview.oracle.com
```

Obtaining an Oracle Exam Attempt

An *exam attempt* (previously called a *certification voucher*) to take the exam is sold by Oracle.

```
https://education.oracle.com/buy-exam
```

Be sure to obtain an exam attempt for *Oracle Technology Exams*, which covers Java certification exams. Credit card information is usually required to arrange payment. The cost of the exam attempt may vary depending on the country you live in and on any offers that might apply at the time. For US residents, the regular price is around $245 at the time of writing this book.

Note that the exam attempt has an expiration date, which is usually six months after it is acquired. Oracle will not replace lost or expired exam attempts, neither will they offer refunds for unused exam attempts.

Scheduling for the Online Proctored Exam

After obtaining the exam attempt, candidates can schedule to take the online proctored exam when they are ready at the *Oracle MyLearn* portal. Be sure to schedule for the right exam. Candidates can reschedule an exam without penalty up to 48 hours before the appointment time.

```
https://mylearn.oracle.com
```

Candidate Agreement

Before taking the exam, candidates will have to agree to the terms and conditions of the *Oracle Certification Program Candidate Agreement* found at this site:

```
https://education.oracle.com/file/general/ocp_candidate_agreement.pdf
```

After Taking the Exam

After taking the exam, candidates will receive an email from Oracle within 30 minutes informing them that their exam results are available in CertView. Candidates who pass the exam will receive an email informing them that an eCertificate is available in CertView. Instructions for requesting a printed copy of the certificate are included in this email.

Candidates who fail the exam can register to retake the exam after a 14-day waiting period.

A.3 How the Online Proctored Exam Is Conducted

The English-language exam is conducted as an online proctored exam. Comprehensive instructions for the online exam can be found at the *Oracle MyLearn* portal.

Requirements for the Online Proctored Exam

Specific requirements are stipulated at the Oracle MyLearn portal for the computer equipment, required ID proofs, and test space in order to take the online exam. A proctor will ensure that these requirements are met before the exam begins and during the exam.

Well before the exam, it is important that candidates familiarize themselves with and prepare for the exam, including making sure all exam requirements are met. Candidates should consult the Oracle MyLearn portal for the requirements that are in effect at any given time. The following is a short summary of these requirements at the time of writing this book.

- *Computer equipment*

  Minimum requirements are spelled out for computer equipment (personal desktop/laptop) with regard to Internet connectivity, audio, and webcam capabilities. Candidates will need to prepare their equipment in advance so that it meets the minimum requirements.

- *Proof of identity*

  The Oracle MyLearn portal states the exact requirements regarding two forms of government-issued identifications that may be required to take the exam.

- *Testing space*

  Apart from checking in 30 minutes before the exam and taking it in a quiet, distraction-free room, there are strict requirements as to what is *not* allowed during the exam. Considering the mode of exam delivery, these restrictions are not surprising as they create a test space where the only communication allowed is that between the candidate and the exam delivery software.

The Exam Program

The computer program used to conduct the exam will select a set of questions at random, and present them through a graphical user interface. The interface is designed in such a way that candidates are able to move back and forth through the questions for reviewing purposes. Questions can be temporarily left unanswered, and the candidate can return to them later. The candidate can also mark questions for later review during the exam.

Before the exam starts, the candidate is allowed a test run with the test interface. A demo test that has nothing to do with the Java exam is used. Its sole purpose is to acquaint the candidate with the program being used to conduct the exam.

Utilizing the Allotted Time

The exam consists of a fixed number of questions that must be answered within the allocated time. As candidates have limited time to answer each question, they cannot afford to get stuck on a question. If the answer does not become apparent within a reasonable time, it is advisable to move on to the next question. Time permitting, it is possible to return to the unanswered questions later. It is important to answer *all* questions, however a wrong answer and a blank answer carry the same penalty: loss of points. Therefore, it is better to guess an answer and hope that it is correct rather than leaving blank. The process of elimination can sometimes be useful in narrowing down the answer to a question. Eliminating obvious incorrect choices increases the chances of arriving at the right answer.

An experienced Java programmer used to taking exams should be able to complete the exam within the allotted time. Any remaining time is best used to review one's answers.

The Exam Result

The exam results are presented on the screen after the exam. Afterwards, candidates should log on to the CertView certification portal to see details about their performance:

- An indication of whether they passed or failed.
- The total score. Only the scored questions on the exam contribute to the final score. All the scored questions are weighted equally, and the score is calculated based on the percentage of correct answers. No credit is given for partially correct answers for the scored questions.
- Indications on how well the candidate did on each category within the objectives. Candidates who fail the exam should pay close attention to this information. If the candidate is planning to retake the exam, it may give a good indication of which topics need closer attention.

The result will not divulge which questions were answered correctly.

A.4   The Questions

Assumptions About the Exam Questions

Candidates should be aware of certain assumptions made about the questions on the *Java SE 17 Developer Exam*. In the following list, we provide a short explanation of these assumptions.

- *Missing package and import statements*
  Unless explicitly provided, stated, or referred to in the question, assume that the code is in the same package/module and all necessary import statements are given.

- *No file or directory pathnames for classes*

  In this case, assume that either all classes are in the same file or each class is in a separate file and these files are in the same directory.

- *Unintended line breaks*

  Line breaks that make the code lines appear to be wrapped unintentionally should be ignored, and the code should be assumed to compile without errors.

- *Code fragments*

  Assume that the necessary context exists to compile and execute the code, if such context is not explicitly specified by the question.

- *Descriptive comments*

  Such comments should be taken at their face value, providing the intent described in the comment.

Types of Questions Asked

Most of the questions follow a common format that requires candidates to apply their knowledge in a special way.

- Analyzing program code. The question provides some source code, and asks a specific question pertaining to the code. Will running the program provide the expected result? What will be written to the standard output when the program is run? Will the code compile? Choosing a code snippet to insert in the given code in order for it to exhibit specific behavior.

- Identifying true or false statements.

When analyzing program code, it is useful to try to apply the same rules as the compiler: examining the exact syntax used, rather than making assumptions on what the code tries to accomplish.

The wording of the questions is precise, and the responses selected in multiple-choice questions are likewise expected to be precise. This often causes the test to be perceived as fastidious. Close attention should be paid to the wording of the responses in a multiple-choice question.

None of the questions is intentionally meant to be a trick question. Exam questions have been reviewed by both Java experts and language experts to remove as much ambiguity from their wording as possible.

Since the program used in the exam will select and present the questions in a random fashion, there is no point in trying to guess the form of the questions. The order of the answers in multiple-choice questions has been randomized, and therefore, has no significance.

Types of Answers Expected

All exam questions are multiple choice. The correct number of alternatives to select is designated in the question, and all must be selected for the question as a whole to be considered correctly answered.

There should be no problem identifying which form of answer each question requires. The wording of the questions will indicate this, and the software used will present the candidate with an input method corresponding to the form of answer expected.

For multiple-choice questions, the program will ask the candidate to select a specific number of answers from a list. Where a single correct answer is expected, radio buttons will allow selection of only one answer. The most appropriate response should be selected.

In questions where all appropriate responses should be selected, check boxes will allow the selection of each response individually. In this case, all choices should be considered on their own merits; that is, responses should not be weighed against each other. It can be helpful to think of each of the choices as an individual true–false question.

Topics Covered by the Questions

Topics covered by the exam are basically derived from the set of exam objectives defined by Oracle. Not all topics may appear on an actual exam session, due to the limited number of questions comprising the exam. The objectives for the *Java SE 17 and 11 Developer* exams are included in Appendix B and Appendix C, respectively, with references to where the topics are covered in the book.

Many of the questions will require intimate knowledge of core Java APIs. This book covers the most important classes and methods of the Java SE Platform API, but it does not go as far as listing every member of every class. The Java SE Platform API documentation should be consulted, as it is essential that candidates familiarize themselves with the relevant parts of the API documentation.

Exam Topics: Java SE 17 Developer

●●

Please note that all information presented in this appendix is valid as of November 2022. It is imperative that readers visit the exam website mentioned in this appendix regularly while preparing for the exam, as Oracle is known to change the exam objectives intermittently.

Exam Name: *Java SE 17 Developer*	Duration: *90 minutes*
Exam Number: *1Z0-829*	Number of Questions: *50*
Certification: *Oracle Certified*	Passing Score: *68%*
Professional: *Java SE 17 Developer*	Exam Format: *Multiple Choice*
	Exam Price: *$245*

Candidates must pass the *Java SE 17 Developer* exam in order to qualify as an *Oracle Certified Professional: Java SE 17 Developer*. Pertinent information about this exam can be found at:

> https://education.oracle.com/java-se-17-developer/pexam_1Z0-829

The web page also lists the exam topics defined by Oracle. The topics are organized in *sections*, and each section is *reproduced verbatim* in this appendix. For each section, we have provided references to where in the book the exam topics (we call them *objectives*) in the section are covered. In addition, the extensive index at the end of the book can also be used to look up specific topics.

General information about taking the exam can be found in Appendix A, p. 1615. Oracle has also specified certain important assumptions about the exam questions, which can also be found in Appendix A, p. 1619. In addition to the exam objectives and the assumptions, the exam web page lists a number of topics that the candidate is expected to know, but the exam will not include any direct questions on these topics. We have classified them as *supplementary topics* (p. 1627).

Section 1: Handling date, time, text, numeric and boolean values	Chapters: 2, 8, 17
[1.1] Use primitives and wrapper classes including Math API, parentheses, type promotion, and casting to evaluate arithmetic and boolean expressions	§2.2, p. 41 to §2.19, p. 92 §8.3, p. 429 §8.6, p. 478
[1.2] Manipulate text, including text blocks, using String and StringBuilder classes	§8.4, p. 439 §8.5, p. 464
[1.3] Manipulate date, time, duration, period, instant and time-zone objects using Date-Time API	§17.1, p. 1024 to §17.7, p. 1072
Section 2: Controlling Program Flow	**Chapter 4**
[2.1] Create program flow control constructs including if/else, switch statements and expressions, loops, and break and continue statements	§4.1, p. 152 to §4.13, p. 184
Section 3: Utilizing Java Object-Oriented Approach	**Chapters: 3, 5, 6, 9, 10, 14**
[3.1] Declare and instantiate Java objects including nested class objects, and explain the object life-cycle including creation, reassigning references, and garbage collection	§9.1, p. 491 to §9.6, p. 521 §10.1, p. 533 to §10.4, p. 537
[3.2] Create classes and records, and define and use instance and static fields and methods, constructors, and instance and static initializers	§3.1, p. 99 to §3.8, p. 112 §5.14, p. 299 §10.5, p. 540 to §10.9, p. 555
[3.3] Implement overloading, including var-arg methods	§3.6, p. 108 §3.11, p. 136 §5.1, p. 202
[3.4] Understand variable scopes, use local variable type inference, apply encapsulation, and make objects immutable	§3.13, p. 142 §6.1, p. 324 §6.6, p. 352 §6.7, p. 356

[3.5]	Implement inheritance, including abstract and sealed classes. Override methods, including that of Object class. Implement polymorphism and differentiate object type versus reference type. Perform type casting, identify object types using instanceof operator and pattern matching	*§5.1, p. 191 to §5.4, p. 218 §5.11, p. 269 §5.12, p. 278 §5.15, p. 311 §14.1, p. 743 to §14.3, p. 753*
[3.6]	Create and use interfaces, identify functional interfaces, and utilize private, static, and default interface methods	*§5.6, p. 237*
[3.7]	Create and use enumerations with fields, methods and constructors	*§5.13, p. 287*
Section 4: Handling Exceptions		**Chapter 7**
[4.1]	Handle exceptions using try/catch/finally, try-with-resources, and multi-catch blocks, including custom exceptions	*§7.2, p. 375 §7.3, p. 375 §7.6, p. 397 §7.7, p. 407*
Section 5: Working with Arrays and Collections		**Chapters: 3, 11, 12, 14, 15**
[5.1]	Create Java arrays, List, Set, Map and Deque collections, and add, remove, update, retrieve and sort their elements	*§3.9, p. 117 §11.1, p. 565 to §11.13, p. 623 §12.1, p. 644 to §12.8, p. 662 §14.4, p. 761 §14.5, p. 769 §15.1, p. 783 to §15.12, p. 864*
Section 6: Working with Streams and Lambda expressions		**Chapters: 13, 16**
[6.1]	Use Java object and primitive Streams, including lambda expressions implementing functional interfaces, to supply, filter, map, consume, and sort data	*§13.1, p. 675 to §13.14, p. 733 §16.3, p. 884 to §16.7, p. 946*
[6.2]	Perform decomposition, concatenation and reduction, and grouping and partitioning on sequential and parallel streams	*§16.7, p. 946 §16.8, p. 978 §16.9, p. 1009*

Section 7: Package and deploy Java code and use the Java Platform Module System	Chapter 19
[7.1] Define modules and their dependencies, expose module content including for reflection. Define services, producers, and consumers	§19.1, p. 1163 to §19.5, p. 1179 §19.8, p. 1191 §19.9, p. 1196
[7.2] Compile Java code, produce modular and non-modular jars, runtime images, and implement migration using unnamed and automatic modules	§19.6, p. 1186 §19.7, p. 1189 §19.10, p. 1204 to §19.14, p. 1218
Section 8: Manage concurrent code execution	**Chapters: 16, 22, 23**
[8.1] Create worker threads using Runnable and Callable, manage the thread lifecycle, including automations provided by different Executor services and concurrent API	§22.1, p. 1367 to §22.5, p. 1408 §23.2, p. 1423
[8.2] Develop thread-safe code, using different locking mechanisms and concurrent API	§23.4, p. 1451 to §23.7, p. 1482
[8.3] Process Java collections concurrently including the use of parallel streams	§16.9, p. 1009 §23.7, p. 1482
Section 9: Use Java I/O API	**Chapters: 20, 21**
[9.1] Read and write console and file data using I/O Streams	§20.1, p. 1233 to §20.4, p. 1256
[9.2] Serialize and de-serialize Java objects	§20.5, p. 1261
[9.3] Create, traverse, read, and write Path objects and their properties using java.nio.file API	§21.1, p. 1287 to §21.8, p. 1345
Section 10: Access databases using JDBC	**Chapter 24**
[10.1] Create connections, create and execute basic, prepared and callable statements, process query results and control transactions using JDBC API	§24.1, p. 1512 to §24.8, p. 1545

Section 11: Implement Localization	Chapter 18
[11.1] Implement localization using locales, resource bundles, parse and format messages, dates, times, and numbers including currency and percentage values	*§18.1, p. 1096 to §18.7, p. 1139*
Section 12: Supplementary Topics	**Chapters: 11, 25**
[12.1] Understand the basics of Java Logging API.	*See Appendix G, p. 1747.*
[12.2] Use Annotations such as Override, FunctionaInterface, Deprecated, SuppressWarnings, and SafeVarargs.	*Standard annotations are covered in §25.5, p. 1577, and are used throughout the book. See also the index.*
[12.3] Use generics, including wildcards.	*Generics are covered in Chapter 11, p. 563.*

Exam Topics: Java SE 11 Developer

Please note that all information presented in this appendix is valid as of November 2022. It is imperative that readers visit the exam website mentioned in this appendix regularly while preparing for the exam, as Oracle is known to change the exam objectives intermittently.

Exam Name: *Java SE 11 Developer*	Duration: *90 minutes*
Exam Number: *1Z0-819*	Number of Questions: *50*
Certification: *Oracle Certified*	Passing Score: *68%*
Professional: Java SE 11 Developer	Exam Format: *Multiple Choice*
	Exam Price: *$245*

Candidates must pass the *Java SE 11 Developer* exam in order to qualify as an *Oracle Certified Professional: Java SE 11 Developer*. Pertinent information about this exam can be found at:

https://education.oracle.com/java-se-11-developer/pexam_1Z0-819

The web page also lists the exam topics defined by Oracle. The topics are organized in *sections*, and each section is *reproduced verbatim* in this appendix. For each section, we have provided references to where in the book the exam topics (we call them *objectives*) in the section are covered. In addition, the extensive index at the end of the book can also be used to look up specific topics. General information about taking the exam can be found in Appendix A, p. 1615. Oracle has also specified certain important assumptions about the exam questions, which can also be found in Appendix A.

Section 1: Working with Java data types	Chapters: 2, 3, 8
[1.1] Use primitives and wrapper classes, including, operators, the use of parentheses, type promotion and casting	§2.2, p. 41 to §2.19, p. 92 §8.3, p. 429

[1.2]	Handle text using String and StringBuilder classes	§8.4, p. 439 §8.5, p. 464
[1.3]	Use local variable type inference, including as lambda parameters	§3.13, p. 142
Section 2: Controlling Program Flow		**Chapter 4**
[2.1]	Create and use loops, if/else, and switch statements	§4.1, p. 152 to §4.8, p. 176
Section 3: Java Object-Oriented Approach		**Chapters: 3, 5, 6, 9, 10, 13**
[3.1]	Declare and instantiate Java objects including nested class objects, and explain objects' lifecycles (including creation, dereferencing by reassignment, and garbage collection)	§9.1, p. 491 to §9.6, p. 521 §10.1, p. 533 to §10.4, p. 537
[3.2]	Define and use fields and methods, including instance, static and overloaded methods	§3.1, p. 99 to §3.8, p. 112
[3.3]	Initialize objects and their members using instance and static initialiser statements and constructors	§3.4, p. 102 §3.7, p. 109 §10.5, p. 540 to §10.9, p. 555
[3.4]	Understand variable scopes, applying encapsulation and make objects immutable	§6.1, p. 324 §6.6, p. 352 §6.7, p. 356
[3.5]	Create and use subclasses and superclasses, including abstract classes	§5.1, p. 191 to §5.4, p. 218
[3.6]	Utilize polymorphism and casting to call methods, differentiating object type versus reference type	§5.11, p. 269 §5.12, p. 278
[3.7]	Create and use interfaces, identify functional interfaces, and utilize private, static, and default methods	§5.6, p. 237 §13.1, p. 675
[3.8]	Create and use enumerations	§5.13, p. 287

[7.2]	Declare, use, and expose modules, including the use of services	*§19.3, p. 1168* *§19.4, p. 1177* *§19.5, p. 1179* *§19.8, p. 1191* *§19.9, p. 1196*
Section 8: Concurrency		**Chapters: 22, 23**
[8.1]	Create worker threads using Runnable and Callable, and manage concurrency using an ExecutorService and java.util.concurrent API	*§22.3, p. 1371* *§23.2, p. 1423*
[8.2]	Develop thread-safe code, using different locking mechanisms and java.util.concurrent API	*§23.4, p. 1451* *to* *§23.7, p. 1482*
Section 9: Java I/O API		**Chapters: 20, 21**
[9.1]	Read and write console and file data using I/O Streams	*§20.1, p. 1233* *to* *§20.4, p. 1256*
[9.2]	Implement serialization and deserialization techniques on Java objects	*§20.5, p. 1261*
[9.3]	Handle file system objects using java.nio.file API	*§21.1, p. 1287* *to* *§21.8, p. 1345*
Section 10: Secure Coding in Java SE Application		**Chapter 26**
[10.1]	Develop code that mitigates security threats such as denial of service, code injection, input validation and ensure data integrity	*§26.1, p. 1600* *§26.2, p. 1602*
[10.2]	Secure resource access including filesystems, manage policies and execute privileged code	*§26.3, p. 1608* *§26.4, p. 1610*
Section 11: Database Applications with JDBC		**Chapter 24**
[11.1]	Connect to and perform database SQL operations, process query results using JDBC API	*§24.1, p. 1512* *to* *§24.8, p. 1545*
Section 12: Localization		**Chapter 18**
[12.1]	Implement Localization using Locale, resource bundles, and Java APIs to parse and format messages, dates, and numbers	*§18.1, p. 1096* *to* *§18.7, p. 1139*

Section 13: Annotations	Chapter 25
[13.1] Create, apply, and process annotations	§25.1, p. 1557 to §25.6, p. 1587

Annotated Answers
to Review Questions

●●●

1   Basics of Java Programming

1.1   *(c)*

A method is an operation defining a particular behavior of an abstraction. Java implements abstractions using classes that have properties and behaviors. Behaviors are defined by the operations of the abstraction.

1.2   *(b)*

An object is an instance of a class. Objects are created from classes that implement abstractions. The objects that are created are concrete realizations of those abstractions. An object is neither a reference nor a variable.

1.3   *(b)*

(2) is the first line of a constructor declaration. A constructor in Java is declared like a method that does not return a value. It has the same name as the class name, but it does not specify a return type and therefore does not return a value. (1) is the header of a class declaration, (3) is the first statement in the constructor body, and (4), (5), and (6) are instance method declarations.

1.4   *(b) and (f)*

Two objects are created and three references are declared by the code. Objects are normally created by using the new operator. The declaration of a reference creates a variable regardless of whether a reference value is assigned to it or not.

1.5   *(d)*

An instance member is a field or an instance method. These members belong to all instances of the class. Members that are not explicitly declared static in a class declaration are instance members.

1.6   *(c)*

An object communicates with another object by calling an instance method of the other object, passing and receiving any information that might be necessary.

1.7   *(d) and (f)*

Given the declaration class B extends A {...}, we can conclude that class B extends class A, class A is the superclass of class B, class B is a subclass of class A, and class B inherits from class A, which means that objects of class B inherit the field value1 from class A.

1.8   *(d)*

The compiler supplied with the JDK is named javac. The names of the source files to be compiled are listed on the command line after the command javac. (c) will compile and execute the program, but will not create a class file.

1.9   *(a)*

Java programs are executed by the Java Virtual Machine (JVM). In the JDK, the command java is used to start the execution by the JVM. The java command requires the name of a class that has a valid main() method. The JVM starts the program execution by calling the main() method of the given class. The exact name of the class should be specified, and not the name of the class file—that is, the .class extension in the class file name should not be specified. Since it is specified that the source file is compiled creating a class file, (c) would not work.

1.10   *(a) and (d)*

The file with a single-file source-code program can contain more than one class declaration and the first class declaration must provide a valid main() method. Such a program cannot access previously compiled user-defined classes, only those in the standard library. It cannot consist of multiple files obviously, but program arguments can be supplied on the command line.

1.11   *(e)*

(a) is incorrect because the JVM must be compatible with the Java Platform on which the program was developed.

(b) is incorrect because the JIT feature of the JVM translates bytecode to machine code.

(c) is incorrect because other languages, like Scala, also compile to bytecode and can be executed by the JVM.

(d) is incorrect because a Java program can only create objects, but destroying objects is at the discretion of the automatic garbage collector.

2 Basic Elements, Primitive Data Types, and Operators

2.1   *(e)*

Everything from the start sequence (/*) of a multiple-line comment to the first occurrence of the end sequence (*/) of a multiple-line comment is ignored by the compiler. Everything from the start sequence (//) of a single-line comment to the end of the line is ignored by the compiler. In (e), the multiple-line comment ends with the first occurrence of the end sequence (*/), leaving the second occurrence of the end sequence (*/) unmatched.

2.2 *(d)*

An assignment statement is an expression statement. The value of the expression statement is the value of the expression on the right-hand side. Since the assignment operator is right associative, the statement a = b = c = 20 is evaluated as follows: (a = (b = (c = 20))). This results in the value 20 being assigned to c, then the same value being assigned to b and finally to a. The program will compile and print 20 at runtime.

2.3 *(c)*

In an assignment statement, the reference value of the source reference is assigned to the destination reference. Assignment does not create a copy of the object denoted by the source reference. After the assignment, both references denote the same object—that is, they are aliases.

The variables a, b, and c are references of type String. The reference value of the "cat" object is first assigned to a, then to b, and later to c. Just before the print statement, a denotes "dog", whereas both b and c denote "cat". The program prints the string denoted by c—that is, "cat".

2.4 *(a), (d), and (e)*

A binary expression with any floating-point operand will be evaluated using floating-point arithmetic. Expressions such as 2/3, where both operands are integers, will use integer arithmetic and evaluate to an integer value. In (e), the result of (0x10 * 1L) is promoted to a floating-point value.

2.5 *(b)*

The / operator has higher precedence than the + operator. This means that the expression is evaluated as ((1/2) + (3/2) + 0.1). The associativity of the binary operators is from left to right, giving (((1/2) + (3/2)) + 0.1). Integer division results in ((0 + 1) + 0.1), which evaluates to 1.1.

2.6 *(b)*

The expression evaluates to -6. The whole expression is evaluated as (((-(-1)) - ((3 * 10) / 5)) - 1) according to the precedence and associativity rules.

2.7 *(d)*

The expression ++k + k++ + + k is evaluated as ((++k) + (k++)) + (+k) → ((2) + (2) + (3)), resulting in the value 7.

2.8 *(d)*

The types char and int are both integral. A char value can be assigned to an int variable since the int type is wider than the char type and an implicit widening conversion will be done. An int type cannot be assigned to a char variable because the char type is narrower than the int type. The compiler will report an error about a possible loss of precision at (4).

2.9 *(a)*

First, the expression ++i is evaluated, resulting in the value 2. Now the variable i also has the value 2. The target of the assignment is now determined to be the element array[2]. Evaluation of the right-hand expression, --i, results in the value 1.

The variable i now has the value 1. The value of the right-hand expression 1 is then assigned to the array element array[2], resulting in the array contents to become {4, 8, 1}. The program computes and prints the sum of these values—that is, 13.

2.10   *(c) and (e)*

The remainder operator is not limited to integral values, but can also be applied to floating-point operands. Short-circuit evaluation occurs with the conditional operators (&&, ||). The operators *, /, and % have the same level of precedence. The data type short is a 16-bit signed two's complement integer, thus the range of values is from -32768 to +32767, inclusive. (+15) is a legal expression using the unary + operator.

2.11   *(a), (c), and (e)*

The != and ∧ operators, when used on boolean operands, will return true if and only if one operand is true, and false otherwise. This means that d and e in the program will always be assigned the same value, given any combination of truth values in a and b. The program will, therefore, print true four times.

2.12   *(b)*

The element referenced by a[i] is determined based on the current value of i, which is 0—that is, the element a[0]. The expression i = 9 will evaluate to the value 9, which will be assigned to the variable i. The value 9 is also assigned to the array element a[0]. After execution of the statement, the variable i will contain the value 9, and the array a will contain the values 9 and 6. The program will print 9 9 6 when run.

2.13   *(c) and (d)*

Note that the logical and conditional operators have lower precedence than the relational operators. Unlike the & and | operators, the && and || operators short-circuit the evaluation of their operands if the result of the operation can be determined from the value of the first operand. The second operand of the || operator in the program is never evaluated because the value of t remains true. All the operands of the other operators are evaluated. Variable i ends up with the value 3, which is the first digit printed, and j ends up with the value 1, which is the second digit printed.

2.14   *(b)*

Both || and && are short-circuit conditional operators. In the conditional expression (x < y || ++z > 4) of the first if statement, since the first operand x < y evaluates to true, the second operand ++z > 4 is not evaluated, as the conditional operator is ||. The if condition is true and the if block is executed, printing a123.

In the conditional expression (x < y || ++z > 4) of the second if statement, since the first operand x < y evaluates to true, the second operand ++z > 4 is evaluated, as the conditional operator is &&. The second operand is false (4 > 4); therefore, the if condition is false and the if block is not executed.

2.15   *(c), (e), and (f)*

In (a), the third operand has the type `double`, which is not assignment compatible with the type `int` of the variable `result1`. Blocks are not legal operands in the conditional operator, as in (b). In (c), the last two operands result in wrapper objects with type `Integer` and `Double`, respectively, which are assignment compatible with the type `Number` of the variable `number`. The evaluation of the conditional expression results in the reference value of an `Integer` object with value 20 being assigned to the `number` variable. All three operands of the operator are mandatory, which is not the case in (d). In (e), the last two operands are of type `int`, and the evaluation of the conditional expression results in an `int` value (21), whose text representation is printed. In (f), the value of the second operand is boxed into a `Boolean`. The evaluation of the conditional expression results in a string literal ("i not equal to j"), which is printed. The `println()` method creates and prints a text representation of any object whose reference value is passed as a parameter.

2.16   *(d)*

The condition in the outer conditional expression is `false`. The condition in the nested conditional expression is `true`, resulting in the value of `m1` (i.e., 20) being printed.

3   Declarations

3.1   *(c)*

The local variable of type `float` will remain uninitialized. Fields and static variables are initialized with a default value. An instance variable of type `int[]` is a reference variable that will be initialized with the `null` value. Local variables remain uninitialized unless explicitly initialized.

3.2   *(e)*

The program will compile. The compiler can figure out that the local variable `price` will always be initialized, since the value of the condition in the `if` statement is `true`. The two instance variables and the two static variables are all initialized to the respective default value of their type.

3.3   *(a) and (e)*

The first and the third pairs of methods will compile. The second pair of methods will fail to compile, since their method signatures do not differ. The compiler has no way of differentiating between the two methods. Note that the return type and the names of the parameters are not a part of the method signature. Both methods in the first pair are named `fly` and have a different number of parameters, thus overloading this method name. The methods in the last pair do not overload the method name `glide`, since only one method has that name. The method named `Glide` is distinct from the method named `glide`, as identifiers are case sensitive in Java.

3.4   *(b) and (e)*

A constructor can be declared `private`, but this means that this constructor can only be used within the class. Constructors need not initialize all the fields when a class is instantiated. A field will be assigned a default value if not explicitly initialized. A constructor is non-static, and as such it can directly access both the static and non-static members of the class.

3.5   *(c)*

A compile-time error will occur at (3), since the class does not have a constructor accepting a single argument of type `int`. The declaration at (1) declares a method, not a constructor, since it is declared as `void`. The method happens to have the same name as the class, but that is irrelevant. The class has the default constructor, since the class contains no constructor declarations. This constructor will be invoked to create a `MyClass` object at (2).

3.6   *(b)*

The keyword `this` can only be used in non-`static` code, as in non-`static` methods, constructors, and instance initializer blocks. Only one occurrence of each `static` variable of a class is created, when the class is loaded by the JVM. This occurrence is shared among all the objects of the class (and for that matter, by other clients). Local variables are only accessible within the local scope, regardless of whether the local scope is defined within a static context.

3.7   *(e)*

The `[]` notation can be placed both after the type name and after the variable name in an array declaration. Multidimensional arrays are created by constructing arrays that can contain references to other arrays. The expression `new int[4][]` will create an array of length 4, which can contain references to arrays of `int` values. The expression `new int[4][4]` will also create a two-dimensional array, but will in addition create four more one-dimensional arrays, each of length 4 and of the type `int[]`. References to each of these arrays are stored in the two-dimensional array. The expression `int[][4]` will not work, because the arrays for the dimensions must be created from left to right.

3.8   *(a), (c), and (d)*

The size of the array cannot be specified, as in (b) and (e). The size of the array is given implicitly by the initialization code. The size of the array is never specified in the declaration of an array reference. The size of an array is always associated with the array instance (on the right-hand side), not the array reference (on the left-hand side).

3.9   *(e)*

The array declaration is valid, and will declare and initialize an array of length 20 containing `int` values. All the values of the array are initialized to their default value of 0. The `for(;;)` loop will print all the values in the array—that is, it will print 0 twenty times.

3.10   (d)

The program will print 0 false 0 null when run. All the instance variables, and the array element, will be initialized to their default values. When concatenated with a string, the values are converted to their text representation. Notice that the null literal is converted to the string "null", rather than throwing a NullPointerException.

3.11   (b)

Evaluation of the actual parameter i++ yields 0, and increments i to 1 in the process. The value 0 is copied into the formal parameter i of the method addTwo() during method invocation. However, the formal parameter is local to the method, and changing its value does not affect the value in the actual parameter. The value of the variable i in the main() method remains 1.

3.12   (d)

The variables a and b are local variables of type int. When these variables are passed as arguments to another method, the method receives copies of the primitive values in the variables. The actual variables are unaffected by operations performed on the copies of the primitive values within the called method. The variable bArr contains a reference value that denotes an array object containing primitive values. When the variable is passed as a parameter to another method, the method receives a copy of the reference value. Using this reference value, the method can manipulate the object that the reference value denotes. This allows the elements in the array object referenced by bArr to be accessed and modified in the method inc2().

3.13   (c)

In (a) and (b), the arguments are encapsulated as elements in the implicitly created array that is passed to the method. In (c), the int array object itself is encapsulated as an element in the implicitly created array that is passed to the method. (a), (b), and (c) are fixed arity calls. Note that int[] is not a subtype of Object[]. In (d), (e), and (f), the argument is a subtype of Object[], and the argument itself is passed without the need for an implicitly created array—that is, these are fixed arity method calls. However, in (d) and (e), the compiler issues a warning that both fixed arity and variable arity method calls are feasible, but chooses fixed arity method calls.

3.14   (b)

Local variable type inference with var is not allowed in a multiple-declaration statement, as at (2).

3.15   (d), (e), and (f)

The restricted keyword var cannot be used as a return type or as the type of a formal parameter, ruling out (a), (b), and (c).

The signature of the method call divide(int, int) is assignment compatible with the method signatures divide(int, int), divide(int, double), and divide(double, int) in (d), (e), and (f), respectively. The double value of the expression in the return statement in the divide() method is assignment compatible with the return type double of the method headers in (d), (e), and (f).

4 Control Flow

4.1   *(d)*

The program will display the letter b when run. The second if statement is evaluated since the boolean expression of the first if statement is true. The else clause belongs to the second if statement. Since the boolean expression of the second if statement is false, the if block is skipped and the else clause is executed.

4.2   *(c)*

The case label value 2 * iLoc is a constant expression whose value is 6, the same as the switch expression. Fall-through results in the program output shown in (c).

4.3   *(c)*

(a) contains a switch statement. Note that there is no break statement associated with the first case label, thus execution falls through to the second case label and assigns the string "Composite" to the reference result, which is then printed.

(b) uses a switch expression to yield a result. However, it does not provide an exhaustive set of case labels and will fail to compile without the default label.

(c) uses the identifier yield as both a variable name and a contextual keyword in the yield statement. There is no fall-through, and the switch expression yields the string "Prime" which is printed.

(d) is mixing two different types of notations for the switch constructs: the arrow notation and the colon notation, which is not permitted.

4.4   *(a)*

The value 1 of the price variable matches the case constant 1 in the first case label, and in this case the discount is calculated by subtracting 1 from the value of price, which results in the value of 0. This code uses a switch expression with the arrow notation, so no fall-through to the next case label can occur. Case labels do not need to be listed in any particular order. The switch expression is exhaustive, because the case labels and the default label cover the range of int values. Code will compile and when executed will yield the value 0.

4.5   *(e)*

The loop body is executed twice and the program will print 3. The first time the loop is executed, the variable i changes value from 1 to 2 and the variable b changes value from false to true. Then the loop condition is evaluated. Since b is true, the loop body is executed again. This time the variable i changes value from 2 to 3 and the variable b changes value from true to false. The loop condition is now evaluated again. Since b is now false, the loop terminates and the current value of i is printed.

4.6   *(b) and (e)*

Both the first and the second numbers printed will be 10. Both the loop body and the update expression will be executed exactly 10 times. Each execution of the loop body will be directly followed by an execution of the update expression. Afterwards, the condition j < 10 is evaluated to see whether the loop body should be executed again.

4.7   *(f)*

The code will compile without error, but will never terminate when run. All the sections in the for header are optional and can be omitted (but not the semicolons). An omitted loop condition is interpreted as being true. Thus a for(;;) loop with an omitted loop condition will never terminate, unless an appropriate control transfer statement is encountered in the loop body. The program will enter an infinite loop at (4).

4.8   *(a) and (d)*

"i=1, j=0" and "i=2, j=1" are part of the output. The variable i iterates through the values 0, 1, and 2 in the outer loop, while j toggles between the values 0 and 1 in the inner loop. If the values of i and j are equal, the printing of the values is skipped and the execution continues with the next iteration of the outer loop. The following can be deduced when the program is run: variables i and j are both 0 and the execution continues with the update expression of the outer loop. "i=1, j=0" is printed and the next iteration of the inner loop starts. Variables i and j are both 1 and the execution continues with the update expression of the outer loop. "i=2, j=0" is printed and the next iteration of the inner loop starts. "i=2, j=1" is printed, j is incremented, j < 2 is false, and the inner loop ends. Variable i is incremented, i < 3 is false, and the outer loop ends.

4.9   *(c) and (d)*

The element type of the array nums must be assignment compatible with the type of the loop variable (i.e., int). Only the element type in (c), Integer, can be automatically unboxed to an int. The element type in (d) is int.

4.10   *(d) and (e)*

In the header of a for(:) loop, we can only declare one local variable. This rules out (a) and (b), as they specify two local variables. Also, the array expression in (a), (b), and (c) is not valid. Only (d) and (e) specify a legal for(:) header.

4.11   *(a), (b), and (c)*

Changing the value of the *variable* does not affect the data structure being iterated over. The for(:) loop cannot run backwards. We cannot iterate over several data structures simultaneously in a for(:) loop, as the syntax does not allow it.

5   Object-Oriented Programming

5.1   *(a) and (c)*

Bar is a subclass of Foo that overrides the method g(). The statement a.j = 5 is not legal, since the member j in the class Bar cannot be accessed through a Foo reference. The statement b.i = 3 is not legal either, since the private member i cannot be accessed from outside of the class Foo.

5.2   *(g)*

It is not possible to invoke the doIt() method in A from an instance method in class C. The method in C needs to call a method in a superclass two levels up in the inheritance hierarchy. The super.super.doIt() strategy will not work, since super is a keyword and cannot be used as an ordinary reference, nor accessed like a field. If the member to be accessed had been a field or a static method, the solution would be to cast the this reference to the class of the field and use the resulting reference to access the field, as illustrated in (f). Field access is determined by the declared type of the reference, whereas the instance method to execute is determined by the actual type of the object denoted by the reference at runtime.

5.3   (e)

The code will compile without errors. None of the calls to a max() method are ambiguous. When the program is run, the main() method will call the max() method on the C object referred to by the reference b with the parameters 13 and 29. This method will call the max() method in B with the parameters 23 and 39. The max() method in B will in turn call the max() method in A with the parameters 39 and 23. The max() method in A will return 39 to the max() method in B. The max() method in B will return 29 to the max() method in C. The max() method in C will return 29 to the main() method.

5.4   (g)

In the class Car, the static method getModelName() hides the static method of the same name in the superclass Vehicle. In the class Car, the instance method get-RegNo() overrides the instance method of the same name in the superclass Vehicle. The declared type of the reference determines the method to execute when a static method is called, but the actual type of the object at runtime determines the method to execute when an overridden method is called.

5.5   (e)

The class MySuper does not have a no-argument constructor. This means that constructors in subclasses must explicitly call the superclass constructor and provide the required parameters. The supplied constructor accomplishes this by calling super(num) in its first statement. Additional constructors can accomplish this either by calling the superclass constructor directly using the super() call, or by calling another constructor in the same class using the this() call which in turn calls the superclass constructor. (a) and (b) are not valid, since they do not call the superclass constructor explicitly. (d) fails, since the super() call must always be the first statement in the constructor body. (f) fails, since the super() and this() calls cannot be combined.

5.6   (b)

In a subclass without any declared constructors, the implicit default constructor will call super(). Use of the super() and this() statements is not mandatory as long as the superclass has a no-argument constructor. If neither super() nor this() is declared as the first statement in the body of a constructor, then the default super() will implicitly be the first statement. A constructor body cannot have both a super() and a this() statement. Calling super() will not always work, since a superclass might not have a no-argument constructor.

5.7 *(d)*

The program will print 12 followed by Test. When the main() method is executed, it will create a new instance of B by passing "Test" as an argument. This results in a call to the constructor of B that has one String parameter. The constructor does not explicitly call any superclass constructor nor any overloaded constructor in B using a this() call, but instead the no-argument constructor of the superclass A is called implicitly. The no-argument constructor of A calls the constructor in A that has two String parameters, passing it the argument list ("1", "2"). This constructor calls the constructor with one String parameter, passing the argument "12". This constructor prints the argument, after implicitly invoking the no-argument constructor of the superclass Object. Now the execution of all the constructors in A is completed, and execution continues in the constructor of B. This constructor now prints the original argument "Test" and returns to the main() method.

5.8 *(c)*

Any non-final class can be declared abstract. A class cannot be instantiated if the class is declared abstract. The declaration of an abstract method cannot provide an implementation. The declaration of a non-abstract method must provide an implementation. If any method in a class is declared abstract, then the class must be declared abstract, so (a) is invalid. The declaration in (b) is not valid, since it omits the keyword abstract in the method declaration. The declaration in (d) is not valid, since it omits the keyword class. In (e), the return type of the method is missing.

5.9 *(b)*

Since the method is abstract, it cannot be inserted at (1) because class Animal is not abstract—thus ruling out (a) and (c). Class Cat is abstract, and the method can be inserted at (2)—thus ruling out (d).

5.10 *(d)*

We cannot create an object of an abstract class with the new operator.

5.11 *(d)*

An instance of Bacteria can be assigned to the org variable at (2), since a supertype reference can refer to a subtype object. There is no @Overload annotation.

5.12 *(a) and (b)*

The extends clause is used to specify that a class extends another class. A subclass can be declared abstract regardless of whether the superclass was declared abstract. Private, overridden, and hidden members from the superclass are not inherited by the subclass. A class cannot be declared both abstract and final, since an abstract class needs to be extended to be useful, and a final class cannot be extended. The accessibility of the class is not limited by the accessibility of its members. A class with all members declared private can still be declared public.

5.13 *(c)*

Only a final class cannot be extended, as in (c). (d) will fail to compile. A class cannot be declared both final and abstract, as in (d).

5.14 *(c)*

Line (3), `void k() { i++; }`, can be re-inserted without introducing errors. Re-inserting line (1) will cause the compilation to fail, since `MyOtherClass` will try to override a `final` method. Re-inserting line (2) will fail, since `MyOtherClass` will no longer have the no-argument constructor. The `main()` method needs to call the no-argument constructor. Re-inserting line (3) will work without any problems, but reinserting line (4) will fail, since the method will try to access a `private` member of the superclass.

5.15 *(a) and (c)*

Abstract classes can declare both `final` methods and non-abstract methods. Non-abstract classes cannot, however, contain abstract methods. Nor can abstract classes be `final`. Only interfaces can declare `default` methods.

5.16 *(d)*

There is no problem compiling the code.

5.17 *(a)*

A `final` class cannot have abstract methods, as a `final` class is a concrete class, providing implementation for all methods in the class.

5.18 *(b) and (g)*

The keywords `protected` and `final` cannot be applied to interface methods. The keyword `public` is implied, but can be specified for abstract and default interface methods. The keywords `private`, `default`, `abstract`, and `static` can be specified for private, default, abstract, and static methods, respectively. The keywords `private`, `default`, and `static` are required for private, default, and static methods, respectively, but the keyword `abstract` is optional as an abstract method is understood to be implicitly abstract.

5.19 *(e)*

The static method `printSlogan()` is *not* inherited by the class `Firm`. It can only be invoked by using a static reference—that is, the name of the interface in which it is declared, regardless of whether the call is in a static or a non-static context.

5.20 *(c)*

The instance method at (3) overrides the `default` method at (1). The `static` method at (2) is not inherited by the class `RaceA`. The instance method at (4) does not override the `static` method at (2).

The method to invoke by the call at (5) is determined at runtime by the object type of the reference, which in this case is `Athlete`, resulting in the method at (3) being invoked. Similarly, the call at (6) will invoke the instance method at (4).

5.21 *(d)*

The code will compile without errors. The class `MyClass` declares that it implements the interfaces `Interface1` and `Interface2`. Since the class is declared abstract, it does not need to implement all abstract method declarations defined in these interfaces. Any non-abstract subclasses of `MyClass` must provide the missing method implementations. The two interfaces share a common abstract method declaration, `void g()`. `MyClass` provides an implementation for this `abstract` method declaration that satisfies both `Interface1` and `Interface2`. Both interfaces provide declarations of constants named `VAL_B`. This can lead to ambiguity when referring to `VAL_B` by its simple name from `MyClass`. The ambiguity can be resolved by using the qualified names `Interface1.VAL_B` and `Interface2.VAL_B`. However, there are no problems with the code as it stands.

5.22 *(b)*

The compiler will allow the statement, as the cast is from the supertype (`Super`) to the subtype (`Sub`). However, if at runtime the reference x does not denote an object of the type `Sub`, a `ClassCastException` will be thrown.

5.23 *(b)*

The expression (`o instanceof B`) will return `true` if the object referred to by o is of type B or a subtype of B. The expression (`!(o instanceof C)`) will return `true` unless the object referred to by o is of type C or a subtype of C. Thus the expression (`o instanceof B`) && (`!(o instanceof C)`) will only return `true` if the object is of type B or a subtype of B that is not C or a subtype of C. Given objects of the classes A, B, and C, this expression will only return `true` for objects of class B.

5.24 *(d)*

The program will print all the letters I, J, C, and D at runtime. The object referred to by the reference x is of class D. Class D extends class C and implements J, and class C implements interface I. This makes I, J, and C supertypes of class D. The reference value of an object of class D can be assigned to any reference of its supertypes and is, therefore, an `instanceof` these types.

5.25 *(c)*

The calls to the `compute()` method in the method declarations at (2) and at (3) are to the `compute()` method declaration at (1), as the argument is always an `int[]`.

The method call at (4) calls the method at (2). The signature of the call at (4) is

   `compute(int[], int[])`

which matches the signature of the method at (2). No implicit array is created.

The method call at (5) calls the method at (1). An implicit array of `int` is created to store the argument values.

The method calls at (6) and (7) call the method at (3). Note the type of the variable arity parameter at (3): an `int[][]`. The signature of the calls at (6) and (7) is

   `compute(int[], int[][])`

which matches the signature of the method at (3). No implicit array is created.

5.26 *(f)*

The `instanceof` pattern match operator can introduce a pattern variable in certain boolean expressions. In the conditional of the `if` statement, both operands of the short-circuit && operator must be `true` for the pattern variable s to be introduced in the `if` block—the scope of variable s is then the `if` block, and s is not accessible in the `else` block. The variable s is thus out of scope in the `else` block, and the code will not compile.

5.27   (d)

For the instanceof pattern match operator, the pattern type (i.e., the type specified for the right operand) must be a subtype of the expression type (i.e., the type of the left operand). This is not the case in (a), (b), or (e). In (a) and (b), both the pattern type and the expression type are Integer, and in (e), the pattern type Number is a supertype of the expression type Integer. Thus (a), (b), and (e) will result in a compile-time error.

In (c), the expression type Integer is incompatible with the pattern type String for comparing types, as one cannot be cast to the other, thus resulting in a compile-time error.

In (d), the pattern type Integer is a subtype of the expression type Number and will compile without any problem.

5.28   (a) and (c)

An instanceof pattern match operator returns false if the reference is null; therefore, it will not throw a NullPointerException. A pattern variable is only introduced when the instanceof pattern match operator returns true.

5.29   (e)

The program will print 2 when System.out.println(ref2.f()) is executed. The object referenced by ref2 is of class C, but the reference is of type B. Since B contains a method f(), the method call will be allowed at compile time. During execution, it is determined that the object is of class C, and dynamic method lookup will cause the overriding method in C to be executed.

5.30   (c)

The program will print 1 when run. The f() methods in A and B are private, and are not accessible by the subclasses. Because of this, the subclasses cannot overload or override these methods, but simply define new methods with the same signature. The object being called is of class C. The reference used to access the object is of type B. Since B contains a method g(), the method call will be allowed at compile time. During execution, it is determined that the object is of class C, and dynamic method lookup will cause the overriding method g() in B to be executed. This method calls a method named f. It can be determined during compilation that this can only refer to the f() method in B, since the method is private and cannot be overridden. This method returns the value 1, which is printed.

5.31   (b), (c), and (d)

The code as it stands will compile. The use of inheritance in this code defines a Planet is-a Star relationship. The code will fail if the name of the field starName is changed in the Star class, since the subclass Planet tries to access it using the name starName. An instance of Planet is not an instance of HeavenlyBody. Neither Planet nor Star implements HeavenlyBody.

5.32   (d)

An enum type can be run as a standalone application, if it provides the appropriate main() method. The constants need not be qualified when referenced inside the enum type declaration. The constants *are* static members. The toString() method always returns the name of the constant, unless it is overridden.

5.33 *(b)*

(1), (2), and (3) define *constant-specific class bodies* that override the toString() method. For constants that do not override the toString() method, the name of the constant is returned.

5.34 *(c)*

An enum type cannot be instantiated to create more objects than those already created implicitly for its constants. All enum types override the equals() method from the Object class. The equals() method of an enum type compares its constants for equality according to reference equality (the same as with the == operator) based on their ordinal values. This equals() method is final.

5.35 *(d) and (e)*

In (a), the compiler recognizes a non-canonical constructor with no parameters in the record class definition. The first statement in such a non-canonical constructor must be an explicit invocation of the canonical constructor using the this() expression. For example, the following constructor declaration will compile, but it will not give the desired result.

```
public Product() {
    this(0, "No name", 0.00);
}
```

However, specifying the required parameters in the constructor header will result in the normal canonical constructor that will compile, and the code will print the right result:

```
public Product(int id, String name, double price) {
    ...
}
```

(b) does not compile because the parameter names in the normal canonical constructor do not match the ones defined in the header of the record class.

In (c), the compiler recognizes a record class that has no component fields. The constructor declared is a non-canonical constructor that must have an explicit invocation of the no-argument implicit canonical constructor using the this() expression. For example, the following constructor declaration will compile, but will not give the desired result.

```
public Product(int id, String name, double price) {
    this();
}
```

However, specifying the field components in the record class header will make the code compile and give the right result:

```
public record Product(int id, String name, double price) {
    ...
}
```

(d) correctly initializes a record using the compact constructor. The name will be stored in uppercase.

(e) correctly initializes a record using the implicit canonical constructor. The record class overrides the method toString() that returns the name field value represented as an uppercase String.

(f) correctly initializes a record using the implicit canonical record constructor, but its overridden toString() method accesses the fields directly, without converting the name field to uppercase. It does not invoke the name() method.

5.36   (d)

The compiler automatically generates an implementation of the equals() method for a record class, if one is not provided. The equals() method added by the compiler will compare all component fields of the record class. This means that the equals() method will return true, but the equality operator == will return false, as the two records that are created are distinct objects that have the same state.

5.37   (c)

All component fields defined by a record class are immutable. A record class can only declare static fields in addition to the component fields specified in its header. The compiler automatically generates the get methods for the component fields of the record class, but not the set methods, since such fields are immutable. Record classes implicitly extend the java.lang.Record class. Record classes cannot have an explicit extends clause.

5.38   (c)

Sealed classes can be abstract. In fact, this is often the case, as the abstract sealed class is intended to be extended by its permitted subclasses. A non-sealed class can also be abstract and can be freely extended. However, a sealed class can only be extended by its permitted subclasses. A class that extends a sealed class must be either final, sealed, or non-sealed.

5.39   (c)

In the code, subtypes Y and Z can be interfaces or classes that can either extend or implement the sealed interface X. A class or an interface that is marked sealed must be defined with the permits clause that specifies its permitted subtypes, unless the permitted subtypes are specified in the same compilation unit. Since the classes and interfaces are all public, each is defined in its own compilation unit.

In (a), interface Z is marked sealed, but does not provide the permits clause or its permitted subtypes in the same compilation unit.

A permitted subtype of a sealed supertype must be explicitly marked as either final, non-sealed, or sealed. In (b), interface Z is not marked with any of these markers, so it will not compile. (d) has the exact same problem with class Y.

In (c), interface Z is correctly marked as sealed, with the appropriate permits clause, and class Y correctly implements both its sealed superinterfaces X and Z.

6 Access Control

6.1 *(a) and (c)*

Bytecode of all reference type declarations in the file is placed in the designated package, and all reference type declarations in the file can access the imported types.

6.2 *(e)*

Both classes are in the same package app, so the first 2 import statements are unnecessary. The package java.lang is always imported in all compilation units, so the next two import statements are unnecessary. The last static import statement is necessary to access the static variable frame in the Window class by its simple name.

6.3 *(b), (c), (d), and (e)*

In (a), the import statement imports types from the mainpkg package, but Window is not one of them.

In (b), the import statement imports types from the mainpkg.subpkg1 package, and Window is one of them.

In (c), the import statement imports types from the mainpkg.subpkg2 package, and Window is one of them.

In (d), the first import statement is a type-import-on-demand statement and the second import statement is a single-type-import statement. Both import the type Window. The second one overrides the first one.

In (e), the first import statement is a single-type-import statement and the second import statement is a type-import-on-demand statement. Both import the type Window. The first one overrides the second one.

In (f), both import statements import the type Window, making the import ambiguous.

In (g), both single-type-import statements import the type Window. The second import statement causes a conflict with the first one.

6.4 *(c) and (e)*

The name of the class must be fully qualified. A parameter list after the method name is not permitted. (c) illustrates single static import, and (e) illustrates static import on demand.

6.5 *(b) and (d)*

In (a) and (c), class A cannot be found. In (e) and (f), class B cannot be found—there is no package under the current directory /top/wrk/pkg to search for class B. Note that specifying pkg in the classpath in (d) is superfluous. The *parent* directory of the package must be specified—that is, the *location* of the package.

6.6 *(d) and (e)*

Static field y in class a.b.X is accessed in the method xyz() of class a.b.c.Z. Static import allows static members from reference type declarations in other packages to be accessed by their simple names.

This rules out (a) as it is a type-import-on-demand statement for all reference type declarations in package a.b, and also (b) as it is a type-import-on-demand statement from class a.b.X. (a) imports class X, but (b) does not import any type, as class X does not declare any non-static inner class members.

(d) is a static import-on-demand statement, meaning it imports all static members of the class a.b.X, including y which can be accessed by its simple name. (e) is a single-static-import statement, meaning only the designated static member y from class a.b.X is imported and can be accessed by its simple name.

6.7 *(a) and (d)*

The class Farm in package habitat accesses classes Cat and Cow by their simple names from package life.animals. (a) is a type-import-on-demand of all reference type declarations from package life.animals, including Cat and Cow. (b) and (c) are ruled out as these are static imports. (d) imports the classes Cat and Cow individually.

6.8 *(d)*

Packages are typically mapped to directories in a file system. A subpackage is an autonomous package that just happens to map to a subdirectory of a directory that represents some other package. There is no relationship between a package and its subpackages. Each package is treated independently, regardless of whether it appears to be implemented as a subdirectory, ruling out (a) and (b).

(c) is incorrect because reference types and static members of types in other packages can be accessed by their fully qualified names, rather than using import statements.

Import statements are not present in the compiled code at all, as type names are always replaced with fully qualified names by the compiler.

6.9 *(b) and (e)*

If no access modifier (public, protected, or private) is given in the member declaration of a class, the member is only accessible by classes in the same package.

A subclass does not have access to members with package accessibility declared in a superclass, unless they are in the same package.

Local variables cannot be declared static or have an access modifier.

6.10 *(b)*

Outside the package, the member j is accessible to any class, whereas the member k is only accessible to subclasses of MyClass.

The field i has package access, and is only accessible by classes inside the package. The field j has public access, and is accessible from anywhere. The field k has protected access, and is accessible from any class inside the package and from subclasses anywhere. The field l has private access, and is only accessible within the class itself.

6.11 *(b)*

A private member is only accessible in the class in which it is declared. If no access modifier has been specified for a member, the member has package accessibility. The keyword default is not an access modifier. A member with package access is only accessible from classes in the same package. Subclasses in other packages cannot access a member with package accessibility.

6.12   (d)

A class that is declared as final cannot be extended. Making a class final is not enough to prevent its state from being modified. A static modifier can be applied to inner classes, but this is not relevant to the question of immutability. A field within an immutable object can refer to a mutable object, which means that members of an immutable object are not automatically immutable.

6.13   (a)

In (a), marking the field name private means it can only be accessible in the class. It can only be initialized once by the constructor when the object is created, and removing the setName() method means the value of private field name cannot be changed. The state of the object is thus immutable.

In (b), the assignment in the setName() method will not compile as it changes the value of the final field name which has already been initialized in the constructor.

In (c), the assignment in the constructor will not compile as it changes the value of the final field name which has already been initialized in its declaration.

7   Exception Handling

7.1   (d)

The program will only print 1, 4, and 5, in that order. The expression 5/k will throw an ArithmeticException, since k equals 0. Control is transferred to the first catch clause, since it is the first catch clause that can handle the arithmetic exceptions. This exception handler simply prints 1. The exception has now been caught and normal execution can resume. Before leaving the try statement, the finally clause is executed. This finally clause prints 4. The last statement of the main() method prints 5.

7.2   (b) and (e)

If run with no program arguments, the program will print The end. If run with one program argument, the program will print the specified argument followed by The end. The finally clause will always be executed, no matter how control leaves the try block.

7.3   (c) and (d)

Normal execution will only resume if the exception is caught by the method. The uncaught exception will propagate up the JVM stack until some method handles it. An overriding method need only declare that it can throw a subset of the checked exceptions the overridden method can throw. The main() method can declare that it throws checked exceptions just like any other method. The finally clause will always be executed, no matter how control leaves the try block.

7.4   (b)

The only thing that is wrong with the code is the ordering of the catch and finally clauses. If present, the finally clause must always appear last in a try-catch-finally construct. Note that since B is a subclass of A, catching A is sufficient to catch exceptions of type B.

7.5   (b)

An invocation of the average() method throws an ArithmeticException, which is then caught in the main() method. The catch block prints "error". This means that the execution of the average() method is stopped, and the method does not return any value, leaving the local variable value still initialized to 1, which is printed.

7.6   (e)

A null value is passed as an argument to the reaction() method, resulting in a PlayerException being thrown, containing the "Invalid action" message. This exception is then caught in the main() method, where its error message is assigned to the local variable message in the catch block. As this exception was successfully handled, normal execution resumes. The print statement prints the error message "Invalid action".

7.7   (c)

As a null value is passed to the readFile() method, it throws a FileNotFound-Exception, which is a subclass of IOException. This exception is caught by the corresponding catch block in the main() method, printing "IO error: invalid file name". Upon resumption of normal execution, the finally block prints " finally", followed by the last print statement printing " the end".

7.8   (g)

The readFile() method executes normally, which means that no catch block is executed in the main() method. The finally block prints "finally" and the last print statement prints " the end".

7.9   (d)

A null value is passed to the readFile() method which then throws an unchecked NullPointerException, which is a subclass of RuntimeException. It is not required to explicitly specify unchecked exceptions in the throws clause or to handle them. The NullPointerException is propagated to the invoking method main(), where it is caught by the catch block that catches an Exception, since RuntimeException is a subclass of Exception. The catch block prints "Other error: invalid file name". Although this catch block contains a return statement, the finally block is executed first, printing " finally", before returning from the main() method. Thus the last print statement in the main() method is not executed.

7.10   (b), (c), and (e)

(b), (c), and (e) correspond to (2), (3), and (5). FileNotFoundException is thrown by the constructor call FileReader(filename). The close() method of the Buffered-Reader throws an IOException. Either the try-with-resources statement must catch it or the exception must be specified in the throws clause of the method—the catch-or-declare rule. (1), (4), and (6) do not fulfill this criteria. Also, the resource variables are final and cannot be assigned to in the body of the try-with-resources statement, ruling out (7). At (5), the resource declaration statements are valid.

7.11   (h)

The top-level try block in the method justDoIt() throws an IOException. The nested try block in the finally clause throws an EOFException that is caught and associated as a suppressed exception with the IOException. It is the IOException that is propagated. The IOException is caught in the catch clause in the main() method and its information is printed, including its suppressed exception EOFException. The supertype exception references are used polymorphically to handle objects of subtype exceptions.

7.12   (f)

In (a), the program does not compile because the checked Exception thrown in the close() method does not comply with the catch-or-declare rule.

In (b), although the close() method will abide by the catch-or-declare rule, the main() method does not.

In (c), adding throws Exception clause only to the main() method does not change the fact that the close() method does not abide by the catch-or-declare rule.

In (d), both methods abide by the catch-or-declare rule. When run, the program will throw an Exception that is not caught.

In (e), adding catch (Exception e) {} clause to the try statement in the main() method does not change the fact that the close() method does not abide by the catch-or-declare rule.

In (f), the close() method will abide by the catch-or-declare rule, and the main() method will catch and handle the exception thrown at runtime.

7.13   (a), (b), and (c)

In (a), the exception parameter e is implicitly final and cannot be reassigned in the multi-catch clause.

In (b), in the two assignments to the exception parameter e, objects of the superclass IOException cannot be assigned to references of subtypes EOFException and FileNotFoundException.

In (c), in the assignment to the exception parameter e of type Exception, an object of the subtype IOException is assigned to e, but an exception of type Exception is thrown in the catch clause. This exception is not covered by the subtype IOException specified in the throws clause. In other words, Exception thrown in the catch clause is not handled.

In (d), the compiler can infer that only FileNotFoundException can be thrown in the try statement. Such an exception can only be thrown in the catch clause, as the parameter e of type Exception can be inferred to be effectively final, and can thus only refer to a FileNotFoundException. This exception is covered by the throws clause.

In (e), the compiler can infer that only FileNotFoundException can be thrown in the try statement. This exception is caught by parameter e of the superclass IOException. IOException is covered by the throws clause that specifies its supertype Exception.

7.14   (a)

In this code example, the Resource object is used in a try-with-resources statement. Its action() method will print "action " and it will be closed by the implicit finally block by invoking the close() method that prints "closure ". There are no exceptions thrown. The last print statement prints " the end".

7.15   (b)

The Resource object is used in the try-with-resources statement, which means it will be closed by the implicit finally block invoking the close() method after the execution of the try block.

There are two exceptions thrown in the code: The first is an IOException that is thrown by the action() method, and the second is thrown by the close() method of the Resource class. The IOException is then caught in the main() method. However, notice that the IOException handler does not attempt to retrieve and print information about suppressed exceptions thrown by the implicit finally block of the try-with-resources statement. The catch block prints "IO action error ". Once the exception is handled, execution of the rest of the method main() resumes. The last print statement prints " the end".

7.16   (b)

There is no reason why explicit and implicit finally blocks cannot coexist. If an explicit finally block is added after the try-with-resources statement, its code is executed after the implicit finally block.

8 Selected API Classes

8.1   (e)

Neither the hashCode() method nor the equals() method is declared final in the Object class, and it cannot be guaranteed that implementations of these methods will differentiate between *all* objects. All arrays are genuine objects and inherit from the Object class, including the clone() method.

8.2   (b)

Values in the range –128 to +127, inclusive, are boxed in Integer objects and cached by the method Integer.valueOf().

8.3   (c)

There is a minor performance penalty associated with the conversion of a primitive value to a wrapper object and vice versa. Wrapper references can be assigned the null value, but they cannot be assigned to a variable of a primitive type. An attempt to convert an uninitialized wrapper reference to a primitive value will result in a NullPointerException. However, if the reference is a local variable then the code will not compile.

8.4 *(b)*

Integer objects with a value between –128 and +127 are interned. Therefore, two references that reference the same interned Integer object will return true when compared with the == operator—that is, they are aliases. The reference i1 is assigned the reference value of a new Integer object with value 10. This Integer object is interned. The reference i2 is assigned the reference value of this interned Integer object, instead of creating a new Integer object. The expression i1 == i2 is thus true, resulting in A being printed. The expression i1 == i3 is also true, since the Integer object referenced by i1 is unboxed to the int value 10 which is also the value in i3, resulting in B being printed.

However, values boxed by the references x1 and x2 are greater than 127, and therefore these references refer to two different Integer objects which are not interned. The expression x1 == x2 returns the value false. The expression x1 == x3 returns true, since the Integer object referenced by x1 is unboxed to the int value 1000 which is also the value in x3, resulting in D being printed.

8.5 *(d)*

The expression str.substring(2,5) will extract the substring "kap". The method extracts the characters from index 2 to index 4, inclusive.

8.6 *(d)*

The program will print str3str1 when run. The concat() method will create and return a new String object, which is the concatenation of the current String object and the String object passed as an argument. The expression statement str1.concat(str2) creates a new String object, but its reference value is not stored after the expression is evaluated. Therefore, this String object gets discarded.

8.7 *(d)*

The constant expressions "ab" + "12" and "ab" + 12 will, at compile time, be evaluated to the string-valued constant "ab12". Both variables s and t are assigned a reference to the same interned String object containing "ab12". The variable u is assigned a new String object, created by using the new operator.

8.8 *(b)*

The reference value in the reference str1 never changes and it refers to the string literal "lower" all the time. The calls to toUpperCase() and replace() return a new String object whose reference value is ignored.

8.9 *(d)*

The call to the put0() method does not change the String object referred to by the s1 reference in the main() method. The reference value returned by the call to the concat() method is ignored.

8.10 *(b)*

The reference value in the reference str1 never changes and it refers to the string literal "lower" all the time. The calls to toUpperCase() and replace() return a new String object whose reference value is ignored.

8.11   *(b)*

The substring() method returns the characters from the start index inclusive to the end index exclusive. The start index is returned by the indexOf(' ') method call, which is the first occurrence of a space character ' ' within the string, namely index 4. The expression s.indexOf(' ', s.indexOf(' ') + 1) finds the next occurrence of the space character ' ', where the search starts after the first occurrence of the space character (' '), returning the index 7. As 1 is added to this index, the end index passed to the substring() method is 8. The resulting substring is from index 4 inclusive to index 8 exclusive—that is, " is ". The strip() method removes both leading and trailing whitespace from this string, resulting in the string "is". To this string, the character '-' is concatenated at either end.

8.12   *(a)*

This text block does not have any incidental whitespace because the last line has no leading whitespace before the closing delimiter of the text block. The while loop splits the text block into individual lines, extracting a substring from the start to the line terminator (\n) of each line. The length of each line does not include the line terminator. The lengths are 3, 5, and 3, as no incidental whitespace is removed. The length of each line is then printed.

8.13   *(d)*

In (a) and (b), the content of the text block does not start after the line terminator of the opening delimiter (""").

In (c), the text block does not end with the closing delimiter ("""), but with four double quotes. Note that there is no requirement that double quotes should be balanced in a text block, and can be specified with or without escaping.

In (d), the text block ends correctly, as it uses the \" escape character for the double quote that should be part of the text block, allowing it to be distinguished from the closing delimiter. However, the last line of the block will not end with a line terminator. The resulting string literal is "\"a\"\"b\"". When printed, the output will be a single line containing the characters "a""b".

(e) is syntactically correct because the text block is correctly terminated. However, in this case the closing delimiter is on a line on its own, resulting in the last line of the text block content to end with a line terminator. The resulting string literal is "\"a\"\"b\"\n". When printed, the output will be a line containing the characters "a""b" followed by a newline.

(f) is incorrect because the last \" escape character results in the subsequent two double quotes also to be escaped, resulting in no closing delimiter being found—that is, \""" results in \"\"\".

8.14   *(a) and (e)*

The content of a text block starts on a new line of text immediately after the line that contains the opening delimiter, and ends just before the closing delimiter. This makes (a) correct, but not (b).

A text block is not a subtype of the String class, as the String class is final, and the type of a text block is String.

Although trailing whitespace is removed from the end of each line in the text block, only incidental whitespace is removed from the start of each line in the text block.

8.15 *(a)*

The code will fail to compile, since the expression (s == sb) is illegal. It compares references of two classes that are not related. Also, the StringBuffer class does not override the equals() method from the Object class, but inherits it.

8.16 *(e)*

The program will compile without errors and will print Have a when run. The contents of the string buffer are truncated to six characters by the method call sb.setLength(6).

8.17 *(c)*

The trimtoSize() only changes the capacity to match the length of the string builder. It does not the change the length of the string builder. The methods append(), reverse(), and setLength() change the string builder successively by appending "!" (" 1234 !"), reversing the string builder ("! 4321 "), and setting the length to 5 ("! 43"). The print statement prints |! 43|.

8.18 *(b)*

The references sb1 and sb2 are not aliases. The StringBuilder class does not override the equals() method so the result will be the same as with the == operator. The correct answer is (b).

8.19 *(a)*

The StringBuilder class does not override the hashCode() method, but the String class does. The references s1 and s2 refer to a String object and a StringBuilder object, respectively. The hash values of these objects are computed by the hashCode() method in the String and the Object class, respectively—giving different results. The references s1 and s3 refer to two different String objects that are equal, hence they have the same hash value.

8.20 *(b)*

String builders are mutable. When created, the string builder s1 has the sequence "W". The call to the append() method in the put0() method appends "0", resulting in "W0". On return from the put0() method, the call to the append() method in the main() method appends "W!" to the string builder. The string builder s1 now contains the sequence "WOW!" which is printed.

8.21 *(i)*

A StringBuilder is manipulated by different methods. First, the string "12" is appended, then the string "34" is inserted at index 1, resulting in the string "1342" in the StringBuilder object. Next, the delete() method does not modify the contents because the start and the end indexes are the same. Finally, the replace() method replaces the characters between the start indices 0 inclusive and the end index 1 exclusive with an empty string—that is, effectively removing the character '1' from index 0. The resulting string is "342".

8.22   *(b)*

Remember that the default capacity of the empty `StringBuilder` is 16 characters, which can change as its contents are modified. The string "42" is appended first, then the second character is deleted from this string, resulting in the `StringBuilder` object containing the string "4". The print statement concatenates the string "4" in the `StringBuilder` with the sum of its capacity (which still has the default value 16) and its length (which is 1)—in other words, the string "4" is concatenated with 17. The resulting string "417" is printed.

8.23   *(b) and (d)*

The method call `Math.ceil(v)` returns the `double` value 11.0, which is printed as 11.0 at (1), but as 11 at (4) after conversion to an `int`.

The method call `Math.round(v)` returns the `long` value 11, which is printed as 11 at (2).

The method call `Math.floor(v)` returns the `double` value 10.0, which is printed as 10.0 at (3), but as 10 at (5) after conversion to an `int`.

(b) and (d), corresponding to (2) and (4), will print 11.

8.24   *(b)*

The value –0.5 is rounded up to 0 and the value 0.5 is rounded up to 1.

8.25   *(b), (c), and (d)*

The expression will evaluate to one of the numbers 0, 1, 2, or 3. Each number has an equal probability of being returned by the expression.

9   Nested Type Declarations

9.1   *(e)*

The code will compile and print 123 at runtime. An instance of the `Outer` class will be created and the field `secret` will be initialized to 123. A call to the `createInner()` method will return the reference value of the newly created `Inner` instance. This object is an instance of a non-static member class and is associated with the outer instance. This means that an object of a non-static member class has access to the members within the outer instance. Since the `Inner` class is nested in the class containing the field `secret`, this field is accessible to the `Inner` instance, even though the field `secret` is declared `private`.

9.2   *(b) and (e)*

A static member class is in many respects like a top-level class, and can contain non-`static` fields. Instances of non-static member classes are created in the context of an outer instance. The inner instance is associated with the outer instance. Several non-static member class instances can be created and associated with the same outer instance. Static member classes do not have any implicit outer instance. A static member interface, just like top-level interfaces, cannot contain non-static fields. Nested interfaces are always `static`.

9.3   *(d)*

The program will compile without error, and will print 1, 3, 4, in that order, at run-time. The expression B.this.val will access the value 1 stored in the field val of the (outer) B instance associated with the (inner) C object referenced by the reference obj. The expression C.this.val will access the value 3 stored in the field val of the C object referenced by the reference obj. The expression super.val will access the field val from A, the superclass of C.

9.4   *(c) and (d)*

The class Inner is a non-static member class of the Outer class, and its qualified name is Outer.Inner. The Inner class does not inherit from the Outer class. The method named doIt is, therefore, neither overridden nor overloaded. Within the scope of the Inner class, the doIt() method of the Outer class is hidden by the doIt() method of the Inner class.

9.5   *(e)*

Non-static member classes, unlike top-level classes, can have any access modifier. Static member classes can be declared in a top-level class and any nested class. Methods in all nested classes can be declared static. Only static member classes can be declared static. Declaring a class static only means that instances of the class are created without having an outer instance. This has no bearing on whether the members of the class can be static or not.

9.6   *(c), (d), and (e)*

The method at (1) will not compile, since the parameter i is neither final nor effectively final, and therefore not accessible from within the inner class. The syntax of the anonymous class in the method at (2) is not correct, as the empty argument list is missing. The parameter i at (3) is effectively final, and at (4) it is final. The method at (5) is legally declared.

9.7   *(d)*

Other static members, not only static final fields declared as constant variables, can be declared within a non-static member class. Members in outer instances are directly accessible using simple names (provided they are not hidden). Fields in nested static member classes need not be final. Anonymous classes cannot have constructors, since they have no names. Nested classes define types that are distinct from the enclosing class, and the instanceof type comparison operator does not take the type of the outer instance into consideration.

9.8   *(d)*

Note that the nested classes are locally declared in a static context.

(a) and (b) refer to the field str1 in Inner. (c) refers to the field str1 in Access. (e) requires the Helper class to be in the Inner class in order to compile, but this will not print the right answer. (f), (g), and (h) will not compile, as the Helper local class cannot be accessed using the enclosing class name.

9.9   *(c)*

The field t denotes an instance of the anonymous inner class that extends the Test class. The toString() method is implicitly called on t in the print statement. The anonymous inner class overrides the toString() method, which is invoked. It returns the result of the following return statement:

```
return this.x + super.toString() + x;
```

Here, both this.x and x refer to the field x declared in the anonymous class, which has the character value '>'. This field shadows the local variable x in the main() method, which in turn shadows the field x in the Test class.

The call super.toString() results in the toString() method in the superclass Test to be invoked. It returns the result of the following statement:

```
return x + "42";
```

Here, the x refers to the field x in the Test class, which has the character value '='. The statement returns the string "=42".

The print statement concatenates the following expression to print ">=42>"—that is, (c):

```
'>' + "=42" + '>'
```

9.10   *(d)*

The String class is final, and therefore, cannot be extended. An anonymous inner class tries to extend the String class, but it will be flagged as an error by the compiler.

10   Object Lifetime

10.1   *(d)*

An object is only eligible for garbage collection if all remaining references to the object are from other objects that are also eligible for garbage collection. Therefore, if object obj2 is eligible for garbage collection and object obj1 contains a reference to it, then object obj1 must also be eligible for garbage collection. Java does not have a keyword delete. An object will not necessarily be garbage collected immediately after it becomes unreachable. However, the object will be eligible for garbage collection. Circular references do not prevent objects from being garbage collected, only reachable references do. An object is not eligible for garbage collection as long as the object can be accessed by any live thread.

10.2   *(b)*

Before (1), the String object initially referenced by arg1 is denoted by both msg and arg1. After (1), the String object is only denoted by msg. At (2), the reference msg is assigned a new reference value. This reference value denotes a new String object created by concatenating the contents of several other String objects. After (2), there are no references to the String object initially referenced by arg1. The String object is now eligible for garbage collection.

10.3   *(a)*

The only object created is the array, and it is reachable when control reaches (1).

10.4   *(a)*

All the objects created in the loop are reachable via p, when control reaches (1).

10.5   *(a)*

It may seem that since the method removeAll() sets the songs array reference to null, there would be three objects (i.e., the array itself and its two Song objects) eligible for garbage collection when control reaches (1). However, prior to this method invocation, this array reference is also assigned to a local array variable songs declared in the main() method. As a result, even though the songs array field in the Album object no longer references the Song array, the local array variable songs still references this array object, which is thus reachable.

10.6   *(c), (e), and (f)*

The static initializer blocks (a) and (b) are not legal, since the fields alive and STEP are non-static and final, respectively. (d) is not a syntactically legal static initializer block. The static block in (e) will have no effect, as its body is an empty block. The static block in (f) will change the value of the static field count from 5 to 1.

10.7   *(c)*

The program will compile and print 50, 70, 0, 20, 0 at runtime. All fields are given default values unless they are explicitly initialized. Field i is assigned the value 50 in the static initializer block that is executed when the class is initialized. This assignment will override the explicit initialization of field i in its declaration statement. When the main() method is executed, the static field i is 50 and the static field n is 0. When an instance of the class is created using the new operator, the value of the static field n (i.e., 0) is passed to the constructor. Before the body of the constructor is executed, the instance initializer block is executed, which assigns the values 70 and 20 to the fields j and n, respectively. When the body of the constructor is executed, the fields i, j, k, and n, and the parameter m, have the values 50, 70, 0, 20, and 0, respectively.

10.8   *(f)*

This class has a blank final boolean instance variable active. This variable must be initialized when an instance is constructed, or else the code will not compile. This also applies to blank final static variables. The keyword static is used to signify that a block is a static initializer block. No keyword is used to signify that a block is an instance initializer block. (a) and (b) are not instance initializer blocks, and (c), (d), and (e) fail to initialize the blank final variable active.

10.9   *(c)*

The program will compile and print 2, 3, and 1 at runtime. When the object is created and initialized, the instance initializer block is executed first as it is declared first, printing 2. Then the instance initializer expression is executed, printing 3. Finally, the constructor body is executed, printing 1. The forward reference in the instance initializer block is legal, as the use of the field m is on the left-hand side of the assignment.

10.10   *(c)*

This question tests understanding of execution order of initializers and constructors when an object is created. First the static initializers are executed, when classes Music and Song are loaded into memory. Therefore, the string "-C--F-" is printed first. The static initializers are invoked only once, so neither "-C-" nor "-F-" is printed again. This excludes (a) and (b).

When the first new Song() object is created, it first triggers initialization starting from its superclass instance initializer and constructor, which prints "-D--E-", after which the instance initializer and constructor in the Song class are executed, printing "-G--A-". This process is repeated for the second new song, resulting in "-D--E--G--A-" being printed. The final printout is "-C--F--D--E--G--A--D--E--G--A-".

10.11   *(c) and (e)*

Line (1) will cause illegal redefinition of the field width. Line (2) uses an illegal forward reference to the fields width and height. The assignment in line (3) is legal. Line (4) is an assignment statement, and therefore illegal in this context. Line (5) declares a local variable inside an initializer block with the same name as the instance variable width, which is allowed. The simple name in this block will refer to the local variable. To access the instance variable width, the this reference must be used in this block.

11   Generics

11.1   *(b)*

The type of intList is List of Integer and the type of numList is List of Number. The compiler issues an error because List<Integer> is *not* a subtype of List<Number>.

11.2   *(c)*

With a reference of type List<? super Integer>, a set/put/write/add operation can only add an Integer or a subtype of Integer to the list. Calls to the add() method in the code are not a problem, as an Integer is added to the list.

With a reference of type List<? super Integer>, a get/read operation can only get an Object from the list. This object is not assignable to a reference of type Number. (3) will not compile.

11.3   *(b)*

The compiler issues an unchecked conversion warning at (1), as we are assigning a raw list to a generic list.

11.4   *(b), (f), and (g)*

We cannot create an array of a type parameter, as at (2). We cannot refer to the type parameters of a generic class in a static context—for example, in static initializer blocks, static field declarations, and as types of local variables in static methods, as at (6) and (7).

11.5   *(b), (c), (e), and (f)*

In (b), (c), (e), and (f), the parameterized type in the object creation expression is a subtype of the type of the reference. This is not the case in (a): Just because HashMap<Integer, String> is a subtype of Map<Integer, String>, it does not follow that HashMap<Integer, HashMap<Integer, String>> is a subtype of Map<Integer, Map<Integer, String>>—there is no subtype covariance relationship between concrete parameterized types. In (d) and (g), wild cards cannot be used to instantiate the class.

11.6   *(b)*

ArrayList<Fruit> is not a subtype of List<? extends Apple> at (1), and ArrayList<Apple> is not a subtype of List<? super Fruit> at (4). Any generic list can be assigned to a raw list reference. A raw list and an unbounded wildcard list are assignment compatible.

11.7   *(d)*

The compiler issues unchecked warnings for calls to the add() method. The TreeSet class orders elements according to their natural ordering. A ClassCastException is thrown at runtime when the statement set.add(2) is executed, as an Integer is not comparable to a String.

11.8   *(a) and (b)*

The type of reference g is of raw type Garage. We can put any object in such a Garage, but only get Objects out. The type of value returned by the get() method at (6) through (8) is Object, and therefore, is not assignment compatible with Vehicle, Car, or Sedan.

11.9   *(d), (e), and (f)*

In (a), the arguments in the call are (List<Number>, List<Integer>). No type inferred from the arguments satisfies the formal parameters (List<? extends T>, List<? super T>).

In (b), the arguments in the call are (List<Number>, List<Integer>). The actual type parameter is Number. The arguments do not satisfy the formal parameters (List<? extends Number>, List<? super Number>). List<Number> is a subtype of List<? extends Number>, but List<Integer> is not a subtype of List<? super Number>.

In (c), the arguments in the call are (List<Number>, List<Integer>). The actual type parameter is Integer. The arguments do not satisfy the formal parameters (List<? extends Integer>, List<? super Integer>). List<Number> is not a subtype of List<? extends Integer>, although List<Integer> is a subtype of List<? super Integer>.

In (d), the arguments in the call are (List<Integer>, List<Number>). The inferred type is Integer. The arguments satisfy the formal parameters (List<? extends Integer>, List<? super Integer>).

In (e), the arguments in the call are (List<Integer>, List<Number>). The actual type parameter is Number. The arguments satisfy the formal parameters (List<? extends Number>, List<? super Number>).

In (f), the arguments in the call are (List<Integer>, List<Number>). The actual type parameter is Integer. The arguments satisfy the formal parameters (List<? extends Integer>, List<? super Integer>).

11.10　*(f)*

(a) invokes the zero-argument constructor at (1).

(b) invokes the constructor at (2) with T as String and V as String.

(c) invokes the constructor at (2) with T as String and V as Integer.

(d) invokes the constructor at (3) with T as Integer and V as String.

(e) invokes the constructor at (3) with T as String and V as Integer.

(f) cannot infer type arguments for Box<>. From the constructor call signature (String, Integer) one would assume that T was String and V was Integer. The parameterized type Box<Integer> of the reference on the left-hand side implies T is Integer, which contradicts that T is String on the right-hand side.

11.11　*(b)*

It is the fully qualified name of the class after erasure that is printed at runtime. Note that it is the type of the object, not the reference, that is printed. The erasure of all the lists in the program is ArrayList.

11.12　*(e)*

(a) contains incompatible types for assignment in the main() method. The method will return a Collection whose element type is some unknown subtype of CharSequence (Collection<? extends CharSequence>). As it is not known which subtype, assignment to Collection<String> cannot be allowed.

(b) contains an incompatible return value in the delete4LetterWords() method. The declared return type is List<E> but the return statement returns a Collection<E>. It cannot convert from Collection<E> to List<E>.

In (c), the reference words denotes a Collection whose element type is some unknown subtype of CharSequence (Collection<? extends CharSequence>). In the for(:) loop, the loop variable word is of type E. The unknown element type of words cannot be converted to E.

(d) contains an incompatible return value in the delete4LetterWords() method: It cannot convert from Collection<E> to List<E>, as explained in (b). In the for(:) loop, the unknown element type of words cannot be converted to an element of type E, as explained in (c).

(e) is OK.

In (f), the keyword super cannot be used in a constraint. It can only be used with a wildcard (?).

11.13　*(b) and (f)*

After erasure, the method at (1) has the signature overloadMe(List, List). Since all methods are declared void, they must differ in their parameter list after erasure in order to be overloaded with the method at (1). All methods have different parameter lists from that of the method at (1), except for the declarations (b) and (f). In other words, all methods have signatures that are not override equivalent to the signature of the method at (1), except for (b) and (f).

11.14   *(b)*

Passing or assigning a raw list to either a list of Integers or to a list of type parameter T is not type-safe. Passing or assigning a raw List to a List<?> is always permissible.

11.15   *(c), (f), (i), and (k)*

The type parameter N in SubC1 does *not* parameterize the supertype SupC. The erasure of the signature at (3) is the same as the erasure of the signature at (1) (i.e., it is a name clash). Therefore, of the three alternatives (a), (b), and (c), only (c) is correct.

The type parameter N in SubC1 cannot be guaranteed to be a subtype of the type parameter T in SupC—that is, incompatible return types for the get() methods at (4) and (2), which are not overridden. Also, methods cannot be overloaded if only return types are different. Therefore, of the three alternatives (d), (e), and (f), only (f) is correct.

The type parameter N in SubC2 is a subtype of the type parameter M, which parameterizes the supertype SupC. The erasure of the signature at (5) is still the same as the erasure of the signature at (1) (i.e., it is a name clash). Therefore, of the three alternatives (g), (h), and (i), only (i) is correct.

The type parameter N in SubC1 is a subtype of the type parameter T (through M) in SupC—that is, covariant return types for the get() methods at (6) and (2), which are overridden. Therefore, of the three alternatives (j), (k), and (l), only (k) is correct.

11.16   *(a), (c), and (e)*

In (a), because of the way an enum type E is implemented as a subtype of the java.lang.Enum<E> class in Java, we cannot define a generic enum type.

In (c), generic exceptions or error types are not allowed because the exception handling mechanism is a runtime mechanism and the JVM is oblivious to generics.

In (e), anonymous classes do not have a name, but a class name is needed for declaring a generic class and specifying its formal type parameters. A *parameterized* anonymous class can always to declared.

11.17   *(d)*

Casts are permitted, as at (2) through (6), but can result in an unchecked warning. The *assignment* at (5) is from a raw type (List) to a parameterized type (List<Integer>), resulting in an unchecked assignment conversion warning. Note that at (5) the cast does not pose any problem. It is the assignment from generic code to legacy code that can be a potential problem, and flagged as an unchecked warning.

At (6), the cast is against the erasure of List<Integer>—that is, List. The compiler cannot guarantee that obj is a List<Integer> at runtime, and therefore flags the cast with an unchecked warning.

Only reifiable types in casts do not result in an unchecked cast warning.

11.18   *(e)*

Instance tests in the scuddle() method use the reified type List<?>. All assignments in the main() method are type-safe.

11.19   *(c)*

The erasure of E[] in the method copy() is Object[]. The array type Object[] is actually cast to Object[] at runtime—that is, an identity cast. The method copy() returns an array of Object. In the main() method, the assignment of this array to an array of Strings results in a ClassCastException.

11.20   *(e)*

The method header at (1) is valid. The type of the variable arity parameter can be generic. The type of the formal parameter aols is an array of Lists of T. However, the compiler issues a potential heap pollution warning because of variable arity parameter aols.

The main() method at (2) can be declared as String..., as it is equivalent to String[], but no potential heap pollution warning is issued, as it is a reifiable type.

The statement at (3) creates an array of Lists of Strings. However, the compiler issues an unchecked conversion warning, since a raw type (List[]) is being assigned to a parameterized type (List<String>[]).

The formal type parameter T is inferred to be String in the method call at (4).

The method doIt() prints each list in its variable arity parameter aols.

12   Collections, Part I: ArrayList<E>

12.1   *(e)*

The for(;;) loop correctly increments the loop variable so that all the elements in the list are traversed. Removing elements using the for(;;) loop does not throw a ConcurrentModificationException at runtime.

12.2   *(b) and (c)*

In the method doIt1(), one of the common elements ("Ada") between the two lists is reversed. The value null is added to one of the lists but not the other.

In the method doIt2(), the two lists have common elements. Swapping the elements in one does not change their position in the other.

12.3   *(c)*

The element at index 2 has the value null. Calling the equals() method on this element throws a NullPointerException.

12.4   *(f)*

Deleting elements when iterating over a list requires care, as the size changes and any elements to the right of the deleted element are shifted left. Incrementing the loop variable after deleting an element will miss the next element (i.e., the last occurrence of "Bob"). Removing elements using the for(;;) loop does not throw a ConcurrentModificationException at runtime.

12.5   *(f)*

The while loop will execute as long as the remove() method returns true—that is, as long as there is an element with the value "Bob" in the list. The while loop body is the empty statement. The remove() method does not throw an exception if an element value is null, or if it is passed a null value.

12.6 *(b)*

An ArrayList object is populated with the content from the String array. Just like with an array, an array list has a 0-based index. The item at index 1 in this array list is replaced with the string "X", making this array list content [A,X,B,A]. Then a new item is added at the same index position, causing all other items in the list to be shifted by one position, making this array list content [A,X,X,B,A]. Lastly, an item at index 2 is removed, giving the result [A,X,B,A].

12.7 *(a)*

The method Arrays.asList() creates a fixed-size list, which does not allow items to be added or removed, but its content can be changed, which is what the set() operations do, replacing items at index 1 and 2 with "X".

12.8 *(c)*

The two arrays and the list in the main() method contain references to the same Song objects. These are not independent copies, so modifications on a shared Song object will be visible no matter how this object is accessed.

12.9 *(b)*

A list that is created using the List.of() method shares the elements with the original array. However, changes applied to the original array are not reflected in the list.

12.10 *(a)*

The method toArray() returns an array with all the elements in the list. The type of the array is given by the array passed as a parameter. If the length of the argument array is equal to the size of the list, the argument array is used. The argument array is also used if its length is greater than the size of the list, but after copying the elements to the array, the remaining elements in the array are filled with null values. Otherwise, a new array of appropriate size is created. In the sample code, the length of the array is equal to the size of the list. Therefore, the argument array is used. Afterwards, the lowercase version of the element at index 0 in the original list is assigned to the element at index 1 in the array.

12.11 *(b)*

An empty ArrayList object is created to store Character objects, using a constructor with a capacity of 3. Five char values from 'a' to 'e' are boxed as Character objects and added to this list. Remember that a list auto-expands its capacity as required.

13 Functional-Style Programming

13.1 *(e)*

A functional interface can be implemented by lambda expressions and classes. A functional interface declaration can only have one abstract method declaration. In the body of a lambda expression, all members in the enclosing class can be accessed. In the body of a lambda expression, only final or effectively final local variables in the enclosing scope can be accessed.

13.2   *(e), (f), (g), and (i)*

The assignments at (5), (6), (7), and (9) will not compile. We must check whether the function type of the target type and the type of the lambda expression are compatible. The function type of the target type p1 in the assignment statements from (1) to (5) is String -> void (i.e., a void return). The function type of the target type p2 in the assignment statements from (6) to (10) is String -> String (i.e., a non-void return). Below, the functional type of the target type is shown in a comment with the prefix LHS (left-hand side), and the type of the lambda expression for each assignment from (1) to (10) is shown in a comment with the prefix RHS (right-hand side).

```
    Funky1 p1;                                  //    LHS: String -> void
    p1 = s -> System.out.println(s);            // (1) RHS: String -> void
    p1 = s -> s.length();                       // (2) RHS: String -> int
    p1 = s -> s.toUpperCase();                  // (3) RHS: String -> String
    p1 = s -> { s.toUpperCase(); };             // (4) RHS: String -> void
//  p1 = s -> { return s.toUpperCase(); };      // (5) RHS: String -> String

    Funky2 p2;                                  //    LHS: String -> String
//  p2 = s -> System.out.println(s);            // (6) RHS: String -> void
//  p2 = s -> s.length();                       // (7) RHS: String -> int
    p2 = s -> s.toUpperCase();                  // (8) RHS: String -> String
//  p2 = s -> { s.toUpperCase(); };             // (9) RHS: String -> void
    p2 = s -> { return s.toUpperCase(); };      // (10)RHS: String -> String
```

Remember that the non-void return of a lambda expression with an *expression statement* as the body can be interpreted as a void return, if the function type of the target type returns void. This is the case at (2) and (3). The return value is ignored. The type String -> String of the lambda expression at (5) is not compatible with the function type String -> void of the target type p1.

The type of the lambda expression at (6), (7), and (9) is not compatible with the function type String -> String of the target type p2.

13.3   *(d)*

The three interfaces are functional interfaces. AgreementB explicitly provides an abstract method declaration of the public method equals() from the Object class, but such declarations are excluded from the definition of a functional interface. Thus AgreementB effectively has only one abstract method. A functional interface can be implemented by a concrete class, such as Beta. The function type of the target type in the assignments (1) to (3) is void -> void. The type of the lambda expression at (1) to (3) is also void -> void. The assignments (1) to (3) are legal.

The assignment at (4) is legal. Subtype references are assigned to supertype references. References o, a, and c refer to the lambda expression at (3).

The assignment at (5) is legal. The reference b has the type AgreementB and class Beta implements this interface.

The code at (6), (7), and (8) invokes the method doIt(). The code at (6) evaluates the lambda expression at (3), printing Jingle|. The code at (7) invokes the doIt()

method on an object of class Beta, printing Jazz|. The code at (8) also evaluates the lambda expression at (3), printing Jingle|.

At (9), the reference o is cast down to AgreementA. The reference o actually refers to the lambda expression at (3), which has target type AgreementC. This interface is a subtype of AgreementA. A subtype is cast to a supertype, which is allowed, so no ClassCastException is thrown at runtime. Invoking the doIt() method again results in evaluation of the lambda expression at (3), printing Jingle|.

Apart from the declarations of the lambda expressions, the rest of the code is plain-vanilla Java. Note also that the following assignment that defines a lambda expression would not be valid, since the Object class is not a functional interface and therefore cannot provide a target type for the lambda expression:

```
Object obj = () -> System.out.println("Jingle");  // Compile-time error!
```

13.4   (c)

The method removeIf() accepts as an argument a lambda expression that implements a Predicate<E> interface. This method removes all strings of length 3 from the list. The for (:) loop calculates the sum of the lengths of the remaining strings in the list, producing a result of 9.

13.5   (c)

The method removeIf() accepts a lambda expression that first converts a string to lowercase and then tests whether the resulting string starts with the character 'a'. Note that the predicate only performs the test, and it does not actually modify the strings in the list. Only the strings "ANNA" and "ALICE" pass the test and are removed.

13.6   (i)

The lambda expression uses identifier s as a parameter name, which is illegal because a variable called s is already defined in the enclosing context of the lambda expression.

13.7   (c)

There are two predicates defined in this code. The first predicate determines whether a string contains the letter O, and the second one determines whether a string ends with the letter P. The composed predicate filter1.and(filter2).negate() determines whether a string does *not* contain an O *or* it does *not* end with a P. Only the strings "PLOT" and "LEAP" pass this test and are removed from the list by the removeIf() method, leaving only the strings "FLOP" and "LOOP" in the list.

13.8   (d)

The compose() method is inherited by the UnaryOperator<T> from its superinterface Function<T, T>. This method returns a Function<T, T>. As an instance of a supertype (Function<T, T>) cannot be assigned to a subtype (UnaryOperator<T>), the assignment to f3 results in a compile-time error.

13.9   (b)

All String values in the list are replaced with their lowercase equivalents using the replaceAll() method which accepts a lambda expression that implements a Unary-Operator<String>. The two consumers are applied to the values in this List.

Consumer c1 is changing the first letter of every string in the list to uppercase, but it does not replace actual `String` objects stored within this list. Next, consumer c2 prints the content of this list, which has been produced by the `replaceAll()` method.

13.10   *(b)*

Regarding method references, the method `isEven()` is static and therefore should be referred to using the class name `Test`, while the method `printValue()` is an instance method, and therefore should be referred to using a reference of the class `Test`.

13.11   *(a)*

The target reference for the bounded instance method reference is set explicitly. The unbounded instance method reference interprets the first argument as the target reference.

13.12   *(d)*

Notice that the `BiFunction` in this example is using raw type. Therefore, the x and y parameters are of the `Object` type. This means that a division operator cannot be applied in this case.

13.13   *(a)*

Functions f1 and f2 are combined to concatenate the prefix and the postfix around the value supplied to the `apply()` method argument. Notice that conversion to `String` works for any object in Java. Therefore, `Function` objects can use raw types.

14 Object Comparison

14.1   *(b) and (d)*

It is recommended that (a) is fulfilled, but it is not a requirement. (c) is also not required, but such objects will lead to collisions in the hash table, as they will map to the same bucket.

14.2   *(a), (b), (d), and (h)*

(c) is eliminated, since the `hashCode()` method cannot claim inequality if the `equals()` method claims equality. (e) and (f) are eliminated, since the `equals()` method must be reflexive, and (g) is eliminated, since the `hashCode()` method must consistently return the same hash code during execution.

14.3   *(b), (d), and (e)*

(a) and (c) fail to satisfy the properties of an equivalence relation. (a) is not transitive, and (c) is not symmetric.

14.4   *(a) and (e)*

(b) is not correct, since it will throw an `ArithmeticException` when called on a newly created `Measurement` object. (c) and (d) are not correct, since they may return unequal hash codes for two objects that are equal according to the `equals()` method.

14.5   *(c)*

The generic static method `cmp()` returns a comparator (implemented as a lambda expression) that reverses the natural ordering of a `Comparable` type. The natural ordering of the class `Person` is ordering by name first and then by age, using the reverse comparators `strCmp` and `intCmp`. p1 is *less* than p2 because of name, and p1 is *greater* than p3, because of age, as their names are equal.

14.6   *(d)*

All methods implement reverse natural ordering, except the method at (4). The method reference `Comparable::compareTo` is equivalent to the lambda expression `(e1, e2) -> e1.compareTo(e2)`—that is, natural ordering.

14.7   *(b)*

A lambda expression that implements the `Comparator<String, String>` is used to sort the array in ascending order based on the text representation of `Integer` objects. Basically, each array element is converted to a `String` before it is compared. The ordering is that of `String` objects, where "-23" is less than "-41" lexicographically.

14.8   *(a)*

The lambda expression that implements the `Comparator<Album>` interface defines a total ordering of `Album`s based on the difference between the lengths of the album titles, resulting in the list being sorted in ascending order by `title` length. The resulting list is then printed using the lambda expression that implements the `Consumer<Album>` interface.

14.9   *(b)*

The `equals()` method of the `Album1` class checks whether the object is not `null` and of the same type as the current object before comparing album titles. This is a strict check that verifies whether the object with which the current object is compared is of exactly the same type, using the following condition: `(getClass() != obj.getClass())`. Alternatively, a less strict check that allows type substitution is also possible: `(obj instanceof Album1)`. The difference between these two approaches is that the `instanceof` operator can return `true` when comparing this object to another object that is an instance of the subtype. Of course, this would not be the case if specific class types are compared.

Note that the logic in the `main()` method compares an `Album1` to an `LP`, which is actually a subclass of `Album1`. This means that even though both of these objects have the same title, they would not be considered equal because the logic of the `equals()` method implements a strict type comparison.

14.10   *(b) and (d)*

The `Comparator<A>` interface defines the `compare()` method that is designed to compare two argument objects of class A to establish their ordering. Each `Comparator<A>` implementation can define a different total ordering for the objects.

15   Collections: Part II

15.1   *(a)*

The expression in the for(:) loop header (in this case the call to the makeCollection() method) is only evaluated once.

15.2   *(c) and (d)*

The for(:) loop does not allow the list to be modified structurally. In (a) and (b), the code will throw a java.util.ConcurrentModificationException. Note that the iterator in (d) is less restrictive than the for(:) loop, allowing elements to be removed in a controlled way.

15.3   *(d)*

The iterator implemented will iterate over the elements of the list in the reverse order, and so will the for(:) loop. The Iterable<E> and the Iterator<E> interfaces are implemented correctly. Note that the anonymous class that implements the iterator is parameterized by the formal type parameter T of the generic class AnotherListIterator<T>.

15.4   *(b) and (d)*

Some operations on a collection may throw an UnsupportedOperationException. This exception type is unchecked, and the user code is not required to explicitly handle unchecked exceptions. A List<E> allows duplicate elements. An Array-List<E> is implemented using a resizable array. The capacity of the array will be expanded automatically when needed. The Set<E> allows at most one null element.

15.5   *(d)*

The program will compile without error, and will print all primes below 25 at runtime. All collection implementations used in the program implement the Collection<E> interface. The implementation instances are interchangeable when denoted by Collection references. None of the operations performed on the implementations will throw an UnsupportedOperationException. The program finds the primes below 25 by removing all values divisible by 2, 3, and 5 from the set of values from 2 through 25.

15.6   *(b)*

The remove() method removes the last element returned by either the next() or previous() method. The four next() calls return A, B, C, and D. D is subsequently removed. The two previous() calls return C and B. B is subsequently removed.

15.7   *(c), (d), (e), and (f)*

Sets cannot have duplicates. HashSet<E> does not guarantee the order of the elements in (a) and (b), so there is no guarantee that the program will print [1, 9]. Because LinkedHashSet<E> maintains elements in insertion order in (c) and (d), the program is guaranteed to print [1, 9]. Because TreeSet<E> maintains elements sorted according to the natural ordering in (e) and (f), the program is guaranteed to print [1, 9].

15.8   *(c) and (d)*

The output from each statement is shown below.

(a) [sea, shell, soap]

(b) [sea, shell]

(c) [soap, swan]

(d) [swan]

(e) [shell, soap]

(f) [sea, shell]

15.9   *(b) and (d)*

Although all *keys* in a map must be unique, duplicate *values* can occur. Since values are not unique, the values() method returns a Collection<V> and not a Set<V>. The collections returned by the keySet(), entrySet(), and values() methods are backed by the underlying map. This means that changes made in one are reflected in the other. Although implementations of the SortedMap<K, V> interface maintain the entries sorted according to key-sort order, this is not a requirement for classes that implement the Map<K, V> interface. For instance, the entries in a HashMap<K, V> are not sorted.

15.10   *(a), (c), and (d)*

The key of a Map.Entry<K, V> cannot be changed, since the key is used for locating the entry within the map. There is no set() method. The setValue() method is optional.

15.11   *(b)*

A set is a collection of unique elements, so an attempt to insert the same element twice is ignored, with no exception raised. The ordering of elements in the set is determined by the Comparator<E> passed to the TreeSet constructor. The comparator passed compares the element strings in the *reverse natural ordering*.

15.12   *(b)*

The set1 object sorts elements according to the *reverse natural ordering*. The set2 object retains that ordering. In the statement

    NavigableSet<String> set2 = new TreeSet<>(set1);

the signature of the constructor called is the following:

    TreeSet<String>(SortedSet<String> set)

resulting in the same ordering for the elements in set2 as in set1 (i.e., reverse natural ordering). Note that class NavigableSet<E> is a subclass of class SortedSet<E> class.

15.13   *(a)*

The set1 object sorts the elements according to reverse natural ordering.

In the statement

    NavigableSet<String> set2 = new TreeSet<>((Collection<String>)set1);

the signature of the constructor called is

    TreeSet<String>(Collection<? extends String> collection)

resulting in the elements in set2 being sorted according to *natural ordering*, and not according to the reverse natural ordering of set1.

15.14 *(a)*

The set1 object sorts its elements in reverse natural ordering. It is polled from the tail, so its elements are fetched according to natural ordering. On the other hand, the elements in set2 are sorted according to natural ordering. set2 is polled from the head, so its elements are fetched according to natural ordering.

15.15 *(b)*

A map view method creates half-open intervals (i.e., the upper bound is not included), unless the inclusion of the bounds is explicitly specified. Clearing a map view clears the affected entries from the underlying map. The argument to the sumValues() method can be any subtype of Map<K, V>, where the type of the value is Integer.

15.16 *(b), (e), and (f)*

(a) throws a ConcurrentModificationException. We cannot remove an entry in a for(:) loop. (c) throws a ConcurrentModificationException as well, even though we use an iterator. The remove() method is called on the map, not on the iterator. The argument to the remove() method of the map must implement Comparable. Map.Entry<K, V> does not, resulting in a ClassCastException in (d).

We can remove an entry from the underlying map when iterating over the key set using an iterator, as in (b). (e) creates a map view of one entry and clears it, thereby clearing it also from the underlying map. (f) removes the entry for "Shampoo" from the map, since the lambda expression returns the value null.

15.17 *(e)*

The variable sumVal is not effectively final when referenced in the lambda expression body, as it is incremented for each entry in the map.

15.18 *(c)*

The computeIfAbsent() method returns an empty TreeSet if the key is not found in the map. If the key is found, it returns the associated TreeSet. The add() method is invoked on the TreeSet that is returned by the computeIfAbsent() method. The add() method adds its argument to this TreeSet. The resulting map is a *multimap*— that is, a key can be associated with a collection of values.

15.19 *(b)*

The BiFunction<Integer, String, String> implemented by the lambda expression computes a new value for the key of an entry in the map. The switch statement determines the new value based on the key. The lambda expression returns the value "FIRST" for key 1, the value "SECOND" for key 2, and so on. The replaceAll() method replaces the value of each entry in the map with the new value computed for the key by the BiFunction<T, U, R>.

15.20   *(b)*

The class `StringBuilder` implements the `Comparable<E>` interface. The `sort()` method sorts the elements in reverse natural ordering: [C, B, A]. The method `subList()` returns the elements in the open interval [1, 2)—that is, the element at index 1, which is "B".

15.21   *(b), (c), (f), and (g)*

The `Collections.addAll()` method adds the elements to an existing list when it is called. All three elements are in `list1` when (1) is executed. The `Arrays.asList()` method returns a new list every time it is called. Only the string "Howdy" is in `list2` when (2) is executed. The `Collection.addAll()` method adds the elements of its argument collection to the collection on which it is called. In this case, `list3` has the same elements as `list1`. Calling the constructor with a collection as an argument initializes the new list with the elements of the specified collection. In this case, `list4` has the same elements as `list2`.

Creating a new list by calling the constructor with a collection as an argument returns an `ArrayList` initialized with the elements of the collection.

15.22   *(a) and (f)*

The largest value a match can return is the largest index—that is, *array.length – 1* (==3). The key must be equal to the largest element in the array. If no match is found, a negative value is returned, which is computed as follows: *– (insertion point + 1)*. The smallest value is returned for a key that is greater than the largest element in the array. This key must obviously be placed at the index *array.length (==4)*, after the largest element—that is, the insertion point is 4. The value of the expression *– (insertion point + 1)* is -5, which is the smallest value printed by the method.

15.23   *(c)*

The operation `pollFirst()` does not throw an exception, but rather returns `null` when the `Deque` object is empty. The operations `peekFirst()` and `peekLast()` return the first and last elements from the `Deque` object, respectively, but do not remove elements from the `Deque`. The operations `pollFirst()` and `pollLast()` return the first and last elements from the `Deque` object, respectively, and remove them from the `Deque`. The operation `offerFirst()` inserts elements at the head of the `Deque`. The operation `offerLast()` inserts elements at the tail of the `Deque`.

15.24   *(b)*

A set cannot have duplicates. This means that object x was only added once to the set. The `add()` method does not throw an exception, but rather returns `false` when an element cannot be added to the set.

15.25   *(d)*

The first two add operations result in the list [1, 2]. Next, a `null` value is inserted at index 2, and the value 3 is inserted at index 3, which results in the list [1, 2, null, 3]. Next, the value 4 is inserted at index 2, shifting elements towards the end of the list, resulting in the list [1, 2, 4, null, 3]. The element at index 2 is replaced with the value 3, giving the list [1, 2, 3, null, 3], and then the element at index 2 is removed, giving the list [1, 2, null, 3]. Finally, the value 2 is inserted at index 2, which results in the list [1, 2, 2, null, 3].

16 Streams

16.1 *(b)*

The mapToInt() operation converts a Stream<String> to an IntStream whose elements are the length of the strings in its input stream. The int stream will contain the values 1, 3, 2, and 4, corresponding to the length of the strings. The filter() operation discards strings of length 4. Its output stream will only contain the values 1, 3, and 2. The reduce() method performs a functional reduction, starting with the initial value of 1. Its accumulator multiplies the cumulative result with the current value in the int stream, with the computation proceeding as follows:

```
(x, y) -> x * y
(1, 1) -> 1 * 1 => 1
(1, 3) -> 1 * 3 => 3
(3, 2) -> 3 * 2 => 6
```

16.2 *(d)*

The filter() intermediate operation is designed to return a stream whose elements match the given Predicate. The findFirst() terminal operation does not necessarily return the first element from the stream when this stream is processed in parallel mode. The reduce() terminal operation performs a functional reduction on the elements of the stream, and it uses an accumulator and not a Predicate. The sorted() intermediate operation sorts the elements according to their natural order, or according to the total order specified by a Comparator.

16.3 *(d) and (e)*

(a) performs a functional reduction starting with the initial value 0 and adding all values in the stream to compute the sum of the values.

(b) performs the same functional reduction as in (a) but in parallel mode.

(c) performs the same functional reduction as in (a), but does not use the initial value of 0. It uses the value of the first element in the stream, if there is one. Since the stream can be empty, it returns an OptionalInt object. The orElse() operation on this OptionalInt object retrieves an int value if it has one; otherwise, the operation returns the value 0.

(d) uses 0 as the initial value, which means that this value will be returned if the steam is empty. Therefore, the operation is guaranteed to return an int value, and not an OptionalInt. The orElse() operation cannot be invoked on an int value, so this code will not compile.

(e) refers to the variable sum within the lambda expression. As it has not been initialized, the code will fail to compile. Note that only final or effectively final variables can be referenced within a lambda expression.

(f) computes the sum of all values in the stream.

16.4   *(b) and (d)*

The stream will contain the following values: 0, 1, 2, 3, and 4. Note that x designates the cumulative value and y designates the current element.

(a) performs functional reduction using the identity value 0 as the initial value and the accumulator adds 1 to the cumulative result for each element. The reduction proceeds as follows:

```
(x, y) -> x + 1
(0, 0) -> 0 + 1 => 1
(1, 1) -> 1 + 1 => 2
(2, 2) -> 2 + 1 => 3
(3, 3) -> 3 + 1 => 4
(4, 4) -> 4 + 1 => 5
```

(b) performs a similar functional reduction as in (a), but uses the value of the first element (0) as the initial value. So it would result in one addition less than (a). The reduction proceeds as follows:

```
(x, y) -> x + 1
(0, 1) -> 0 + 1 => 1
(1, 2) -> 1 + 1 => 2
(2, 3) -> 2 + 1 => 3
(3, 4) -> 3 + 1 => 4
```

(c) performs a functional reduction similar to (a), but now the accumulator increases the value of the stream element y by 1. The reduction proceeds as follows:

```
(x, y) -> y + 1
(0, 0) -> 0 + 1 => 1
(1, 1) -> 1 + 1 => 2
(2, 2) -> 2 + 1 => 3
(3, 3) -> 3 + 1 => 4
(4, 4) -> 4 + 1 => 5
```

(d) performs a functional reduction using the initial value 0 and where the accumulator returns the value of the stream element y. The reduction proceeds as follows:

```
(x, y) -> y
(0, 0) -> 0 => 0
(0, 1) -> 1 => 1
(1, 2) -> 2 => 2
(2, 3) -> 3 => 3
(3, 4) -> 4 => 4
```

(e) performs a function reduction which is similar to (c), except that it uses the identity value of 1 as the initial value. The reduction proceeds as follows:

```
(x, y) -> y + 1
(1, 0) -> 0 + 1 => 1
(1, 1) -> 1 + 1 => 2
(2, 2) -> 2 + 1 => 3
(3, 3) -> 3 + 1 => 4
(4, 4) -> 4 + 1 => 5
```

(f) performs a functional reduction of the stream elements using the count() operation, which in this case results in the value 5.

16.5   (d)

(a) produces three groups based on the Integer values corresponding to the lengths of String objects in the stream. The Predicate expression discards any value containing the string "C".

```
1 []
2 [AA, DD]
3 [BBB, EEE]
```

(b) produces three groups based on the Integer values corresponding to the lengths of String objects in the stream. The filter() operation discards all values except those that contain the string "C".

```
1 [C]
2 []
3 []
```

(c) produces two groups based on the Integer values corresponding to the lengths of String objects in the stream. However, the filter() operation discards any values containing the string "C", before the groups are created.

```
2 [AA, DD]
3 [BBB, EEE]
```

(d) results in a single group based on the Integer values corresponding to the length of String objects in the stream. The filter() operation discards any values except those that contain the string "C", before any groups are created.

```
1 [C]
```

16.6   (d)

An infinite stream of string "A" is generated. The first peek() operation prints the string "B". The Predicate of the takeWhile() operation returns false immediately on encountering the first element in the stream which is "A". The takeWhile() operation only takes an element if it is not "A". It short-circuits the stream processing, resulting in an output stream that is empty. The Consumer of the second peek() operation does not execute, as the stream is empty. The anyMatch() terminal operation returns false on encountering an empty stream.

16.7   (a)

A stream of int values that correspond to character codes for letters 'a', 'b', 'c', and 'd' is generated. These values are mapped to single-letter strings that are converted to uppercase. The filter() operation discards a letter if it does not match a vowel, which results in an output stream with only the element "A", which is printed.

16.8   (b) and (c)

A stream of int values 0, 1, 2, 3, and 4 is generated. The filter() operation discards all even numbers from this stream, retaining only the odd numbers 1 and 3, which are then printed.

(a) generates a stream of int values 0, 1, 2, 3, 4, and 5 which is one value more than in the program. Even numbers are discarded, retaining only the odd numbers 1, 3, and 5 which are then printed.

(b) generates a stream of int values between 0 and 10. The takeWhile() operation only takes values less than 5. It truncates the stream when the element is greater than or equal to 5. The filter() operation discards all even numbers from the truncated stream, retaining only the odd numbers 1 and 3, which are then printed.

(c) generates a stream of int values between 0 and 10, which is then truncated to the first five values. The filter() operation discards all even numbers from this truncated stream, retaining only the odd numbers 1 and 3, which are then printed.

(d) generates an infinite stream of 0s. The expression x++ will always evaluate to 0, when x is initialized to 0. The takeWhile() operation will continue to take elements from the stream, as its Predicate will always return true. The filter() operation will continue to discard each element, as its value will always be 0. The terminal operation will never get to process an element. This state of affairs will continue indefinitely, with nothing being printed.

(e) does not compile because the variable x referred to in the lambda expression is not final. The expression x++ will change the value in x, which is not permitted.

16.9   *(d)*

Two streams of String objects containing the values "A", "B", "C" and the values "X", "Y", "Z" are concatenated into a single stream. The resulting stream has the values "X", "Y", "Z", "A", "B", "C".

The functional reduction concatenates the elements from this new stream into a single string. This operation returns an Optional<String>, as the reduction uses the first element as the initial value. The result string in the Optional<String> is returned by the get() method of the Optional class.

Note that a denotes the cumulative result and b denotes the current element in the stream. The reduction operation is performed as follows:

```
(a,           b)  ->  b + a
("X",       "Y")  ->  "Y" + "X" => "YX"
("YX",      "Z")  ->  "Z" + "YX" => "ZYX"
("ZYX",     "A")  ->  "A" + "ZYX" => "AZYX"
("AZYX",    "B")  ->  "B" + "AZYX" => "BAZYX"
("BAZYX",   "C")  ->  "C" + "BAZYX" => "CBAZYX"
```

16.10   *(a)*

All process a stream of String objects that are one-letter strings from "A" to "E". Grouping is done based on a classifier which is a Function, whereas partitioning is done based on a Predicate. Identical lambda expressions implement the classifier and the predicate in all options. The lambda expression returns true if the single-letter string is a vowel. The map created by both operations will have the type Map<Boolean, List<String>>, where the keys are Boolean and the value associated with a key is a List<String>. The list is created implicitly, as in (a) and (b), or explicitly in a downstream collector, as in (c) and (d).

The filtering is done by the same predicate in all options, discarding any one-letter string that is greater than the string "A". Effectively, the only element processed by the stream is the string "A".

The `partitioningBy()` operation always creates entries for the `Boolean.TRUE` and `Boolean.FALSE` keys in the result map, even if no values can be computed for these keys from the stream elements. On the other hand, the `groupingBy()` operation creates entries for keys computed by its classifier—that is, an entry is created for the key `Boolean.TRUE` or `Boolean.FALSE` depending on the elements in the stream. However, when the `filtering()` operation is used as a downstream collector in the grouping operation, entries for both the `Boolean.TRUE` and `Boolean.FALSE` keys are created, regardless of whether any value is associated with these keys.

In (a), grouping creates only one entry for the `Boolean.TRUE` key in the result map based on its `Predicate` being `true`, since the only element "A" in the stream is a vowel. The output is the following:

```
true [A]
```

In (b), partitioning creates two entries in the result map: one for the `Boolean.TRUE` key (vowels) and one for the `Boolean.FALSE` key (consonants). The only element "A" is associated with the `true` key as it a vowel. The output is the following:

```
false []
true [A]
```

In (c), grouping creates two entries: one for the `Boolean.TRUE` key (vowels) and one for the `Boolean.FALSE` key (consonants), as its downstream collector is a `filtering()` operation. Since the string "A" is a vowel, it is accumulated in the list associated with the `Boolean.TRUE` key. The list associated with the `Boolean.FALSE` key remains empty. The output is the following:

```
false []
true [A]
```

In (d), partitioning creates two entries: one for the `Boolean.TRUE` key (vowels) and one for the `Boolean.FALSE` key (consonants), regardless of its downstream collector. Since the string "A" is a vowel, it is accumulated in the list associated with the `Boolean.TRUE` key. The list associated with the `Boolean.FALSE` key remains empty. The output is the following:

```
false []
true [A]
```

This means that (a) resulted in only one entry in the map, while the other resulted in two identical entries.

16.11   *(d)*

It is important to note that the stream of strings is not processed separately from the stream of chars, but rather they are fused into a single stream pipeline. This is because only one terminal operation exists in the stream pipeline. This means that the parallel processing applies to the entire pipeline. The `sort()` operation sorts the characters in the flattened stream, but the `forEach()` operation cannot be relied upon to respect the order, especially in a parallel stream. The `forEachOrdered()` operation will give a deterministic result regardless of the execution mode of a stream. The result from the program is therefore unpredictable.

16.12   *(c) and (d)*

The filter() method accepts a Predicate. The methods peek() and forEach() accept a Consumer. map() accepts a Function, max() accepts a Comparator, and findAny() does not accept any parameters.

16.13   *(b) and (f)*

The methods peek(), map(), filter(), and sorted() are all intermediate operations. The methods forEach() and min() are terminal operations.

16.14   *(b) and (d)*

Short-circuit methods may produce finite results for potentially an infinite stream. For example, the operations limit() and anyMatch() are short-circuit operations. A short-circuit operation terminates the stream pipeline, whether or not all elements in the stream have been processed.

16.15   *(f)*

These statements all perform an equivalent functional reduction of counting the number of elements in the stream. Empty string or null elements are still counted as elements. Thus all of these operations return the value 6. Counting the number of elements in the stream can be achieved using the count() method of the Stream interface, or the counting() method provided by the Collectors class. Another solution is to map all stream elements to the value 1, and then summing up the 1s will give the same result.

16.16   *(b) and (d)*

In (a), a set of String objects is constructed that contains the values "XX", "XXXX", "", and "X" because the filter() method removes all null elements from the stream. Notice the absence of the duplicate values due to the fact that a Set does not allow duplicates. All strings of this set are then processed in another stream that maps the strings to int values according to the length of each string. This results in the output 0124, because sorting of values is done before printing.

In (b), another set of Integer objects is constructed based on the same values. However, in this case all null elements and empty strings are converted to the int value of 0, and then removed from the stream by the filter() method. All values in the result set are then processed in another stream that sorts the elements and prints the output 124.

(c) applies similar logic to that in (b), except that it uses a collector that assembles the values in a List rather than a Set. Duplicate elements are allowed in lists, resulting in the output 1224.

(d) is similar to (c), but it applies the distinct() operation to the stream elements, removing any duplicates, and resulting in the output 124.

17 Date and Time

17.1   *(b)*

The first `LocalDate` object represents the date January 31, 2021, thus representing 31 days since the start of the year. The second `LocalDate` object is the result of adding exactly one month to the first `LocalDate` object. Since 2021 is not a leap year, it represents the date February 28, 2021, which is 59 days from the start of the year. The third `LocalDate` object is the result of subtracting one month from the second `LocalDate` object, resulting in the date January 28, 2021.

17.2   *(a)*

A `LocalDate` object is initially constructed to represent the date January 1, 2021. A new `LocalDate` object is then constructed based on this date, by first changing the day of the month to be 31, which is the last day of this month. Next, the month in this date is changed to February. It is important to remember that February in 2021 has only 28 days, so the resulting `LocalDate` object would have to represent the last day of February.

17.3   *(d)*

The `LocalDateTime` denoted by d1 represents 2021-04-01T00:00.

The method `toInstant()` converts d1 by applying zone offset +18:00—that is, 18 hours ahead of the time at UTC.

To convert d1 to an `Instant` denoted by i1 at zero UTC offset, we must subtract 18 hours, resulting in the instant 2021-03-31T06:00:00Z.

The `ofInstant()` method converts i1 to `LocalDate`, but no offset adjustment is necessary to the date represented in i1 as it represents a point in time on the UTC timeline.

17.4   *(c)*

Two `ZonedDateTime` objects are constructed exactly one hour apart. However, two new zoned date-time objects are create from these two, and the duration between them is calculated. These new zoned data-time objects are an extra hour apart because one subtracts and the other one adds 30 minutes, thus increasing the time difference to two hours between 23:30CET and 00:30GMT. Another way to view this is to convert the time in one time zone (23:30CET) to the other time zone (22:30GMT). The difference between 22:30GMT and 00:30GMT is two hours.

17.5   *(d)*

Both `Instant` and `LocalTime` can express values with nanosecond precision. The `between()` method of the `Duration` can be used to calculate the time difference between two temporal objects—that is, between objects of the classes `LocalDate`, `LocalTime`, `LocalDateTime`, `ZonedDateTime`, and `Instant`. The `between()` method of the `Period` can be used to calculate the date-based amount of time between two `LocalDate` objects.

17.6   *(c)*

A LocalDateTime object is created that represents 2021-04-01T08:15. Thirty minutes are subtracted from this date-time object, returning a new date-time object. The day of the month is set to 12 for the resulting date-time object. However, the reference value of the final object is not assigned to any reference. LocalDateTime objects are immutable, thus the date-time object denoted by dt is never modified.

17.7   *(e)*

Unlike Period, when Duration is applied to a ZonedDateTime object, it disregards daylight savings.

A Period is a date-based amount of time (in terms of years, months, and days), and therefore cannot express an amount of time smaller than one day. A Period of one hour cannot be created.

Unlike ZonedDateTime objects, LocalTime and LocalDateTime objects have no time zone, so they do not take into consideration daylight savings.

A Period of one day may or may not be treated the same as a Duration of 24 hours, when using these objects with ZonedDateTime because of the differences in the handling of daylight savings.

Finally, both Period and Duration can express positive and negative amounts of time.

17.8   *(e)*

The plus() method of the LocalDate class returns a LocalDate. The plus() method of the LocalDateTime class returns a LocalDateTime.

17.9   *(d)*

The plus() method of the LocalDate class can accept a Duration object, but in this scenario it will throw an exception at runtime. The reason for this is that Duration is expressed in seconds and nanoseconds, which cannot be applied to a LocalDate object.

17.10 *(a) and (e)*

In order to compute the desired result, a time of 30 minutes and two days should be added to the given LocalDate object.

(a) combines a LocalTime object with a value of 30 minutes to the LocalDate object using the atTime() method, returning a LocalDateTime object. Then a duration of 48 hours is added to this LocalDateTime object.

(b) attempts to add a Duration of 48 hours to the LocalDate object, which will result in an UnsupportedTemporalTypeException. The reason for this is that Duration is expressed in seconds and nanoseconds, which cannot be applied to a LocalDate object.

(c) attempts to create a LocalTime object, with an amount of time greater than 23 hours, which is invalid for a LocalTime object, and will result in a DateTimeException.

(d) attempts to create a LocalTime object with a negative number of hours, which is also invalid, and would result in a DateTimeException.

(e) combines a value of 30 minutes to the `LocalDate` object using the `atTime()` method and returning a `LocalDateTime` object. Then a duration of 48 hours is added to this `LocalDateTime` object. The `atTime()` method is an overloaded method.

17.11 *(c)*

Five `LocalDate` objects are created in this example. The `atTime()` method creates a `LocalDateTime` object. The other five methods create a new `LocalDate` object.

17.12 *(d)*

The method `between()` calculates the amount of time that has elapsed between a `LocalTime` object and a `LocalDateTime` object. A `LocalTime` object is derived from the second argument, which is a `LocalDateTime` object. The result would have been a runtime exception if the two arguments had been interchanged: We cannot derive a `LocalDateTime` object from a `LocalTime` object.

The value of the first argument of the `between()` method represents a time that is after the time represented by the derived `LocalTime` object. Therefore, the resulting `Duration` object will have negative values. The time difference between 17:30 and 15:15 is two hours and 15 minutes.

17.13 *(d)*

The required `LocalDateTime` object is exactly 25 hours (one day and one hour) ahead of the initial `LocalDateTime` object.

(a) adds one hour to the initial `LocalDateTime` object and changes the date to the next day.

(b) adds one day to the initial `LocalDateTime` object and changes the time by one hour.

(c) adds two days to the initial `LocalDateTime` object and subtracts 23 hours, which results in the required 25 hours being added to the initial `LocalDateTime` object.

(d) adds two days to the initial `LocalDateTime` object and subtracts 16 hours and 15 minutes, which results in the `LocalDateTime` object having the value 2021-04-03T23:15.

(e) and (f) both adds a `Duration` of 25 hours (60 * 25 minutes) to the initial `Local-DateTime` object.

18 Localization

18.1 *(a)*

For the French locale, the resource bundle for the default locale (US) is loaded, as there is no resource bundle file named `MyResources_fr_FR.properties`. The values of the keys in this resource bundle are printed. The key "farewell" has duplicates. The last value ("Bye!") specified for this key is returned.

18.2 *(b)*

The resource bundles loaded for `Locale.ENGLISH` are:

```
MyResources_en.properties
MyResources.properties
```

The method `getString()` returns the value `"Have a good one!"` for the key `"farewell"` in the resource bundle file `MyResources_en.properties`.

18.3 *(b)*

The code prints all available key–value pairs in the resource bundle for the English locale. The resource bundles loaded for the English locale are:

```
resources_en.properties
resources.properties (parent)
```

The key set contains the keys from both bundles: k1 and k2. The key k1 is found in the `resources_en.properties` bundle with the value c, and the key k2 is found in the `resources.properties` bundle with the value b. Only if a key is not found in the current resource bundle, will it be looked up in its parent bundle, and so on. The `resource_en_GB.properties` bundle is not loaded by this code.

18.4 *(b)*

The code sets the default locale to the Russian locale, but then prints all available key–value pairs in the resource bundle for the English locale. The resource bundles loaded for the English locale are:

```
resources_en.properties
resources.properties (parent)
```

As appropriate bundles were found for the English locale, the default locale Russian bundle is not loaded.

The key set contains the keys from both bundles: k1 and k2. The key k1 is found in the `resources_en.properties` bundle with the value c, and the key k2 is found in the `resources.properties` bundle with the value b. Only if a key is not found in the current resource bundle, will it be looked up in its parent bundle, and so on.

18.5 *(a), (b), (c), (d), and (e)*

The patterns produce the following output:

Pattern		Output
(a)	.00	|.46|
(b)	.##	|.46|
(c)	.0#	|.46|
(d)	#.00	|.46|
(e)	#.0#	|.46|
(f)	#.##	|0.46|
(g)	.#0	Throws java.lang.IllegalArgumentException.

18.6 *(c)*

Notice that the code sets the number of decimal digits to two. First, the rounding mode is set to `HALF_UP`, which would round a double value of 9876.54321 to 9876.54. Then the same number is formatted again, but this time with the rounding mode set to `HALF_DOWN`, which would actually produce the same result. Because the third digit after the decimal point is 3 and not 5, it has no effect on the rounding by the `HALP_UP` or `HALF_DOWN` rounding mode.

18.7   *(d)*

Notice that the code sets the number of decimal digits to two. The value is a `Big-Decimal` and therefore is represented with a higher precision than it would be in a `double` value. The third digit after the decimal point is 5; therefore, the discarded fraction is 0.5. In this case, `HALF_DOWN` mode rounds up if the discarded fraction is > 0.5, which it is not, resulting in the formatted value `$9,876.54`. `HALF_UP` mode rounds up if the discarded fraction is >= 0.5, resulting in the formatted value `$9,876.55`.

18.8   *(d)*

The default short date format for the British locale is dd/MM/YYYY. However, this is not relevant in this case, because a `DateTimeFormatter` is used to format a `LocalDate` object, which has no time part, and thus results in an `UnsupportedTemporalType-Exception`.

18.9   *(h)*

A `DateTimeFormatter` object is configured to use a pattern, where d stand for the day of the month, a for an am/pm marker and y for a year. It is configured to use the UK locale. Notice that the time value in the `LocalDateTime` object is 14:30, which makes it pm.

18.10   *(e)*

In the code, the default locale is initially set to UK (British). A `DateTimeFormatter` is created to format a date according to the `MEDIUM` style format (MMM d, yyyy). This formatter formats the date to the string "Apr 1, 2021". The reference s1 denotes this string.

Next, the default locale is set to France. However, the `DateTimeFormatter` is immutable, and the date is formatted to the string "Apr 1, 2021". The reference s2 denotes this string.

Lastly, the `localizedBy()` method returns a new `DateTimeFormatter` object with the US locale, but it is not assigned to any reference. The date is again formatted by the previous `DateTimeFormatter` to the string "Apr 1, 2021". The reference s3 denotes this string. This means that only the condition in the first `if` statement is true.

18.11   *(d)*

`NumberFormat` interprets a floating-point number as a percentage, considering 1.0 to be equal to 100%. The default percentage format object rounds the value to two decimal digits, so it would round the double value 0.987654321 to 0.99. The value 0.99 represents 99%.

18.12   *(a)*

The code creates a `LocalDateTime` object (date1) first and adds a London time zone to it to create a `ZonedDateTime` object (date2).

Next, two `DateTimeFormatter` objects, df1 and df2, are created based on the same pattern "hz", and the time zones for London (GMT) and Paris (CET) are associated with them, respectively. The "hz" pattern stands for hour and time zone. Both date1 and date2 are formatted by each `DateTimeFormatter`.

The DateTimeFormatter df1 will format the hour in date1, but will supply the time zone, as this date object has no time zone, creating the string "1GMT". It will format date2 as "1GMT", as the ZonedDateTime date2 and the DateTimeFormatter df1 have the London time zone.

The DateTimeFormatter df2 will format the hour in date1, but will supply the time zone, as a date object has no time zone, creating the string "1CET". It will format date2 as "2CET", as the ZonedDateTime date2 and the DateTimeFormatter df2 have different time zones. Therefore, the London time (1h) in date2 is interpreted as Paris time (2h) by the DateTimeFormatter.

18.13 *(d)*

Values in single quotes are treated as verbatim text, rather than format elements. Only two values are actually supplied for the message pattern, so the format element with index 3 receives no value and will thus be formatted as text.

18.14 *(b)*

During the format operation, elements of the values array are interpreted by the MessageFormat and ChoiceFormat objects to determine the limit value that affects the selection of the appropriate choice format and the value that should be substituted into a message pattern. In this code, the value 4 in values[0] is the limit value, and the value 5 in values[1] is the value to format, resulting in the choice pattern "{1}th" at formats[4] to be chosen to format the value 5. The formatted result is "5th".

18.15 *(b)*

The limit values are given by the limits array. Note that the limit values are not ordered.

```
limits[0]   limits[1]   limits[2]
   0           -1           1
```

The corresponding choice formats are given by the formats array:

```
formats[0]   formats[1]   formats[2]
 "zero"      "negative"   "positive"
```

The supplied value 0.9 is greater than 0, and of course also greater than –1, but less than 1. It satisfies the following relation, determining index 1 in the limits array to choose the choice format.

```
limits[1]  <= 0.9 <  limits[2]
  -1       <= 0.9 <     1
```

Index 1 in the formats array determines the choice format to be the string "negative".

The value 0.9 results in the choice format at index 1 in the formats array to be chosen.

18.16 *(a)*

The default locale is set to the US locale and a DateTimeFormatter object is created to format dates in the MEDIUM style format (MMM d, yyyy).

At (1), a string is parsed using the dtf formatter, according to the MEDIUM date format style and the default locale (in this case, US). The string is specified in the MEDIUM format style for the US locale.

At (2), a string is parsed to a date. As no formatter is specified, the string is expected to be in the ISO format, which it is.

At (3), the LocalDate d is formatted using the dtf formatter that uses the MEDIUM format style and the default locale (in this case, US).

18.17 *(c)*

The default locale is set to the US locale and a DateTimeFormatter object is created to format dates in the SHORT style format (M-d-yy).

At (1), a string is parsed to a date. As no formatter is used, the string is expected to be in the ISO format, which it is.

At (2), a string is parsed using the dtf formatter, according to the SHORT date format style and the default locale (in this case, US). The string is specified in the SHORT format style for the US locale.

Finally, this date is printed using the default ISO format.

18.18 *(d)*

The default locale can be defined explicitly; otherwise, it is the platform locale that is supplied by the runtime environment. The default locale is not necessarily the US locale. The default format for LocalDate objects is ISO_DATE.

19 Java Module System

19.1 *(b)*

Code in the module ui can access public types defined in the packages store.frontend and store.backend via direct dependency, but also public types defined in the package product.data via transitive dependency. However, module ui does not require module customer, thus it cannot access public types from the customer.data package. This means that (a) is false, but (b) is true.

Code in the module customer cannot access public types from the product.data package, despite the presence of transitive dependency via the modules ui and store. This is because module customer does not have a direct dependency on module store, which has a transitive dependency on module product. This means that (c) and (d) are both false.

Code in the module product cannot access public types from the customer.data package because of the absence of a dependency between these modules. This means (e) is false.

19.2 *(e)*

Only public types in the exported packages of a module are accessible to code in modules that require this module.

19.3 *(e)*

The java.se module is at the root of the module graph, as it depends on the highest number of modules in the graph. The java.base module is at the bottom of the module graph, and does not depend on any module. The java.logging module depends on the java.base module.

19.4   *(c) and (f)*

Only public types in the exported package animals.primates are accessible to code in module zoo.

19.5   *(a) and (d)*

Module music should declare a requires directive that should specify module production. Also, module production should export package production.company.

19.6   *(c) and (d)*

An automatic module is a plain JAR that is loaded from the module path. Plain JARs loaded from the class path are included in the unnamed module.

19.7   *(a)*

In (a), code in module store can access types defined in package product.data because this package is exported by module product, which module store actually requires. Code in module store can access types defined in package marketing.offers by reflection as this package is opened by module marketing.

(b) is incorrect because code in module marketing cannot access types defined in packages product.data and product.pricing because it does not require module product.

(c) is incorrect because code in module marketing cannot access types defined in package product.data as it does not require module product. However, code in module marketing can access types defined in package store.frontend, as module marketing requires module store.

(d) is incorrect because code in module store can access types defined in package product.data, but not in package product.pricing, as this package is only exported to module marketing.

(e) is incorrect because code in module product cannot access types defined in package store.frontend as module product does not have a dependency on module store. However, code in module product can access types in the open package marketing.offers.

19.8   *(b)*

The requires directive specifies module names, not package names, which disqualifies (a) and (d). In (c), module music does not depend on module artist, and therefore cannot access types in package artist.recoding. This leaves (b), which works because module music has a direct dependency on module production, and also has a dependency on module artist via the requires-transitive directive in module production.

19.9   *(b)*

Service consumer module player does not need to declare any dependency on service provider module brass. Service consumer module player needs to declare a dependency on service module music, and specify which abstract type (in this case music.sound.Instrument) defines the service.

19.10   *(b) and (e)*

The jlink tool creates platform-specific runtime images that can be deployed. Runtime images contain application code, as well as the necessary JDK modules and tools, among other artifacts. However, no installation of a separate JVM is required to run the application.

19.11   *(a) and (b)*

Module music requires module instrument, which in turn requires module music. This results in a cyclic dependency, and thus is illegal and would cause these module declarations not to compile. Both modules music and artist export the same package preferences.style, which implies that this package is a split package, which is illegal and would cause this module declaration not to compile. It is allowed to declare the opens directive in a module declaration. It is also allowed to declare a qualified exports directive even if the specified module does not require this module.

19.12   *(e)*

Both modular and plain JARs can be used in the context of the class path as well as the module path. A listing of modules using the --list-modules of the java tool includes all observable modules, but not the unnamed module, as it has no name. The name of an automatic module is derived from the JAR file name, unless it is specified in the MANIFEST.MF file. There is only one unnamed module, and it obviously does not have a name, which makes the JAR file name irrelevant in this case.

19.13   *(c) and (d)*

An automatic module implicitly requires all other modules. An explicit module cannot access code in the unnamed module using the requires directive, since the unnamed module has no name. If an explicit module needs to access code in an automatic module, it must declare a requires directive to specify this automatic module.

20   Java I/O: Part I

20.1   *(d)*

The read() method will return -1 when the end of the stream has been reached. Normally an unsigned 8-bit int value is returned (range from 0 to 255). I/O errors result in an IOException being thrown.

20.2   *(d)*

The print() methods of the PrintWriter do not throw an IOException when the end of the file is reached, but instead sets an error status that can be checked.

20.3   *(d)*

The read() method of an InputStreamReader returns -1 when the end of the stream is reached.

20.4   *(b)*

The `readLine()` method of a `BufferedReader` returns `null` when the end of the file is reached.

20.5   *(c)*

An `ObjectOutputStream` can write both objects and Java primitive types, as it implements the `ObjectInput` and the `DataInput` interfaces. The serialization mechanism will follow references in objects and write the complete object graph.

20.6   *(a), (b), (d), and (i)*

Static fields and `transient` instance fields are not serialized—they are treated the same way when it comes to serialization. The accessibility modifier `private` does not determine whether an instance field should be serialized or not. `Serializable` is a marker interface. Subclass objects are serializable if the superclass is serializable. The modifier `final` of a class does not determine whether the class is serializable or not.

20.7   *(b)*

(a) is incorrect because there is no requirement that all versions of a serializable class must provide a declaration of a `serialVersionUID`.

In (b), there is no guarantee that a streamed object based on one version can be deserialized based on the other, even if the two versions of the class have the same `serialVersionUID`. It depends on whether the changes in the class versions are compatible with deserialization. For example, changing the type of a field is an incompatible change.

(c) is incorrect because `serialVersionUID` in two unrelated serializable classes is also unrelated and need not be unique.

(d) is incorrect because there is no requirement that the `serialVersionUID` of a serializable class must be incremented every time a new version of the class is created.

(e) is incorrect because any class can declare a `static final` field of type `long` having the name `serialVersionUID`, but it has meaning for serialization only in a serializable class.

20.8   *(e)*

During deserialization, the zero-argument constructor of the superclass `Person` is called because this superclass is not `Serializable`.

20.9   *(c)*

If the superclass is `Serializable`, then the subclass is also `Serializable`—resulting in the printout in (c).

20.10   *(e)*

Note that only `GraduateStudent` is `Serializable`. The field `name` in the `Person` class is `transient`. During serialization of a `GraduateStudent` object, the fields `year` and `studNum` are included as part of the serialization process, but not the field `name`. During deserialization, the private method `readObject()` in the `GraduateStudent` class is called. This method first deserializes the GraduateStudent object calling the no-argument constructor in the superclasses, but then initializes the fields with new values. Without the private readObject() method, the output would be as in (d).

20.11   *(a)*

Constructors for Product and Food are triggered when a new Food object is created. These constructors print "product food ". After that, the product object is serialized. Product is a superclass of Food and is marked as Serializable, which implies that all of its subclasses, such as Food, are also serializable. Values of Product name and Food calories are included in the serialization of the product object.

No constructors are triggered during deserialization, thus Product and Food constructors do not print any values. No errors are triggered during deserialization, and values of Product name and Food calories are restored and printed.

20.12   *(c)*

A buffer (a char array of length 4) is used to read and write characters to files. In the while loop, this buffer is filled with characters from the test1.txt file and written to the text2.txt file. On the first iteration, the characters a, b, c, and d are read from the text1.txt file, filling the buffer to full capacity, and then written to the test2.txt file. On the second iteration, the remaining characters e, f, and g are read from the test1.txt file into the buffer. These characters are read into the first three elements of the buffer. The fourth element in the buffer still contains the character d from the previous read operation. The buffer contains the characters e, f, g, and d, which are written to the text2.txt file. The next read operation returns -1 since the end of the file has been reached in the text1.txt file, thereby terminating the loop.

20.13   *(c)*

Both fields numberOfTracks and currentTrack are not included when an Album object is serialized, as the field numberOfTracks is static and the instance field current-Track is transient. Only the instance field title (having the value "Songs") is included in the serialization of the Album object.

The readObject() method of the Album class is not private, but public, and is never called during deserialization to change the state of the Album object created at deserialization.

The Album object created at deserialization is initialized with the instance field title having the value "Songs" and the transient field currentTrack initialized to the default int value 0.

Deserialization requires definition of the class, thus an Album object created at deserialization can access the static field numberOfTracks in its class that has the value 5.

21   Java I/O: Part II

21.1   *(b) and (c)*

Compiling and running the program results in the following output:

```
/wrk/./document/../book/../chapter1
/wrk/chapter1
chapter1
./document/../book/../chapter1
./document/../book/..
```

Note that only the `Path.toRealPath()` method requires that the file exists; other wise, it throws a `java.io.IOException`.

21.2   *(c)*

Compiling and running the program results in the following output:

```
./wrk/src


./wrk
./wrk/src
./wrk/src/readme.txt


./wrk
./wrk/src
./wrk/src/readme.txt
```

The `Files.list()` method creates a stream based on the *immediate* entries of the directory path passed as a parameter. The `Files.walk()` method traverses depth-first every entry in the hierarchy of the directory passed as a parameter. The `Files.find()` method will find every entry in the hierarchy of the directory passed as a parameter, since the matcher argument is always `true` and will traverse to depth 2 (i.e., equal to the actual depth of the directory).

21.3   *(a)*

There are three absolute `Path` objects (starting at the root (`/`) of the file system) constructed in this example:

`Path earth` is defined as `"/planets/earth"`.

`Path moonOrbit` is defined as `"/planets/earth/moon/orbit.param"`—that is, as a child of `Path earth`.

`Path mars` is defined as `"/planets/mars"`—that is, as a sibling of `Path earth`.

There is one relative path:

`Path fromMarsToMoon` is defined as `"../earth/moon/orbit.param "`—that is, as a relative path between `Path mars` and `Path moonOrbit`.

These `Path` objects do not have to actually exist in the file system, so long as a program makes no attempt to validate or access these paths. Thus no runtime exception will be thrown.

21.4   *(b)*

First, a `Path` object is created with the relative path `"./mars/../earth"`, that has four name elements. Next, this `Path` is normalized, resulting in a `Path` object with the path string "earth" that has one name element. Then it is converted to the absolute path "/planets/earth" which has two name elements. If this path had not have been normalized, then the absolute path would be "/planets/./mars/../earth", which has five name elements. Whether the paths exists in the file system is irrelevant, since this program makes no attempts to actually validate or access any of these paths.

21.5 (d)

The list() method of the Files class creates a stream of Path objects denoting the immediate entries in the given directory. Unlike the method walk(), the list() method does not traverse the contents of the subdirectories. The stream created by the list() method will include the Path objects that denote the following paths:

```
/test/a.txt
/test/c
/test/e.txt
/test/f.txt
```

A filter is applied to this stream of Path objects, which uses the method getFileName() of the Path interface to return the last name element of the Path. The filter will discard any entry whose file name does not end with "txt". This leaves only the following paths in the stream:

```
/test/a.txt
/test/e.txt
/test/f.txt
```

These paths are then printed to the console.

21.6 (g)

The walk() method of the Files class creates a stream of Path objects that denote all entries in the given directory, including its subdirectories, by traversing the directory hierarchy depth-first. The stream will include Path objects that denote the following paths:

```
/test/a.txt
/test/a.txt/b.txt
/test/c
/test/c/d.txt
/test/e.txt
/test/f.txt
```

A map operation is applied to this stream of Path objects, converting it to a stream of String objects, where each String represents the last name element of the path—that is, the file name:

```
a.txt
b.txt
c
d.txt
e.txt
f.txt
```

A filter is applied to this stream of String objects which excludes strings that do not end in the file extension "txt". This leaves only the following paths in the stream (notice that these strings are sorted):

```
a.txt
b.txt
d.txt
e.txt
f.txt
```

These String objects are then printed to the console.

21.7 *(b)*

The method Files.createDirectories() does not throw an exception when trying to create a directory that already exists. However, the method Files.createDirectory() does.

Method Files.delete() does throw an exception when trying to delete a non-existent directory.

Method Files.move() does throw an exception when moving a non-empty directory, but only if it actually needs to move all files within this directory to another file system. Moving a directory within the same file system does not actually perform any move operations for the directory. It only changes the path of the directory.

Method Files.exists() returns a boolean value to indicate the existence or non-existence of a path.

21.8 *(c)*

Two Path objects are initialized. However, both of these Path objects reference the same file. This is because p1.getName(1) returns a relative path to directory joe, which is the second component in this path, considering that the first component is directory users with index 0. This path is then used to resolve another relative path test/a.jpg, which results in the path joe/test/a.jpg. And finally, the path /users is used as a root directory to resolve this path, resulting in the path /users/joe/test/a.jpg, which is identical to the path referenced by p1.

Next, an attempt is made to move the entry at path p1 to path p2, where both denote the same directory entry. In this scenario, Files.move() method performs no action because it can detect that both the source and the destination path are the same.

21.9 *(c)*

In this example, the p1 reference represents an absolute path, and the p2 reference represents a relative path. Keep in mind that an absolute path starts from the root of a file system, in this case designated by the slash character (/).

The purpose of the method resolve() is to construct a path where a relative path is appended to another relative path, or to an absolute path. p1.resolve(p2) results in the relative path store being appended to the absolute path /test. As it is not possible to append an absolute path to another path, p2.resolve(p1) returns the absolute path /test denoted by the reference p2.

21.10 *(d)*

This question assumes the existence of the destination file, yet this code example does not specify the replace-existing file copy option:

```
Files.copy(p1, p2, StandardCopyOption.REPLACE_EXISTING);
```

Therefore, the code will throw a java.nio.file.FileAlreadyExistsException.

21.11 (d)

The code reads lines of text from a file as a stream of strings. A filter operation discards lines that do not start with <. Then each line in the stream is mapped by the map operation to a >. The reduction operation is applied to concatenate each >. The resulting string ">>>>>" is printed as there are five lines that are mapped to >.

21.12 (d)

Only permissions explicitly added to the set are applied, all other permissions are removed. In order to be able to access files inside a directory, the directory needs to have execute permission. However, the permissions for the /test/data directory are changed to read-only in the code. Therefore, an attempt to access the info.txt file in this directory by the walk() method will throw an AccessDeniedException, that will terminate the stream processing.

21.13 (d)

The thing to note is that a PosixFileAttributeView can be used to set permissions for the file that is associated with it. However, the PosixFileAttributes object obtained from the PosixFileAttributeView will only reflect the file attribute values at the time it was obtained from the view. It is not updated automatically when the file attribute values change in the file. A new PosixFileAttributes object must be obtained from the view to reflect any changes in the file attribute values.

The program first removes all permissions from the file. A PosixFileAttributeView is created on the file, and the PosixFileAttributes object associated with the view is obtained. This PosixFileAttributes object is used in the rest of the program, and it will always reflect that the file has no permissions, regardless of any permissions set in the file through the view.

Note also that removing an element (OWNER_WRITE permission) from an empty set does not throw an exception. The permissions of the file are changed as follows, but the changes are not reflected by the PosixFileAttributes object:

```
---------
r---w-r--
-w-------
```

21.14 (a)

First, this program converts a URI object to a Path object. Path p1 references the same file as path p2. No action is taken by the copy() method when the source file and the destination file are the same. Lastly, a Path object is converted to a legacy File object. This program runs successfully and produces no output.

22 Concurrency: Part I

22.1 (e)

The program will compile without errors, and will simply terminate without any output when run. Two thread objects will be created, but they will never be started. The start() method must be called on the thread objects to make the threads execute the run() method asynchronously.

22.2   *(d)*

Note that calling the `run()` method on a `Thread` object does not start a thread. In the statement:

```
new Thread(new R1(),"|R1a|").run();
```

the `run()` method of the `Thread` class will invoke the `run()` method of the `Runnable` object (R1) that is passed as an argument in the constructor call. In other words, the `run()` method of the R1 class is executed in the R2 thread—that is, the thread that called the `run()` method of the `Thread` class and whose name will be printed.

However, the statement:

```
new Thread(new R1(),"|R1b|").start();
```

starts the |R1b| thread, and the `run()` method of the `Thread` class will invoke the `run()` method of the `Runnable` object (R1) that is passed as an argument in the constructor call, but it is executed by the |R1b| thread whose name will be printed.

The last statement in the `run()` method of the R2 class is executed by the |R2| thread whose name will be printed.

22.3   *(c)*

Note that the complete signature of the `run()` method does not specify a `throws` clause, meaning it does not throw any *checked* exceptions. However, a method can always be implemented with a `throws` clause that specifies *unchecked* exceptions, as in the case of the `run()` method.

22.4   *(a) and (e)*

Because the exact behavior of the thread scheduler is undefined, the text A, B, and End can be printed in any order. The thread printing B is a daemon thread, which means that the program may terminate before the thread manages to print the letter.

22.5   *(a) and (e)*

The lock is also released when an uncaught exception occurs in the statement.

22.6   *(c) and (d)*

First note that a call to `sleep()` does not release the lock on the `Smiley.class` object once a thread has acquired this lock. Even if a thread sleeps, it does not release any locks it might possess.

(a) does not work, as `run()` is not called directly by the client code.

(b) does not work, as the infinite `while` loop becomes the critical region and the lock will never be released. Once a thread has the lock, other threads cannot participate in printing smileys.

(c) works, as the lock will be released between each iteration, giving other threads the chance to acquire the lock and print smileys.

(d) works for the same reason as (c), since the three print statements will be executed as one atomic operation.

(e) may not work, as the three print statements may not be executed as one atomic operation, since the lock will be released after each print statement.

Synchronizing on `this` does not help, as the printout from each of the three print statements executed by each thread can be interspersed.

22.7   *(d)*

A thread terminates when the execution of the run() method ends. The call to the start() method is asynchronous—that is, it returns immediately, and it moves the thread to the *READY* substate. Calling the sleep() or wait() method will block the thread.

22.8   *(b) and (d)*

The nested createThread() call is evaluated first, and will print 23 as the first number. The last number the main thread prints is 14. After the main thread ends, the thread created by the nested createThread() completes its join() call and prints 22. After this thread ends, the thread created by the outer createThread() call completes its join() call and prints the number 12 before the program terminates.

22.9   *(e)*

The exact behavior of the scheduler is not defined. There is no guarantee that a call to the yield() method will grant other threads use of the CPU.

22.10   *(b)*

The final method notify() is defined in the Object class.

22.11   *(c)*

An IllegalMonitorStateException will be thrown if the wait() method is called and the current thread does not hold the lock of the object.

22.12   *(d)*

Since the two methods emptying() and filling() are synchronized, only one operation at a time can take place on the tank that is a shared resource between the two threads.

The method emptying() waits to empty the tank if it is already empty (i.e., isEmpty is true). When the tank becomes full (i.e., isEmpty becomes false), it empties the tank and sets the condition that the tank is empty (i.e., isEmpty is true).

The method filling() waits to fill the tank if it is already full (i.e., isEmpty is false). When the tank becomes empty (i.e., isEmpty becomes true), it fills the tank and sets the condition that the tank is full (i.e., isEmpty is false).

Since the tank is empty to start with (i.e., isEmpty is true), it will be filled first. Once started, the program will continue to print the string "filling" followed by the string "emptying".

Note that the while loop in the pause() method must always check against the field isEmpty.

23 Concurrency: Part II

23.1   *(c)*

A single thread executor service does not allow scheduling of tasks, but a scheduled executor service allows a task to be scheduled with a specified delay, and also allows a task to be executed periodically. The work stealing mechanism is specific to the work stealing thread pool, and the work stealing thread pool is designed to maintain enough threads to support a given level of parallelism.

23.2   (b)

The shutdown() method of the executor service initiates the shutdown of the executor service, allowing currently running tasks to continue, but preventing new tasks from being submitted. It does not wait for the termination of currently running tasks. The awaitTermination() method can throw an InterruptedException. The shutdownNow() method also initiates the shutdown of the executor service, but it cancels all running tasks and returns.

23.3   (b)

The read lock does not prevent other operations from reading data. Methods that acquire read and write locks can throw an InterruptedException. The write lock is designed to allow only a single exclusive write operation on the data, preventing other read and write operations to be performed, thus preserving memory consistency and preventing data corruption.

23.4   (b)

The contents of list1 are created by spawning a number of threads, concurrently writing data to the copy-on-write list. There is no guarantee that these threads would actually complete copying all elements from the initial list by the time list1 is printed.

The contents of list2 are created by processing elements from the initial list using a parallel stream with a list collector reduction operation combining processed data into a single list. The collect() terminal operation ensures that the stream is exhausted and the collector ensures that all data is assembled into the list. When printed, list2 has the same contents as the initial list.

The contents of list3 are created by processing elements from the initial list using a parallel stream, but manually adding elements into list3. This does not guarantee the consistency of list3 because of potential contention between threads trying to access list3, and is likely to corrupt data.

23.5   (d)

Synchronized collections provide blocking (synchronized) methods that modify collection content. However, synchronized collections do not provide a synchronized iterator. It is the programmer's responsibility to implement synchronized iteration behavior for such collections.

Copy-on-write collections achieve concurrency by creating a copy of a collection for each thread that tries to modify the collection, and then automatically merging these copies without any need to implement thread synchronization.

Immutable collections are read only, and thus are automatically considered to be memory safe, without any need for synchronization.

23.6   (d)

Atomic variables are designed to be thread-safe without the use of synchronization and intrinsic locking. Methods provided for atomic variables do not throw an InterruptedException.

23.7   *(a) and (b)*

The Atomic API provides operations that guarantee object consistency. However, no specific order is enforced when a number of atomic operations are performed concurrently. In this example, a number of incrementAndGet() calls are executed on an AtomicLong object, resulting in the consistent increment of its value. This means that the last value in this example would always be 3. The order of the Future objects is the same as that of the invoked tasks, but the stream iterating through the list of these Future objects can print the numbers 1, 2, and 3 in any order, as the order of the concurrent increment operations is unpredictable.

23.8   *(a)*

In this example, an attempt is made to upgrade a read lock to a write lock, which is not possible. It should be noted that a write lock can be downgraded to a read lock. Consider the following scenarios:

Attempting to obtain the read lock using the lock() method after the write lock has been acquired is allowed:

```
writeLock.lock();
readLock.lock();
```

Attempting to obtain a write lock using the lock() method after the read lock has been acquired will not succeed:

```
readLock.lock();
writeLock.lock();
```

Attempting to obtain a write lock using the tryLock() method after the read lock has been acquired will return false—that is, the write lock is not acquired:

```
readLock.lock();
writeLock.tryLock();
```

In the finally block, the isWriteLocked() method checks whether the write lock has been acquired, but we have already established that this would not be the case. So only the "Read lock acquired" and "The end" messages will be printed in this scenario.

23.9   *(d)*

In this example, the variable counter is declared as volatile. A volatile variable guarantees visibility of write operations. It does not guarantee memory consistency when several concurrent threads attempt to modify this volatile variable with a non-atomic operation (--). There is a danger of interleaving of read and write operations on the variable by different threads; thus the results are unpredictable.

23.10   *(e)*

The submit() method does not throw an exception. It is possible to submit both a Callable (() -> "acme") that returns a value and a Runnable (() -> {}) that does not.

The shutdown() method does not throw an exception. An invocation of the shutdown() method initiates the shutdown of the executor service, but the two already submitted tasks are allowed to complete. However, the shutdown() method does not wait for the tasks to complete execution.

Although the get() method can throw checked exceptions, no exceptions are thrown in this case. Invocation of the get() method on a Future blocks until the task represented by the `Future` completes execution. The first `get()` method call returns the result of executing the `Callable`, which in this case returns the string `"acme"`. Since a `Runnable` does not return a value, the second `get()` method call returns the `null` value to indicate normal completion of the task represented by the `Runnable`.

The print statement does not throw an exception. It prints `"acme null"`, which is the concatenation of the results `"acme"` and the `null` value returned by the `get()` methods, respectively.

23.11   *(f) and (h)*

In the `for(;;)` loop, there is no guarantee that a task will actually be cancelled before it completes. Cancelled or not, each task is added to the `results` list. The `shutdown()` method initiates the shutdown of the executor service, allowing those tasks that are already running to complete execution.

The method `isDone()` only returns `true` if the task completed due to normal termination, an exception, or cancellation. If any task was still running, the `allMatch(r->r.isDone())` expression will return `false`, causing the letter `Z` to be printed.

If all tasks completed, then there could be some among them that were cancelled. An attempt to get the value of a `Future` whose task has been cancelled will result in an exception. In order to concatenate the values returned by the tasks in the `Future` objects, all cancelled tasks are filtered from the stream by calling the `isCancelled()` method. Since it is unpredictable which tasks were cancelled and which terminated normally, the output from the program may contain any of the letters `A`, `B`, `C`, `D`, or `E`.

24   Database Connectivity

24.1   *(c)*

When no rows are returned by the query, invoking the `next()` method simply returns `false` to indicate the absence of the next row in the result set. This is considered normal behavior and does not cause an exception, ruling out (a) and (b). The first row in the result set has index 1.

24.2   *(c)*

Programmers should ensure that result sets are closed first, then statements, and only then the connection. The closure order is important because unclosed result sets and statements can cause a memory leak on the database side. This has nothing to do with the transactional behavior of the program, and thus is not related to auto-commit mode.

24.3   *(b)*

In this code example, the marker parameter in the select statement is set to match rows that start with the string `"Where"`. The table contains exactly two rows that match the where clause, so these rows will be retrieved and printed by the program. When retrieving a column value, the column might not have a value—that is, it might be `null`. Testing a reference for `null` before using the reference avoids the `NullPointerException` at (3).

24.4   *(b)*

Notice that in this code example, the value 103 that is set for the id column in the query does not match any id in the rows in the table. Therefore, when executed, this query will not return any rows. This is not an error, so it would not cause any exceptions. Instead, the method next() will return false, as the result set is empty. As a result, the body of the if statement will not be executed and nothing will be printed.

24.5   *(b)*

First note that the auto-commit mode has been disabled for the connection. Next, this program sets the marker parameters and executes an update statement. However, when it sets the marker parameter for the select statement, it uses index 2, but there is only one marker parameter in this select statement, so the line of code ps1.setInt(2, id) will throw an exception. This will interrupt normal program execution and control will be transferred directly to the catch block. This means that the explicit commit statement will not be executed.

However, the catch block does not attempt to roll back this transaction, so once the exception is handled by the catch block, the program will resume its normal execution, which will correctly close the statements and the connection in the implicit finally block of the outer try-with-resources statement. Therefore, the database will not have any indication that it is supposed to perform a rollback, as no rollback is executed in the catch block. Its reaction to a normal connection closure is to commit any outstanding changes.

24.6   *(b)*

The resources will be closed in the following order: result set, statement, and connection.

24.7   *(b)*

Marker parameters in a prepared statement are set with the setXXX() methods, not with the executeQuery() method, which rules out (a). Each prepared statement represents a single SQL statement, which can be parameterized and executed multiple times, contradicts (c) and (d).

24.8   *(a) and (b)*

The SQL query in this example selects rows from the questions table, using a where clause that selects rows that do not have any value (null) for the answer column. Then the code iterates through the result set containing these rows and updates the answer column value to be "no answer".

(c) is incorrect because the SELECT statement will return some, but not necessarily all, rows from the questions table. (d) is incorrect because potential exceptions will be caught by the catch block, which does not invoke the rollback() method. Therefore, once an exception is caught, the program will resume normal execution and will correctly close the connection in the implicitly finally block of the outer try-with-resources statement. Databases assume that if a program has correctly closed its JDBC connection, then there is no reason not to commit any outstanding changes made within the context of this connection.

24.9　(c)

There are two problems with the code.

First, only one of the marker parameters is actually set before the statement is executed.

And second, an update SQL operation cannot be executed using the execute-Query() method.

Either one of these issues would cause the executeQuery() method to throw an exception.

24.10　(a)

Marker parameters in a prepared statement need not be set in any specific order, as long as they are all set before the statement is executed. In the given code, all marker parameters are set before the statement is executed, so the code executes normally.

24.11　(b), (c), and (d)

A prepared statement can be executed multiple times, making (b) a correct option. If a statement is a SELECT statement, then it can be executed using either the execute() or executeQuery() methods; otherwise, it can be executed using the execute() and executeUpdate() methods, making (c) and (d) correct options. Statements executed by the executeQuery() method and the executeUpdate() method are mutually exclusive—the former executes SELECT statements and the latter non-SELECT statements like INSERT, UPDATE, and DELETE. The execute() method can execute all statements.

24.12　(a)

The default navigation direction in a result set is forward only, meaning starting with the first row and successively proceeding to the last row each time the next() method is called. Forward-only navigation is supported by all databases. Other result set options, such as reflection of changes, scroll sensitivity, and cursor closure on commit, may or may not be supported by different databases.

24.13　(a)

The relative(int rows) method moves the cursor a specified number of rows in relation to the current row in the result set. The parameter value can be a positive or a negative int value.

Calling the method relative(1) moves the cursor forward by one row, which is the same as calling the method next().

Calling the method relative(0) does not move the cursor from its current position.

Calling the method relative(-1) moves the cursor backward by one row, which is the same as calling the method previous().

Calling the method absolute(1) moves the cursor to the first row in the result set, which is the same as calling the method first().

Calling the method absolute(0) moves the cursor to before the first row in the result set.

Calling the method absolute(-1) moves the cursor to the last row in the result set, which is the same as calling the method last().

25 Annotations

25.1   *(a) and (b)*

Annotations are compiled into classes just like any other classes or interfaces. The purpose of an annotation is to provide metadata for program elements in the code (like Java classes, interfaces, methods, and variables). Annotations can be applied to other annotations, and can also be used as a type of an annotation element.

25.2   *(c)*

Annotations having the target `ElementType.TYPE` can be applied to classes, interfaces, enums, and other annotations. Annotations having the target `Element-Type.TYPE_PARAMETER` can be applied to type parameters in generic code. Annotations having the target `ElementType.FIELD` can be applied to constants, as constants are static fields. Annotations having the target `ElementType.METHOD` can be applied to only methods, but annotations having the target `ElementType.CONSTRUCTOR` can be applied to constructors.

25.3   *(a) and (c)*

The annotation in question is applied to the class, and requires no parameters to be supplied. This means that its target must be either default, or explicitly declared to be applicable to `ElementType.TYPE`. This would exclude (b) and (d).

25.4   *(b) and (g)*

The annotation type declaration defines a single element type of `int` array called `value`, and provides a default value for this element. This question asks to identify incorrect ways of applying this annotation. (a) and (f) supply a single value for this annotation element, in which case no {} are required to enclose the value, and it is not required to specify the element name `value` when only one value is specified. (c) is legal because the element name `value` does not have to be specified when it is the only element specified in the annotation type declaration. (d) and (e) are legal because the `value` element does not have to be set, since it has a default value, and parentheses () are optional when no value is specified. (b) and (g) are illegal because they are missing the block notation {} to enclose the list of values specified.

25.5   *(b)*

The annotation type `Test5Annotation` should be defined to be applicable to at least the targets of `TYPE`, `TYPE_PARAMETER`, and `FIELD`. It should also define an element named `value` (and not `values`), whose type should be a `String` array and have a default value.

25.6   *(d)*

Annotations are not reflected in the documentation of the class in which they are applied, unless the `@Documented` meta-annotation is applied to its annotation type.

25.7   *(b) and (e)*

Default values are not mandatory for annotation type elements, and a default value cannot be `null`. An annotation element of an array type can be assigned a single default value, in which case it does not need to be enclosed in block notation {}. Annotation element names must be specified as method names with no parameters, but mandatory parentheses ().

25.8   *(a), (b), and (c)*

The annotation type can be applied to Java types—that is, classes, enums, and interfaces. It can also be applied to fields and constructors.

(a) applies annotation to an interface, which is valid because it is defined as applicable to a type. It provides a string value for the `value()` element, and it does not set any other elements, relying instead on their default values. This means it does not have to explicitly qualify the element `value()` name.

(b) applies annotation to enum fields, which is allowed by this annotation definition. It provides both `value()` and `details()` element values for the first three fields, and relies on the default value of the `details()` element for the fourth field.

(c) applies the annotation to a field, explicitly qualifying the element `value` and relying on the default value of the `details()` element.

(d) applies annotation to a class, which is allowed by this annotation type. However, it does not qualify the name of the `value()` element, which must be qualified when it is not the only element specified.

(e) applies annotation to a method, which is not allowed by this annotation type.

(f) applies annotation to an expression (i.e., in a *type context*), which is not allowed by this annotation type.

25.9   *(b)*

The `Containee` annotation type is defined as a repeatable annotation type. Thus it can be used as an array type of the mandatory `value()` element declared in the `Container` annotation type. However, in order for this construct to work, any other elements specified in the `Container` annotation type must be declared with default values.

25.10   *(c)*

The way in which the annotation `@Folder` is applied to the `Storage` class requires the `Folder` annotation type to be repeatable—that is, its type declaration must be marked with the `@Repeatable` meta-annotation having the argument `Folders.class`. Because of the way the `@Folder` annotation is applied to the `Storage` class, its type declaration must define two elements: a `value()` element and a `temp()` element. The `temp()` element of the `Folder` annotation type must be defined with a default value. The container annotation type `Folders` must define a `value()` element of type `Folder[]`.

26 Secure Coding

26.1   *(c)*

Data obfuscation is considered to be an important measure for securing sensitive information. Sanitizing input values is a countermeasure that helps preventing code injections. Encapsulation helps to prevent code corruption. Terminating recursive data references helps to prevent a type of denial-of-service attack that attempts to cause a program to start an infinite data processing loop.

26.2   *(d)*

Encapsulation is a software design strategy that only allows access to an object's state through specifically defined operations. Mutable objects are those whose state can be modified. Code corruption is a category of threats that can be used to corrupt application logic. A code injection allows executable code to be passed as an input parameter.

26.3   *(d)*

Normally an addition of 1 to a maximum value of a primitive type would result in the value wrapping around to the minimum value. The maximum value of the int type is 2147483647 and the minimum value is -2147483648. However, in this case, the addition is performed by the addExact() method, which actually checks value boundaries and will throw an ArithmeticException to prevent the value wrapping around.

26.4   *(c)*

The Secure Hash Algorithm (SHA) is designed to produce a fixed-length result, known as a message digest, from a variable-length input. The number 256 is the length of the digest—that is, the result produced by the hash algorithm.

26.5   *(a)*

Java security policies are specified as a grant, defining restrictions and permissions on code execution and on access to resources.

26.6   *(c)*

Any checked exceptions thrown within the PrivilegedAction.run() method must be handled within this method. Alternatively, if checked exceptions need to be propagated outside the run() method, then the PrivilegedExceptionAction interface should be implemented instead.

Mock Exam: Java SE 17 Developer

This is a mock exam for the *Java SE 17 Developer* exam. It comprises brand-new questions, which are similar to the questions that can be expected on the real exam. Working through this exam will give a good indication of how well you are prepared for the real exam, and whether any topics need further study.

Considering the vast number of Java topics in the exam objectives and only 50 multiple-choice questions on the exam, this mock exam contains questions on a selected number of topics, as on the real exam.

Annotated answers to the questions can be found in Appendix F, p. 1737.

Questions

Q1   What will be printed when the following program is run?

```java
class Base {
  protected int i;
  Base() { add(1); }
  void add(int v) { i += v; }
  void print() { System.out.println(i); }
}
class Extension extends Base {
  Extension() { add(2); }
  void add(int v) { i += v*2; }
}
public class Qd073 {
  public static void main(String[] args) {
    bogo(new Extension());
  }
  static void bogo(Base b) {
    b.add(8);
```

```
        b.print();
    }
}
```

Select the one correct answer.

(a) 9
(b) 11
(c) 13
(d) 21
(e) 22

Q2   What will be printed when the following program is executed?

```
public class Qcb90 {
    private int a;
    private int b;
    public void f() {
        a = 0;
        b = 0;
        int[] c = { 0 };
        g(b, c);
        System.out.println(a + " " + b + " " + c[0] + " ");
    }
    public void g(int b, int[] c) {
        a = 1;
        b = 1;
        c[0] = 1;
    }
    public static void main(String[] args) {
        Qcb90 obj = new Qcb90();
        obj.f();
    }
}
```

Select the one correct answer.

(a) 0 0 0
(b) 0 0 1
(c) 0 1 0
(d) 1 0 0
(e) 1 0 1

Q3   Given the following interface declaration, which declaration is valid?

```
interface I {
    void setValue(int val);
    int getValue();
}
```

Select the one correct answer.

```
(a) class A extends I {
        int value;
        void setValue(int val) { value = val; }
        int getValue() { return value; }
    }
```

(b) interface B extends I {
```
    void increment();
  }
```
(c) abstract class C implements I {
```
    int getValue() { return 0; }
    abstract void increment();
  }
```
(d) interface D implements I {
```
    void increment();
  }
```
(e) class E implements I {
```
    int value;
    public void setValue(int val) { value = val; }
  }
```

Q4 What will be the result of compiling and running the following program?

```
public class Q200A80 {
  public static void main(String[] args) {
    callType(10);
  }

  private static void callType(Number num){
    System.out.println("Number passed");
  }

  private static void callType(Object obj){
    System.out.println("Object passed");
  }
}
```

Select the one correct answer.

(a) The program will compile and will print Object passed.
(b) The program will compile and will print Number passed.
(c) The program will fail to compile, because the call to the callType() method is ambiguous.
(d) The program will compile, but it will throw a ClassCastException at runtime.

Q5 Given the following code:

```
class MyClass {
  public static void main(String[] args) {
    int k = 0;
    int 1 = 0;
    for (int i = 0; i <= 3; i++) {
      k++;
      if (i == 2) break;
      1++;
    }
    System.out.println(k + ", " + 1);
  }
}
```

Which of the following statements is true?

Select the one correct answer.

(a) The program will fail to compile.

(b) The program will print 3, 3 at runtime.

(c) The program will print 4, 3 at runtime if the break statement is replaced by the continue statement.

(d) The program will fail to compile if the break statement is replaced by the return statement.

(e) The program will fail to compile if the break statement is replaced by an empty statement.

Q6 Given the declaration:

```
int[][] nums = {{20}, {30}, {40}};
```

Which code will compile and print 90 at runtime?
Select the one correct answer.

(a)
```
{
    int sum = 0;
    for (int[] row : nums[])
        for (int val : nums[row])
            sum += val;
    System.out.println(sum);
}
```

(b)
```
{
    int sum = 0;
    for (int[] row : nums[][])
        for (int val : nums[row])
            sum += val;
    System.out.println(sum);
}
```

(c)
```
{
    int sum = 0;
    for (int[] row : nums)
        for (int val : nums[row])
            sum += val;
    System.out.println(sum);
}
```

(d)
```
{
    int sum = 0;
    for (int[] row : nums)
        for (int val : row)
            sum += val;
    System.out.println(sum);
}
```

(e)
```
{
    int sum = 0;
    for (Integer[] row : nums)
        for (int val : row)
            sum += val;
    System.out.println(sum);
}
```

Q7 What will be the result from running the following program?

```java
public class Q1408b {
  public static void main(String[] args) {
    int i = 0;
    while (++i == i) {
      System.out.println(i++);
    }
  }
}
```

Select the one correct answer.

(a) The program will execute and terminate normally, but it will not print anything.
(b) The program will execute indefinitely, printing all numbers from 1 onward.
(c) The program will execute indefinitely, printing all numbers from 2 onward.
(d) The program will execute indefinitely, printing all even numbers from 2 onward.
(e) The program will execute indefinitely, printing all odd numbers from 1 onward.
(f) The program will execute indefinitely, printing all odd numbers from 3 onward.

Q8 What will be the result from running the following program?

```java
public class RemainderFun {
  public static void main(String[] args) {
    int i = 24, k = 7;
    System.out.print( i % k + "|");
    System.out.print( i % -k + "|");
    System.out.print(-i % k + "|");
    System.out.println(-i % -k);
  }
}
```

Select the one correct answer.

(a) The program will fail to compile.
(b) The program will compile, but it will throw an exception at runtime.
(c) 3|-3|-3|3
(d) 3|3|-3|-3
(e) 3|-3|-3|-3
(f) 3|-3|3|-3

Q9 Which statement is true about the following program?

```java
public class Switchy {
  public static void main(String[] args) {
    final String s1 = "January";
    final String yr = " 2022";
    s1.concat(yr);
    switch (s1) {
      default -> System.out.println("Sorry.");
      case "January" + yr, s1 + " 2023" -> System.out.println("OK.");
    }
  }
}
```

Select the one correct answer.

(a) The program will fail to compile.
(b) The program will compile. When run, it will print:
    Sorry.
    OK.
(c) The program will compile. When run, it will print:
    Sorry.
(d) The program will compile. When run, it will print:
    OK.

Q10 What will be the result from the following program?

```java
public class CodeMe {
  public static void main(String[] args) {
    boolean flag = false;
    if (false)            // (1)
      flag = !flag;
    System.out.println(flag);
  }
}
```

Select the two correct answers.

(a) The program, as it stands, does not compile.
(b) The program will compile without errors. When run, it will print false.
(c) The program will compile without errors. When run, it will print true.
(d) If the keyword if at (1) is replaced with the keyword while, the program will compile without errors. When run, it will print false.
(e) If the keyword if at (1) is replaced with the keyword while, the program will compile without errors. When run, it will print true.
(f) If the keyword if at (1) is replaced with the keyword while, the program will fail to compile.

Q11 What will be the result from the following program?

```java
import java.util.List;

class Person implements Comparable<Person> {
  public int compareTo(Person p) {
    return 1;
  }
}

class Student extends Person {
  public int compareTo(Student s) {
    return 2;
  }
}

public class Calling {
  public static void main(String[] args) {
    Person  p1 = new Person();
    Student s1 = new Student();
    Student s2 = new Student();
```

```
        Person   p2 = s1;
        System.out.println(List.of(
            p1.compareTo(s1), p1.compareTo(p2),
            p2.compareTo(s1), p2.compareTo(p1),
            s1.compareTo(p1), s1.compareTo(p2),
            s1.compareTo(s2)));
    }
}
```

Select the one correct answer.

(a) [1, 1, 2, 1, 1, 1, 2]

(b) [1, 1, 1, 1, 1, 1, 2]

(c) [1, 1, 2, 1, 1, 2, 2]

(d) [1, 1, 1, 1, 1, 2, 2]

(e) [1, 1, 1, 1, 2, 2, 2]

Q12   What will be the result of compiling and running the following program?

```
import java.util.ArrayList;
import java.util.List;

public class Q12A56 {
    public static void main(String[] args) {
        List<String> strList = new ArrayList<>();
        strList.add(0, "Ada");
        strList.add("Alyla");
        strList.set(strList.size()-1, "Otto");
        strList.add(strList.size()-1, "Anna");
        System.out.println(strList);                      // (1)
        int size = strList.size();
        for (int i = 0; i < size; ++i) {
            strList.add(strList.get(size-1-i));
        }
        System.out.println(strList);                      // (2)
    }
}
```

Select the two correct answers.

(a) (1) will print [Ada, Alyla, Anna].

(b) (1) will print [Ada, Anna, Otto].

(c) (1) will print [Ada, Otto, Alyla].

(d) (2) will print [Ada, Alyla, Anna, Anna, Alyla, Ada].

(e) (2) will print [Ada, Anna, Otto, Otto, Anna, Ada].

(f) (2) will print [Ada, Otto, Alyla, Alyla, Otto, Ada].

Q13   What will be the result of compiling and running the following program?

```
import java.util.ArrayList;
import java.util.List;

public class Q12A55 {
    public static void main(String[] args) {
        List<String> strList = new ArrayList<>();
        strList.add(strList.size(), "Anna");
```

```
        strList.add(strList.size()-1, "Ada");
        strList.add(strList.size()-1, "Otto");
        strList.add(0, "Alyla");
        System.out.println(strList);
        int size = strList.size();
        for (int i = 0; i < size/2; ++i) {
          String strTemp = strList.get(i);
          strList.set(i, strList.get(size-1-i));
          strList.set(size-1-i, strTemp);
        }
        System.out.println(strList);
      }
    }
```

Select the one correct answer.

(a) The program will fail to compile.

(b) The program will throw an IndexOutOfBoundsException.

(c) The program will throw a NullPointerException.

(d) The program will print:
```
[Alyla, Ada, Otto, Anna]
[Anna, Otto, Ada, Alyla]
```

(e) The program will print:
```
[Ada, Otto, Alyla, Anna]
[Anna, Alyla, Otto, Ada]
```

Q14 Given the following code:
```
import java.util.function.Predicate;
public class Test {
  public static void main(String[] args) throws IOException  {
    Stream<String> shapes = Stream.of("Circle","Cube");
    // (1) INSERT CODE HERE
    shapes.filter(p).forEach(v->System.out.println(v));
  }
}
```

Which code option can be inserted at (1) so that the program prints "Circle" and "Cube"?

Select the one correct answer.

(a) `Predicate<String> p = s -> {`
```
        s.toLowerCase();
        return s.contains("c");
    };
```

(b) `Predicate p = s -> {`
```
        s = s.toString().toLowerCase();
        return s.contains("c");
    };
```

(c) `Predicate<String> p = s -> s.contains("c");`

(d) `Predicate<Object> p = s -> s.toString().toLowerCase().contains("c");`

(e) `Predicate p = s -> s.contains("c");`

(f) `Predicate p = s -> s.toLowerCase().contains("c");`

Q15 Which statement is true about the following interfaces?

```
interface IA              { boolean equals(Object obj); }
interface IB extends IA { boolean doIt(String str); }
interface IC extends IB { boolean doIt(String str); }
interface ID extends IC { boolean equals(Object obj);}
```

Select the one correct answer.

(a) IA is a functional interface.
(b) IB is a functional interface.
(c) IC is not a functional interface.
(d) ID is not a functional interface.

Q16 What will be the result of compiling and running the following program?

```
import java.time.LocalDate;

public class Q11A35 {
  public static void main(String[] args) {
    LocalDate date = LocalDate.of(2015, 1, 1);
    date.withYear(5);
    System.out.println(date.plusMonths(12));
  }
}
```

Select the one correct answer.

(a) The program will fail to compile.
(b) The program will throw an exception at runtime.
(c) The program will print 0006-01-01.
(d) The program will print 2021-01-01.
(e) The program will print 2015-01-01.
(f) The program will print 2016-01-01.

Q17 Which code, when inserted at (1), will make the program compile and execute normally?

```
import java.time.*;
import java.time.format.*;

public class Q11A95 {
  public static void main(String[] args) {
    String inputStr = "The time is 15 minutes past 10PM.";
    String pattern = "'The time is 'm' minutes past 'ha.";
    DateTimeFormatter dtf = DateTimeFormatter.ofPattern(pattern);
    // (1) INSERT CODE HERE
  }
}
```

Select the three correct answers.

(a) LocalTime time = LocalTime.parse(inputStr, dtf);
(b) LocalDate date = LocalDate.parse(inputStr, dtf);
(c) LocalDateTime dateTime = LocalDateTime.parse(inputStr, dtf);
(d) String timeStr = LocalTime.of(9, 20).format(dtf);
(e) String dateStr = LocalDate.of(2015, 12, 24).format(dtf);
(f) String dateTimeStr = LocalDateTime.of(2015, 12, 24, 22, 15).format(dtf);

Q18 Given that a static method doIt() in the class Work represents work to be done,
which lines of code will succeed in starting a new thread that will do the work?
Select the one correct answer.

(a)
```java
Runnable r = new Runnable() {
  public void run() {
    Work.doIt();
  }
};
Thread t = new Thread(r);
t.start();
```

(b)
```java
Thread t = new Thread() {
  public void start() {
    Work.doIt();
  }
};
t.start();
```

(c)
```java
Runnable r = new Runnable() {
  public void run() {
    Work.doIt();
  }
};
r.start();
```

(d)
```java
Thread t = new Thread(new Work());
t.start();
```

(e)
```java
Runnable t = new Runnable() {
  public void run() {
    Work.doIt();
  }
};
t.run();
```

Q19 Which of the following statements are true about the following program?

```java
public class Q100A82 {
  public static void main(String[] args) {
    Object o = choose(991, "800");                        // (1)
    Number n1 = choose(991, 3.14);                        // (2)
    Number n2 = Q100A82.<Double>choose((double)991, 3.14); // (3)
    int k = (int) choose(1.3, 3.14);                      // (4)
    int l = (int) (double) choose(1.3, 3.14);             // (5)
  }

  public static <T extends Comparable<T>> T choose(T t1, T t2) {
    return t1.compareTo(t2) >= 0 ? t1 : t2;
  }
}
```

Select the two correct answers.

(a) The class must be declared as a generic type:
    `public class Q100A82<T extends Comparable<T>> { ... }`
(b) The compiler reports errors at (1).
(c) The compiler reports no errors at (2).
(d) The compiler reports no errors at (3).

(e) The compiler reports no errors at (4).

(f) The compiler reports errors at (5).

Q20 Which of the following statements, when inserted at (1), will make the program print 1 when executed?

```java
public class Outer {
    private int a = 1;
    private int b = 1;
    private int c = 1;

    class Inner {
        private int a = 2;

        int get() {
            int c = 3;
            // (1) INSERT CODE HERE
            return c;
        }
    }

    Outer() {
        Inner i = new Inner();
        System.out.println(i.get());
    }

    public static void main(String[] args) {
        new Outer();
    }
}
```

Select the two correct answers.

(a) `c = b;`

(b) `c = this.a;`

(c) `c = this.b;`

(d) `c = Outer.this.a;`

(e) `c = c;`

Q21 What will be the result of compiling and running the following code?

```java
public enum FrequentFlyer {
    PLATINUM(20), GOLD(10), SILVER(5), BASIC(0);
    private double extra;

    FrequentFlyer(double extra) {
        this.extra = extra;
    }

    public static FrequentFlyer max(FrequentFlyer c1, FrequentFlyer c2) {
        return c1.compareTo(c2) < 0 ? c2 : c1;
    }

    public static FrequentFlyer max2(FrequentFlyer c1, FrequentFlyer c2) {
        return c1.extra < c2.extra ? c2 : c1;
    }

    public static void main (String[] args) {
        System.out.println(GOLD.ordinal() > SILVER.ordinal());
```

```
      System.out.println(max(GOLD, SILVER));
      System.out.println(max2(GOLD, SILVER));
    }
  }
```

Select the one correct answer.

(a) The program will compile and print:
```
false
SILVER
GOLD
```

(b) The program will compile and print:
```
true
GOLD
SILVER
```

(c) The program will compile and print:
```
true
GOLD
GOLD
```

(d) The program will fail to compile, since the enum type FrequentFlyer does not implement the Comparable interface.

Q22 Which of the following statements are true about the following code?

```
public class Vertical {
  private int alt;
  public synchronized void up() {
    ++alt;
  }
  public void down() {
    --alt;
  }
  public synchronized void jump() {
    int a = alt;
    up();
    down();
    System.out.println(a == alt);
  }
}
```

Select the two correct answers.

(a) The code will fail to compile.
(b) Different threads can execute the up() method concurrently.
(c) Different threads can execute the down() method concurrently.
(d) Different threads can execute both the up() and the down() methods concurrently.
(e) The jump() method will always print true.

Q23 Which parameter declarations can be inserted at (1) so that the program will compile without warnings?

```
interface Wagger{}
class Pet implements Wagger{}
class Dog extends Pet {}
class Cat extends Pet {}
```

```
public class Q100A51 {
  public static void main(String[] args) {
    List<Pet> p = new ArrayList<>();
    List<Dog> d = new ArrayList<>();
    List<Cat> c = new ArrayList<>();
    examine(p);
    examine(d);
    examine(c);
  }

  static void examine(/* INSERT PARAMETER TYPE HERE */ pets) {        // (1)
    System.out.print("Your pets need urgent attention.");
  }
}
```

Select the three correct answers.

(a) List<? extends Pet>
(b) List<? super Pet>
(c) List<? extends Wagger>
(d) List<? super Wagger>
(e) List<?>

Q24   Given the following code:

```
package p1;
public enum Format {
  JPEG, GIF, TIFF;
}
```

```
package p1;
public class Util {
  public enum Format {
    JPEG { public String toString() {return "Jpeggy"; }},
    GIF  { public String toString() {return "Giffy"; }},
    TIFF { public String toString() {return "Tiffy"; }};
  }
  public static <T> void print(T t) {
    System.out.print("|" + t + "|");
  }
}
```

```
import static p1.Util.Format;
import static p1.Util.print;

public class Importing {
  static final int JPEG = 200;
  public static void main(String[] args) {
    final int JPEG = 100;
    print(JPEG);
    // (1) INSERT CODE HERE
  }
}
```

Which lines of code when inserted at (1) will result in the following output:

|100||200||Jpeggy||JPEG|

Select the one correct answer.

(a) `print(Format.JPEG);`
     `print(p1.Format.JPEG);`
     `print(Importing.JPEG);`

(b) `print(Format.JPEG);`
     `print(Importing.JPEG);`
     `print(p1.Format.JPEG);`

(c) `print(Importing.JPEG);`
     `print(Format.JPEG);`
     `print(p1.Format.JPEG);`

Q25 What will be the result of compiling and running the following program?

```java
import java.util.ArrayList;
import java.util.List;
public class Q400A70 {
  public static void main(String[] args) {
    List<Integer> list = new ArrayList<>();
    list.add(2019); list.add(2020); list.add(2021);
    System.out.println("Before: " + list);
    for (int i : list) {
      int index = list.indexOf(i);
      list.set(index, ++i);
    }
    System.out.println("After:  " + list);
  }
}
```

Select the one correct answer.

(a) The program will print:
     ```
     Before: [2019, 2020, 2021]
     After:  [2020, 2021, 2022]
     ```

(b) The program will print:
     ```
     Before: [2019, 2020, 2021]
     After:  [2022, 2020, 2021]
     ```

(c) The program will print:
     ```
     Before: [2019, 2020, 2021]
     After:  [2019, 2020, 2021]
     ```

(d) The program will print:
     ```
     Before: [2019, 2020, 2021]
     After:  [2020, 2021, 2019]
     ```

(e) The program will throw a `java.util.ConcurrentModificationException` at
     runtime.

Q26 Given the following code:

```java
public class Person {
  protected transient String name;
  Person() { this.name = "NoName"; }
  Person(String name) { this.name = name; }
}
```

and

```java
public class Student extends Person {
  protected long studNum;
  Student() { }
  Student(String name, long studNum) {
    super(name);
    this.studNum = studNum;
  }
}
```

and

```java
import java.io.Serializable;
public class GraduateStudent extends Student implements Serializable {
  private int year;
  GraduateStudent(String name, long studNum, int year) {
    super(name, studNum);
    this.year = year;
  }

  public String toString() {
    return "(" + name + ", " + studNum + ", " + year + ")";
  }
}
```

and

```java
import java.io.*;
public class Q800A60 {
  public static void main(String args[])
      throws IOException, ClassNotFoundException {
    try (FileOutputStream outputFile = new FileOutputStream("storage.dat");
        ObjectOutputStream outputStream = new ObjectOutputStream(outputFile)) {
      GraduateStudent stud1 = new GraduateStudent("Aesop", 100, 1);
      System.out.print(stud1);
      outputStream.writeObject(stud1);
    }

    try (FileInputStream inputFile = new FileInputStream("storage.dat");
        ObjectInputStream inputStream = new ObjectInputStream(inputFile)) {
      GraduateStudent stud2 = (GraduateStudent) inputStream.readObject();
      System.out.println(stud2);
    }
  }
}
```

Which statement is true about the program?
Select the one correct answer.

(a) It will fail to compile.
(b) It will compile, but it will throw an exception at runtime.
(c) It will print (Aesop, 100, 1)(NoName, 0, 1).
(d) It will print (Aesop, 100, 1)(Aesop, 100, 1).
(e) It will print (Aesop, 100, 1)(null, 0, 1).

Q27   Which of the following statements are true about the classes SupA, SubB, and SubC?

```java
public class SupA<T> {
  public List<?> fuddle() { return null; }
  public List scuddle(T t) { return null; }
}

public class SubB<U> extends SupA<U> {
  public List fuddle() { return null;}
  public List<?> scuddle(U t) { return null; }
}

public class SubC<V> extends SupA<V> {
  public List<V> fuddle() { return null;}
  public List<? extends Object> scuddle(V t) { return null; }
}
```

Select the four correct answers.

(a) Class SubB will fail to compile.
(b) Class SubC will fail to compile.
(c) Class SubB will compile.
(d) Class SubC will compile.
(e) Class SubB overloads the methods in class SupA.
(f) Class SubC overloads the methods in class SupA.
(g) Class SubB overrides the methods in class SupA.
(h) Class SubC overrides the methods in class SupA.

Q28   Which of the following statements is true?

Select the one correct answer.

(a) If a method does not handle an exception that is thrown, it must declare the exception in a throws clause.
(b) A try block cannot be followed by both a catch and a finally clause.
(c) An empty catch clause is not allowed.
(d) A catch clause cannot follow a finally clause.
(e) A finally clause must always follow one or more catch clauses.

Q29   Which import statements, when inserted at (4) in package p3, will result in a program that can be compiled and run?

```java
package p2;
enum March {LEFT, RIGHT;                       // (1)
  public String toString() {
    return "Top-level enum";
  }
}
public class DefenceInDepth {
  public enum March {LEFT, RIGHT;              // (2)
    public String toString() {
      return "Static enum";
    }
  }
  public enum Military { INFANTRY, AIRFORCE;
    public static enum March {LEFT, RIGHT;     // (3)
```

```
          public String toString() {
            return "Statically nested enum";
          }
        }
      }
    }
}
```

```
package p3;
// (4) INSERT IMPORTS HERE
public class MarchingOrders {
  public static void main(String[] args) {
    System.out.println(March.LEFT);
    System.out.println(DefenceInDepth.March.LEFT);
    System.out.println(p2.DefenceInDepth.March.LEFT);
    System.out.println(Military.March.LEFT);
    System.out.println(DefenceInDepth.Military.March.LEFT);
    System.out.println(p2.DefenceInDepth.Military.March.LEFT);
    System.out.println(LEFT);
  }
}
```

Select the three correct answers.

(a) `import p2.*;`
    `import p2.DefenceInDepth.*;`
    `import static p2.DefenceInDepth.Military.March.LEFT;`

(b) `import p2.*;`
    `import static p2.DefenceInDepth.*;`
    `import static p2.DefenceInDepth.Military.March.LEFT;`

(c) `import p2.DefenceInDepth;`
    `import static p2.DefenceInDepth.*;`
    `import static p2.DefenceInDepth.Military.March.LEFT;`

(d) `import static p2.DefenceInDepth;`
    `import static p2.DefenceInDepth.*;`
    `import static p2.DefenceInDepth.Military.March.LEFT;`

(e) `import p2.*;`
    `import static p2.DefenceInDepth.*;`
    `import static p2.DefenceInDepth.Military.*;`

(f) `import p2.*;`
    `import static p2.DefenceInDepth.*;`
    `import static p2.DefenceInDepth.Military.March;`

Q30   Which statement is true about the following code?

```
public class A {
  public A() {}
  public A(int i) { this(); }
}
public class B extends A {
  public boolean B(String msg) { return false; }
}
public class C extends B {
  private C() { super(); }
```

```
    public C(String msg) { this(); }
    public C(int i) {}
}
```

Select the one correct answer.

(a) The code will fail to compile.

(b) The constructor in A that takes an int as an argument will never be called as a result of constructing an object of class B or C.

(c) Objects of class B cannot be constructed.

(d) At most, one constructor of each class is called as a result of constructing an object of class C.

Q31   Given the following class declarations, which expression identifies whether the object referenced by obj was created by instantiating class B rather than classes A, C, and D?

```
    class A {}
    class B extends A {}
    class C extends B {}
    class D extends A {}
```

Select the one correct answer.

(a) obj instanceof B

(b) obj instanceof A && !(obj instanceof C)

(c) obj instanceof B && !(obj instanceof C)

(d) !(obj instanceof C || obj instanceof D)

(e) !(obj instanceof A) && !(obj instanceof C) && !(obj instanceof D)

Q32   What will be the result of compiling and running the following code?

```
    public enum Scale5 {
      GOOD, BETTER, BEST;

      public char getGrade() {
        return switch (this) {
          case GOOD   -> 'C';
          case BETTER -> 'B';
          case BEST   -> 'A';
        };
      }

      public static void main (String[] args) {
        System.out.println(GOOD.getGrade());
      }
    }
```

Select the one correct answer.

(a) The program will fail to compile, as the switch expression is not compatible with the case labels.

(b) The program will fail to compile, as enum constants cannot be used as case labels.

(c) The program will fail to compile, as the case labels must be qualified with the enum type name.

(d) The program will compile, and when run, will print C.

(e) The program will compile, and when run, will print GOOD.

Q33 Which method declarations, when inserted at (7), will not result in a compile-time error?

```java
// File: MyClass.java
package p4;
class MySuperclass {
    public         Integer step1(int i)                      { return 1; }     // (1)
    protected      String  step2(String str1, String str2)   { return str1; }  // (2)
    public         String  step2(String str1)                { return str1; }  // (3)
    public static String   step2()                           { return "Hi"; }  // (4)

    public MyClass       makeIt()  { return new MyClass(); }                    // (5)
    public MySuperclass makeIt2() { return new MyClass(); }                     // (6)
}

public class MyClass extends MySuperclass {
    // (7) INSERT METHOD DECLARATION HERE
}
```

Select the two correct answers.

(a) `public int step1(int i) { return 1; }`

(b) `public String step2(String str2, String str1) { return str1; }`

(c) `private void step2() { }`

(d) `private static void step2() { }`

(e) `private static String step2(String str) { return str; }`

(f) `public MySuperclass makeIt() { return new MySuperclass(); }`

(g) `public MyClass makeIt2() { return new MyClass(); }`

Q34 What is the result of compiling and running the following program?

```java
public class Q800A60 {
    static void printFirst(Integer... ints) {
        System.out.println("Integer...: " + ints[0]);
    }

    static void printFirst(Number... nums) {
        System.out.println("Number...: " + nums[0]);
    }

    static void printFirst(Object... objs) {
        System.out.println("Object...: " + objs[0]);
    }

    public static void main(String[] args) {
        printFirst(10);
        printFirst((byte)20);
        printFirst('3', '0');
        printFirst("40");
        printFirst((short)50, 55);
        printFirst((Number[])new Integer[] {70, 75});
    }
}
```

Select the one correct answer.

(a) The program does not compile because of ambiguous method calls.

(b) The program will compile and will print:
```
Integer...: 10
Integer...: 20
Integer...: 3
Object...: 40
Integer...: 50
Number...: 70
```

(c) The program will compile and will print:
```
Integer...: 10
Number...: 20
Object...: 3
Object...: 40
Number...: 50
Number...: 70
```

(d) The program will compile and will print:
```
Integer...: 10
Integer...: 20
Integer...: 3
Object...: 40
Number...: 50
Number...: 70
```

Q35 What will be the result of compiling and running the following program?
```java
public class Initialization {
  private static String msg(String msg) {
    System.out.println(msg);
    return msg;
  }
  static String m = msg("1");
  { m = msg("2"); }
  static { m = msg("3"); }
  public static void main(String[] args) {
    Object obj = new Initialization();
  }
}
```

Select the one correct answer.

(a) The program will fail to compile.

(b) The program will compile and print 1, 2, and 3 at runtime.

(c) The program will compile and print 2, 3, and 1 at runtime.

(d) The program will compile and print 3, 1, and 2 at runtime.

(e) The program will compile and print 1, 3, and 2 at runtime.

Q36 Given the following resource bundle:
```
# File: MyResources_en_US.properties
greeting = Long time no see!
```

Assuming that the current default locale is "en_US", what will be the result of compiling and running the following program?

```
import java.util.*;
public class LocatingBundlesForDefaultLocale {
  public static void main(String[] args) {
    Locale norLocale = new Locale("no", "NO");
    ResourceBundle rbs = ResourceBundle.getBundle("MyResources", norLocale);
    System.out.println(rbs.getString("greeting"));
    Locale.setDefault(norLocale);
    System.out.println(rbs.getString("greeting"));
  }
}
```

Select the one correct answer.

(a) When run, the program will print the following and terminate normally.
```
Long time no see!
Long time no see!
```

(b) When run, the program will print `Long time no see!` and terminate normally.

(c) When run, the program will print `Long time no see!` and then throw a `Missing-ResourceException`.

(d) When run, the program will immediately throw a `MissingResourceException`.

(e) When run, the program will terminate normally without printing anything.

Q37 What will be the result of compiling and running the following program?

```
public class Syncher2 {
  static final int[] intArray = new int[2];

  private static void pause() {
    while (intArray[0] == 0) {
      try { intArray.wait(); }
      catch (InterruptedException ie) {
        System.out.println(Thread.currentThread() + " interrupted.");
      }
    }
  }

  public static void main (String[] args) {
    Thread runner = new Thread() {
      public void run() {
        synchronized (intArray) {
          pause();
          System.out.println(intArray[0] + intArray[1]);
    }}};

    runner.start();
    intArray[0] = intArray[1] = 10;
    synchronized(intArray) {
      intArray.notify();
    }
  }
}
```

Select the one correct answer.

(a) The program will fail to compile.

(b) The program will compile. When run, it will throw an exception.

(c) The program will compile and continue running once started, but will not print anything.

(d) The program will compile. When run, it will print 0 and terminate normally.

(e) The program will compile. When run, it will print 20 and terminate normally.

(f) The program will compile. When run, it will print some number other than 0 or 20, and terminate normally.

Q38   Given the following code:

```java
public class Thingy<T> implements Comparable<T> {
  private T value;
  public Thingy(T value) {
    this.value = value;
  }
  public String toString() {
    return value.toString();
  }
  public int compareTo(T obj) {
    return this.value.toString().compareTo(obj.toString());
  }
}
```

and

```java
import java.math.*;
import java.util.*;
public class TestThingy {
  public static void main(String[] args) {
    Thingy[] values  = {
      new Thingy<BigDecimal>(BigDecimal.valueOf(12.99)),
      new Thingy<BigDecimal>(BigDecimal.valueOf(7.99)),
      new Thingy<BigDecimal>(BigDecimal.valueOf(7)),
      new Thingy<BigDecimal>(BigDecimal.valueOf(9.99))};
    Arrays.sort(values);
    for (Thingy t: values) {
      System.out.print(t + " ");
    }
  }
}
```

What is the result?

Select the one correct answer.

(a) 12.99 7.99 7 9.99

(b) 12.99 7 7.99 9.99

(c) 7 7.99 9.99 12.99

(d) 12.99 9.99 7.99 7

(e) The code will throw an exception at runtime.

(f) The code will fail to compile.

Q39   Given the following code:

```java
public class Widget<T> {
  private T value;
  private static int result;
  public Widget(T value) { this.value = value; }
  public void compute(Comparable<T> c) {
    result += c.compareTo(value);
  }
  public static int getResult() { return result; }
}
```

and

```java
import java.time.*;
public class TestWidget {
  public static void main(String[] args) {
    Widget<String> t1 = new Widget<>("ACME");
    t1.compute(v -> v.length());
    t1.compute(v -> v.indexOf("C"));
    Widget<LocalDate> t2 = new Widget<>(LocalDate.of(2020, 10, 20));
    t2.compute(v -> v.getDayOfMonth());
    System.out.println(Widget.getResult());
  }
}
```

What is the result?

Select the one correct answer.

(a) 23
(b) 24
(c) 25
(d) 13
(e) 14
(f) 15
(g) The code will throw an exception at runtime.
(h) The code will fail to compile.

Q40   Given the following code:

```java
import java.util.*;
public class Test13A10 {
  public static void main(String[] args) {
    Integer[] values = {4, 2, 6, 3, 5};
    Arrays.sort(values, (x, y) -> x - y);
    System.out.println(Arrays.toString(values));
  }
}
```

What is the result?

Select the one correct answer.

(a) [4, 2, 6, 3, 5]
(b) [2, 3, 4, 5, 6]
(c) [6, 5, 4, 3, 2]
(d) [2, -4, 3, -2]
(e) The code will throw an exception at runtime.
(f) The code will fail to compile.

Q41   Given the following code:

```
import java.time.*;
import java.time.format.DateTimeFormatter;
public class Q700A12 {
  public static void main(String[] args) {
    LocalDate d = LocalDate.of(0, 1, 1);
    DateTimeFormatter dtf = DateTimeFormatter.ofPattern("dd MM yy G");
    System.out.println(d.format(dtf));
  }
}
```

What is the result?

Select the one correct answer.

(a) 01 01 01 BC
(b) 00 01 01 BC
(c) 01 01 01 AD
(d) 00 01 01 AD

Q42   Given the following code:

```
Comparable<?>[] values = { LocalDate.of(2022, Month.JANUARY, 1),
    LocalDate.of(2022, Month.FEBRUARY, 5),
    Integer.valueOf(3),
    LocalDateTime.of(2022, Month.JANUARY, 22, 1, 12, 2),
    "4"};
long result = Arrays.stream(values)
    .mapToInt(v -> (v instanceof LocalDateTime ldt)
                    ? ldt.toLocalTime().getSecond() : 1)
    .sum();
System.out.println(result);
```

What is the result?

Select the one correct answer.

(a) 2
(b) 4
(c) 6
(d) 8
(e) The code will throw an exception at runtime.

Q43   Given the following code:

```
String txt = """
  a
    b
  c
  """;

txt.lines().map(String::length).forEachOrdered(System.out::print);
```

The first line of the text block has two leading spaces, the second line has four leading spaces, and the third line has two leading spaces. There are two leading whitespace on the line with the closing delimiter of the text block.

What is the result of executing the code?

Select the one correct answer.

(a) 353
(b) 3530
(c) 1510
(d) 131

Q44 Given the following code:

```java
import java.nio.file.*;
public class Test {
  public static void main(String[] args) {
    Path p1 = Path.of("/users/joe");
    Path p2 = Path.of("/users/bob");
    Path p3 = p1.resolve(p1.relativize(p2));
    Path p4 = p3.normalize();
    System.out.println(p3.getName(1) + " " + p4.getName(1));
  }
}
```

What is the result?
Select the one correct answer.

(a) users bob
(b) joe users
(c) joe bob
(d) users users

Q45 Given the following code:

```java
import java.util.*;
public class Localizing {  public static void main(String[] args) {
    ResourceBundle rb = ResourceBundle.getBundle("resources", new Locale("en"));
    DateTimeFormatter fmt = DateTimeFormatter.ofPattern(rb.getString("f1"),
                                            new Locale("en","GB"));
    LocalDate d = LocalDate.of(2022, 4, 1);
    System.out.println(fmt.format(d));
  }
}
```

and

```
// File: resources.properties
f1=yy-MMM-dd
```

and

```
// File: resources_en.properties
f2=MMM-dd-yy
```

and

```
// File: resources_en_GB.properties
f1=dd-MMM-yy
```

What is the result?
Select the one correct answer.

(a) 01-Apr-22
(b) 22-Apr-01
(c) Apr-01-22
(d) The code will throw an exception at runtime.

Q46   Given the following code:

```
public class TestX {
  public static void main(String[] args) {
    System.out.println(action(Integer.valueOf("1")));
  }
  public static boolean action(Object obj) {
    return (obj instanceof String value1 && value1.contains("1") ||
            obj instanceof Integer value2 && value2.intValue() < 1);
  }
}
```

What is the result?
Select the one correct answer.

(a) true
(b) false
(c) The program will throw an exception at runtime.
(d) The program will fail to compile.

Q47   Given the following code:

```
import java.time.Duration;
public record Song(String title, Duration duration) {
  // (1) INSERT CODE HERE
}
```

and

```
public class TestY {
  public static void main(String[] args) {
    Song song = new Song("Imagine", 106);
    System.out.println(song);
  }
}
```

Which option can be inserted into the Song record declaration at (1), so that the program will print Song[title=IMAGINE, duration=PT1M46S]?
Select the one correct answer.

(a) ```
    public Song(int seconds) {
      this(this.title.toUpperCase(), Duration.ofSeconds(seconds));
    }
    ```

(b) ```
    public Song(int seconds) {
      this(title.toUpperCase(), Duration.ofSeconds(seconds));
    }
    ```

(c) ```
    public Song(String title, int seconds) {
      this(title.toUpperCase(), Duration.ofSeconds(seconds));
    }
    ```

(d) ```
    public Song(String title, int seconds) {
      this.title = title.toUpperCase();
      this.duration = Duration.ofSeconds(seconds);
    }
    ```

(e) ```
    public Song {
      this.title.toUpperCase();
      this.duration = Duration.ofSeconds(seconds));
    }
    ```
    ```

Q48   Given the following directory structure under the directory ./Sun:

```
./Sun/1_Mercury
./Sun/2_Venus
./Sun/3_Earth
./Sun/3_Earth/1_Moon
./Sun/4_Mars
./Sun/4_Mars/1_Phobos
./Sun/4_Mars/2_Deimos
./Sun/5_Jupiter
./Sun/5_Jupiter/1_Io
./Sun/5_Jupiter/2_Europa
./Sun/5_Jupiter/3_Ganymede
./Sun/5_Jupiter/4_Calisto
./Sun/6_Saturn
./Sun/7_Uranus
./Sun/8_Neptune
```

and the code:

```
try {
    Path sun = Path.of("./Sun");
    Files.walk(sun)
        .map(p->p.getName(p.getNameCount()-1).toString())
        .sorted()
        .limit(3)
        .forEach(p->System.out.println(p.substring(2)));
} catch (IOException e) {
    e.printStackTrace();
}
```

What is the result?
Select the one correct answer.

(a) Io
     Mercury

(b) Io
     Mercury
     Moon

(c) Io
     Mercury
     Moon
     Phobos

(d) Earth
     Ganymede

(e) Venus
     Deimos
     Europa

Q49   Given the text file data.txt that contains following lines:

```
Apple:1.99
Pear:1.70
Apple:1.70
Apple:1.75
Orange:1.99
```

and the following code:

```
try {
    Path test = Path.of("data.txt");
    Map<String, List<String>> values
        = Files.lines(test).collect(Collectors.groupingBy(
                                    ln -> ln.substring(ln.indexOf(":") + 1)));
    System.out.println(values);
} catch (IOException e) {
    e.printStackTrace();
}
```

What is the result?

Select the one correct answer.

(a) {1.70=[1.70, 1.70], 1.99=[1.99, 1.99], 1.75=[1.75]}

(b) {1.70=[Pear:1.70, Apple:1.70], 1.99=[Apple:1.99, Orange:1.99], 1.75=[Apple:1.75]}

(c) {1.70=[Pear, Apple], 1.99=[Apple, Orange], 1.75=[Apple]}

(d) {Apple=[Apple:1.99, Apple:1.70, Apple:1.75], Pear=[Pear:1.70], Orange=[Orange:1.99]}

(e) {Apple=[1.99, 1.70, 1.75], Pear=[1.70], Orange=[1.99]}

(f) {Apple=[Apple, Apple, Apple], Pear=[Pear], Orange=[Orange]}

Q50   Given the following code:

```
module travel {
    requires transport;
    uses transport.mode.TransportType;
}
```

and

```
module transport {
    exports transport.mode;
}
```

What is the correct declaration for a module named basic that implements the TransportType service?

Select the one correct answer.

(a) ```
module basic {
    requires travel;
    provides travel.mode.TransportType with basic.mode.Horse;
}
```

(b) ```
module basic {
    requires transport.mode;
    provides TransportType with Horse;
}
```

(c) ```
module basic {
    requires transport;
    provides transport.mode.TransportType with basic.mode.Horse;
}
```

(d) ```
module basic {
    requires travel.mode;
    provides TransportType with Horse;
}
```

Annotated Answers to Mock Exam

This appendix provides annotated answers to the questions in the mock exam for the *Java SE 17 Developer* exam found in Appendix E, p. 1709.

Annotated Answers

Q1 *(e)*
An object of the class Extension is created. The first thing the constructor of Extension does is invoke the constructor of Base, using an implicit super() call. All calls to the method void add(int) are dynamically bound to the add() method in the Extension class, since the actual object is of type Extension. Therefore, this method is called by the constructor of Base, the constructor of Extension, and the bogo() method with the parameters 1, 2, and 8, respectively. The instance field i changes value accordingly: 2, 6, and 22. The final value of 22 is printed.

Q2 *(e)*
Method g() modifies field a. Method g() modifies parameter b, not field b, since the parameter declaration shadows the field. Variables are passed by value, so the change of value in parameter b is confined to the method g(). Method g() modifies the array whose reference value is passed as a parameter. A change to the first element is visible after return from the method g().

Q3 *(b)*
Classes cannot extend interfaces; they can implement them. Interfaces can extend, but not implement other interfaces. A class must be declared as abstract if it does not provide an implementation for all abstract methods of the interfaces that it implements. Instance methods that have no implementation in an interface are implicitly public and abstract. Classes that implement these methods must explicitly declare these methods to be public.

Q4   (b)

The method with the most specific signature is chosen. In this case the int argument 10 is boxed to an Integer, which is passed to the Number formal parameter, as type Number is more specific than Object.

Q5   (c)

As it stands, the program will compile correctly and will print 3, 2 at runtime. If the break statement is replaced with a continue statement, the loop will perform all four iterations and will print 4, 3. If the break statement is replaced with a return statement, the whole method will end when i equals 2, before anything is printed. If the break statement is simply removed, leaving the empty statement (;), the loop will complete all four iterations and will print 4, 4.

Q6   (d)

The type of nums is int[][]. The outer loop iterates over the rows, so the type of the loop variable in the outer loop must be int[], and the loop expression is nums. The inner loop iterates over each row, int[]. The loop variable in the inner loop must be int, and the loop expression in the inner loop is a row given by the loop variable of the outer loop. Only in the loop headers in (d) are both element types compatible.

Q7   (e)

The loop condition ++i == i is always true, as we are comparing the value of i to itself, and the loop will execute indefinitely. The evaluation of the loop condition proceeds as follows: ((++i) == i), with the operands having the same value. For each iteration, the loop variable i is incremented twice: once in the loop condition and a second time in the parameter expression i++. However, the value of i is printed before it is incremented the second time, resulting in odd numbers from 1 onward being printed. If the prefix operator is also used in the println statement, all even numbers from 2 onward would be printed.

Q8   (d)

The expression i % k evaluates to the remainder value 3. The expression i % -k also evaluates to the remainder value 3. We ignore the sign of the operands, and negate the remainder only if the dividend (i in this case) is negative.

Q9   (c)

Strings are immutable, so the method concat() does not change the state of the s1 string. The default case is executed in the switch statement. There is no fall-through in the switch statement, as the switch statement uses arrow notation in which the case labels are mutually exclusive.

Q10   (b) and (f)

In both cases, the code in the if statement and the while loop is unreachable, so it can never be executed. In the case of the while loop, the compiler flags an error. The if statement is treated as a special case by the compiler to simulate conditional compilation, allowing code that should not be executed.

Q11   *(b)*

The thing to note is that the method compareTo() is overloaded in the subclass Student, and is not overridden. Thus objects of class Student have two methods with the same name: compareTo. For overloaded methods, the method to be executed is determined at compile time, depending on the type of the reference used to invoke the method, and the type of the actual parameters. When the type of the reference is Person (as is the case for p1 and p2), the method compareTo() in Person will always be executed. When the type of the reference is Student and the argument type is Person, the overridden method compareTo() in Person will always be executed. The overloaded method compareTo() defined in the subclass Student is executed by the last call s1.compareTo(s2) in the main() method, where the type of the reference is Student and the argument type is also Student.

Q12   *(b) and (e)*

The add(element) method adds an element at the end of the list. The add(index, element) method adds the element at the specified index in the list, shifting elements to the right from the specified index. The index satisfies (index >= 0 && index <= size()). The set(index, element) method replaces the element at the specified index in the list with the specified element. The index satisfies (index >= 0 && index < size()). The for(;;) loop adds the elements currently in the list at the end of the list. The list changes as follows:

```
[Ada]
[Ada, Alyla]
[Ada, Otto]
[Ada, Anna, Otto]
[Ada, Anna, Otto, Otto, Anna, Ada]
```

Q13   *(d)*

The add(index, element) method accepts an index that satisfies the condition (index >= 0 && index <= size()). The for(;;) loop swaps elements to reverse the elements in the list.

Q14   *(d)*

In (a), the type of parameter s is inferred to be String. The new string returned by calling the toLowerCase() method is discarded. Only the string element "Circle" contains the substring "c" and is printed.

In (b), the raw type Predicate is used. The type of parameter s is inferred to be Object. The expression s.contains("c") in the return statement fails to compile since the method contains() is not defined in the class Object.

In (c), the type of parameter s is inferred to be String. Only the string element "Circle" contains the substring "c" and is printed.

In (d), the type of parameter s is inferred to be Object. The string elements are referenced by the parameter s of type Object. However, the chain of method calls is invoked on objects of type String, resulting in both stream elements being selected and printed.

In (e), the raw type `Predicate` is used. The type of parameter s is inferred to be `Object`. The statement fails to compile since the method `contains()` is not defined in the class `Object`.

In (f), the raw type `Predicate` is used. The type of parameter s is inferred to be `Object`. The class `Object` does not define the method `toLowerCase()` and the statement fails to compile.

Q15   *(b)*

A functional interface is an interface that has only one abstract method, aside from the abstract method declarations of `public` methods from the `Object` class. This single abstract method declaration can be the result of inheriting multiple declarations of the abstract method from superinterfaces.

All except `IA` are functional interfaces. `IA` does not define an abstract method, as it provides only an abstract method declaration of the concrete `public` method `equals()` from the `Object` class. `IB` defines a single abstract method, `doIt()`. `IC` overrides the abstract method from `IB`, so effectively it has only one abstract method. `IC` inherits the abstract method `doIt()` from `IB` and overrides the `equals()` method from `IA`, so effectively it also has only one abstract method.

Q16   *(f)*

The date value `2015-01-01` in the date reference never changes. The `withYear()` method returns a new `LocalDate` object (with the date value `0005-01-01`) that is ignored. The `plusMonths()` method also returns a new `LocalDate` object whose value is printed. The calculation of `date.plusMonths(12)` proceeds as follows:

`2021-01-01 + 12 months (i.e., 1 year) ==> 2022-01-01`

Q17   *(a), (d), and (f)*

The input string matches the pattern. The input string specifies the time-based values that can be used to construct a `LocalTime` object in (a) by a formatter, based on the time-related pattern letters in the pattern. No date-based values can be interpreted from the input string, as this pattern has only time-related pattern letters. (b) and (c), which require a date part, will throw a `DateTimeParseException`.

To use the pattern for formatting, the temporal object must provide values for the parts corresponding to the pattern letters in the pattern. The `LocalTime` object in (d) has the time part required by the pattern. The `LocalDate` object in (e) does not have the time part required by the pattern, so an `UnsupportedTemporalTypeException` will be thrown. The `LocalDateTime` object in (f) has the time part required by the pattern. In (f), only the time part of the `LocalDateTime` object is formatted.

Q18   *(a)*

A `Thread` object executes the `run()` method of a `Runnable` object in a separate thread. A `Runnable` object can be provided when constructing a `Thread` object. If no `Runnable` object is supplied, the `run()` method of the `Thread` object (which implements the Runnable interface) is executed. A thread is initiated by calling the `start()` method of the `Thread` object.

Q19 *(b) and (d)*

In (a), the class need not be declared as a generic type if it defines any generic methods.

In (b), the method choose(T, T), where T extends Comparable<T>, is not applicable to the arguments (Integer, String). Note that Object is not Comparable<Object>.

In (c), the method choose(T, T), where T extends Comparable<T>, is not applicable to the arguments (Integer, Double). Note that Number is not Comparable<Number>.

In (d), the actual type parameter Double specified in the method call also requires that the int argument is cast to a double in order for the call to be valid. The method choose(T, T), where T extends Comparable<T>, is then applicable to the argument list (Double, Double).

(e) cannot convert the Double returned by the method to an int using a cast.

In (f), the method returns a Double that is first converted to a double, which in turn is converted to an int.

Q20 *(a) and (d)*

Field b of the outer class is not shadowed by any local or inner class variables; therefore, (a) will work. Using this.a will access field a in the inner class. Using this.b will result in a compile-time error, since there is no field b in the inner class. Using Outer.this.a will successfully access the field of the outer class. The statement c = c will only reassign the current value of the local variable c to itself.

Q21 *(a)*

All enum types implement the Comparable interface. Comparison is based on natural order, which in this case is the order in which the constants are specified, with the first one being the smallest. The ordinal value of the first enum constant is 0, the next one has the ordinal value 1, and so on.

Q22 *(c) and (d)*

Executing synchronized code does not guard against executing non-synchronized code concurrently.

Q23 *(a), (c), and (e)*

Lists of type Pet, Dog, and Cat are subtypes of List<? extends Pet>, List<? extends Wagger> and List<?>.

List<? super Pet> is a supertype for a list of Pet itself or a supertype of Pet—for example, Wagger, but not Dog or Cat.

List<? super Wagger> is a supertype for a list of Wagger itself or a supertype of Wagger—for example, Object, but not Pet, Dog, or Cat.

Q24 *(c)*

We need to access the following:

- Importing.JPEG (to print 200).
- p1.Util.Format.JPEG (to print Jpeggy). Since p1.Util.Format is statically imported by the second import statement, we need only specify Format.JPEG.
- p1.Format.JPEG (to print JPEG), which is explicitly specified to distinguish it from other JPEG declarations.

Q25   *(b)*
First, note that the indexOf() method returns the index of the *first* occurrence of its argument in the list. Although the value of variable i is successively changing during the execution of the loop, it is the *first* occurrence of this value that is replaced in each iteration:

```
                   0     1     2
                 [2019, 2020, 2021]
After iteration 1: [2020, 2020, 2021]
After iteration 2: [2021, 2020, 2021]
After iteration 3: [2022, 2020, 2021]
```

Note also that we are not removing or adding elements to the list, only changing the reference values stored in the elements of the list.

Q26   *(c)*
Note that only GraduateStudent is Serializable. The field name in the Person class is transient. During serialization of a GraduateStudent object, the fields year and studNum are included as part of the serialization process, but not the field name. During deserialization, the default constructors of the superclasses up the inheritance hierarchy of the GraduateStudent class are called, as none of the superclasses are Serializable.

Q27   *(c), (d), (g), and (h)*
The method header signature of the corresponding methods is the same after erasure—that is, List fuddle() and List scuddle(Object). The return type of overriding methods can be a raw type or a parameterized type.

Q28   *(d)*
A try block must be followed by at least one catch or finally clause. No catch clause can follow a finally clause. Methods must declare any checked exceptions in a throws clause, if they do not catch the exceptions.

Q29   *(a), (b), and (c)*
First, note that nested packages or nested static members are not automatically imported.

In (d), p2.DefenceInDepth is not a static member and therefore cannot be imported statically.

With (e), March.LEFT becomes ambiguous because both the second and the third import statements statically import March. The enum constant LEFT cannot be resolved either, as its enum type March cannot be resolved.

With (f), the enum constant LEFT cannot be resolved, as none of the static import statements specify it.

The enum type p2.March is also not visible outside the package.

Q30   *(b)*
Statement (c) is false, since an object of B can be created using the implicit default constructor of the class. B has a default constructor since no constructor has been defined. Statement (d) is false, since the second constructor of C will call the first constructor of C.

Q31 *(c)*
The important thing to remember is that an instance of a class is also an instance of its superclasses in the inheritance hierarchy.

Q32 *(d)*
Enum constants can be used as case labels and are not qualified with the enum type name in the case label declaration. The switch selector expression is compatible with the case labels, as the reference this will refer to objects of the enum type Scale5, which is the type of the case labels. The call to the method getGrade() returns a char value, which in this case is 'C'.

Q33 *(b) and (g)*
The method in (a) and the method at (1) do not have the same or covariant return types required for overriding.

The method in (b) overrides the method at (2).

The instance method in (c) cannot override the static method at (4).

The static method in (d) and the static method at (4) do not have compatible return types for overriding.

The static method in (e) cannot hide the instance method at (3).

The instance method in (f) and the instance method at (5) do not have compatible return types for overriding.

The instance method in (g) overrides the instance method at (6), and they have covariant return types.

Q34 *(c)*
A primitive value cannot be widened and then boxed implicitly. The primitive value is boxed to its corresponding wrapper type, and an attempt is made to find a corresponding formal parameter with the most specific type to which it can be passed. The varargs value is passed in the method calls as follows:

```
printFirst(10);         // new Integer[] {Integer.valueOf(10)}
printFirst((byte)20);   // new Number[] {Byte.valueOf(20)}
printFirst('3', '0');   // new Object[] {Character.valueOf('3'),
                        //               Character.valueOf('0')}
printFirst("40");       // new Object[] {"40"}
printFirst((short)50, 55);// new Number[] {Short.valueOf(50),
                        //               Integer.valueOf(55)}
printFirst((Number[])new Integer[] {70, 75}); // Passed as array of Number
```

Q35 *(e)*
The program will compile and print 1, 3, and 2 at runtime. First, the static initializers are executed when the class is initialized, printing 1 and 3. When the object is created and initialized, the instance initializer block is executed, printing 2.

Q36 *(a)*
As there is no appropriate resource bundle file for the no_NO locale, the resource bundle for the default locale (US) is loaded. The value of the key "greeting" from this resource bundle is printed. Changing the default locale of the application does not change the locale associated with the resource bundle rbs. The value of the key "greeting" from this resource bundle is printed one more time.

Q37   *(e)*

The runner thread can only proceed if `intArray[0]` is not 0. If this element is not 0, it has been initialized to 10 by the main thread. If this element is 0, the runner thread is put into the wait set of the `intArray` object, and must wait for notification. The main thread only notifies after initializing both elements of the array to 10. Calling the `notify()` method on an object with no threads in its wait set does not pose any problems. A thread can only call `notify()` on an object whose lock it holds. Therefore, the last `synchronized` statement in the `main()` method is necessary.

Q38   *(b)*

Notice that the array is declared as a raw type, yet the objects that are placed into this array are of a parameterized type. This is a legal assignment because an object of a parameterized type can be assigned to a raw type variable, in this case an element within the raw type array. However, in this case the `compareTo()` method accepts an argument of type parameter `T`, which allows invocation of any `Object` method using a reference of this type parameter. The code in the `compareTo()` method invokes the `toString()` method to convert each value into a `String` object and then compare these strings. The order of the comparison is therefore not numeric, but lexicographical. Note that the raw type `Thingy` is also used in the `for(:)` loop.

Q39   *(c)*

Each lambda expression implements a `Comparable` that returns an `int` value. These `int` values are accumulated and stored in the static field `result` of class `Widget`. The first lambda expression returns the length of the `"ACME"` string (i.e., 4), the second lambda expression returns the index of letter `"C"` within the string `"ACME"` (i.e., 1), and the third expression returns the day of the month in the `LocalDate` object (i.e., 20). The sum in the `result` field is thus 25, which is printed.

Q40   *(b)*

The `sort()` method of the `Arrays` class sorts the elements of the `Integer` array according to the total ordering defined by the `Comparator<Integer>` that is implemented by the lambda expression. The difference `x - y` between two values `x` and `y` determines whether `x` is less than, equal to, or greater than `y`, according to the contract of the `compare()` method of the `Comparator<E>` interface. The elements of the array are sorted in ascending order.

Q41   *(a)*

The `LocalDate` class uses the ISO-8601 standard, where year 0 corresponds to 1 BC. The pattern `"dd MM yy G"` results in the number of the day in the month, the short name of the month, the two-digit value of the year, and BC/AD being used to format the local date.

Q42   *(c)*

Stream processing distinguishes `LocalDateTime` objects from all other objects. It extracts the number of seconds from a `LocalDateTime` object, substitutes 1 for all other elements in the stream, and calculates the sum for all the elements. There is only one `LocalDateTime` object in this stream, which yields the value of 2; the other four objects are substituted with a value of 1 in the stream. Thus the result is 6.

Q43 (d)

The text block has two incidental leading whitespace on each line that are removed. After the removal of the two incidental spaces from all lines, the line lengths in the text block are 1, 3, and 1. The resulting string literal is "a\n b\nc\n".

Q44 (c)

The paths constructed by the code are as follows:

```
p1: /users/joe
p2: /users/bob
p1.relativize(p2):                      ../bob
p3 = p1.resolve(p1.relativize(p2)): /users/joe/../bob
p4 = p3.normalize():                    /users/bob
```

Since the first component of a path has index 0, index 1 refers to joe in p3 and bob in p4.

Q45 (b)

The resource bundles are loaded from the files resources_en.properties (which has an entry for key f2) and resources.properties (which has an entry for key f1). The resources_en_GB bundle is not loaded by the getBundle() method.

When the value for key f1 is not present in the resources_en bundle, the parent bundle resources is searched for the value of key f1. The en_GB locale is applied to the formatter, which uses the value "yy-MMM-dd" of key f1 to format the date.

Q46 (b)

The action() method uses short-circuit conditional operators || and && to test whether the parameter obj is a String or an Integer. The instanceof pattern match operator only introduces a pattern variable if it evaluates to true. If it is a String, it checks whether this string contains the character '1'. Otherwise, it checks whether the parameter obj is an Integer, and if it is, it determines whether its value is less than 1. The object passed to the method is an Integer object with a value of 1, which is not less than 1, and thus the boolean expression returns false.

Q47 (c)

A non-canonical constructor is required, since the arguments passed in the constructor are of type String and int, and not String and Duration, as in the declaration. The first statement in a non-canonical constructor must be an explicit invocation of a constructor with the this() expression that leads to the canonical constructor being invoked so that the component fields title and duration are initialized.

(a) and (b) are incorrect because they do not provide a value for the title field. Moreover, in (a), the this reference cannot be used in a this() expression.

(d) and (e) do not invoke the canonical record constructor with the this() expression.

(c) fulfills all the requirements.

Q48   *(b)*

The walk() method navigates the directory structure for the directory ./Sun. The map() method extracts the name of the leaf element from each Path that is encountered in this depth-first walk in the directory tree. The names are sorted. Notice that although the names start with a character that represents a number, the natural ordering is that for strings.

The limit() method limits the length of the stream to just the first three elements. Given the natural ordering for strings, the first three elements in the list are 1_Io, 1_Mercury, and 1_Moon. The forEach() operation prints a substring extracted from the name starting at index 2.

Q49   *(b)*

The method lines() creates a stream of text lines read from the text file. Lines are grouped on the substring extracted from each line after the ':' character. The map created by grouping has these substrings as keys and the lines containing the key as values. All lines that end with 1.70 will be grouped together, all lines that end with 1.99 will be in another group, and so on.

Q50   *(c)*

Module basic is the service provider as it implements the service defined by the service interface TransportType in module transport. Module basic requires module transport and must declare that it provides an implementation (basic.mode.Horse) of the service interface transport.mode.TransportType.

The requires directive must specify modules, not packages, as in (b) and (d). (a) requires the wrong service module and implements the wrong service interface.

Java Logging API Overview

●●

The Java Logging API is a supplementary topic, and *not* an exam objective. However, there could be some exam questions that utilize the Logging API to facilitate non-blocking parallel processing, such as in parallel streams. Also, an understanding of the Logging API principals and capabilities is an important practical programming skill.

G.1 Purpose of the Logging API

The purpose of the Java Logging API is to provide a simple yet flexible mechanism for writing logs to different destinations, while minimizing the effects of writing these logs on the overall performance of a Java application. A program can write messages to the standard output or standard error using System.out or System.err, respectively. However, this approach is not particularly flexible, because such write operations block the current thread. Thus they adversely affect program performance, and are totally unsuitable in any concurrent or parallel execution of code—for example, in parallel stream processing. Using standard out and standard error is also not very flexible because they do not allow a programmer to reconfigure the target destination for the log messages, nor do they provide a flexible dynamic mechanism to filter or format log messages.

The Logging API addresses the following issues:

- Provides a *configuration properties file* to configure:
  - *Log handlers*, which write log messages to different destinations
  - *Log message format* for each destination
  - *Logging levels*, which control how detailed logging should be done
- Minimizes performance implications with:
  - *Non-blocking* log writing operations
  - *Guarded logging*, which avoids unnecessary message formatting when the logger level is set in a way that a particular message is not going to reach the actual log destination

G.2 Configuring Logging

By default, the file `logging.properties` is used to configure Java logging. It is located in the JAVA_HOME/conf folder. (For Java version 8 or earlier, this was JAVA_HOME/jre/lib folder.) A different configuration file can be specified using the `java.util.logging` `.config.file` system property. For example:

```
java -Djava.util.logging.config.file=another-config
```

Log handlers are classes that are responsible for writing log messages to different destinations. The package `java.util.logging` provides a number of handler classes. A *logger configuration file* can be used to enable one or more handlers specified as a comma-separated list. By default, the logger configuration only sets up the *console handler*, but other handlers can be enabled as required. For example:

```
handlers = java.util.logging.FileHandler, java.util.logging.ConsoleHandler
```

Each handler has its own specific configurable properties. For example, a file handler allows setting up a naming pattern for log file names, minimum size of the file, log rollover to the next file, and so on. For example:

```
java.util.logging.FileHandler.pattern = %h/java%u.log
java.util.logging.FileHandler.limit   = 50000
java.util.logging.FileHandler.count   = 1
```

Obviously, such properties are not applicable to other types of handlers, such as the console handler. However, all handlers provided by the Java Logging API allow a logger format to be set; for example, as a simple plain text or xml format.

```
java.util.logging.ConsoleHandler.formatter = java.util.logging.SimpleFormatter
java.util.logging.FileHandler.formatter    = java.util.logging.XMLFormatter
```

It is possible to implement customized handlers by extending the `java.util.logging.` `Handler` class or one of its subclasses: `MemoryHandler` or `StreamHandler`. Also, it is possible to implement a customized formatter by extending the `java.util.logging.` `Formatter` class.

Level configuration is used to control the number of messages that are actually written to a log destination. *Logging levels* are defined by the `java.util.logging.Level` class using the following constants:

```
SEVERE (highest value)
WARNING
INFO
CONFIG
FINE
FINER
FINEST (lowest value)
```

In addition, there is a level `OFF` that can be used to turn off logging, and a level `ALL` that can be used to enable logging of all messages.

When logging is set to a certain logging level, any log message that is associated with this logging level and levels above it will be written to the log destination. However, messages that are associated with any logging levels below the one that was set in the configuration will essentially be ignored by the logger.

For example, when the log level is set to INFO, the INFO, SEVERE, and WARNING level messages will be written to the log, but the CONFIG, FINE, FINER, and FINEST level messages will be ignored by the logger.

It is possible to implement additional logging levels by subclassing the java.util.logging.Level class.

Log level configuration defines a *global log level property*, but also allows overriding the level for specific loggers. For example:

```
.level=INFO
org.foo.level=SEVERE
```

It is important to note that by convention, logger names are essentially Java packages and class names. So this example implies that everywhere in the program, the global logger level is INFO, except for the package org.foo, where it is set to SEVERE.

It is also possible to set the logging level for a specific handler. For example:

```
java.util.logging.ConsoleHandler.level = WARNING
```

Suppose that logging has been configured to use a file logger and the console logger, and the console logger is restricted to the WARNING level, but no such restriction is imposed on the file logger. Also, assume that the global log level is set to INFO. This would mean that log messages associated with a level below INFO would all be ignored; only WARNING and SEVERE level message would be written to the console logger; and INFO, WARNING, and SEVERE level messages would be written to the file logger.

G.3 Writing Log Messages

To set up logging for a program requires a few basic steps. First, a logger object must be initialized, using the java.util.logging.Logger.getLogger(String name) method. By convention, the name of a logger object should correspond to the fully qualified class name from which the log is written. This way, it will match the logger naming convention used by the logger configuration file. For example:

```
package org.foo;
import java.util.logging.*;
public class Test {
  private static Logger logger = Logger.getLogger(org.foo.Test.class.getName());
  public static void main(String[] args) {
    ...
  }
}
```

Notice that the logger name could theoretically be any string. However, using package and class names really helps to organize logger configuration. In this case, a logger config file can associate the org.foo logger name with a particular level of logging, which is going to affect log messages written from the org.foo.Test class.

Once the logger object is initialized, it can be used to write messages, using the logger.log() method. Each message is associated with a specific logger level and may contain any text. The log() method is overloaded to allow the program to pass an exception object as an additional argument so that exception details can be passed to the logger as part of the message. For example:

```
package org.foo;
import java.util.logging.*;
public class Test {
  private static Logger logger = Logger.getLogger(org.foo.Test.class.getName());
  public static void main(String[] args) {
    try {
      // any actions that may potentially throw an exception
    }catch(Exception e) {
      logger.log(Level.ERROR, "Some error message", e);
    }
    logger.log(Level.INFO, "Some other message");
  }
}
```

The Logger class provides a number of additional convenience methods that are equivalent to the log() method:

logp()

The *log precise* method takes additional parameters that specify a class and a method name.

logrb()

The *log with resource bundle* method takes a resource bundle name that may be used to localize log messages.

entering(), exiting(), throwing()

These are convenience methods used to log method entry, method exit, and any exception thrown at the FINER level.

severe(), warning(), config(), info(), fine(), finer(), finest()

These are convenience methods, each hardcoded to use a specific log level, rather than indicating the log level as an argument. In other words, logger.info("My message") is equivalent to logger.log(Level.INFO, "My message").

All of these log methods are *non-blocking*. This means that when any of these log methods are invoked in the program, the current thread is not blocked, as the method call returns immediately. The logger accumulates messages produced by the different program threads, and writes these messages to the actual destinations in another thread of its own. As a result, the log messages can reach their destinations with a minimum of delay, but the performance impact on the overall program execution is minimized. This allows loggers to be utilized in concurrent and parallel execution scenarios.

G.4 Applying Guarded Logging

Finally, it is a good idea not to format log messages ahead of time. This is because it is not known whether the message would or would not be written into a log because of the possible changes to the logger configuration. This means that code in the following example is not advisable:

```
logger.log(Level.FINE, "This is " + someVar + " value");
```

In the preceding code, message concatenation is going to be performed even if the log level could be set in a way that would ignore this message. In order to prevent such unnecessary processing, it is advised to use *guarded logging*. Basically, the aim is not to do message formatting when the message is going to be discarded because of the log level settings. This could be achieved with an if statement or by using *message value substitution*. For example, the following if statement:

```
if(logger.isLoggable(Level.FINER)) {                        // (1)
  logger.log(Level.FINE, "This is " + someVar + " value");
}
```

can be witten using message value substitution:

```
logger.log(Level.FINE, "This is {0} value", someVar);       // (2)
```

Notice that the code at (2) looks much cleaner than the code at (1) and is thus probably the best way to handle log messages.

G.5 Summary

The Logging API provides a simple, yet flexible non-blocking mechanism to write information about program execution, including general information as well as error messages. The certification exam does not ask any direct questions about logging, but use of loggers may be encountered in the context of other questions, specifically where non-blocking output is important, such as in the context of the Concurrency API or execution of parallel streams.

Index

Index includes entries for Vol. I and Vol. II. References to pp. 1–878 refer to items in Vol. I (Chapters 1–15).

●●●

J

N

#1 programming language for today's tech trends

www.oracle.com/java